Gleim Publications, Inc., offers five university-level study systems:

Auditing & Systems Exam Questions and Explanations with Test Prep Software
Business Law/Legal Studies Exam Questions and Explanations with Test Prep Software
Federal Tax Exam Questions and Explanations with Test Prep Software
Financial Accounting Exam Questions and Explanations with Test Prep Software
Cost/Managerial Accounting Exam Questions and Explanations with Test Prep Software

The following is a list of Gleim examination review systems:

CIA Review: Part 1, The Internal Audit Activity's Role in Governance, Risk, and Control
CIA Review: Part 2, Conducting the Internal Audit Engagement
CIA Review: Part 3, Business Analysis and Information Technology
CIA Review: Part 4, Business Management Skills
CIA Review: A System for Success

CMA Review: Part 1, Financial Planning, Performance, and Control
CMA Review: Part 2, Financial Decision Making
CMA Review: A System for Success

CPA Review: Financial
CPA Review: Auditing
CPA Review: Business
CPA Review: Regulation
CPA Review: A System for Success

EA Review: Part 1, Individuals
EA Review: Part 2, Businesses
EA Review: Part 3, Representation, Practices, and Procedures
EA Review: A System for Success

An order form is provided at the back of this book or contact us at www.gleim.com or (800) 874-5346.

REVIEWERS AND CONTRIBUTORS

Garrett Gleim, B.S., CPA (not in public practice), is a graduate of the Wharton School at the University of Pennsylvania. Mr. Gleim coordinated the production staff, reviewed the manuscript, and provided production assistance throughout the project.

Grady M. Irwin, J.D., is a graduate of the University of Florida College of Law, and he has taught in the University of Florida College of Business. Mr. Irwin provided substantial editorial assistance throughout the project.

John F. Rebstock, B.S.A., is a graduate of the Fisher School of Accounting at the University of Florida. He has passed the CIA and CPA exams. Mr. Rebstock reviewed portions of the manuscript.

Kristina M. Rivet, CPA, graduated *cum laude* from Florida International University. She has extensive public accounting experience in the areas of financial accounting, tax, and consulting. Ms. Rivet provided substantial editorial assistance throughout the project.

Stewart B. White, B.M., *cum laude*, University of Richmond, B.S., Virginia Commonwealth University, has passed the CPA, CIA, and CISA exams and has worked in the fields of retail management, financial audit, IT audit, COBOL programming, and data warehouse management. Mr. White provided substantial editorial assistance throughout the project.

A PERSONAL THANKS

This manual would not have been possible without the extraordinary effort and dedication of Jacob Brunny, Julie Cutlip, Kate Devine, Eileen Nickl, Teresa Soard, Joanne Strong, and Candace Van Doren, who typed the entire manuscript and all revisions and drafted and laid out the diagrams and illustrations in this book.

The authors appreciate the production and editorial assistance of Katie Anderson, Alexander Karnazes, Katie Larson, Cary Marcous, Jean Marzullo, Shane Rapp, Drew Sheppard, Katie Wassink, and Martha Willis.

The authors also appreciate the critical reading assistance of Brett Babir, Ellen Buhl, Lauren Bull, Reed Daines, Lawrence Lipp, and Kristina Schoen.

Finally, we appreciate the encouragement, support, and tolerance of our families throughout this project.

SIXTEENTH EDITION

GLEIM

CMA Review

Part 1
Financial Planning, Performance, and Control

by

Irvin N. Gleim, Ph.D., CPA, CIA, CMA, CFM

and

Dale L. Flesher, Ph.D., CPA, CIA, CMA, CFM

ABOUT THE AUTHORS

Irvin N. Gleim is Professor Emeritus in the Fisher School of Accounting at the University of Florida and is a member of the American Accounting Association, Academy of Legal Studies in Business, AICPA, Association of Government Accountants, Florida Institute of CPAs, The IIA, and the IMA. He has had articles published in the *Journal of Accountancy*, *The Accounting Review*, and *The American Business Law Journal* and is author/coauthor of numerous accounting and aviation books and CPE courses.

Dale L. Flesher is the Arthur Andersen Alumni Professor in the School of Accountancy at the University of Mississippi and has written over 300 articles for business and professional journals, including *Management Accounting*, *Journal of Accountancy*, and *The Accounting Review*, as well as numerous books. He is a member of the IMA, AICPA, The IIA, American Accounting Association, and American Taxation Association. He is a past editor of *The Accounting Historians' Journal* and is a trustee and past president of the Academy of Accounting Historians. He is currently the vice president of finance for the American Accounting Association. In 2011, he received the AICPA's highest award for educators, The Distinguished Performance in Accounting Education Award, which is a lifetime achievement award. Previously, in 1990, he received The Institute of Internal Auditors Radde Award as the Outstanding Auditing Educator worldwide.

Gleim Publications, Inc.
P.O. Box 12848
University Station
Gainesville, Florida 32604
(800) 87-GLEIM or (800) 874-5346
(352) 375-0772
Fax: (352) 375-6940
Internet: www.gleim.com
Email: admin@gleim.com

For updates to the first printing of the sixteenth edition of *CMA Review: Part 1*

Go To: www.gleim.com/updates

Or: Scan code with your mobile device

Or: Email update@gleim.com with **CMA 1 16-1** in the subject line. You will receive our current update as a reply.

Updates are available until the next edition is published.

ISSN: 2152-6427

ISBN: 978-1-58194-200-2

First Printing: July 2012

ACKNOWLEDGMENTS

The authors are indebted to the Institute of Certified Management Accountants (ICMA) for permission to use problem materials from past CMA examinations. Questions and unofficial answers from the Certified Management Accountant Examinations, copyright © 1982 through 2008 by the Institute of Certified Management Accountants, are reprinted and/or adapted with permission.

The authors are also indebted to The Institute of Internal Auditors, Inc., for permission to use Certified Internal Auditor Examination Questions and Suggested Solutions, copyright © 1985 through 1996 by The Institute of Internal Auditors, Inc.

The authors also appreciate and thank the American Institute of Certified Public Accountants, Inc. Material from Uniform Certified Public Accountant Examination questions and unofficial answers, copyright © 1981-2012 by the American Institute of Certified Public Accountants, Inc., is reprinted and/or adapted with permission.

This publication was printed and bound by Corley Printing Company, St. Louis, MO, a registered ISO-9002 company. More information about Corley Printing Company is available at www.corleyprinting.com or by calling (314) 739-3777.

Visit www.gleim.com for the latest updates and information on all of our products.

This publication is designed to provide accurate and authoritative information with regard to the subject matter covered. It is sold with the understanding that the publisher is not engaged in rendering legal, accounting, or other professional service.

If legal advice or other expert assistance is required, the services of a competent professional person should be sought.

(From a declaration of principles jointly adopted by a Committee of the American Bar Association and a Committee of Publishers.)

TABLE OF CONTENTS

Page

Preface for CMA Part 1 Candidates vi

Preparing for and Taking the CMA Exam 1

Study Unit 1. Ethics for Management Accountants and Cost Management Concepts 17

Study Unit 2. Cost Accumulation Systems 53

Study Unit 3. Cost Allocation Techniques 89

Study Unit 4. Operational Efficiency and Business Process Performance 133

Study Unit 5. Budgeting Concepts and Forecasting Techniques 167

Study Unit 6. Budget Methodologies and Budget Preparation 207

Study Unit 7. Cost and Variance Measures 255

Study Unit 8. Responsibility Accounting and Performance Measures 291

Study Unit 9. Internal Controls -- Risk and Procedures for Control 325

Study Unit 10. Internal Controls -- Internal Auditing and Systems Controls 363

Appendix A: ICMA Content Specification Outlines and Cross-References 399

Appendix B: ICMA Suggested Reading List 405

Appendix C: Types and Levels of Exam Questions 407

Index 413

Order Form 425

PREFACE FOR CMA PART 1 CANDIDATES

The purpose of this book is to help **you** prepare **yourself** to pass Part 1 of the two-part CMA examination. The overriding consideration is to provide an inexpensive, effective, and easy-to-use study program. This manual

1. Explains how to optimize your grade by focusing on Part 1 of the CMA exam.

2. Defines the subject matter tested on Part 1 of the CMA exam.

3. Outlines all of the subject matter tested on Part 1 in 10 easy-to-use-and-complete study units.

4. Presents multiple-choice and essay questions from past CMA examinations to prepare you for questions in future CMA exams. The multiple-choice answer explanations are presented to the immediate right of each question for your convenience. Use a piece of paper to cover our explanations as you study the questions.

5. Suggests exam-taking and question-answering techniques to help you maximize your exam score.

The outline format, the spacing, and the question-and-answer formats in this book are designed to facilitate readability, learning, understanding, and success on the CMA exam. Our most successful candidates use the Gleim CMA Review System*, which includes books, Test Prep Software, Audio Review, Gleim Online, Essay Wizard, FREE Practice Exams (available Summer 2012), and access to a Personal Counselor; or a group study CMA review program. (Check our website for live courses we recommend.) This review book and all Gleim CMA Review materials are compatible with other CMA review materials and courses that are based on the ICMA's Content Specification Outlines.

To maximize the efficiency and effectiveness of your CMA review program, augment your studying with *CMA Review: A System for Success*. This booklet has been carefully written and organized to provide important information to assist you in passing the CMA examination.

Thank you for your interest in our materials. We deeply appreciate the thousands of letters and suggestions we have received from CIA, CMA, CPA, and EA candidates and accounting students and faculty during the past 5 decades.

If you use Gleim materials, we want YOUR feedback immediately after the exam and as soon as you have received your grades. The CMA exam is NONDISCLOSED, and you must maintain the confidentiality and agree not to divulge the nature or content of any CMA question or answer under any circumstances. We ask only for information about our materials, i.e., the topics that need to be added, expanded, etc.

Please go to www.gleim.com/feedbackCMA1 to share your suggestions on how we can improve this edition.

Good Luck on the Exam,

Irvin N. Gleim
Dale L. Flesher
July 2012

PREPARING FOR AND TAKING THE CMA EXAM

Transition to Two-Part Exam 1
Follow These Steps to PASS the Exam 2
Introduction to CMA 3
Overview of the CMA Examination 3
Subject Matter for Part 1 4
Learning Outcome Statements 4
Which Pronouncements are Tested? 4
How Ethics Are Tested 4
Nondisclosed Exam 4
The ICMA's Requirements for CMA Designations 5
CMA Exam Fees 5
Maintaining Your CMA Designation 6
Eligibility Period 6
Steps to Become a CMA 6
Preliminary Testing: Gleim CMA Diagnostic Quizzes 8
How to Study a Study Unit Using the Gleim Review System 8
CMA Gleim Online 9
Gleim Essay Wizard 9
Gleim Books 10
CMA Test Prep Software 11
Studying with Books and Software 11
Gleim Audio Reviews 12
Final Review: Gleim CMA Practice Exam 12
Time-Budgeting and Question-Answering Techniques for the Exam 12
Essay Questions 14
Essay Grading 16
How to Be in Control while Taking the Exam 16
If You Have Questions about Gleim Materials 16

TRANSITION TO TWO-PART EXAM

In 2010, the ICMA changed the CMA program from a four-part to a two-part exam. Candidates are now able to enter only into the two-part program; i.e., old exam Parts 1, 2, 3, and 4 are no longer available to complete.

Candidates who previously began the four-part exam process can transition to the new exam. If they passed old Part 2, they only have to pass new Part 2 to complete the CMA. If they passed old Part 3, they only have to pass new Part 1 to complete the CMA. If both old Parts 2 and 3 were passed, a 2-hour transition exam must be taken to complete the CMA. The Transition Exam will be available until February 28, 2013.

FOLLOW THESE STEPS TO PASS THE EXAM

1. Read this **Introduction** to familiarize yourself with the content and structure of Part 1 of the CMA exam. In the following pages, you will find

   a. An **overview of Part 1** and what it generally tests, including the ICMA's Content Specification Outlines (CSOs)

   b. A detailed plan with **steps to obtain your CMA certification**, including

      1) The order in which you should apply, register, schedule your exam, and buy your study materials

      2) The studying tactics on which you should focus

      3) How to organize your study schedule to make the most out of each resource in the Gleim CMA Review System (i.e., books, Test Prep Software Download, Audio Review, Gleim Online, Essay Wizard, Diagnostic Quizzes, Practice Exams, etc.)

   c. Tactics for your **actual test day**, including

      1) Time budgeting, so you complete all questions with time to review

      2) Question-answering techniques to obtain every point you can

      3) An explanation of how to be in control of your CMA exam

2. Scan the Gleim *CMA Review: A System for Success* booklet and note where to revisit later in your studying process to obtain a deeper understanding of the CMA exam.

   a. *CMA Review: A System for Success* has seven study units:

      Study Unit 1: The CMA Examination: An Overview and Preparation Introduction
      Study Unit 2: ICMA Content Specification Outlines
      Study Unit 3: Content Preparation, Test Administration, and Performance Grading
      Study Unit 4: Multiple-Choice Questions
      Study Unit 5: Essay Questions
      Study Unit 6: Preparing to Pass the CMA Exam
      Study Unit 7: How to Take the CMA Exam

3. BEFORE you begin studying, take a **Diagnostic Quiz** at www.gleim.com/cmadiagnosticquiz or use our **Gleim Diagnostic Quiz App** for iPhone, iPod Touch, and Android.

   a. The Diagnostic Quiz includes a representative sample of 40 multiple-choice questions and will determine your weakest areas in Part 1.

   b. When you are finished, one of our **Personal Counselors** will consult with you to better focus your review on any areas in which you have less confidence.

4. Follow the steps outlined on page 8, "How to Study a Study Unit Using the Gleim CMA Review System." This is the **study plan** that our most successful candidates adhere to. Study until you have reached your **desired proficiency level** (e.g., 75%) for each study unit in Part 1.

   a. As you proceed, be sure to check any **Updates** that may have been released.

      1) Gleim Online and Essay Wizard are updated automatically.

      2) Test Prep Software is updated by the Online Library Updates system in the Tools menu of your Test Prep. You can (and should) set your Test Prep to automatically update at least once a month.

      3) Book updates can be viewed at www.gleim.com/updates, or you can have them emailed to you. See the information box in the top right corner of page iv for details.

   b. **Review the *CMA Review: A System for Success* booklet** and become completely comfortable with what will be expected from you on test day.

5. Shortly before your test date, take a **Practice Exam** (complimentary with the purchase of the complete Gleim CMA Review System!) at www.gleim.com/cmapracticeexam (available Summer 2012).

   a. This timed and scored exam emulates the actual CMA exam and tests you not only on the content you have studied, but also on the question-answering and time-management techniques you have learned throughout the Gleim study process.

   b. When you have completed the exam, study your results to discover where you should **focus your review during the final days before your exam**.

6. **Take and PASS** Part 1 of the CMA exam!

   a. When you have completed the exam, please contact Gleim with your **suggestions, comments, and corrections**. We want to know how well we prepared you for your testing experience.

INTRODUCTION TO CMA

CMA is the acronym for Certified Management Accountant. The CMA examination is developed and offered by the Institute of Certified Management Accountants (ICMA) in numerous domestic and international locations.

According to the IMA, the "CMA is the advanced professional certification specifically designed to measure the accounting and financial management skills that drive business performance."

OVERVIEW OF THE CMA EXAMINATION

The total exam is 8 hours of testing. It is divided into two parts, as follows:

Part 1 – Financial Planning, Performance, and Control
Part 2 – Financial Decision Making

Each part consists of 100 multiple-choice questions and 2 essay scenarios, and testing lasts 4 hours (3 hours for the multiple-choice questions plus 1 hour for the essays). The exams are only offered during the following three testing windows: January/February, May/June, and September/October.

The CMA exam is computerized to facilitate easier testing. Prometric, the testing company that the IMA contracts to proctor the exams, has hundreds of testing centers worldwide. The Gleim Test Prep Software, Gleim Online, Gleim Essay Wizard, and Gleim CMA Practice Exams provide exact exam emulations of the Prometric computer screens and procedures to prepare you to PASS.

SUBJECT MATTER FOR PART 1

Below, we have provided the ICMA's abbreviated Content Specification Outline (CSO) for Part 1. The percentage coverage of each topic is indicated to its right. We adjust the content of our materials to any changes in the CSO.

Candidates for the CMA designation are expected to have a minimum level of business knowledge that transcends both examination parts. This minimum level includes knowledge of basic financial statements, time value of money concepts, and elementary statistics. Specific discussion of the ICMA's Levels of Performance (A, B, and C) is provided in Appendix C, which is a reprint of the ICMA's discussion of "Types and Levels of Exam Questions."

Part 1: Financial Planning, Performance, and Control

Planning, Budgeting, and Forecasting	30%
Performance Management	25%
Cost Management	25%
Internal Controls	15%
Professional Ethics	5%

Appendix A contains the CSOs in their entirety as well as cross-references to the subunits in our text where topics are covered. Remember that we have studied and restudied the CSOs in developing our *CMA Review* materials. Accordingly, you do not need to spend time with Appendix A. Rather, it should give you confidence that Gleim *CMA Review* is the best review source available to help you PASS the CMA exam.

LEARNING OUTCOME STATEMENTS

In addition to the Content Specification Outlines, the ICMA has published Learning Outcome Statements (LOSs) that specify in detail what skills a candidate should possess. Before you study our knowledge transfer outline, read the LOS at the beginning of each study unit. This will alert you to what is expected and required of you.

WHICH PRONOUNCEMENTS ARE TESTED?

New pronouncements are eligible to be tested on the CMA exam in the testing window beginning 1 year after a pronouncement's effective date.

HOW ETHICS ARE TESTED

Ethical issues and considerations are tested from the perspective of the individual in Part 1 and from the perspective of the organization in Part 2. Candidates will be expected to evaluate the issues involved and make recommendations for the resolution of the situation.

NONDISCLOSED EXAM

As part of the ICMA's nondisclosure policy and to prove each candidate's willingness to adhere to this policy, a confidentiality agreement must be accepted by each candidate before each part is taken. This statement is reproduced here to remind all CMA candidates about the ICMA's strict policy of nondisclosure, which Gleim consistently supports and upholds.

I hereby attest that I will not divulge the content of this examination, nor will I remove any examination materials, notes or other unauthorized materials from the examination room. I understand that failure to comply with this attestation may result in invalidation of my grades and disqualification from future examinations. For those already certified by the Institute of Certified Management Accountants, failure to comply with the statement will be considered a violation of the IMA's Statement of Ethical Professional Practice and could result in revocation of the certification.

THE ICMA'S REQUIREMENTS FOR CMA DESIGNATIONS

The CMA designation is granted only by the ICMA. Candidates must complete the following steps to become a CMA:

1. Become a member of the IMA, enter the certification program, and register for the part(s) you are going to take. The *CMA Review: A System for Success* booklet contains concise instructions on the membership and certification application and registration processes and a useful worksheet to help you keep track of your process and organize what you need for exam day. Detailed instructions and screenshots for those steps can also be found at www.gleim.com/accounting/cma/steps.
2. Pass both parts of the exam within 3 years.
3. Satisfy the education requirement.
4. Satisfy the experience requirement.
5. Comply with the IMA's *Statement of Ethical Professional Practice*.

Upon completion of all requirements, the ICMA will issue a numbered CMA certificate. To keep the certificate, a CMA must (1) maintain active membership in the IMA and pay the annual CMA maintenance fee, (2) fulfill the requirements for continuing professional education, and (3) continue to comply with the IMA's *Statement of Ethical Professional Practice* and all applicable state laws.

CMA EXAM FEES

1. IMA Membership Fees: IMA membership is required for all CMA candidates. There are four types of membership: Regular, Student, Young Professional, and Academic. Fees for IMA members include a one-time membership application fee (for all new members except Students and Young Professionals) and an annual membership renewal fee. Members who have passed the CMA exam will also need to pay an annual maintenance fee, due at the same time as the renewal fee.

   Go to www.gleim.com/CMAfees for the most current IMA membership fees.
2. CMA Certification Fees:

	Entrance Fee	Exam Fee One Part/Window	Exam Fee Both Parts/Window	Rescheduling/ Cancelation Fee *
Regular	$225	$350	$300	$50
Student	$75	$175	$125	$50
Academic	$75	$175	$125	$50

*This fee is applicable to candidates who reschedule/cancel their exam within 30 days of their appointment. Prior to 30 days, there is no penalty.

MAINTAINING YOUR CMA DESIGNATION

When you have completed all requirements, you will be issued a numbered CMA certificate. This certificate is the property of the ICMA and must be returned upon request. To maintain your certificate, membership in the IMA is required. The annual CMA maintenance fee for regular members is $30. You are also required to comply with the IMA's *Statement of Ethical Professional Practice*. The final requirement is continuing professional education (CPE).

Beginning the calendar year after successful completion of the CMA exams, 30 hours of CPE must be completed, which is about 4 days per year. Qualifying topics include management accounting, corporate taxation, statistics, computer science, systems analysis, management skills, marketing, business law, and insurance. All CMAs are required to complete 2 hours of CPE on the subject of ethics as part of their 30-hour annual requirement.

ELIGIBILITY PERIOD

Candidates must register for an exam part within the first 12 months after being admitted to the Certification Program. In addition, all candidates are required to pass both parts of the exam within 3 years of being admitted to the CMA program. If a candidate is not able to pass both parts within this time period, the Certification Entrance Fee will have to be repaid and the passed part will have to be retaken.

STEPS TO BECOME A CMA

1. Become knowledgeable about the exam, and decide which part you will take first.
2. Purchase the Gleim CMA Review System (including books, Test Prep Software Download, Audio Review, Gleim Online, Essay Wizards, Practice Exams, and access to a Personal Counselor) to thoroughly prepare for the CMA exam. Commit to systematic preparation for the exam as described in our review materials, including *CMA Review: A System for Success*.
3. Communicate with your Personal Counselor to design a study plan that meets your needs. Call (800) 874-5346 or email CMA@gleim.com.
4. Apply for membership in the IMA and the Certification Program.
5. Register online to take the desired part of the exam in the next available window.
6. Upon receipt of authorization to take the exam, schedule your test with Prometric.
7. Work systematically through each study unit in the Gleim CMA Review System.
8. Sit for and PASS the CMA exam while you are in control, as described in Study Unit 7 of *CMA Review: A System for Success*. Gleim will make it easy.
9. Contact Gleim with your comments on our study materials and how well they prepared you for the exam.
10. Enjoy your career, pursue multiple certifications (CIA, CPA, EA, etc.), recommend Gleim to others who are also taking these exams, and stay up-to-date on your continuing professional education with Gleim CPE.

More specifically, you should focus on the following **system for success** on the CMA exam:

1. **Understand the exam, including its purpose, coverage, preparation, format, administration, grading, and pass rates.**

    a. The better you understand the examination process from beginning to end, the better you will perform.

    b. Study the Gleim *CMA Review: A System for Success.* Please be sure you have a copy of this useful booklet (also available online at www.gleim.com/sfs).

2. **Learn and understand the subject matter tested.** The ICMA's CSOs for Part 1 are the basis for the study outlines that are presented in each of the 10 study units that make up this book.* You will also learn and understand the material tested on the CMA exam by answering numerous multiple-choice and essay questions from previous CMA exams.

3. **Practice answering past exam questions to perfect your question-answering techniques.** Answering past exam questions helps you understand the standards to which you will be held. This motivates you to learn and understand while studying (rather than reading) the outlines in each of the 10 study units.

    a. Question-answering techniques are suggested for multiple-choice and essay questions in Study Unit 4 and Study Unit 5, respectively, of *CMA Review: A System for Success.*

    b. Our **CMA Test Prep** Software contains thousands of additional multiple-choice questions that are not offered in our books. Additionally, CMA Test Prep Software has many useful features, including documentation of your performance and the ability to simulate the CMA exam environment.

    c. Our **CMA Gleim Online** is a powerful Internet-based program that allows CMA candidates to learn in an interactive environment and provides feedback to candidates to encourage learning. It includes multiple-choice and essay questions in Prometric's format. Each CMA Gleim Online candidate has access to a Personal Counselor, who helps organize study plans that work with busy schedules.

    d. Additionally, each candidate should utilize the Gleim CMA Essay Wizard online courses for even more practice on essays in an exam-like environment. The Essay Wizard courses provide 40 additional essays that can be answered and graded for an accurate indication of how well-prepared you are for the CMA's essays.

4. **Plan and practice exam execution.** Anticipate the exam environment and prepare yourself with a plan: When to arrive? How to dress? What exam supplies to bring? How many questions and what format? Order of answering questions? How much time to spend on each question? See Study Unit 7 in *CMA Review: A System for Success.*

    a. Expect the unexpected and adjust! Remember, your sole objective when taking an examination is to maximize your score. You must outperform your peers, and being as comfortable and relaxed as possible gives you an advantage!

5. **Be in control.** Develop confidence and ensure success with a controlled preparation program followed by confident execution during the examination.

---

*Please fill out our online feedback form (www.gleim.com/feedbackCMA1) IMMEDIATELY after you take the CMA exam so we can adapt to changes in the exam. Our approach has been approved by the ICMA.

PRELIMINARY TESTING: GLEIM CMA DIAGNOSTIC QUIZZES

The five Gleim CMA Diagnostic Quizzes provide a representative sample of 40 multiple-choice questions for each exam part to identify your preliminary strengths and any weaknesses before you start preparing in earnest for the CMA exam. They also provide you with the actual exam experience, i.e., what you will encounter when you take the CMA exam at Prometric.

When you have completed each quiz, one of our Personal Counselors will consult with you to better focus your review on any areas in which you have less confidence. After your consultation, you will be able to access a Review Session, where you can study answer explanations for the correct and incorrect answer choices of the questions you answered incorrectly.

For smart phone users, there is also a Gleim Diagnostic Quiz App for iPhone, iPod Touch, and Android. See our website (www.gleim.com/cmadiagnosticquiz) for more information.

HOW TO STUDY A STUDY UNIT USING THE GLEIM REVIEW SYSTEM

To ensure that you are using your time effectively, we recommend that you follow the steps listed below when using all of the CMA Review System materials together (books, Test Prep Software, Audio Review, Gleim Online, and Essay Wizard):

1. (30 minutes, plus 10 minutes for review) In the CMA Gleim Online course, complete Multiple-Choice Quiz #1 in 30 minutes. It is expected that your scores will be lower on the first quiz.

    a. Immediately following the quiz, you will be prompted to review the questions you marked and/or answered incorrectly. For each question, analyze and understand why you were unsure or answered it incorrectly. This step is an essential learning activity.

2. (30 minutes) Use the audiovisual presentation for an overview of the study unit. The Gleim CMA Review Audios can be substituted for audiovisual presentations and can be used while driving to work, exercising, etc.

3. (45 minutes) Complete the 30-question True/False quiz. It provides immediate feedback and is most effective if used prior to studying the Knowledge Transfer Outline.

4. (60 minutes) Study the Knowledge Transfer Outline, particularly the troublesome areas identified from the multiple-choice questions in the Gleim Online course. The Knowledge Transfer Outlines can be studied either online or from the books.

5. (30 minutes, plus 10 minutes for review) Complete Multiple-Choice Quiz #2 in the Gleim Online course.

    a. Immediately following the quiz, you will be prompted to review the questions you marked and/or answered incorrectly. For each question, analyze and understand why you were unsure or answered it incorrectly. This step is an essential learning activity.

6. (60 minutes) Complete two 20-question quizzes while in Test Mode from the CMA Test Prep Software. Review as needed.

7. (30 minutes) Complete and review the essay question in Gleim Online.

When following these steps, you will complete all 10 units in about 50 hours. Then spend about 10-20 hours using the CMA Test Prep Software to create customized tests for the problem areas that you identified. When you are ready, create 20-question quizzes that draw questions from all 10 study units. Continue taking 20-question quizzes until you approach a 75%+ proficiency level.

The times mentioned above are recommendations based on prior candidate feedback and how long you will have to answer questions on the actual exam. Each candidate's time spent in any area will vary depending on proficiency and familiarity with the subject matter.

CMA GLEIM ONLINE

CMA Gleim Online is a versatile, interactive, self-study review program delivered via the Internet. It is divided into two courses (one for each part of the CMA exam) and emulates the CMA exam.

Each course is broken down into 10 individual, manageable study units. Completion time per study unit will be about 4 hours. Each study unit in the course contains an audiovisual presentation, 30 true/false study questions, 10-20 pages of Knowledge Transfer Outlines, two 20-question multiple-choice quizzes, and an essay question.

CMA Gleim Online provides you with a Personal Counselor, a real person who will provide support to ensure your competitive edge. CMA Gleim Online is a great way to get confidence as you prepare with Gleim. This confidence will continue during and after the exam.

GLEIM ESSAY WIZARD

The Gleim Essay Wizard is a training program that focuses on the essay questions that appear in both parts of the CMA exam. This online course provides two essay questions per study unit, as well as test-taking tips from Dr. Gleim to help you stay in control.

I wouldn't have passed the CMA exams without the help of Gleim.

- Gary Caccamise

GLEIM BOOKS

This edition of the CMA Part 1 Review book has the following features to make studying easier:

1. **Examples:** Longer, illustrative examples, both hypothetical and those drawn from actual events, are set off in shaded, bordered boxes.

EXTENDED EXAMPLE of Normal Costing

Instead of using a different overhead application rate for each budget period, the company uses a single average figure for the entire year.

- The company expects to produce 24,000 units during the year, for an average of 8,000 units per budget period.
- Dividing the fixed overhead of $20,000 for each budget period by 8,000 units yields a fixed overhead application rate of $2.50.
- The new total overhead application rate per unit is thus $3.50 ($1.00 variable cost + $2.50 fixed cost), and the new per-unit cost for all 3 budget periods is $10.50 ($3.00 direct materials + $4.00 direct labor + $3.50 overhead application rate).

The revised income statements prepared using a normalized overhead rate reveal the smoothing effect on gross margin:

	Jan-Apr	May-Aug	Sep-Dec	Totals
Sales:				
Produced in Jan-Apr	7,000	3,000		
Produced in May-Aug		4,000	2,000	
Produced in Sep-Dec			5,000	
Expected unit sales	7,000	7,000	7,000	
Expected selling price	× $12	× $12	× $12	
Total expected sales	$84,000	$84,000	$84,000	$252,000
Cost of goods sold:				
From Jan-Apr	$73,500	$31,500		
From May-Aug		42,000	$21,000	
From Sep-Dec			52,500	
Total expected COGS	$73,500	$73,500	$73,500	$220,500
Gross margin	**$10,500**	**$10,500**	**$10,500**	**$ 31,500**

---

2. **Gleim Success Tips:** These tips supplement the core exam material by suggesting how certain topics might be presented on the exam or how you should prepare for an issue.

Management accountants are expected to know the theory and how to complete detailed calculations for the topics covered in this study unit. To provide a more focused approach to studying, Gleim has broken up the theoretical questions and computational questions of the different cost allocation techniques into separate subunits. CMA candidates should expect a mix of both theory and computational questions on the CMA exam.

---

3. **Core Concepts:** Core concepts are included at the end of each subunit. The core concepts provide an overview of the key points of each subunit that serve as the foundation for learning. As part of your review, you should make sure that you understand each of them.

CMA TEST PREP SOFTWARE

Twenty-question tests in the **CMA Test Prep** Software will help you to focus on your weaker areas. Make it a game: How much can you improve?

Our CMA Test Prep (in test mode) forces you to commit to your answer choice before looking at answer explanations; thus, you are preparing under true exam conditions. It also keeps track of your time and performance history for each study unit, which is available in either a table or graphical format.

STUDYING WITH BOOKS AND SOFTWARE

Simplify the exam preparation process by following our suggested steps listed below. DO NOT omit the step in which you diagnose the reasons for answering questions incorrectly; i.e., learn from your mistakes while studying so you avoid making similar mistakes on the CMA exam.

1. In test mode, answer a 20-question diagnostic test from each study unit before studying any other information.

2. Study the Knowledge Transfer Outline for the corresponding study unit in your Gleim book.

   a. Place special emphasis on the weaker areas that you identified with the initial diagnostic test in Step 1.

3. Take two or three 20-question tests in test mode after you have studied the Knowledge Transfer Outline.

4. Immediately following each practice test, you will be prompted to review the questions you marked and/or answered incorrectly. For each question, analyze and understand why you were unsure or answered it incorrectly. This step is an essential learning activity.

5. Continue this process until you approach a predetermined proficiency level, e.g., 75%+.

6. Modify this process to suit your individual learning process.

   a. Learning from questions you answer incorrectly is very important. Each question you answer incorrectly should be viewed as an **opportunity** to avoid missing actual test questions on your CMA exam. Thus, you should carefully study the answer explanations provided until you understand why you chose the incorrect answer so you can avoid similar errors on your exam. This study technique is clearly the difference between passing and failing for many CMA candidates.

   b. Also, you **must** determine why you answered questions incorrectly and learn how to avoid the same error in the future. Reasons for missing questions include:

      1) Misreading the requirement (stem)
      2) Not understanding what is required
      3) Making a math error
      4) Applying the wrong rule or concept
      5) Being distracted by one or more of the answers
      6) Incorrectly eliminating answers from consideration
      7) Not having any knowledge of the topic tested
      8) Employing bad intuition when guessing

   c. It is also important to verify that you answered correctly for the right reasons (i.e., read the discussion provided for the correct answer). Otherwise, if the material is tested on the CMA exam in a different manner, you may not answer it correctly.

   d. It is imperative that you complete your predetermined number of study units per week so you can review your progress and realize how attainable a comprehensive CMA review program is when using Gleim CMA Review System. Remember to meet or beat your schedule to give yourself confidence.

GLEIM AUDIO REVIEWS

Gleim CMA Audio Reviews provide an average of 30 minutes of quality review for each study unit. Each review provides an overview of the Knowledge Transfer Outline for each study unit in the *CMA Review* book. The purpose is to get candidates "started" so they can relate to the questions they will answer before reading the study outlines in each study unit.

The audios get to the point, as does the entire Gleim System for Success. We are working to get you through the CMA exam with the minimum time, cost, and frustration. You can listen to two short sample audio reviews on our website at www.gleim.com/accounting/demos/.

FINAL REVIEW: GLEIM CMA PRACTICE EXAM - available Summer 2012

Take a CMA Practice Exam (complimentary with your complete CMA Review System) shortly before you take the actual exam to gain experience in the computer-based exam environment. The Practice Exam is 4 hours (240 minutes) long and contains 100 multiple-choice and 2 essay questions, just like the CMA exam. Therefore, it tests you not only on the content you have studied, but also on the question-answering and time-management techniques you have learned.

For the most realistic practice exam experience, we suggest you complete the entire exam in one sitting, just like the actual CMA exam. Once you have completed the Practice Exam and received your grade, you will be provided with a Review Session that shows which questions were answered incorrectly. Additionally, you will be able to study answer explanations and suggested essay responses to assist you in learning the topics.

TIME-BUDGETING AND QUESTION-ANSWERING TECHNIQUES FOR THE EXAM

Expect 100 multiple-choice questions and 2 essay questions on each part with a 240-minute total time allocation (180 minutes max for multiple-choice questions and at least 60 minutes for the essays). See Study Units 4 and 5 in *CMA Review: A System for Success* for additional discussion of how to maximize your score on multiple-choice questions and essays.

1. **Budget your time.**
   a. We make this point with emphasis. Just as you would fill up your gas tank prior to reaching empty, so too should you finish your exam before time expires.
   b. You have 180 minutes to answer the 100 multiple-choice questions, i.e., 1.8 minutes per question. We suggest you allocate 1.5 minutes per question. This would result in completing 100 questions in 150 minutes to give you 30 minutes to review questions that you have marked.
   c. Before beginning the multiple-choice questions, prepare a Gleim Time Management Sheet as recommended in Study Unit 7 of *CMA Review: A System for Success*.

2. **Answer the questions in consecutive order.**
   a. Do **not** agonize over any one item. Stay within your time budget.
   b. Mark any questions you are unsure of and return to them later as time allows.
   c. Never leave a multiple-choice question unanswered. Make your best educated guess in the time allowed. Remember that your score is based on the number of correct responses. You will not be penalized for guessing incorrectly.

3.   **For each multiple-choice question,**

    a.   **Try to ignore the answer choices.** Do not allow the answer choices to affect your reading of the question.

        1)   If four answer choices are presented, three of them are incorrect. These choices are called **distractors** for good reason. Often, distractors are written to appear correct at first glance until further analysis.

        2)   In computational items, the distractors are carefully calculated such that they are the result of making common mistakes. Be careful, and double-check your computations if time permits.

    b.   **Read the question** carefully to determine the precise requirement.

        1)   Focusing on what is required enables you to ignore extraneous information, to focus on the relevant facts, and to proceed directly to determining the correct answer.

            a)   Be especially careful to note when the requirement is an **exception**; e.g., "All of the following statements regarding a company's internal rate of return are true **except**:"

    c.   **Determine the correct answer** before looking at the answer choices.

    d.   **Read the answer choices carefully.**

        1)   Even if the first answer appears to be the correct choice, do **not** skip the remaining answer choices. Questions often ask for the "best" of the choices provided. Thus, each choice requires your consideration.

        2)   Treat each answer choice as a true/false question as you analyze it.

    e.   **Click on the best answer.**

        1)   You have a 25% chance of answering the question correctly by blindly guessing.

        2)   For many multiple-choice questions, two answer choices can be eliminated with minimal effort, thereby increasing an educated guess to a 50-50 proposition.

    f.   As you answer a question, you can mark it by pressing the "Mark" button or unmark a marked question by pressing the "Marked" button. After you have answered, marked, or looked at and not answered all 100 questions, you will be presented with a review screen that shows how many questions you did not answer and how many you marked. You then have the option of revisiting all of the unanswered questions and "marked" questions.

        1)   Go back to the marked questions and finalize your answer choices.

        2)   Verify that all questions have been answered.

    g.   **If you don't know the answer:**

        1)   Again, guess; but make it an educated guess, which means select the best possible answer. First, rule out answers that you think are incorrect. Second, speculate on what the ICMA is looking for and/or the rationale behind the question. Third, select the best answer or guess between equally appealing answers. Your first guess is usually the most intuitive. If you cannot make an educated guess, read the stem and each answer and pick the best or most intuitive answer. It's just a guess!

        2)   Make sure you accomplish this step within your predetermined time budget per testlet.

ESSAY QUESTIONS

Each part of the CMA exam contains two essays. You have at least 1 hour to complete both. If you finish your multiple-choice questions section in less than 3 hours, your remaining time will be carried over to the essay section and added to the standard 1-hour allocation. Essay questions that require a purely written answer will have a box in which to type your response. For certain problems that require quantitative responses, you will be able to use a spreadsheet tool to present your calculations. Complete instructions and the ICMA's recommendations regarding the use of the spreadsheet function can be found at www.prometric.com/ICMA/demo.htm.

The following example shows a typical essay question that does not require a quantitative answer.

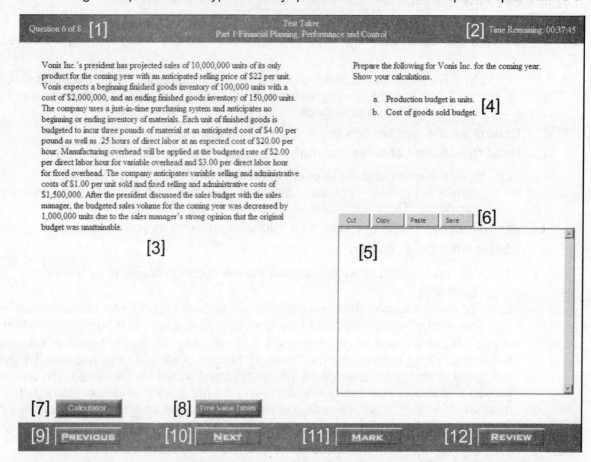

1. Question Number: The question number indicates which question the candidate is answering out of the total questions in both scenarios.

2. Time Remaining: This information box displays to the candidate how long (s)he has remaining to complete and review the essays. Consistently check the amount of time remaining in order to stay on schedule.

3. Scenario: This section displays the content of the current essay's scenario.

4. Question: This section displays the content of the current question the candidate is answering.

5. Answer Box: This area is where the candidate types in his/her response to the current question.

6. Word Processing Tools: These icons, when selected, enable the candidate to cut, copy, paste, and save the content of his/her response (much like a standard word processing program).

7. Calculator: The calculator provided is a basic tool for simple computations. It is similar to calculators used in common software programs.

8. Time Value Tables: This function allows the examinee to access Present/Future Time Value Tables as needed.

9. Previous: This navigation button allows the candidate to move back to the previous question.

10. Next: This navigation button allows the candidate to move ahead to the next question.

11. Mark: This button allows the candidate to mark a question for later review.

12. Review: Clicking this button takes the candidate to the Review screen, which contains a scrollable listing of all the question numbers and indicates if the question has been marked for review, completed, or skipped.

The following example shows a typical essay question that requires a quantitative answer. Note that many of the buttons and functions are the same as in the non-quantitative questions; these have not been explained again below.

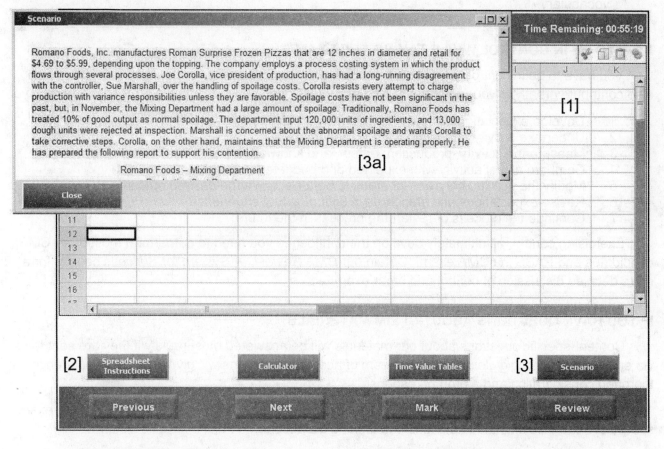

1. CMA Spreadsheet: This is the area where the candidate types in his/her response to a question that requires computations. Remember that the CMA spreadsheet is NOT Excel. Therefore, even candidates who are extremely proficient in Excel need to practice with the CMA spreadsheets.

2. Spreadsheet Instructions: The spreadsheet instructions detail the different functions and tools available in the CMA spreadsheet.

3. Scenario: Clicking this button opens a pop-up window (see [3a]) that shows the content of the current essay's scenario.

DING

en-response questions will not be graded online, and therefore, you will not immediately ... grade. The questions will be graded by subject matter experts, and partial credit will be given. For example, if you are asked to give three reasons why a selected alternative action is good for a business and you provide only two correct reasons, you will receive partial credit for these two responses. Likewise, for questions requiring a calculated response, partial credit will be given for a correct formula even though a mathematical error may have been made in the final number.

The ICMA grades candidates on both subject matter and writing skills on the essay portion of the CMA exam. For writing skills to be graded, the response must be relevant to the question asked. The specific criteria for the ICMA's grading are as follows:

Use of standard English – includes proper grammar, punctuation, and spelling.

Organization – response is arranged logically and coherently.

Clarity – analysis is clearly communicated with well-constructed sentences and appropriate vocabulary.

HOW TO BE IN CONTROL WHILE TAKING THE EXAM

You have to be in control to be successful during exam preparation and execution. Control can also contribute greatly to your personal and other professional goals. Control is a process whereby you

1. Develop expectations, standards, budgets, and plans
2. Undertake activity, production, study, and learning
3. Measure the activity, production, output, and knowledge
4. Compare actual activity with expected and budgeted activity
5. Modify the activity, behavior, or study to better achieve the desired outcome
6. Revise expectations and standards in light of actual experience
7. Continue the process or restart the process in the future

Exercising control will ultimately develop the confidence you need to outperform most other CMA candidates and PASS the CMA exam! Obtain our *CMA Review: A System for Success* booklet for a more detailed discussion of control and other exam tactics.

IF YOU HAVE QUESTIONS ABOUT GLEIM MATERIALS

Content-specific questions about our materials will be answered most rapidly if they are sent to us via email to accounting@gleim.com. Our team of accounting experts will give your correspondence thorough consideration and a prompt response.

Questions regarding the information in this Introduction (study suggestions, studying plans, exam specifics) should be emailed to personalcounselor@gleim.com.

Questions concerning orders, prices, shipments, or payments should be sent via email to customerservice@gleim.com and will be promptly handled by our competent and courteous customer service staff.

For technical support, you may use our automated technical support service at www.gleim.com/support, email us at support@gleim.com, or call us at (800) 874-5346.

STUDY UNIT ONE
ETHICS FOR MANAGEMENT ACCOUNTANTS
AND COST MANAGEMENT CONCEPTS

(21 pages of outline)

1.1	Ethics for Management Accountants	18
1.2	Cost Management Terminology	21
1.3	Cost Behavior and Relevant Range	24
1.4	Cost of Goods Calculations	27
1.5	Cost Classification	28
1.6	Costing Techniques	31
1.7	Core Concepts	35
1.8	Essay Questions	51

Ethics for Management Accountants

Global competition and economic uncertainty are placing stress on accounting and finance professionals to compromise ethical principles. A report released in May 2012 by the American Institute of Certified Public Accountants and the Chartered Institute of Management Accountants (UK) found a weakened "tone from the top" and more pressure on financial professionals – especially in emerging economies – to act unethically.

Maintaining a sense of ethical commitment is an extremely serious responsibility for Certified Management Accountants. The IMA's requirements for all members in this area are found in its *Statement on Ethical Professional Practice*, issued in August 2005. The CMA exam tests not only the contents of the Statement itself, but also requires the candidate to imagine him or herself in a realistic ethical dilemma and determine how best to resolve it.

Cost Management

Cost management is at the heart of the field of management accounting. Thus, the CMA exam places great emphasis on this area of study. The candidate will face many questions involving numerical calculations and others requiring a knowledge of cost terminology and the implications of cost management decisions.

This study unit is the **first of four** on **cost management**. The relative weight assigned to this major topic in Part 1 of the exam is **25%**. The four study units are

Study Unit 1: Ethics for Management Accountants and Cost Management Concepts
Study Unit 2: Cost Accumulation Systems
Study Unit 3: Cost Allocation Techniques
Study Unit 4: Operational Efficiency and Business Process Performance

After studying the outline and answering the questions in this study unit, you will have the skills necessary to address the following topics listed in the ICMA's Learning Outcome Statements:

<u>Part 1 – Section E. Ethical considerations for management accounting and financial management professionals</u>

Ethics may be tested in conjunction with any topic area.

1.   Provisions of IMA's *Statement of Ethical Professional Practice*
2.   Evaluation and resolution of ethical issues

Using the standards outlined in IMA's *Statement of Ethical Professional Practice*, the candidate should be able to:

a.   identify and describe the four overarching ethical principles

b.   evaluate a given business situation for its ethical implications

c.   identify and describe relevant standards that may have been violated in a given business situation and explain why the specific standards are applicable

d.   recommend a course of action for management accountants or financial managers to take when confronted with an ethical dilemma in the business environment

e.   evaluate and propose resolutions for ethical issues such as fraudulent reporting, manipulation of analyses, results, and budgets

<u>Part 1 – Section C.1. Measurement concepts</u>

The candidate should be able to:

a.   demonstrate an understanding of the behavior of fixed and variable costs in the long and short terms and how a change in assumptions regarding cost type or relevant range affects these costs

> *Statements b. through d. are covered in Study Unit 2.*
> *Statements e. through l. are covered in Study Unit 3.*

1.1 ETHICS FOR MANAGEMENT ACCOUNTANTS

> CMA candidates need to be prepared to answer ethics questions that will be integrated with any of the other topics tested on Part 1: Financial Planning, Performance, and Control. Ethics may be tested in either or both the multiple-choice and essay sections of Part 1. In the essay format, these questions will not only require the candidate to identify the exact nature of the ethical dilemma, but also how the professional facing the dilemma should resolve it. It is thus imperative that candidates memorize IMA's *Statement on Ethical Professional Practice*. Like all other topics, ethics is eligible for testing at all three levels of difficulty.

1.   **IMA's *Statement of Ethical Professional Practice***

a.   The *Statement* contains four overarching principles, which can be remembered with the mnemonic HFOR.

1)   Honesty
2)   Fairness
3)   Objectivity
4)   Responsibility

b.   The *Statement* also contains four specific standards, which can be remembered with the mnemonic CCIC.

1)   Competence
2)   Confidentiality
3)   Integrity
4)   Credibility

    c.   The final section, Resolution of Ethical Conflict, is especially significant and has been the subject of many CMA examination questions over the years.

        1)   One of the most common questions asked deals with the individual to whom an ethical challenge should be reported.

        2)   The IMA has an ethics hotline for members who wish to discuss ethical conflicts. It is reached at 800-245-1383.

    d.   Adherence to these provisions is integral to achieving the objectives of management accounting.

        1)   Management accountants shall not commit acts contrary to the *Statement*, nor shall they condone the commission of such acts by others within their organization.

2.   **Conflicts of Interest**

    a.   One of the provisions of the IMA *Statement* enjoins members to mitigate actual, and to avoid apparent, conflicts of interest.

        1)   A conflict of interest is a conflict between the personal and the official responsibilities of a person in a position of trust, sufficient to affect judgment, independence, or objectivity in conducting the affairs of the business.

    b.   Examples of a conflict of interest include

        1)   Having a substantial financial interest in a supplier, customer, or distributor; and

        2)   Using privileged information gained from one's official position to enter transactions for personal gain.

    c.   Methods for control of a conflict of interest include the following:

        1)   Provide a code of conduct provision applying to conflicts of interest. The code of conduct should say that employees are to refrain from engaging in any activity that would prejudice their ability to carry out their duties ethically.

        2)   Require full financial disclosure by all managers.

        3)   Require prior notification of any transaction that may raise a question about a possible conflict of interest. The Code says that all parties should be notified of the potential conflict.

        4)   Prohibit financial ties to any supplier, customer, or distributor.

        5)   Encourage adherence to strong ethical behavior in corporate actions, policies, and public communications.

        6)   Employees should refuse any gift, favor, or hospitality that would influence or would appear to influence their actions.

            a)   For example, in one case, an auditor accepted a loan from an auditee. The auditee was not trying to influence the auditor, but when it later was discovered that the auditee had committed a fraud and the auditor had not caught the fraud, the court's conclusion was that the auditor was guilty. To have refused the favor would have kept the auditor out of prison, but once he accepted the favor, there was a perception that he had allowed his judgment to be influenced.

3.   **Ethics on Part 1 of the CMA Exam**

    a.   CMA candidates should essentially memorize the entire contents of IMA's *Statement of Ethical Professional Practice* and be able to apply its provisions in evaluating and proposing resolutions for ethical issues, such as fraudulent reporting, manipulation of financial analyses, financial statement results, and/or budgets.

IMA STATEMENT OF ETHICAL PROFESSIONAL PRACTICE

Members of IMA shall behave ethically. A commitment to ethical professional practice includes: overarching principles that express our values, and standards that guide our conduct.

PRINCIPLES

IMA's overarching ethical principles include: Honesty, Fairness, Objectivity, and Responsibility. Members shall act in accordance with these principles and shall encourage others within their organizations to adhere to them.

STANDARDS

A member's failure to comply with the following standards may result in disciplinary action.

I. COMPETENCE

Each member has a responsibility to:

1. Maintain an appropriate level of professional expertise by continually developing knowledge and skills.
2. Perform professional duties in accordance with relevant laws, regulations, and technical standards.
3. Provide decision support information and recommendations that are accurate, clear, concise, and timely.
4. Recognize and communicate professional limitations or other constraints that would preclude responsible judgment or successful performance of an activity.

II. CONFIDENTIALITY

Each member has a responsibility to:

1. Keep information confidential except when disclosure is authorized or legally required.
2. Inform all relevant parties regarding appropriate use of confidential information. Monitor subordinates' activities to ensure compliance.
3. Refrain from using confidential information for unethical or illegal advantage.

III. INTEGRITY

Each member has a responsibility to:

1. Mitigate actual conflicts of interest. Regularly communicate with business associates to avoid apparent conflicts of interest. Advise all parties of any potential conflicts.
2. Refrain from engaging in any conduct that would prejudice carrying out duties ethically.
3. Abstain from engaging in or supporting any activity that might discredit the profession.

IV. CREDIBILITY

Each member has a responsibility to:

1. Communicate information fairly and objectively.
2. Disclose all relevant information that could reasonably be expected to influence an intended user's understanding of the reports, analyses, or recommendations.
3. Disclose delays or deficiencies in information, timeliness, processing, or internal controls in conformance with organization policy and/or applicable law.

RESOLUTION OF ETHICAL CONFLICT

In applying the Standards of Ethical Professional Practice, you may encounter problems in identifying unethical behavior or in resolving an ethical conflict. When faced with ethical issues, you should follow your organization's established policies on the resolution of such conflict. If these policies do not resolve the ethical conflict, you should consider the following courses of action:

1. Discuss the issue with your immediate superior except when it appears that the supervisor is involved. In that case, present the issue to the next level. If you cannot achieve a satisfactory resolution, submit the issue to the next management level. If your immediate superior is the chief executive officer or equivalent, the acceptable reviewing authority may be a group such as the audit committee, executive committee, board of directors, board of trustees, or owners. Contact with levels above the immediate superior should be initiated only with your superior's knowledge, assuming he or she is not involved. Communication of such problems to authorities or individuals not employed or engaged by the organization is not considered appropriate, unless you believe there is a clear violation of the law.

2. Clarify relevant ethical issues by initiating a confidential discussion with an IMA Ethics Counselor or other impartial advisor to obtain a better understanding of possible courses of action.

3. Consult your own attorney as to legal obligations and rights concerning the ethical conflict.

IMA Ethics Helpline Number: 800-245-1383

---

    b.   CMA candidates should be able to apply the provisions of IMA's *Statement of Ethical Professional Practice* in recommending a course of action for management accountants to follow when confronted with an ethical dilemma in the business environment.

        1)   A memorization of the "resolution" section of the *Statement* will enable the candidate to answer questions of this nature.

Stop and review! You have completed the outline for this subunit. Study multiple-choice questions 1 through 6 beginning on page 38.

1.2 COST MANAGEMENT TERMINOLOGY

1.   **Subdisciplines of Accounting**

    a.   **Financial accounting** is concerned principally with reporting to external users, usually through a set of financial statements produced in accordance with GAAP. Financial accounting thus has a historical focus.

    b.   **Management accounting** is concerned principally with reporting to internal users. The management accountant's goal is to produce reports that improve organizational decision making. Management accounting is thus future-oriented.

    c.   **Cost accounting** supports both financial and management accounting. Information about the cost of resources acquired and consumed by an organization underlies effective reporting for both internal and external users.

2.   **Basic Definitions**

    a.   A cost is defined by the IMA in two senses:

        1)   "In management accounting, a measurement in monetary terms of the amount of resources used for some purpose. The term by itself is not operational. It becomes operational when modified by a term that defines the purpose, such as acquisition cost, incremental cost, or fixed cost."

2)   "In financial accounting, the sacrifice measured by the price paid or required to be paid to acquire goods or services. The term 'cost' is often used when referring to the valuation of a good or service acquired. When 'cost' is used in this sense, a cost is an asset. When the benefits of the acquisition (the goods or services) expire, the cost becomes an expense or loss."

b.   A **cost object** is any entity to which costs can be attached.

1)   Examples are products, processes, employees, departments, and facilities.

c.   A **cost driver** is the basis used to assign costs to a cost object.

1)   Cost driver is defined by the IMA as "a measure of activity, such as direct labor hours, machine hours, beds occupied, computer time used, flight hours, miles driven, or contracts, that is a causal factor in the incurrence of cost to an entity."

2)   The key aspect of a cost driver is the existence of a direct cause-and-effect relationship between the quantity of the driver consumed and the amount of total cost.

3.   **Manufacturing vs. Nonmanufacturing**

a.   The costs of manufacturing a product can be classified as one of three types:

1)   **Direct materials** are those tangible inputs to the manufacturing process that can practicably be traced to the product, e.g., sheet metal welded together for a piece of heavy equipment.

   a)   In addition to the purchase price, all costs of bringing raw materials to the production line, e.g., transportation-in, are included in the cost of direct materials.

2)   **Direct labor** is the cost of human labor that can practicably be traced to the product, e.g., the wages of the welder.

3)   **Manufacturing overhead** consists of all costs of manufacturing that are not direct materials or direct labor.

   a)   **Indirect materials** are tangible inputs to the manufacturing process that cannot practicably be traced to the product, e.g., the welding compound used to put together a piece of heavy equipment, or staples used in a stapling machine.

   b)   **Indirect labor** is the cost of human labor connected with the manufacturing process that cannot practicably be traced to the product, e.g., the wages of assembly line supervisors and janitorial staff.

   c)   **Factory operating costs**, such as utilities, real estate taxes, insurance, depreciation on factory equipment, etc.

b.   Manufacturing costs are often grouped into the following classifications:

1)   **Prime cost** equals direct materials plus direct labor, i.e., those costs directly attributable to a product.

2)   **Conversion cost** equals direct labor plus manufacturing overhead, i.e., the costs of converting raw materials into the finished product.

c.   Operating a manufacturing concern requires the incurrence of nonmanufacturing costs:

1)   **Selling (marketing) expenses** are those costs incurred in getting the product from the factory to the consumer, e.g., sales personnel salaries, advertising, and product transportation.

2)   **Administrative expenses** are those costs incurred by a company not directly related to producing or marketing the product, e.g., executive salaries and depreciation on the headquarters building.

4. **Product vs. Period**

   a.   One of the most important classifications a management accountant can make is whether to capitalize a cost as part of finished goods inventory or to expense it as incurred.

      1) **Product costs** (also called inventoriable costs) are capitalized as part of finished goods inventory. They eventually become a component of cost of goods sold.

      2) **Period costs** are expensed as incurred, i.e., they are not capitalized in finished goods inventory and are thus excluded from cost of goods sold.

         a) The theory is that period costs are caused by the passage of time and would occur even if production was zero.

   b.   This distinction is crucial because of the required treatment of manufacturing costs for external financial reporting purposes.

      1) For **external financial reporting**, all manufacturing costs (direct materials, direct labor, variable overhead, and fixed overhead) must be treated as product costs, and all selling and administrative (S&A) costs must be treated as period costs.

         a) This approach is called **absorption costing** (also called full costing).

      2) For **internal reporting**, a more informative accounting treatment is often to capitalize only variable manufacturing costs as product costs, and treat all other costs (variable S&A and the fixed portion of both production and S&A expenses) as period costs.

         a) This approach is called **variable costing** (also called direct costing).

      3) The following table summarizes these two approaches:

	Absorption Costing (Required under GAAP)	**Variable Costing (For Internal Reporting Only)**
Product Costs (Included in Cost of Goods Sold)	Variable production costs	
	Fixed production costs	
Period Costs		Fixed production costs
	Variable S&A expenses	
(Excluded from Cost of Goods Sold)	Fixed S&A expenses	

         a) These treatments are explained more fully in item 1. in Subunit 6.

5. **Direct vs. Indirect**

   a.   Costs can be classified by how they are assigned to cost objects.

      1) **Direct costs** are ones that can be associated with a particular cost object in an economically feasible way, i.e., they can be traced to that object.

         a) Examples are the direct materials and direct labor inputs to a manufacturing process discussed in item 3.a. on the previous page.

      2) **Indirect costs** are ones that cannot be associated with a particular cost object in an economically feasible way and thus must be allocated to that object.

         a) Examples are the indirect materials and indirect labor inputs to a manufacturing process discussed in item 3.a.3) on the previous page.

            i) To simplify the allocation process, indirect costs are often collected in cost pools.

         b) A **cost pool** is an account into which a variety of similar cost elements with a common cause are accumulated.

            i) It is preferable for all the costs in a cost pool to have the same cost driver.

            ii) Manufacturing overhead is a commonly used cost pool into which various untraceable costs of the manufacturing process are accumulated prior to being allocated.

3) **Common costs** are another notable type of indirect cost. A common cost is one shared by two or more users.

   a) The key to common costs is that, since they cannot be directly traced to the users that generate the costs, they must be allocated using some systematic and rational basis.

   b) An example is depreciation or rent on the headquarters building. This is a direct cost when treating the building as a whole, but is a common cost of the departments located in the building, and thus must be allocated when treating the individual departments.

Stop and review! You have completed the outline for this subunit. Study multiple-choice questions 7 through 13 beginning on page 40.

1.3 COST BEHAVIOR AND RELEVANT RANGE

1. **Relevant Range**

   a. The relevant range defines the limits within which per-unit variable costs remain constant and fixed costs are not changeable. It is synonymous with the short run.

   b. The relevant range is established by the efficiency of a company's current manufacturing plant, its agreements with labor unions and suppliers, etc.

2. **Variable Costs**

   a. **Variable cost per unit** remains constant in the short run regardless of the level of production.

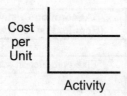

   b. **Variable costs in total**, on the other hand, vary directly and proportionally with changes in volume.

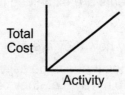

   c. EXAMPLE: A company requires one unit of direct material to be used in each finished good it produces.

Number of Outputs Produced	Input Cost per Unit	Total Cost of Inputs
0	$10	$ 0
100	$10	$ 1,000
1,000	$10	$ 10,000
5,000	$10	$ 50,000
10,000	$10	$100,000

3. **Fixed Costs**

   a. **Fixed costs in total** remain unchanged in the short run regardless of production level, e.g., the amount paid for an assembly line is the same even if production is halted entirely.

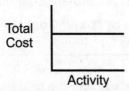

   b. **Fixed cost per unit**, on the other hand, varies indirectly with the activity level.

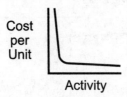

   c. EXAMPLE: The historical cost of the assembly line is settled, but its cost per unit decreases as production increases.

Number of Outputs Produced	Cost of Assembly Line	Per Unit Cost of Assembly Line
1	$1,000,000	$1,000,000
100	$1,000,000	$ 10,000
1,000	$1,000,000	$ 1,000
5,000	$1,000,000	$ 200
10,000	$1,000,000	$ 100

4. **Mixed (Semivariable) Costs**

   a. Mixed (semivariable) costs combine fixed and variable elements, e.g., rental expense on a car that carries a flat fee per month plus an additional fee for each mile driven.

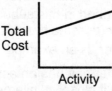

   b. EXAMPLE: The company rents a piece of machinery to make its production line more efficient. The rental is $150,000 per year plus $1 for every unit produced.

Number of Outputs Produced	Fixed Cost of Extra Machine	Variable Cost of Extra Machine	Total Cost of Extra Machine
0	$150,000	$ 0	$150,000
100	$150,000	$ 100	$150,100
1,000	$150,000	$ 1,000	$151,000
5,000	$150,000	$ 5,000	$155,000
10,000	$150,000	$10,000	$160,000

   c. Two methods of estimating mixed costs are in general use.

      1) The regression, or scattergraph, method is by far the more complex (and accurate) of the two and is beyond the scope of the CMA exam.

      2) The high-low method is the less accurate but quicker of the two methods.

d.   The first step in applying the high-low method is to isolate the variable portion of the cost.

1)   The difference in cost between the highest and lowest levels of activity for a group of periods is divided by the difference in the cost drivers (activity level) at the two levels (cost drivers are defined in item 2.c. in Subunit 1.2).

Variable Portion of Mixed Cost Using High-Low Method

$$\frac{\text{Cost at highest activity level} - \text{Cost at lowest activity level}}{\text{Driver at highest activity level} - \text{Driver at lowest activity level}}$$

2)   EXAMPLE: A company has the following cost data:

Month	Machine Hours	Maintenance Costs
April	1,000	$2,275
May	1,600	$3,400
June	1,200	$2,650
July	800	$1,900
August	1,200	$2,650
September	1,000	$2,275

$$\text{Variable portion} = \frac{\text{May cost} - \text{July cost}}{\text{May driver} - \text{July driver}} = \frac{\$3,400 - \$1,900}{1,600 - 800} = \frac{\$1,500}{800} = \$1.875 \text{ per machine hour}$$

e.   The fixed portion can now be calculated by inserting the appropriate values for either the high or low period in the range:

$$\begin{aligned}\text{Fixed portion} &= \text{Total cost} - \text{Variable portion} \\ &= \$1,900 - (800 \text{ machine hours} \times \$1.875 \text{ per hour}) \\ &= \$1,900 - \$1,500 \\ &= \$400\end{aligned}$$

f.   The firm can now use this information to project total cost at any level of activity; e.g., the expenditure of 1,300 machine hours will generate a probable total cost of $2,837.50 [$400 + (1,300 × $1.875)].

5.   **Linear vs. Nonlinear Cost Functions**

a.   Four of the five costs described in this subunit are linear-cost functions; i.e., they change at a constant rate (or remain unchanged) over the short run.

b.   Fixed cost per unit, however, is an example of a nonlinear-cost function.

1)   Note that fixed cost per unit has an asymptotic character with respect to the x-axis, approaching it closely while never intersecting it (it does intersect the y-axis at the zero level of activity). The function shows a high degree of variability over its range taken as a whole (see item 3.b. on the previous page).

2)   Another type of nonlinear-cost function is a step-cost function, one that is constant over small ranges of output but increases by steps (discrete amounts) as levels of activity increase.

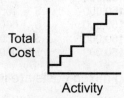

a)   Both fixed and variable costs can display step-cost characteristics. If the steps are relatively narrow, these costs are usually treated as variable. If the steps are wide, they are more akin to fixed costs.

3)   An example of a step cost would be the salary of production foremen. Operating at one shift per day might require one foreman, while two shifts would require two foremen.

6. **Relevant Range and Marginal Cost**

    a. Marginal cost is the cost incurred by a one-unit increase in the activity level of a particular cost driver.

        1) Necessarily then, marginal cost remains constant across the relevant range.

    b. Management accountants capture the concept of relevant range when they say that "All costs are variable in the long run."

        1) Investment in new, more productive equipment results in higher total fixed costs but may result in lower total and per-unit variable costs.

Stop and review! You have completed the outline for this subunit. Study multiple-choice questions 14 through 21 beginning on page 41.

1.4 COST OF GOODS CALCULATIONS

1. **Cost of Goods Sold**

    a. Cost of goods sold is a straightforward computation for a **retailer** because retailers have only a **single class of inventory**.

Beginning inventory	$XX,XXX
Add: purchases	X,XXX
Less: ending inventory	(X,XXX)
Cost of goods sold	**$XX,XXX**

2. **Cost of Goods Manufactured**

    a. The calculation is more complex for a **manufacturer** because manufacturers have **three distinct classes of inventory**.

    b. Cost of goods sold contains an additional component called cost of goods manufactured, analogous to the retailer's purchases account.

Beginning work-in-process inventory	$XX,XXX
Add: total manufacturing costs	X,XXX
Less: ending work-in-process inventory	(X,XXX)
Cost of goods manufactured	**$XX,XXX**

    c. Total manufacturing costs are calculated on a separate statement called a Cost of Goods Manufactured Statement (or sometimes simply the Manufacturing Statement). The statement compiles the three major elements of manufacturing cost: new materials, direct labor, and factory overhead.

3. **Comparison**

Cost of goods sold for a retailer:

Beginning inventory		$ XXX,XXX
Add: Purchases	$X,XXX,XXX	
Less: Returns and discounts	(XX,XXX)	
Net purchases	X,XXX,XXX	
Add: Freight-in	XX,XXX	X,XXX,XXX
Goods available for sale		X,XXX,XXX
Less: Ending inventory		(XXX,XXX)
Costs of goods sold		**$X,XXX,XXX**

Cost of goods sold for a manufacturer:

Beginning raw materials inventory			$ XXX,XXX
Add: Purchases	$X,XXX,XXX		
Less: Returns and discounts	(XX,XXX)		
Net purchases	X,XXX,XXX		
Add: Freight-in	XX,XXX	X,XXX,XXX	
Raw materials available for use		X,XXX,XXX	
Less: Ending raw materials inventory		(XXX,XXX)	
Direct materials used in production			$X,XXX,XXX
Direct labor costs			X,XXX,XXX
Manufacturing overhead costs			XXX,XXX
Total manufacturing costs for the period			**X,XXX,XXX**
Add: Beginning work-in-process inventory			XXX,XXX
Less: Ending work-in-process inventory			(XXX,XXX)
Costs of goods manufactured			**X,XXX,XXX**
Add: Beginning finished goods inventory			XXX,XXX
Goods available for sale			**X,XXX,XXX**
Less: Ending finished goods inventory			(XXX,XXX)
Costs of goods sold			**$X,XXX,XXX**

    a. Note that in the comparison above, the calculations down through cost of goods manufactured would appear on the Manufacturing Statement. That total and the remainder of the illustration would be on the income statement.

Stop and review! You have completed the outline for this subunit. Study multiple-choice questions 22 through 27 beginning on page 44.

1.5 COST CLASSIFICATION

1. **Controllable vs. Noncontrollable**

    a. **Controllable costs** are those that are under the discretion of a particular manager. **Noncontrollable costs** are those to which another level of the organization has committed, removing the manager's discretion.

    b. In other words, controllability is determined at different levels of the organization; it is not inherent in the nature of a given cost.

        1) For example, an outlay for new machinery may be controllable to the division vice president but noncontrollable to a plant manager or lower-level manager.

2. **Avoidable vs. Committed**

    a. **Avoidable costs** are those that may be eliminated by not engaging in an activity or by performing it more efficiently. An example is direct materials cost, which can be saved by ceasing production.

    b. **Committed costs** arise from holding property, plant, and equipment. Examples are insurance, real estate taxes, lease payments, and depreciation. They are by nature long-term and cannot be reduced by lowering the short-term level of production.

3. **Incremental vs. Differential**

    a. **Incremental cost** is the additional cost inherent in a given decision. **Differential cost** is the difference in total cost between two decisions.

    b. EXAMPLE: A company must choose between introducing two new product lines.

        1) The incremental choice of the first option is the initial investment of $1.5 million; the incremental choice of the second option is the initial investment of $1.8 million.

        2) The differential cost of the two choices is $300,000.

    c. In practice, these two terms are often used interchangeably.

4. **Engineered vs. Discretionary**

    a. **Engineered costs** are those having a direct, observable, quantifiable cause-and-effect relationship between the level of output and the quantity of resources consumed.

        1) Examples are direct materials and direct labor.

    b. **Discretionary costs** are those characterized by an uncertainty in the degree of causation between the level of output and the quantity of resources consumed. They tend to be the subject of a periodic (e.g., annual) outlay decision.

        1) Examples are advertising and R&D costs. Some routine maintenance costs might also fit this classification.

5. **Outlay vs. Opportunity**

    a. **Outlay costs** require actual cash disbursements. They are also called explicit, accounting, or out-of-pocket costs.

        1) An example is the tuition payment required to attend college.

    b. **Opportunity cost** is the maximum benefit forgone by using a scarce resource for a given purpose and not for the next-best alternative. It is also called implicit cost.

        1) An example is the wages foregone by attending college instead of working full-time.

    c. **Economic cost** is the sum of explicit and implicit costs.

    d. **Imputed costs** are those that should be involved in decision making even though no transaction has occurred that would be routinely recognized in the accounts. They are a type of opportunity cost.

        1) An example is the profit lost as a result of being unable to fill orders because the inventory level is too low.

6. **Relevant vs. Sunk**

    a. **Relevant costs** are those future costs that will vary depending on the action taken. All other costs are assumed to be constant and thus have no effect on (are irrelevant to) the decision.

        1) An example is tuition that must be spent to attend a fourth year of college.

    b. **Sunk costs** are costs either already paid or irrevocably committed to incur. Because they are unavoidable and will therefore not vary with the option chosen, they are not relevant to future decisions.

        1) An example is 3 years of tuition already spent. The previous 3 years of tuition make no difference in the decision to attend a fourth year.

    c. **Historical cost** is the actual (explicit) price paid for an asset. Financial accountants rely heavily on it for balance sheet reporting.

        1) Because historical cost is a sunk cost, however, management accountants often find other (implicit) costs to be more useful in decision making.

7. **Joint vs. Separable**

    a. Often a manufacturing process involves processing a single input up to the point at which multiple end products become separately identifiable, called the **split-off point**.

        1) **Joint costs** are those costs incurred before the split-off point; i.e., since they are not traceable to the end products, they must be allocated.

           a) For example, the cost of a tree would be a joint cost for a lumber yard.

        2) **Separable costs** are those incurred beyond the split-off point, i.e., once separate products become identifiable.

        3) **By-products** are products of relatively small total value that are produced simultaneously from a common manufacturing process with products of greater value and quantity (joint products).

           a) For example, a lumber yard might have leftover lumber and sawdust that could be sold as by-products for a small amount.

    b. An example where joint costing is very important is petroleum refining.

        1) Costs incurred in bringing crude oil to the fractionating process are joint costs. The fractionating process is the split-off point.

        2) Once the oil has been refined into its separately identifiable end products (asphalt, diesel fuel, kerosene, etc.), all further costs are separable costs.

        3) If selling costs are lower than disposal costs, the sludge left over after the high-value products have been processed may be sold as a cheap lubricant. It is considered a by-product.

8.   **Normal vs. Abnormal Spoilage**

    a.   **Normal spoilage** is the spoilage that occurs under normal operating conditions. It is essentially uncontrollable in the short run.

        1)   Since normal spoilage is expected under efficient operations, it is treated as a product cost; that is, it is absorbed into the cost of the good output.

    b.   **Abnormal spoilage** is spoilage that is not expected to occur under normal, efficient operating conditions. The cost of abnormal spoilage should be separately identified and reported to management.

        1)   Abnormal spoilage is typically treated as a period cost (a loss) because of its unusual nature.

9.   **Rework, Scrap, and Waste**

    a.   **Rework** consists of end products that do not meet standards of salability but can be brought to salable condition with additional effort.

        1)   The decision to rework or discard is based on whether the marginal revenue to be gained from selling the reworked units exceeds the marginal cost of performing the rework.

    b.   **Scrap** consists of raw material left over from the production cycle but still usable for purposes other than those for which it was originally intended.

        1)   Scrap may be used for a different production process or may be sold to outside customers, usually for a nominal amount.

    c.   **Waste** consists of raw material left over from the production cycle for which there is no further use.

        1)   Waste is not salable at any price and must be discarded.

10.   **Other Costs**

    a.   **Carrying costs** are the costs of storing or holding inventory. Examples include the cost of capital, insurance, warehousing, breakage, and obsolescence.

    b.   **Transferred-in costs** are those incurred in a preceding department and received in a subsequent department in a multi-departmental production setting.

    c.   **Value-adding costs** are the costs of activities that cannot be eliminated without reducing the quality, responsiveness, or quantity of the output required by a customer or the organization.

11.   **Manufacturing Capacity**

    a.   **Normal capacity** is the long-term average level of activity that will approximate demand over a period that includes seasonal, cyclical, and trend variations. Deviations in a given year will be offset in subsequent years.

    b.   **Practical capacity** is the maximum level at which output is produced efficiently. It allows for unavoidable delays in production for maintenance, holidays, etc. Use of practical capacity as a denominator value usually results in underapplied overhead because it always exceeds the actual level of use.

    c.   **Theoretical (ideal) capacity** is the maximum capacity assuming continuous operations with no holidays, downtime, etc.

Stop and review! You have completed the outline for this subunit. Study multiple-choice questions 28 through 35 beginning on page 47.

1.6 COSTING TECHNIQUES

1. **Absorption vs. Variable Costing**

   a. **Absorption costing** (sometimes called full costing or full absorption costing) treats all manufacturing costs as product costs.

      1) The inventoried cost of the product thus includes all production costs, whether variable or fixed. This technique is required for external financial reporting and for income tax purposes.

      2) **Gross margin** (also called gross profit) is the net difference between sales revenue and absorption cost of goods sold. It represents the amount available to cover selling and administrative expenses.

   b. **Variable costing** (also called direct costing) considers only variable manufacturing costs to be product costs, i.e., inventoriable (the phrase "direct costing" is considered misleading because it implies traceability).

      1) Fixed manufacturing costs are considered period costs and are thus expensed as incurred. This technique is not allowed for external financial reporting but is very useful for internal decision making.

      2) **Contribution margin** is the net of sales revenue minus all variable costs (both manufacturing and S&A). It represents the amount available to cover fixed costs.

   c. The illustration below highlights the differing treatment of the four main categories of cost.

      1) The accounting for variable production costs and fixed selling and administrative expenses is identical under the two methods.

      2) The difference lies in the varying treatment of fixed production costs and variable selling and administrative expenses.

Legend	Cost Component
(a)	Variable production costs
(b)	Fixed production costs
(c)	Variable selling and administrative expenses
(d)	Fixed selling and administrative expenses

		Absorption Costing (Required for ext. rptg.)	Variable Costing (For internal reporting only)
	Sales	$X,XXX	$X,XXX
	Beg. finished goods inventory	$X,XXX	$X,XXX
Product Costs	Add: variable production costs	X,XXX (a)	X,XXX (a)
	Add: fixed production costs	X,XXX (b)	-
	Goods available for sale	$X,XXX	$X,XXX
	Less: end. finished goods inventory	(X,XXX)	(XXX)
	Cost of goods sold	**$(X,XXX)**	**$(X,XXX)**
	Less: variable S&A expenses	-	(XXX) (c)
	Gross margin (abs.) / Contribution margin (var.)	**$X,XXX**	**$X,XXX**
Period Costs	Less: fixed production costs	-	(X,XXX) (b)
	Less: variable S&A expenses	(XXX) (c)	-
	Less: fixed S&A expenses	(XXX) (d)	(XXX) (d)
	Operating income	**$X,XXX**	**$X,XXX**

   d. Note that operating income will differ between the two methods due to the different treatment of fixed production costs.

2.   **Actual vs. Normal Costing**

    a.   **Actual costing** is the most accurate method of accumulating costs in a cost accounting system. However, it is also the least timely and most volatile method.

        1)   After the end of the production period, all actual costs incurred for a cost object are totaled; indirect costs are allocated.

        2)   Because per-unit costs depend on the level of production in a period, large fluctuations arise from period to period. This volatility can lead to the reporting of misleading financial information.

    b.   **Normal costing** charges actual direct materials and direct labor to a cost object (i.e., a specific product or a production department) but applies overhead on the basis of budgeted (normalized) rates. This compensates for the fluctuations in unit cost inherent in actual costing.

    c.   **Extended normal costing** extends the use of normalized rates to direct material and direct labor, so that all three major input categories use normalized rates.

3.   **Accumulating Manufacturing Costs**

    a.   **Job-order costing** is appropriate when producing products with individual characteristics or when identifiable groupings are possible.

        1)   Costs are attached to specific "jobs." Each job will result in a single, identifiable end product.

        2)   Examples are any industry that generates custom-built products, such as shipbuilding or a sign shop.

    b.   **Process costing** is used when similar products are mass produced on a continuous basis.

        1)   Costs are attached to specific departments or phases of production. Examples are automobile and candy manufacturing.

        2)   Since costs are attached to streams of products rather than individual items, process costing involves calculating an average cost for all units. The two widely used methods are weighted-average and first-in, first-out (FIFO).

        3)   Some units remain unfinished at the end of the period. For each department to adequately account for the costs attached to its unfinished units, the units, called work-in-process, must be restated in terms of equivalent units of production (EUP).

    c.   **Activity-based costing (ABC)** attaches costs to activities rather than to physical goods.

        1)   ABC is a response to the distortions of product cost information brought about by peanut-butter costing, which is the inaccurate averaging or spreading of costs like peanut butter over products or service units that use different amounts of resources.

            a)   A major cause of the problems associated with peanut-butter costing is the significant increase in indirect costs brought about by the increasing use of technology.

2) The difference between traditional (that is, volume-based) costing systems and ABC can be summarized as follows:

    a) Under volume-based systems, a single pool collects all indirect costs and the total cost in the pool is then allocated to production.

    b) Under ABC, by contrast, every activity that bears on the production process has its own cost pool. The costs in each pool are assigned based on a cost driver specific to the activity.

        i) For example, with a single pool, all costs may be assigned based on a single driver, such as machine hours or direct-labor hours.

        ii) Under ABC, a dozen different cost pools might be assigned on the basis of a dozen different cost drivers.

  d. **Life-cycle costing** emphasizes the need to price products to cover all the costs incurred over the lifespan of a product, not just the immediate costs of production.

    1) Costs incurred before production, such as R&D and product design, are referred to as upstream costs.

    2) Costs incurred after production, such as marketing and customer service, are called downstream costs.

4. **Standard Costing, Flexible Budgeting, and Variance Analysis**

  a. **Standard costing** is a system designed to alert management when the actual costs of production differ significantly from target ("standard") costs.

    1) Standard costs are predetermined, attainable unit costs. A standard cost is not just an average of past costs, but an objectively determined estimate of what a cost should be. It is similar to "par" on a golf course.

    2) Standard costs can be used with both job-order and process-costing systems.

  b. **Flexible budgeting** is the calculation of the quantity and cost of inputs that should have been consumed given the achieved level of production.

    1) Flexible budgeting supplements the **static budget**, which is the company's best projection of the resource consumption and levels of output that will be achieved for an upcoming period.

  c. The static and flexible budgets are compared to the actual results and the differences are calculated. These differences are referred to as variances.

    1) Variance analysis enables **management by exception**, the practice of giving attention primarily to significant deviations from expectations (whether favorable or unfavorable).

5. **Allocating Joint Costs**

  a. The **physical unit method** is the simplest. The total joint cost is allocated to the separable products in proportion to some physical measure, such as volume or weight. Total joint costs are multiplied by the following:

(Units of each product ÷ Total units)

  b. The **sales-value at split-off method** is based upon each of the separable products' relative proportion of total sales value ultimately attributable to the period's production. Total joint costs are multiplied by the following:

(Estimated selling price at split-off ÷ Total selling price at split-off)

c. The **estimated net realizable value method** is a variation of the relative sales value method. The significant difference is that, under the estimated NRV method, all separable costs necessary to make the product salable are subtracted before the allocation is made. Total joint costs are multiplied by the following:

[(Estimated final price – Separable costs) ÷ Total estimated final price]

d. The **constant gross-margin percentage NRV method** is based on using the same gross margin percentage for all of the products. There are three steps under this method:

1) Determine the overall gross-margin percentage.

2) Subtract the appropriate gross margin from the final sales value of each product to calculate total costs for that product.

3) Subtract the separable costs to arrive at the joint cost amount.

6. **Allocating Service Department Costs**

a. The **direct method** is the simplest but least accurate of the methods.

1) All service department costs are allocated directly to production departments. No allocation is made of the cost of services rendered to other service departments.

Direct Method

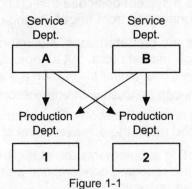

Figure 1-1

b. The **step-down method** is a sequential process. It is slightly more involved than the direct method but is more accurate.

1) The service departments are allocated in order, from the one that provides the most service to other service departments down to the one that provides the least.

2) As each allocation is performed, the costs of the service departments are allocated to both the remaining service departments and the production departments.

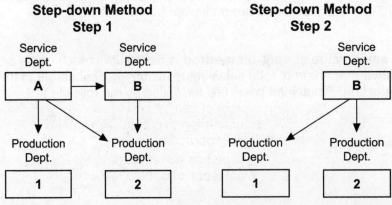

Figure 1-2

    c.   The **reciprocal method** is by far the most complex and most accurate of the three methods.

        1)   Simultaneous equations are used to allocate each service department's costs among all other service departments and production departments.

Reciprocal Method

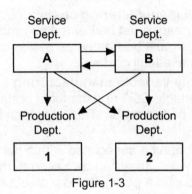

Figure 1-3

7. **Miscellaneous**

    a.   **Target costing** is the practice of calculating the price for a product by adding the desired unit profit margin to the total unit cost. It is an adjunct concept of target pricing.

        1)   For example, a furniture manufacturer might want to produce a sofa that sells for $600 and has a $200 profit margin. That means the cost can be no more than $400.

        2)   If the new-product development team says the expected cost will be more than $400, then the product will not be manufactured because, under target costing, the product is not a "sofa" but a "$600 sofa."

Stop and review! You have completed the outline for this subunit. Study multiple-choice questions 36 through 42 beginning on page 49.

1.7 CORE CONCEPTS

Ethics for Management Accountants

- IMA's *Statement of Ethical Professional Practice* requires members to act in accordance with four principles.

   - Competence, which requires expertise in the performance of the member's duties.
   - Confidentiality, which requires members not to share or divulge information gained during the course of their duties unless legally or professionally required to do so.
   - Integrity, which requires members to avoid actual and report potential conflicts of interest.
   - Credibility, which requires members to communicate information fairly and objectively.

Cost Management Terminology

- A **cost object** is any entity to which costs can be attached. A **cost driver** is the basis used to assign costs to a cost object. The cost driver is the cause of the cost.
- The **costs of manufacturing** a product can be classified as one of **three types**: direct materials, direct labor, and manufacturing overhead. Overhead typically consists of indirect materials, indirect labor, and factory operating costs.
- Manufacturing costs are often grouped as either **prime costs** (direct materials plus direct labor) or **conversion costs** (direct labor plus manufacturing overhead).

- ■ Operating a manufacturing concern also requires the incurrence of **nonmanufacturing costs**, consisting of selling (marketing) costs and administrative expenses.
- ■ **Product costs** (also called inventoriable costs) are capitalized as part of finished goods inventory. They eventually become a component of cost of goods sold. **Period costs** are expensed as incurred; i.e., they are not capitalized in finished goods inventory and are thus excluded from cost of goods sold.
- ■ For **external reporting, all manufacturing costs** (direct materials, direct labor, variable overhead, and fixed overhead) must be treated as product costs, and all selling and administrative (S&A) costs must be treated as period costs. This approach is called absorption costing (also called full costing).
- ■ For **internal reporting, only variable manufacturing costs** are capitalized as product costs. All other costs (variable S&A and the fixed portion of both production and S&A expenses) are treated as period costs. This approach is called variable costing (also called direct costing).
- ■ **Direct costs** are ones that can be associated with a particular cost object in an economically feasible way, i.e., they can be traced to that object. **Indirect costs** are ones that cannot be associated with a particular cost object in an economically feasible way and thus must be allocated to that object.
- ■ To simplify the allocation process, **indirect costs** are often collected in **cost pools**. A cost pool is an account into which a variety of similar cost elements with a common cause are accumulated. Manufacturing overhead is a commonly used example.

Cost Behavior and Relevant Range

- ■ The **relevant range** defines the limits within which per-unit variable costs remain constant and fixed costs are not changeable. It is synonymous with the short run.
  - • **Variable cost** per unit remains constant in the short run regardless of the level of production. Variable costs in total, on the other hand, vary directly and proportionally with changes in volume.
  - • **Fixed costs** in total remain unchanged in the short run regardless of production level. Fixed cost per unit, on the other hand, varies indirectly with the activity level.
  - • **Mixed (semivariable) costs** combine fixed and variable elements. The high-low method is used to separate the fixed and variable elements.
- ■ **Marginal cost** is the cost incurred by a one-unit increase in the activity level of a particular cost driver. Necessarily then, marginal cost remains constant across the relevant range.

Cost of Goods Calculations

- ■ Cost of goods sold is a straightforward computation for a **retailer** because retailers have only a single class of inventory.
- ■ The calculation is more complex for a **manufacturer** because manufacturers have three distinct classes of inventory: raw materials, work-in-process, and finished goods.
  - • The manufacturer's cost of goods manufactured is analogous to the retailer's purchases account.

Cost Classification

- Costs can be defined in **conceptual groupings**.

  - Controllable vs. noncontrollable costs
  - Avoidable vs. committed costs
  - Incremental vs. differential cost
  - Engineered vs. discretionary costs
  - Outlay vs. opportunity cost (explicit vs. implicit)
  - Economic vs. imputed cost
  - Relevant vs. sunk costs (historical cost is a sunk cost)

- **Manufacturing processes** their own particular cost groups.

  - Joint costs, separable costs, and by-products
  - Normal vs. abnormal spoilage
  - Rework, scrap, and waste

Costing Techniques

- **Absorption vs. Variable Costing**

  - Absorption costing treats all manufacturing costs as product costs. The inventoried cost of the product thus includes all production costs, whether variable or fixed. This technique is required for external reporting.

  - Variable costing considers only variable manufacturing costs to be product costs, i.e., inventoriable. Fixed manufacturing costs are considered period costs and are thus expensed as incurred. This technique is permitted for internal reporting only.

- **Normalized Costing**

  - Actual costing is the most accurate, but also the least timely and most volatile, method of accumulating costs.

  - Normal costing charges actual direct materials and direct labor to a cost object, but applies overhead on the basis of budgeted (normalized) rates.

  - Extended normal costing extends the use of normalized rates from only manufacturing overhead to include direct materials and direct labor, so that all three major input categories use normalized rates.

- **Cost Accumulation Systems**

  - Job-order costing for manufacturing customized products
  - Process costing for mass production
  - Activity-based costing (ABC) when overhead is a high proportion of the total cost
  - Life-cycle costing to track a product's lifetime costs

- **Standard costing** is a system designed to alert management when the actual costs of production differ significantly from target ("standard") costs. Standard costs are predetermined, attainable unit costs.

- Four methods for **allocating joint costs** are

  - Physical unit method
  - Sales-value at split-off method
  - Estimated net realizable value (NRV) method
  - Constant gross-margin percentage NRV method

- Three methods for **allocating service department costs** are in common use:

  - Direct method, which is the easiest to use
  - Step-down method, which is more reliable than the direct method
  - Reciprocal method, which is the most accurate but also the most complicated

QUESTIONS

1.1 Ethics for Management Accountants

1. At Key Enterprises, the controller is responsible for directing the budgeting process. In this role, the controller has significant influence with executive management as individual department budgets are modified and approved. For the current year, the controller was instrumental in the approval of a particular line manager's budget without modification, even though significant reductions were made to the budgets submitted by other line managers. As a token of appreciation, the line manager in question has given the controller a gift certificate for a popular local restaurant. In considering whether or not to accept the certificate, the controller should refer to which section of IMA's *Statement of Ethical Professional Practice*?

A. Competence.

B. Confidentiality.

C. Integrity.

D. Credibility.

Answer (C) is correct. *(CMA, adapted)*
REQUIRED: The ethical standard relevant to the controller's acceptance of a gift from a line manager.
DISCUSSION: The integrity standard requires an IMA member to "refrain from engaging in any conduct that would prejudice carrying out duties ethically."
Answer (A) is incorrect. The competence standard pertains to an IMA member's responsibility to maintain his/her professional skills and knowledge. It also pertains to the performance of activities in a professional manner. Answer (B) is incorrect. The confidentiality standard concerns an IMA member's responsibility not to disclose or use the firm's confidential information. Answer (D) is incorrect. Credibility is the fourth standard of IMA's *Statement of Ethical Professional Practice*. It requires that information be communicated "fairly and objectively," and that all information that could reasonably influence users be disclosed.

2. In accordance with IMA's *Statement of Ethical Professional Practice*, a member who fails to perform professional duties in accordance with relevant standards is acting contrary to which one of the following standards?

A. Competence.

B. Confidentiality.

C. Integrity.

D. Credibility.

Answer (A) is correct. *(CMA, adapted)*
REQUIRED: The ethical standard violated by a management accountant who fails to perform professional duties in accordance with relevant standards.
DISCUSSION: One of the responsibilities of an IMA member under the competence standard is to "maintain an appropriate level of professional expertise by continually developing knowledge and skills." (S)he must also "perform professional duties in accordance with relevant laws, regulations, and technical standards." The third requirement under this standard is to "provide decision support information and recommendations that are accurate, clear, concise, and timely."
Answer (B) is incorrect. The confidentiality standard concerns an IMA member's responsibility not to disclose or use the firm's confidential information. Answer (C) is incorrect. The integrity standard pertains to conflicts of interest, avoidance of acts discreditable to the profession, and refraining from activities that prejudice the ability to carry out duties ethically. Answer (D) is incorrect. Credibility is the fourth standard of IMA's *Statement of Ethical Professional Practice*. It requires that information be communicated "fairly and objectively," and that all information that could reasonably influence users be disclosed.

3. According to IMA's *Statement of Ethical Professional Practice*, a member has a responsibility to recognize professional limitations. Under which standard of ethical conduct would this responsibility be included?

A. Competence.

B. Confidentiality.

C. Integrity.

D. Credibility.

Answer (A) is correct. *(CMA, adapted)*
REQUIRED: The standard of ethical conduct related to the responsibility to recognize professional limitations.
DISCUSSION: The competence standard pertains to an IMA member's responsibility to "recognize and communicate professional limitations or other constraints that would preclude responsible judgment or successful performance of an activity."
Answer (B) is incorrect. The confidentiality standard concerns an IMA member's responsibility not to disclose or use the firm's confidential information. Answer (C) is incorrect. The integrity standard deals with conflicts of interest, avoidance of acts discreditable to the profession, and refraining from activities that prejudice the ability to carry out duties ethically. Answer (D) is incorrect. Credibility is the fourth standard of IMA's *Statement of Ethical Professional Practice*. It requires that information be communicated "fairly and objectively," and that all information that could reasonably influence users be disclosed.

4. If an IMA member has a problem in identifying unethical behavior or resolving an ethical conflict, the first action (s)he should normally take is to

   A. Consult the board of directors.

   B. Discuss the problem with his/her immediate superior.

   C. Notify the appropriate law enforcement agency.

   D. Resign from the company.

Answer (B) is correct. *(Publisher, adapted)*
   REQUIRED: The proper ethical behavior by an IMA member.
   DISCUSSION: IMA's *Statement of Ethical Professional Practice* states that the member should first discuss an ethical problem with his/her immediate superior. If the superior is involved, the problem should be taken initially to the next higher managerial level.
   Answer (A) is incorrect. The board would be consulted initially only if the immediate superior is the chief executive officer and that person is involved in the ethical conflict. Answer (C) is incorrect. An IMA member should keep information confidential except when disclosure is authorized or legally required. Answer (D) is incorrect. Resignation is a last resort.

5. If an IMA member discovers unethical conduct in his/her organization and fails to act, (s)he will be in violation of which of IMA's ethical standard(s)?

   A. "Refrain from engaging in any conduct that would prejudice carrying out duties correctly."

   B. "Communicate information fairly and objectively."

   C. "Disclose all relevant information that could reasonably be expected to influence an intended user's understanding of reporting analyses or recommendations."

   D. All of the answers are correct.

Answer (D) is correct. *(Publisher, adapted)*
   REQUIRED: The ethical standard(s) violated by failure to disclose unethical behavior.
   DISCUSSION: An IMA member displays his/her competence and credibility and maintains integrity by taking the appropriate action within the organization to resolve an ethical problem. All of these activities should be a part of an IMA member's normal job processes.

6. IMA's *Statement of Ethical Professional Practice* requires an IMA member to follow the established policies of the organization when faced with an ethical conflict. If these policies do not resolve the conflict, the member should

   A. Consult the board of directors immediately.

   B. Discuss the problem with the immediate superior if (s)he is involved in the conflict.

   C. Communicate the problem to authorities outside the organization.

   D. Contact the next higher managerial level if initial presentation to the immediate superior does not resolve the conflict.

Answer (D) is correct. *(CIA, adapted)*
   REQUIRED: The proper action when organizational policies do not resolve an ethical conflict.
   DISCUSSION: In these circumstances, the problem should be discussed with the immediate superior unless (s)he is involved. In that case initial presentation should be to the next higher managerial level. If the problem is not satisfactorily resolved after initial presentation, the question should be submitted to the next higher level.
   Answer (A) is incorrect. This course of action would be appropriate only for the chief executive officer or for his/her immediate subordinate when the CEO is involved in the conflict. Answer (B) is incorrect. The proper action would be to present the matter to the next higher managerial level. Answer (C) is incorrect. Such action is inappropriate unless legally prescribed.

1.2 Cost Management Terminology

7. The terms direct cost and indirect cost are commonly used in accounting. A particular cost might be considered a direct cost of a manufacturing department but an indirect cost of the product produced in the manufacturing department. Classifying a cost as either direct or indirect depends upon

    A. The behavior of the cost in response to volume changes.

    B. Whether the cost is expensed in the period in which it is incurred.

    C. The cost object to which the cost is being related.

    D. Whether an expenditure is unavoidable because it cannot be changed regardless of any action taken.

Answer (C) is correct. *(CMA, adapted)*
    REQUIRED: The factor that influences whether a cost is classified as direct or indirect.
    DISCUSSION: A direct cost can be specifically associated with a single cost object in an economically feasible way. An indirect cost cannot be specifically associated with a single cost object. Thus, the specific cost object influences whether a cost is direct or indirect. For example, a cost might be directly associated with a single plant. The same cost, however, might not be directly associated with a particular department in the plant.
    Answer (A) is incorrect. Behavior in response to volume changes is a factor only if the cost object is a product. Answer (B) is incorrect. The timing of an expense is not a means of classifying a cost as direct or indirect. Answer (D) is incorrect. Both direct and indirect costs can be either avoidable or unavoidable, depending upon the cost object.

8. Which one of the following best describes direct labor?

    A. A prime cost.

    B. A period cost.

    C. A product cost.

    D. Both a product cost and a prime cost.

Answer (D) is correct. *(CMA, adapted)*
    REQUIRED: The best description of direct labor.
    DISCUSSION: Direct labor is both a product cost and a prime cost. Product costs are incurred to produce units of output and are deferred to future periods to the extent that output is not sold. Prime costs are defined as direct materials and direct labor.
    Answer (A) is incorrect. Direct labor is also a product cost. Answer (B) is incorrect. A period cost is expensed when incurred. Direct labor cost is inventoriable. Answer (C) is incorrect. Direct labor is also a prime cost.

9. Inventoriable costs

    A. Include only the prime costs of manufacturing a product.

    B. Include only the conversion costs of manufacturing a product.

    C. Are expensed when products become part of finished goods inventory.

    D. Are regarded as assets before the products are sold.

Answer (D) is correct. *(CMA, adapted)*
    REQUIRED: The true statement about inventoriable costs.
    DISCUSSION: Under an absorption costing system, inventoriable (product) costs include all costs necessary for good production. These include direct materials and conversion costs (direct labor and overhead). Both fixed and variable overhead is included in inventory under an absorption costing system. Inventoriable costs are treated as assets until the products are sold because they represent future economic benefits. These costs are expensed at the time of sale.
    Answer (A) is incorrect. Overhead costs as well as prime costs (direct materials and labor) are included in inventory. Answer (B) is incorrect. Materials costs are also included. Answer (C) is incorrect. Inventory costs are expensed when the goods are sold, not when they are transferred to finished goods.

10. In cost terminology, conversion costs consist of

    A. Direct and indirect labor.

    B. Direct labor and direct materials.

    C. Direct labor and factory overhead.

    D. Indirect labor and variable factory overhead.

Answer (C) is correct. *(CMA, adapted)*
    REQUIRED: The components of conversion costs.
    DISCUSSION: Conversion costs consist of direct labor and factory overhead. These are the costs of converting raw materials into a finished product.
    Answer (A) is incorrect. All factory overhead is included in conversion costs, not just indirect labor. Answer (B) is incorrect. Direct materials are not an element of conversion costs; they are a prime cost. Answer (D) is incorrect. Direct labor is also an element of conversion costs.

11. Costs are allocated to cost objects in many ways and for many reasons. Which one of the following is a purpose of cost allocation?

    A. Evaluating revenue center performance.

    B. Measuring income and assets for external reporting.

    C. Budgeting cash and controlling expenditures.

    D. Aiding in variable costing for internal reporting.

Answer (B) is correct. *(CMA, adapted)*
    REQUIRED: The purpose of cost allocation.
    DISCUSSION: Cost allocation is the process of assigning and reassigning costs to cost objects. It is used for those costs that cannot be directly associated with a specific cost object. Cost allocation is often used for purposes of measuring income and assets for external reporting purposes. Cost allocation is less meaningful for internal purposes because responsibility accounting systems emphasize controllability, a process often ignored in cost allocation.
    Answer (A) is incorrect. A revenue center is evaluated on the basis of revenue generated, without regard to costs. Answer (C) is incorrect. Cost allocation is not necessary for cash budgeting and controlling expenditures. Answer (D) is incorrect. Allocations are not needed for variable costing, which concerns direct, not indirect, costs.

12. Cost drivers are

    A. Activities that cause costs to increase as the activity increases.

    B. Accounting techniques used to control costs.

    C. Accounting measurements used to evaluate whether or not performance is proceeding according to plan.

    D. A mechanical basis, such as machine hours, computer time, size of equipment, or square footage of factory, used to assign costs to activities.

Answer (A) is correct. *(CMA, adapted)*
    REQUIRED: The definition of a cost driver.
    DISCUSSION: A cost driver is "a measure of activity, such as direct labor hours, machine hours, beds occupied, computer time used, flight hours, miles driven, or contracts, that is a causal factor in the incurrence of cost to an entity" (IMA). It is a basis used to assign costs to cost objects.
    Answer (B) is incorrect. Cost drivers are measures of activities that cause the incurrence of costs. Answer (C) is incorrect. Cost drivers are not accounting measurements but measures of activities that cause costs. Answer (D) is incorrect. Although cost drivers may be used to assign costs, they are not necessarily mechanical. For example, a cost driver for pension benefits is employee salaries.

13. Which one of the following is **least** likely to be an objective of a cost accounting system?

    A. Product costing.

    B. Department efficiency.

    C. Inventory valuation.

    D. Sales commission determination.

Answer (D) is correct. *(CMA, adapted)*
    REQUIRED: The item that is the least likely to be an objective of a cost accounting system.
    DISCUSSION: A cost accounting system has numerous objectives, including product costing, assessing departmental efficiency, inventory valuation, income determination, and planning, evaluating, and controlling operations. Determining sales commissions is not an objective of a cost accounting system because such commissions are based on sales, not costs.
    Answer (A) is incorrect. Product costing is an objective of a cost accounting system. Answer (B) is incorrect. Department efficiency is an objective of a cost accounting system. Answer (C) is incorrect. Inventory valuation is an objective of a cost accounting system.

1.3 Cost Behavior and Relevant Range

14. Which one of the following categories of cost is most likely **not** considered a component of fixed factory overhead?

    A. Rent.

    B. Property taxes.

    C. Depreciation.

    D. Power.

Answer (D) is correct. *(CMA, adapted)*
    REQUIRED: The item of cost most likely not considered a component of fixed factory overhead.
    DISCUSSION: A fixed cost is one that remains unchanged within the relevant range for a given period despite fluctuations in activity. Such items as rent, property taxes, depreciation, and supervisory salaries are normally fixed costs because they do not vary with changes in production. Power costs, however, are at least partially variable because they increase as usage increases.
    Answer (A) is incorrect. Rent is an example of fixed factory overhead. Answer (B) is incorrect. Property taxes are an example of fixed factory overhead. Answer (C) is incorrect. Depreciation is an example of fixed factory overhead.

15. The controller of JoyCo has requested a quick estimate of the manufacturing supplies needed for the Morton Plant for the month of July when production is expected to be 470,000 units to meet the ending inventory requirements and sales of 475,000 units. JoyCo's budget analyst has the following actual data for the last 3 months:

Month	Production in Units	Manufacturing Supplies
March	450,000	$723,060
April	540,000	853,560
May	480,000	766,560

Using these data and the high-low method to develop a cost estimating equation, the estimate of needed manufacturing supplies for July would be

  A. $652,500

  B. $681,500

  C. $749,180

  D. $752,060

Answer (D) is correct. *(CMA, adapted)*
  REQUIRED: The estimate of needed manufacturing supplies using the high-low method.
  DISCUSSION: The fixed and variable portions of mixed costs may be estimated by identifying the highest and the lowest costs within the relevant range. The difference in cost divided by the difference in activity is the variable rate. Once the variable rate is found, the fixed portion is determinable. April and March provide the highest and lowest amounts. The difference in production was 90,000 units (540,000 April – 450,000 March), and the difference in the cost of supplies was $130,500 ($853,560 – $723,060). Hence, the unit variable cost was $1.45 ($130,500 ÷ 90,000 units). The total variable costs for March must have been $652,500 (450,000 units × $1.45 VC per unit), and the fixed cost must therefore have been $70,560 ($723,060 – $652,500). The probable costs for July equal $681,500 (470,000 units × $1.45 VC per unit), plus $70,560 of fixed costs, a total of $752,060.
  Answer (A) is incorrect. The total variable costs for March equal $652,500. Answer (B) is incorrect. The variable portion of the total costs is $681,500. Answer (C) is incorrect. The amount of $749,180 is a nonsense answer.

16. Butteco has the following cost components for 100,000 units of product for the year:

Direct materials	$200,000
Direct labor	100,000
Manufacturing overhead	200,000
Selling and administrative expense	150,000

All costs are variable except for $100,000 of manufacturing overhead and $100,000 of selling and administrative expenses. The total costs to produce and sell 110,000 units for the year are

  A. $650,000

  B. $715,000

  C. $695,000

  D. $540,000

Answer (C) is correct. *(CMA, adapted)*
  REQUIRED: The flexible budget costs for producing and selling a given quantity.
  DISCUSSION: Direct materials unit costs are strictly variable at $2 ($200,000 ÷ 100,000 units). Similarly, direct labor has a variable unit cost of $1 ($100,000 ÷ 100,000 units). The $200,000 of manufacturing overhead for 100,000 units is 50%. The variable unit cost is $1. Selling costs are $100,000 fixed and $50,000 variable for production of 100,000 units, and the variable unit selling expenses is $.50 ($50,000 ÷ 100,000 units). The total unit variable cost is therefore $4.50 ($2 + $1 + $1 + $.50). Fixed costs are $200,000. At a production level of 110,000 units, variable costs are $495,000 (110,000 units × $4.50). Hence, total costs are $695,000 ($495,000 + $200,000).
  Answer (A) is incorrect. The cost at a production level of 100,000 units is $650,000. Answer (B) is incorrect. The amount of $715,000 assumes a variable unit cost of $6.50 with no fixed costs. Answer (D) is incorrect. Total costs are $695,000 based on a unit variable cost of $4.50 each.

17. The difference between variable costs and fixed costs is

  A. Variable costs per unit fluctuate and fixed costs per unit remain constant.

  B. Variable costs per unit are fixed over the relevant range and fixed costs per unit are variable.

  C. Total variable costs are variable over the relevant range and fixed in the long term, while fixed costs never change.

  D. Variable costs per unit change in varying increments, while fixed costs per unit change in equal increments.

Answer (B) is correct. *(CMA, adapted)*
  REQUIRED: The difference between variable and fixed costs.
  DISCUSSION: Fixed costs remain unchanged within the relevant range for a given period despite fluctuations in activity, but per unit fixed costs do change as the level of activity changes. Thus, fixed costs are fixed in total but vary per unit as activity changes. Total variable costs vary directly with activity. They are fixed per unit, but vary in total.
  Answer (A) is incorrect. Variable costs are fixed per unit; they do not fluctuate. Fixed costs per unit change as production changes. Answer (C) is incorrect. All costs are variable in the long term. Answer (D) is incorrect. Unit variable costs are fixed in the short term.

18. Which of the following is the best example of a variable cost?

- A. The corporate president's salary.
- B. Cost of raw material.
- C. Interest charges.
- D. Property taxes.

Answer (B) is correct. *(CMA, adapted)*
REQUIRED: The item that is a variable cost.
DISCUSSION: Variable costs vary directly with the level of production. As production increases or decreases, material cost increases or decreases, usually in a direct relationship.
Answer (A) is incorrect. The president's salary usually does not vary with production levels. Answer (C) is incorrect. Interest charges are independent of production levels. They are called "fixed" costs and are elements of overhead. Answer (D) is incorrect. Property taxes are independent of production levels. They are called "fixed" costs and are elements of overhead.

19. A fixed cost that would be considered a direct cost is

- A. A cost accountant's salary when the cost objective is a unit of product.
- B. The rental cost of a warehouse to store inventory when the cost objective is the Purchasing Department.
- C. A production supervisor's salary when the cost objective is the Production Department.
- D. Board of directors' fees when the cost objective is the Marketing Department.

Answer (C) is correct. *(CMA, adapted)*
REQUIRED: The fixed cost that would be considered a direct cost.
DISCUSSION: A direct cost is one that can be specifically associated with a single cost objective in an economically feasible way. Thus, a production supervisor's salary can be directly associated with the department (s)he supervises.
Answer (A) is incorrect. A cost accountant's salary cannot be directly associated with a single product. Cost accountants work with many different products during a pay period. Answer (B) is incorrect. Warehouse rent is not directly traceable to the Purchasing Department. Other departments have influence over the level of inventories stored. Answer (D) is incorrect. Directors' fees cannot be directly associated with the Marketing Department. Directors provide benefits to all departments within a corporation.

20. Which one of the following is correct regarding a relevant range?

- A. Total variable costs will not change.
- B. Total fixed costs will not change.
- C. Actual fixed costs usually fall outside the relevant range.
- D. The relevant range cannot be changed after being established.

Answer (B) is correct. *(CMA, adapted)*
REQUIRED: The true statement about a relevant range.
DISCUSSION: The relevant range is the range of activity over which unit variable costs and total fixed costs are constant. The incremental cost of one additional unit of production will be equal to the variable cost.
Answer (A) is incorrect. Variable costs will change in total, but unit variable costs will be constant. Answer (C) is incorrect. Actual fixed costs should not vary greatly from budgeted fixed costs for the relevant range. Answer (D) is incorrect. The relevant range can change whenever production activity changes; the relevant range is merely an assumption used for budgeting and control purposes.

21. Jackson Co. has the following information for the first quarter of its year:

	Machine Hours	Cleaning Expense
January	2,100	$ 900
February	2,600	1,200
March	1,600	800
April	2,000	1,000

Using the high-low method, what is Jackson's fixed cost?

- A. $160
- B. $320
- C. $640
- D. $1,040

Answer (A) is correct. *(Publisher, adapted)*
REQUIRED: The fixed cost using the high-low method.
DISCUSSION: Once the variable portion of a mixed cost has been determined using the high-low method (in this case, $400 cost difference ÷ 1,000 machine hours difference = $.40 per machine hour), it can be substituted in the total cost formula for one of the months to isolate the fixed portion.

Variable costs + Fixed costs= Total cost
(2,600 × $.40) + Fixed costs= $1,200
Fixed costs= $1,200 – $1,040
Fixed costs= $160

Answer (B) is incorrect. The fixed cost is not $320.
Answer (C) is incorrect. The fixed cost is not $640. Answer (D) is incorrect. The variable cost at 2,600 machine hours is $1,040.

1.4 Cost of Goods Calculations

Questions 22 through 25 are based on the following information.

Madtack Company's beginning and ending inventories for the month of November are

	November 1	November 30
Direct materials	$ 67,000	$ 62,000
Work-in-process	145,000	171,000
Finished goods	85,000	78,000

Production data for the month of November follows:

Direct labor	$200,000
Actual factory overhead	132,000
Direct materials purchased	163,000
Transportation in	4,000
Purchase returns and allowances	2,000

Madtack uses one overhead control account and charges overhead to production at 70% of direct labor cost. The company does not formally recognize over- or underapplied overhead until year end.

22. Madtack Company's prime cost for November is

A. $370,000

B. $168,000

C. $363,000

D. $170,000

Answer (A) is correct. *(CMA, adapted)*
REQUIRED: The prime cost.
DISCUSSION: Prime costs are the combined costs of direct materials and direct labor.

Beginning materials inventory	$ 67,000
Add: purchases	163,000
Add: transportation in	4,000
Less: purchase returns	(2,000)
Materials available	$232,000
Less: ending materials inventory	(62,000)
Materials used in production	$170,000

Direct materials	$170,000
Direct labor	200,000
Total prime costs	$370,000

Answer (B) is incorrect. The amount of $168,000 equals purchases of materials adjusted for the change in inventories. Answer (C) is incorrect. The amount of $363,000 incorporates the change in finished goods inventories. Answer (D) is incorrect. The amount of $170,000 equals the materials used.

23. Madtack Company's total manufacturing cost for November is

A. $502,000

B. $503,000

C. $363,000

D. $510,000

Answer (D) is correct. *(CMA, adapted)*
REQUIRED: The total manufacturing costs for the month.
DISCUSSION: Total manufacturing cost is the sum of direct materials cost, direct labor cost, and manufacturing overhead.

Beginning materials	$ 67,000
Add: purchases	163,000
Add: transportation in	4,000
Less: purchase returns	(2,000)
Materials available	$232,000
Less: ending materials	(62,000)
Materials used in production	$170,000

Direct materials	$170,000
Direct labor	200,000
Manufacturing overhead (DL × 70%)	140,000
Total manufacturing costs	$510,000

Answer (A) is incorrect. The amount of $502,000 is based on actual overhead. Answer (B) is incorrect. The amount of $503,000 incorporates the change in finished goods inventories. Answer (C) is incorrect. The amount of $363,000 excludes overhead but includes the change in finished goods inventory.

24. Madtack Company's cost of goods transferred to finished goods inventory for November is

A. $469,000

B. $477,000

C. $495,000

D. $484,000

Answer (D) is correct. *(CMA, adapted)*
REQUIRED: The cost of goods transferred to finished goods inventory during the month.
DISCUSSION: This solution requires a series of computations. Total manufacturing cost is the sum of direct materials cost, direct labor cost, and manufacturing overhead.

Beginning materials	$ 67,000
Add: purchases	163,000
Add: transportation in	4,000
Less: purchase returns	(2,000)
Materials available	$232,000
Less: ending materials	(62,000)
Materials used in production	$170,000

Direct materials	$170,000
Direct labor	200,000
Manufacturing overhead (DL × 70%)	140,000
Total manufacturing costs	$510,000

Total manufacturing costs	$510,000
Add: beginning work-in-process	145,000
Less: ending work-in-process	(171,000)
Costs transferred to finished goods	$484,000

Answer (A) is incorrect. The amount of $469,000 uses actual overhead and adjusts the figures for the change in finished goods inventory. Answer (B) is incorrect. The amount of $477,000 includes the change in finished goods inventory in the calculation. Answer (C) is incorrect. The amount of $495,000 uses materials purchased rather than materials used and also fails to adjust properly for transportation in.

25. Madtack Company's cost of goods sold for November is

A. $484,000

B. $491,000

C. $502,000

D. $476,000

Answer (B) is correct. *(CMA, adapted)*
REQUIRED: The cost of goods sold for the month.
DISCUSSION: This solution requires a series of computations. Total manufacturing cost is the sum of direct materials cost, direct labor cost, and manufacturing overhead.

Beginning materials	$ 67,000
Add: purchases	163,000
Add: transportation in	4,000
Less: purchase returns	(2,000)
Materials available	$232,000
Less: ending materials	(62,000)
Materials used in production	$170,000

Direct materials	$170,000
Direct labor	200,000
Manufacturing overhead (DL × 70%)	140,000
Total manufacturing costs	$510,000

Total manufacturing costs	$510,000
Add: beginning work-in-process	145,000
Less: ending work-in-process	(171,000)
Costs transferred to finished goods	$484,000

Beginning finished goods inventory	$ 85,000
Add: cost of goods manufactured	484,000
Goods available for sale	$569,000
Less: ending finished goods inventory	(78,000)
Cost of goods sold	$491,000

Answer (A) is incorrect. The amount of $484,000 is the cost of goods manufactured. Answer (C) is incorrect. The amount of $502,000 is based on cost of goods manufactured of $495,000. Answer (D) is incorrect. The amount of $476,000 is based on actual overhead costs and fails to adjust for the change in finished goods inventories.

Questions 26 and 27 are based on the following information. Alex Company had the following inventories at the beginning and end of the month of January:

	January 1	January 31
Finished goods	$125,000	$117,000
Work-in-process	235,000	251,000
Direct materials	134,000	124,000

The following additional manufacturing data were available for the month of January:

Direct materials purchased	$189,000
Purchase returns and allowances	1,000
Transportation-in	3,000
Direct labor	300,000
Actual factory overhead	175,000

Alex Company applies factory overhead at a rate of 60% of direct labor cost, and any overapplied or underapplied factory overhead is deferred until the end of the year, December 31.

---

26. Alex Company's prime cost for January was

A. $199,000

B. $501,000

C. $489,000

D. $201,000

Answer (B) is correct. *(CMA, adapted)*
REQUIRED: The amount of prime cost for the month.
DISCUSSION: Prime cost is defined as those costs directly traceable to specific units of production, specifically direct labor and direct materials. According to the following statement of cost of goods manufactured, total prime cost was $501,000.

Beginning direct materials inventory	$ 134,000
Add: purchases	189,000
Less: purchase returns	(1,000)
Add: transportation-in	3,000
Total direct materials available	$ 325,000
Less: ending direct materials inventory	(124,000)
Direct materials used	$ 201,000
Direct labor	300,000
Total prime costs	$ 501,000

Answer (A) is incorrect. Direct materials used without adjustments for purchase returns and transportation-in equals $199,000. Answer (C) is incorrect. Direct materials purchased plus direct labor equals $489,000. Answer (D) is incorrect. Direct materials used equals $201,000.

27. Alex Company's total manufacturing cost for January was

A. $681,000

B. $665,000

C. $489,000

D. $673,000

Answer (A) is correct. *(CMA, adapted)*
REQUIRED: The total manufacturing cost for the month.
DISCUSSION: The sum of direct materials used, direct labor, and factory overhead applied (60% of direct labor) is $681,000.
Answer (B) is incorrect. The cost of goods manufactured equals $665,000. Answer (C) is incorrect. The direct materials purchased plus direct labor equals $489,000. Answer (D) is incorrect. The cost of goods sold equals $673,000.

1.5 Cost Classification

28. "Committed costs" are

   A. Costs that management decides to incur in the current period to enable the company to achieve objectives other than the filling of orders placed by customers.

   B. Costs that are likely to respond to the amount of attention devoted to them by a specified manager.

   C. Costs that are governed mainly by past decisions that established the present levels of operating and organizational capacity and that only change slowly in response to small changes in capacity.

   D. Amortization of costs that were capitalized in previous periods.

Answer (C) is correct. *(CMA, adapted)*
   REQUIRED: The definition of committed costs.
   DISCUSSION: Committed costs are those that are required as a result of past decisions.
   Answer (A) is incorrect. Costs incurred in a current period to achieve objectives other than the filling of orders by customers are known as discretionary costs. Answer (B) is incorrect. Costs that are likely to respond to the amount of attention devoted to them by a specified manager are controllable costs. Answer (D) is incorrect. Amortization of costs capitalized in previous periods is depreciation.

29. "Discretionary costs" are costs that

   A. Management decides to incur in the current period to enable the company to achieve objectives other than the filling of orders placed by customers.

   B. Are likely to respond to the amount of attention devoted to them by a specified manger.

   C. Are governed mainly by past decisions that established the present levels of operating and organizational capacity and that only change slowly in response to small changes in capacity.

   D. Will be unaffected by current managerial decisions.

Answer (A) is correct. *(CMA, adapted)*
   REQUIRED: The definition of discretionary costs.
   DISCUSSION: Discretionary costs are those that are incurred in the current period at the "discretion" of management and are not required to fill orders by customers.
   Answer (B) is incorrect. Costs that are likely to respond to the amount of attention devoted to them by a specified manager are controllable costs. Answer (C) is incorrect. Costs required as a result of past decisions are committed costs. Answer (D) is incorrect. Costs unaffected by managerial decisions are costs such as committed costs and depreciation that were determined by decisions of previous periods.

30. "Controllable costs" are costs that

   A. Management decides to incur in the current period to enable the company to achieve objectives other than the filling of orders placed by customers.

   B. Are likely to respond to the amount of attention devoted to them by a specified manger.

   C. Fluctuate in total in response to small changes in the rate of utilization of capacity.

   D. Will be unaffected by current managerial decisions.

Answer (B) is correct. *(CMA, adapted)*
   REQUIRED: The definition of controllable costs.
   DISCUSSION: Controllable costs can be affected by the efforts of a manager.
   Answer (A) is incorrect. Costs incurred in a current period to achieve objectives other than the filling of orders by customers are known as discretionary costs. Answer (C) is incorrect. Costs that fluctuate with small changes in volume are variable costs. Answer (D) is incorrect. Costs that are unaffected by managerial decisions are costs such as committed costs and depreciation that was determined by decisions of previous periods.

31. In joint-product costing and analysis, which one of the following costs is relevant when deciding the point at which a product should be sold to maximize profits?

   A. Separable costs after the split-off point.

   B. Joint costs to the split-off point.

   C. Sales salaries for the period when the units were produced.

   D. Purchase costs of the materials required for the joint products.

Answer (A) is correct. *(CMA, adapted)*
   REQUIRED: The cost relevant to deciding when a joint product should be sold.
   DISCUSSION: Joint products are created from processing a common input. Joint costs are incurred prior to the split-off point and cannot be identified with a particular joint product. As a result, joint costs are irrelevant to the timing of sale. However, separable costs incurred after the split-off point are relevant because, if incremental revenues exceed the separable costs, products should be processed further, not sold at the split-off point.
   Answer (B) is incorrect. Joint costs have no effect on the decision as to when to sell a product. Answer (C) is incorrect. Sales salaries for the production period do not affect the decision. Answer (D) is incorrect. Purchase costs are joint costs.

32. Practical capacity as a plant capacity concept

   A. Assumes all personnel and equipment will operate at peak efficiency and total plant capacity will be used.

   B. Does not consider idle time caused by inadequate sales demand.

   C. Includes consideration of idle time caused by both limited sales orders and human and equipment inefficiencies.

   D. Is the production volume that is necessary to meet sales demand for the next year.

Answer (B) is correct. *(CMA, adapted)*
   REQUIRED: The true statement about practical capacity.
   DISCUSSION: Practical capacity is the maximum level at which output is produced efficiently. It includes consideration of idle time caused by human and equipment inefficiencies but not by inadequate sales demand. Practical capacity exceeds the other commonly used denominator levels included in the calculation of the fixed factory overhead rate. Because practical capacity will almost always exceed the actual use of capacity, it will result in an unfavorable production volume variance. Moreover, this variance (the difference between budgeted fixed overhead and the fixed overhead applied based on standard input allowed for the actual output) will be greatest given a practical capacity measure. The unfavorable production volume variance is charged to income summary, so the effect of using a larger denominator volume is the more rapid write-off of fixed overhead (practical capacity may be used for federal income tax purposes).
   Answer (A) is incorrect. Theoretical capacity assumes all personnel and equipment will operate at peak efficiency and total plant capacity will be used. Answer (C) is incorrect. Practical capacity ignores demand. Answer (D) is incorrect. The production volume to meet a given production level may be more or less than practical capacity. Horngren, Foster, and Datar call this volume the master-budget volume.

33. A cost that bears an observable and known relationship to a quantifiable activity base is a(n)

   A. Engineered cost.

   B. Indirect cost.

   C. Sunk cost.

   D. Target cost.

Answer (A) is correct. *(CMA, adapted)*
   REQUIRED: The cost that bears an observable and known relationship to a quantifiable activity base.
   DISCUSSION: A cost that bears an observable and known relationship to a quantifiable activity base is known as an engineered cost. Engineered costs have a clear relationship to output. Direct materials would be an example of an engineered cost.
   Answer (B) is incorrect. An indirect cost does not have a clear relationship to output. Answer (C) is incorrect. A sunk cost is the result of a past irrevocable action; it is not important to future decisions. Answer (D) is incorrect. A target cost is the maximum allowable cost of a product and is calculated before the product is designed or produced.

34. The cost associated with abnormal spoilage ordinarily is charged to

   A. Inventory.

   B. A material variance account.

   C. Manufacturing overhead.

   D. A special loss account.

Answer (D) is correct. *(CMA, adapted)*
   REQUIRED: The method of accounting for abnormal spoilage.
   DISCUSSION: Abnormal spoilage is usually charged to a special loss account because it is not expected to occur under normal, efficient operating conditions. Because it is unusual, it should be separately reported as a period cost.
   Answer (A) is incorrect. Normal spoilage, not abnormal spoilage, costs are charged to inventory. Answer (B) is incorrect. Material variance accounts are only charged for the variances in material usage or material price, not the spoilage of product. Answer (C) is incorrect. While charging abnormal spoilage to manufacturing overhead is an occasional practice, it is not the ordinary practice.

35. An imputed cost is

   A. The difference in total costs that results from selecting one alternative instead of another.

   B. A cost that cannot be avoided because it has already been incurred.

   C. A cost that does not entail any dollar outlay but is relevant to the decision-making process.

   D. A cost that continues to be incurred even though there is no activity.

Answer (C) is correct. *(CMA, adapted)*
   REQUIRED: The definition of an imputed cost.
   DISCUSSION: An imputed cost does not entail any dollar outlay but is relevant to the decision-making process.
   Answer (A) is incorrect. The difference in total costs that results from selecting one alternative instead of another is an incremental cost. Answer (B) is incorrect. A cost that cannot be avoided because it has already been incurred is a sunk cost. Answer (D) is incorrect. A cost that continues to be incurred even though there is no activity is a fixed cost.

1.6 Costing Techniques

36. Which one of the following alternatives correctly classifies the business application to the appropriate costing system?

Job Costing System	Process Costing System
A. Wallpaper manufacturer	Oil refinery
B. Aircraft assembly	Public accounting firm
C. Paint manufacturer	Retail banking
D. Print shop	Beverage manufacturer

Answer (D) is correct. *(CMA, adapted)*
REQUIRED: The appropriate matching of business applications with costing systems.
DISCUSSION: A job costing system is used when products differ from one customer to the next, that is, when products are heterogeneous. A process costing system is used when similar products are mass produced on a continuous basis. A print shop, for example, would use a job costing system because each job will be unique. Each customer provides the specifications for the product desired. A beverage manufacturer, however, would use a process costing system because homogenous units are produced continuously.
Answer (A) is incorrect. A wallpaper manufacturer would use a process costing system. Answer (B) is incorrect. A public accounting firm would use a job costing system. Answer (C) is incorrect. A paint manufacturer would use a process costing system.

37. Which one of the following considers the impact of fixed overhead costs?

A. Full absorption costing.

B. Marginal costing.

C. Direct costing.

D. Variable costing.

Answer (A) is correct. *(CMA, adapted)*
REQUIRED: The method of costing that considers the impact of fixed overhead costs.
DISCUSSION: Full absorption costing treats fixed factory overhead costs as product costs. Thus, inventory and cost of goods sold include (absorb) fixed factory overhead.
Answer (B) is incorrect. Marginal costing considers only the incremental costs of producing an additional unit of product. In most cases marginal costs are variable costs. Answer (C) is incorrect. Direct (variable) costing treats only variable costs as product costs. Answer (D) is incorrect. Direct (variable) costing treats only variable costs as product costs.

38. An accounting system that collects financial and operating data on the basis of the underlying nature and extent of the cost drivers is

A. Direct costing.

B. Activity-based costing.

C. Cycle-time costing.

D. Variable costing.

Answer (B) is correct. *(CMA, adapted)*
REQUIRED: The accounting system that collects data on the basis of cost drivers.
DISCUSSION: An activity-based costing (ABC) system identifies the causal relationship between the incurrence of cost and the underlying activities that cause those costs. Under an ABC system, costs are applied to products on the basis of resources consumed (drivers).
Answer (A) is incorrect. Direct costing is a system that treats fixed costs as period costs; in other words, production costs consist only of variable costs, while fixed costs are expensed as incurred. Answer (C) is incorrect. Cycle time is the period from the time a customer places an order to the time that product is delivered. Answer (D) is incorrect. Variable costing is the same as direct costing, which expenses fixed costs as incurred.

39. Because this allocation method recognizes that service departments often provide each other with interdepartmental service, it is theoretically considered to be the most accurate method for allocating service department costs to production departments. This method is the

A. Direct method.

B. Variable method.

C. Reciprocal method.

D. Linear method.

Answer (C) is correct. *(CMA, adapted)*
REQUIRED: The most accurate method for allocating service department costs to production departments.
DISCUSSION: The three most common methods of allocating service department costs are the direct method, the step method, and the reciprocal method (also called the simultaneous equations method). The reciprocal method is theoretically the preferred method because it recognizes reciprocal services among service departments.
Answer (A) is incorrect. The direct method does not recognize the fact that service departments might provide services to each other; all costs are assigned directly to production departments. Answer (B) is incorrect. The variable method is a nonsense term as used here. Answer (D) is incorrect. The linear method is not one of the methods used to allocate departmental costs.

40. Which of the following statements is true for a firm that uses variable costing?

A. The cost of a unit of product changes because of changes in number of units manufactured.

B. Profits fluctuate with sales.

C. An idle facility variation is calculated.

D. Product costs include variable administrative costs.

Answer (B) is correct.   *(CMA, adapted)*
   REQUIRED: The true statement about variable costing.
   DISCUSSION: In a variable costing system, only the variable costs are recorded as product costs. All fixed costs are expensed in the period incurred. Because changes in the relationship between production levels and sales levels do not cause changes in the amount of fixed manufacturing cost expensed, profits more directly follow the trends in sales.
   Answer (A) is incorrect. The cost of a unit of product changing owing to a change in the number of units manufactured is a characteristic of absorption costing systems. Answer (C) is incorrect. Idle facility variation is a characteristic of absorption costing systems. Answer (D) is incorrect. Neither variable nor absorption costing includes administrative costs in inventory.

41. A difference between standard costs used for cost control and budgeted costs

A. Can exist because standard costs must be determined after the budget is completed.

B. Can exist because standard costs represent what costs should be, whereas budgeted costs represent expected actual costs.

C. Can exist because budgeted costs are historical costs, whereas standard costs are based on engineering studies.

D. Cannot exist because they should be the same amounts.

Answer (B) is correct.   *(CMA, adapted)*
   REQUIRED: The true statement about the difference between standard costs and budgeted costs.
   DISCUSSION: Standard costs are predetermined, attainable unit costs. Standard cost systems isolate deviations (variances) of actual from expected costs. One advantage of standard costs is that they facilitate flexible budgeting. Accordingly, standard and budgeted costs should not differ when standards are currently attainable. However, in practice, budgeted (estimated actual) costs may differ from standard costs when operating conditions are not expected to reflect those anticipated when the standards were developed.
   Answer (A) is incorrect. Standard costs are determined independently of the budget. Answer (C) is incorrect. Budgeted costs are expected future costs, not historical costs. Answer (D) is incorrect. Budgeted and standard costs should in principle be the same, but in practice they will differ when standard costs are not expected to be currently attainable.

42. A standard costing system is most often used by a firm in conjunction with

A. Management by objectives.

B. Target (hurdle) rates of return.

C. Participative management programs.

D. Flexible budgets.

Answer (D) is correct.   *(CMA, adapted)*
   REQUIRED: The manner in which a standard costing system is most often used.
   DISCUSSION: A standard cost is an estimate of what a cost should be under normal operating conditions based on accounting and engineering studies. Comparing actual and standard costs permits an evaluation of the effectiveness of managerial performance. Because of the impact of fixed costs in most businesses, a standard costing system is usually not effective unless the company also has a flexible budgeting system. Flexible budgeting uses standard costs to prepare budgets for multiple activity levels.
   Answer (A) is incorrect. MBO is a behavioral, communication-oriented, responsibility approach to employee self-direction. Although MBO can be used with standard costs, the two are not necessarily related. Answer (B) is incorrect. Rates of return relate to revenues as well as costs, but a standard costing system concerns costs only. Answer (C) is incorrect. Participative management stresses multidirectional communication. It has no relationship to standard costs.

Use Gleim **CMA Test Prep** Software for interactive testing with **additional multiple-choice questions!**

1.8 ESSAY QUESTIONS

Scenario for Essay Questions 1, 2, 3

The external auditors for Heart Health Procedures (HHP) are currently performing the annual audit of HHP's financial statements. As part of the audit, the external auditors have prepared a representation letter to be signed by HHP's Chief Executive Officer (CEO) and Chief Financial Officer (CFO). The letter provides, among other items, a representation that appropriate provisions have been made for

- Reductions of any excess or obsolete inventories to net realizable values, and
- Losses from any purchase commitments for inventory quantities in excess of requirements or at prices in excess of market.

HHP began operations by developing a unique balloon process to open obstructed arteries to the heart. In the last several years, HHP's market share has grown significantly because its major competitor was forced to cease its balloon operations by the Food and Drug Administration (FDA). HHP purchases the balloon's primary and most expensive component from a sole supplier. Two years ago, HHP entered into a 5-year contract with this supplier at the then current price with inflation escalators built into each of the 5 years. The long-term contract was deemed necessary to ensure adequate supplies and discourage new competition. However, during the past year, HHP's major competitor developed a technically superior product, which utilizes an innovative, less costly component. This new product was recently approved by the FDA and has been introduced to the medical community, receiving high acceptance. It is expected that HHP's market share, which has already seen softness, will experience a large decline, and that the primary component used in the HHP balloon will decrease in price as a result of the competitor's use of its recently developed superior, cheaper component. The new component has been licensed by the major competitor to several outside sources of supply to maintain available quantity and price competitiveness. At this time, HHP is investigating the purchase of this new component.

HHP's officers are on a bonus plan that is tied to overall corporate profits. Jim Honig, vice president of manufacturing, is responsible for both manufacturing and warehousing. During the course of the audit, he advised the CEO and CFO that he was not aware of any obsolete inventory nor any inventory or purchase commitments where current, or expected prices, were significantly below acquisition or commitment prices. Honig took this position even though Marian Nevins, assistant controller, had apprised him of both the existing excess inventory attributable to the declining market share and the significant loss associated with the remaining years of the 5-year purchase commitment.

Nevins has brought this situation to the attention of her superior, the controller, who also participates in the bonus plan and reports directly to the CFO. Nevins works closely with the external audit staff and subsequently ascertains that the external audit manager was unaware of the inventory and purchase commitment problems. Nevins is concerned about the situation and is not sure how to handle the matter.

Questions

1. Assuming that the controller did not apprise the CEO and CFO of the situation, explain the ethical considerations of the controller's apparent lack of action by discussing specific standards (competence, confidentiality, integrity, and credibility) of IMA's *Statement of Ethical Professional Practice.*

2. Assuming Marian Nevins believes the controller has acted unethically and not apprised the CEO and CFO of his findings, describe the steps that she should take to resolve the situation. Use IMA's *Statement* to support your answer.

3. Describe actions that Heart Health Procedures can take to improve the ethical situation within the company.

Essay Questions 1, 2, 3 — Unofficial Answers

1. Assuming the controller did not apprise the CEO and CFO of the situation, the ethical considerations of the controller's apparent lack of action, as covered in IMA's *Statement of Ethical Professional Practice*, are as follows:

    a. **Competence.** Management accountants have a responsibility to perform their professional duties in accordance with the relevant laws, regulations, and technical standards, and to provide decision support information and recommendations that are accurate, clear, concise, and timely. The controller's apparent lack of action regarding the overstatement of inventory and lack of provision for potential purchase commitment losses do not comply with generally accepted accounting principles.

    b. **Confidentiality.** This standard does not apply to the situation.

    c. **Integrity.** Management accountants have a responsibility to mitigate actual conflicts of interest, to refrain from engaging in any activity that would prejudice carrying out duties ethically, and to abstain from engaging in or supporting any activity that might discredit the profession.

    d. **Credibility.** Management accountants have a responsibility to communicate information fairly and objectively; to disclose all relevant information that could reasonably be expected to influence an intended user's understanding of the reports, analyses, or recommendations; and to disclose delays or deficiencies in information, timeliness, processing, or internal controls in conformance with organization policy and/or applicable law.

2. The recommended course of action that Marian Nevins should take, as described in IMA's *Statement of Ethical Professional Practice*, is as follows:

    a. Consult company policies and procedures regarding ethical conflict. If the company does not have adequate procedures in place to resolve the conflict, then Nevins should discuss the problem with her immediate supervisor, the controller. However, as the controller is apparently involved in the matter and she has already spoken to him, it would not be necessary to inform him that she is taking the situation to the CFO.

    b. As the issue is still not resolved, she should consult the next higher level of management, the CFO, particularly since he will be one of the signers of the representation letter.

    c. During this process Nevins could clarify relevant concepts by confidential discussion with an objective adviser to obtain an understanding of possible courses of action.

    d. If the issue remains unresolved, Nevins should continue to take the problem to the next higher levels of authority, which may include the audit committee, executive committee, and/or the board of directors.

    e. If the ethical conflict still exists, after exhausting all levels of internal review, Nevins should resign and submit an informative memorandum to an appropriate representative of the organization.

    f. Except where legally prescribed, communication of these issues to outsiders (the media, regulatory bodies, etc.) by Nevins is not considered appropriate.

3. The actions that Heart Health Procedures can take to improve the ethical situation within the company include

    a. Setting the tone at the top for control consciousness of the people in the organization

    b. Establishing an audit committee within the board of directors and providing an avenue for communication free of reprisals within the company

    c. Adopting performance-based, long-term financial incentive plans

---

Use **CMA Gleim Online** and **Essay Wizard** to practice additional essay questions in an exam-like environment.

STUDY UNIT TWO
COST ACCUMULATION SYSTEMS

(22 pages of outline)

2.1	Job-Order Costing	54
2.2	Process Costing	57
2.3	Activity-Based Costing	63
2.4	Life-Cycle Costing	70
2.5	Core Concepts	72
2.6	Essay Questions	87

This study unit is the **second of four** on **cost management**. The relative weight assigned to this major topic in Part 1 of the exam is **25%**. The four study units are

Study Unit 1: Ethics for Management Accountants and Cost Management Concepts
Study Unit 2: Cost Accumulation Systems
Study Unit 3: Cost Allocation Techniques
Study Unit 4: Operational Efficiency and Business Process Performance

After studying the outline and answering the questions in this study unit, you will have the skills necessary to address the following topics listed in the ICMA's Learning Outcome Statements:

Part 1 – Section C.1. Measurement concepts

The candidate should be able to:

Statement a. is covered in Study Unit 1.

b. identify cost objects and cost pools and assign costs to appropriate activities
c. demonstrate an understanding of the nature and types of cost drivers and the causal relationship that exists between cost drivers and costs incurred
d. demonstrate an understanding of the various methods for measuring costs and accumulating work-in-process and finished goods inventories

Statements e. through l. are covered in Study Unit 3.

Part 1 – Section C.2. Costing systems

For each cost accumulation system identified (job-order costing, process costing, activity-based costing, life-cycle costing), the candidate should be able to:

a. define the nature of the system, understand the cost flows of the system, and identify its appropriate use
b. calculate inventory values and cost of goods sold
c. demonstrate an understanding of the proper accounting for normal and abnormal spoilage
d. discuss the strategic value of cost information regarding products and services, pricing, overhead allocations, and other issues
e. identify and describe the benefits and limitations of each cost accumulation system

For the following specific cost accumulation systems, the candidate should be able to:

f. demonstrate an understanding of the concept of equivalent units in process costing and calculate the value of equivalent units
g. define the elements of activity-based costing such as cost pool, cost driver, resource driver, activity driver, and value-added activity

h. calculate product cost using an activity-based system and compare and analyze the results with costs calculated using a traditional system

i. explain how activity based costing can be utilized in service firms

j. demonstrate an understanding of the concept of the life-cycle costing and the strategic value of including upstream costs, manufacturing costs, and downstream costs

2.1 JOB-ORDER COSTING

1. **Use of Job-Order Costing**

    a. Job-order costing is concerned with accumulating costs by specific job.

        1) This method is appropriate when producing products with individual characteristics (e.g., yachts), or when identifiable groupings are possible (e.g., jewelry). Units (jobs) should be dissimilar enough to warrant the special record keeping required by job-order costing. Products are usually custom made for a specific customer.

2. **Steps in Job-Order Costing**

    a. The first step in the process is the receipt of a sales order from a customer requesting a product or special group of products.

    b. The sales order is approved and a production order is issued.

    c. Costs are recorded by classification, such as direct materials, direct labor, and manufacturing overhead, on a job cost sheet (may be manual or electronic), which is specifically prepared for each job.

        1) The physical inputs required for the production process are obtained from suppliers. The journal entry to record the acquisition of inventory would be

Raw materials	$XXX	
Accounts payable		$XXX

        2) Production commences and three "documents" feed cost amounts into the costing system:

            a) Materials requisition forms request direct materials to be pulled from the warehouse and sent to the production line.

Work-in-process -- Job 1015	$XXX	
Raw materials		$XXX

            b) Time tickets track the direct labor that workers expend on various jobs.

Work-in-process -- Job 1015	$XXX	
Wages payable		$XXX

            c) These two major components of product cost are charged to work-in-process using the actual amounts incurred.

        3) Under job-order costing, the third component, manufacturing overhead, is charged using an estimated rate.

            a) The application of an estimated overhead rate is necessary under job-order costing because the outputs are customized and the processes vary from period to period.

                i) Contrast this with the treatment of overhead under process costing (item 2.f. in Subunit 2.2) in which actual overhead costs incurred are charged to work-in-process at the end of the period.

b) As indirect costs are paid throughout the year, they are collected in the manufacturing overhead control account.

  i) Note that work-in-process is not affected when actual overhead costs are incurred.

Manufacturing overhead control	$XXX	
Property taxes payable		$XXX
Manufacturing overhead control	$XXX	
Prepaid insurance		$XXX
Manufacturing overhead control	$XXX	
Accumulated depreciation -- factory equipment		$XXX

c) Overhead costs are applied to ("absorbed" by) each job based on a predetermined overhead application rate for the year (such as $5 per direct labor hour, or machine hour, etc., or based on an activity-based costing system).

  i) At the beginning of the year, an estimate is made of the total amount that will be spent for manufacturing overhead during that year.

  ii) This total is divided by the allocation base, such as direct labor hours or machine hours, to arrive at the application rate.

  iii) The amount applied equals the number of units of the allocation base used during the period times the application rate.

  - The credit is to manufacturing overhead applied, a contra-account for manufacturing overhead control.

Work-in-process -- Job 1015	$XXX	
Manufacturing overhead applied		$XXX

  iv) By tracking the amounts applied to the various jobs in a separate account, the actual amounts spent on overhead are preserved in the balance of the overhead control account.

  - In addition, the firm can determine at any time how precise its estimate of overhead costs for the period was by comparing the balances in the two accounts. The closer they are (in absolute value terms), the better the estimate was.

d) At the end of the period, the overhead control and applied accounts are netted.

  i) If the result is a credit, overhead was overapplied for the period. If the result is a debit, overhead was underapplied.

  - If the variance is immaterial, it can be closed directly to cost of goods sold.

  - If the variance is material, it should be allocated based on the relative values of work-in-process, finished goods, and cost of goods sold.

4) The amounts from the input documents are accumulated on job-cost sheets. These serve as a subsidiary ledger page for each job.

  a) The total of all job-cost sheets for jobs in progress will equal the balance in the general ledger work-in-process inventory account.

  b) Once the job is completed, but before it is delivered to the customer, the job cost sheet serves as the subsidiary ledger for the finished goods inventory account.

    d.   When a job order is completed, all the costs are transferred to finished goods.

Finished goods	$X,XXX	
Work-in-process -- Job 1015		$X,XXX

    e.   When the output is sold, the appropriate portion of the cost is transferred to cost of goods sold.

Cost of goods sold	$X,XXX	
Finished goods		$X,XXX

3. Job-Order Cost Flow Diagram

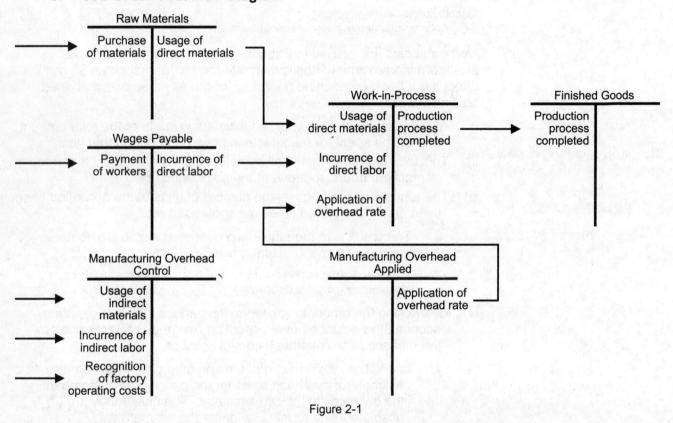

Figure 2-1

4. Spoilage

CMA candidates will be expected to understand the proper accounting procedure for normal and abnormal spoilage under both job-order costing and process costing. In job-order costing, normal spoilage is treated as a product cost while abnormal spoilage is treated as a period cost. It is important to understand not only that they are treated differently, but why. When answering questions pertaining to spoilage, pay attention to the question stem, what system is being used, and whether the product can be sold or not.

    a.   Output that does not meet the quality standards for salability is considered spoilage.

          1)   If the spoilage is the amount expected in the ordinary course of production, it is considered normal spoilage.

               a)   The accounting treatment is to include normal spoilage as a product cost.

               b)   This is accomplished by allowing the net cost of the spoilage to remain in the work-in-process account of the job that generated it.

                    i)   If the normal spoilage is worthless and must be discarded, no entry is made.

                    ii)   If the normal spoilage can be sold, the entry is

Spoiled inventory (at fair market value)	$XX	
Work-in-process -- Job 1015		$XX

2) If the spoilage is over and above the amount expected in the ordinary course of production, it is considered abnormal spoilage.

    a) The accounting treatment is to highlight abnormal spoilage as a period cost so that management can address the deficiency that caused it.

    b) This is accomplished by charging a loss account for the net cost of the spoilage.

        i) If the abnormal spoilage is worthless and must be discarded, the entry is

```
Loss from abnormal spoilage
  (costs up to point of inspection)          $XX
    Work-in-process -- Job 1015                       $XX
```

        ii) If the abnormal spoilage can be sold, the entry is

```
Spoiled inventory                            $XX
Loss from abnormal spoilage (difference)      XX
    Work-in-process -- Job 1015                       $XX
      (costs up to point of inspection)
```

Stop and review! You have completed the outline for this subunit. Study multiple-choice questions 1 through 4 beginning on page 75.

2.2 PROCESS COSTING

1. **Use of Process Costing**

    a. Process cost accounting is used to assign costs to inventoriable goods or services. It is applicable to relatively homogeneous products that are mass produced on a continuous basis (e.g., petroleum products, thread, computer monitors).

        1) Assigning an exact amount of materials, labor, and indirect costs to thousands, or even millions, of individual end products is simply not cost-effective. For this reason, process costing involves averaging the costs of production and allocating them to work-in-process and finished goods.

2. **Accumulation of Costs**

    a. The accumulation of costs under a process costing system is by department rather than by project. There will normally be a work-in-process inventory account for each department.

        1) This reflects the continuous, homogeneous nature of the manufacturing process.

    b. As in job-order costing, the physical inputs required for the production process are obtained from suppliers.

```
Raw materials                                $XXX
    Accounts payable                                 $XXX
```

    c. Direct materials are used by the first department in the process.

```
Work-in-process -- Department A              $XXX
    Raw materials                                    $XXX
```

d. Because of the machine-intensive nature of process costing, direct labor tends to form a smaller proportion of overall costs than under job-order costing.

1) For this reason, cost accounting under process costing sometimes combines direct labor and manufacturing overhead and treats them as conversion costs.

2) Actual amounts are used. Standard costs are applied at a later stage for purposes of variance analysis.

Work-in-process -- Department A	$XXX	
Wages payable (direct and indirect labor)		$XXX
Manufacturing supplies (indirect materials)		XXX
Property taxes payable		XXX
Prepaid insurance		XXX
Accumulated depreciation -- factory equipment		XXX

e. The products move from one department to the next.

Work-in-process -- Department B	$XXX	
Work-in-process -- Department A		$XXX

f. The second department adds more direct materials and more conversion costs.

Work-in-process -- Department B	$XXX	
Raw materials		$XXX
Work-in-process -- Department B	$XXX	
Wages payable (direct and indirect labor)		$XXX
Manufacturing supplies (indirect materials)		XXX
Property taxes payable		XXX
Prepaid insurance		XXX
Accumulated depreciation -- factory equipment		XXX

g. If a standard costing system is used, standard costs are applied at this point to work-in-process, with the differences going to a direct materials variance and a conversion costs variance account.

h. When processing is finished in the last department, all the costs are transferred to finished goods.

Finished goods	$X,XXX	
Work-in-process -- Department B		$X,XXX

i. As products are sold, the costs are transferred to cost of goods sold.

Cost of goods sold	$X,XXX	
Finished goods		$X,XXX

3. **Process Costing Cost Flow Diagram**

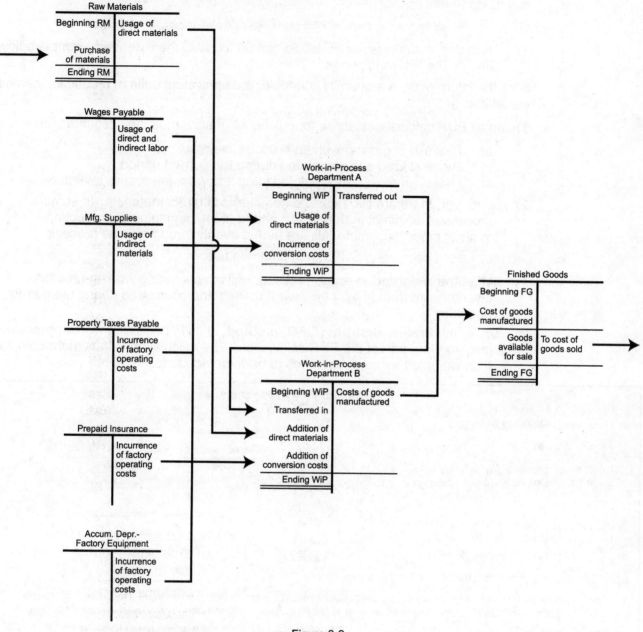

Figure 2-2

4. **Equivalent Units of Production (EUP)**

   a. Some units remain unfinished at the end of the period. For each department to account adequately for the costs attached to its unfinished units, the units must be restated in terms of equivalent units of production.

       1) The EUP is the number of complete goods that could have been produced using the inputs consumed during the period.

   b. The EUP conversion is a two-phase process: First, the equivalent units are determined, then the per-unit cost is calculated.

       1) The two calculations are made separately for direct materials and conversion costs (transferred-in costs are by definition 100% complete). Conversion costs are assumed to be uniformly incurred. Occasionally, a company will have to make three calculations: one for raw materials, another for direct labor, and a third for overhead.

c.   The first step is to prepare the quantity schedule. The quantity schedule is based on this fundamental relationship:

Beginning WIP + Units started = Units transferred out + Ending WIP

   1)   An example of a quantity schedule can be found in the extended example below and on the following pages.

d.   Using the information in a quantity schedule, the equivalent units of production can be calculated.

   1)   In all EUP calculations, three "populations" of units must be accounted for:

      a)   Those in beginning work-in-process inventory
      b)   Those started and completed during the current period
      c)   Those remaining uncompleted in ending work-in-process inventory

   2)   Moreover, there are two possible treatments of direct materials. In some processes, all direct materials are added at the beginning of production. In other processes, materials are added evenly throughout the process.

e.   Two methods of calculating EUP are in common use:

   1)   Under the **weighted-average method**, units in beginning work-in-process inventory are treated as if they were started and completed during the current period.

   2)   Under the **first-in, first-out (FIFO) method**, units in beginning work-in-process inventory are part of the EUP calculation. The calculation is thus more complex than weighted-average but tends to be more accurate.

EXTENDED EXAMPLE

Quantity Schedule

	Units	Completed for Direct Materials	Completed for Conversion Costs
Beginning work-in-process	2,000	80%	40%
Units started during period	8,000		
Units to account for	10,000		
Units transferred to next department	9,000		
Ending work-in-process	1,000	90%	70%
Units accounted for	10,000		

When direct materials are added at the beginning of the process

- Under weighted-average, prior period and current period costs are both considered. Thus, direct materials costs embedded in beginning WIP, as well as those added during the period, are used in the calculation.

- Under FIFO, only current period activity is considered. Since all DM were added in the previous period, no DM costs are added in the current period.

- Under both methods, ending WIP is by definition 100% complete with respect to materials. Notice that the ending inventory is only 70% complete with respect to conversion costs.

EUP for direct materials -- added at beginning of process:

	Weighted Average				FIFO			
Beginning WIP	2,000 units	× 100% (a)	=	2,000	2,000 units	× 0% (c)	=	0
Started and completed	7,000 units	× 100%	=	7,000	7,000 units	× 100%	=	7,000
Ending WIP	1,000 units	× 100% (b)	=	1,000	1,000 units	× 100% (d)	=	1,000
Totals	10,000			10,000	10,000			8,000

(a) Always 100%   (c) Needed to complete
(b) Degree of completeness   (d) Degree of completeness

-- **Continued on next page** --

EXTENDED EXAMPLE -- Continued

One way to remember the difference between weighted average and FIFO is to consider the theoretical implications of the calculation for beginning inventory. Under weighted average, costs will be the average for two periods, so you look at the work done for both periods -- in this case, 2,000 units. Under FIFO, you look at layers. Since this year's layer was zero, that is your EUP.

When direct materials are added evenly throughout the process

- Under weighted-average, the treatment of beginning WIP is the same as that when materials are added at the beginning (i.e., all units treated as started and completed in the current period).
- Under FIFO, the costs incurred in the current period for beginning WIP are only those needed to complete them.
- Under both methods, ending WIP uses the percentage of completion.

EUP for direct materials -- added throughout process:

Ending inventory is 90% complete, while beginning inventory is 80% complete.

	Weighted Average					FIFO				
Beginning WIP	2,000 units	×	100% (a)	=	2,000	2,000 units	×	20% (c)	=	400
Started and completed	7,000 units	×	100%	=	7,000	7,000 units	×	100%	=	7,000
Ending WIP	1,000 units	×	90% (b)	=	900	1,000 units	×	90% (d)	=	900
Totals	10,000				**9,900**	10,000				**8,300**

(a) Always 100%   (c) Needed to complete
(b) Degree of completeness   (d) Degree of completeness

Conversion costs by their nature are added evenly throughout the process. Based on the quantity schedule, ending inventory is 70% complete with respect to conversion costs.

EUP for conversion costs:

	Weighted Average					FIFO				
Beginning WIP	2,000 units	×	100% (a)	=	2,000	2,000 units	×	60% (c)	=	1,200
Started and completed	7,000 units	×	100%	=	7,000	7,000 units	×	100%	=	7,000
Ending WIP	1,000 units	×	70% (b)	=	700	1,000 units	×	70% (d)	=	700
Totals	10,000				**9,700**	10,000				**8,900**

(a) Always 100%   (c) Needed to complete
(b) Degree of completeness   (d) Degree of completeness

Assume that the costs to be allocated are as follows:

	Direct Materials	Conversion Costs		Total
Beginning work-in-process	$25,000	$10,000	=	$ 35,000
Added during the month	55,000	50,000	=	105,000
				$140,000

The per-unit costs under each of the two methods can now be derived.

- Under the weighted-average method, all direct materials and conversion costs are averaged in, both those incurred in the current period and those in beginning work-in-process. In other words, divide costs for both periods by all units worked on in both periods.
- Under the FIFO method, only the costs incurred in the current period are included in the calculation because only the work performed in the current period is included in EUP.

-- Continued on next page --

EXTENDED EXAMPLE -- Continued

Per-unit costs -- direct materials added at beginning of process:

Conversion costs are 70% complete on ending WIP.

	Weighted-average		FIFO	
Direct materials:	$\dfrac{\$25,000 + \$55,000}{10,000 \text{ EUP}}$	= $8.000	$\dfrac{\$55,000}{8,000 \text{ EUP}}$	= $6.875
Conversion costs:	$\dfrac{\$10,000 + \$50,000}{9,700 \text{ EUP}}$	= $6.186	$\dfrac{\$50,000}{8,900 \text{ EUP}}$	= $5.618
Total per-unit cost		**$14.186**		**$12.493**

Per-unit costs -- direct materials added throughout process:

	Weighted-average		FIFO	
Direct materials:	$\dfrac{\$25,000 + \$55,000}{9,900 \text{ EUP}}$	= $8.081	$\dfrac{\$55,000}{8,300 \text{ EUP}}$	= $6.627
Conversion costs:	$\dfrac{\$10,000 + \$50,000}{9,700 \text{ EUP}}$	= $6.186	$\dfrac{\$50,000}{8,900 \text{ EUP}}$	= $5.618
Total per-unit cost		**$14.267**		**$12.245**

The final step is the valuation of ending inventory. Equivalent units are used:

Ending inventory valuation -- direct materials added at beginning:

    Weighted-average $14.186 × 1,000 units = $14,186
    FIFO $12.493 × 1,000 units = $12,493

Ending inventory valuation -- direct materials added throughout:

    Weighted-average $14.267 × 1,000 units = $14,267
    FIFO $12.245 × 1,000 units = $12,245

5. **Spoilage in Process Costing**

    a. As with job-order costing, the cost of a normal level of spoilage is left in cost of goods sold; abnormal spoilage is recognized separately as a loss.

    b. Recognizing the loss resulting from abnormal spoilage under process costing is a multi-step process.

        1) The manufacturer establishes inspection points, that is, the places in the production process where those goods not meeting specifications are pulled from the process. This is in contrast to job-order costing, in which a unit can be judged to be spoiled at any time.

            a) The typical arrangement is to inspect units as they are being transferred from one department to the next. This way, each department has its own amount of spoilage, calculated using its own equivalent-unit costs.

        2) The loss is equal to the number of units of abnormal spoilage multiplied by the department's equivalent-units costs, whether weighted-average or FIFO.

            Loss on abnormal spoilage $XXX
                Work-in-process -- Department A $XXX

3) The following calculations serve as a check that all costs have been accounted for:

Weighted-Average

Costs in beginning WiP:				
Direct materials	$XX,XXX			
Conversion costs	XX,XXX			
Total costs in beginning WiP		$ XX,XXX		
Costs added in current period:			Cost of good units transferred out	$XXX,XXX
Direct materials	XX,XXX		Normal spoilage	XX,XXX
Conversion costs	XX,XXX		Abnormal spoilage	XX,XXX
Total costs added in current period		XX,XXX	Ending WiP	XX,XXX
Total costs to account for		$XXX,XXX	Total costs accounted for	$XXX,XXX

FIFO

Costs in beginning WiP		$ XX,XXX	Total from beginning WiP	$ XX,XXX
Costs added in current period:			Started and completed	XX,XXX
Direct materials	$XX,XXX		Normal spoilage	XX,XXX
Conversion costs	XX,XXX		Abnormal spoilage	XX,XXX
Total costs added in current period		XX,XXX	Ending WiP	XX,XXX
Total costs to account for		$XXX,XXX	Total costs accounted for	$XXX,XXX

Stop and review! You have completed the outline for this subunit. Study multiple-choice questions 5 through 20 beginning on page 76.

2.3 ACTIVITY-BASED COSTING

1. **Use of Activity-Based Costing**

    a. Activity-based costing (ABC) is a response to the significant increase in the incurrence of indirect costs resulting from the rapid advance of technology.

    1) ABC is a refinement of an existing costing system (job-order or process).

        a) Under a traditional (volume-based) costing system, overhead is simply dumped into a single cost pool and spread evenly across all end products.

        b) Under ABC, indirect costs are attached to activities that are then rationally allocated to end products.

    2) ABC may be used by manufacturing, service, or retailing entities.

2. **Traditional (Volume-Based) Costing System**

    a. The inaccurate averaging or spreading of indirect costs over products or service units that use different amounts of resources is called **peanut-butter costing**.

    1) Peanut-butter costing results in **product-cost cross-subsidization**, the condition in which the miscosting of one product causes the miscosting of other products.

    2) The peanut-butter effect of using a traditional (i.e., volume-based) costing system can be summarized as follows:

        a) Direct labor and direct materials are traced to products or service units.

        b) A single pool of indirect costs (overhead) is accumulated for a given organizational unit.

        c) Indirect costs from the pool are assigned using an allocative (rather than a tracing) procedure, such as using a single overhead rate for an entire department, e.g., $3 of overhead for every direct labor hour.

            i) The effect is an averaging of costs that may result in significant inaccuracy when products or service units do not use similar amounts of resources.

EXAMPLE of Product-Cost Cross-Subsidization

A company produces two similar products. Both products require one unit of raw material and one hour of direct labor. Raw materials costs are $14 per unit, and direct labor is $70 per hour. During the month just ended, the company produced 1,000 units of Product A and 100 units of Product B. Manufacturing overhead for the month totaled $20,000.

Using direct labor hours as the overhead allocation base, per-unit costs and profits are calculated as follows:

	Product A	Product B	Total
Raw materials	$ 14,000	$ 1,400	
Direct labor	70,000	7,000	
Overhead {$20,000 × [$70,000 ÷ ($70,000 + $7,000)]}	18,182		
Overhead {$20,000 × [$7,000 ÷ ($70,000 + $7,000)]}		1,818	
Total costs	**$102,182**	**$ 10,218**	**$112,400**
Selling price	$ 119.99	$ 119.99	
Cost per unit	(102.18)	(102.18)	
Profit per unit	**$ 17.81**	**$ 17.81**	

The company's management accountants have determined that overhead consists almost entirely of production line setup costs, and that the two products require equal setup times. Allocating overhead on this basis yields vastly different results.

	Product A	Product B	Total
Raw materials	$14,000	$ 1,400	
Direct labor	70,000	7,000	
Overhead ($20,000 × 50%)	10,000		
Overhead ($20,000 × 50%)		10,000	
Total costs	**$94,000**	**$18,400**	**$112,400**
Selling price	$119.99	$119.99	
Cost per unit	(94.00)	(184.00)	
Profit per unit	**$ 25.99**	**$ (64.01)**	

Rather than the comfortable profit the company believed it was making on both products using peanut-butter costing, it becomes clear that the company is losing money on every unit of Product B that it sells. The high-volume Product A has been heavily subsidizing the setup costs for the low-volume Product B.

    b.   The previous example assumed a single component of overhead for clarity. In reality, overhead is made up of many components.

        1)   The peanut-butter effect of traditional overhead allocation is illustrated in the following diagram:

Overhead Allocation in a Traditional (Volume-Based) Cost Accumulation System

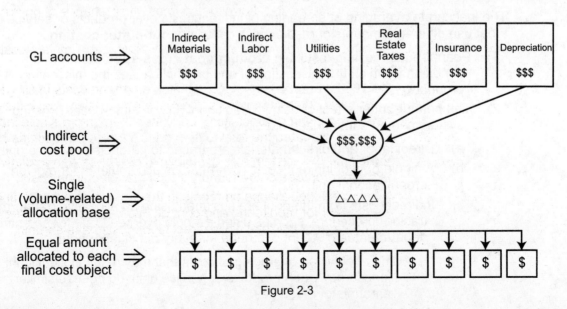

Figure 2-3

3. **Volume-Based Systems vs. Activity-Based Systems**

    a. Volume-based systems were appropriate throughout the decades when direct costs were the bulk of manufacturing costs. With increasing automation, however, overhead became an ever greater percentage of the total. ABC was developed to deal with this increasing complexity of overhead costs.

        1) **Volume-based systems**, as illustrated on the previous page, involve

            a) Accumulating costs in general ledger accounts (utilities, taxes, etc.),
            b) Using a single cost pool to combine the costs in all the related accounts,
            c) Selecting a single driver to use for the entire indirect cost pool, and
            d) Allocating the indirect cost pool to final cost objects.

        2) **Activity-based systems**, by contrast, involve

            a) Identifying organization activities that constitute overhead,
            b) Assigning the costs of resources consumed by the activities, and
            c) Assigning the costs of the activities to final cost objects, based on the activity that drives (causes) the costs.

4. **Steps in Activity-Based Costing**

    a. **Step 1 – Activity Analysis**

        1) An activity is a set of work actions undertaken within the entity, and a cost pool is established for each activity.

        2) Activities are classified in a hierarchy according to the level of the production process at which they take place.

            a) **Unit-level activities** are performed for each unit of output produced. Examples are using direct materials and using direct labor.

            b) **Batch-level activities** occur for each group of outputs produced. Examples are materials ordering, materials handling, and production line setup.

            c) **Product-sustaining** (or service-sustaining) **activities** support the production of a particular product (or service), irrespective of the level of production. Examples are product design, engineering changes, and testing.

            d) **Facility-sustaining activities** concern overall operations and therefore cannot be traced to products at any point in the production process. Examples are accounting, human resources, maintenance of physical plant, and safety/security arrangements.

        3) EXAMPLE: Fabulous Foundry uses a job-order system to accumulate costs for the custom pipe fittings of all sizes that it produces.

            a) Since the 1950s, Fabulous has accumulated overhead costs in six general ledger accounts (indirect materials, indirect labor, utilities, real estate taxes, insurance, and depreciation), combined them into a single indirect cost pool, and allocated the total to its products based on machine hours.

               i) At the time this system was established, overhead was a relatively small percentage of the foundry's total manufacturing costs.

               ii) With increasing reliance on robots in the production process and computers for monitoring and control, overhead is now a greater percentage of the total while direct labor costs have shrunk.

b)   To obtain better data about product costs, Fabulous has decided to refine its job-order costing system by switching to activity-based costing for the allocation of overhead.

  i)   The foundry's management accountants conducted extensive interviews with production and sales personnel to determine how the incurrence of indirect costs can be viewed as activities that consume resources.

  ii) The accountants identified five activities and created a cost pool for each to capture the incurrence of indirect costs:

Activity	Hierarchy
Product design	Product-sustaining
Production setup	Batch-level
Machining	Unit-level
Inspection & testing	Unit-level
Customer maintenance	Facility-sustaining

b. **Step 2 – Assign Resource Costs to Activities**

  1)   Once the activities are designated, the next step in enacting an ABC system is to assign the costs of resources to the activities. This is termed first-stage allocation.

  2)   Identifying resource costs is not the simple matter it is in volume-based overhead allocation (where certain GL accounts are designated for combination into a single cost pool).

    a)   A separate accounting system may be necessary to track resource costs separately from the general ledger.

  3)   Once the resources have been identified, resource drivers are designated to allocate resource costs to the activity cost pools.

    a)   Resource drivers (causes) are measures of the resources consumed by an activity.

  4)   EXAMPLE: Fabulous Foundry's management accountants identified the following resources used by its indirect cost processes:

Resource	Driver
Computer processing	CPU cycles
Production line	Machine hours
Materials management	Hours worked
Accounting	Hours worked
Sales & marketing	Number of orders

c. **Step 3 – Allocate Activity Cost Pools to Final Cost Objects**

  1)   The final step in enacting an ABC system is allocating the activity cost pools to final cost objects. This is termed second-stage allocation.

  2)   Costs are reassigned to final-stage (or, if intermediate cost objects are used, next-stage) cost objects on the basis of activity drivers.

    a)   Activity drivers are measures of the demands made on an activity by next-stage cost objects, such as the number of parts in a product used to measure an assembly activity.

    b)   EXAMPLE: Fabulous Foundry's management accountants have designated these drivers to associate with their corresponding activities:

Activity	Driver
Product design	Number of products
Production setup	Number of setups
Machining	Number of units produced
Inspection & testing	Number of units produced
Customer maintenance	Number of orders

5. **Indirect Cost Assignment Diagram**

   a. The differences between traditional overhead allocation and activity-based costing are illustrated in the following diagram:

Indirect Cost Assignment in an Activity-Based Costing System

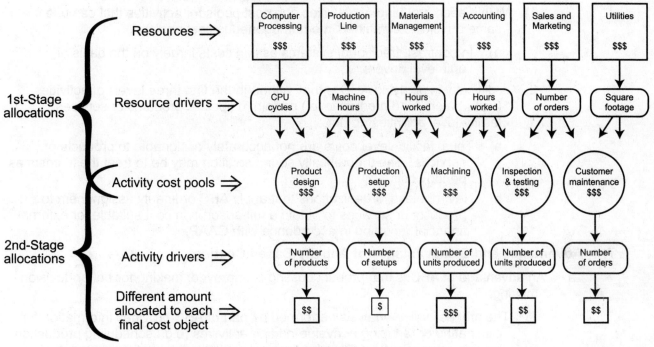

Figure 2-4

6. **Cost Drivers**

   a. Drivers (both resource and activity) must be chosen on the basis of a cause-and-effect relationship with the resource or activity cost being allocated, not simply a high positive correlation.

      1) A cost object may be a job, product, process, activity, service, or anything else for which a cost measure is desired.

      2) Intermediate cost objects receive temporary accumulations of costs as the cost pools move from their originating points to the final cost objects.

         a) For example, work-in-process is an intermediate cost object, and finished salable goods are final cost objects.

   b. Design of an ABC system starts with process value analysis, a comprehensive understanding of how an organization generates its output.

      1) A process value analysis involves a determination of which activities that use resources are value-adding or nonvalue-adding and how the latter may be reduced or eliminated.

         a) A value-adding activity contributes to customer satisfaction or meets a need of the entity. The perception is that it cannot be omitted without a loss of the quantity, quality, or responsiveness of output demanded by the entity or its customers.

         b) A nonvalue-adding activity does not make such a contribution. It can be eliminated, reduced, or redesigned without impairing the quantity, quality, or responsiveness of the product or service desired by customers or the entity.

      2) The linkage of product costing and continuous improvement of processes is activity-based management (ABM). It encompasses driver analysis, activity analysis, and performance measurement.

  c. Using a four-level driver-analysis model, activities are grouped, and drivers are determined for the activities.

      1) Within each grouping of activities, the cost pools for activities that can use the same driver are combined into homogeneous cost pools.

         a) In contrast, traditional systems assign costs largely on the basis of unit-level drivers.

      2) A difficulty in applying ABC is that, although the first three levels of activities (unit-, batch-, and product-level) pertain to specific products or services, facility-level activities do not.

         a) Thus, facility-level costs are not accurately assignable to products or services. The theoretically sound solution may be to treat these costs as period costs.

         b) Nevertheless, organizations that apply ABC ordinarily assign them to products or services to obtain a full-absorption cost suitable for external financial reporting in accordance with GAAP.

7. **Advantages and Disadvantages of Activity-Based Costing**

  a. An advantage of ABC is that product costing is improved, making for better decision making.

      1) The process value analysis performed as part of ABC provides information for eliminating or reducing nonvalue-adding activities (e.g., scheduling production, moving components, waiting for the next operating step, inspecting output, or storing inventories).

         a) The result is therefore not only more accurate cost assignments, especially of overhead, but also better cost control and more efficient operations.

  b. A disadvantage of ABC is the increased time and effort needed to

      1) Maintain a separate accounting system to capture resource costs.

      2) Design and implement drivers and cost pools.

      3) ABC-derived costs of products or services may not conform with GAAP; for example, ABC may assign research costs to products but not such traditional product costs as plant depreciation, insurance, or taxes.

8. **Organizational Benefits**

  a. Organizations most likely to benefit from using ABC are those with products or services that vary significantly in volume, diversity of activities, and complexity of operations; relatively high overhead costs; or operations that have undergone major technological or design changes.

      1) Although the previous illustrations have assumed a manufacturing operation, service organizations can also use ABC and most of the advantages will be similar. However, service organizations may have some difficulty in implementing ABC because they tend to have relatively high facility-level costs that are difficult to assign to specific service units.

         a) Service organizations also engage in many nonuniform human activities for which information is not readily accumulated.

         b) Moreover, output measurement is more problematic in service than in manufacturing entities.

         c) Nevertheless, ABC has been adopted by various insurers, banks, railroads, and healthcare providers.

b. Direct labor (hours or dollars) has long been the most common base for allocating overhead because of the simplicity of the calculation, but it is not always relevant.

1) Companies now use dozens of different allocation bases depending upon how activity affects overhead costs. One company reported that it used 37 different bases to allocate overhead, some of which were averages of several activities.

2) In principle, a separate overhead account or subsidiary ledger account should be used for each type of overhead.

3) In the past, "people were cheap and machines were expensive." This meant that direct labor was ordinarily a larger component of total production cost than overhead and was the activity that drove (caused) overhead costs.

a) Due to the lowered cost of computers and robotics and the expansion of employee benefits ("machines are cheap and people are expensive"), overhead is more likely to be a large component of total production cost, with direct labor often a small percentage.

b) Most overhead costs vary in proportion to product diversity and the complexity of an operation.

i) Direct labor is not a cost driver for most overhead costs.

c) Allocating a very large cost (overhead) using a very small cost (direct labor) as a base is irrational.

i) A small change in direct labor on a product can make a significant difference in total production cost, an effect that may rest on an invalid assumption about the relationship of the cost and the allocation base.

4) As previously noted, ABC is more useful when overhead costs are relatively high.

a) Also, the more diverse a company's line of products or services or the more significant the volume differences among its products or services, the more beneficial ABC will be.

b) Simple averaging procedures such as direct-labor-based costing are valid only when products or services are absolutely uniform. For example, a simple allocation basis in a factory with large and small machines and high-priced and low-cost labor that work together would not be very exact.

c. Companies use ABC because of its ability to solve costing problems that conventional cost accounting either creates or fails to address.

1) These problems include suboptimal pricing, poor allocation of costs, and incorrect direction by management.

2) For example, if overhead is allocated at 700% of direct labor, managers may try to reduce direct labor costs by $1 to reduce the amount of overhead allocated by $7.

a) But the better decision may be to ignore direct labor and concentrate on such cost-cutting efforts as eliminating setups, engineering changes, and movement of materials.

d. ABC is the theoretically preferred method of overhead allocation, but its disadvantage is its cost of implementation.

1) Initial costs are quite high, and continuing costs of application can also be significant. Thus, if a company has a low level of fixed costs, there is little or no advantage to using ABC as compared to a simple overhead application method, such as a fixed amount per direct labor hour.

2) Similarly, if a company produces a single product, there is no advantage. Also, if volume levels among various products do not vary too much, there is little advantage.

3) The real benefits of ABC occur when a company has a high level of fixed costs and produces a wide variety of products with widely varying levels of production.

Stop and review! You have completed the outline for this subunit. Study multiple-choice questions 21 through 27 beginning on page 82.

2.4 LIFE-CYCLE COSTING

1. **Life-Cycle Approach**

    a. A life-cycle approach to budgeting estimates a product's revenues and expenses over its entire sales life cycle beginning with research and development, proceeding through the introduction and growth stages into the maturity stage, and finally into the harvest or decline stage.

        1) Accordingly, life-cycle costing takes a long-term view of the entire cost life cycle, also known as the value chain.

Value Chain for a Manufacturer

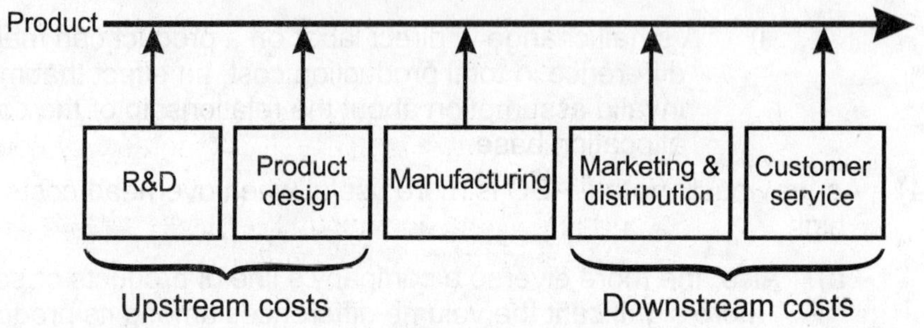

Figure 2-5

        2) This information is important for pricing decisions because revenues must cover costs incurred in each stage of the value chain, not just production.

2. **Potential Benefits**

    a. Life-cycle costing emphasizes the relationships among costs incurred at different value-chain stages, for example, the effect of reduced design costs on future customer-service costs.

        1) Because it makes a distinction between incurring costs (actually using resources) and locking in (designing in) costs, life-cycle costing highlights the potential for cost reduction activities during the upstream phase of the value chain.

        2) It is in this phase that the greatest opportunity exists to minimize downstream costs. Indeed, it has been estimated that 90% or more of costs are committed (not incurred) before production begins.

3. **Life-Cycle vs. Other Costing Methods**

    a. In contrast, traditional approaches focus on cost control (as opposed to cost reduction) during production and treat pre- and postproduction (upstream and downstream) costs as period costs that are largely ignored in determining the profitability of specific products.

        1) Other costs that traditional methods ignore are the after-purchase costs (operating, support, repair, and disposal) incurred by customers.

2) Accordingly, whole-life cost is a concept closely associated with life-cycle cost.

    a) Whole-life cost equals the life-cycle cost plus after-purchase costs.

    b) Attention to the reduction of all whole-life costs through analysis and management of all value-chain activities is a powerful competitive tool because of the potential for increasing customer satisfaction.

3) Life-cycle and whole-life cost concepts are associated with target costing and target pricing.

    a) A firm may determine that market conditions require that a product sell at a given target price.

    b) Hence, a target cost can be determined by subtracting the desired unit profit margin from the target price.

    c) The cost reduction objectives of life-cycle and whole-life cost management can therefore be determined using target costing.

4) Value engineering is a means of reaching targeted cost levels.

    a) Value engineering is a systematic approach to assessing all aspects of the value chain cost buildup for a product.

        i) The purpose is to minimize costs without reducing customer satisfaction.

    b) For this purpose, distinguishing between value-adding and nonvalue-adding activities is useful.

        i) A value-adding activity contributes to customer value or satisfies a need of the entity. A nonvalue-adding activity does not make such a contribution.

        ii) Accordingly, value engineering seeks to minimize nonvalue-adding activities and their costs by reducing the cost drivers of those activities.

        iii) Value engineering also attempts to minimize the costs of value-adding activities by improving their efficiency.

4. **Internal and External Reporting Effects**

    a. For external financial statement purposes, costs during the upstream phase must be expensed in the period incurred.

    1) For internal management accounting purposes, the costs (such as R&D) that result in marketable products represent a life-cycle investment and must be capitalized.

        a) As a result, organizations that focus on a product's life cycle must develop an accounting system consistent with GAAP for external financial reporting purposes.

        b) It should also allow for capitalization and subsequent allocation of upstream costs for management accounting purposes.

    2) Essentially, life-cycle costing requires the accumulation of all costs over a product's lifetime, from inception of the idea to the abandonment of the product.

        a) These costs are then allocated to production on an expected unit-of-output basis.

3)   The internal income statement for a product will report total sales for all periods, minus all expenses to date.

    a)   A risk reserve may be established as an account contra to the capitalized costs.

    b)   The reserve consists of any deferred product costs that might not be recovered if sales are less than planned.

4)   The overall advantage of life-cycle costing is that it provides a better measure for evaluating the performance of product managers.

    a)   Traditional financial statements, however, might report that certain products were extremely profitable because upstream costs were expensed in previous periods.

    b)   For example, if a substantial investment is made in the development of a new product, but that product quickly becomes obsolete due to new technology, how worthwhile was the investment?

    c)   Life-cycle costing combines all costs and revenues for all periods to provide a better view of a product's overall performance.

Stop and review! You have completed the outline for this subunit. Study multiple-choice questions 28 through 31 beginning on page 85.

2.5 CORE CONCEPTS

Job-Order Costing

■   **Job-order costing** is concerned with accumulating costs by specific job. This method is appropriate when producing products with individual characteristics or when identifiable groupings are possible, e.g., yachts, jewelry.

    ●   **Direct costs** (direct materials and direct labor) are charged at the actual amounts incurred.

    ●   **Manufacturing overhead** is charged using an estimated rate. Overhead costs are applied to ("absorbed" by) each job based on a predetermined overhead application rate for the year. At the end of the period, overhead may have been overapplied or underapplied.

■   Output that does not meet the quality standards for salability is considered spoilage.

    ●   If the spoilage is the amount expected in the ordinary course of production, it is considered **normal spoilage** and treated as a product cost.

    ●   If the spoilage is over and above the amount expected in the ordinary course of production, it is considered **abnormal spoilage** and is treated as a period cost.

Process Costing

■   Process cost accounting is used to assign costs to relatively **homogeneous products** that are mass produced on a continuous basis (e.g., petroleum products, thread, computer monitors).

■   Direct materials are used by the first department in the process. Conversion costs are the sum of direct labor and manufacturing overhead. The products move from one department to the next. Each department adds more direct materials and more conversion costs.

■   **Equivalent units of production (EUP)** is the number of complete goods that could have been produced using the inputs consumed during the period.

    ●   The EUP conversion is a two-phase process: First, the equivalent units are determined, then the per-unit cost is calculated.

    ●   The two calculations are made separately for direct materials and conversion costs (transferred-in costs are by definition 100% complete). Conversion costs are assumed to be uniformly incurred.

- **Two methods** of calculating EUP are in common use:
  - Under the **weighted-average** method, units in beginning work-in-process inventory are treated as if they were started and completed during the current period.
  - Under the **first-in, first-out (FIFO)** method, units in beginning work-in-process inventory are part of the EUP calculation. The calculation is thus more complex than weighted-average but tends to be more accurate.

Activity-Based Costing

- Activity-based costing (ABC) is a response to the significant increase in the incurrence of indirect costs resulting from the rapid advance of technology. ABC is a refinement of an existing costing system (job-order or process).
- Volume-based systems involve accumulating costs in general ledger accounts (utilities, taxes, etc.), using a single cost pool to combine the costs in all the related accounts, selecting a single driver to use for the entire indirect cost pool, and allocating the indirect cost pool to final cost objects.
- Activity-based systems, by contrast, involve identifying organization activities that constitute overhead, assigning the costs of resources consumed by the activities, and assigning the costs of the activities to final cost objects.
- Activities are classified in a hierarchy according to the level of the production process at which they take place: unit-level activities, batch-level activities, product-sustaining (or service-sustaining) activities, and facility-sustaining activities.
- Once the activities are designated, the next step in enacting an ABC system is to assign the costs of resources to the activities. This is termed first-stage allocation. A separate accounting system may be necessary to track resource costs separately from the general ledger.
- Once the resources have been identified, resource drivers are designated to allocate resource costs to the activity cost pools. Resource drivers are measures of the resources consumed by an activity.
- The final step in enacting an ABC system is allocating the activity cost pools to final cost objects. This is termed second-stage allocation. Costs are reassigned to final-stage (or, if intermediate cost objects are used, next-stage) cost objects on the basis of activity drivers. Activity drivers are measures of the demands made on an activity by next-stage cost objects, such as the number of parts in a product used to measure an assembly activity.
- A cost object may be a job, product, process, activity, service, or anything else for which a cost measure is desired. Intermediate cost objects receive temporary accumulations of costs as the cost pools move from their originating points to the final cost objects. For example, work-in-process is an intermediate cost object, and finished salable goods are final cost objects.

Life-Cycle Costing

- A life-cycle approach to budgeting estimates a product's revenues and expenses over its entire sales life cycle beginning with research and development, proceeding through the introduction and growth stages into the maturity stage, and finally into the harvest or decline stage. Accordingly, life-cycle costing takes a long-term view of the entire cost life cycle, also known as the value chain.
- Life-cycle costing emphasizes the relationships among costs incurred at different value-chain stages, for example, the effect of reduced design costs on future customer-service costs. Because it makes a distinction between incurring costs (actually using resources) and locking in (designing in) costs, life-cycle costing highlights the potential for cost reduction activities during the upstream phase of the value chain.
- Essentially, life-cycle costing requires the accumulation of all costs over a product's lifetime, from inception of the idea to the abandonment of the product. These costs are then allocated to production on an expected unit-of-output basis.

*Page
Intentionally
Left Blank*

QUESTIONS

2.1 Job-Order Costing

1. Lucy Sportswear manufactures a specialty line of T-shirts using a job-order costing system. During March, the following costs were incurred in completing job ICU2: direct materials, $13,700; direct labor, $4,800; administrative, $1,400; and selling, $5,600. Overhead was applied at the rate of $25 per machine hour, and job ICU2 required 800 machine hours. If job ICU2 resulted in 7,000 good shirts, the cost of goods sold per unit would be

A. $6.50

B. $6.30

C. $5.70

D. $5.50

Answer (D) is correct. *(CMA, adapted)*
REQUIRED: The cost of goods sold per unit using job-order costing.
DISCUSSION: Cost of goods sold is based on the manufacturing costs incurred in production but does not include selling or general and administrative expenses. Manufacturing costs equal $38,500 [$13,700 DM + $4,800 DL + (800 hours × $25) OH]. Thus, per-unit cost is $5.50 ($38,500 ÷ 7,000 units).
Answer (A) is incorrect. The amount of $6.50 includes selling and administrative expenses. Answer (B) is incorrect. The amount of $6.30 includes selling costs. Answer (C) is incorrect. The amount of $5.70 includes administrative expenses.

2. Kepler Optics makes lenses for telescopes. Because Kepler will only sell lenses of the highest quality, the normal spoilage during a reporting period is 1,000 units. At the beginning of the current reporting period, Kepler had 2,200 units in inventory, and during the period, production was started and completed on 4,000 units. Units in inventory at the end of the current reporting period were 1,500, and the units transferred out were 3,000. During this period, the abnormal spoilage for Kepler's lens production was

A. 700 units.

B. 1,000 units.

C. 1,700 units.

D. 3,200 units.

Answer (A) is correct. *(CMA, adapted)*
REQUIRED: The abnormal spoilage for the period.
DISCUSSION: Kepler's abnormal spoilage for the period can be calculated as follows:

Beginning work-in-process	2,200
Add: started and completed	4,000
Less: transferred out	(3,000)
Less: ending work-in-process	(1,500)
Total spoilage for period	1,700
Less: normal spoilage	(1,000)
Abnormal spoilage for period	700

Answer (B) is incorrect. The normal spoilage for the period is 1,000 units. Answer (C) is incorrect. The total spoilage for the period is 1,700 units. Answer (D) is incorrect. Failing to subtract the ending work-in-process to arrive at total spoilage results in 3,200 units.

3. What is the journal entry to record the purchase of materials on account?

A. Raw materials inventory   XX
     Accounts payable   XX

B. Accounts payable   XX
     Raw materials inventory   XX

C. Accounts receivable   XX
     Accounts payable   XX

D. Raw materials inventory   XX
     Cash   XX

Answer (A) is correct. *(Publisher, adapted)*
REQUIRED: The journal entry to record the purchase of materials on account.
DISCUSSION: The correct entry to record a purchase of materials on account is to increase the appropriate asset and liability accounts. Materials are charged to an inventory; the corresponding liability is accounts payable. The asset account(s) could be stores control and/or supplies or a number of other accounts. Also, subsidiary ledgers may be used to account for various individual items (a perpetual inventory system). The term control implies that a subsidiary ledger is being used.
Answer (B) is incorrect. The entry to record the return of materials to suppliers debits accounts payable and credits raw materials inventory. Answer (C) is incorrect. This entry reclassifies credit balances in accounts receivable as liabilities or debit balances in accounts payable as assets. Answer (D) is incorrect. This entry would record the purchase of materials for cash.

4. Darden Manufacturing, a calendar-year corporation, had $17,000 of spoilage during April that production management characterized as abnormal. The spoilage was incurred on Job No. 532, which was sold 3 months later for $459,000. Which of the following correctly describes the impact of the spoilage on Darden's unit manufacturing cost for Job No. 532 and on the year's operating income?

	Unit Manufacturing Cost	Operating Income
A.	Increase	No effect
B.	Increase	Decrease
C.	No effect	Decrease
D.	No effect	Not enough information to judge

Answer (C) is correct. *(CMA, adapted)*
REQUIRED: The impact abnormal spoilage has on unit manufacturing cost and operating income.
DISCUSSION: Under job-order costing, unit manufacturing cost is unaffected by abnormal spoilage. Also, the difference between the disposal value of the spoiled goods and the value of the goods in work-in-process control must be recognized as a loss, which will decrease operating income.
Answer (A) is incorrect. Under job-order costing, the difference between the disposal value of the spoiled goods and the value of the goods in work-in-process control must be recognized as a loss. Answer (B) is incorrect. Under job-order costing, unit manufacturing cost is unaffected by abnormal spoilage. Answer (D) is incorrect. Under job-order costing, the difference between the disposal value of the spoiled goods and the value of the goods in work-in-process control must be recognized as a loss.

2.2 Process Costing

Questions 5 through 8 are based on the following information.

Levittown Company employs a process cost system for its manufacturing operations. All direct materials are added at the beginning of the process and conversion costs are added proportionately. Levittown's production quantity schedule for November is reproduced in the next column.

Units work-in-process November 1 (60% complete as to conversion costs)	1,000
Units started during November	5,000
Total units to account for	6,000
Units completed and transferred out from beginning inventory	1,000
Units started and completed during November	3,000
Work-in-process on November 30 (20% complete as to conversion costs)	2,000
Total units accounted for	6,000

5. Using the FIFO method, Levittown's equivalent units for direct materials for November are

A. 5,000 units.

B. 6,000 units.

C. 4,400 units.

D. 3,800 units.

Answer (A) is correct. *(CMA, adapted)*
REQUIRED: The equivalent units for direct materials under the FIFO method.
DISCUSSION: The computation of equivalent units for a period using the FIFO method of process costing includes only the conversion costs and material added to the product in that period and excludes any work done in previous periods. Accordingly, FIFO equivalent units include work and material to complete BWIP, plus work and material to complete units started this period, minus work and material needed to complete EWIP. Given that all materials are added at the beginning of the process, only those units started during November would have received materials in that month. Because 5,000 units were started, the equivalent units for direct materials equal 5,000.
Answer (B) is incorrect. The total units to account for is 6,000. Answer (C) is incorrect. The number of units completed and transferred out from BI plus units started and completed in November plus 20% of work-in-process on November 30 equals 4,400 (1,000 + 3,000 + 400). Answer (D) is incorrect. The equivalent units for direct materials is not 3,800. Only those units started during November would have received materials in that month. Therefore, equivalent units for direct materials equal 5,000.

6. Using the FIFO method, Levittown's equivalent units for conversion costs for November are

   A. 3,400 units.

   B. 3,800 units.

   C. 4,000 units.

   D. 4,400 units.

Answer (B) is correct. *(CMA, adapted)*
REQUIRED: The equivalent units for conversion costs under the FIFO method.
DISCUSSION: Given that BWIP (1,000 units) was already 60% complete, 400 equivalent units were needed for completion. In addition, 3,000 units were started and completed during the period. The 2,000 units in EWIP equal 400 equivalent units since they are 20% complete. Total equivalent units are 3,800 (400 + 3,000 + 400).
Answer (A) is incorrect. The units started and completed during November plus the 20% of work-in-process complete as to conversion costs equals 3,400 units (3,000 + 400). Answer (C) is incorrect. The number of units started and completed in November and the units completed and transferred out from BI equals 4,000 units (3,000 + 1,000). Answer (D) is incorrect. The number of units started and completed in November, plus the units completed and transferred out from BI, plus the 20% of work-in-process complete as to conversion costs equals 4,400 units (3,000 + 1,000 + 400).

7. Using the weighted-average method, Levittown's equivalent units for direct materials for November are

   A. 3,400 units.

   B. 4,400 units.

   C. 5,000 units.

   D. 6,000 units.

Answer (D) is correct. *(CMA, adapted)*
REQUIRED: The equivalent units for direct materials using the weighted-average method.
DISCUSSION: The difference between the weighted-average and FIFO methods of process costing is how BWIP is handled. FIFO makes a distinction between the costs in BWIP and the costs of goods started this period. Weighted average does not. Thus, when there is no BWIP, there is no difference between the two costing methods. Because 6,000 units have been started (1,000 BWIP + 5,000 started this period), and all materials are added at the beginning of the process, equivalent units for materials equal 6,000.
Answer (A) is incorrect. Units started and completed in November plus 20% of ending work-in-process equals 3,400 units (3,000 + 400). Answer (B) is incorrect. The number of units started and completed in November plus units completed and transferred out from BI plus 20% of ending work-in-process equals 4,400 units (3,000 + 1,000 + 400). Answer (C) is incorrect. The number of units started in November is 5,000.

8. Using the weighted-average method, Levittown's equivalent units for conversion costs for November are

   A. 3,400 units.

   B. 3,800 units.

   C. 4,000 units.

   D. 4,400 units.

Answer (D) is correct. *(CMA, adapted)*
REQUIRED: The equivalent units for conversion costs using the weighted-average method.
DISCUSSION: Under the weighted-average method, work in the previous period on the beginning inventories is included along with the work added this period. Thus, the only difference between the FIFO calculations and the weighted-average calculation is the equivalent units for the beginning inventory. The 4,000 completed units (1,000 BWIP + 3,000 started this period) equal 4,000 equivalent units. The 2,000 units in EWIP are equivalent to 400 units (2,000 units × 20% complete). Thus, there are 4,400 conversion cost equivalent units.
Answer (A) is incorrect. The number of 3,400 units consist of the units started and completed in November plus the 20% of work-in-process complete as to conversion costs (3,000 + 400). Answer (B) is incorrect. The number of 3,800 units equal the 400 units in BWIP needed for completion plus the units started and completed in November plus the 20% of work-in-process complete as to conversion costs (400 + 3,000 + 400). Answer (C) is incorrect. The number of 4,000 units equal the units completed and transferred out from BI plus units started and completed during November (1,000 + 3,000).

Questions 9 through 15 are based on the following information.

Kimbeth Manufacturing uses a process cost system to manufacture Dust Density Sensors for the mining industry. The following information pertains to operations for the month of May.

	Units
Beginning work-in-process inventory, May 1	16,000
Started in production during May	100,000
Completed production during May	92,000
Ending work-in-process inventory, May 31	24,000

The beginning inventory was 60% complete for materials and 20% complete for conversion costs. The ending inventory was 90% complete for materials and 40% complete for conversion costs.

Costs pertaining to the month of May are as follows:

• Beginning inventory costs are materials, $54,560; direct labor, $20,320; and overhead, $15,240.
• Costs incurred during May are materials used, $468,000; direct labor, $182,880; and overhead, $391,160.

9. Using the first-in, first-out (FIFO) method, Kimbeth's equivalent units of production (EUP) for materials are

A. 97,600 units.

B. 104,000 units.

C. 107,200 units.

D. 108,000 units.

Answer (B) is correct. *(CMA, adapted)*
REQUIRED: The equivalent units of production for materials under FIFO.
DISCUSSION: Under FIFO, EUP are based solely on work performed during the current period. The EUP equals the sum of the work done on the beginning work-in-process inventory, units started and completed in the current period, and the ending work-in-process inventory. Given that beginning work-in-process was 60% complete as to materials, the current period is charged for 6,400 EUP (16,000 units × 40%). Because 92,000 units were completed during the period, 76,000 (92,000 – 16,000 in BWIP) must have been started and completed during the period. They represent 76,000 EUP. Finally, the EUP for ending work-in-process equal 21,600 (24,000 units × 90%). Thus, total EUP for May are 104,000 (6,400 + 76,000 + 21,600).
Answer (A) is incorrect. This number of units omits the 6,400 EUP added to beginning work-in-process. Answer (C) is incorrect. This number of units assumes beginning work-in-process was 40% complete. Answer (D) is incorrect. This number of units equals the sum of the physical units in beginning work-in-process and the physical units completed.

10. Using the FIFO method, Kimbeth's equivalent units of production for conversion costs are

A. 85,600 units.

B. 88,800 units.

C. 95,200 units.

D. 98,400 units.

Answer (D) is correct. *(CMA, adapted)*
REQUIRED: The equivalent units of production for conversion costs under FIFO.
DISCUSSION: The beginning inventory was 20% complete as to conversion costs. Hence, 12,800 EUP (16,000 units × 80%) were required for completion. EUP for units started and completed equaled 76,000 [(92,000 completed units – 16,000 units in BWIP) × 100%]. The work done on ending work-in-process totaled 9,600 EUP (24,000 units × 40%). Thus, total EUP for May are 98,400 (12,800 + 76,000 + 9,600).
Answer (A) is incorrect. This number of units omits the work done on beginning work-in-process. Answer (B) is incorrect. This number of units omits the work done on ending work-in-process. Answer (C) is incorrect. This number of units assumes the beginning work-in-process was 40% complete as to conversion costs.

11. Using the FIFO method, Kimbeth's equivalent unit cost of materials for May is

A. $4.12

B. $4.50

C. $4.60

D. $4.80

Answer (B) is correct. *(CMA, adapted)*
REQUIRED: The equivalent unit cost of materials under FIFO.
DISCUSSION: Under the FIFO method, EUP for materials equal 104,000 [(16,000 units in BWIP × 40%) + (76,000 units started and completed × 100%) + (24,000 units in EWIP × 90%)]. Consequently, the equivalent unit cost of materials is $4.50 ($468,000 total materials cost in May ÷ 104,000 EUP).
Answer (A) is incorrect. The amount of $4.12 is based on EUP calculated under the weighted-average method. Answer (C) is incorrect. The amount of $4.60 is the weighted-average cost per equivalent unit. Answer (D) is incorrect. The amount of $4.80 omits the 6,400 EUP added to beginning work-in-process.

12. Using the FIFO method, Kimbeth's equivalent unit conversion cost for May is

A. $5.65

B. $5.83

C. $6.00

D. $6.20

Answer (B) is correct. *(CMA, adapted)*
REQUIRED: The conversion cost per equivalent unit under FIFO.
DISCUSSION: Under the FIFO method, EUP for conversion costs equal 98,400 [(16,000 units in BWIP × 80%) + (76,000 units started and completed × 100%) + (24,000 units in EWIP × 40%)]. Conversion costs incurred during the current period equal $574,040 ($182,880 DL + $391,160 FOH). Hence, the equivalent unit cost for conversion costs is $5.83 ($574,040 ÷ 98,400).
Answer (A) is incorrect. The amount of $5.65 is based on EUP calculated under the weighted-average method. Answer (C) is incorrect. The amount of $6.00 is the cost per equivalent unit calculated under the weighted-average method. Answer (D) is incorrect. The amount of $6.20 results from combining conversion costs for May with those in beginning work-in-process and dividing by 98,400 EUP.

13. Using the FIFO method, Kimbeth's total cost of units in the ending work-in-process inventory at May 31 is

A. $153,168

B. $154,800

C. $155,328

D. $156,960

Answer (A) is correct. *(CMA, adapted)*
REQUIRED: The total cost of units in ending work-in-process under FIFO.
DISCUSSION: The FIFO costs per equivalent unit for materials and conversion costs are $4.50 and $5.83, respectively. EUP for materials in ending work-in-process equal 21,600 (24,000 × 90%). Thus, total FIFO materials cost is $97,200 (21,600 EUP × $4.50). EUP for conversion costs in ending work-in-process equal 9,600 (24,000 × 40%). Total conversion costs are therefore $55,968 (9,600 EUP × $5.83). Consequently, total work-in-process costs are $153,168 ($97,200 + $55,968).
Answer (B) is incorrect. The amount of $154,800 is based on a FIFO calculation for materials and a weighted-average calculation for conversion costs. Answer (C) is incorrect. The amount of $155,328 is based on a weighted-average calculation for materials and a FIFO calculation for conversion costs. Answer (D) is incorrect. The amount of $156,960 is the weighted-average cost of ending work-in-process.

14. Using the weighted-average method, Kimbeth's equivalent unit cost of materials for May is

A. $4.12

B. $4.50

C. $4.60

D. $5.02

Answer (C) is correct. *(CMA, adapted)*
REQUIRED: The weighted-average equivalent unit cost for materials.
DISCUSSION: The weighted-average method averages the work done in the prior period with the work done in the current period. There are two layers of units to analyze: those completed during the period, and those still in ending inventory. The units completed totaled 92,000. The 24,000 ending units are 90% complete as to materials, so EUP equal 21,600. Hence, total EUP for materials are 113,600 (92,000 + 21,600). The total materials costs incurred during the period and accumulated in beginning work-in-process is $522,560 ($468,000 + $54,560). Thus, weighted-average unit cost is $4.60 ($522,560 ÷ 113,600 EUP).
Answer (A) is incorrect. The amount of $4.12 equals materials costs for May divided by weighted-average EUP. Answer (B) is incorrect. The amount of $4.50 is the equivalent unit cost based on the FIFO method. Answer (D) is incorrect. The amount of $5.02 is based on a FIFO calculation of equivalent units and a weighted-average calculation of costs.

15. Refer to the information on the preceding page(s). Using the weighted-average method, Kimbeth's equivalent unit conversion cost for May is

A. $5.65

B. $5.83

C. $6.00

D. $6.20

Answer (C) is correct. *(CMA, adapted)*
REQUIRED: The weighted-average conversion cost per equivalent unit.
DISCUSSION: The weighted-average method does not distinguish between the work done in the prior period and the work done in the current period. Accordingly, the 92,000 completed units represent 92,000 weighted-average EUP. The 24,000 units in ending work-in-process are 40% complete as to conversion costs, so they equal 9,600 EUP. Hence, total EUP for conversion costs are 101,600 (92,000 + 9,600). The sum of the conversion costs accumulated in beginning work-in-process and incurred during the period is $609,600 ($20,320 + $15,240 + $182,880 + $391,160). Thus, weighted-average unit cost is $6.00 ($609,600 ÷ 101,600 EUP).
Answer (A) is incorrect. The amount of $5.65 omits the conversion costs in beginning work-in-process. Answer (B) is incorrect. The amount of $5.83 is the equivalent unit conversion cost based on FIFO. Answer (D) is incorrect. The amount of $6.20 is based on a FIFO calculation of equivalent units and a weighted-average calculation of costs.

Questions 16 and 17 are based on the following information.

Goggle-eyed Old Snapping Turtle, a sporting goods manufacturer, buys wood as a direct material for baseball bats. The Forming Department processes the baseball bats, and the bats are then transferred to the Finishing Department where a sealant is applied. The Forming Department began manufacturing 10,000 "Casey Sluggers" during the month of May. There was no beginning inventory.

Costs for the Forming Department for the month of May were as follows:

Direct materials	$33,000
Conversion costs	17,000
Total	$50,000

A total of 8,000 bats were completed and transferred to the Finishing Department; the remaining 2,000 bats were still in the forming process at the end of the month. All of the Forming Department's direct materials were placed in process, but, on average, only 25% of the conversion cost was applied to the ending work-in-process inventory.

16. The cost of the units transferred to Snapping Turtle's Finishing Department is

A. $50,000

B. $40,000

C. $53,000

D. $42,400

Answer (D) is correct. *(CMA, adapted)*
REQUIRED: The cost of the units transferred to the Finishing Department.
DISCUSSION: The total equivalent units for raw materials equals 10,000 because all materials for the ending work-in-process had already been added to production. Hence, the materials cost per unit was $3.30 ($33,000 ÷ 10,000). For conversion costs, the total equivalent units equals 8,500 [8,000 completed + (2,000 in EWIP × 25%)]. Thus, the conversion cost was $2.00 per unit ($17,000 ÷ 8,500). The total cost transferred was therefore $42,400 [8,000 units × ($3.30 + $2.00)].
Answer (A) is incorrect. A portion of the total costs is still in work-in-process. Answer (B) is incorrect. The amount of $40,000 assumes that work-in-process is 100% complete as to conversion costs. Answer (C) is incorrect. The amount of $53,000 exceeds the actual costs incurred during the period. Given no beginning inventory, the amount transferred out cannot exceed the costs incurred during the period.

17. The cost of the work-in-process inventory in Snapping Turtle's Forming Department at the end of May is

A. $10,000

B. $2,500

C. $20,000

D. $7,600

Answer (D) is correct. *(CMA, adapted)*
REQUIRED: The cost of the work-in-process inventory.
DISCUSSION: The equivalent units for raw materials would be 10,000 (8,000 + 2,000) since the work-in-process is 100% complete as to materials. Therefore, dividing the $33,000 by 10,000 units results in a unit cost for materials of $3.30. The equivalent units for conversion costs would be 8,500 units [8,000 + (2,000 units × .25)]. Dividing the $17,000 of conversion costs by 8,500 equivalent units results in a unit cost of $2 per bat. Therefore, the total cost of goods transferred out would be $5.30, consisting of $3.30 for materials and $2 for conversion costs. Multiplying $5.30 times the 8,000 bats completed results in a total transfer of $42,400. Consequently, the cost of the ending work-in-process must have been $7,600 ($50,000 total costs incurred – $42,400).
Answer (A) is incorrect. The amount of $10,000 assumes that work-in-process inventory is 100% complete as to conversion costs. Answer (B) is incorrect. The amount of $2,500 assumes that work-in-process inventory is 100% complete as to conversion costs and that 500 bats are in inventory. Answer (C) is incorrect. The amount of $20,000 assumes that work-in-process is 100% complete as to conversion costs and that 6,000 units were transferred out.

Questions 18 through 20 are based on the following information. Marlan Manufacturing produces a product that passes through two departments. The units from the molding department are completed in the assembly department. The units are completed in assembly by adding the remaining direct materials when the units are 60% complete with respect to conversion costs. Conversion costs are added proportionately in assembly. The production activity in the assembly department for the current month is presented as follows. Marlan uses the FIFO (first-in, first-out) inventory method in its process cost system.

Beginning inventory units (25% complete with respect to conversion costs)	8,000
Units transferred in from the molding department during the month	42,000
Units to account for	50,000
Units completed and transferred to finished goods inventory	38,000
Ending inventory units (40% complete with respect to conversion costs)	12,000
Units accounted for	50,000

18. The equivalent units transferred from Marlan's molding department to the assembly department for the current month are

A. 30,000 units.

B. 38,000 units.

C. 40,800 units.

D. 42,000 units.

Answer (D) is correct. *(CMA, adapted)*
REQUIRED: The equivalent units transferred from the molding department to the assembly department.
DISCUSSION: This problem seemingly asks a technical question, but in reality was designed to test the candidate's alertness. The equivalent units transferred from the molding department are simply the total units transferred from the molding department (42,000 units).
Answer (A) is incorrect. The number of units started and completed during the period was 30,000. Answer (B) is incorrect. The number of units transferred out, not to, the assembly department was 38,000. Answer (C) is incorrect. The equivalent units for conversion costs equals 40,800.

19. The equivalent units in Marlan's assembly department for conversion costs for the current month are

A. 34,800 units.

B. 40,800 units.

C. 42,800 units.

D. 43,200 units.

Answer (B) is correct. *(CMA, adapted)*
REQUIRED: The equivalent units for conversion costs.
DISCUSSION: The equivalent units for conversion costs equal total units to account for, minus work done on beginning inventory, minus work not done on ending inventory. Hence, the equivalent units for conversion costs equal 40,800 units [50,000 units – (25% × 8,000 units) – (60% × 12,000 units)].
Answer (A) is incorrect. The number of 34,800 units assumes the beginning inventory was 100% complete. Answer (C) is incorrect. Conversion-cost EUP based on the weighted-average method is 42,800 units. Answer (D) is incorrect. The ending inventory was 40% complete, resulting in subtracting 60%, not 40%, of the 12,000 items in ending inventory to determine work not on ending inventory.

20. Refer to the information on the preceding page(s). The equivalent units in Marlan's assembly department for direct materials for the current month are

    A. 30,000 units.

    B. 38,000 units.

    C. 40,800 units.

    D. 42,000 units.

Answer (B) is correct. *(CMA, adapted)*
    REQUIRED: The equivalent units in the assembly department for direct materials.
    DISCUSSION: Direct materials are added when the units are 60% complete as to conversion costs. The beginning inventory of 8,000 units was only 25% complete at the start of the period, and 42,000 units were transferred in. Given that the ending inventory of 12,000 units was only 40% complete, neither beginning nor ending inventory had received direct materials in the assembly department. Accordingly, the equivalent units in the assembly department for direct materials must have been 38,000 units (8,000 units BI + 42,000 units transferred in – 12,000 units EI).
    Answer (A) is incorrect. The number of 30,000 units ignores the 8,000 units in process at the beginning of the period. Answer (C) is incorrect. Equivalent units for conversion costs, not direct materials, is 40,800. Answer (D) is incorrect. The 42,000 units were transferred in during the month. Not all received an input of direct materials.

2.3 Activity-Based Costing

21. The series of activities in which customer usefulness is added to the product is the definition of

    A. A value chain.

    B. Process value analysis.

    C. Integrated manufacturing.

    D. Activity-based costing.

Answer (A) is correct. *(CMA, adapted)*
    REQUIRED: The series of activities in which customer usefulness is added to the product.
    DISCUSSION: Value-chain analysis for assessing competitive advantage is an integral part of the strategic planning process. Value-chain analysis is a continuous process of gathering, evaluating, and communicating information for business decision making. A value chain depicts how customer value accumulates along a chain of activities that lead to an end product or service. A value chain consists of the activities required to research and develop, design, produce, market, deliver, and support its product. Extended value-chain analysis expands the view of the parties involved to include those upstream (e.g., suppliers) and downstream (e.g., customers).
    Answer (B) is incorrect. Process value analysis relates to a single process. Answer (C) is incorrect. Computer-integrated manufacturing uses computers to control all aspects of manufacturing in a single location. Answer (D) is incorrect. Activity-based costing identifies the activities associated with cost incurrence and the drivers of those activities. Costs are then assigned to cost objects based on the demands they make on activities.

22. The use of activity-based costing (ABC) normally results in

    A. Substantially greater unit costs for low-volume products than is reported by traditional product costing.

    B. Substantially lower unit costs for low-volume products than is reported by traditional product costing.

    C. Decreased setup costs being charged to low-volume products.

    D. Equalizing setup costs for all product lines.

Answer (A) is correct. *(CMA, adapted)*
    REQUIRED: The true statement about ABC.
    DISCUSSION: ABC differs from traditional product costing because it uses multiple allocation bases and therefore allocates overhead more accurately. The result is that ABC often charges low-volume products with more overhead than a traditional system. For example, the cost of machine setup may be the same for production runs of widely varying sizes. This relationship is reflected in an ABC system that allocates setup costs on the basis of the number of setups. However, a traditional system using an allocation base such as machine hours may underallocate setup costs to low-volume products. Many companies adopting ABC have found that they have been losing money on low-volume products because costs were actually higher than originally thought.
    Answer (B) is incorrect. Low-volume products are usually charged with greater unit costs under ABC. Answer (C) is incorrect. Greater setup costs are usually charged to low-volume products under ABC. Answer (D) is incorrect. Setup costs will not be equalized unless setup time is equal for all products.

Questions 23 and 24 are based on the following information.

Zeta Company is preparing its annual profit plan. As part of its analysis of the profitability of individual products, the controller estimates the amount of overhead that should be allocated to the individual product lines from the information given in the next column:

	Wall Mirrors	Specialty Windows
Units produced	25	25
Material moves per product line	5	15
Direct labor hours per unit	200	200
Budgeted materials handling costs		$50,000

23. Under a costing system that allocates overhead on the basis of direct labor hours, Zeta Company's materials handling costs allocated to one unit of wall mirrors would be

A. $1,000

B. $500

C. $2,000

D. $5,000

Answer (A) is correct. *(CMA, adapted)*
REQUIRED: The amount of materials handling costs allocated to one unit of wall mirrors when direct labor hours is the activity base.
DISCUSSION: If direct labor hours are used as the allocation base, the $50,000 of costs is allocated over 400 hours of direct labor. Multiplying the 25 units of each product times 200 hours results in 5,000 labor hours for each product, or a total of 10,000 hours. Dividing $50,000 by 10,000 hours results in a cost of $5 per direct labor hour. Multiplying 200 hours times $5 results in an allocation of $1,000 of overhead per unit of product.
Answer (B) is incorrect. The amount of $500 is the allocation based on number of material moves. Answer (C) is incorrect. The amount of $2,000 assumes that all the overhead is allocated to the wall mirrors. Answer (D) is incorrect. The amount of $5,000 assumes overhead of $250,000.

24. Under activity-based costing (ABC), Zeta's materials handling costs allocated to one unit of wall mirrors would be

A. $1,000

B. $500

C. $1,500

D. $2,500

Answer (B) is correct. *(CMA, adapted)*
REQUIRED: The amount of materials handling costs allocated to one unit of wall mirrors under ABC.
DISCUSSION: An activity-based costing (ABC) system allocates overhead costs on the basis of some causal relationship between the incurrence of cost and activities. Because the moves for wall mirrors constitute 25% (5 ÷ 20) of total moves, the mirrors should absorb 25% of the total materials handling costs. Thus, $12,500 ($50,000 × 25%) is allocated to mirrors. The remaining $37,500 is allocated to specialty windows. Dividing the $12,500 by 25 units produces a cost of $500 per unit of mirrors.
Answer (A) is incorrect. The amount of $1,000 uses direct labor as the allocation basis. Answer (C) is incorrect. The amount of $1,500 is the allocation per unit of specialty windows. Answer (D) is incorrect. The amount of $2,500 is not based on the number of material moves.

25. Because of changes that are occurring in the basic operations of many firms, all of the following represent trends in the way indirect costs are allocated **except**

A. Treating direct labor as an indirect manufacturing cost in an automated factory.

B. Using throughput time as an application base to increase awareness of the costs associated with lengthened throughput time.

C. Preferring plant-wide application rates that are applied to machine hours rather than incurring the cost of detailed allocations.

D. Using several machine cost pools to measure product costs on the basis of time in a machine center.

Answer (C) is correct. *(CMA, adapted)*
REQUIRED: The item not a trend in the way indirect costs are being allocated.
DISCUSSION: With the automation of factories and the corresponding emphasis on activity-based costing (ABC), companies are finding new ways of allocating indirect factory overhead. One change is that plant-wide application rates are being used less often because a closer matching of costs with cost drivers provides better information to management. ABC results in a more accurate application of indirect costs because it provides more refined data. Instead of a single cost goal for a process, a department, or even an entire plant, an indirect cost pool is established for each identified activity. The related cost driver, the factor that changes the cost of the activity, also is identified.
Answer (A) is incorrect. Computerization has decreased the amount of direct labor to the point that some companies are treating direct labor as an indirect factory overhead cost. Answer (B) is incorrect. Throughput time (the rate of production over a stated time), clearly drives (influences) costs. Answer (D) is incorrect. Multiple cost pools are preferable. They permit a better matching of indirect costs with cost drivers.

26. Multiple or departmental overhead rates are considered preferable to a single or plantwide overhead rate when

    A. Manufacturing is limited to a single product flowing through identical departments in a fixed sequence.

    B. Various products are manufactured that do not pass through the same departments or use the same manufacturing techniques.

    C. Cost drivers, such as direct labor, are the same over all processes.

    D. Individual cost drivers cannot accurately be determined with respect to cause-and-effect relationships.

Answer (B) is correct. *(CMA, adapted)*
REQUIRED: The situation in which multiple or departmental overhead rates are considered preferable.
DISCUSSION: Multiple rates are appropriate when a process differs substantially among departments or when products do not go through all departments or all processes. The trend in cost accounting is toward activity-based costing, which divides production into numerous activities and identifies the cost driver(s) most relevant to each. The result is a more accurate tracing of costs.
Answer (A) is incorrect. One rate may be cost beneficial when a single product proceeds through homogeneous processes. Answer (C) is incorrect. If cost drivers are the same for all processes, multiple rates are unnecessary. Answer (D) is incorrect. Individual cost drivers for all relationships must be known to use multiple application rates.

27. New-Rage Cosmetics has used a traditional cost accounting system to apply quality control costs uniformly to all products at a rate of 14.5% of direct labor cost. Monthly direct labor cost for Satin Sheen makeup is $27,500. In an attempt to distribute quality control costs more equitably, New-Rage is considering activity-based costing. The monthly data shown in the chart below have been gathered for Satin Sheen makeup.

Activity	Cost Driver	Cost Rates	Quantity for Satin Sheen
Incoming material inspection	Type of material	$11.50 per type	12 types
In-process inspection	Number of units	$0.14 per unit	17,500 units
Product certification	Per order	$77 per order	25 orders

The monthly quality control cost assigned to Satin Sheen makeup using activity-based costing (ABC) is

    A. $88.64 per order.

    B. $525.50 lower than the cost using the traditional system.

    C. $8,500.50

    D. $525.50 higher than the cost using the traditional system.

Answer (D) is correct. *(CMA, adapted)*
REQUIRED: The monthly quality control cost assigned using activity-based costing.
DISCUSSION: ABC identifies the causal relationship between the incurrence of cost and activities, determines the drivers of the activities, establishes cost pools related to the drivers and activities, and assigns costs to ultimate cost objects on the basis of the demands (resources or drivers consumed) placed on the activities by those cost objects. Hence, ABC assigns overhead costs based on multiple allocation bases or cost drivers. Under the traditional, single-base system, the amount allocated is $3,987.50 ($27,500 × 14.5%). Under ABC, the amount allocated is $4,513 [(12 × $11.50) + (17,500 × $.14) + (25 × $77)], or $525.50 more than under the traditional system.
Answer (A) is incorrect. The ABC assignment of $4,513 is at a rate of $180.52 for each of the 25 orders. Answer (B) is incorrect. ABC yields a higher allocation. Answer (C) is incorrect. The total is $4,513 on the ABC basis.

2.4 Life-Cycle Costing

28. Life-cycle costing

- A. Is sometimes used as a basis for cost planning and product pricing.
- B. Includes only manufacturing costs incurred over the life of the product.
- C. Includes only manufacturing cost, selling expense, and distribution expense.
- D. Emphasizes cost savings opportunities during the manufacturing cycle.

Answer (A) is correct. *(CMA, adapted)*
REQUIRED: The true statement about life-cycle costing.
DISCUSSION: Life-cycle costing estimates a product's revenues and expenses over its expected life cycle. This approach is especially useful when revenues and related costs do not occur in the same periods. It emphasizes the need to price products to cover all costs, not just those for production. Hence, costs are determined for all value-chain categories: upstream (R&D, design), manufacturing, and downstream (marketing, distribution, and customer service). The result is to highlight upstream and downstream costs in the cost planning process that often receive insufficient attention.
Answer (B) is incorrect. The life-cycle model includes the upstream (R&D and design) and downstream (marketing, distribution, and customer service) elements of the value chain as well as manufacturing costs. Answer (C) is incorrect. The life-cycle model includes the upstream (R&D and design) and downstream (marketing, distribution, and customer service) elements of the value chain as well as manufacturing costs. Answer (D) is incorrect. Life-cycle costing emphasizes the significance of locked-in costs, target costing, and value engineering for pricing and cost control. Thus, cost savings at all stages of the life cycle are important.

29. Target pricing

- A. Is more effective when applied to mature, long-established products.
- B. Considers short-term variable costs and excludes fixed costs.
- C. Is often used when costs are difficult to control.
- D. Is a pricing strategy used to create competitive advantage.

Answer (D) is correct. *(CMA, adapted)*
REQUIRED: The definition of target pricing.
DISCUSSION: Target pricing and costing may result in a competitive advantage because it is a customer-oriented approach that focuses on what products can be sold at what prices. It is also advantageous because it emphasizes control of costs prior to their being locked in during the early links in the value chain. The company sets a target price for a potential product reflecting what it believes consumers will pay and competitors will do. After subtracting the desired profit margin, the long-run target cost is known. If current costs are too high to allow an acceptable profit, cost-cutting measures are implemented or the product is abandoned. The assumption is that the target price is a constraint.
Answer (A) is incorrect. Target pricing is used on products that have not yet been developed. Answer (B) is incorrect. Target pricing considers all costs in the value chain. Answer (C) is incorrect. Target pricing can be used in any situation, but it is most likely to succeed when costs can be well controlled.

30. In target costing,

- A. The market price of the product is taken as a given.
- B. Only raw materials, labor, and variable overhead cannot exceed a threshold target.
- C. Only raw materials cannot exceed a threshold target.
- D. Raw materials are recorded directly to cost of goods sold.

Answer (A) is correct. *(CMA, adapted)*
REQUIRED: The true statement about target costing.
DISCUSSION: Target costing begins with a target price, which is the expected market price given the company's knowledge of its customers and competitors. Subtracting the unit target profit margin determines the long-term target cost. If this cost is lower than the full cost, the company may need to adopt comprehensive cost-cutting measures. For example, in the furniture industry, certain price points are popular with buyers: A couch might sell better at $400 than at $200 because consumers question the quality of a $200 couch and thus will not buy the lower-priced item. The result is that furniture manufacturers view $400 as the target price of a couch, and the cost must be lower.
Answer (B) is incorrect. All product cost categories are addressed by target costing. Answer (C) is incorrect. All product cost categories are addressed by target costing. Answer (D) is incorrect. The manner in which raw materials costs are accounted for is irrelevant.

31. Claremont Company has been asked to evaluate the profitability of a product that it manufactured and sold from Year 7 through Year 10. The product had a one-year warranty from date of sale. The following information appears in the financial records.

Research, development, and design cost Yr 5 & Yr 6	Manufacturing and distribution costs Yr 7 - Yr 10	Warranty costs Yr 7 - Yr 10	Warranty cost Yr 11
$5,000,000	$7,000,000	$200,000	$100,000

The life-cycle cost for this product is

   A. $10,000,000

   B. $12,000,000

   C. $12,200,000

   D. $12,300,000

Answer (D) is correct. *(CMA, adapted)*
REQUIRED: The cost of a product calculated on a life-cycle basis.
DISCUSSION: Life-cycle costing takes into account costs incurred at all stages of the value-chain, not just manufacturing. The life-cycle cost for this product is thus $12,300,000 ($5,000,000 + $7,000,000 + $200,000 + $100,000).
Answer (A) is incorrect. The amount of $10,000,000 is not supported by the information given. Answer (B) is incorrect. The amount of $12,000,000 improperly excludes future warranty costs. Answer (C) is incorrect. The amount of $12,200,000 improperly excludes the $100,000 of warranty costs for Year 11.

Use Gleim **CMA Test Prep** Software for interactive testing with **additional multiple-choice questions**!

2.6 ESSAY QUESTIONS

Scenario for Essay Questions 1, 2, 3

Kristina Company, which manufactures quality paint sold at premium prices, uses a single production department. Production begins with the blending of various chemicals, which are added at the beginning of the process, and ends with the canning of the paint. Canning occurs when the mixture reaches the 90% stage of completion. The gallon cans are then transferred to the Shipping Department for crating and shipment. Labor and overhead are added continuously throughout the process. Factory overhead is applied on the basis of direct labor hours at the rate of $3.00 per hour.

Prior to May, when a change in the process was implemented, work-in-process inventories were insignificant. The change in the process enables greater production but results in material amounts of work-in-process for the first time. The company has always used the weighted average method to determine equivalent production and unit costs. Now, production management is considering changing from the weighted average method to the first-in, first-out method.

The following data relate to actual production during the month of May:

Costs for May

Work-in-process inventory, May 1 (4,000 gallons 25% complete):	
Direct materials -- chemicals	$ 45,600
Direct labor ($10 per hour)	6,250
Factory overhead	1,875
May costs added	
Direct materials -- chemicals	228,400
Direct materials -- cans	7,000
Direct labor ($10 per hour)	35,000
Factory overhead	10,500

Units for May

	Gallons
Work-in-process inventory, May 1 (25% complete)	4,000
Sent to Shipping Department	20,000
Started in May	21,000
Work-in-process inventory, May 31 (80% complete)	5,000

Questions

1. Prepare a schedule of equivalent units for each cost element for the month of May using the

    a. Weighted-average method
    b. First-in, first-out method

2. Calculate the cost (to the nearest cent) per equivalent unit for each cost element for the month of May using the

    a. Weighted-average method
    b. First-in, first-out method

3. Discuss the advantages and disadvantages of using the weighted-average method versus the first-in, first-out method, and explain under what circumstances each method should be used.

Essay Questions 1, 2, 3 — Unofficial Answers

1. a. The equivalent units for each cost element, using the weighted-average method, are presented below.

	Direct Materials		
	Chemicals	Cans	Conversion
Units completed and transferred to Shipping	20,000	20,000	20,000
Work-in-process at 5/31			
Chemicals (100%)	5,000		
Cans (0%)		0	
Conversion costs (80%)			4,000
Equivalent units	25,000	20,000	24,000

 b. The equivalent units for each cost element, using the first-in, first-out method, are presented below.

	Direct Materials		
	Chemicals	Cans	Conversion
Transferred to Shipping from 5/1 work-in-process			
(4,000 @ 25%)			
Chemicals (0%)	0		
Cans (100%)		4,000	
Conversion costs (75%)			3,000
Current production transferred to Shipping (100%)	16,000	16,000	16,000
5/31 work-in-process (5,000 @ 80%)			
Chemicals (100%)	5,000		
Cans (0%)		0	
Conversion costs (80%)			4,000
Equivalent units	21,000	20,000	23,000

2. a. The cost per equivalent unit for each cost element, using the weighted-average method, is presented below.

	Direct Materials		
	Chemicals	Cans	Conversion*
Work-in-process at 5/1	$ 45,600	$ 0	$ 8,125
Plus: May costs incurred	228,400	7,000	45,500
Total costs	$274,000	$ 7,000	$53,625
Divided by: EUP	÷ 25,000	÷20,000	÷24,000
Weighted-average unit costs	$ 10.96	$ .35	$ 2.23

Conversion cost = Direct labor + Factory overhead

 b. The cost per equivalent unit for each cost element, using the first-in, first-out method, is presented below.

	Direct Materials		
	Chemicals	Cans	Conversion
May costs incurred	$228,400	$ 7,000	$45,500
Divided by: EUP	÷ 21,000	÷20,000	÷23,000
FIFO unit costs	$ 10.88	$ .35	$ 1.98

3. The weighted-average method is easier to use, as the calculations are simpler. This method tends to obscure current period costs, as the cost per equivalent unit includes both current costs and prior costs that were in the beginning inventory. This method is most appropriate when conversion costs, inventory levels, and raw material prices are stable.

   The first-in, first-out method is based on the work done in the current period only. This method is most appropriate when conversion costs, inventory levels, or raw material prices fluctuate. In addition, this method should be used when accuracy in current equivalent unit costs is important or when a standard cost system is used.

Use **CMA Gleim Online** and **Essay Wizard** to practice additional essay questions in an exam-like environment.

STUDY UNIT THREE
COST ALLOCATION TECHNIQUES

(26 pages of outline)

3.1	Absorption and Variable Costing -- Theory	90
3.2	Absorption and Variable Costing -- Calculations	97
3.3	Joint Product and By-Product Costing	97
3.4	Overhead Allocation and Normal Costing -- Theory	101
3.5	Overhead Allocation and Normal Costing -- Calculations	108
3.6	Allocating Service Department Costs -- Theory	108
3.7	Allocating Service Department Costs -- Calculations	112
3.8	Core Concepts	113
3.9	Essay Questions	131

This study unit is the **third of four** on **cost management**. The relative weight assigned to this major topic in Part 1 of the exam is **25%**. The four study units are:

Study Unit 1: Ethics for Management Accountants and Cost Management Concepts
Study Unit 2: Cost Accumulation Systems
Study Unit 3: Cost Allocation Techniques
Study Unit 4: Operational Efficiency and Business Process Performance

After studying the outline and answering the questions in this study unit, you will have the skills necessary to address the following topics listed in the ICMA's Learning Outcome Statements:

Part 1 – Section C.1. Measurement concepts

The candidate should be able to:

> Statement a. is covered in Study Unit 1.
> Statements b. through d. are covered in Study Unit 2.

e. identify and define cost measurement techniques such as actual costing, normal costing, and standard costing; calculate costs using each of these techniques; identify the appropriate use of each technique; and describe the benefits and limitations of each technique

f. demonstrate an understanding of the characteristics of variable (direct) costing and absorption (full) costing and the benefits and limitations of these measurement concepts

g. calculate inventory costs, cost of goods sold, and operating profit using both variable costing and absorption costing

h. demonstrate an understanding of how the use of variable costing or absorption costing affects the value of inventory, cost of goods sold, and operating income

i. prepare summary income statements using variable costing and absorption costing

j. determine the appropriate use of joint product and by-product costing

k. demonstrate an understanding of concepts such as split-off point and separable costs

l. determine the allocation of joint product and by-product costs using the physical measure method, the sales value at split-off method, constant gross profit (gross margin) method, and the net realizable value method; and describe the benefits and limitations of each method

Part 1 – Section C.3. Overhead costs

The candidate should be able to:

    a.   distinguish between fixed and variable overhead expenses

    b.   determine the appropriate time frame for classifying both variable and fixed overhead expenses

    c.   demonstrate an understanding of the different methods of determining overhead rates, e.g., plant-wide rates, departmental rates, and individual cost driver rates

    d.   describe the benefits and limitations of each of the methods used to determine overhead rates

    e.   identify the components of variable overhead expense

    f.   determine the appropriate allocation base for variable overhead expenses

    g.   calculate the per-unit variable overhead expense

    h.   identify the components of fixed overhead expense

    i.   identify the appropriate allocation base for fixed overhead expense

    j.   calculate the fixed overhead application rate

    k.   describe how fixed overhead can be over- or underapplied and how this difference should be accounted for in the cost of goods sold, work-in-process, and finished goods accounts

    l.   compare and contrast traditional overhead allocation with activity-based overhead allocation

    m.   calculate overhead expense in an activity-based costing setting

    n.   identify and describe the benefits derived from activity-based overhead allocation

    o.   explain why companies allocate the cost of service departments, such as human resources or information technology, to divisions, departments, or activities

    p.   calculate service or support department cost allocations using the direct method, the reciprocal method, the step-down method, and the dual allocation method

    q.   estimate fixed costs using the high-low method and demonstrate an understanding of how regression can be used to estimate fixed costs

3.1 ABSORPTION AND VARIABLE COSTING -- THEORY

1.   **Two Ways of Treating Fixed Production Costs**

    a.   For external reporting purposes, the cost of a product must include <u>all</u> the costs of manufacturing it: direct labor, direct materials, and all factory overhead (both fixed and variable).

        1)   This method is commonly known as absorption costing or full costing.

    b.   For internal purposes, decision making is improved by treating fixed overhead as a period cost so that only costs that are variable in the short run are included in the cost of the product.

        1)   Fixed overhead costs are considered as period costs and are deducted in the period in which they are incurred.

        2)   This practice is termed variable, or direct, costing. Variable costing is the preferred term because it describes what is really happening – namely that product costs are based only on variable costs.

2. **Absorption Costing**

    a.   Under absorption costing (sometimes called full or full absorption costing), the fixed portion of manufacturing overhead is "absorbed" into the cost of each unit of product.

        1)   Product cost thus includes all manufacturing costs, both fixed and variable.

        2)   Absorption-basis cost of goods sold is subtracted from sales to arrive at gross margin.

        3)   Total selling and administrative (S&A) expenses (i.e., both fixed and variable) are then subtracted from gross margin to arrive at operating income.

    b.   This method is required for external reporting purposes and for tax purposes.

3. **Variable Costing**

    a.   This method (sometimes called direct costing) is more appropriate for internal reporting.

        1)   Product cost includes only the variable portion of manufacturing costs.

        2)   Variable-basis cost of goods sold and the variable portion of S&A expenses are subtracted from sales to arrive at contribution margin.

            a)   This figure (sales – total variable costs) is an important element of the variable costing income statement because it is the amount available for covering fixed costs (both manufacturing and S&A).

            b)   For this reason, some accountants call the method contribution margin reporting.

        3)   The term "direct costing" is somewhat misleading because it suggests traceability, which is not what is meant in this context. "Variable costing" is more suitable.

        4)   Contribution margin is an important metric internally but is generally considered irrelevant to outside financial statement users.

4. **Justification for Variable Costing**

    a.   Under variable costing, fixed overhead cost is considered a cost of maintaining capacity, not a cost of producing a product.

        1)   To illustrate, a company has a fixed rental expense of $10,000 per month on its factory building. That cost will be $10,000 regardless of whether there is any production.

            a)   If the company produces zero units, the cost will be $10,000; if the company produces 10,000 units, the cost will be $10,000.

        2)   Therefore, the $10,000 is not viewed as a cost of production and is not added to the cost of the inventories produced. That $10,000 was a cost of maintaining a certain level of production capacity.

    b.   To emphasize, variable costing is used only for internal decision making purposes; it is not permitted for external financial reporting or for tax calculation.

        1)   The main advantage of the variable costing method is that income cannot be manipulated by management action, whereas management can manipulate income when using the absorption method (this is explained in item 7. on page 95).

c. EXAMPLE: A firm, during its first month in business, produced 100 units and sold 80 while incurring the following costs:

Direct materials	$1,000
Direct labor	2,000
Variable overhead	1,500
Manufacturing costs used in variable costing	**$4,500**
Fixed overhead	3,000
Manufacturing costs used in absorption costing	**$7,500**

1) The impact on the financial statements from using one method over the other can be seen in these calculations:

	Absorption Basis	Variable Basis
Manufacturing costs	$7,500	$4,500
Divided by: units produced	÷ 100	÷ 100
Per-unit cost	$ 75	$ 45
Times: ending inventory	× 20	× 20
Value of ending inventory	**$1,500**	**$ 900**

2) The per-unit selling price of the finished goods was $100, and the company incurred $200 of variable selling and administrative expenses and $600 of fixed selling and administrative expenses.

d. The following are partial income statements prepared using the two methods:

		Absorption Costing (Required under GAAP)	Variable Costing (For internal reporting only)
	Sales	$ 8,000	$ 8,000
	Beginning finished goods inventory	$ 0	$ 0
Product Costs	Plus: variable production costs	4,500 (a)	4,500 (a)
	Plus: fixed production costs	3,000 (b)	
	Goods available for sale	$7,500	$4,500
	Less: ending finished goods inventory	(1,500)	(900)
	Cost of goods sold	$(6,000)	$(3,600)
	Less: variable S&A expenses		(200) (c)
	Gross margin (abs.) / Contribution margin (var.)	**$ 2,000**	**$ 4,200**
Period Costs	Less: fixed production costs		(3,000) (b)
	Less: variable S&A expenses	(200) (c)	
	Less: fixed S&A expenses	(600) (d)	(600) (d)
	Operating income	**$ 1,200**	**$ 600**

1) The $600 difference in operating income ($1,200 – $600) is the difference between the two ending inventory values ($1,500 – $900).

a) In essence, the absorption method carries 20% of the fixed overhead costs ($3,000 × 20% = $600) on the balance sheet as an asset because 20% of the month's production (100 available – 80 sold = 20 on hand) is still in inventory.

2) This calculation is for illustrative purposes only. The difference in operating income is exactly the difference in ending inventory only when beginning inventory is $0.

5. **Impact on Operating Income**

   a. As production and sales levels change, the two methods have varying impacts on operating income.

      1) When everything produced during a period is sold that period, the two methods report the same operating income.

         a) Total fixed costs budgeted for the period are charged to sales revenue in the period under both methods.

      2) When production and sales are not equal for a period, the two methods report different operating income.

   b. ILLUSTRATION:

When production	**When production**
△ △ △ △ △ △ △	△ △ △
exceeds sales,	**is less than sales,**
△ △ △	△ △ △ △ △ △ △
ending inventory expands.	**ending inventory contracts.**
↑↑↑↑↑↑↑↑↑↑↑↑↑↑↑	↓↓↓↓↓↓
Under absorption costing, some fixed costs are still embedded in ending inventory.	**Under absorption costing,** fixed costs embedded in beginning inventory get expensed.
Under variable costing, all fixed costs have been expensed.	**Under variable costing,** only the current period's fixed costs are expensed.
Therefore,	Therefore,
operating income is higher under <u>absorption</u> costing.	**operating income is higher under <u>variable</u> costing.**

   c. The diagram above illustrates the perverse incentive inherent to absorption costing and reveals why many companies prefer variable costing for internal reporting.

      1) Whenever production exceeds sales, fewer fixed costs are expensed under the absorption basis, and operating income always increases.

      2) A production manager can thus increase absorption-basis operating income merely by increasing production, whether there is any customer demand for the additional product or not.

         a) The company must also deal with the increased carrying costs resulting from swelling inventory levels.

      3) This practice, called producing for inventory, can be effectively discouraged by using variable costing for performance reporting and consequent bonus calculation.

EXTENDED EXAMPLE of Absorption and Variable Operating Income

A company has the following sales and cost data:

	Year 1	Year 2	Year 3
Production in units	40,000	50,000	0
Sales in units	30,000	30,000	30,000
Ending inventory in units (FIFO)	10,000	30,000	0

Unit sales price	$1.00
Unit variable cost	$0.50
Fixed manufacturing costs	$4,000 per year
Variable S&A expenses	$0.03 per unit
Fixed S&A expenses	$1,000 per year

Compare the 3-year income statements prepared under the two methods:

Absorption Costing (Required for external reporting)				Variable Costing (For internal reporting only)			
	Year 1	Year 2	Year 3		Year 1	Year 2	Year 3
Sales	**$30,000**	**$30,000**	**$30,000**	**Sales**	**$30,000**	**$30,000**	**$30,000**
Beginning inventory	$ 0	$ 6,000	$17,500	Beginning inventory	$ 0	$ 5,000	$15,000
Variable mfg. costs	20,000	25,000	0	Variable mfg. costs	20,000	25,000	0
Fixed mfg. costs	4,000	4,000	4,000				
Goods available for sale	$24,000	$35,000	$21,500	Goods avail. for sale	$20,000	$30,000	$15,000
Less: ending inventory	(6,000)	(17,500)	0	Less: ending inventory	(5,000)	(15,000)	0
Absorption COGS	**$18,000**	**$17,500**	**$21,500**	**Variable COGS**	**$15,000**	**$15,000**	**$15,000**
				Variable S&A exps.	(900)	(900)	(900)
Gross margin	**$12,000**	**$12,500**	**$ 8,500**	**Contribution margin**	**$14,100**	**$14,100**	**$14,100**
				Fixed mfg. costs	(4,000)	(4,000)	(4,000)
Variable S&A expenses	(900)	(900)	(900)				
Fixed S&A expenses	(1,000)	(1,000)	(1,000)	Fixed S&A expenses	(1,000)	(1,000)	(1,000)
Operating income	**$10,100**	**$10,600**	**$ 6,600**	**Operating income**	**$ 9,100**	**$ 9,100**	**$ 9,100**

Note that, assuming zero inventory at the beginning of Year 1 and at the end of Year 3, the total operating income for the 3-year period is the same under either costing method.

	Absorption Costing	Variable Costing
Year 1	$10,100	$ 9,100
Year 2	10,600	9,100
Year 3	6,600	9,100
3-Year Total	**$27,300**	**$27,300**

Absorption costing shows a higher operating income than variable costing in Years 1 and 2 because fixed overhead has been capitalized and does not get expensed until Year 3. Variable costing, on the other hand, treats fixed overhead as an expense of the period in which the cost is incurred. In Year 2, despite the same cash flow, there is a $1,400 difference between the final operating income figures. There is an even greater difference in Year 3.

If fixed costs increase relative to variable costs, the differences become more dramatic (here, 50% of the selling price is variable manufacturing cost, and fixed overhead is no more than 20% of the variable manufacturing cost).

From an internal point of view, a manager can manipulate absorption income by changing production levels. But, with variable costing, a manager cannot manipulate simply by changing production levels.

Note that, under the absorption method, management was able to show higher incomes in Years 1 and 2 by overproducing. If the manager was being given a bonus for a higher level of income, (s)he could obtain the bonus by producing more units than could be sold. As a result, some fixed costs would be added to the balance sheet as inventories. Thus, the income statement and balance sheet both look good, despite the fact that the production manager has done a bad thing: (S)he has produced excessive inventories, which require the company to incur storage and financing costs. Spoilage may also be a result.

6. **Summary of Effects on Income and Ending Inventory**

    a. Since fixed manufacturing costs are excluded from inventories under the variable costing method, the amount shown on the balance sheet for inventories will be lower.

    b. Income and inventory levels will differ whenever sales and production differ.

        1) Income will be higher or lower under variable costing depending upon whether inventories are increased during the period or liquidated.

        2) If inventories increase during a period, the variable costing method will show a lower income because all fixed costs are being subtracted on the income statement, while under the absorption method, some fixed costs are being capitalized as inventories.

        3) Variable costing will show a higher income in periods when inventories decline because the absorption method forces the subtraction of all of the current period fixed costs, plus some fixed costs incurred (and capitalized) in prior periods.

    c. Under variable costing, profits always move in the same direction as sales volume. Profits reported under absorption costing behave erratically and sometimes move in the opposite direction from sales trends.

    d. In the long run, the two methods will report the same total profits if sales equal production. The inequalities between production and sales are usually minor over an extended period.

7. **Benefits of Variable Costing**

    a. Although the use of variable costing for financial statements is prohibited, most agree about its superiority for internal reporting. It is far better suited than absorption costing to the needs of management.

        1) Management requires a knowledge of cost behavior under various operating conditions. For planning and control, management is more concerned with treating fixed and variable costs separately than with calculating full costs.

        2) Full costs are usually of dubious value because they contain arbitrary allocations of fixed cost.

    b. First and foremost, under the variable costing method, a production manager cannot manipulate income levels by overproducing. Given the same cost structure every year, the income levels will be based on sales, not the level of production.

    c. Under variable costing, the cost data for profit planning and decision making are readily available from accounting records and statements. Reference to auxiliary records and supplementary analyses is not necessary.

        1) For example, cost-volume-profit relationships and the effects of changes in sales volume on net income can easily be computed from the income statement prepared under the variable costing concept, but not from the conventional absorption cost income statement based on the same data.

    d. Profits and losses reported under variable costing have a relationship to sales revenue and are not affected by inventory or production variations.

    e. Absorption cost income statements may show decreases in profits when sales are rising and increases in profits when sales are decreasing, which may be confusing to management. Attempts at explanation by means of volume variances often compound rather than clarify the confusion.

        1) Production volume variances not only are unnecessary but also are frustrating and confusing to management.

f.   When variable costing is used, the favorable margin between selling prices and variable cost should provide a constant reminder of profits forgone because of lack of sales volume. A favorable margin justifies a higher production level.

g.   The full impact of fixed costs on net income, partially hidden in inventory values under absorption costing, is emphasized by the presentation of costs on an income statement prepared under variable costing.

h.   Proponents of variable costing maintain that fixed factory overhead is more closely correlated to capacity to produce than to the production of individual units.

8.   **Further Aspects of Variable Costing**

a.   Variable costing is also preferred over absorption costing for studies of relative profitability of products, territories, and other segments of a business. It concentrates on the contribution that each segment makes to the recovery of fixed costs that will not be altered by decisions to make and sell. Under variable costing procedures,

1)   The marginal income concept leads to better pricing decisions, which are the principal advantage of variable costing.

2)   The impact of fixed costs on net income is emphasized by showing the total amount of such costs separately in financial reports.

3)   Out-of-pocket expenditures required to manufacture products conform closely with the valuation of inventory.

4)   The relationship between profit and the major factors of selling price, sales mix, sales volume, and variable manufacturing and nonmanufacturing costs is measured in terms of a single index of profitability.

a)   This profitability index, expressed as a positive amount or as a ratio, facilitates the analysis of cost-volume-profit relationships, compares the effects of two or more contemplated courses of action, and aids in answering many questions that arise in profit planning.

5)   Inventory changes have no effect on the breakeven computations.

6)   Marginal income figures facilitate appraisal of products, territories, and other business segments without having the results hidden or obscured by allocated joint fixed costs.

7)   Questions regarding whether a particular part should be made or bought can be more effectively answered if only variable costs are used.

a)   Management must consider whether to charge the product being made with variable costs only or to charge a percentage of fixed costs as well.

b)   Management must also consider whether the making of the part will require additional fixed costs and a decrease in normal production.

8)   Disinvestment decisions are facilitated because whether a product or department is recouping its variable costs can be determined.

a)   If the variable costs are being covered, operating a department at an apparent loss may be profitable.

9)   Management is better able to judge the differences between departments if certain fixed costs are omitted from the statements instead of being allocated arbitrarily.

10) Cost figures are guided by the sales figures.

    a) Under variable costing, cost of goods sold will vary directly with sales volume, and the influence of production on gross profit is avoided.

    b) Variable costing also eliminates the possible difficulties of having to explain over- or underapplied factory overhead to higher management.

Stop and review! You have completed the outline for this subunit. Study multiple-choice questions 1 through 6 beginning on page 115.

3.2 ABSORPTION AND VARIABLE COSTING -- CALCULATIONS

 Management accountants are expected to know the theory and how to complete detailed calculations for the topics covered in this study unit. To provide a more focused approach to studying, Gleim has broken up the theoretical questions and computational questions of the different cost allocation techniques into separate subunits. CMA candidates should expect a mix of both theory and computational questions on the CMA exam.

Some of the questions concerning absorption and variable costing that a candidate will encounter on the CMA exam focus on the detailed calculations required under the two methods. This subunit consists entirely of such questions. Please review Subunit 3.1 before attempting to answer the questions in this subunit.

Stop and review! You have completed the outline for this subunit. Study multiple-choice questions 7 through 11 beginning on page 116.

3.3 JOINT PRODUCT AND BY-PRODUCT COSTING

1. **Joint Processing and the Split-Off Point**

    a. When two or more separate products are produced by a common manufacturing process from a common input, the outputs from the process are joint products.

    b. **Joint (common) costs** are those costs incurred up to the point where the products become separately identifiable, called the split-off point.

        1) Joint costs include direct materials, direct labor, and manufacturing overhead. Because they are not separately identifiable, they must be allocated to the individual joint products.

        2) EXAMPLE: Crude oil can be refined into multiple salable products. All costs incurred in getting the crude oil to the distilling tower are joint costs.

    c. At the split-off point, the joint products acquire separate identities. Costs incurred after split-off are separable costs.

        1) **Separable costs** can be identified with a particular joint product and allocated to a specific unit of output.

        2) EXAMPLE: Once crude oil has been distilled into asphalt, fuel oil, diesel fuel, kerosene, and gasoline, costs incurred in further refining and distributing these individual products are separable costs.

d.   Since joint costs cannot be traced to individual products, they must be allocated. The methods available for this allocation can be classified in two conceptual groupings.

   1)   The physical-measure-based approach employs a physical measure, such as volume, weight, or a linear measure.

   2)   Market-based approaches assign a proportionate amount of the total cost to each product on a monetary basis.

      a)   Sales-value at split-off method
      b)   Estimated net realizable value method
      c)   Constant-gross-margin percentage NRV method

2.   **Physical-Measure-Based Approach**

a.   The **physical-unit method** allocates joint production costs to each product based on their relative proportions of the measure selected.

   1)   EXAMPLE: A refinery processes 1,000 barrels of crude oil and incurs $100,000 of processing costs. The process results in the following outputs. Under the physical unit method, the joint costs up to split-off are allocated as follows:

Asphalt	$100,000 × (300 barrels ÷ 1,000 barrels) =	$ 30,000
Fuel oil	$100,000 × (300 barrels ÷ 1,000 barrels) =	30,000
Diesel fuel	$100,000 × (200 barrels ÷ 1,000 barrels) =	20,000
Kerosene	$100,000 × (100 barrels ÷ 1,000 barrels) =	10,000
Gasoline	$100,000 × (100 barrels ÷ 1,000 barrels) =	10,000
Joint costs allocated		$100,000

b.   The physical-unit method's simplicity makes it appealing, but it does not match costs with the individual products' revenue-generating potential.

   1)   Basically, there is almost no situation where the physical-unit method is beneficial. Its advantage is that it is easy to use.

   2)   However, its limitations are that it treats low-value products that are large in size as if they were valuable. As a result, a large, low-value product might always show a loss, whereas small, high-value products will always show a profit.

3.   **Market-Based Approaches**

a.   These allocations are performed using the entire production run for an accounting period, not units sold. This is because the joint costs were incurred on all the units produced, not just those sold.

b.   The **sales-value at split-off method** is based on the relative sales values of the separate products at split-off.

   1)   EXAMPLE: The refinery estimates that the five outputs can sell for the following prices at split-off:

Asphalt	300 barrels @ $ 60/barrel =	$ 18,000
Fuel oil	300 barrels @ $180/barrel =	54,000
Diesel fuel	200 barrels @ $160/barrel =	32,000
Kerosene	100 barrels @ $ 80/barrel =	8,000
Gasoline	100 barrels @ $180/barrel =	18,000
Total sales value at split-off		$130,000

The total expected sales value for the entire production run at split-off is thus $130,000. Multiply the total joint costs to be allocated by the proportion of the total expected sales of each product:

Asphalt	$100,000 × ($18,000 ÷ $130,000) =	$ 13,846
Fuel oil	$100,000 × ($54,000 ÷ $130,000) =	41,539
Diesel fuel	$100,000 × ($32,000 ÷ $130,000) =	24,615
Kerosene	$100,000 × ($ 8,000 ÷ $130,000) =	6,154
Gasoline	$100,000 × ($18,000 ÷ $130,000) =	13,846
Joint costs allocated		$100,000

c.   The **estimated net realizable value (NRV)** method also allocates joint costs based on the relative market values of the products.

   1)   The significant difference is that, under the estimated NRV method, all separable costs necessary to make the product salable are subtracted before the allocation is made.

   2)   EXAMPLE: The refinery estimates final sales prices as follows:

Asphalt	300 barrels @ $ 70/barrel =	$ 21,000
Fuel oil	300 barrels @ $200/barrel =	60,000
Diesel fuel	200 barrels @ $180/barrel =	36,000
Kerosene	100 barrels @ $ 90/barrel =	9,000
Gasoline	100 barrels @ $190/barrel =	19,000

From these amounts, separable costs are subtracted (these costs are given):

Asphalt	$21,000 – $1,000 =	$ 20,000
Fuel oil	$60,000 – $1,000 =	59,000
Diesel fuel	$36,000 – $1,000 =	35,000
Kerosene	$ 9,000 – $2,000 =	7,000
Gasoline	$19,000 – $2,000 =	17,000
Total net realizable value		$138,000

Multiply the total joint costs to be allocated by the proportion of the final expected sales of each product:

Asphalt	$100,000 × ($20,000 ÷ $138,000) =	$ 14,493
Fuel oil	$100,000 × ($59,000 ÷ $138,000) =	42,754
Diesel fuel	$100,000 × ($35,000 ÷ $138,000) =	25,362
Kerosene	$100,000 × ($ 7,000 ÷ $138,000) =	5,072
Gasoline	$100,000 × ($17,000 ÷ $138,000) =	12,319
Joint costs allocated		$100,000

d.   The **constant-gross-margin percentage NRV** method is based on allocating joint costs so that the gross-margin percentage is the same for every product.

   1)   The three steps under this method are

   a)   Determine the overall gross-margin percentage.

   b)   Subtract the appropriate gross margin from the final sales value of each product to calculate total costs for that product.

   c)   Subtract the separable costs to arrive at the joint cost amount.

2) EXAMPLE: The refinery uses the same calculation of expected final sales price as under the estimated NRV method:

Asphalt	300 barrels @ $ 70/barrel =	$ 21,000
Fuel oil	300 barrels @ $200/barrel =	60,000
Diesel fuel	200 barrels @ $180/barrel =	36,000
Kerosene	100 barrels @ $ 90/barrel =	9,000
Gasoline	100 barrels @ $190/barrel =	19,000
	Total of final sales prices	$145,000

The final sales value for the entire production run is thus $145,000. From this total, the joint costs and total separable costs are deducted to arrive at a total gross margin for all products:

$$\$145,000 - \$100,000 - \$7,000 = \$38,000$$

The gross margin percentage can then be derived:

$$\$38,000 \div \$145,000 = 26.21\%$$

Deduct gross margin from each product to arrive at a cost of goods sold:

Asphalt	$21,000 – ($21,000 × 26.21%) =	$15,497
Fuel oil	$60,000 – ($60,000 × 26.21%) =	44,276
Diesel fuel	$36,000 – ($36,000 × 26.21%) =	26,565
Kerosene	$ 9,000 – ($ 9,000 × 26.21%) =	6,641
Gasoline	$19,000 – ($19,000 × 26.21%) =	14,021

Deduct the separable costs from each product to arrive at the allocated joint costs:

Asphalt	$15,497 – $1,000 =	$ 14,497
Fuel oil	$44,276 – $1,000 =	43,276
Diesel fuel	$26,566 – $1,000 =	25,565
Kerosene	$ 6,641 – $2,000 =	4,641
Gasoline	$14,021 – $2,000 =	12,021
	Joint costs allocated	$100,000

e. The three market-based approaches are far superior to the physical-measure-based approach, although they do require more work and more record keeping. However, they produce more usable results.

4. **Accounting for By-Products**

a. By-products are one or more products of relatively small total value that are produced simultaneously from a common manufacturing process with products of greater value and quantity.

b. The first question that must be answered in regard to by-products is: Do the benefits of further processing and bringing them to market exceed the costs?

Selling price	$X,XXX
Less: additional processing costs	(XXX)
Less: selling costs	(XXX)
Net realizable value	**$X,XXX**

1) If the net realizable value is zero or negative, the by-products should be discarded as scrap.

  c. If the by-products are material, they are capitalized in a separate inventory account, as in this example:

Finished goods inventory – Asphalt (allocated costs)	$XX,XXX
Finished goods inventory – Fuel oil (allocated costs)	XX,XXX
Finished goods inventory – Diesel fuel (allocated costs)	XX,XXX
Finished goods inventory – Kerosene (allocated costs)	XX,XXX
Finished goods inventory – Gasoline (allocated costs)	XX,XXX
By-product inventory – Sludge (estimated net realizable value)	X,XXX
Work-in-process (total manufacturing costs for period)	$XXX,XXX

    1) The amount capitalized is the entire estimated net realizable value of the by-products generated during the period.

      a) This treatment is justifiable when a ready market for the by-products is available.

    2) By proportionally reducing the amounts capitalized for the major finished goods, this treatment of by-product inventory effectively reduces cost of goods sold. Thus, when the by-products are sold, the income statement effects have already been recognized.

Cash	$X,XXX
By-product inventory – Sludge	$X,XXX

  d. If the by-products are immaterial, they are not recognized until the time of sale.

    1) The amount of miscellaneous revenue (or reduction to cost of goods sold) reported is the actual proceeds from the sale of the by-products.

  e. Regardless of the timing of their recognition in the accounts, by-products usually do not receive an allocation of joint costs because the cost of this accounting treatment ordinarily exceeds the benefit.

 5. **Sell-or-Process-Further Decisions**

  a. The decision to sell or process further is made based on whether the incremental revenue to be gained by further processing exceeds the incremental cost thereof.

    1) The joint cost of the product is irrelevant because it is a sunk cost.

Stop and review! You have completed the outline for this subunit. Study multiple-choice questions 12 through 17 beginning on page 119.

3.4 OVERHEAD ALLOCATION AND NORMAL COSTING -- THEORY

 1. **Components of Manufacturing Overhead**

  a. Manufacturing overhead consists of all costs of manufacturing that are not direct materials or direct labor.

  b. Indirect materials are tangible inputs to the manufacturing process that cannot practicably be traced to the product, e.g., the welding compound used to put together a piece of heavy equipment.

  c. Indirect labor is the cost of human labor connected with the manufacturing process that cannot practicably be traced to the product, e.g., the wages of assembly line supervisors and janitorial staff.

  d. Factory operating costs, such as utilities, real estate taxes, insurance, depreciation on factory equipment, etc.

    1) Overhead thus consists of all costs of manufacturing that are not direct materials or direct labor.

2.   **Variable and Fixed Components**

    a.   Unlike direct materials and direct labor, which are purely variable costs, overhead contains both variable and fixed components

        1)   Variable overhead costs include indirect materials, indirect labor, utilities, and depreciation expense under any method that ties depreciation to the level of output.

            a)   The time frame for planning variable overhead is the short run, i.e., the period within which per-unit variable costs remain constant and therefore predictable.

        2)   Fixed overhead costs include real estate taxes, insurance, and depreciation expense under any method that is not tied to the level of output.

            a)   The time frame for planning fixed overhead is the long run. Such cost elements as real estate taxes and depreciation are determined by capital expenditures, i.e., those that by their nature span multiple years.

    b.   Estimated overhead for the year is accumulated in two indirect cost pools (one for variable costs and one for fixed), which will then be allocated to production using an approximate allocation base for each.

    c.   EXAMPLE: A manufacturer is preparing its budget for the upcoming year and has compiled the following estimates of total costs:

Cost Element	Estimated Variable Overhead	Estimated Fixed Overhead
Indirect materials	$ 80,000	
Indirect labor	46,000	
Utilities	155,000	
Real estate taxes		$ 81,000
Insurance		54,000
Straight-line depreciation		240,000
Totals	$281,000	$375,000

3.   **Selecting an Allocation Base**

    a.   The crucial quality of an allocation base is that it be a cost driver of the costs in the pool to be allocated.

        1)   Recall that a cost driver should capture a cause-and-effect relationship between the level of the driver and the level of the cost being allocated.

    b.   In labor-intensive industries, direct labor hours or cost is an appropriate driver. In capital-intensive industries, machine hours is more appropriate.

        1)   It is therefore possible that variable and fixed overhead will employ the same allocation base.

        2)   Overhead is usually not allocated on the basis of units produced because of the lack of a cause-and-effect relationship.

    c.   EXAMPLE: The variable elements of overhead vary directly with the level of production, so the company has chosen to use units of output as the allocation base for variable overhead. The fixed elements of overhead are related directly to the level of productive capacity, such as factory space and amount of machinery, so the company has decided that it will use machine hours as the allocation base for fixed overhead.

4. **Calculating the Application Rate**

   a. Once appropriate allocation bases have been selected, the predetermined overhead application rates are calculated.

      1) The estimates made of the total amounts of overhead will be the numerators.
      2) Estimates are then made of the total quantity of each allocation base that will be expended; these will be the denominators.
      3) The quotients are the application rates for that budget period.

   b. EXAMPLE: The company's best projection for the upcoming year is that 1,110,000 units will be produced and 57,000 machine hours will be expended. The overhead allocation rates can thus be calculated as follows:

   Variable overhead application rate: $281,000 ÷ 1,110,000 units of output = $0.253 per unit
   Fixed overhead application rate: $375,000 ÷ 57,000 machine hours = $6.579 per hour

   c. A significant conceptual challenge is understanding the need to apply fixed overhead using an allocation base rather than simply to recognize one-twelfth of the estimated total every month.

      1) Since fixed costs are by their nature unchanging within the relevant range, using an allocation base at first appears to unnecessarily complicate the bookkeeping process. But, one way or another, fixed costs must be covered by selling products to customers.
      2) The advantage of applying fixed overhead at a predetermined rate is that an allocation base, even if only indirectly, reflects the level of productive activity.

         a) If production is way down or way up in a particular month, using an allocation base will result in a fixed overhead production-volume variance, also called the denominator-level variance (this is discussed in more detail in Study Unit 7, Subunit 6).
         b) The existence of a production-volume/denominator-level variance alerts management to the fact that fixed costs are being spread among fewer or more units, respectively, than anticipated.

   d. Under activity-based costing, individual overhead costs are assigned based on the level of an associated activity rather than lumped in a single (or double) pool (see Study Unit 2, Subunit 3, for a fuller discussion).

5. **Recording Actual Overhead Costs**

   a. During the budget period, actual overhead costs are accumulated in the control accounts as they are incurred.

   b. EXAMPLE: At the end of October, the company recorded the following journal entries to recognize actual overhead costs incurred during the month:

Variable overhead control	$22,050	
Raw materials (withdrawals for indirect materials)		$ 6,059
Wages payable (indirect labor)		4,120
Utilities (bill from utility provider)		11,871
Fixed overhead control	$31,250	
Real estate taxes ($81,000 ÷ 12 months)		$ 6,750
Insurance expense ($54,000 ÷ 12 months)		4,500
Depreciation expense ($240,000 ÷ 12 months)		20,000

6. **Allocating Overhead to Work-in-Process**

   a. At the end of the period, overhead is applied to work-in-process based on the actual level of the driver.

   b. EXAMPLE: During October, the company produced 91,000 units and expended 4,000 machine hours. The journal entry to apply overhead for October is as follows:

Work-in-process	$49,339	
Variable overhead applied (91,000 units × $0.253)		$23,023
Fixed overhead applied (4,000 hours × $6.579)		26,316

7. **Over- and Underapplied Overhead**

   a. Inevitably, the overhead amounts applied throughout the year will vary from the amount actually incurred, which is only determinable once the job is complete. This variance is called over- or underapplied overhead.

      1) Overapplied overhead (a credit balance in overhead applied) results when product costs are overstated because the

         a) Activity level was higher than expected, or
         b) Actual overhead costs were lower than expected.

      2) Underapplied overhead (a debit balance in overhead applied) results when product costs are understated because the

         a) Activity level was lower than expected, or
         b) Actual overhead costs were higher than expected.

   b. Over- and underapplied overhead is subject to one of two treatments:

      1) If the variance is considered immaterial, it can be closed directly to cost of goods sold.

         a) EXAMPLE:

If overapplied:		
Variable overhead applied (balance)	$23,023	
Cost of goods sold (difference)		$ 973
Variable overhead control (balance)		22,050
If underapplied:		
Fixed overhead applied (balance)	$26,316	
Cost of goods sold (difference)	4,934	
Fixed overhead control (balance)		$31,250

      2) If the variance is considered material, it should be allocated based on the relative values of work-in-process, finished goods, and cost of goods sold.

         a) EXAMPLE: Work-in-process, finished goods, and cost of goods sold bear a 20:20:60 cost relationship.

If overapplied:		
Variable overhead applied (balance)	$23,023	
Work-in-process (overapplied amount × allocation %)		$ 195
Finished goods (overapplied amount × allocation %)		195
Cost of goods sold (overapplied amount × allocation %)		583
Variable overhead control (balance)		22,050
If underapplied:		
Fixed overhead applied (balance)	$26,316	
Work-in-process (underapplied amount × allocation %)	987	
Finished goods (underapplied amount × allocation %)	987	
Cost of goods sold (underapplied amount × allocation %)	2,960	
Fixed overhead control (balance)		$31,250

8. **Overhead Allocation under Activity-Based Costing**

    a. The example on the previous page was prepared using a traditional (volume-based) overhead allocation system, i.e., one where only two indirect cost pools were used, one for variable overhead and one for fixed overhead.

        1) Activity-based costing (ABC) arose in response to the significant increase in the incurrence of indirect costs resulting from the rapid advance of technology. ABC is a refinement of an existing costing system, such as job-order or process.

    b. Under ABC, indirect costs are attached to activities rather than simply dumped in one or two indirect cost pools (see Subunit 3 in Study Unit 2 for a fuller discussion).

        1) EXAMPLE: A foundry has reengineered its indirect cost assignment system using activity-based costing principles. It now uses five pools for overhead instead of two:

Indirect cost pool	Driver
Product design	Engineering hours
Production setup	Number of batches
Machining	Machine hours
Inspection & testing	Number of valves
Customer maintenance	Salesperson hours

    c. Since ABC employs multiple indirect cost pools, it provides far greater detail regarding overhead than does traditional functional or spending-category budgeting.

        1) EXAMPLE: Activity-based costing allows the foundry to calculate much more accurate cost data about its two products:

Cost Category	Actual Driver Level	Cost per Unit of Driver		Simple Valve	Complex Valve	Total
Direct materials				$ 438,716	$288,017	$ 726,733
Direct labor				241,505	78,885	320,390
Total direct costs				**$ 680,221**	**$366,902**	**$1,047,123**
Indirect cost assignment:						
Product design:						
Simple valve	1,101	× $23.75	=	$26,149		$89,941
Complex valve	2,686	× 23.75	=		$63,793	
Production setup:						
Simple valve	200	× 21.00	=	4,200		4,620
Complex valve	20	× 21.00	=		420	
Machining:						
Simple valve	2,155	× 3.2581	=	7,021		68,612
Complex valve	18,904	× 3.2581	=		61,591	
Inspection & testing:						
Simple valve	50,000	× 12.50	=	625,000		750,000
Complex valve	10,000	× 12.50	=		125,000	
Customer maintenance:						
Simple valve	1,600	× 17.70	=	28,320		40,834
Complex valve	707	× 17.70	=		12,514	
Total indirect costs				**$ 690,690**	**$263,318**	**$ 954,007**
Total manufacturing costs				**$1,370,911**	**$630,220**	**$2,001,130**

9.   **Timeframe for Calculating Application Rates**

    a.   Calculating new overhead application rates each month can result in misleading unit costs. Thus, overhead rates are normally calculated no more often than annually.

        1)   This is because, during months of low production, per-unit overhead charges will skyrocket. This leads to higher product costs during months of lower production and to distortions in the financial statements.

        2)   The example below illustrates this phenomenon.

EXTENDED EXAMPLE of Unit-Cost Distribution

A manufacturing firm divides its reporting year into 3 budget periods. The company is expecting the following units of production and sales during the upcoming year. Note that production is expected to fluctuate but sales are expected to be even:

	Jan-Apr	May-Aug	Sep-Dec	Totals
Production	10,000	6,000	8,000	24,000
Sales	7,000	7,000	7,000	21,000

Variable overhead costs are calculated at $1 per unit:

	Jan-Apr	May-Aug	Sep-Dec	Totals
Variable overhead cost	$10,000	$ 6,000	$ 8,000	$24,000
Fixed overhead cost	20,000	20,000	20,000	60,000
Total overhead cost	**$30,000**	**$26,000**	**$28,000**	**$84,000**

For simplicity, a single overhead application rate is used in this example:

	Jan-Apr	May-Aug	Sep-Dec
Estimated total overhead / Estimated production	$\frac{\$30,000}{10,000} = \$3.00$	$\frac{\$26,000}{6,000} = \$4.33$	$\frac{\$28,000}{8,000} = \$3.50$

These fluctuations in the applied overhead rate will lead to fluctuations in unit cost:

	Jan-Apr	May-Aug	Sep-Dec
Direct materials	$ 3.00	$ 3.00	$ 3.00
Direct labor	4.00	4.00	4.00
Manufacturing overhead	3.00	4.33	3.50
Total unit cost	**$10.00**	**$11.33**	**$10.50**

The comparative income statements make clear the distorting effect:

	Jan-Apr	May-Aug	Sep-Dec	Totals
Sales:				
Produced in Jan-Apr	7,000	3,000		
Produced in May-Aug		4,000	2,000	
Produced in Sep-Dec			5,000	
Expected unit sales	7,000	7,000	7,000	
Expected selling price	× $12	× $12	× $12	
Total expected sales	$84,000	$84,000	$84,000	$252,000
Cost of goods sold:				
From Jan-Apr	$70,000	$30,000		
From May-Aug		45,333	$22,667	
From Sep-Dec			52,500	
Total expected COGS	$70,000	$75,333	$75,167	$220,500
Gross margin	**$14,000**	**$ 8,667**	**$ 8,833**	**$ 31,500**

Large fluctuations in gross margin are reported during a period when there was no change at all in the company's underlying cost structure, and sales were the same throughout.

b. To prevent these distortions in the financial statements, **normal costing** derives a single overhead application rate by looking at the entire year.

EXTENDED EXAMPLE of Normal Costing

Instead of using a different overhead application rate for each budget period, the company uses a single average figure for the entire year.

- The company expects to produce 24,000 units during the year, for an average of 8,000 units per budget period.
- Dividing the fixed overhead of $20,000 for each budget period by 8,000 units yields a fixed overhead application rate of $2.50.
- The new total overhead application rate per unit is thus $3.50 ($1.00 variable cost + $2.50 fixed cost), and the new per-unit cost for all 3 budget periods is $10.50 ($3.00 direct materials + $4.00 direct labor + $3.50 overhead application rate).

The revised income statements prepared using a normalized overhead rate reveal the smoothing effect on gross margin:

	Jan-Apr	May-Aug	Sep-Dec	Totals
Sales:				
Produced in Jan-Apr	7,000	3,000		
Produced in May-Aug		4,000	2,000	
Produced in Sep-Dec			5,000	
Expected unit sales	7,000	7,000	7,000	
Expected selling price	× $12	× $12	× $12	
Total expected sales	$84,000	$84,000	$84,000	$252,000
Cost of goods sold:				
From Jan-Apr	$73,500	$31,500		
From May-Aug		42,000	$21,000	
From Sep-Dec			52,500	
Total expected COGS	$73,500	$73,500	$73,500	$220,500
Gross margin	**$10,500**	**$10,500**	**$10,500**	**$ 31,500**

---

c. **Extended normal costing** applies a normalized rate to direct costs as well as to manufacturing overhead.

1) The following table summarizes the use of rates in the three costing methods described:

	Actual Costing	Normal Costing	Extended Normal Costing
Direct Materials	Actual	Actual	Budgeted
Direct Labor	Actual	Actual	Budgeted
Manufacturing Overhead	Actual	Budgeted	Budgeted

10. **Departmental vs. Plantwide Rates**

a. All the examples of overhead application so far have employed a single plantwide rate. This method has the benefit of simplicity.

1) However, some production departments may be labor-intensive while others are machine-intensive. In these cases, the use of a single driver for applying overhead to every phase of the production results in the miscosting of products.

2) A more accurate method is the use of departmental rates.

b. EXAMPLE: A company is preparing its overhead budget for the coming year and has selected direct labor hours as the allocation base.

	Budgeted Overhead		Allocation Base		Overhead Application Rate
Department A	$ 60,000				
Department B	40,000				
Total process	$100,000	÷	20,000	=	$5.00 per direct labor hour

A study by the company's management accountants reveals that Department A heavily employs direct labor while Department B is far more automated.

● Of the total direct labor hours budgeted for the year, 15,000 are projected for Department A and only 5,000 for Department B.

● At the same time, Department A is projected to consume 8,000 machine hours while Department B is projected to use 16,000.

Instead of applying a single plantwide application rate, then, a more accurate allocation can be obtained by using a different allocation base for each production department.

	Budgeted Overhead		Allocation Base		Overhead Application Rate
Department A	$ 60,000	÷	15,000	=	$4.00 per direct labor hour
Department B	$ 40,000	÷	16,000	=	$2.50 per machine hour

c. When indirect costs represent a large proportion of total production costs, activity-based costing, which uses cost pools for all costs (not just overhead), may be the most appropriate cost accumulation system.

Stop and review! You have completed the outline for this subunit. Study multiple-choice questions 18 through 23 beginning on page 121.

3.5 OVERHEAD ALLOCATION AND NORMAL COSTING -- CALCULATIONS

Some of the questions concerning overhead allocation and normal costing that a candidate will encounter on the CMA exam focus on the detailed calculations required. This subunit consists entirely of such questions. Please review Subunit 3.4 before attempting to answer the questions in this subunit.

Stop and review! You have completed the outline for this subunit. Study multiple-choice questions 24 through 29 beginning on page 123.

3.6 ALLOCATING SERVICE DEPARTMENT COSTS -- THEORY

1. **Reasons for Allocation**

a. Service (support) department costs are considered part of overhead (indirect costs). Thus, they cannot feasibly be traced to cost objects and therefore must be allocated to the operating departments that use the services.

1) When service departments also render services to each other, their costs may be allocated to each other before allocation to operating departments.

b. Four criteria are used to allocate costs:

1) Cause and effect should be used if possible because of its objectivity and acceptance by operating management.

2) Benefits received is the most frequently used alternative when a cause-and-effect relationship cannot be determined.

   a) However, it requires an assumption about the benefits of costs, for example, that advertising that promotes the company but not specific products was responsible for increased sales by the various divisions.

3) Fairness is sometimes mentioned in government contracts but appears to be more of a goal than an objective allocation base.

4) Ability to bear (based on profits) is usually unacceptable because of its dysfunctional effect on managerial motivation.

c. Three methods of service department allocation are in general use.

2. Direct Method

a. The direct method is the simplest. Under the direct method, service department costs are allocated directly to the producing departments without regard for services rendered by service departments to each other.

1) Service department costs are allocated to production departments based on an allocation base appropriate to each service department's function.

b. EXAMPLE: A company has the following service department costs and allocation bases:

Service Department	Costs to Be Allocated	Allocation Base
Information Technology	$120,000	CPU cycles
Custodial Services	40,000	Floor space
Total	**$160,000**	

The production departments have the following preallocation costs and allocation base amounts:

Production Department	Preallocation Costs	CPU Cycles Used	%	Floor Space in Sq. Ft.	%
Milling	$300,000	60,000,000	62.5%	56,000	70.0%
Finishing	200,000	36,000,000	37.5%	24,000	30.0%
Totals	**$500,000**	**96,000,000**	**100.0%**	**80,000**	**100.0%**

The direct method allocates the service department costs to the production departments as follows:

	Information Technology	Custodial Services	Milling	Finishing	Total
Totals before allocation	$120,000	$40,000	$300,000	$200,000	$660,000
Allocate IT (62.5%, 37.5%)	(120,000)	--	75,000	45,000	0
Allocate Custodial (70.0%, 30.0%)	--	(40,000)	28,000	12,000	0
Totals after allocation	**$ 0**	**$ 0**	**$403,000**	**$257,000**	**$660,000**

3.   **Step (Step-Down) Method**

a.   Under the step, or step-down method, some of the costs of services rendered by service departments are allocated to each other.

1)   This method derives its name from the procedure involved: The service departments are allocated in order, from the one that provides the most service to other service departments down to the one that provides the least.

b.   EXAMPLE: The services that each service department provides the other must be ascertained:

	Provided by IT		Provided by CS	
	CPU Cycles		Floor Space	
Service Department	Used	%	in Sq. Ft.	%
Information Technology	196,000,000	98.0%	20,000	80.0%
Custodial Services	4,000,000	2.0%	5,000	20.0%
Totals	**200,000,000**	**100.0%**	**25,000**	**100.0%**

Looking just at reciprocal service department activity, custodial services provides 80% of its services to information technology, but IT only provides 2% of its services to custodial. Thus, custodial will be allocated first.

The next step is to determine the relative proportions of the three departments that will receive the first allocation (the second allocation will only be distributed to the two production departments, whose allocation bases were determined under the direct method on the preceding page).

Allocate Custodial Services:	Floor Space in Sq. Ft.	%	Amount to Be Allocated	Departmental Allocations
To Milling	56,000	56.0%	$40,000	$22,400
To Finishing	24,000	24.0%	40,000	9,600
To Information Technology	20,000	20.0%	40,000	8,000
Totals	**100,000**	**100.0%**		**$40,000**

The step-down allocation is performed as follows:

	Service Departments		Production Departments		
	Custodial Services	Information Technology	Milling	Finishing	Total
Totals before allocation	$ 40,000	$120,000	$300,000	$200,000	$660,000
Allocate Custodial	(40,000)	8,000	22,400	9,600	0
Totals after first allocation	**$ 0**	**$128,000**	**$322,400**	**$209,600**	**$660,000**

Allocate IT:	CPU Cycles Used	%	Amount to Be Allocated	Departmental Allocations
To Milling	60,000,000	62.5%	$128,000	$ 80,000
To Finishing	36,000,000	37.5%	128,000	48,000
Totals	**96,000,000**	**100.0%**		**$128,000**

		Production Departments		
	Information Technology	Milling	Finishing	Total
Totals after first allocation	$128,000	$322,400	$209,600	$660,000
Allocate IT	(128,000)	80,000	48,000	0
Totals after second allocation	**$ 0**	**$402,400**	**$257,600**	**$660,000**

4. **Reciprocal Method**

    a.   The reciprocal method is the most complex and the most theoretically sound of the three methods. It is also known as the simultaneous solution method, cross allocation method, matrix allocation method, or double distribution method.

        1)   Under the reciprocal method, services rendered by all service departments to each other are recognized.

    b.   EXAMPLE: The reciprocal method requires calculating the allocation base amounts for information technology; i.e., the service department that was not allocated to the other service department under the step method.

Allocate Information Technology:	CPU Cycles Used	%
To Milling	60,000,000	60.0%
To Finishing	36,000,000	36.0%
To Custodial Services	4,000,000	4.0%
Totals	**100,000,000**	**100.0%**

Use linear algebra to calculate fully reciprocated information technology costs (FRITC) and fully reciprocated custodial services costs (FRCSC):

FRITC   = Preallocation IT costs + (FRCSC × Portion of custodial effort used by IT)
           = $120,000 + (FRCSC × 20%)

FRCSC   = Preallocation custodial costs + (FRITC × Portion of IT effort used by custodial)
           = $40,000 + (FRITC × 4%)

These algebraic equations can be solved simultaneously.

FRITC	= $120,000 + (FRCSC × 20%)
	= $120,000 + {[$40,000 + (FRITC × 4%)] × 20%}
	= $120,000 + [($40,000 + .04FRITC) × .2]
	= $120,000 + $8,000 + .008FRITC
.992FRITC	= $128,000
FRITC	= $129,032
FRCSC	= $40,000 + (FRITC × 4%)
	= $40,000 + ($129,032 × .04)
	= $40,000 + $5,161
	= $45,161

The reciprocal allocation is performed as follows:

	Service Departments		Production Departments		
	Custodial Services	Information Technology	Milling	Finishing	Total
Totals before allocation	$40,000	$120,000	$300,000	$200,000	$ 660,000
Allocate Custodial Services (20.0%, 56.0%, 24.0%)	(45,161)	9,032	25,290	10,839	0
Allocate Information Technology (4.0%, 60.0%, 36.0%)	5,161	(129,032)	77,419	46,452	0
Totals after allocation	**$ 0**	**$ 0**	**$402,709**	**$257,291**	**$ 660,000**

5.   **Single-Rate vs. Dual-Rate Allocation**

a.   The examples presented employed a single rate to allocate the costs of each support department. Some firms find that employing dual-rate allocation provides more useful information.

b.   EXAMPLE: The company has decided to allocate the IT department's costs using a dual-rate method, one rate for the costs of IT's investment in hardware and software (fixed), and another rate for the costs of services provided (variable).

- The IT department has determined that $40,000 of its total allocable costs are associated with variable costs. These will henceforth be allocated using technician and programmer hours.

- The company's technicians and programmers worked a total of 1,600 hours on projects for the Milling and Finishing Departments during the period. Variable IT costs will thus be applied at the rate of $25 per hour ($40,000 ÷ 1,600).

- The remaining $80,000 of allocable IT costs are associated with the department's investment in fixed plant. These costs will continue to be allocated using CPU cycles.

- Since the company's central computers consumed a total of 96 million CPU cycles doing processing for the Milling and Finishing Departments during the period, fixed IT costs will be applied at the rate of $0.00083 per cycle ($80,000 ÷ 96,000,000).

The dual-rate allocations will be made as follows:

Allocate to Milling:	Driver Units Consumed		Application Rate		Totals
Variable IT costs	640 hours	×	$25.00	=	$16,000
Fixed IT costs	60,000,000 cycles	×	$0.00083	=	$50,000
Total					**$66,000**

Allocate to Finishing:	Driver Units Consumed		Application Rate		Totals
Variable IT costs	960 hours	×	$25.00	=	$24,000
Fixed IT costs	36,000,000 cycles	×	$0.00083	=	$30,000
Total					**$54,000**

1)   The total amount of IT department costs has been allocated ($66,000 + $54,000 = $120,000).

c.   The dual-rate method can be used to refine a system currently using a single rate under any of the other methods (direct, step-down, reciprocal).

Stop and review! You have completed the outline for this subunit. Study multiple-choice questions 30 through 35 beginning on page 125.

3.7 ALLOCATING SERVICE DEPARTMENT COSTS -- CALCULATIONS

Some of the questions concerning service department allocation costing that a candidate will encounter on the CMA exam focus on the detailed calculations required. This subunit consists entirely of such questions. Please review Subunit 3.6 before attempting to answer the questions in this subunit.

Stop and review! You have completed the outline for this subunit. Study multiple-choice questions 36 through 42 beginning on page 128.

3.8 CORE CONCEPTS

Absorption and Variable Costing

- Under **absorption costing** (sometimes called full or full absorption costing), the fixed portion of manufacturing overhead is "absorbed" into the cost of each product. Product cost thus includes all manufacturing costs, both fixed and variable.

    - Absorption-basis cost of goods sold is subtracted from sales to arrive at **gross margin**.
    - This method is required for external reporting purposes and for tax purposes.

- **Variable costing** (sometimes called direct costing) is more appropriate for internal reporting. Product cost includes only the variable portion of manufacturing costs.

    - Variable-basis cost of goods sold and the variable portion of S&A expenses are subtracted from sales to arrive at **contribution margin**.

- When production exceeds sales, operating income is higher under absorption costing. This is the **perverse incentive** inherent in absorption costing and reveals why many companies prefer variable costing for internal reporting.

    - A production manager can increase absorption-basis operating income merely by increasing production, whether there is any customer demand for the additional product or not.

Joint Product and By-Product Costing

- When two or more separate products are produced by a common manufacturing process from a common input, the outputs from the process are joint products.

    - **Joint (common) costs** are those costs incurred up to the point where the products become separately identifiable, called the **split-off point**.
    - At the split-off point, the joint products acquire separate identities. Costs incurred after split-off are **separable costs**.

- A physical measure-based approach employs a physical measure such as volume, weight, or a linear measure.

    - The **physical-unit method** allocates joint production costs to each product based on their relative proportions of the measure selected.

- Market-based approaches assign a proportionate amount of the total cost to each product on a monetary basis.

    - The **sales-value at split-off method** is based on the relative sales values of the separate products at split-off.
    - The **estimated net realizable value (NRV) method** also allocates joint costs based on the relative market values of the products.
    - The **constant-gross-margin percentage NRV method** is based on allocating joint costs so that the gross-margin percentage is the same for every product.

- **By-products** are one or more products of relatively small total value that are produced simultaneously from a common manufacturing process with products of greater value and quantity. They can be sold or discarded.

Overhead Allocation and Normal Costing

- Whenever overhead is to be allocated, as in job-order costing and activity-based costing, an **appropriate allocation base** must be chosen.

    - In traditional cost accounting, allocation bases include direct labor hours, direct labor cost, machine hours, materials cost, and units of production. The crucial quality of an allocation base is that it be a cost driver of (i.e., have a cause-and-effect relationship with) the costs in the pool to be allocated.

- Overhead is usually allocated to products based upon the level of activity. For example, if overhead is largely made up of machine maintenance, the activity base may be machine hours.

    - The predetermined **overhead application rate** equals budgeted overhead divided by the budgeted activity level (measure of capacity).

- Inevitably, the overhead amounts applied throughout the year will vary from the amount actually incurred, which is only determinable once the job is complete. This **variance** is called **over- or underapplied overhead**.

    - If immaterial, it can be closed directly to cost of goods sold. If material, it should be allocated based on the relative values of work-in-process, finished goods, and cost of goods sold.

- Calculating new overhead application rates each month can result in misleading unit costs. This is because, during months of low production, per-unit overhead charges will skyrocket. This leads to higher product costs during months of lower production and to distortions in the financial statements.

    - To prevent these distortions in the financial statements, **normal costing** derives a single overhead application rate by looking at the entire year.
    - Extended normal costing applies the use of a normalized rate to direct costs as well as to manufacturing overhead.

Allocating Service Department Costs

- **Service (support) department** costs are considered part of overhead (indirect costs). Thus, they cannot feasibly be traced to cost objects and therefore **must be allocated** to the operating departments that use the services.

- The **direct method** is the simplest. Service department costs are allocated directly to the producing departments without regard for services rendered by service departments to each other.

    - Service department costs are allocated to production departments based on an allocation base appropriate to each service department's function.

- Under the **step, or step-down, method**, some of the costs of services rendered by service departments are allocated to each other.

    - The step method derives its name from the procedure involved: The service departments are allocated in order, from the one that provides the most service to other service departments down to the one that provides the least.
    - The **reciprocal method** is the most complex and the most theoretically sound of the three methods. It is also known as the simultaneous solution method, cross allocation method, matrix allocation method, or double distribution method. The reciprocal method recognizes services rendered by all service departments to each other.

QUESTIONS

3.1 Absorption and Variable Costing -- Theory

1. Which of the following statements is true for a firm that uses variable costing?

A. The cost of a unit of product changes because of changes in number of units manufactured.

B. Profits fluctuate with sales.

C. An idle facility variation is calculated.

D. Product costs include variable administrative costs.

Answer (B) is correct. *(CMA, adapted)*
REQUIRED: The true statement about variable costing.
DISCUSSION: In a variable costing system, only the variable costs are recorded as product costs. All fixed costs are expensed in the period incurred. Because changes in the relationship between production levels and sales levels do not cause changes in the amount of fixed manufacturing cost expensed, profits more directly follow the trends in sales.
Answer (A) is incorrect. The cost of a unit of product changing owing to a change in the number of units manufactured is a characteristic of absorption costing systems. Answer (C) is incorrect. Idle facility variation is a characteristic of absorption costing systems. Answer (D) is incorrect. Neither variable nor absorption costing includes administrative costs in inventory.

2. Which method of inventory costing treats direct manufacturing costs and manufacturing overhead costs, both variable and fixed, as inventoriable costs?

A. Direct costing.

B. Variable costing.

C. Absorption costing.

D. Conversion costing.

Answer (C) is correct. *(CMA, adapted)*
REQUIRED: The method of inventory costing that treats direct manufacturing costs and all manufacturing overhead as inventoriable.
DISCUSSION: Absorption (full) costing considers all manufacturing costs to be inventoriable as product costs. These costs include variable and fixed manufacturing costs, whether direct or indirect. The alternative to absorption is known as variable (direct) costing.
Answer (A) is incorrect. Variable (direct) costing does not inventory fixed overhead. Answer (B) is incorrect. Variable (direct) costing does not inventory fixed overhead. Answer (D) is incorrect. Conversion costs include direct labor and overhead but not direct materials.

3. The difference between the sales price and total variable costs is

A. Gross operating profit.

B. Net profit.

C. The breakeven point.

D. The contribution margin.

Answer (D) is correct. *(CMA, adapted)*
REQUIRED: The difference between sales price and total variable costs.
DISCUSSION: The contribution margin is calculated by subtracting all variable costs from sales revenue. It represents the portion of sales that is available for covering fixed costs and profit.
Answer (A) is incorrect. Gross operating profit is the net result after deducting all manufacturing costs from sales, including both fixed and variable costs. Answer (B) is incorrect. Net profit is the remainder after deducting from revenue all costs, both fixed and variable. Answer (C) is incorrect. The breakeven point is the level of sales that equals the sum of fixed and variable costs.

4. Which one of the following statements is true regarding absorption costing and variable costing?

A. Overhead costs are treated in the same manner under both costing methods.

B. If finished goods inventory increases, absorption costing results in higher income.

C. Variable manufacturing costs are lower under variable costing.

D. Gross margins are the same under both costing methods.

Answer (B) is correct. *(CMA, adapted)*
REQUIRED: The true statement regarding absorption costing and variable costing.
DISCUSSION: Under variable costing, inventories are charged only with the variable costs of production. Fixed manufacturing costs are expensed as period costs. Absorption costing charges to inventory all costs of production. If finished goods inventory increases, absorption costing results in higher income because it capitalizes some fixed costs that would have been expensed under variable costing. When inventory declines, variable costing results in higher income because some fixed costs capitalized under the absorption method in prior periods are expensed in the current period.
Answer (A) is incorrect. Fixed overhead is treated differently under the two methods. Answer (C) is incorrect. Variable costs are the same under either method. Answer (D) is incorrect. Gross margins will be different. Fixed factory overhead is expensed under variable costing and capitalized under the absorption method.

5. The costing method that is properly classified for both external and internal reporting purposes is

		External Reporting	Internal Reporting
A.	Activity-based costing	No	Yes
B.	Job-order costing	No	Yes
C.	Variable costing	No	Yes
D.	Process costing	No	No

Answer (C) is correct. *(CMA, adapted)*
REQUIRED: The costing method that is properly classified for both internal and external reporting purposes.
DISCUSSION: Activity-based costing, job-order costing, process costing, and standard costing can all be used for both internal and external purposes. Variable costing is not acceptable under GAAP for external reporting purposes.
Answer (A) is incorrect. ABC is appropriate for external as well as internal purposes. Answer (B) is incorrect. Job-order costing is acceptable for external reporting purposes. Answer (D) is incorrect. Process costing is acceptable for external reporting purposes.

6. Absorption costing and variable costing are two different methods of assigning costs to units produced. Of the four cost items listed below, identify the one that is **not** correctly accounted for as a product cost.

		Part of Product Cost Under	
		Absorption Costing	Variable Costing
A.	Manufacturing supplies	Yes	Yes
B.	Insurance on factory	Yes	No
C.	Direct labor cost	Yes	Yes
D.	Packaging and shipping costs	Yes	Yes

Answer (D) is correct. *(CMA, adapted)*
REQUIRED: The cost not correctly accounted for.
DISCUSSION: Under absorption costing, all manufacturing costs, both fixed and variable, are treated as product costs. Under variable costing, only variable costs of manufacturing are inventoried as product costs. Fixed manufacturing costs are expensed as period costs. Packaging and shipping costs are not product costs under either method because they are incurred after the goods have been manufactured. Instead, they are included in selling and administrative expenses for the period.
Answer (A) is incorrect. Manufacturing supplies are variable costs inventoried under both methods. Answer (B) is incorrect. Factory insurance is a fixed manufacturing cost inventoried under absorption costing but written off as a period cost under variable costing. Answer (C) is incorrect. Direct labor cost is a product cost under both methods.

3.2 Absorption and Variable Costing -- Calculations

Questions 7 and 8 are based on the following information. At the end of its fiscal year, Jubal Manufacturing recorded the data below:

Prime cost	$800,000
Variable manufacturing overhead	100,000
Fixed manufacturing overhead	160,000
Variable selling and other expenses	80,000
Fixed selling and other expenses	40,000

7. If Jubal uses variable costing, the inventoriable costs for the fiscal year are

A. $800,000

B. $900,000

C. $980,000

D. $1,060,000

Answer (B) is correct. *(CMA, adapted)*
REQUIRED: The inventoriable costs using the variable costing method.
DISCUSSION: The only costs capitalized are the variable costs of manufacturing. Prime costs (direct materials and direct labor) are variable.

Prime costs (direct materials and direct labor)	$800,000
Variable manufacturing overhead	100,000
Total inventoriable costs	$900,000

Answer (A) is incorrect. The amount of $800,000 equals only the prime costs. Answer (C) is incorrect. The amount of $980,000 includes the variable selling and other expenses. Answer (D) is incorrect. The amount of $1,060,000 equals inventoriable costs under absorption costing.

8. Using absorption (full) costing, Jubal's inventoriable costs are

A. $800,000

B. $900,000

C. $1,060,000

D. $1,180,000

Answer (C) is correct. *(CMA, adapted)*
REQUIRED: The inventoriable costs using the absorption costing method.
DISCUSSION: The absorption method is required for financial statements prepared according to GAAP. It charges all costs of production to inventories. The prime costs of $800,000, variable manufacturing overhead of $100,000, and the fixed manufacturing overhead of $160,000 are included. They total $1,060,000.
Answer (A) is incorrect. The amount of $800,000 equals only prime costs. Answer (B) is incorrect. The amount of $900,000 equals inventoriable costs under variable costing. Answer (D) is incorrect. The amount of $1,180,000 includes the fixed and variable selling and other expenses.

9. A manufacturing company employs variable costing for internal reporting and analysis purposes. However, it converts its records to absorption costing for external reporting. The Accounting Department always reconciles the two operating income figures to assure that no errors have occurred in the conversion. The fixed manufacturing overhead cost per unit was based on the planned level of production of 480,000 units. Financial data for the year are presented below:

	Budget	Actual
Sales (in units)	495,000	510,000
Production (in units)	480,000	500,000

	Variable Costing	Absorption Costing
Variable costs	$10.00	$10.00
Fixed manufacturing overhead	0	6.00
Total unit manufacturing costs	$10.00	$16.00

The difference between the operating income calculated under the variable costing method and the operating income calculated under the absorption costing method would be

A. $57,600

B. $60,000

C. $90,000

D. $120,000

Answer (B) is correct. *(CIA, adapted)*
REQUIRED: The difference between variable costing and absorption costing operating income.
DISCUSSION: The difference between variable costing and absorption costing is that the former treats fixed manufacturing overhead as a period cost. The latter method treats it as a product cost. Given that sales exceeded production, both methods expense all fixed manufacturing overhead incurred during the year. However, 10,000 units (510,000 sales – 500,000 production) manufactured in a prior period were also sold. These units presumably were recorded at $10 under variable costing and $16 under absorption costing. Consequently, absorption costing operating income is $60,000 (10,000 units × $6) less than that under variable costing.
Answer (A) is incorrect. The amount of $57,600 equals 10,000 units times $5.76 per unit (total budgeted fixed manufacturing overhead ÷ 500,000 units). Answer (C) is incorrect. The amount of $90,000 is the difference between planned sales (495,000 units) and actual sales (510,000 units), times the fixed manufacturing overhead per unit ($6). Answer (D) is incorrect. The amount of $120,000 is the volume variance under absorption costing.

Questions 10 and 11 are based on the following information. Osawa, Inc., planned and actually manufactured 200,000 units of its single product during its first year of operations. Variable manufacturing costs were $30 per unit of product. Planned and actual fixed manufacturing costs were $600,000, and selling and administrative costs totaled $400,000. Osawa sold 120,000 units of product at a selling price of $40 per unit.

10. Osawa's operating income using absorption (full) costing is

A. $200,000

B. $440,000

C. $600,000

D. $840,000

Answer (B) is correct. *(CMA, adapted)*
REQUIRED: The operating income under absorption costing.
DISCUSSION: Absorption costing net income is computed as follows:

Sales (120,000 units × $40)		$4,800,000
Variable production costs		
(200,000 units × $30)	$6,000,000	
Fixed production costs	600,000	
Total production costs	$6,600,000	
Ending inventory (80,000 units × $33)	(2,640,000)	
Cost of goods sold		(3,960,000)
Gross profit		$ 840,000
Selling and administrative expenses		(400,000)
Operating income		$ 440,000

Answer (A) is incorrect. The amount of $200,000 is the operating income under variable costing. Answer (C) is incorrect. The amount of $600,000 is the operating income that results from capitalizing $240,000 fixed manufacturing costs and $160,000 of selling and administrative costs (the $160,000 is incorrect as all selling and administrative costs should be expensed). Answer (D) is incorrect. The amount of $840,000 is the gross profit under absorption costing, i.e., before selling and administrative expenses.

11. Osawa's operating income for the year using variable costing is

A. $200,000

B. $440,000

C. $800,000

D. $600,000

Answer (A) is correct. *(CMA, adapted)*
REQUIRED: The operating income under variable costing.
DISCUSSION: The contribution margin from manufacturing (sales – variable costs) is $10 ($40 – $30) per unit sold, or $1,200,000 (120,000 units × $10). The fixed costs of manufacturing ($600,000) and selling and administrative costs ($400,000) are deducted from the contribution margin to arrive at an operating income of $200,000. The difference between the absorption income of $440,000 and the $200,000 of variable costing income is attributable to capitalization of the fixed manufacturing costs under the absorption method. Because 40% of the goods produced are still in inventory (80,000 ÷ 200,000), 40% of the $600,000 in fixed costs, or $240,000, was capitalized under the absorption method. That amount was expensed under the variable costing method.

Answer (B) is incorrect. The amount of $440,000 is the operating income under absorption costing. Answer (C) is incorrect. The amount of $800,000 is the operating income if fixed costs of manufacturing are not deducted. Answer (D) is incorrect. The amount of $600,000 is the operating income that results from capitalizing 40% of both fixed manufacturing costs and selling and administrative costs.

3.3 Joint Product and By-Product Costing

Questions 12 through 16 are based on the following information.

Atlas Foods produces the following three supplemental food products simultaneously through a refining process costing $93,000.

The joint products, Alfa and Betters, have a final selling price of $4 per pound and $10 per pound, respectively, after additional processing costs of $2 per pound of each product are incurred after the split-off point. Morefeed, a by-product, is sold at the split-off point for $3 per pound.

Alfa	10,000 pounds of Alfa, a popular but relatively rare grain supplement having a caloric value of 4,400 calories per pound
Betters	5,000 pounds of Betters, a flavoring material high in carbohydrates with a caloric value of 11,200 calories per pound
Morefeed	1,000 pounds of Morefeed, used as a cattle feed supplement with a caloric value of 1,000 calories per pound

12. Assuming Atlas Foods inventories Morefeed, the by-product, the joint cost to be allocated to Alfa using the net realizable value method is

A. $3,000

B. $30,000

C. $31,000

D. $60,000

Answer (B) is correct. *(CMA, adapted)*
REQUIRED: The joint cost allocated to Alfa based on net realizable values if the by-product is inventoried.
DISCUSSION: The NRV at split-off for each of the joint products must be determined. Given that Alfa has a $4 selling price and an additional $2 of processing costs, the value at the split-off is $2 per pound. The total value at split-off for 10,000 pounds is $20,000. Betters has a $10 selling price and an additional $2 of processing costs. Thus, the value at split-off is $8 per pound. The total value of 5,000 pounds of Betters is therefore $40,000. The 1,000 pounds of Morefeed has a split-off value of $3 per pound, or $3,000. Assuming that Morefeed (a by-product) is inventoried (recognized in the accounts when produced) and treated as a reduction of joint costs, the allocable joint cost is $90,000 ($93,000 – $3,000). (NOTE: Several other methods of accounting for by-products are possible.) The total net realizable value of the main products is $60,000 ($20,000 Alfa + $40,000 Betters). The allocation to Alfa is $30,000 [($20,000 ÷ $60,000) × $90,000].
Answer (A) is incorrect. The amount of $3,000 is the value of the by-product. Answer (C) is incorrect. The amount of $31,000 fails to adjust the joint processing cost for the value of the by-product. Answer (D) is incorrect. The amount of $60,000 is the amount allocated to Betters.

13. Assuming Atlas Foods inventories Morefeed, the by-product, the joint cost to be allocated to Alfa, using the physical quantity method is

A. $3,000

B. $30,000

C. $31,000

D. $60,000

Answer (D) is correct. *(CMA, adapted)*
REQUIRED: The joint cost allocated to Alfa based on the physical quantity method if the by-product is inventoried.
DISCUSSION: Joint cost is $93,000 and Morefeed has a split-off value of $3,000 (1,000 pounds × $3 split-off value per pound). Assuming the latter amount is treated as a reduction in joint cost, the allocable joint cost is $90,000. The total physical quantity (volume) of the two joint products is 15,000 pounds (10,000 Alfa + 5,000 Betters). Hence, $60,000 of the net joint costs [(10,000 ÷ 15,000) × $90,000] should be allocated to Alfa.
Answer (A) is incorrect. The figure of $3,000 is the value of the by-product. Answer (B) is incorrect. The figure of $30,000 is based on the net realizable value method. Answer (C) is incorrect. The figure of $31,000 is based on the net realizable value method and fails to adjust the joint processing cost for the value of the by-product.

14. Refer to the information on the preceding page(s). Assuming Atlas Foods inventories Morefeed, the by-product, the joint cost to be allocated to Betters using the weighted-quantity method based on caloric value per pound is

A. $39,208

B. $39,600

C. $40,920

D. $50,400

Answer (D) is correct. *(CMA, adapted)*
    REQUIRED: The joint cost allocated to Betters based on weighted quantities if the by-product is inventoried.
    DISCUSSION: The net allocable joint cost is $90,000, assuming the value of Morefeed is inventoried and treated as a reduction in joint costs. The caloric value of Alfa is 44,000,000 (4,400 × 10,000 pounds), the caloric value of Betters is 56,000,000 (11,200 × 5,000 pounds), and the total is 100,000,000. Of this total volume, Alfa makes up 44% and Betters 56%. Thus, $50,400 ($90,000 × 56%) should be allocated to Betters.
    Answer (A) is incorrect. The figure of $39,208 is the amount allocated to Alfa if the 1,000,000 calories attributable to Morefeed is included in the computation. Answer (B) is incorrect. The figure of $39,600 is the allocation to Alfa. Answer (C) is incorrect. The figure of $40,920 is the allocation to Alfa if the sales value of the by-product is not treated as a reduction of joint cost.

15. Refer to the information on the preceding page(s). Assuming Atlas Foods inventories Morefeed, the by-product, and that it incurs no additional processing costs for Alfa and Betters, the joint cost to be allocated to Alfa using the gross market value method is

A. $36,000

B. $40,000

C. $41,333

D. $50,000

Answer (B) is correct. *(CMA, adapted)*
    REQUIRED: The joint cost allocated to Alfa using the gross market value method if the by-product is inventoried.
    DISCUSSION: The gross market value of Alfa is $40,000 (10,000 pounds × $4), Betters has a total gross value of $50,000 (5,000 pounds × $10), and Morefeed has a split-off value of $3,000. If the value of Morefeed is inventoried and treated as a reduction in joint cost, the allocable joint cost is $90,000 ($93,000 – $3,000). The total gross value of the two main products is $90,000 ($40,000 + $50,000). Of this total value, $40,000 should be allocated to Alfa [($40,000 ÷ $90,000) × $90,000].
    Answer (A) is incorrect. The amount of $36,000 is based on 40%, not 4/9. Answer (C) is incorrect. The amount of $41,333 fails to adjust the joint cost by the value of the by-product. Answer (D) is incorrect. The amount of $50,000 is the joint cost allocated to Betters.

16. Refer to the information on the preceding page(s). Assuming Atlas Foods does not inventory Morefeed, the by-product, the joint cost to be allocated to Betters using the net realizable value method is

A. $30,000

B. $31,000

C. $52,080

D. $62,000

Answer (D) is correct. *(CMA, adapted)*
    REQUIRED: The joint cost allocated to Betters based on net realizable values if the by-product is not inventoried.
    DISCUSSION: The NRV of Alfa is $20,000 [10,000 pounds × ($4 selling price – $2 additional processing costs)] , and the NRV of Betters is $40,000 [5,000 pounds × ($10 selling price – $2 additional processing costs)]. If the joint cost is not adjusted for the value of the by-production, the amount allocated to Betters is $62,000 {[$40,000 ÷ ($20,000 + $40,000)] × $93,000}.
    Answer (A) is incorrect. The amount of $30,000 is the amount allocated to Alfa when the by-product is inventoried. Answer (B) is incorrect. The amount of $31,000 is the amount allocated to Alfa when the by-product is not inventoried. Answer (C) is incorrect. The amount of $52,080 assumes that a weighting method using caloric value is used.

17. A company produces three main joint products and one by-product. The by-product's relative sales value is quite low compared with that of the main products. The preferable accounting for the by-product's net realizable value is as

A. An addition to the revenues of the other products allocated on the basis of their respective net realizable values.

B. Revenue in the period it is sold.

C. A reduction in the common cost to be allocated to the three main products.

D. A separate net realizable value upon which to allocate some of the common costs.

Answer (C) is correct. *(CIA, adapted)*
    REQUIRED: The preferable accounting method for by-products.
    DISCUSSION: Because of the relatively small sales value, a cost-effective allocation method is used for by-products. The net realizable value of by-products is usually deducted from the cost of the main products.
    Answer (A) is incorrect. Treating the net realizable value of a by-product as an addition to the revenues of the other products attributes the allocation characteristics of main products to by-products. Answer (B) is incorrect. The NRV is ordinarily recognized as a contra cost in the period the by-product is produced. Answer (D) is incorrect. Recognition of a separate net realizable value upon which to allocate some of the common costs attributes the allocation characteristics of main products to by-products.

3.4 Overhead Allocation and Normal Costing -- Theory

18. Units of production is an appropriate overhead allocation base when

A. Several well-differentiated products are manufactured.

B. Direct labor costs are low.

C. Direct material costs are large relative to direct labor costs incurred.

D. Only one product is manufactured.

Answer (D) is correct. *(CMA, adapted)*
REQUIRED: The situation in which units of production is an appropriate overhead allocation base.
DISCUSSION: Allocating overhead on the basis of the number of units produced is usually not appropriate. Costs should be allocated on the basis of some plausible relationship between the cost object and the incurrence of the cost, preferably cause and effect. The fixed portion of overhead costs is incurred regardless of the level of production. When multiple products are involved, the number of units of production may bear no relationship to the incurrence of the allocated cost. If overhead is correlated with machine hours but different products require different quantities of that input, the result may be an illogical allocation. However, if a firm manufactures only one product, this allocation method may be acceptable because all costs are to be charged to the single product.
Answer (A) is incorrect. The number of units of production may have no logical relationship to overhead when several different products are made. Answer (B) is incorrect. A low level of direct labor costs means that fixed overhead is substantial, and an appropriate cost driver should be used to make the allocation. Answer (C) is incorrect. The allocation should be made on the basis of the appropriate cost drivers without regard to the relationship between direct materials and labor costs.

19. Generally, individual departmental rates rather than a plantwide rate for applying manufacturing overhead are used if

A. A company wants to adopt a standard cost system.

B. A company's manufacturing operations are all highly automated.

C. Manufacturing overhead is the largest cost component of its product cost.

D. The manufactured products differ in the resources consumed from the individual departments in the plant.

Answer (D) is correct. *(CMA, adapted)*
REQUIRED: The circumstance in which individual departmental overhead application rates are used.
DISCUSSION: Overhead is usually assigned to products based on a predetermined rate or rates. The activity base for overhead allocation should have a high degree of correlation with the incurrence of overhead. Given only one cost driver, one overhead application rate is sufficient. If products differ in the resources consumed in individual departments, multiple rates are preferable.
Answer (A) is incorrect. A standard cost system can be based on individual or multiple application rates. Answer (B) is incorrect. Whether production is machine intensive affects the nature but not necessarily the number of cost drivers.
Answer (C) is incorrect. A single plant-wide application rate is acceptable, even with high overhead, if all overhead is highly correlated with a single application base.

20. The appropriate method for the disposition of underapplied or overapplied overhead of a manufacturer

A. Is to cost of goods sold only.

B. Is to finished goods inventory only.

C. Is apportioned to cost of goods sold and finished goods inventory.

D. Depends on the significance of the amount.

Answer (D) is correct. *(CMA, adapted)*
REQUIRED: The appropriate treatment of underapplied or overapplied overhead at the end of a period.
DISCUSSION: Overapplied or underapplied overhead should be disposed of at the end of an accounting period by transferring the balance either to cost of goods sold (if the amount is not material) or to cost of goods sold, finished goods inventory, and work-in-process inventory. Theoretically, the allocation is preferred, but, because the amount is usually immaterial, the entire balance is often transferred directly to cost of goods sold. Thus, the entry depends upon the significance of the amount.

Question 21 is based on the following information.

Nash Glassworks Company has budgeted fixed manufacturing overhead of $100,000 per month. The company uses absorption costing for both external and internal financial reporting purposes. Budgeted overhead rates for cost allocations for the month of April using alternative unit output denominator levels are shown in the next column.

Capacity Levels	Budgeted Denominator Level (units of output)	Budgeted Overhead Cost Rate
Theoretical	1,500,000	$.0667
Practical	1,250,000	.0800
Normal	775,000	.1290
Master-budget	800,000	.1250

Actual output for the month of April was 800,000 units of glassware.

21. When Nash Glassworks Company allocates fixed costs, management will select a capacity level to use as the denominator volume. All of the following are appropriate as the capacity level that approximates actual volume levels **except**

   A. Normal capacity.

   B. Expected annual activity.

   C. Theoretical capacity.

   D. Master-budget capacity.

Answer (C) is correct. *(CMA, adapted)*
   REQUIRED: The item not an approximation of actual volume levels.
   DISCUSSION: Theoretical (ideal) capacity is the maximum capacity given continuous operations with no holidays, downtime, etc. It assumes perfect efficiency at all times. Consequently, it can never be attained and is not a reasonable estimate of actual volume.
   Answer (A) is incorrect. Normal capacity is the long-term average level of activity that will approximate demand over a period that includes seasonal, cyclical, and trend variations. Answer (B) is incorrect. Expected annual activity is an approximation of actual volume levels for a specific year. Answer (D) is incorrect. Master-budget capacity is the expected level of activity used for budgeting for a given year.

22. In determining next year's overhead application rates, a company desires to focus on manufacturing capacity rather than output demand for its products. To derive a realistic application rate, the denominator activity level should be based on

   A. Practical capacity.

   B. Maximum capacity.

   C. Normal capacity.

   D. Master-budget (expected annual) capacity.

Answer (A) is correct. *(CMA, adapted)*
   REQUIRED: The proper denominator level of activity for selecting an overhead application rate.
   DISCUSSION: Practical capacity is based on realistic, attainable levels of production and input efficiency and is the most appropriate denominator level to use in selecting an overhead application rate.
   Answer (B) is incorrect. Using maximum capacity assumes no downtime, an unrealistic assumption in any case. Answer (C) is incorrect. Normal capacity may be lower than the equipment is capable of with proper maintenance and attention to efficiency. Answer (D) is incorrect. Master-budget (expected) capacity cannot be determined until the application base is selected.

23. When the amount of overapplied factory overhead is significant, the entry to close overapplied factory overhead will most likely require

   A. A debit to cost of goods sold.

   B. Debits to cost of goods sold, finished goods inventory, and work-in-process inventory.

   C. A credit to cost of goods sold.

   D. Credits to cost of goods sold, finished goods inventory, and work-in-process inventory.

Answer (D) is correct. *(CIA, adapted)*
   REQUIRED: The most likely entry to close overapplied factory overhead.
   DISCUSSION: Under a normal costing system, overhead is applied to all jobs worked on during the period at a predetermined rate. Because cost of goods sold, finished goods inventory, and work-in-process inventory all relate to these jobs, each should be adjusted by its proportionate share of over- or underapplied overhead. This apportionment may be based on either the percentage of total overhead (theoretically preferable) or the percentage of total cost. The entry to close overapplied overhead requires credits to these three accounts.
   Answer (A) is incorrect. Cost of goods sold should be credited (not debited) for its share of overapplied overhead. Answer (B) is incorrect. Cost of goods sold, finished goods inventory, and work-in-process inventory should be credited (not debited). Answer (C) is incorrect. Although commonly used, the immediate write-off method is not as conceptually sound as the allocation among cost of goods sold, finished goods inventory, and work-in-process inventory.

3.5 Overhead Allocation and Normal Costing -- Calculations

24. A manufacturer allocates overhead to jobs in process using direct labor costs, direct materials costs, and machine hours. The overhead application rates for the current year are

> 100% of direct labor
> 20% of direct materials
> $117 per machine hour

A particular production run incurred the following costs:

> Direct labor, $8,000
> Direct materials, $2,000
> A total of 140 machine hours were required for the production run.

What is the total cost charged to the production run?

A. $18,000

B. $18,400

C. $34,780

D. None of the answers are true.

Answer (C) is correct. *(CIA, adapted)*
REQUIRED: The total cost for a production run given overhead application rates.
DISCUSSION: The total cost charged to the production run is calculated as follows:

Direct labor			$ 8,000
Direct materials			2,000
Manufacturing overhead:			
$8,000 of direct labor × 100%	=	$ 8,000	
$2,000 of direct materials × 20%	=	400	
140 machine hours × $117	=	16,380	24,780
Total charged to production			$34,780

Answer (A) is incorrect. The amount of $18,000 includes only $8,000 for overhead (based on 100% of direct labor). Answer (B) is incorrect. The amount of $18,400 includes only $8,400 for overhead (based on 100% of direct labor and 20% of direct materials). Answer (D) is incorrect. Total cost is $34,780.

25. Pane Company uses a job costing system and applies overhead to products on the basis of direct labor cost. Job No. 75, the only job in process on January 1, had the following costs assigned as of that date: direct materials, $40,000; direct labor, $80,000; and factory overhead, $120,000. The following selected costs were incurred during the year:

Traceable to jobs:
Direct materials	$178,000
Direct labor	345,000
Total	$523,000

Not traceable to jobs:
Factory materials and supplies	$ 46,000
Indirect labor	235,000
Plant maintenance	73,000
Depreciation on factory equipment	29,000
Other factory costs	76,000
Total	$459,000

Pane's profit plan for the year included budgeted direct labor of $320,000 and overhead of $448,000. Assuming no work-in-process on December 31, Pane's overhead for the year was

A. $11,000 overapplied.

B. $24,000 overapplied.

C. $11,000 underapplied.

D. $24,000 underapplied.

Answer (B) is correct. *(CMA, adapted)*
REQUIRED: The extent to which overhead was under- or overapplied.
DISCUSSION: Pane applies overhead to products on the basis of direct labor cost. The rate is 1.4 ($448,000 budgeted OH ÷ $320,000 budgeted DL cost). Thus, $483,000 ($345,000 actual DL cost × 1.4) of overhead was applied, of which $24,000 ($483,000 – $459,000 actual OH) was overapplied.

Answer (A) is incorrect. The amount of $11,000 equals the difference between budgeted and actual overhead. Answer (C) is incorrect. The amount of $11,000 equals the difference between budgeted and actual overhead. Answer (D) is incorrect. The overhead was overapplied.

26. During the current accounting period, a manufacturing company purchased $70,000 of raw materials, of which $50,000 of direct materials and $5,000 of indirect materials were used in production. The company also incurred $45,000 of total labor costs and $20,000 of other manufacturing overhead costs. An analysis of the work-in-process control account revealed $40,000 of direct labor costs. Based upon the above information, what is the total amount accumulated in the overhead control account?

A. $25,000

B. $30,000

C. $45,000

D. $50,000

Answer (B) is correct. *(CIA, adapted)*
REQUIRED: The total amount accumulated in the overhead control account.
DISCUSSION: Overhead consists of all costs, other than direct materials and direct labor, that are associated with the manufacturing process. The overhead control account should have the following costs:

Indirect materials	$ 5,000
Indirect labor ($45,000 – $40,000)	5,000
Other overhead	20,000
Total overhead	$30,000

Answer (A) is incorrect. The amount of $25,000 excludes the indirect materials. Answer (C) is incorrect. The amount of $45,000 is the total labor cost. Answer (D) is incorrect. The amount of $50,000 is the direct materials cost.

Question 27 is based on the following information.

Nash Glassworks Company has budgeted fixed manufacturing overhead of $100,000 per month. The company uses absorption costing for both external and internal financial reporting purposes. Budgeted overhead rates for cost allocations for the month of April using alternative unit output denominator levels are shown in the next column.

Capacity Levels	Budgeted Denominator Level (units of output)	Budgeted Overhead Cost Rate
Theoretical	1,500,000	$.0667
Practical	1,250,000	.0800
Normal	775,000	.1290
Master-budget	800,000	.1250

Actual output for the month of April was 800,000 units of glassware.

27. The choice of a production volume level as a denominator in the computation of fixed overhead rates can significantly affect reported net income. Which one of the following statements is true for Nash Glassworks Company if its beginning inventory is zero, production exceeded sales, and variances are adjustments to cost of goods sold? The choice of

A. Practical capacity as the denominator level will result in a lower net income amount than if master-budget capacity is chosen.

B. Normal capacity as the denominator level will result in a lower net income amount than if any other capacity volume is chosen.

C. Master-budget capacity as the denominator level will result in a lower net income amount than if theoretical capacity is chosen.

D. Practical capacity as the denominator level will result in a higher net income amount than if normal capacity is chosen.

Answer (A) is correct. *(CMA, adapted)*
REQUIRED: The true statement about choosing a denominator volume for computing fixed overhead application rates.
DISCUSSION: The choice of practical rather than master budget capacity as the denominator level will result in a lower absorption costing net income. Practical capacity is the maximum level at which output is produced efficiently, with an allowance for unavoidable interruptions, for example, for holidays and scheduled maintenance. Because this level will be higher than master-budget (expected) capacity, its use will usually result in the underapplication of fixed overhead. For example, given costs of $100,000 and master-budget capacity of 800,000 units, $.125 per unit is the application rate. If practical capacity is 1,250,000 units, the application rate is $.08 per unit. If actual production is 800,000 units, fixed overhead will not be over- or underapplied given the use of master-budget capacity. However, there will be $36,000 (450,000 units × $.08) of underapplied fixed overhead if practical capacity is the denominator level. Consequently, given that the beginning inventory is zero and that production exceeded sales, less fixed overhead will be inventoried at the lower practical capacity rate than at the master-budget rate. Thus, master-budget net income will be greater.
Answer (B) is incorrect. A normal capacity rate results in a larger ending inventory and a greater net income than a theoretical or practical capacity rate. Answer (C) is incorrect. The master-budget rate exceeds the theoretical capacity rate. It results in a greater ending inventory and a greater net income. Answer (D) is incorrect. A practical capacity rate results in a lower ending inventory and a lower net income than a normal capacity rate.

28. A review of the year-end accounting records of Elk Industries discloses the following information:

Raw materials	$ 80,000
Work-in-process	128,000
Finished goods	272,000
Cost of goods sold	1,120,000

The company's underapplied overhead equals $133,000. On the basis of this information, Elk's cost of goods sold is most appropriately reported as

A. $987,000

B. $1,213,100

C. $1,218,000

D. $1,253,000

Answer (C) is correct. *(CMA, adapted)*
REQUIRED: The reported year-end balance of cost of goods sold.
DISCUSSION: Given the amounts involved, $133,000 is material; thus, over- or underapplied overhead should be allocated to all work-in-process, finished goods, and cost of goods sold. The proportion of the total of these three accounts represented by cost of goods sold is 73.68% [$1,120,000 ÷ ($128,000 + $272,000 + $1,120,000)]. The amount of underapplied overhead assigned to cost of goods sold is thus $98,000 ($133,000 × 73.68%), making the total reported amount of cost of goods sold $1,218,000 ($1,120,000 + $98,000)
Answer (A) is incorrect. The amount of $987,000 results from improperly subtracting the entire amount of underapplied overhead from the balance of cost of goods sold instead of allocating it across three inventory accounts. Answer (B) is incorrect. The amount of $1,213,100 improperly includes raw materials in the allocation base for underapplied overhead. Answer (D) is incorrect. The amount of $1,253,000 results from improperly allocating the entire amount of underapplied overhead to cost of goods sold.

29. Wagner Corporation applies factory overhead based upon machine hours. At the beginning of the year, Wagner budgeted factory overhead at $250,000 and estimated that 100,000 machine hours would be used to make 50,000 units of product. During the year, the company produced 48,000 units using 97,000 machine hours. Actual overhead for the year was $252,000. Under a standard cost system, the amount of factory overhead applied during the year was

A. $240,000

B. $242,500

C. $250,000

D. $252,000

Answer (A) is correct. *(CMA, adapted)*
REQUIRED: The amount of applied factory overhead given relevant information.
DISCUSSION: Wagner's application rate for overhead is $2.50 per machine hour ($250,000 budgeted total ÷ 100,000 estimated machine hours), and each unit of output is estimated to require 2 machine hours (100,000 estimated machine hours ÷ 50,000 units budgeted output). Under a standard cost system, the amount of overhead applied during the year was therefore $240,000 (48,000 units actual output × $2.50 per machine hour application rate × 2 machine hours standard per unit).
Answer (B) is incorrect. The amount of $242,500 results from improperly multiplying by 48,500 units of product (half the number of machine hours). Answer (C) is incorrect. The amount of $250,000 results from improperly multiplying by the 50,000 budgeted units of product instead of by the 48,000 actual units. Answer (D) is incorrect. The amount of $252,000 was the actual overhead incurred.

3.6 Allocating Service Department Costs -- Theory

30. In allocating factory service department costs to producing departments, which one of the following items would most likely be used as an activity base?

A. Units of product sold.

B. Salary of service department employees.

C. Units of electric power consumed.

D. Direct materials usage.

Answer (C) is correct. *(CMA, adapted)*
REQUIRED: The item most likely used as an activity base when allocating factory service department costs.
DISCUSSION: Service department costs are considered part of factory overhead and should be allocated to the production departments that use the services. A basis reflecting cause and effect should be used to allocate service department costs. For example, the number of kilowatt hours used by each producing department is probably the best allocation base for electricity costs.
Answer (A) is incorrect. Making allocations on the basis of units sold may not meet the cause-and-effect criterion. Answer (B) is incorrect. The salary of service department employees is the cost allocated, not a basis of allocation. Answer (D) is incorrect. Making allocations on the basis of materials usage may not meet the cause-and-effect criterion.

31. The two most appropriate factors for budgeting manufacturing overhead expenses would be

A. Machine hours and production volume.

B. Management judgment and contribution margin.

C. Management judgment and production volume.

D. Management judgment and sales dollars.

Answer (C) is correct. *(CMA, adapted)*
REQUIRED: The two most important factors for budgeting manufacturing overhead expenses.
DISCUSSION: The most important factor in budgeting manufacturing overhead is production volume. Many overhead items have variable costs, and those that are fixed with a relevant range of output may increase if production exceeds that range. The other essential consideration is management's judgment with respect to the nature and amount of costs to be incurred and expectations for production volume. Because overhead is applied based on predetermined rates, accurate judgment is important.
Answer (A) is incorrect. Machine hours may not be the appropriate activity base. Moreover, some overhead is fixed regardless of the activity base. Answer (B) is incorrect. The contribution margin can be calculated only after variable costs and sales prices are determined. Some overhead is variable. Answer (D) is incorrect. Sales volume (or dollars) is less significant because overhead is based on production volume.

32. When allocating service department costs to production departments, the method that does **not** consider different cost behavior patterns is the

A. Step method.

B. Reciprocal method.

C. Direct method.

D. Single-rate method.

Answer (D) is correct. *(CMA, adapted)*
REQUIRED: The method of service department cost allocation that does not consider cost behavior patterns.
DISCUSSION: The single-rate method combines fixed and variable costs. However, dual rates are preferable because they allow variable costs to be allocated on a different basis from fixed costs.
Answer (A) is incorrect. The step method can be used on a single- or dual-rate basis. Answer (B) is incorrect. The reciprocal method can be used on a single- or dual-rate basis. Answer (C) is incorrect. The direct method can be used on a single- or dual-rate basis.

33. Allocation of service department costs to the production departments is necessary to

A. Control costs.

B. Coordinate production activity.

C. Determine overhead rates.

D. Maximize efficiency.

Answer (C) is correct. *(CMA, adapted)*
REQUIRED: The reason service department costs are allocated to production departments.
DISCUSSION: Service department costs are indirect costs allocated to production departments to better determine overhead rates when the measurement of full (absorption) costs is desired. Overhead should be charged to production on some equitable basis to provide information useful for such purposes as allocation of resources, pricing, measurement of profits, and cost reimbursement.
Answer (A) is incorrect. Costs can be controlled by the service departments without allocation. However, allocation encourages cost control by the production departments. If the costs are allocated, managers have an incentive not to use services indiscriminately. Answer (B) is incorrect. Allocation does not affect the coordination of production activity.
Answer (D) is incorrect. Allocation of costs has no effect on the efficiency of the provision of services when the department that receives the allocation has no control over the costs being controlled.

34. A corporation allocates indirect corporate overhead costs to its operating divisions. The company uses a cause-and-effect criterion in the selection of appropriate allocation bases. Which of the following would be an appropriate allocation base to assign the costs of the corporate personnel department to the operating divisions using a cause-and-effect criterion?

A. Number of employees in each division.

B. Square footage of space occupied by each division.

C. Total service years of employees in each division.

D. Total book value of identifiable division assets.

Answer (A) is correct. *(CIA, adapted)*
REQUIRED: The appropriate allocation base to assign the costs of a personnel department using a cause-and-effect criterion.
DISCUSSION: The cause-and-effect criterion seeks a relationship between cost and the cost objective (for example, an operating division) such that changes in total costs can be predicted based on activities of the cost objective. Thus, the number of employees in an operating division is likely to correlate with incurrence of costs by the personnel department.
Answer (B) is incorrect. Square footage would be more appropriate for allocating building and maintenance costs than personnel costs. Answer (C) is incorrect. Total service years of employees in each division is not a basis for predicting changes in personnel department costs. Answer (D) is incorrect. Total book value of identifiable division assets is not a basis for predicting changes in personnel department costs.

35. A public accounting firm has two departments, Management Consulting Services (MCS) and Tax Advisory Services (TAS). These two departments use the services of two service departments, Computer Programming (CP) and Computer Operations (CO). The percentages of each service used by each department for a typical period are

	CP	CO	MCS	TAS
CP	--	30%	50%	20%
CO	25%	--	45%	30%

The company prices its management consulting and tax advisory services on the basis of estimated costs of providing those services. Based upon this information, the most appropriate method for allocating service department costs is the

A. Physical-units method.

B. Step-down method.

C. Estimated NRV method.

D. Reciprocal method.

Answer (D) is correct. *(CIA, adapted)*
REQUIRED: The most appropriate method for allocating service department costs.
DISCUSSION: The reciprocal method uses simultaneous equations to allocate costs by explicitly recognizing the mutual services rendered among all departments. Because it acknowledges all sources of cost, it should be used when management is using the results of allocations to make decisions on pricing products.
Answer (A) is incorrect. The physical units method is not a service department cost allocation method. It is a method for allocating joint costs. Answer (B) is incorrect. The step-down method gives only partial recognition to services rendered by service departments to other service departments. Once a service department's costs have been allocated, the costs of subsequent service departments are not reallocated to it. Answer (C) is incorrect. Estimated NRV method is applicable to joint product costing, not service department allocation.

3.7 Allocating Service Department Costs -- Calculations

Questions 36 through 40 are based on the following information. The managers of Rochester Manufacturing are discussing ways to allocate the cost of service departments, such as Quality Control and Maintenance, to the production departments. To aid them in this discussion, the controller has provided the following information:

	Quality Control	Maintenance	Machining	Assembly	Total
Budgeted overhead costs before allocation	$350,000	$200,000	$400,000	$300,000	$1,250,000
Budgeted machine hours	--	--	50,000	--	50,000
Budgeted direct labor hours	--	--	--	25,000	25,000
Budgeted hours of service:					
Quality Control	--	7,000	21,000	7,000	35,000
Maintenance	10,000	--	18,000	12,000	40,000

36. If Rochester uses the direct method of allocating service department costs, the total service costs allocated to the assembly department would be

A. $80,000

B. $87,500

C. $120,000

D. $167,500

Answer (D) is correct. *(CMA, adapted)*
   REQUIRED: The total service costs allocated to the Assembly Department using the direct method.
   DISCUSSION: Under the direct method, service department costs are allocated directly to the production departments, with no allocation to other service departments. The total budgeted hours of service by the Quality Control Department to the two production departments is 28,000 (21,000 + 7,000). Given that the Assembly Department is expected to use 25% (7,000 ÷ 28,000) of the total hours budgeted for the production departments, it will absorb 25% of total quality control costs ($350,000 × 25% = $87,500). The total budgeted hours of service by the Maintenance Department to the production departments is 30,000 (18,000 + 12,000). The Assembly Department is expected to use 40% (12,000 ÷ 30,000) of the total maintenance hours budgeted for the production departments. Thus, the Assembly Department will be allocated 40% of the $200,000 of maintenance costs, or $80,000. The total service department costs allocated to the Assembly Department is $167,500 ($87,500 + $80,000).

37. Using the direct method, the total amount of overhead allocated to each machine hour at Rochester would be

A. $2.40

B. $5.25

C. $8.00

D. $15.65

Answer (D) is correct. *(CMA, adapted)*
   REQUIRED: The total overhead allocated to each machine hour.
   DISCUSSION: Machining uses 75% (21,000 ÷ 28,000) of the total quality control hours and 60% (18,000 ÷ 30,000) of the total maintenance hours budgeted for the production departments. Under the direct method, it will therefore be allocated $262,500 ($350,000 × 75%) of quality control costs and $120,000 ($200,000 × 60%) of maintenance costs. In addition, Machining is expected to incur another $400,000 of overhead costs. Thus, the total estimated Machining overhead is $782,500 ($262,500 + $120,000 + $400,000), and the overhead cost per machine hour is $15.65 ($782,500 ÷ 50,000 hours).

38. If Rochester uses the step-down method of allocating service costs beginning with quality control, the maintenance costs allocated to the assembly department would be

A. $70,000

B. $108,000

C. $162,000

D. $200,000

Answer (B) is correct. *(CMA, adapted)*
   REQUIRED: The maintenance costs allocated to the Assembly Department if the step-down method is applied beginning with quality control costs.
   DISCUSSION: The step-down method allocates service costs to both service and production departments but does not involve reciprocal allocations among service departments. Accordingly, Quality Control will receive no allocation of maintenance costs. The first step is to allocate quality control costs to the Maintenance Department. Maintenance is expected to use 20% (7,000 ÷ 35,000) of the available quality control hours and will be allocated $70,000 ($350,000 × 20%) of quality control costs. Thus, total allocable maintenance costs equal $270,000 ($70,000 + $200,000). The Assembly Department is estimated to use 40% (12,000 ÷ 30,000) of the available maintenance hours. Consequently, it will be allocated maintenance costs of $108,000 ($270,000 × 40%).

39. If Rochester uses the reciprocal method of allocating service costs, the total amount of quality control costs (rounded to the nearest dollar) to be allocated to the other departments would be

A. $284,211

B. $336,842

C. $350,000

D. $421,053

Answer (D) is correct. *(CMA, adapted)*
   REQUIRED: The total quality control costs to be allocated to the other departments using the reciprocal method.
   DISCUSSION: The reciprocal method involves mutual allocations of service costs among service departments. For this purpose, a system of simultaneous equations is necessary. The total costs for the Quality Control Department consist of $350,000 plus 25% (10,000 hours ÷ 40,000 hours) of maintenance costs. The total costs for the Maintenance Department equal $200,000 plus 20% (7,000 hours ÷ 35,000 hours) of quality control costs. These relationships can be expressed by the following equations:

$$Q = \$350,000 + .25M$$
$$M = \$200,000 + .2Q$$

To solve for Q, the second equation can be substituted into the first as follows:

$$Q = \$350,000 + .25(\$200,000 + .2Q)$$
$$Q = \$350,000 + \$50,000 + .05Q$$
$$.95Q = \$400,000$$
$$Q = \$421,053$$

40. If Rochester decides not to allocate service costs to the production departments, the overhead allocated to each direct labor hour in the Assembly Department would be

A. $3.20

B. $3.50

C. $12.00

D. $16.00

Answer (C) is correct. *(CMA, adapted)*
   REQUIRED: The overhead cost per direct labor hour in the Assembly Department if no service costs are allocated to production departments.
   DISCUSSION: With no allocation of service department costs, the only overhead applicable to the Assembly Department is the $300,000 budgeted for that department. Hence, the overhead cost applied per direct labor hour will be $12 ($300,000 budgeted overhead ÷ 25,000 hours).

Questions 41 and 42 are based on the following information. Longstreet Company's Photocopying Department provides photocopy services for both Departments A and B and has prepared its total budget using the following information for next year:

Fixed costs	$100,000
Available capacity	4,000,000 pages
Budgeted usage	
Department A	1,200,000 pages
Department B	2,400,000 pages
Variable cost	$0.03 per page

41. Assume that Longstreet uses the single-rate method of cost allocation and the allocation base is budgeted usage. How much photocopying cost will be allocated to Department B in the budget year?

A. $72,000

B. $122,000

C. $132,000

D. $138,667

Answer (D) is correct. *(CMA, adapted)*
REQUIRED: The service cost allocated to Department B using a single rate based on budgeted usage.
DISCUSSION: Department B is budgeted to use 66 2/3% of total production (2,400,000 ÷ 3,600,000), so it should be allocated fixed costs of $66,667 ($100,000 × 66 2/3%). The variable cost allocation is $72,000 (2,400,000 pages × $.03 per page), and the total allocated is therefore $138,667 ($66,667 + $72,000).
Answer (A) is incorrect. The amount of $72,000 is the variable cost allocation. Answer (B) is incorrect. The amount of $122,000 assumes that fixed costs are allocated equally between A and B. Answer (C) is incorrect. The amount of $132,000 assumes fixed costs are allocated at a per-page rate based on available capacity ($100,000 ÷ 4,000,000 pages = $.025 per page), not on budgeted usage ($100,000 ÷ 3,600,000 pages = $.0278 per page).

42. Assume that Longstreet uses the dual-rate cost allocation method, and the allocation basis is budgeted usage for fixed costs and actual usage for variable costs. How much cost would be allocated to Department A during the year if actual usage for Department A is 1,400,000 pages and actual usage for Department B is 2,100,000 pages?

A. $42,000

B. $72,000

C. $75,333

D. $82,000

Answer (C) is correct. *(CMA, adapted)*
REQUIRED: The service cost allocated to Department A if a dual-rate allocation method is used.
DISCUSSION: Based on budgeted usage, Department A should be allocated 33 1/3% [1,200,000 pages ÷ (1,200,000 pages + 2,400,000 pages)] of fixed costs, or $33,333 ($100,000 × 33 1/3%). The variable costs are allocated at $.03 per unit for 1,400,000 pages, or $42,000. The sum of the fixed and variable elements is $75,333.
Answer (A) is incorrect. The amount of $42,000 equals the variable costs allocated to Department A. Answer (B) is incorrect. The amount of $72,000 is the allocation to Department B using a single rate. Answer (D) is incorrect. The amount of $82,000 assumes fixed costs are allocated at a per-page rate based on actual usage ($100,000 ÷ 3,500,000 pages = $.0286 per page).

Use Gleim **CMA Test Prep** Software for interactive testing with **additional multiple-choice questions!**

3.9 ESSAY QUESTIONS

Scenario for Essay Questions 1, 2, 3

The Daniels Tool & Die Corporation has been in existence for a little over 3 years; sales have been increasing each year. A job order cost system is used. Factory overhead is applied to jobs based on direct labor hours, utilizing the absorption (full) costing method. Overapplied or underapplied overhead is treated as an adjustment to cost of goods sold. The company's income statements for the last 2 years are presented below.

Daniels Tool & Die Corporation
Year 3-Year 4 Comparative Income Statements

	Year 3	Year 4
Sales	$840,000	$1,015,000
Cost of goods sold:		
Finished goods, 1/1	$ 25,000	$ 18,000
Cost of goods manufactured	548,000	657,600
Total available	$573,000	$ 675,600
Finished goods, 12/31	18,000	14,000
Cost of goods sold before overhead adjustment	$555,000	$ 661,600
Underapplied factory overhead	36,000	14,400
Cost of goods sold	$591,000	$ 676,000
Gross profit	$249,000	$ 339,000
Selling expenses	$ 82,000	$ 95,000
Administrative expenses	70,000	75,000
Total operating expenses	$152,000	$ 170,000
Operating income	$ 97,000	$ 169,000

Daniels Tool & Die Corporation
Inventory Balances

	1/1/Year 3	12/31/Year 3	12/31/Year 4
Raw material	$22,000	$30,000	$10,000
Work-in-process costs	$40,000	$48,000	$64,000
Direct labor hours	1,335	1,600	2,100
Finished goods costs	$25,000	$18,000	$14,000
Direct labor hours	1,450	1,050	820

Daniels used the same predetermined overhead rate in applying overhead to production orders in both Year 3 and Year 4. The rate was based on the following estimates:

Fixed factory overhead	$ 25,000
Variable factory overhead	$155,000
Direct labor hours	25,000
Direct labor costs	$150,000

In Year 3 and Year 4, actual direct labor hours expended were 20,000 and 23,000, respectively. Raw materials put into production were $292,000 in Year 3 and $370,000 in Year 4. Actual fixed overhead was $37,400 for Year 4 and $42,300 for Year 3, and the planned direct labor rate was the direct labor rate achieved.

For both years, all of the reported administrative costs were fixed, while the variable portion of the reported selling expenses result from a commission of 5% of sales revenue.

Questions

1. For the year ended December 31, Year 4, prepare a revised income statement utilizing the variable (direct) costing method. Be sure to include contribution margin.

2. Prepare a numerical reconciliation of the difference in operating income between Daniels' Year 4 income statement prepared on the basis of absorption costing and the revised Year 4 income statement prepared on the basis of variable costing.

3. Describe both the advantages and disadvantages of using variable costing.

Essay Questions 1, 2, 3 — Unofficial Answers

1.

Daniels Tool & Die Corporation
Variable Costing Income Statement
For the Year Ended December 31, Year 4

Sales		$1,015,000
Finished goods, 1/1/Year 4 ($18,000 – $1,050 fixed overhead)	$ 16,950	
Work-in-process, 1/1/Year 4 ($48,000 – $1,600 fixed overhead)	46,400	
Manufacturing costs incurred*	650,600	
Total available	$713,950	
Work-in-process, 12/31/Year 4 ($64,000 – $2,100 fixed overhead)	(61,900)	
Finished goods, 12/31/Year 4 ($14,000 – $820 fixed overhead)	(13,180)	
Variable manufacturing cost of goods sold	$638,870	
Variable selling expenses ($1,015,000 × .05)	50,750	
Total variable costs		(689,620)
Contribution margin		$ 325,380
Fixed factory overhead (given)	$ 37,400	
Fixed selling expenses ($95,000 – $50,750)	44,250	
Fixed administrative expenses (all)	75,000	
Total fixed costs		(156,650)
Operating income		$ 168,730

*Raw materials	$370,000	(same as under absorption method)
Direct labor	138,000	(23,000 hours × $6.00 [same as under absorption method])
Variable overhead	142,600	(23,000 hours × $6.20 [same as under absorption method])
Mfg. costs incurred	$650,600	

2. The difference in the operating income of $270 is caused by the different treatment of fixed manufacturing overhead. Under absorption costing, fixed overhead costs are assigned to inventory and are not expensed until the goods are sold. Under variable costing, these costs are treated as expenses in the period incurred. Since the direct labor hours in the work-in-process and finished goods inventories had a net increase of 270 hours, the absorption costing operating profit is higher because the fixed factory overhead associated with the increased labor hours in inventory is not expensed under absorption costing.

	1/1/Year 4 Inventories	12/31/Year 4 Inventories	Difference
Work-in-process	1,600	2,100	500
Finished goods	1,050	820	(230)
Total	2,650	2,920	270

3. The advantages of using variable costing follow:

   a. The fixed manufacturing costs are reported at incurred values, not at absorbed values, which increases the likelihood of better control over fixed costs.

   b. Profits are directly influenced by changes in sales volume and not by changes in inventory levels.

   c. Contribution margin by product line, territory, department, or division is emphasized.

The disadvantages of using variable costing follow:

   d. Variable costing is not acceptable for tax reporting, for SEC reporting, nor for external financial reporting; therefore, companies need to keep two sets of records.

   e. Costs other than variable costs, i.e., fixed costs and total production costs, may be ignored when making decisions, especially long-term decisions.

   f. With the movement toward a fully automated factory, fixed factory overhead may be a significant portion of production costs. To ignore these significant costs in inventory valuation may not be acceptable.

STUDY UNIT FOUR
OPERATIONAL EFFICIENCY
AND BUSINESS PROCESS PERFORMANCE

(23 pages of outline)

4.1	Just-in-Time Inventory and Lean Operation	134
4.2	Materials Requirements Planning and Outsourcing	137
4.3	Theory of Constraints and Throughput Costing	139
4.4	Capacity Management	143
4.5	Value Chain Analysis	145
4.6	Other Process Improvement Tools	148
4.7	Core Concepts	153
4.8	Essay Questions	165

This study unit is the **last of four** on **cost management**. The relative weight assigned to this major topic in Part 1 of the exam is **25%**. The four study units are:

Study Unit 1: Ethics for Management Accountants and Cost Management Concepts
Study Unit 2: Cost Accumulation Systems
Study Unit 3: Cost Allocation Techniques
Study Unit 4: Operational Efficiency and Business Process Performance

After studying the outline and answering the questions in this study unit, you will have the skills necessary to address the following topics listed in the ICMA's Learning Outcome Statements:

Part 1 – Section C.4. Operational efficiency

The candidate should be able to:

a. define a just-in-time system and describe its central purpose

b. identify and describe the operational benefits of implementing a just-in-time system

c. define the term kanban and describe how kanban is used in a just-in-time system

d. demonstrate an understanding of work cells and how they relate to just-in-time processes

e. define material requirements planning (MRP)

f. identify and describe the benefits of an MRP system

g. calculate subunits needed to complete an order for a finished product using MRP

h. explain the concept of outsourcing and identify the benefits and limitations of choosing this option

i. demonstrate a general understanding of the theory of constraints

j. identify the five steps involved in theory of constraints analysis

k. define throughput costing (supervariable costing) and calculate inventory costs using throughput costing

l. define and calculate throughput contribution

m. discuss how the theory of constraints and activity-based costing are complementary analytical tools

n. describe how capacity level affects product costing, capacity management, pricing decisions, and financial statements

o. explain how using practical capacity as the denominator for fixed costs rate enhances capacity management

p. calculate the financial impact of implementing the above-mentioned methods

<u>Part 1 – Section C.5. Business process performance</u>

The candidate should be able to:

    a.   define value chain analysis

    b.   identify the steps in value chain analysis

    c.   explain how value chain analysis is used to better understand a firm's competitive advantage

    d.   define, identify, and provide examples of a value-added activity and explain how the value-added concept is related to improving performance

    e.   demonstrate an understanding of process analysis and business process reengineering

    f.   demonstrate an understanding of benchmarking process performance

    g.   identify the benefits of benchmarking in creating a competitive advantage

    h.   apply activity-based management principles to recommend process performance improvements

    i.   explain the relationship among continuous improvement techniques, activity-based management, and quality performance

    j.   explain the concept of continuous improvement and how it relates to implementing ideal standards and quality improvements

    k.   define best practice analysis and discuss how it can be used by an organization to improve performance

    l.   describe and identify the components of the costs of quality, commonly referred to as prevention costs, appraisal costs, internal failure costs, and external failure costs

    m.   calculate the financial impact of implementing the above-mentioned processes

4.1 JUST-IN-TIME INVENTORY AND LEAN OPERATION

    1.   **Overview**

        a.   Modern inventory planning favors the **just-in-time (JIT)** model. Many companies have traditionally built parts and components for subsequent operations on a preset schedule. Such a schedule provides a cushion of inventory so that the next operation will always have parts to work with – a just-in-case method.

            1)   In contrast, JIT limits output to the demand of the subsequent operation. Reductions in inventory levels result in less money invested in idle assets; reduction of storage space requirements; and lower inventory taxes, pilferage, and obsolescence risks.

        b.   JIT is a reaction to the trends of global competition and rapid technological progress that have resulted in shorter product life-cycles and greater consumer demand for product diversity.

            1)   High inventory levels often mask production problems because defective parts can be overlooked when plenty of good parts are available. If only enough parts are made for the subsequent operation, however, any defects will immediately halt production.

            2)   The focus of quality control under JIT shifts from the discovery of defective parts to the prevention of quality problems, so zero machine breakdowns (achieved through preventive maintenance) and zero defects are ultimate goals. Higher quality and lower inventory go together.

        c.   **Lean operation** is often used as a synonym for JIT.

            1)   Lean implies a demand-driven (i.e., pull) system, a focus on waste reduction, and a commitment to low- or zero-defect production.

2. **Objectives**

    a.   Higher productivity, reduced order costs as well as carrying costs, faster and cheaper setups, shorter manufacturing cycle times, better due date performance, improved quality, and more flexible processes are objectives of JIT methods.

        1)   The ultimate goal is increased competitiveness and higher profits.

3. **Features**

    a.   JIT/lean systems are based on a manufacturing philosophy devised by Japanese industry that affects production, inventory control, and purchasing.

        1)   JIT is a **pull system**, i.e., items are pulled through production by current demand, not pushed through by anticipated demand. One operation produces only what is needed by the next operation, and components and raw materials arrive just in time to be used.

        2)   Demand-driven production allows **inventory levels to be minimized**. Counting, handling, and storing inventory are viewed as nonvalue-added.

            a)   Indeed, carrying inventory is regarded as a symptom of correctable problems, such as poor quality, long cycle times, and lack of coordination with suppliers.

        3)   The **dependability of suppliers** is crucial. Organizations that adopt JIT systems therefore develop close relationships with a few carefully chosen suppliers who are extensively involved in the buyer's processes.

            a)   Buyer-supplier relationships are further facilitated by electronic data interchange (EDI), a technology that allows the supplier access to the buyer's online inventory management system. Thus, electronic messages replace paper documents (purchase orders and sales invoices), and the production schedules and deliveries of the parties can be more readily coordinated.

4. **Results**

    a.   One consequence of the lower inventory levels associated with a JIT/lean system is elimination of the need for certain internal controls.

        1)   Frequent receipt of deliveries from suppliers often means less need for a sophisticated inventory control system and for control personnel.

    b.   JIT also may eliminate central receiving areas, hard copy receiving reports, and storage areas. A central warehouse is not needed because deliveries are made by suppliers directly to the area of production.

    c.   The quality of parts provided by suppliers is verified by use of statistical controls rather than inspection of incoming goods. Storage, counting, and inspecting are eliminated in an effort to perform only value-adding work.

5. **Role of Kanban**

The Japanese term kanban and JIT are often confused. For the purpose of this exam, CMA candidates will be required to understand the benefits of implementing just-in-time (JIT) systems and how kanban is used in the process.

    a.   JIT is a total system of purchasing, production, and inventory control. Kanban is one of the many elements in the JIT system and was developed by the Toyota Motor Corporation (kanban is not characteristic of Japanese industry as a whole).

    b.   Kanban means tickel. Tickets (also described as cards or markers) control the flow of production or parts so that they are produced or obtained in the needed amounts at the needed times. A basic kanban system includes

        1)   A withdrawal kanban that states the quantity that a later process should withdraw from its predecessor,

        2)   A production kanban that states the output of the preceding process, and

        3)   A vendor kanban that tells a vendor what, how much, where, and when to deliver.

    c.   Kanban is essentially a visual workflow management system.

        1)   When a worker sees a kanban, it acts as authorization to release inventory to the next step. Work cannot move to the next stage until a kanban indicates that stage is ready for it.

    d.   U.S. companies have not been comfortable with controlling production using tickets on the production floor. **Computerized information systems** have been used for many years, and U.S. companies have been reluctant to give up their computers in favor of the essentially manual kanban system. Instead, U.S. companies have integrated their existing systems, which are complex computerized planning systems, with the JIT system.

6.   **Changes to Production Process**

    a.   To implement a JIT inventory/lean production system, the factory is reorganized around what are called **manufacturing cells**.

        1)   In a conventional plant layout, each department or function operates specialized machines that perform one task. All work moves from department to department.

        2)   In a cellular layout, each cell is a miniature manufacturing plant. Cells are sets of machines, often grouped in semicircles, that produce a given product or product family.

    b.   Each worker in a cell must be able to operate all machines and, possibly, to perform support tasks, such as setup activities, preventive maintenance, movement of work-in-process within the cell, and quality inspection.

        1)   In such a pull system, workers might often be idle if they are not multi-skilled.

    c.   Central support departments are reduced or eliminated, space is saved, fewer and smaller factories may be required, and materials and tools are brought close to the point of use.

        1)   Manufacturing cycle time and setup time are also reduced. As a result, on-time delivery performance and response to changes in markets are enhanced, and production of customized goods in small lots becomes feasible.

    d.   A cellular organization requires workers to operate as effective teams, so employee empowerment is crucial in a JIT inventory/lean production system.

        1)   Greater participation by employees is needed to achieve the objectives of continuous improvement and zero defects, so they may, for example, have the power to stop production to correct a problem, be consulted about changes in processes, or become involved in hiring co-workers. Thus, managers in such a system usually play more of a facilitating than a support role.

Stop and review! You have completed the outline for this subunit. Study multiple-choice questions 1 through 7 beginning on page 155.

4.2 MATERIALS REQUIREMENTS PLANNING AND OUTSOURCING

1. **Overview**

   a. Short-range (tactical or operational) plans must be converted into specific production targets for finished goods. The raw materials going into the creation of these end products must be carefully scheduled for delivery.

      1) The yearly/quarterly/monthly numbers and styles of finished goods called for in the demand forecasts included in the operational plans must be turned into specific dates for completion and availability for shipment to the customer. This is the task of the **master production schedule (MPS)**.

   b. A **materials requirements planning (MRP)** system enables a company to efficiently fulfill the requirements of the MPS by coordinating both the manufacture of component parts for finished goods and the arrival of the raw materials necessary to create the intermediate components.

      1) As computers were introduced into manufacturing, it was common for firms to have a production scheduling system and an inventory control system. MRP joins the two into a single application.

      2) The three overriding goals of MRP are the arrival of the right part in the right quantity at the right time.

   c. MRP is a push system; i.e., the demand for raw materials is driven by the forecasted demand for the final product, which can be programmed into the computer.

      1) For example, an automobile manufacturer need only tell the computer how many autos of each type are to be manufactured.

   d. MRP, in effect, creates schedules of when items of inventory will be needed in the production departments.

      1) If parts are not in stock, the system automatically generates a purchase order on the proper date (considering lead times) so that deliveries will arrive on time.

      2) The timing of deliveries is vital to avoid both production delays AND a pileup of raw materials inventory that must be stored.

   e. Some benefits of MRP are

      1) Reduced idle time
      2) Lower setup costs
      3) Lower inventory carrying costs
      4) Increased flexibility in responding to market changes

2.   **Bill of Materials**

    a.   The MRP system consults the bill of materials (BOM), a record of which (and how many) subassemblies go into the finished product. The system then generates a complete list of every part and component needed.

EXAMPLE of a Bill of Materials Calculation

A manufacturer has the following bill of materials for its product:

Subunit	Quantity
CM12	1
PR75	5

The bill of materials for the component subunits is as follows:

Subunit	Contains	Quantity
CM12	TT413	2
	XH511	3
PR75	LQ992	1

Current inventory quantities are as follows:

Subunit	On Hand
CM12	25
PR75	35
LQ992	50
TT413	30
XH511	40

The company has 20 units of the finished product in inventory and wishes to maintain this level throughout the year. Production of 40 units is scheduled for the upcoming month. The quantities of the principal subunits that must be produced are calculated below:

Subunit	Quantity per Finished Product		Production Run		Quantity Needed		Quantity On Hand		To Be Built
CM12	1	×	40	=	40	−	25	=	15
PR75	5	×	40	=	200	−	35	=	165

The parts that must be ordered from vendors can thus be calculated as follows:

Subunit	Components	Component Quantity		Subunits To Be Built		Quantity Needed		Quantity On Hand		To Be Purchased
CM12	TT413	2	×	15	=	30	−	30	=	0
	XH511	3	×	15	=	45	−	40	=	5
PR75	LQ992	1	×	165	=	165	−	50	=	115

---

3.   **Manufacturing Resource Planning (MRP II)**

    a.   MRP II is a closed-loop manufacturing system that integrates all facets of a manufacturing business, including production, sales, inventories, schedules, and cash flows.

        1)   The same system is used for both the financial reporting and managing operations (both use the same transactions and numbers).

        2)   Because manufacturing resource planning encompasses materials requirements planning, MRP is a component of an MRP II system.

4. **Outsourcing**

    a.   Outsourcing is the management or day-to-day execution of an entire business function by a third-party service provider. Outsourced services may be provided on or off premises, in the same country, or in a separate country.

        1)   Outsourcing enables a company to focus on its core business rather than having to be concerned with marginal activities. For example, payroll preparation is often outsourced because a company does not want to maintain a full-time staff to perform what is only a weekly or monthly activity.

    b.   Business process outsourcing is the outsourcing of back office and front office functions typically performed by white collar and clerical workers. Examples of these functions include data processing, accounting, human resources, and medical coding and transcription.

        1)   **Insourcing** is the transfer of an outsourced function to an internal department of a company to be managed entirely by company employees. The term has also been used to describe a foreign company's locating of facilities in a host country where it employs local workers.

        2)   **Cosourcing** is performance of a business function by both internal staff and external resources, such as consultants or outsourcing vendors, who have specialized knowledge of the business function.

    c.   Benefits of outsourcing include reliable service, reduced costs, avoidance of the risk of obsolescence, and access to technology. Disadvantages include dependence on an outside party and loss of control over a necessary function.

Stop and review! You have completed the outline for this subunit. Study multiple-choice questions 8 through 11 beginning on page 157.

4.3 THEORY OF CONSTRAINTS AND THROUGHPUT COSTING

1. **Overview**

    a.   The theory of constraints (TOC), devised by Israeli physicist and business consultant Eliyahu Goldratt (b. 1948), is a system to improve human thinking about problems. It has been greatly extended to include manufacturing operations.

    b.   The basic premise of TOC as applied to business is that improving any process is best done not by trying to maximize efficiency in every part of the process, but by focusing on the slowest part of the process, called the **constraint**.

        1)   EXAMPLE: During the early days of the American Civil War, several units calling themselves legions were formed, consisting of combined infantry, artillery, and cavalry. This arrangement did not last because the entire unit could only maneuver as fast as the slowest part. The artillery was the constraint.

        2)   Increasing the efficiency of processes that are not constraints merely creates backup in the system.

    c.   The **steps in a TOC analysis** are as follows (they are described in more detail under items 2. – 6.):

        1)   Identify the constraint.
        2)   Determine the most profitable product mix given the constraint.
        3)   Maximize the flow through the constraint.
        4)   Increase capacity at the constraint.
        5)   Redesign the manufacturing process for greater flexibility and speed.

2.   **Step 1 -- Identify the Constraint**

   a.   The bottleneck operation can usually be identified as the one where work-in-process backs up the most.

   b.   A more sophisticated approach is to analyze available resources (number and skill level of employees, inventory levels, time spent in other phases of the process) and determine which phase has negative slack time, i.e., the phase without enough resources to keep up with input.

3.   **Step 2 -- Determine the Most Profitable Product Mix Given the Constraint**

   a.   A basic principle of TOC analysis is that short-term profit maximization requires maximizing the contribution margin through the constraint, called the **throughput margin** or throughput contribution.

   1)   TOC thus helps managers to recognize that the product they should produce the most of is not necessarily the one with the highest contribution margin per unit, but the one with the highest throughput margin per unit; i.e., managers must make the most profitable use of the bottleneck operation.

   b.   **Throughput costing**, sometimes called **supervariable costing**, recognizes only direct materials costs as being truly variable and thus relevant to the calculation of throughput margin. All other manufacturing costs are ignored because they are considered fixed in the short run.

   1)   Even direct labor is considered a fixed cost, which makes sense considering that many companies have union contracts or paternalistic policies that involve employing laborers, or at least paying them, even when no work is available.

   Throughput margin = Sales - Direct materials

   c.   EXAMPLE: (Note: This is the same example as that used in item 4. in Study Unit 3, Subunit 1, with a subtotal for supervariable costing added.)

   1)   During its first month in business, a firm produced 100 units and sold 80 while incurring the following costs:

Direct materials	$1,000
Manufacturing costs used in supervariable costing	**$1,000**
Direct labor	2,000
Variable overhead	1,500
Manufacturing costs used in variable costing	**$4,500**
Fixed overhead	3,000
Manufacturing costs used in absorption costing	**$7,500**

   2)   The impact on the financial statements of using one method over another can be seen in the following calculations. Note that, because throughput costing capitalizes so few costs as product costs, ending inventory and cost of goods sold are lower than under variable costing and much lower than under absorption costing.

   Cost per unit:
   Absorption ($7,500 ÷ 100 units) $75
   Variable ($4,500 ÷ 100 units)   45
   Supervariable ($1,000 ÷ 100 units)   10

   Ending inventory:
   Absorption ($75 × 20 units) $1,500
   Variable ($45 × 20 units)   900
   Supervariable ($10 × 20 units)   200

3) Below is a comparison of the calculation of operating income under two of the methods.

    a) The units were sold at a price of $100 each.

    b) The company incurred $200 of variable selling and administrative expenses and $600 of fixed selling and administrative expenses.

    c) Note the drastic reduction in operating income resulting from the treatment of so many costs as period costs under throughput costing.

Variable Costing			Supervariable Costing		
Sales		$ 8,000	Sales		$ 8,000
Beginning inventory	$ 0		Beginning inventory	$ 0	
Variable manufacturing costs	4,500		Direct materials costs	1,000	
Goods available for sale	$ 4,500		Goods available for sale	$1,000	
Less: ending inventory	(900)		Less: ending inventory	(200)	
Variable cost of goods sold		(3,600)	**Supervariable cost of goods sold**		(800)
Variable S&A expenses		(200)			
Contribution margin		$ 4,200	**Throughput margin**		$7,200
			Direct labor		(2,000)
			Variable overhead		(1,500)
			Variable S&A expenses		(200)
Fixed overhead		(3,000)	Fixed overhead		(3,000)
Fixed S&A expenses		(600)	Fixed S&A expenses		(600)
Operating income		$ 600	**Operating loss**		$ (100)

d. To determine the most profitable use of the bottleneck operation, a manager next calculates the throughput margin per unit of time spent in the constraint.

    1) Profitability is maximized by keeping the bottleneck operation busy with the product with the highest throughput margin per unit of time.

4. Step 3 -- Maximize the Flow Through the Constraint

a. Production flow through a constraint is managed using the **drum-buffer-rope (DBR)** system.

    1) The drum (i.e., the beat to which a production process marches) is the bottleneck operation. The constraint sets the pace for the entire process.

    2) The buffer is a minimal amount of work-in-process input to the drum that is maintained to ensure that it is always in operation.

    3) The rope is the sequence of activities preceding and including the bottleneck operation that must be coordinated to avoid inventory buildup.

5. Step 4 -- Increase Capacity at the Constraint

a. In the short-run, TOC encourages a manager to make the best use of the bottleneck operation. The medium-term step for improving the process is to increase the bottleneck operation's capacity.

6. Step 5 -- Redesign the Manufacturing Process for Greater Flexibility and Speed

a. The long-term solution is to reengineer the entire process. The firm should take advantage of new technology, product lines requiring too much effort should be dropped, and remaining products should be redesigned to ease the manufacturing process.

    1) Value engineering is useful for this purpose because it explicitly balances product cost and the needs of potential customers (product functions).

EXTENDED EXAMPLE of a TOC Calculation

Step 1 -- Identify the Constraint

A company makes three products: an airborne radar unit, a seagoing sonar unit, and a ground sonar unit. Under the current setup, the hours spent by each product in the two phases of the manufacturing process are as follows:

Product	Assembly	Testing
Airborne Radar	3	4
Seagoing Sonar	8	10
Ground Sonar	5	5

The company has 150 hours available every month for testing. Under the current setup, therefore, the testing phase is the constraint.

Step 2 -- Determine the Most Profitable Product Mix Given the Constraint

The company calculates the throughput margin on each product and divides by the hours spent in testing:

	Radar	Seagoing Sonar	Ground Sonar
Price	$200,000	$600,000	$300,000
Less: materials costs	(100,000)	(400,000)	(250,000)
Throughput margin	$100,000	$200,000	$ 50,000
Divided by: constraint time	÷ 4	÷ 10	÷ 5
Throughput margin per hour	**$ 25,000**	**$ 20,000**	**$ 10,000**

The crucial factor in determining the optimal product mix is not which product is the most profitable product in terms of absolute throughput margin (the seagoing sonar), but which one generates the highest margin per time spent in the bottleneck operation (the radar).

To derive the most profitable product mix given finite resources, customer demand must be taken into account. The company has determined that it can sell 12 units of radar, 6 units of seagoing sonar, and 22 units of ground sonar per month.

The available time in the bottleneck operation is first devoted to the product with the highest throughput margin (TM), then in descending order until the company is unable to meet demand.

In the calculation below, the hours remaining after assignment to each product are the hours that can be devoted to the next product.

	Highest TM:		2nd Highest TM:		Lowest TM:	
			Seagoing		Ground	
	Radar		Sonar		Sonar	
Hours available	150		102		42	
Hours needed to fulfill demand:						
Demand in units	12		6		22	
Hours per unit in bottleneck	× 4	(48)	× 10	(60)	× 5	(110)
Hours remaining		102		42		(68)

Applying the principles of TOC, the company will forgo some sales of the ground sonar in favor of products that are more profitable given the current constraint.

Step 3 -- Maximize the Flow Through the Bottleneck Operation

The company will apply a drum-buffer-rope system to ensure that the bottleneck operation stays busy on high-TM products while keeping work-in-process inventory to a minimum.

Step 4 -- Increase Capacity at the Bottleneck Operation

The company will hire and train more employees for the testing department.

Step 5 -- Redesign the Manufacturing Process for Greater Flexibility and Speed

The company will examine its markets and new manufacturing technology to determine which products it wants to continue selling, whether to add new ones, and whether to retool the production line.

7. **TOC Analysis Complements Activity-Based Costing**

    a. TOC and ABC (see Study Unit 2, Subunit 3) focus on different aspects of process improvement.

        1) TOC has a short-term focus based on costs of materials and product mix; ABC has a long-term focus that considers all product costs and is concerned with strategic pricing and profit planning.

    b. TOC analysis, unlike ABC, addresses the issues of resource constraints and operational capacity.

        1) TOC ignores cost drivers, focusing mainly on process time; ABC requires defining cost drivers in every part of the organization.

Stop and review! You have completed the outline for this subunit. Study multiple-choice questions 12 through 17 beginning on page 158.

4.4 CAPACITY MANAGEMENT

1. **Capacity Planning**

    a. Capacity planning is an element of strategic planning that is closely related to capital budgeting. The IMA's Statement on Management Accounting *Measuring the Cost of Capacity* (issued in March 1996) states that maximizing the value created within an organization starts with understanding the nature and capabilities of all of the company's resources. According to that statement, effective capacity cost management requires:

- In the short run, optimizing capital decisions and the effective and flexible use of investments that have already been made
- Maximizing the value delivered to customers
- Helping minimize requirements for future investment
- Supporting effective matching of a firm's resources with current and future market opportunities
- Closing any gap between market demands and a firm's capabilities
  - At times, the firm may have excess capabilities; at others, shortages may exist. These capabilities may be physical, human, technological, or financial.
- Eliminating waste in the short, intermediate, and long run
- Providing useful costing information on current process costs versus those proposed in current or future investment proposals
- Supporting the establishment of capacity usage measurements that identify the cost of capacity and its impact on business cycles and overall company performance
- Identifying the capacity required to meet strategic and operational objectives and to estimate current available capacity
- Detailing the opportunity cost of unused capacity and suggesting ways to account for that cost
- Supporting change efforts by providing predecision information and analysis on the potential resource and cost implications of a planned change
- Creating a common language for, and understanding of, capacity cost management

        1) Thus, capacity should be defined from several different perspectives. Managing the cost of that capacity starts when a product or process is first envisioned. It continues through the subsequent disposal of resources downstream.

    b. Capacity planning is part of the capital budgeting process.

        1) Estimating capacity levels for future periods allows for the acquisition of more capacity when needed, or disposal of capacity that is not expected to be utilized.

   c.   Capacity level influences product costing, pricing decisions, and financial statements.

      1)   Excess capacity has a cost. Having excess capacity means that a company will either have to charge higher prices for its products or will report lower income on its financial statements.

   d.   Similarly, producing at full capacity can have a cost in the form of opportunity costs. A company that could generate additional sales if it had more capacity needs to address whether the acquisition of additional capacity is warranted.

2. **Capacity Expansion**

   a.   According to business strategy theorist Michael E. Porter, whether to expand capacity is a major strategic decision because of the capital required, the difficulty of forming accurate expectations, and the long timeframe of the lead times and the commitment. The key forecasting problems are long-term demand and behavior of competitors. The key strategic issue is avoidance of industry overcapacity. Capacity expansion is also referred to as market penetration because it involves increasing the amount of an existing product in an existing market.

   b.   Undercapacity in a profitable industry tends to be a short-term issue. Profits ordinarily lure additional investors. Overcapacity tends to be a long-term problem because firms are more likely to compete intensely rather than reverse their expansion.

   c.   The formal capital budgeting process entails predicting future cash flows related to the expansion project, discounting them at an appropriate interest rate, and determining whether the net present value is positive. This process permits comparison with other uses of the firm's resources.

      1)   The apparent simplicity of this process is deceptive because it depends upon, among many other things, which expansion method is chosen, developments in technology, and profitability. The latter factor in turn depends on such uncertainties as total long-term demand and the expansion plans of rival firms.

   d.   Porter's model of the decision process for capacity expansion has the following interrelated steps:

      1)   The firm must identify the options in relation to their size, type, degree of vertical integration (if any), and possible response by competitors.

      2)   The second step is to forecast demand, input costs, and technology developments. The firm must be aware that its technology may become obsolete or that future design changes to allow expansion may or may not be possible. Moreover, the expansion itself may put upward pressure on input prices.

      3)   The next step is analysis of competitors to determine when each will expand. The difficulty is that forecasting their behavior depends on knowing their expectations. Another difficulty is that each competitor's actions potentially affect all other competitors' actions, with the industry leader being most influential.

      4)   Using the foregoing information, the firm predicts total industry capacity and firms' market shares. These estimates, together with the expected demand, permit the firm to predict prices and cash flows.

      5)   The final step is testing for inconsistencies.

   e.   The extent of uncertainty about future demand is a crucial variable in determining the nature of industry expansion. For example, if uncertainty is great, firms willing to take greater risks because of their large cash resources or strategic stake in the industry will act first. Other firms will await events.

      1)   When demand uncertainty is low, firms will tend to adopt a strategy of preemption, usually with strong market signals, to forestall competitors' expansion plans. Excess preemption leads to excess industry capacity because firms overestimate their competitive strengths, misunderstand market signals, or fail to accurately assess competitors' intentions.

3.   **Practical Capacity**

   a.   Using **practical capacity** as the denominator rate for **allocating fixed overhead** can enhance capacity management.

   1)   Practical capacity in the denominator aligns the allocation of fixed costs with normal production activity. Any variance can be a signal for a change in demand for the product.

   2)   A firm that allocates fixed costs based on maximum capacity will consistently underapply fixed overhead during times of normal production.

Stop and review! You have completed the outline for this subunit. Study multiple-choice questions 18 and 19 on page 160.

4.5 VALUE CHAIN ANALYSIS

1.   **Value and Customers' Perceptions**

   a.   To remain on the market, a product must provide value to the customer and a profit to the seller.

   1)   Customers assign value to a product. The producer can affect the customer's perception of value by differentiating the product and lowering its price.

   2)   The producer's profit is the difference between its costs and the price it charges for the product. Thus, by keeping costs low, the producer has more flexibility in pricing.

   b.   The relationship of these three aspects of value creation can be graphically depicted as follows:

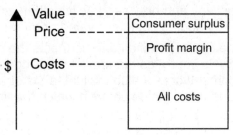

Figure 4-1

2.   **The Value Chain**

   a.   The value chain is a model for depicting the way in which every function in a company adds value to the final product.

   1)   The IMA's Statement on Management Accounting (SMA) *Value Chain Analysis for Assessing Competitive Advantage* (issued in March 1996) says, "The value chain approach for assessing competitive advantage is an integral part of the strategic planning process."

   b.   A value chain depicts how costs and customer value accumulate along a chain of activities that lead to an end product or service.

   1)   A value chain consists of the internal processes or activities a company performs: R&D, design, production, marketing, distribution, and customer service.

   c.   Another view is that the value chain consists of all of the value-creating activities leading to the ultimate end-use product delivered into the final consumers' hands.

   1)   In other words, a value chain is a firm's overall chain of value-creating (value-added) processes.

d.   Primary activities deal with the product directly. Support activities lend aid to the primary activity functions. The value chain can be graphically depicted as follows:

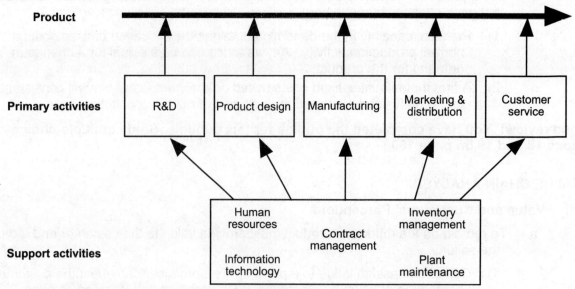

Figure 4-2

3. **Value-Chain Analysis**

a.   Value-chain analysis is a strategic analysis tool that allows a firm to focus on those activities that are consistent with its overall strategy.

1)   Value-chain analysis allows a firm to decide which parts of the value chain it wants to occupy and how each activity then contributes to the firm's competitive advantage by adding customer value or by reducing costs.

b.   Because the value chain identifies and connects the organization's strategic activities, value chain analysis improves the firm's knowledge of its relations with customers, suppliers, and competitors. It also facilitates the strategic determination of the phase(s) of the industry's value chain in which the firm should operate.

1)   The first step in a value-chain analysis is to identify the firm's value-creating activities.

2)   The second step is to determine how each value-creating activity can produce a competitive advantage for the firm. This step has multiple substeps.

a)   Identify the firm's competitive advantage (e.g., cost reduction, product differentiation) so that the firm's position in the industry's value chain can be clarified.

b)   Identify the ways in which the firm's value-creating activities can generate additional customer value.

c)   Identify activities that are candidates for cost reduction or, in the case of non-core competencies, outsourcing.

d)   Identify value-adding ways in which the firm's remaining activities can be linked.

c.   Value-chain analysis is a team effort. Management accountants need to collaborate with engineering, production, marketing, distribution, and customer service professionals to focus on the strengths, weaknesses, opportunities, and threats identified in the value-chain analysis results.

1)   Value-chain analysis offers an excellent opportunity to integrate strategic planning and management accounting to guide the firm to survival and growth.

4. **The Supply Chain**

    a. The supply chain is the flow of materials and services from their original sources to final consumers. Moreover, it usually encompasses more than one firm.

        1) Firms seeking to improve performance and reduce costs must analyze all phases of the supply chain as well as the value chain. Thus, a firm must reduce the cost of, and increase the value added by, its purchasing function.

    b. Purchasing is the management function that concerns the acquisition process. It includes choice of vendors, contract negotiation, the decision whether to purchase centrally or locally, and value analysis. The process is initiated by purchase requisitions issued by the production control function.

        1) Purchase requisitions ultimately result from insourcing vs. outsourcing (make vs. buy) decisions made when production processes were designed.

        2) For a retailer, the purchase decision is the same as the decision about what to sell.

        3) The choice of vendors depends on price, quality, delivery performance, shipping costs, credit terms, and service. Purchasers with a competitive orientation and considerable economic power may be able to extract very favorable terms from vendors.

        4) Purchasers with a cooperative orientation adopt a longer-term approach: supply chain coordination. The purchaser and the vendor are viewed as committed to a partnership involving joint efforts to improve quality.

            a) For example, in the case of a major manufacturer and one of its suppliers, this orientation may include the purchaser's willingness to help develop the vendor's managerial, technical, and productive capacities. Thus, it tends to result in minimizing the number of vendors.

    c. Supply chain analysis and coordination should extend to all parties in the chain, from initial sources of materials to retailers.

        1) Coordination has special relevance to inventory management. By sharing information among all parties, demand uncertainty is reduced at each level, with consequent decreases of inventory at each level, minimization of stockouts, and avoidance of overproduction and rush orders.

        2) For example, such cooperation counteracts what has been called the **bullwhip or backlash effect**. This phenomenon occurs when demand variability increases at each level of the supply chain.

        3) Retailers face only customer demand variability, but the manufacturer must cope with retailer demand variability that is greater than customer demand variability because retailers' purchases vary with additional factors, such as batching of orders and trade promotions.

        4) Similarly, the variability of manufacturer demands on suppliers may be greater than the variability of retailer demands on manufacturers.

    d. Value-chain and supply-chain analysis should be used to meet customer requirements for better performance regarding such critical success factors as

        1) Cost reduction,
        2) Efficiency,
        3) Continuous improvement of quality to meet customer needs and wants,
        4) Minimization or elimination of defects,
        5) Faster product development and customer response times, and
        6) Constant innovation.

5.   **Value Engineering**

    a.   Value engineering is a means of reaching targeted cost levels. It is a systematic approach to assessing all aspects of the value chain cost buildup for a product. The purpose is to minimize costs without sacrificing customer satisfaction.

        1)   Value engineering requires distinguishing between cost incurrence and **locked-in costs**.

    b.   Cost incurrence is the actual use of resources, but locked-in (designed-in) costs will result in use of resources in the future as a result of past decisions. Thus, value engineering emphasizes controlling costs at the design stage, that is, before they are locked in.

    c.   Life-cycle costing is sometimes used as a basis for cost planning and product pricing. Life-cycle costing estimates a product's revenues and expenses over its expected life cycle. The result is to highlight upstream and downstream costs in the cost planning process that often receive insufficient attention. Emphasis is on the need to price products to cover all costs, not just production costs.

Stop and review! You have completed the outline for this subunit. Study multiple-choice questions 20 through 24 beginning on page 160.

4.6 OTHER PROCESS IMPROVEMENT TOOLS

1.   **Process Analysis**

    a.   Process analysis is a means of linking a firm's internal processes to its overall strategy.

    b.   Types of Process

        1)   Continuous, such as candy bars produced by machinery
        2)   Batch, such as beer brewing
        3)   Hybrid, in which both continuous and batch processes are used
        4)   Make-to-stock, such as automobile assembly
        5)   Make-to-order, such as deli sandwich making

    c.   Process Interdependence

        1)   The degree of interdependence among the stages in a process is referred to as "tightness."

        2)   A tight process is one in which a breakdown in one stage brings the succeeding stages to a halt. This is characteristic of continuous processes that do not have buffer work-in-process inventories.

        3)   A loose process is one in which subsequent stages can continue working after a breakdown in a previous stage. This is characteristic of batch processes and any others with extensive work-in-process inventories.

    d.   Bottlenecks

        1)   Very few processes run at the precise same speed in every stage.

        2)   One part of the process is almost always the slowest, referred to as the "bottleneck." If capacity is added at that point, the bottleneck simply shifts to the next slowest operation.

            a)   The theory of constraints was developed to deal with this challenge (see Subunit 4.3).

        3)   The bottleneck issue only arises when demand for the firm's product is sufficient to absorb all of the output. When a production line is running at less than full capacity, bottlenecks can be avoided.

2. **Process Value Analysis**

    a. **Process value analysis** is a comprehensive understanding of how an organization generates its output. It involves a determination of which activities that use resources are value-adding or nonvalue-adding and how the latter may be reduced or eliminated.

        1) This linkage of product costing and continuous improvement of processes is activity-based management (ABM). ABM redirects and improves the use of resources to increase the value created for customers and other stakeholders.

            a) ABM encompasses activity analysis, cost driver analysis, and quality performance measurement.

        2) Kaizen is the Japanese word for the continuous pursuit of improvement in every aspect of organizational operations.

            a) For example, a budget prepared on the kaizen principle projects costs based on future improvements. The possibility of such improvements must be determined, and the cost of implementation and the savings therefrom must be estimated.

    b. An **activity analysis** determines what is done, by whom, at what cost in time and other resources, and the value added by each activity.

        1) A value-added activity is necessary to remain in business. For example, a manufacturer would deem the conversion of raw materials into salable products a value-added activity.

            a) Such an activity may be mandated (e.g., a regulatory requirement) or discretionary. The latter produces some changes not otherwise achievable that enables other activities to occur.

        2) A value-added cost is incurred to perform a value-added activity without waste. Most types of direct labor would be considered value-added cost because the costs are being incurred to directly produce the product.

        3) A nonvalue-added activity is unnecessary and should be eliminated. The act of generating nonsalable final products is a nonvalue-added activity.

            a) An example of a nonvalue-added activity is where inventory has to be moved long distances from one work station to another in a production process. Similarly, inventory that has to wait in line before being processed is a waste. This is why just-in-time inventory systems have proved popular, because JIT eliminates much of the waste in a production process.

        4) A nonvalue-added cost is caused by a nonvalue-added activity or inefficient performance of a value-added activity. The costs of raw materials and direct labor expended on products that fail inspection would be considered nonvalue-added costs.

            a) Thus, managing the causes of cost results in elimination of unnecessary activities as well as greater efficiency of activities.

    c. Financial and nonfinancial **measures of activity performance** address efficiency, quality, and time. The purpose is to assess how well activities meet customer demands.

        1) To satisfy customer needs and wants, activities should be efficient (a favorable input-to-output ratio) so that customers are willing to pay the prices charged.

        2) Activities should produce defect-free output (high quality), and that output should be produced in a timely manner (with less resource usage and in response to customer requirements).

d.   The selection of value-added activities in each place of the value chain reflects the firm's determination of its competitive advantage and its choice of competitive strategy.

    1)   For example, different design strategies require different activities and costs. A firm might choose to be the low-cost producer of an undifferentiated product rather than compete on the basis of superior product quality.

e.   One aspect of process analysis is the management of time. Product development time is a crucial factor in the competitive equation. A company that is first in the market with a new product has obvious advantages.

    1)   Reducing development time is also important because product life cycles are becoming shorter.

    2)   Companies need to respond quickly and flexibly to new technology, changes in consumer tastes, and competitive challenges.

3.   **Business Process Reengineering (BPR)**

a.   BPR is a complete rethinking of how business functions are performed to provide value to customers, that is, radical innovation instead of mere improvement, and a disregard for current jobs, hierarchies, and reporting relationships.

    1)   Technological advances have increased the popularity of business process reengineering.

b.   A process is how something is accomplished in a firm. It is a set of activities directed toward the same objective. Reengineering is process innovation and core process redesign. Instead of improving existing procedures, it finds new ways of doing things. Thus, reengineering should be contrasted with process improvement, which consists of incremental but constant changes that improve efficiency.

    1)   Accordingly, BPR techniques eliminate many traditional controls. They exploit modern technology to improve productivity and decrease the number of clerical workers. Thus, the emphasis is on developing controls that are automated and self-correcting and require minimal human intervention.

c.   The emphasis therefore shifts to monitoring internal control so management can determine when an operation may be out of control and corrective action is needed.

    1)   Most BPR techniques also assume that humans will be motivated to work actively in improving operations when they are full participants in the process.

d.   Monitoring assesses the quality of internal control over time. Management considers whether internal control is properly designed and operating as intended and modifies it to reflect changing conditions. Monitoring may be in the form of separate, periodic evaluations or of ongoing monitoring.

    1)   Ongoing monitoring occurs as part of routine operations. It includes management and supervisory review, comparisons, reconciliations, and other actions by personnel as part of their regular activities.

4.   **Benchmarking**

a.   The IMA's Statement on Management Accounting (SMA) *Effective Benchmarking*, issued in July 1995, describes techniques for improving the effectiveness of benchmarking, which is a means of helping companies with productivity management and business process reengineering.

    1)   "Benchmarking involves continuously evaluating the practices of best-in-class organizations and adapting company processes to incorporate the best of these practices." It "analyzes and measures the key outputs of a business process or function against the best and also identifies the underlying key actions and root causes that contribute to the performance difference."

        2) Benchmarking is an ongoing process that entails quantitative and qualitative measurement of the difference between the company's performance of an activity and the performance by the best in the world. The benchmark organization need not be a competitor.

  b. The first phase in the benchmarking process is to select and prioritize benchmarking projects.

        1) An organization must understand its critical success factors and business environment to identify key business processes and drivers and to develop parameters defining what processes to benchmark.

        2) The criteria for selecting what to benchmark relate to the reasons for the existence of a process and its importance to the entity's mission, values, and strategy. These reasons relate in large part to satisfaction of end users or customer needs.

  c. The next phase is to organize benchmarking teams.

        1) A team organization is appropriate because it permits an equitable division of labor, participation by those responsible for implementing changes, and inclusion of a variety of functional expertise and work experience.

        2) Team members should have knowledge of the function to be benchmarked, respected positions in the company, good communication skills, teaming skills, motivation to innovate and to support cross-functional problem solving, and project management skills.

  d. The benchmarking team must thoroughly investigate and document internal processes.

        1) The organization should be seen as a series of processes, not as a fixed structure. A process is "a network of related and independent activities linked by the outputs they exchange." One way to determine the primary characteristics of a process is to trace the path a request for a product or service takes through the organization.

        2) The benchmarking team must also develop a family of measures that are true indicators of process performance and a process taxonomy, that is, a set of process elements, measures, and phrases that describes the process to be benchmarked.

  e. Researching and identifying best-in-class performance is often the most difficult phase.

        1) The critical steps are setting up databases, choosing information-gathering methods (internal sources, external public domain sources, and original research are the possible approaches), formatting questionnaires (lists of questions prepared in advance), and selecting benchmarking partners.

  f. The data analysis phase entails identifying performance gaps, understanding the reasons they exist, and prioritizing the key activities that will facilitate the behavioral and process changes needed to implement the benchmarking study's recommendations.

        1) Sophisticated statistical analysis and other methods may be needed when the study involves many variables, testing of assumptions, or presentation of quantified results.

  g. Leadership is most important in the implementation phase of the benchmarking process because the team must be able to justify its recommendations.

        1) Moreover, the process improvement teams must manage the implementation of approved changes.

5. **Balanced Scorecard**

    a. The balanced scorecard approach employs multiple measures of performance to permit a determination as to whether the organization is achieving certain objectives at the expense of others that may be equally or more important.

        1) For example, an improvement in operating results at the expense of new product development would be apparent using this approach.

    b. The scorecard is a goal congruence tool that informs managers about the nonfinancial factors that top management believes to be important.

        1) As mentioned previously, measures may be financial or nonfinancial, internal or external, and short term or long term.

    c. The balanced scorecard facilitates best practice analysis.

        1) Best practice analysis is a method of accomplishing a business function or process that is considered to be superior to all other known methods. A lesson learned from one area of a business can be passed on to another area of the business or between businesses.

        2) Thus, the whole concept of benchmarking is aimed at identifying best practices.

    d. A typical scorecard includes measures in four categories:

        1) Financial
        2) Customer
        3) Learning, growth, and innovation
        4) Internal business processes

6. **Costs of Quality**

    a. The IMA's Statement on Management Accounting *Managing Quality Improvements*, issued in 1993, describes four categories of costs of quality: prevention, appraisal, internal failure, and external failure. The organization should attempt to minimize its total cost of quality.

    b. Conformance costs include prevention and appraisal, which are both financial measures of internal performance.

        1) **Prevention** attempts to avoid defective output. These costs include preventive maintenance, employee training, review of equipment design, and evaluation of suppliers.

        2) **Appraisal** encompasses such activities as statistical quality control programs, inspection, and testing.

    c. Nonconformance costs include costs of internal failure (a financial measure of internal performance) and external failure costs (a financial measure of customer satisfaction).

        1) **Internal failure** costs occur when defective products are detected before shipment.

            a) Examples are scrap, rework, tooling changes, downtime, redesign of products or processes, lost output, reinspection and retesting, expediting of operations after delays, lost learning opportunities, and searching for and correcting problems.

        2) The costs of **external failure** or lost opportunity include lost profits from a decline in market share as dissatisfied customers make no repeat purchases, return products for refunds, cancel orders, and communicate their dissatisfaction to others.

            a) Thus, external failure costs are incurred for customer service complaints; rejection, return, repair, or recall of products or services; warranty obligations; products liability claims; and customer losses.

b) Environmental costs are also external failure costs, e.g., fines for nonadherence to environmental law and loss of customer goodwill.

i) To minimize environmental damage and its resulting costs, the International Organization for Standardization has issued ISO 14000 standards to promote the reduction of environmental damage by an organization's products, services, and operations and to develop environmental auditing and performance evaluation systems.

Stop and review! You have completed the outline for this subunit. Study multiple-choice questions 25 through 31 beginning on page 162.

4.7 CORE CONCEPTS

Just-in-Time Systems

- A just-in-time inventory management system limits the output of each function to the immediate demand of the next function. The accompanying reductions in inventory levels result in less money invested in idle assets.
- High inventory levels often mask production problems because defective parts can be overlooked when plenty of good parts are available.
- Higher productivity, reduced order costs as well as carrying costs, faster and cheaper setups, shorter manufacturing cycle times, better due date performance, improved quality, and more flexible processes are objectives of JIT methods.
- Minimization of inventory is a goal because many inventory-related activities are viewed as nonvalue-added. JIT is a **pull or demand-driven system**; items are pulled through production by current demand, not pushed through by anticipated demand.
- **Frequent receipt of deliveries** from suppliers often means less need for a sophisticated inventory control system and for control personnel. JIT also may **eliminate central receiving areas**, hard copy receiving reports, and storage areas. A central warehouse is not needed because deliveries are made by suppliers directly to the area of production.
- **Kanban**, a Japanese term meaning ticket, is one of the many elements in the JIT system and was developed by the Toyota Motor Corporation. Tickets (also described as cards or markers) control the flow of production or parts so that they are **produced or obtained in the needed amounts** at the needed times.
- JIT also encompasses changes in the **production process** itself. To implement this approach and to eliminate waste of materials, labor, factory space, and machine usage, the **factory is reorganized** to permit what is often called **lean production**.

Materials Requirements Planning and Outsourcing

- A **materials requirements planning (MRP)** system enables a company to efficiently fulfill the requirements of the master production schedule by coordinating both the manufacture of component parts for finished goods and the arrival of the raw materials necessary to create the intermediate components.
- MRP is a **push system**, that is, the demand for raw materials is driven by the forecasted demand for the final product, which can be programmed into the computer.
- **Manufacturing resource planning (MRP II)** is a closed-loop manufacturing system that integrates all facets of a manufacturing business, including production, sales, inventories, schedules, and cash flows. The **same system** is used for both the **financial reporting and managing operations** (both use the same transactions and numbers).
- **Outsourcing** is the management or day-to-day execution of an entire business function by a third-party service provider. Outsourced services may be provided on or off premises, in the same country, or in a separate country.

Theory of Constraints and Throughput Costing

- The basic premise of the **theory of constraints (TOC)** as applied to business is that improving any process is best done not by trying to maximize efficiency in every part of the process, but by focusing on the **handful of factors** that are crucial, called **constraints**. Increasing the efficiency of processes that are not constraints merely creates backup in the system.
- The **steps in a TOC analysis** are: identify the bottleneck operation (the constraint), determine the most profitable profit mix given the constraint, maximize product flow through the bottleneck, increase capacity at the bottleneck, and redesign the manufacturing process.
- A basic principle of TOC analysis is that short-term profit maximization requires maximizing the **contribution margin through the constraint**, called the **throughput contribution** or throughput margin.
- **Throughput costing**, sometimes called **supervariable costing**, recognizes **only direct materials costs** as being truly variable and thus relevant to the calculation of throughput contribution. All other manufacturing costs are ignored because they are considered fixed in the short run.
- Production flow is managed using the **drum-buffer-rope** (DBR) system. The drum is the bottleneck operation, the buffer is the minimal amount of work-in-process input to the drum, and the rope is the sequence of activities preceding and including the bottleneck that must be coordinated.

Capacity Planning

- **Capacity planning** is an element of strategic planning that is closely related to capital budgeting. Maximizing the value created within an organization starts with understanding the nature and capabilities of **all of the company's resources**. Thus, capacity should be defined from several different perspectives.
- Whether to expand capacity is a major strategic decision because of the capital required, the difficulty of forming accurate expectations, and the long timeframe of the lead times and the commitment. The key forecasting problems are **long-term demand** and **behavior of competitors**.

Value Chain Analysis

- The **value chain** is a model for depicting the way in which every function in a company adds value to the final product. **Primary activities** (R&D, manufacturing, etc.) deal with the product directly. **Support activities** (human resources, inventory management, etc.) lend aid to the primary activity functions.
- The **supply chain** is the flow of materials and services from their original sources to final consumers. Moreover, it usually encompasses more than one firm.
- **Value engineering** is a means of reaching targeted cost levels. It is a systematic approach to assessing all aspects of the value chain cost buildup for a product. The purpose is to minimize costs without sacrificing customer satisfaction. Value engineering requires distinguishing between **cost incurrence** and **locked-in costs**.
- **Cost incurrence** is the actual use of resources, but **locked-in (designed-in)** costs will result in the use of resources in the future as a result of past decisions. Thus, value engineering emphasizes **controlling costs at the design stage**, that is, before they are locked in.
- **Life-cycle costing** is sometimes used as a basis for cost planning and product pricing. Life-cycle costing estimates a product's revenues and expenses over its expected life cycle. The result is to **highlight upstream and downstream costs** that often receive insufficient attention in the cost planning process.
- **Process value analysis** is a comprehensive understanding of how an organization generates its output. It involves a determination of which activities that use resources are **value-adding** or **nonvalue-adding** and how the latter may be reduced or eliminated.

Other Process Improvement Tools

- Technological advances have increased the popularity of **total quality management (TQM)** techniques and **business process reengineering**. Reengineering should be contrasted with **process improvement**, which consists of incremental but constant changes that improve efficiency.

- **Benchmarking** is an ongoing process that entails quantitative and qualitative measurement of the difference between the company's performance of an activity and the performance by the best in the world.

- **Kaizen** is the Japanese word for the continuous pursuit of improvement in every aspect of organizational operations.

- The trend in managerial performance evaluation is the **balanced scorecard** approach. Multiple measures of performance permit a determination as to whether a manager is achieving certain objectives at the expense of others that may be equally or more important. The scorecard is a **goal congruence tool** that informs managers about the nonfinancial factors that top management believes to be important.

QUESTIONS

4.1 Just-in-Time Inventory and Lean Operation

1. The effectiveness of a JIT system is often facilitated by the elimination of some common forms of internal control. The elimination of which internal control is usually acceptable with a JIT system?

A. Preparation of hard copy receiving reports.

B. Voucher approval prior to paying accounts payable.

C. Two signatures required on large checks.

D. Locked doors on production areas.

Answer (A) is correct. *(Publisher, adapted)*
  REQUIRED: The internal control that is not necessary with a JIT system.
  DISCUSSION: Receiving departments are often eliminated with a JIT system so receiving reports are not needed. Also, the quantity received should be exactly equal to immediate production needs.

2. Just-in-time manufacturing practices are based in part on the belief that

A. High inventory levels provide greater flexibility in production scheduling.

B. Attempting to reduce inventory to a consistently low level can lead to "panic" situations.

C. Goods should be "pulled" through the production process, not "pushed."

D. Beefed-up internal control in the central warehouse can greatly enhance productivity in the production areas.

Answer (C) is correct. *(Publisher, adapted)*
  REQUIRED: The concept that is part of the philosophy of just-in-time manufacturing.
  DISCUSSION: Just-in-time (JIT) manufacturing is a pull system; items are pulled through production by current demand, not pushed through by anticipated demand as in traditional manufacturing setups.
  Answer (A) is incorrect. Under the JIT philosophy, high inventory levels often mask production problems. Answer (B) is incorrect. Attempting to reduce inventory to a consistently low level is a core objective of JIT. Answer (D) is incorrect. Under JIT, central warehouses are often eliminated.

3. Key Co. changed from a traditional manufacturing operation with a job-order costing system to a just-in-time operation with a backflush costing system. What is(are) the expected effect(s) of these changes on Key's inspection costs and recording detail of costs tracked to jobs in process?

	Inspection Costs	Detail of Costs Tracked to Jobs
A.	Decrease	Decrease
B.	Decrease	Increase
C.	Increase	Decrease
D.	Increase	Increase

4. If a worker encounters a production kanban at his/her workstation, the worker should

A. Release the requested item to the next stage in the process.

B. Begin manufacturing the requested item.

C. Initiate a purchase order with the supplier of the requested item.

D. Confirm the amount of the item requested and present the kanban to the production supervisor.

5. A firm that is deploying just-in-time manufacturing for the first time will

A. Establish contracts with many suppliers since an interruption in supply is extremely disruptive of the production process.

B. Establish contracts with a few carefully chosen suppliers since an interruption in supply is extremely disruptive of the production process.

C. Maintain a carefully calibrated safety stock since interruptions in supply are inevitable.

D. Acquire considerable computer processing capability to manage the demands of the data-dependent kanban inventory management system.

6. The physical reconfiguration of equipment that often accompanies the institution of a just-in-time manufacturing regime is described as the creation of

A. Cells.

B. Kanbans.

C. Electronic Data Interchange.

D. Tickets.

Answer (A) is correct. *(CPA, adapted)*
REQUIRED: The expected effects of changing to JIT.
DISCUSSION: In a JIT system, materials go directly into production without being inspected. The assumption is that the vendor has already performed all necessary inspections. The minimization of inventory reduces the number of suppliers, storage costs, transaction costs, etc. Backflush costing eliminates the traditional sequential tracking of costs. Instead, entries to inventory may be delayed until as late as the end of the period. For example, all product costs may be charged initially to cost of sales, and costs may be flushed back to the inventory accounts only at the end of the period. Thus, the detail of cost accounting is decreased.
Answer (B) is incorrect. The detail of costs tracked to jobs will also decrease. Answer (C) is incorrect. Inspection costs will also decrease. Answer (D) is incorrect. Both inspection costs and the detail of costs tracked to jobs will decrease.

Answer (B) is correct. *(Publisher, adapted)*
REQUIRED: The action a worker should take upon being presented with a production kanban.
DISCUSSION: In a kanban inventory control system, a production kanban is an indication to a worker to begin producing the item referred to on the kanban.
Answer (A) is incorrect. Release of an item to a subsequent stage in production is initiated with a withdrawal kanban. Answer (C) is incorrect. A purchase from a supplier is indicated by a vendor kanban. Answer (D) is incorrect. Under a kanban system, a worker is authorized to take action upon being presented with a kanban; involving the production supervisor only slows down the process.

Answer (B) is correct. *(Publisher, adapted)*
REQUIRED: The aspect of employing just-in-time (JIT) inventory management.
DISCUSSION: In a JIT system, the suppliers' dependability is crucial. Organizations that adopt JIT systems develop close relationships with a few carefully chosen suppliers who are extensively involved in the buyer's processes.
Answer (A) is incorrect. In a JIT system, the suppliers' dependability is crucial. Organizations that adopt JIT systems develop close relationships with a few carefully chosen suppliers who are extensively involved in the buyer's processes. Answer (C) is incorrect. The use of safety stock is considered a nonvalue-adding activity under a JIT system, and interruptions in supply are not considered inevitable. Answer (D) is incorrect. A JIT system does not necessarily require the employment of kanban inventory management. Also, kanban is essentially a manual system.

Answer (A) is correct. *(Publisher, adapted)*
REQUIRED: The term referring to the result of equipment reconfiguration that often accompanies just-in-time manufacturing.
DISCUSSION: Plant layout in a JIT-lean production environment is not arranged by functional department or process but by manufacturing cells (work cells). Cells are sets of machines, often group in semicircles, that produce a given product or product type.
Answer (B) is incorrect. While a kanban system is sometimes part of a JIT arrangement, the term does not refer to the physical rearrangement of machinery. Answer (C) is incorrect. While electronic data interchange (EDI) facilitates the vendor relations that make JIT possible, the term does not refer to the physical rearrangement of machinery. Answer (D) is incorrect. Ticket is the meaning of the Japanese term kanban, which does not refer to the physical rearrangement of machinery.

7. Which of the following terms is **not** connected with the employment of just-in-time (JIT) manufacturing?

A. Cells.

B. Kanban.

C. Lean production.

D. Safety stock.

Answer (D) is correct. *(Publisher, adapted)*
REQUIRED: The term that is not connected with just-in-time manufacturing.
DISCUSSION: Safety stock involves always keeping enough raw materials on hand to overcome the effects of an interruption in supply. In a JIT system, manufacturers are completely dependent upon the reliability of their suppliers in delivering raw materials as they are needed. Keeping safety stock undercuts the entire philosophy of JIT.

4.2 Materials Requirements Planning and Outsourcing

8. In contrast to just-in-time manufacturing, materials requirements planning is a

A. Push system.

B. Pull system.

C. Automated system.

D. Manual system.

Answer (A) is correct. *(Publisher, adapted)*
REQUIRED: The description of materials requirements planning (MRP) that stands in contrast to just-in-time manufacturing.
DISCUSSION: MRP is a push system, that is, the demand for raw materials is driven by the forecasted demand for the final product, which can be programmed into the computer. This is in contrast with just-in-time manufacturing, which is a pull system, meaning items are pulled through production by current demand, not pushed through by anticipated demand.
Answer (B) is incorrect. Just-in-time manufacturing is a pull system. Answer (C) is incorrect. Both systems may be automated. Answer (D) is incorrect. Neither system need be manual.

9. Materials requirements planning (MRP) sometimes results in

A. Longer idle periods.

B. Less flexibility in responding to customers.

C. Increased inventory carrying costs.

D. Decreased setup costs.

Answer (D) is correct. *(Publisher, adapted)*
REQUIRED: The result of implementing a materials requirements planning (MRP) system.
DISCUSSION: Among the benefits of MRP are reduced idle time, lower setup costs, lower inventory carrying costs, and increased flexibility in responding to market changes.
Answer (A) is incorrect. MRP often results in reduced idle time. Answer (B) is incorrect. MRP often results in increased flexibility in responding to market changes. Answer (C) is incorrect. MRP often results in lower inventory carrying costs.

10. The manufacturing concept that relates demand forecasts to specific dates for completion is

A. Master production schedule.

B. Materials requirements planning.

C. Manufacturing resource planning.

D. Bill of materials.

Answer (A) is correct. *(Publisher, adapted)*
REQUIRED: The concept that relates demand forecasts to specific dates for completion.
DISCUSSION: The yearly/quarterly/monthly numbers and styles of finished goods called for in the demand forecasts included in the operational plans must be turned into specific dates for completion and availability for shipment to the customer. This is the task of the master production schedule (MPS).
Answer (B) is incorrect. Materials requirements planning is a system that enables a company to efficiently fulfill the goals of the master production schedule. Answer (C) is incorrect. Manufacturing resource planning is a closed-loop manufacturing system that integrates all facets of a manufacturing business, including production, sales, inventories, schedules, and cash flows. Answer (D) is incorrect. A bill of materials is a record of which (and how many) subassemblies go into the finished product. The system then generates a complete list of every part and component needed.

11. Which of the following is **not** a typical benefit of an outsourcing arrangement?

   A. Reduced costs.

   B. Access to technology.

   C. Avoidance of risk of obsolescence.

   D. Increased control over a necessary function.

Answer (D) is correct. *(Publisher, adapted)*
REQUIRED: The item that is not a typical benefit of outsourcing.
DISCUSSION: Outsourcing results in a loss of control over the outsourced function.

4.3 Theory of Constraints and Throughput Costing

12. United Industries manufactures three products at its highly automated factory. The products are very popular, with demand far exceeding the company's ability to supply the marketplace. To maximize profit, management should focus on each product's

   A. Gross margin.

   B. Segment margin.

   C. Contribution margin ratio.

   D. Contribution margin per machine hour.

Answer (D) is correct. *(CMA, adapted)*
REQUIRED: The measure used to determine the profit maximizing output.
DISCUSSION: When demand far exceeds a company's ability to supply the marketplace, management will want to maximize its profits per unit of scarce resource. If the scarce resource is raw materials, the products that provide the greatest contribution margin per unit of raw materials are the products to emphasize. If machine hours are the constraint, profits are maximized by emphasizing the contribution margin per machine hour.
   Answer (A) is incorrect. Focusing on high gross margin products does not maximize profits if those products require an excessive amount of resources. Answer (B) is incorrect. The company can sell as much of each product as it can produce. Thus, sales are limited by production constraints, e.g., machine hours. The company should therefore seek to maximize its return per unit of the constraint. Answer (C) is incorrect. The contribution margin ratio is only important as it translates to dollars. A high margin on a low sales volume will not be profitable.

13. Antler, Inc., produces a single product that sells for $150 per unit. The product is processed through the Cutting and Finishing Departments. Additional data for these departments are as follows:

	Cutting	Finishing
Annual capacity (36,000 direct labor hours available in each department)	180,000 units	135,000 units
Current production rate (annualized)	108,000 units	108,000 units
Fixed manufacturing overhead	$1,296,000	$1,944,000
Fixed selling and administrative expense	864,000	1,296,000
Direct materials cost per unit	45	15

The current production rate is the budgeted rate for the entire year. Direct labor employees earn $20 per hour, and the company has a "no layoff" period in effect. What is the amount of the throughput contribution per unit as computed using the theory of constraints?

   A. $90.00

   B. $76.67

   C. $46.67

   D. $26.67

Answer (A) is correct. *(CMA, adapted)*
REQUIRED: The amount of throughput contribution per unit.
DISCUSSION: Throughput costing, sometimes called supervariable costing, recognizes only direct materials costs as being truly variable and thus relevant to the calculation of throughput margin (throughput contribution). All other manufacturing costs are ignored because they are considered fixed in the short turn. For Antler's single product, the throughput margin is therefore $90 ($150 selling price − $45 direct materials in Cutting − $15 direct materials in Finishing).
   Answer (B) is incorrect. Labor, overhead, and selling and administrative costs are not considered in the calculation of throughput contribution. Answer (C) is incorrect. Labor, overhead, and selling and administrative costs are not considered in the calculation of throughput contribution. Answer (D) is incorrect. Labor, overhead, and selling and administrative costs are not considered in the calculation of throughput contribution.

14. Three of the basic measurements used by the theory of constraints (TOC) are

A. Gross margin (or gross profit), return on assets, and total sales.

B. Number of constraints (or subordinates), number of nonconstraints, and operating leverage.

C. Throughput (or throughput contribution), inventory (or investments), and operational expense.

D. Fixed manufacturing overhead per unit, fixed general overhead per unit, and unit gross margin (or gross profit).

Answer (C) is correct. *(CMA, adapted)*
REQUIRED: The relevant measurements in TOC analysis.
DISCUSSION: Theory of constraints (TOC) analysis describes three basic measurements: throughput contribution (sales – direct materials), investments (raw materials; work-in-process; finished goods; R&D costs; and property, plant, and equipment), and operating costs (all costs except direct materials).
Answer (A) is incorrect. Gross margin, return on assets, and total sales are used in analyzing a firm's profitability; they are not measurements used in TOC analysis. Answer (B) is incorrect. Although the number of constraints/nonconstraints is important under the TOC, these numbers are not basic measurements used in TOC analysis. Operating leverage concerns contribution margin, which is not a basic measurement under TOC. Answer (D) is incorrect. These measurements are used under absorption (full) costing, not in TOC analysis.

15. Under throughput costing, the only cost considered to be truly variable in the short run is

A. Direct materials.

B. Direct labor.

C. Manufacturing overhead.

D. All manufacturing costs are considered variable.

Answer (A) is correct. *(Publisher, adapted)*
REQUIRED: The variable cost under throughput costing.
DISCUSSION: Throughput costing, also called supervariable costing, recognizes only direct materials costs as being truly variable and thus relevant to the calculation of throughput margin.
Answer (B) is incorrect. Under throughput costing, direct labor is considered fixed because of labor contracts and employment levels. Answer (C) is incorrect. Under throughput costing, overhead is considered fixed in the short run. Answer (D) is incorrect. Under throughput costing, only direct materials costs are considered variable in the short run.

16. The immediate goal of a theory of constraints (TOC) analysis is to

A. Maximize the efficiency of the entire production process.

B. Minimize direct materials cost.

C. Maximize contribution margin through the constraint.

D. Smooth production flow to eliminate backup in the system.

Answer (C) is correct. *(Publisher, adapted)*
REQUIRED: The immediate goal of a theory of constraints analysis.
DISCUSSION: A basic principle of TOC analysis is that short-term profit maximization requires maximizing the contribution margin through the constraint, called the throughput margin or throughput contribution.
Answer (A) is incorrect. Under the principles of TOC, maximizing the efficiency of processes that have excess capacity merely creates backup in the system. Answer (B) is incorrect. Holding down direct materials costs, while an important part of improving contribution margin, is not part of a TOC analysis. Answer (D) is incorrect. While eliminating backup is a goal of a TOC analysis, it is not done by simply "smoothing" production flow, since this could mean slowing down the entire process to match the bottleneck.

17. A manufacturer can sell its single product for $660. Below are the cost data for the product:

Direct materials	$170
Direct labor	225
Manufacturing overhead	90

The relevant margin amount when beginning a theory of constraints (TOC) analysis is

A. $490

B. $345

C. $265

D. $175

Answer (A) is correct. *(Publisher, adapted)*
REQUIRED: The relevant margin amount when beginning a theory of constraints (TOC) analysis.
DISCUSSION: A theory of constraints (TOC) analysis proceeds from the assumption that only direct materials costs are truly variable in the short run. This is called throughput, or supervariable, costing. The relevant margin amount is throughput margin, which equals price minus direct materials. Thus, the relevant margin amount for this manufacturer is $490 ($660 – $170).
Answer (B) is incorrect. The amount of $345 results from subtracting conversion cost, rather than throughput cost, from selling price. Answer (C) is incorrect. The amount of $265 results from subtracting prime cost, rather than throughput cost, from selling price. Answer (D) is incorrect. The amount of $175 results from subtracting all manufacturing costs, rather than just throughput cost, from selling price.

4.4 Capacity Management

18. Effective cost capacity management

    A. Minimizes the value delivered to customers.

    B. Maximizes required future investments.

    C. Matches the firm's resources with current and future market opportunities.

    D. Is limited to eliminating short-term worth.

Answer (C) is correct. *(Publisher, adapted)*
    REQUIRED: The true statement about effective cost capacity arrangement.
    DISCUSSION: According to the IMA's Statement on Management Accounting *Measuring the Cost of Capacity*, maximizing the value created within an organization starts with understanding the nature and capabilities of all of the company's resources. Capacity is defined from several different perspectives. Managing capacity cost starts when a product or process is first envisioned. It continues through the subsequent disposal of resources downstream. Effective capacity cost management requires supporting effective matching of a firm's resources with current and future market opportunities.
    Answer (A) is incorrect. Effective capacity management maximizes value delivered to customers. Answer (B) is incorrect. Effective capacity management minimizes required future investments. Answer (D) is incorrect. Effective capacity management minimizes waste in the short, intermediate, and long run.

19. Capacity expansion is also referred to as

    A. Market penetration.

    B. Market development.

    C. Product development.

    D. Diversification.

Answer (A) is correct. *(CIA, adapted)*
    REQUIRED: The term used for capacity expansion.
    DISCUSSION: Market penetration is growth of existing products or development of existing markets. It occurs in mature firms within an industry.
    Answer (B) is incorrect. Market development seeks new markets for current products. Answer (C) is incorrect. Product development is launching new products in existing markets. Answer (D) is incorrect. Diversification is launching new products for new markets.

4.5 Value Chain Analysis

20. Process value analysis is a key component of activity-based management that links product costing and

    A. Reduction of the number of cost pools.

    B. Continuous improvement.

    C. Accumulation of heterogeneous cost pools.

    D. Overhead rates based on broad averages.

Answer (B) is correct. *(Publisher, adapted)*
    REQUIRED: The element of process value analysis.
    DISCUSSION: Design of an ABC system starts with process value analysis, a comprehensive understanding of how an organization generates its output. It involves a determination of which activities that use resources are value-adding or nonvalue-adding and how the latter may be reduced or eliminated. This linkage of product costing and continuous improvement of processes is activity-based management (ABM). It encompasses driver analysis, activity analysis, and performance measurement.
    Answer (A) is incorrect. ABC tends to increase the number of cost pools and drivers used. Answer (C) is incorrect. ABC's philosophy is to accumulate homogeneous cost pools. Thus, the cost elements in a pool should be consumed by cost objects in proportion to the same driver. Homogenizing cost pools minimizes broad averaging of costs that have different drivers. Answer (D) is incorrect. ABC's philosophy is to accumulate homogeneous cost pools. Thus, the cost elements in a pool should be consumed by cost objects in proportion to the same driver. Homogenizing cost pools minimizes broad averaging of costs that have different drivers.

21. A systematic approach to reaching targeted cost levels during value chain analysis is known as

    A. Value engineering.

    B. Life-cycle costing.

    C. Process value analysis.

    D. Activity analysis.

Answer (A) is correct. *(Publisher, adapted)*
    REQUIRED: The term referring to a systematic approach to reaching targeted cost levels during value chain analysis.
    DISCUSSION: Value engineering is a means of reaching targeted cost levels. It is a systematic approach to assessing all aspects of the value chain cost buildup for a product.
    Answer (B) is incorrect. Life-cycle costing is a basis for cost planning and product pricing. Answer (C) is incorrect. Process value analysis is a way of understanding how a company generates its output. Answer (D) is incorrect. Activity analysis determines what is done, by whom, at what cost in time and other resources, and the value added by each activity.

22. Gram Co. develops computer programs to meet customers' special requirements. How should Gram categorize payments to employees who develop these programs?

	Direct Costs	Value-Adding Costs
A.	Yes	Yes
B.	Yes	No
C.	No	No
D.	No	Yes

Answer (A) is correct. *(CPA, adapted)*
　　REQUIRED: The proper categorization of employee costs.
　　DISCUSSION: Direct costs may be defined as those that can be specifically associated with a single cost object and can be assigned to it in an economically feasible manner. Wages paid to labor that can be identified with a specific finished good are direct costs. Value-adding costs may be defined as the costs of activities that cannot be eliminated without reducing the quality, responsiveness, or quantity of the output required by a customer or by an organization. Clearly, the amounts paid to programmers add value to computer programs.
　　Answer (B) is incorrect. The activities performed by programmers add value to computer programs. Therefore, the payments to employees who develop these programs is considered a value-adding cost. Answer (C) is incorrect. Payments to programmers are both direct costs and value-adding costs of computer programs. Answer (D) is incorrect. Wages paid to labor that can be identified with a specific finished good are direct costs. Therefore, payments to employees who develop computer programs is a direct cost.

23. The term referring to the excess of the price of a good over its cost is

A. Consumer surplus.

B. Profit margin.

C. Contribution margin.

D. Value-added transfer.

Answer (B) is correct. *(Publisher, adapted)*
　　REQUIRED: The term referring to the excess of the price of a good over its cost.
　　DISCUSSION: To remain in the market, a product must provide value to the customer and a profit to the seller. The producer's profit (profit margin) is the difference between its costs and the price it charges for the product.
　　Answer (A) is incorrect. Consumer surplus is the excess of the value a consumer places on a good over the price (s)he pays for it. Answer (C) is incorrect. Contribution margin is the excess of the sales price over variable costs. Answer (D) is incorrect. Value-added transfer is not a meaningful term in this context.

24. Which of the following is **not** a phase in a value-chain analysis?

A. Identify activities that are candidates for cost reduction.

B. Identify ways to generate additional customer value.

C. Identify means for improving product cost efficiency.

D. Identify the firm's competitive advantage.

Answer (C) is correct. *(Publisher, adapted)*
　　REQUIRED: The item not a phase in a value-chain analysis.
　　DISCUSSION: The second step in a value-chain analysis is to determine how each value-creating activity can produce a competitive advantage for the firm. This step has multiple substeps:

1. Identify the firm's competitive advantage (e.g., cost reduction, product differentiation) so that the firm's position in the industry's value chain can be clarified.

2. Identify the ways in which the firm's value-creating activities can generate additional customer value.

3. Identify activities that are candidates for cost reduction or, in the case of non-core competencies, outsourcing.

4. Identify value-adding ways in which the firm's remaining activities can be linked.

　　Answer (A) is incorrect. Identifying activities that are candidates for cost reduction or, in the case of non-core competencies, outsourcing, is one of the phases of a value-chain analysis. Answer (B) is incorrect. Identifying ways in which the firm's value-creating activities can generate additional customer value is one of the phases of a value-chain analysis. Answer (D) is incorrect. Identifying the firm's competitive advantage (e.g., cost reduction, product differentiation) so that the firm's position in the industry's value chain can be clarified is one of the phases of a value-chain analysis.

4.6 Other Process Improvement Tools

25. Which of the following is **not** a type of process?

A. Make-to-stock.

B. Make-to-order.

C. Buffer.

D. Hybrid.

Answer (C) is correct.   *(Publisher, adapted)*
REQUIRED: The term not referring to a type of process.
DISCUSSION: A buffer in the context of process analysis is a quantity of work-in-process inventory that allows some stage(s) of the overall process to continue operating when an earlier stage breaks down.
Answer (A) is incorrect. Make-to-stock is a type of process, exemplified by automobile assembly. Answer (B) is incorrect. Make-to-order is a type of process, exemplified by deli sandwich making. Answer (D) is incorrect. A hybrid process is one in which both continuous and batch processes are used.

26. Which of the following statements regarding benchmarking is **false**?

A. Benchmarking involves continuously evaluating the practices of best-in-class organization and adapting company processes to incorporate the best of these practices.

B. Benchmarking, in practice, usually involves a company forming benchmarking teams.

C. Benchmarking is an ongoing process that entails quantitative and qualitative measurement of the difference between the company's performance of an activity and the performance by the best in the world or the best in the industry.

D. The benchmarking organization against which a firm is comparing itself must be a direct competitor.

Answer (D) is correct.   *(Publisher, adapted)*
REQUIRED: The false statement about benchmarking.
DISCUSSION: Benchmarking is an ongoing process that entails quantitative and qualitative measurement of the difference between the company's performance of an activity and the performance by a best-in-class organization. The benchmarking organization against which a firm is comparing itself need not be a direct competitor. The important consideration is that the benchmarking organization be an outstanding performer in its industry.

27. An example of an internal nonfinancial benchmark is the

A. Labor rate of comparably skilled employees at a major competitor's plant.

B. Average actual cost per pound of a specific product at the company's most efficient plant becoming the benchmark for the company's other plants.

C. Company setting a benchmark of $50,000 for employee training programs at each of the company's plants.

D. Percentage of customer orders delivered on time at the company's most efficient plant becoming the benchmark for the company's other plants.

Answer (D) is correct.   *(CIA, adapted)*
REQUIRED: The internal nonfinancial benchmark.
DISCUSSION: Benchmarking involves continuously evaluating the principles of best-in-class organizations and adapting company processes to incorporate the best of these practices. It analyzes and measures the key outputs of a business process or function against the best and also identifies the underlying key actions and root causes that contribute to the performance difference. The percentage of orders delivered on time at the company's most efficient plant is an example of an internal nonfinancial benchmark.
Answer (A) is incorrect. The labor rate of a competitor is a financial benchmark. Answer (B) is incorrect. The cost per pound of a product at the company's most efficient plant is a financial benchmark. Answer (C) is incorrect. The cost of a training program is a financial benchmark.

28. The four categories of costs associated with product quality costs are

A. External failure, internal failure, prevention, and carrying.

B. External failure, internal failure, prevention, and appraisal.

C. External failure, internal failure, training, and appraisal.

D. Warranty, product liability, training, and appraisal.

Answer (B) is correct. *(CMA, adapted)*
REQUIRED: The categories of product quality costs.
DISCUSSION: The IMA *Management Accounting Glossary* lists four categories of quality costs: prevention, appraisal, internal failure, and external failure (lost opportunity). Costs of prevention include attempts to avoid defective output, including employee training, review of equipment design, preventive maintenance, and evaluation of suppliers. Appraisal costs include quality control programs, inspection, and testing. Internal failure costs are incurred when detection of defective products occurs before shipment, including scrap, rework, tooling changes, and downtime. External failure costs are incurred after the product has been shipped, including the costs associated with warranties, product liability, and customer ill will.
Answer (A) is incorrect. Carrying cost is not one of the elements of quality costs. Answer (C) is incorrect. Training costs are not a category of quality costs. Answer (D) is incorrect. Warranty, product liability, and training are not cost categories identified by the IMA *Management Accounting Glossary*.

29. The cost of scrap, rework, and tooling changes in a product quality cost system is categorized as a(n)

A. Training cost.

B. External failure cost.

C. Internal failure cost.

D. Prevention cost.

Answer (C) is correct. *(CMA, adapted)*
REQUIRED: The categorization of the cost of scrap, rework, and tooling changes in a product quality cost system.
DISCUSSION: According to the IMA *Management Accounting Glossary*, internal failure costs are incurred when detection of defective products occurs before shipment. Examples of internal failure costs are scrap, rework, tooling changes, and downtime.
Answer (A) is incorrect. Training costs are prevention costs. Answer (B) is incorrect. The costs of external failure, such as warranty expense, product liability, and customer ill will, arise when problems are discovered after products have been shipped. Answer (D) is incorrect. Prevention costs are incurred to avoid defective output. Examples include preventive maintenance, employee training, review of equipment design, and evaluation of suppliers.

30. The cost of statistical quality control in a product quality cost system is categorized as a(n)

A. Internal failure cost.

B. Training cost.

C. External failure cost.

D. Appraisal cost.

Answer (D) is correct. *(CMA, adapted)*
REQUIRED: The cost category that includes statistical quality control.
DISCUSSION: The following are the four categories of quality costs: prevention, appraisal, internal failure, and external failure (lost opportunity). Appraisal costs include quality control programs, inspection, and testing. However, some authorities regard statistical quality and process control as preventive activities because they not only detect faulty work but also allow for adjustment of processes to avoid future defects.
Answer (A) is incorrect. Internal failure costs arise after poor quality has been found; statistical quality control is designed to detect quality problems. Answer (B) is incorrect. Statistical quality control is not a training cost. Answer (C) is incorrect. External failure costs are incurred after the product has been shipped, including the costs associated with warranties, product liability, and customer ill will.

31. Listed below are selected line items from the Cost of Quality Report for Watson Products for last month.

Category	Amount
Rework	$ 725
Equipment maintenance	1,154
Product testing	786
Product repair	695

What is Watson's total prevention and appraisal cost for last month?

A. $786

B. $1,154

C. $1,940

D. $2,665

Answer (C) is correct. *(CMA, adapted)*
   REQUIRED: The total prevention and appraisal costs.
   DISCUSSION: The costs of prevention and appraisal are conformance costs that serve as financial measures of internal performance. Prevention costs are incurred to prevent defective output. These costs include preventive maintenance, employee training, review of equipment design, and evaluation of suppliers. Appraisal costs are incurred to detect nonconforming output. They embrace such activities as statistical quality control programs, inspection, and testing. The equipment maintenance cost of $1,154 is a prevention cost. The product testing cost of $786 is an appraisal cost. Their sum is $1,940.
   Answer (A) is incorrect. The appraisal cost is $786.
Answer (B) is incorrect. The prevention cost is $1,154.
Answer (D) is incorrect. The amount of $2,665 includes rework, an internal failure cost.

Use Gleim **CMA Test Prep** Software for interactive testing with **additional multiple-choice questions**!

4.8 ESSAY QUESTIONS

Scenario for Essay Questions 1, 2, 3

The management at Megafilters, Inc., has been discussing the possible implementation of a just-in-time (JIT) production system at its Illinois plant, where oil filters and air filters for heavy construction equipment and large, off-the-road vehicles are manufactured. The Metal Stamping Department at the Illinois plant has already instituted a JIT system for controlling raw materials inventory, but the remainder of the plant is still discussing how to proceed with the implementation of this concept. Some of the other department managers have grown increasingly cautious about the JIT process after hearing about the problems that have arisen in the Metal Stamping Department.

Robert Goertz, manager of the Illinois plant, is a strong proponent of the JIT production system and recently made the following statement at a meeting of all departmental managers: "Just-in-time is often referred to as a management philosophy of doing business rather than a technique for improving efficiency of the plant floor. We will all have to make many changes in the way we think about our employees, our suppliers, and our customers if we are going to be successful in using just-in-time procedures. Rather than dwelling on some of the negative things you have heard from the Metal Stamping Department, I want each of you to prepare a list of things we can do to make a smooth transition to the just-in-time philosophy of management for the rest of the plant."

Questions

1. The just-in-time (JIT) management philosophy emphasizes objectives for the general improvement of a production system. Describe several important objectives of this philosophy.

2. Discuss several actions that Megafilters can take to ease the transition to a just-in-time (JIT) production system at the Illinois plant.

3. In order for the just-in-time (JIT) production system to be successful, Megafilters must establish appropriate relationships with its vendors, employees, and customers. Describe each of these three relationships.

Essay Questions 1, 2, 3 — Unofficial Answers

1.   The objectives for the general improvement of a production system as emphasized in the just-in-time (JIT) management philosophy include

   a.   Flowing product continuously through the plant and minimizing the investment in raw materials, work-in-process, and finished goods inventories

   b.   Making production operations in the plant more efficient by redesigning work stations, simplifying the environment, and reducing both set-up and lead times

   c.   Increasing the attention to quality control, reducing obsolescence and waste, and identifying non-value-added cost drivers (i.e., nonproductive labor, insurance, taxes) that can be eliminated

2.   Megafilters, Inc., can take the following actions to ease the transition to a just-in-time (JIT) production system at the Illinois plant:

   a.   Communicate to employees, customers, and vendors the corporate objectives and plans for implementing the JIT production system.

   b.   Elicit employee participation in implementing the JIT system and train employees on the necessary tools (i.e., computers).

   c.   Chart the production-process flows through the plant and develop statistical measurement and control procedures. Simplify processing and identify and alleviate cost drivers, non-value-added activities, and waste.

   d.   Obtain competitive bids and JIT proposals from several vendors for each material, selecting the few who will reduce lead times, increase the quality of raw materials, and comply with strict delivery schedules.

3.   Megafilters, Inc., must establish the following appropriate relationships in order to successfully implement the just-in-time (JIT) production system:

   a.   Vendors

      1)   Reduce the number of vendors to those who will be highly dependable and reliable.

      2)   Commit the vendor to high quality standards by shifting responsibility for production problems to the suppliers (i.e., defective parts).

   b.   Employees

      1)   Develop trust and communication with the employees to obtain team participation in the initial plan and elicit feedback in the future.

      2)   Increase the employees' responsibility to assist in improving operations and quality while reducing cost drivers.

      3)   Treat employees as partners in the process, eliciting their commitment.

   c.   Customers

      1)   Develop trust and communication for including the customers' participation in the initial plan and eliciting feedback in the future.

      2)   Ensure that Megafilters is fulfilling the customers' needs and demands.

      3)   Build a team spirit through assurances that the company will meet the customers' demands at a competitive price. Employ the customer as a partner in the process (i.e., wait together for delayed deliveries, in order to keep costs at a minimum).

Use **CMA Gleim Online** and **Essay Wizard** to practice additional essay questions in an exam-like environment.

STUDY UNIT FIVE
BUDGETING CONCEPTS
AND FORECASTING TECHNIQUES

(24 pages of outline)

5.1	Roles of Budgets	169
5.2	The Budgeting Process	172
5.3	Budgeting and Standard Costs	174
5.4	Correlation and Regression	176
5.5	Learning Curve Analysis	180
5.6	Time Series Analysis	181
5.7	Expected Value	184
5.8	Sensitivity Analysis	186
5.9	Core Concepts	188
5.10	Essay Question	205

Planning, Budgeting, and Forecasting

A budget is a realistic plan for the future that is expressed in quantitative terms. A budget is many tools in one; it is a planning tool, a control tool, a communication tool, and a motivational tool. As such, the area of budgeting, as tested on the CMA exam, is a composite of theory and calculations. Some of the calculations have many steps, thus making budgeting problems among the most-missed questions on the exam. Alternatively, budgeting should not be viewed as a difficult area; the concepts are easy, but you need to pay close attention to detail as you work numerical questions.

This study unit is the **first of two** on **planning, budgeting, and forecasting**. The relative weight assigned to this major topic in Part 1 of the exam is **30%**. The two study units are

Study Unit 5: Budgeting Concepts and Forecasting Techniques
Study Unit 6: Budget Methodologies and Budget Preparation

After studying the outline and answering the questions in this study unit, you will have the skills necessary to address the following topics listed in the ICMA's Learning Outcome Statements:

Part 1 – Section A.1. Budgeting concepts

The candidate should be able to:

    a.   describe the role that budgeting plays in the overall planning and performance evaluation process of an organization

    b.   explain the interrelationships between economic conditions, industry situation, and a firm's plans and budgets

    c.   identify the role that budgeting plays in formulating short-term objectives and planning and controlling operations to meet those objectives

    d.   demonstrate an understanding of the role that budgets play in measuring performance against established goals

    e.   identify the characteristics that define successful budgeting processes

    f.   explain how the budgeting process facilitates communication among organizational units and enhances coordination of organizational activities

    g.   describe the concept of a controllable cost as it relates to both budgeting and performance evaluation

h.   explain how the efficient allocation of organizational resources is planned during the budgeting process

i.   identify the appropriate time frame for various types of budgets

j.   identify who should participate in the budgeting process for optimum success

k.   describe the role of top management in successful budgeting

l.   identify best practices guidelines for the budget process

m.   demonstrate an understanding of the use of cost standards in budgeting

n.   differentiate between ideal (theoretical) standards and currently attainable (practical) standards

o.   differentiate between authoritative standards and participative standards

p.   identify the steps to be taken in developing standards for both direct material and direct labor

q.   demonstrate an understanding of the techniques that are used to develop standards such as activity analysis and the use of historical data

r.   discuss the importance of a policy that allows budget revisions that accommodate the impact of significant changes in budget assumptions

s.   explain the role of budgets in monitoring and controlling expenditures to meet strategic objectives

t.   define budgetary slack and discuss its impact on goal congruence

Part 1 – Section A.2. Forecasting techniques

The candidate should be able to:

a.   demonstrate an understanding of a simple regression equation and the measures associated with it

b.   define a multiple regression equation and recognize when multiple regression is an appropriate tool to use for forecasting

c.   calculate the result of a simple regression equation

d.   demonstrate an understanding of learning curve analysis

e.   calculate the results under a cumulative average-time learning model and under an incremental unit-time learning model

f.   demonstrate an understanding of moving averages, weighted moving averages, and exponential smoothing, and calculate forecasts using these methods

g.   demonstrate an understanding of time series analyses, including objectives and patterns, i.e., trend, cyclical, seasonal, and irregular

h.   list the benefits and shortcomings of regression analysis, learning curve analysis, and time series analysis

i.   calculate the expected value of random variables

j.   identify the benefits and shortcomings of expected value techniques

k.   use probability values to estimate future cash flows

l.   identify the uses of sensitivity analysis

m.   perform a sensitivity analysis with different values for the probabilities of the states of nature and/or the payoffs

n.   identify the benefits and shortcomings of sensitivity analysis

5.1 ROLES OF BUDGETS

1. **The Budget as a Tool**

    a. The budget is a **planning** tool.

       1) A budget is a written plan for the future.

       2) Companies that prepare budgets anticipate problems before they occur.

          a) EXAMPLE: If a company runs out of critical raw material, it may have to shut down. At best, it will incur extremely high freight costs to have the needed materials rushed in. The company with a budget will have anticipated the shortage and planned around it.

       3) A firm that has no goals may not always make the best decisions. A firm with a goal in the form of a budget will be able to plan.

    b. The budget is a **control** tool.

       1) A budget helps a firm control costs by setting cost guidelines.

       2) Guidelines reveal the efficient or inefficient use of company resources.

       3) A manager is less apt to spend money for things that are not needed if (s)he knows that all costs will be compared with the budget.

          a) (S)he will be accountable if controllable costs exceed budgeted amounts.

       4) Budgets can also reveal the progress of highly effective managers. Consequently, employees should not view budgets negatively. A budget is just as likely to provide a boost to a manager's career as it is to be detrimental.

       5) Managers can also use a budget as a personal self-evaluation tool.

       6) Budgetary slack (overestimation of expenses) must be avoided, however, if a budget is to have its desired effects. The natural tendency of a manager is to negotiate for a less stringent measure of performance so as to avoid unfavorable variances from expectations.

       7) For the budgetary process to serve effectively as a control function, it must be integrated with the accounting system and the organizational structure. Such integration enhances control by transmitting data and assigning variances to the proper organizational subunits.

    c. The budget is a **motivational** tool.

       1) A budget helps motivate employees to do a good job.

          a) Employees are particularly motivated if they help prepare the budget.

          b) A manager who is asked to prepare a budget for his/her department will work hard to stay within the budget.

       2) A budget must be seen as realistic by employees before it can become a good motivational tool.

       3) Unfortunately, the budget is not always viewed in a positive manner. Some managers view a budget as a restriction.

       4) Employees are more apt to have a positive feeling toward a budget if some degree of flexibility is allowed.

    d. The budget is a means of **communication**.

       1) A budget can help tell employees what goals the firm is attempting to accomplish.

       2) If the firm does not have an overall budget, each department might think the firm has different goals.

3) For example, the sales department may want to keep as much inventory as possible so that no sales will be lost, but the company treasurer may want to keep the inventory as low as possible in order to conserve cash reserves. If the budget specifies the amount of inventory, all employees can work toward the same objectives.

2. **The Budget as a Formal Quantification of Management's Plans**

a. Corporations have goals for market share, profitability, growth, dividend payout, etc. Not-for-profit organizations also have goals, such as increased number of free meals served, lowered recidivism rate among offenders, etc.

1) These goals cannot be achieved without careful planning about the allocation of resources and the expected results.

b. A budget lays out in specific terms an organization's expectations about the consumption of resources and the resulting outcomes.

3. **Budgeting's Role in the Overall Planning and Evaluation Process**

a. **Planning** is the process by which an organization sets specific goals for itself and sets about pursuing those goals. Planning is an organization's response to the saying "If you don't know where you're going, any path will take you there."

1) The starting point for any organization's planning process is the formulation of its **mission statement**. The mission statement, formulated by the board and senior management, embodies the organization's reason for existing.

a) EXAMPLE: Increase shareholder value by providing global telecommunications services.

2) Next, the organization draws up its **strategic plan** containing the means by which the firm expects to fulfill its stated mission.

a) To a great extent, the strategy is made up of **long-term objectives**, a set of specific, measurable goals.

b) EXAMPLE: Hold a 35% market share of U.S. cell phone users within 5 years.

3) Once the long-term objectives are in place, the **priorities** of the organization will be clear.

a) Awareness of priorities is crucial for the **allocation of limited resources**.

b) EXAMPLE: How many cell towers, each of which require the outlay of construction and maintenance costs, will provide the optimum amount of coverage.

4) **Short-term objectives** flow directly from the priorities.

a) EXAMPLE: Determine the appropriate number of cell towers needed and where they can feasibly be placed in the Metro Atlanta region.

b) The planning process coordinates the efficient allocation of organizational resources.

b. To **evaluate progress** toward success in each of these stages, quantification is necessary. This is the role of the various types of budgets.

1) Not all quantification is in monetary terms. To extend the previous example, although cell towers obviously have a dollar cost, they must be simply counted as well.

2) **Comparing actual results to the budget** allows the organization as a whole to evaluate its performance and managers to do the same on an individual level.

4. **Budgeting's Role in Formulating and Controlling Short-term Objectives**

   a. A company's goal of increasing market share, making a steady dividend payout, etc., can only be achieved through the completion of incremental steps.

   b. The budget lays out the specific revenue targets and expense limitations for each functional area and department of the organization on a month-by-month basis.

      1) A budget cannot simply be a lump-sum total for a year. Incremental goals must be achieved each month or week. This is especially true in seasonal businesses, such as agricultural supply.

5. **Role of Budgets in Measuring Performance against Established Goals**

   a. One of the most important reasons for adopting a budget is to provide guideposts for the assessment of success or failure on the part of individual managers and functional areas.

   b. As the fiscal year progresses, revenues, expenses, and other metrics can be compared to the budget to determine where organizational performance is meeting, lagging, or exceeding expectations.

6. **The Role of Budgets in Monitoring and Controlling Expenditures**

   a. The initial budget is a planning tool. To monitor how actual performance compares with the budget, budget reports are produced periodically during the year.

      1) The difference between actual performance and a budgeted amount is called a **variance**. Analysis of variances reveals the efficient or inefficient use of company resources (see Study Unit 7, "Cost and Variance Measures").

7. **Role of Budgeting Process in Facilitating Communication among Organizational Units and Enhancing Coordination of Organizational Activities**

   a. On a detailed level, the budget informs employees at all levels what objectives the firm is attempting to accomplish.

      1) If the firm does not have an overall budget, each department tends to pursue its own objectives without regard to what is good for the firm as a whole. Thus, a budget promotes goal congruence.

   b. The concrete nature of a budget facilitates coordination of the activities of a firm. An example is the purchasing of raw materials.

      1) Materials are needed prior to production, but the proper quantity to buy cannot be determined until the projected level of output is established.

         a) Thus, a production budget (in units) is a prerequisite to the preparation of a materials purchases budget.

      2) Similarly, a direct labor budget is based on how many units are to be produced and how fast the workers are.

         a) Labor standards are also complex in that they must consider the impact of the learning curve on productivity.

Stop and review! You have completed the outline for this subunit. Study multiple-choice questions 1 through 5 beginning on page 190.

5.2 THE BUDGETING PROCESS

1. **Characteristics of a Successful Budgeting Process**

   a. **Sufficient lead time.** For a budget to be useful, it must be finalized when the fiscal year begins. This often calls for months of preparation, since the overall goals and baseline assumptions must be announced before functional areas and individual departments can begin formulating their numbers.

      1) The preparation of a complete organizational budget usually takes several months. A firm with a calendar year end may start the budget process in September, anticipating its completion by the first of December.

      2) The **budget planning calendar** is the schedule of activities for the development and adoption of the budget. It includes a list of dates indicating when specific information is to be provided to others by each information source.

         a) Because all of the individual departmental budgets are based on forecasts prepared by others and the budgets of other departments, it is essential to have a planning calendar to integrate the entire process.

   b. **Budget manual.** Everyone involved in preparing the budget at all levels must be educated on the detailed procedures for preparing and submitting their part of the overall budget.

      1) Because of the number of component departments, budgets must be prepared in a standard format.

         a) In addition, all concerned must be informed of the ultimate goals that are being pursued and the baseline assumptions that have been laid down. A budget may, for example, begin with a blanket mandate to raise revenues by 6.5% or to cut expenses across all departments by 2%.

      2) Distribution instructions are vital because of the interdependencies of a master budget.

         a) One department's budget may be dependent on another's, and functional areas must be aggregated from their constituent department budgets. The distribution instructions coordinate these interdependencies.

   c. **Buy-in at all levels.** Participative budgeting has a much greater chance of acceptance by those affected and thus of achieving ultimate success than does a budget that is imposed from above.

      1) The support of top management is crucial to the budgeting efforts.

2. **Participation in the Budget Process**

   a. Participation in the budget preparation process is up and down the organization.

      1) The budget process begins with the mission statement formulated by the **board of directors**.

      2) **Senior management** translates the mission statement into a strategic plan with measurable, realizable goals.

      3) A **budget committee/department** composed of top management is formed to draft the budget calendar and budget manual. The budget committee/department also reviews and approves the departmental budgets submitted by operating managers.

         a) A budget director's primary responsibility is to compile the budget and manage the budget process.

      4) **Middle and lower management** receive their budget instructions, draw up their departmental budgets in conformity with the guidelines, and submit them to the budget committee.

    b.   **Top-down budgeting** is imposed by upper management and therefore has less of a chance of acceptance by those on whom the budget is imposed.

    c.   **Bottom-up budgeting** is characterized by general guidance from the highest levels of management, followed by extensive input from middle and lower management. Because of this level of participation within the company, there is usually a greater chance of acceptance.

    d.   Participation in developing a budget may result in a **padding** of the budget, also known as budgetary slack.

        1)   **Budgetary slack** is the excess of resources budgeted over the resources necessary to achieve organizational goals.

            a)   The natural tendency of a manager is to negotiate for a less stringent measure of performance so as to avoid unfavorable variances from expectations.

        2)   Management may create slack by overestimating costs and underestimating revenues.

            a)   A firm may decrease slack by emphasizing the consideration of all variables, holding in-depth reviews during budget development, and allowing for flexibility in making additional budget changes.

        3)   The existence of slack can have both positive and negative effects on the budgeting process. The existence of slack can reduce the planning benefits of a budget since the budget may not be entirely accurate.

            a)   For example, a cash budget might show that $500,000 needs to be borrowed this month, whereas that amount is not really needed because managers were just being cautious.

            b)   Alternatively, the lack of slack may discourage managers from implementing new programs, or might cause managers to avoid routine maintenance when the budget does not show funds available in a particular period.

3.   **Time Frames for Budgets**

    a.   Each phase of the organization's planning cycle has its own budget with an appropriate **time frame**.

        1)   **Strategic** plans and budgets most concern senior managers and have time frames of up to 10 years or more.

        2)   **Intermediate** plans and budgets most concern middle managers and have time frames of up to 2 years.

        3)   **Operational** plans and budgets most concern lower-level managers and generally have time frames of 1 month to 1 year.

4.   **Effects of External Factors on the Budgeting Process**

    a.   Decisions about a firm's strategy, and in turn about its budget, are dependent upon **general economic conditions** and their expected trends as well as the availability of financial resources.

        1)   For instance, if the economy is entering a period of lower demand, a manufacturer will not project increased sales. If costs are not changeable, the company may budget losses for the short-term to hold on to market share.

    b.   **Industry situation** includes the company's current market share, governmental regulatory measures, the labor market, and the activities of competitors.

        1)   For instance, if input costs are rising in a firm's industry, the budget must reflect that reality; profit margins and cash flows will not be the same as in prior years. Also, a company in, or near, bankruptcy will face a different financial situation than would the market leader.

5.   **The Concept of Controllability**

    a.   Controllability is a key concept in the use of budgets and other standards to evaluate performance. Controllability is the extent to which a manager can influence activities and related revenues and costs.

    b.   Controllable costs are those that are under the discretion of a particular manager. Noncontrollable costs are those to which another level of the organization has committed, removing the manager's discretion.

    c.   Controllability can be difficult to isolate because few costs or revenues are under the sole influence of one manager. Also, separating the effects of current management's decisions from those of former management is difficult.

        1)   If responsibility exceeds the extent to which a manager can influence an activity, the result may be reduced morale, a decline in managerial effort, and poor performance.

        2)   The principle of controllability must be kept in mind when the budget is used as the basis for managerial evaluation.

6.   **Revisions to the Budget**

    a.   Often an organization will find that the assumptions under which the budget was prepared undergo significant change during the year. A policy must be in place to accommodate revisions to the budget resulting from these changes.

        1)   Accommodation of change is a key characteristic of successful budgeting. If such a policy is not in place, managers can come to believe they are being held to a budget that is no longer possible to achieve, and morale can suffer.

    b.   Information gained during the year as actual results and variances are reported can be used to help the company take corrective action. These steps make up a control loop:

        1)   Establishing standards of performance (the budget)
        2)   Measuring actual performance
        3)   Analyzing and comparing performance with standards
        4)   Devising and implementing corrective actions
        5)   Reviewing and revising the standards

Stop and review! You have completed the outline for this subunit. Study multiple-choice questions 6 through 12 beginning on page 191.

5.3 BUDGETING AND STANDARD COSTS

1.   **The Use of Cost Standards**

    a.   Standard costs are **predetermined expectations** about how much a unit of input, a unit of output, or a given activity should cost.

        1)   The use of standard costs in budgeting allows the standard-cost system to alert management when the actual costs of production differ significantly from the standard.

    b.   A standard cost is not just an average of past costs but an objectively determined estimate of what a cost should be. Standards may be based on accounting, engineering, or statistical quality control studies.

        1)   Because of the impact of fixed costs in most businesses, a standard costing system is usually not effective unless the company also has a flexible budgeting system (see item 2. in Study Unit 6, Subunit 3).

2. **Developing Standards**

    a. **Activity analysis** identifies, describes, and evaluates the activities that go into producing a particular output. Determining the resources and steps that go into the production process aids in the development of standard costs.

        1) Each operation requires its own unique set of inputs and preparations. Activity analysis describes what these inputs are and who performs these preparations.

            a) Inputs include the amounts and kinds of equipment, facilities, materials, and labor. Engineering analysis, cost accounting, time-and-motion study, and other approaches may be useful.

        2) **Historical data** may be used to set standards by firms that lack the resources to engage in the complex task of activity analysis.

    b. For **direct materials**, there is often a direct relationship between unit price and quality. In establishing its cost standards, a manufacturer must decide whether it will use an input that is

        1) Cheaper per unit but will ultimately result in higher consumption because of low quality, or

        2) Pricier but allows more efficient usage because of lower waste and spoilage.

    c. For **direct labor**, the complexity of the production process and the restrictions on pay scales imposed by union agreements have the most impact on formulating cost standards. Human resources also must be consulted to help project the costs of benefits.

3. **Theoretical vs. Practical Standards**

    a. **Ideal (theoretical) standards** are standard costs that are set for production under optimal conditions. For this reason, they are also called perfection or maximum efficiency standards.

        1) They are based on the work of the most skilled workers with no allowance for waste, spoilage, machine breakdowns, or other downtime.

        2) Often called "tight" standards, they can have positive behavioral implications if workers are motivated to strive for excellence. However, they are not widely used because they can have negative behavioral effects if the standards are perceived as impossible to attain.

        3) Ideal standards have been adopted by some companies that apply continuous improvement and other total quality management principles.

        4) Ideal standards are ordinarily replaced by currently attainable standards for cash budgeting, product costing, and budgeting departmental performance. Otherwise, accurate financial planning will be impossible.

    b. **Currently attainable (practical) standards** may be defined as the performance that is expected to be achieved by reasonably well-trained workers with an allowance for normal spoilage, waste, and downtime.

        1) An alternative interpretation is that practical standards represent possible but difficult-to-attain results.

4. **Authoritative vs. Participative Standard Setting**

    a. A purely **authoritative (top-down) approach** to standard setting has the advantage of ensuring total consistency across all functional areas. It is also far less complex and time-consuming than coordinating input from the middle and lower levels.

    b. **Participative (bottom-up)** standard setting uses input from middle- and lower-level employees.

        1) Participation encourages employees to have a sense of ownership of the output of the process. The result is an acceptance of, and commitment to, the goals expressed in the budget.

        2) An imposed budget is much less likely to foster this sense of commitment.

        3) Participation also enables employees to relate performance to rewards or penalties.

            a) A further advantage of participation is that it provides a broader information base. Middle- and lower-level managers are often far more informed about operational realities than senior managers.

        4) Disadvantages of participative standard setting include its cost in terms of time and money. In addition, the quality of participation is affected by the goals, values, beliefs, and expectations of those involved.

            a) A manager who expects his/her request to be reduced may inflate the amount.

            b) If a budget is to be used as a performance evaluator, a manager asked for an estimate may provide one that is easily attained.

Stop and review! You have completed the outline for this subunit. Study multiple-choice questions 13 through 16 beginning on page 194.

5.4 CORRELATION AND REGRESSION

1. **Forecasting Methods**

    a. Forecasts are the basis for business plans. Forecasts are used to project product demand, inventory levels, cash flow, etc.

        1) **Qualitative methods** of forecasting rely on the manager's experience and intuition.

        2) **Quantitative methods** use mathematical models and graphs.

            a) When some factor in the organization's environment is plotted on the x-axis, the technique is causal relationship forecasting.

            b) When time periods are plotted on the x-axis, the technique is time-series analysis.

2. **Correlation Analysis**

    a. Correlation analysis is the foundation of any quantitative method of forecasting.

        1) Correlation is the strength of the linear relationship between two variables, expressed mathematically in terms of the coefficient of correlation (r). It can be graphically depicted by plotting the values for the variables on a graph in the form of a scatter diagram.

            a) The value of r ranges from 1 (perfect direct relationship) to –1 (perfect inverse relationship). The more the scatter pattern resembles a straight line, the greater the absolute value of r.

b) **Perfect direct relationship (r = 1)**

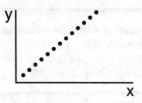

c) **Perfect inverse relationship (r = –1)**

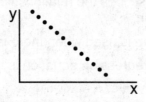

d) **Strong direct relationship (r = 0.7)**

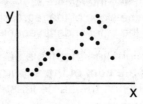

e) **No linear relationship (r = 0)**

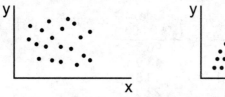 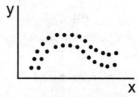

      i) Note from the right-hand graph of the pair above that a coefficient of correlation of zero does not mean there is no relationship at all between the two variables, only that what relationship they may have cannot be expressed as a linear equation.

2) The **coefficient of determination (r^2)**, or the coefficient of correlation squared, is a measure of how good the fit between the two variables is.

    a) Mathematically, the coefficient of determination is the proportion of the total variation in the dependent variable that is accounted for by the independent variable.

    b) EXAMPLE: A car dealership determines that new car sales are a function of disposable income with a coefficient of correlation of .8. This is equivalent to stating that 64% ($.8^2$) of the variation of new car sales from the average can be explained by changes in disposable income.

3.   Regression Analysis

 CMA candidates should be able to demonstrate an understanding of the measures associated with simple regression as well as calculate the result of the equation. They should also be able to identify when it is appropriate to use multiple regression. Therefore, candidates should memorize and fully understand the formulas for both simple and multiple regression analysis.

a.   Regression analysis, also called least-squares analysis, is the process of deriving the linear equation that describes the relationship between two variables with a nonzero coefficient of correlation.

1)   **Simple regression** is used when there is one independent variable.

a)   The simple regression equation is the algebraic formula for a straight line:

$$y = a + bx$$

Where: y = the dependent variable
a = the y intercept
b = the slope of the regression line
x = the independent variable

b)   The best straight line that fits a set of data points is derived using calculus to minimize the sum of the squares of the vertical distances of each point to the line (hence the name least-squares method).

c)   EXAMPLE: A firm has collected observations on advertising expenditures and annual sales.

Advertising ($000s)	Sales ($000,000s)
71	26.3
31	13.9
50	19.8
60	22.9
35	15.1

i)   Solving with the least-squares method reveals that expected sales equal $4.2 million plus 311.741 times the advertising expenditure.

y = $4,200,000 + 311.741x

ii)   The observations are graphed as follows:

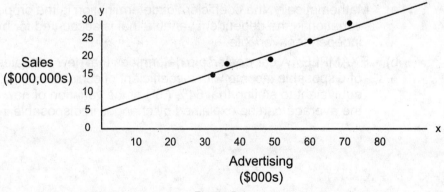

Figure 5-1

iii) The firm can now project the amount it will have to spend on advertising to generate $32,000,000 in sales.

$$y = \$4,200,000 + 311.741x$$
$$\$32,000,000 = \$4,200,000 + 311.741x$$
$$311.741x = \$27,800,000$$
$$x = \$89,177$$

2) Regression analysis is particularly valuable for budgeting and cost accounting purposes.

a) Regression analysis is almost a necessity for computing the fixed and variable portions of mixed costs for flexible budgeting. The y-axis intercept is the fixed portion and the slope of the regression line is the variable portion.

3) **Regression does not determine causality.**

a) Although x and y move together, the apparent relationship may be caused by some other factor. For instance, car wash sales volume and sunny weather are strongly correlated, but car wash sales do not cause sunny weather.

4) **Multiple regression** is used when there is more than one independent variable.

a) The example on the previous page relating advertising to sales is clearly unrealistic. Sales are dependent upon more than just advertising expenditures.

b) Multiple regression allows a firm to identify many factors (independent variables), and to weight each one according to its influence on the overall outcome.

$$y = a + b_1x_1 + b_2x_2 + b_3x_3 + b_4x_4 + etc.$$

5) **Assumptions** of the linear regression model.

a) The linear relationship established for x and y is only valid across the **relevant range**. The user must identify the relevant range and ensure that (s)he does not project the relationship beyond it.

b) Regression analysis assumes that **past relationships** can be validly projected into the future.

c) The distribution of y around the regression line is constant for different values of x, referred to as **homoscedasticity** or **constant variance**. This is known as the *ceteris paribus* assumption, or that all things must remain equal. Thus, a limitation of the regression method is that it can only be used when cost patterns remain unchanged from prior periods.

Stop and review! You have completed the outline for this subunit. Study multiple-choice questions 17 through 25 beginning on page 195.

5.5 LEARNING CURVE ANALYSIS

1. **Learning Curves**

   a. Learning curve analysis reflects the increased rate at which people perform tasks as they gain experience.

   1) The time required to perform a given task becomes progressively shorter during the early stages of production.

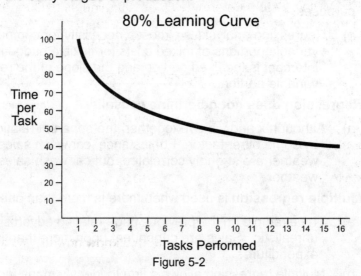

Figure 5-2

   2) The curve is usually expressed as a percentage of reduced time to complete a task for each doubling of cumulative production. In practice, the most common percentage used is 80%. However, on the exam, be prepared to see a variety of percentages.

   a) The following table illustrates this phenomenon for a product whose first unit takes 100 minutes to produce:

Cumulative Units Produced	70% Cumulative Average Time per Unit		80% Cumulative Average Time per Unit		90% Cumulative Average Time per Unit	
1	100		100		100	
2	70	(100 × 70%)	80	(100 × 80%)	90	(100 × 90%)
4	49	(70 × 70%)	64	(80 × 80%)	81	(90 × 90%)
8	34.3	(49 × 70%)	51.2	(64 × 80%)	72.9	(81 × 90%)
16	24.01	(34.3 × 70%)	40.96	(51.2 × 80%)	65.61	(72.9 × 90%)

   b) The time listed in the cumulative average time per unit column is an average of all the units produced up to that point. Note that with an 80% learning curve upon completion of the final batch (units 9 – 16), the average had come down to 40.96 minutes per unit. For it to reach this level from the 51.2 minutes it had reached at the end of the fourth batch (units 5 – 8), the average of the units in the fifth batch alone must have been 30.72 minutes [(40.96 minutes × 2) – 51.2 minutes].

   c) With more sophisticated quantitative techniques, a more accurate average can be calculated of the units within each "batch."

CMA candidates need to be alert as to the nature of the question being asked. Sometimes the question might ask, "What is the average time per unit after two units?" From the table above, you can see that the answer is 80. Alternatively, sometimes the question asks, "What is the time to produce the second unit?" The answer would be 60. Since the first unit took 100 minutes and the average for the two units is 80 minutes (a total of 160), then the second unit must have taken only 60 minutes.

2. **Application**

     a. **Two methods** of applying learning curve analysis are in common use.

         1) The **cumulative average-time learning model** projects the reduction in the cumulative average time it takes to complete a certain number of tasks.

         2) The **incremental unit-time learning model** projects the reduction in the incremental time it takes to complete the last task.

         3) EXAMPLE: A firm determines that 100 minutes of labor are required to complete one unit of product. Assuming an 80% learning curve, the following table illustrates the difference between the two methods.

Learning Curve 80% at Each Doubling		Cumulative Average-Time Model		Incremental Unit-Time Model	
(A)	(B) Cumulative Average Time per Unit	(A) × (B) Cumulative Total Time	Time Spent on Most Recent Unit	Σ(B) Incremental Unit Total Time	Σ (B) / (A) Average Time Spent on Most Recent Unit
Unit Produced					
1	100.00	100.00	100.00	100.00	100.00
2	80.00	160.00	60.00	180.00	90.00
3	70.21	210.63	50.63	250.21	83.40
4	64.00	256.00	45.37	314.21	78.55

           a) CMA candidates will not need to know how to calculate units within a batch. You should know how to calculate the learning curves for 1, 2, and 4 unit(s) produced.

         4) The difference between the two methods is clear in the way each calculates total time. Most CMA questions have historically used the cumulative-average-time method, and it is often called the "traditional" learning curve model.

3. **Limitations**

     a. The limitation of the learning curve in practice is the difficulty in knowing the shape of the learning curve.

         1) There is no question that the learning curve effect exists, but companies typically do not know what percentage they should use in calculations until after it is too late to use the information effectively. As a result, many companies simply assume an 80% learning curve and make decisions based on those results.

Stop and review! You have completed the outline for this subunit. Study multiple-choice questions 26 through 30 beginning on page 198.

5.6 TIME SERIES ANALYSIS

1. **Components**

     a. **Time series analysis** projects future trends based on past experience (for this reason, it is also called trend analysis). Changes in business activity over time may have several possible components.

         1) **Secular trend** is the long-term change in spite of short-term ups and downs.

         2) **Seasonal variations** are common in many businesses, most obviously retail, which experiences a large spike in activity around the winter holidays.

         3) **Cyclical fluctuations** are variations in the level of activity tied to the business cycle, i.e., activity in the overall economy.

         4) **Irregular or random variables** are the unexpected happenings that affect businesses (weather, strikes, fires, etc.).

2.   **Techniques**

    a.   There are three main techniques used in time series/trend analysis: simple moving average, weighted moving average, and exponential smoothing.

        1)   **Simple moving average** is appropriate in situations where the demand for a product is relatively stable and not subject to seasonal variations. It is calculated by summing the data points and dividing them by the number of time periods. This process is repeated for successive groups of time periods.

            a)   EXAMPLE: A convenience store with a fairly uniform sales history wants to project future gasoline sales. The store has determined that it needs 4 months of data to make a sound projection.

Simple Moving Average

Month	Sales	4-Month Cumulative Sales	Divided by: Number of Months	Equals: Next Month's Forecast	Error	Error %
September	$5,480					
October	5,550					
November	5,500					
December	5,520	$22,050	4	$5,513	$53	1.0%
January	5,460	22,030	4	5,508	58	1.1%
February	5,450	21,930	4	5,483	3	0.0%
March	5,480	21,910	4	5,478	(73)	(1.3%)
April	5,550	21,940	4	5,485	(105)	(1.9%)
May	5,590	22,070	4	5,518	(13)	(0.2%)
June	5,530	22,150	4	5,538	(33)	(0.6%)
July	5,570	22,240	4	5,560	50	0.9%
August	5,510	22,200	4	5,550	---	---

        2)   In a **weighted moving average**, each data point is assigned a weight indicating its relative importance in determining the outcome, and then the average is taken to calculate the next period's forecast.

            a)   Typically, more recent data is assigned a greater weight, but this method can also be used to remove seasonal fluctuations from the data.

            b)   EXAMPLE: The store's owners decide that weighting the months will give them better projections. Most recent month, 60%; 2 months ago, 20%; 3 months ago, 10%; 4 months ago, 10%. The results are calculated as follows:

Weighted Moving Average

Month	Sales	January Forecast		February Forecast		March Forecast		April Forecast		May Forecast		June Forecast	
September	$5,480	10%	$ 548										
October	5,550	10%	555	10%	$ 555								
November	5,500	20%	1,100	10%	550	10%	$ 550						
December	5,520	60%	3,312	20%	1,104	10%	552	10%	$ 552				
January	5,460	*P:	$5,515	60%	3,276	20%	1,092	10%	546	10%	$ 546		
February	5,450	**E:	$ 55	*P:	$5,485	60%	3,270	20%	1,090	10%	545	10%	$ 545
March	5,480		1.0%	**E:	$ 35	*P:	$5,464	60%	3,288	20%	1,096	10%	548
April	5,550				0.6%	**E:	$ (16)	*P:	$5,476	60%	3,330	20%	1,110
May	5,590						(0.3%)	**E:	$ (74)	*P:	$5,517	60%	3,354
June	5,530								(1.3%)	**E:	$ (73)	*P:	$5,557
July	5,570										(1.3%)	**E:	$ 27
August	5,510												0.5%

*P = Projected**E = Error

            c)   The smaller error percentages indicate improved forecasting.

3) **Exponential smoothing** is a popular technique for making projections because it requires less data be kept on hand than the moving average methods.

   a) **Step 1 – Develop some forecasts** using a more data-intensive method, such as one of the two moving average methods.

   b) **Step 2 – Set the smoothing factor** (alpha) between 0 and 1. The closer it is set to 1, the more weight is put on recent data.

      i) This feature of exponential smoothing makes it especially appropriate for responding to trends. For instance, if sales are steadily increasing, the smoothing factor can be set near 1 to give the more recent (i.e., higher) data more weight in the calculation.

   c) **Step 3 – Calculate the next period's forecast.** Each forecast is the sum of the following two components:

      i) The current period's actual results multiplied by the smoothing factor, and

      ii) The current period's forecast multiplied by the smoothing factor's complement.

   d) The **general formula** for exponential smoothing is therefore

$$F_t = (\alpha)x_{t-1} + (1 - \alpha)F_{t-1}$$

Where: F = the forecast for a period
        t = the time period
        α = the smoothing factor $(0 < \alpha < 1)$
        x = the actual result for a period

   e) **EXAMPLE:** A convenience store is switching to exponential smoothing from weighted moving average to project its unit sales for each month. Under the old method, $6,000 was forecast for September.

Month	Smoothing Factor	Actual Result	Times: Actual Result Smoothed	Smoothing Factor Complement	What Was Forecast	Times: Forecast Smoothed	Next Month Forecast	Error	Error %
September	0.75	$5,480	$4,110	0.25	$6,000	$1,500	$5,610	$ 60	1.1%
October	0.75	5,550	4,163	0.25	5,610	1,403	5,566	66	1.2%
November	0.75	5,500	4,125	0.25	5,565	1,391	5,516	(4)	(0.0%)
December	0.75	5,520	4,140	0.25	5,516	1,379	5,519	59	1.1%
January	0.75	5,460	4,095	0.25	5,519	1,380	5,475	25	0.5%
February	0.75	5,450	4,088	0.25	5,475	1,369	5,457	(23)	(0.4%)
March	0.75	5,480	4,110	0.25	5,456	1,364	5,474	(76)	(1.4%)
April	0.75	5,550	4,163	0.25	5,474	1,369	5,532	(58)	(1.0%)
May	0.75	5,590	4,193	0.25	5,531	1,383	5,576	46	0.8%
June	0.75	5,530	4,148	0.25	5,575	1,394	5,542	(28)	(0.5%)
July	0.75	5,570	4,178	0.25	5,541	1,385	5,563	53	1.0%
August	0.75	5,510	4,133	0.25	5,563	1,391	5,524	--	--

Stop and review! You have completed the outline for this subunit. Study multiple-choice questions 31 through 33 beginning on page 200.

5.7 EXPECTED VALUE

1. **Expected Value**

   a. Expected value is a means of associating a dollar amount with each of the possible outcomes of a probability distribution.

      1) The outcome yielding the highest expected monetary value (which may or may not be the most likely one) is the optimal alternative.

         a) The **decision** alternative is under the manager's control.

         b) The **state of nature** is the future event whose outcome the manager is attempting to predict.

         c) The **payoff** is the financial result of the combination of the manager's decision and the actual state of nature.

      2) The expected value of an event is calculated by multiplying the probability of each outcome by its payoff and summing the products.

         a) EXAMPLE: An investor is considering the purchase of two identically priced pieces of property. The value of the properties will change if a road, currently planned by the state, is built.

            i)   The following are estimates that road construction will occur:

Future State of Nature (SN)	Event	Probability
SN 1	No road is ever built.	.1
SN 2	A road is built this year.	.2
SN 3	A road is built more than 1 year from now.	.7

            ii) The following are estimates of the values of the properties under each of the three possible events:

Property	SN 1	SN 2	SN 3
Bivens Tract	$10,000	$40,000	$35,000
Newnan Tract	$20,000	$50,000	$30,000

            iii) The expected value of each property is determined by multiplying the probability of each state of nature by the value under that state of nature and adding all of the products.

		Expected Value
Bivens Tract:	.1($10,000) + .2($40,000) + .7($35,000) =	**$33,500**
Newnan Tract:	.1($20,000) + .2($50,000) + .7($30,000)	**$33,000**

            Thus, Bivens Tract is the better investment.

            iv) A calculation such as this is often referred to as a payoff table.

      3) The difficult aspect of constructing a payoff table is the determination of all possible outcomes of decisions and their probabilities. Thus, a probability distribution must be established.

         a) The assigned probabilities may reflect prior experience with similar decisions, the results of research, or highly subjective estimates.

4) The expected value criterion is likely to be adopted by a decision maker who is risk neutral. However, other circumstances may cause the decision maker to be risk averse or even risk seeking.

a) EXAMPLE: A dealer in luxury yachts may order 0, 1, or 2 yachts for this season's inventory.

i) The dealer projects demand for the season as follows:

Demand	Probability
0 yachts	10%
1 yacht	50%
2 yachts	40%

ii) The cost of carrying each excess yacht is $50,000, and the gain for each yacht sold is $200,000. The profit or loss resulting from each combination of decision and outcome is thus as follows:

Decision	States of Nature			Expected Value Without Perfect Info. Totals
	Demand = 0	Demand = 1	Demand = 2	
Stock 0 yachts	$ 0	$ 0	$ 0	$ 0
Stock 1 yacht	(50,000)	200,000	200,000	175,000
Stock 2 yachts	(100,000)	150,000	400,000	225,000

b) In this example, a risk-averse decision maker may not wish to accept the risk of losing $100,000 by ordering two yachts.

5) The benefit of expected value analysis is that it allows a manager to apply scientific management techniques to applications that would otherwise be guesswork.

a) Although exact probabilities may not be known, the use of expected value analysis forces managers to evaluate decisions in a more organized manner. At the least, managers are forced to think of all of the possibilities that could happen with each decision.

6) A criticism of expected value is that it is based on repetitive trials, whereas in reality, most business decisions involve only one trial.

a) EXAMPLE: A company wishes to launch a communications satellite.

i) The probability of launch failure is .2, and the value of the satellite if the launch fails is $0. The probability of a successful launch is .8, and the value of the satellite would then be $25,000,000. The expected value is calculated as follows:

.2($0) + .8($25,000,000) = $20,000,000

ii) But $20,000,000 is not a possible value for a single satellite; either it flies for $25,000,000 or it crashes for $0.

2.   **Perfect Information**

    a.   Perfect information is the certain knowledge of which state of nature will occur.

        1)   The **expected value of perfect information (EVPI)** is the additional expected value that could be obtained if a decision maker knew ahead of time which state of nature would occur.

            a)   EXAMPLE: The yacht dealer on the previous page would maximize profits if (s)he were able to determine exactly what all potential customers intended to do for the season.

                i)   The profit that could be obtained with this perfect knowledge of the market is calculated as follows:

States of Nature	Probability	Best Decision Alternative	Payoff	Expected Value
Demand = 0	0.1	0 Yachts	$ 0	$ 0
Demand = 1	0.5	1 Yacht	200,000	100,000
Demand = 2	0.4	2 Yachts	400,000	160,000
				$260,000

$$(.1 \times \$0) + (.5 \times \$200,000) + (.4 \times \$400,000) = \$260,000$$

                ii)   The difference between this amount and the best choice without perfect information is the EVPI.

Expected value with perfect information	$260,000
Expected value without perfect information	(225,000)
Expected value of perfect information (EVPI)	$ 35,000

                iii)   The dealer is therefore not willing to pay more than $35,000 for perfect information about future demand.

Stop and review! You have completed the outline for this subunit. Study multiple-choice questions 34 through 39 beginning on page 201.

5.8 SENSITIVITY ANALYSIS

1.   Sensitivity analysis reveals how sensitive expected value calculations are to the accuracy of the initial estimates.

    a.   Sensitivity analysis is thus useful in determining whether expending additional resources to obtain better forecasts is justified.

        1)   If a change in the probabilities assigned to the various states of nature results in large changes in the expected values, the decision maker is justified in expending more effort to make better predictions about the outcomes.

        2)   The benefit of sensitivity analysis is that managers can see the effect of changed assumptions on the final objective.

            a)   For example, in a capital budgeting situation, a proposed investment might promise a return of $10,000 per year and a rate of return of 15%. But that $10,000 is based on an estimate. What management needs to know is how acceptable would the investment be if the return was only $6,000 per year.

b.   EXAMPLE: The yacht dealer in the expected value computation illustrated on the previous page is testing different combinations of probabilities. All three of the scenarios depicted here yield the same decision (stock two yachts for the season):

Decision Alternatives	States of Nature	Payoff	Original		First Alternative		Second Alternative	
			Probability	Expected Value	Probability	Expected Value	Probability	Expected Value
Stock	Demand = 0	$ 0	0.1	$ 0	0.5	$ 0	0.333	$ 0
0 Yachts	Demand = 1	0	0.5	0	0.1	0	0.333	0
	Demand = 2	0	0.4	0	0.4	0	0.333	0
				$ 0		$ 0		$ 0
Stock	Demand = 0	(50,000)	0.1	(5,000)	0.5	(25,000)	0.333	(16,650)
1 Yacht	Demand = 1	200,000	0.5	100,000	0.1	20,000	0.333	66,600
	Demand = 2	200,000	0.4	80,000	0.4	80,000	0.333	66,600
				$175,000		$ 75,000		$116,550
Stock	Demand = 0	(100,000)	0.1	(10,000)	0.5	(50,000)	0.333	(33,300)
2 Yachts	Demand = 1	150,000	0.5	75,000	0.1	15,000	0.333	49,950
	Demand = 2	400,000	0.4	160,000	0.4	160,000	0.333	133,200
				$225,000		$125,000		$149,850

1)   However, the following combination indicates that only one yacht should be stocked:

Decision Alternatives	States of Nature	Payoff	Third Alternative	
			Probability	Expected Value
Stock	Demand = 0	$ 0	0.1	$ 0
0 Yachts	Demand = 1	0	0.8	0
	Demand = 2	0	0.1	0
				$ 0
Stock	Demand = 0	(50,000)	0.1	(5,000)
1 Yacht	Demand = 1	200,000	0.8	160,000
	Demand = 2	200,000	0.1	20,000
				$175,000
Stock	Demand = 0	(100,000)	0.1	(10,000)
2 Yachts	Demand = 1	150,000	0.8	120,000
	Demand = 2	400,000	0.1	40,000
				$150,000

2)   Clearly, the more accurately the dealer is able to anticipate demand, the more profit (s)he will make. In this case, the dealer considers it worthwhile to expend further resources gathering more data about market conditions for yachts.

c.   A trial-and-error method inherent in sensitivity analysis is obviously greatly facilitated by the use of computer software.

d.   A major use of sensitivity analysis is in capital budgeting, where small changes in prevailing interest rates or payoff amounts can make a very great difference in the profitability of a project.

Stop and review! You have completed the outline for this subunit. Study multiple-choice questions 40 and 41 on page 204.

5.9 CORE CONCEPTS

Roles of Budgets

- A **budget** is a planning tool, a control tool, a motivational tool, and a communication tool. A budget helps communicate to all employees what goals the firm is trying to accomplish. Without a master budget, each department might think the firm has different goals.
- The planning process **coordinates the efficient allocation** of organizational resources.
- **The budget is a formal quantification of management's plans.** A budget lays out in specific terms an organization's expectations about the consumption of resources and the resulting outcomes.
- The budget lays out the **specific revenue targets** and expense limitations for each functional area and department of the organization on a month-by-month basis. A budget cannot simply be a lump-sum total for a year. **Incremental goals** must be achieved each month or week. This is especially true in seasonal businesses such as agricultural supply.

Budgeting Process

- Characteristics of a successful budgeting process include sufficient lead time, a budget manual, and buy-in at all levels.
- **Participation** in the budget preparation process is up and down the organization.
- **Controllability** is the extent to which a manager can influence activities and related revenues and costs. Controllable costs are those that are under the discretion of a particular manager. Noncontrollable costs are those to which another level of the organization has committed, removing the manager's discretion. The principle of controllability must be kept in mind when the budget is used as the basis for managerial evaluation.
- Often an organization will find that the assumptions under which the budget was prepared undergo **significant change** during the year. A policy must be in place to accommodate revisions to the budget resulting from these changes.

Budgeting and Standard Costs

- **Standard costs** are predetermined expectations about how much a unit of input, a unit of output, or a given activity should cost. The use of standard costs in budgeting allows the standard-cost system to alert management when the actual costs of production differ significantly from the standard.

  - A purely **authoritative (top-down)** approach to standard setting has the advantage of ensuring total consistency across all functional areas. It is also far less complex and time-consuming than coordinating input from the middle and lower levels. **Participative (bottom-up)** standard setting uses input from middle- and lower-level employees. Participation encourages employees to have a sense of ownership of the output of the process. The result is an acceptance of, and commitment to, the goals expressed in the budget.

Forecasting Analysis

- **Forecasts** are the basis for business plans. Forecasts are used to project product demand, inventory levels, cash flow, etc. **Qualitative methods** of forecasting rely on the manager's experience and intuition. **Quantitative methods** use mathematical models and graphs.
- **Correlation analysis** is the foundation of any quantitative method of forecasting. Correlation is the strength of the **linear relationship** between two variables, expressed mathematically in terms of the coefficient of correlation (r). It can be graphically depicted by plotting the values for the variables on a graph in the form of a scatter diagram. The value of r ranges from 1 (perfect direct relationship) to −1 (perfect inverse relationship).

- The **coefficient of determination (r^2)**, or the coefficient of correlation squared, is a measure of how good the fit is between the two variables. Mathematically, the coefficient of determination is the proportion of the total variation in the dependent variable that is accounted for by the independent variable.
- **Regression analysis**, also called least-squares analysis, is the process of deriving the linear equation that describes the relationship between two variables with a nonzero coefficient of correlation. Simple regression is used when there is one independent variable. The simple regression equation is, obviously, the algebraic formula for a straight line: $y = a + bx$. Regression analysis is particularly valuable for budgeting and cost accounting purposes.

Learning Curve Analysis

- **Learning curve analysis** reflects the increased rate at which people perform tasks as they gain experience. The time required to perform a given task becomes progressively shorter during the early stages of production. The curve is usually expressed as a percentage of reduced time to complete a task for each doubling of cumulative production. The most common percentage used in practice is 80%. Two methods of applying learning curve analysis are in common use:

  - The **cumulative average-time learning model** projects the reduction in the cumulative average time it takes to complete a certain number of tasks. The time spent on the most recent unit is treated as if it were the average for all units so far.
  - The **incremental unit-time learning model** projects the reduction in the incremental time it takes to complete the last task. The time spent on all units so far is accumulated and the average taken.

Time Series Analysis

- **Time series analysis** projects future trends based on past experience (for this reason, it is also called trend analysis). Time series/trend analysis encompasses three main techniques:

  - **Simple moving average** is appropriate when, for instance, the demand for a product is relatively stable and not subject to seasonal variations. The data points are summed and divided by the number of time periods. This process is repeated for successive groups of time periods.
  - **Weighted moving average** allows a firm to give each data point a weight indicating its relative importance in determining the outcome.
  - **Exponential smoothing** is a widespread technique for making projections because it requires less data be kept on hand than the moving average methods.

    - Step 1 – Develop some forecasts using a more data-intensive method, such as one of the two moving average methods.
    - Step 2 – Set the smoothing factor (alpha) between 0 and 1. The closer it is set to 1, the more weight is put on recent data.
    - Step 3 – Calculate the next period's forecast. Each forecast is the sum of the current period's actual results multiplied by the smoothing factor, and the current period's forecast multiplied by the smoothing factor's complement.

Expected Value

- **Expected value** is a means of associating a **dollar amount** with each of the possible outcomes of a probability distribution. The outcome yielding the highest expected value (which may or may not be the most likely one) is the optimal alternative. The expected value of an event is calculated by multiplying the probability of each outcome by its payoff and summing the products. A calculation such as this is often referred to as a **payoff table**. A criticism of expected value is that it is based on repetitive trials, whereas many business decisions involve only one trial.

Sensitivity Analysis

- **Sensitivity analysis** reveals how sensitive expected value calculations are to the accuracy of the initial estimates. Sensitivity analysis is thus useful in determining whether expending additional resources to obtain better forecasts is justified. If a change in the probabilities assigned to the various states of nature results in large changes in the expected values, the decision maker is justified in expending more effort to make better predictions about the outcomes.

QUESTIONS

5.1 Roles of Budgets

1. All of the following are advantages of the use of budgets in a management control system **except** that budgets

    A. Force management planning.

    B. Provide performance criteria.

    C. Promote communication and coordination within the organization.

    D. Limit unauthorized expenditures.

Answer (D) is correct. *(CMA, adapted)*
    REQUIRED: The item that is not an advantage of the use of budgets in a management control system.
    DISCUSSION: Budgets serve many roles. They force management to plan ahead, communicate organizational goals throughout the organization, and provide criteria for future performance evaluations.
    Answer (A) is incorrect. Forcing management planning is an advantage of using budgets. Answer (B) is incorrect. Providing performance criteria is an advantage of using budgets. Answer (C) is incorrect. Promoting communication and coordination within the organization is an advantage of using budgets.

2. In the budgeting and planning process for a firm, which one of the following should be completed first?

    A. Sales budget.

    B. Financial budget.

    C. Cost management plan.

    D. Strategic plan.

Answer (D) is correct. *(CMA, adapted)*
    REQUIRED: The phase of the planning and budgeting process completed first.
    DISCUSSION: An organization must complete its strategic plan before any specific budgeting can begin. The strategic plan lays out the means by which a firm expects to fulfill its stated mission.
    Answer (A) is incorrect. The sales budget cannot be started until the strategic plan is finished. Answer (B) is incorrect. The financial budget is a cluster of budgets that cannot be started until the cluster of budgets referred to as the operating budget is finished. Answer (C) is incorrect. A cost management plan is independent of the firm's stated budget.

3. Each organization plans and budgets its operations for slightly different reasons. Which one of the following is **not** a significant reason for planning?

    A. Providing a basis for controlling operations.

    B. Forcing managers to consider expected future trends and conditions.

    C. Ensuring profitable operations.

    D. Checking progress toward the objectives of the organization.

Answer (C) is correct. *(CMA, adapted)*
    REQUIRED: The item that is not a significant reason for planning.
    DISCUSSION: This question is apparently directed toward budgeting. A budget is a realistic plan for the future that is expressed in quantitative terms. It is a planning, control, motivational, and communications tool. A budget promotes goal congruence and coordination among operating units. Unfortunately, a budget does not ensure profitable operations.
    Answer (A) is incorrect. Control of operations is a goal of planning. Answer (B) is incorrect. Forcing managers to consider expected future trends and conditions is a goal of planning. Answer (D) is incorrect. Checking progress toward objectives is a goal of planning.

4. The budget that describes the long-term position, goals, and objectives of an entity within its environment is the

A. Capital budget.

B. Operating budget.

C. Cash management budget.

D. Strategic budget.

Answer (D) is correct. *(CMA, adapted)*
REQUIRED: The budget that describes the long-term position, goals, and objectives of an entity.
DISCUSSION: Strategic budgeting is a form of long-range planning based on identifying and specifying organizational goals and objectives. The strengths and weaknesses of the organization are evaluated and risk levels are assessed. The influences of environmental factors are forecast to derive the best strategy for reaching the organization's objectives.
Answer (A) is incorrect. Capital budgeting involves evaluating specific long-term investment decisions. Answer (B) is incorrect. The operating budget is a short-range management tool. Answer (C) is incorrect. Cash management is a short-range consideration related to liquidity.

5. Which one of the following best describes the role of top management in the budgeting process? Top management

A. Should be involved only in the approval process.

B. Lacks the detailed knowledge of the daily operations and should limit their involvement.

C. Needs to be involved, including using the budget process to communicate goals.

D. Needs to separate the budgeting process and the business planning process into two separate processes.

Answer (C) is correct. *(CMA, adapted)*
REQUIRED: The best description of top management's role in the budgeting process.
DISCUSSION: Among other things, the budget is a tool by which management can communicate goals to lower-level employees. It is also a tool for motivating employees to reach those goals. For the budget to function in these communication and motivating roles, top management must be involved in the process. This involvement does not extend to dictating the exact numerical contents of the budget since top management lacks a detailed knowledge of daily operations.
Answer (A) is incorrect. Top managers can use the budget for motivational and communication purposes; they should do more than merely sign off on the finished document. Answer (B) is incorrect. Top managers should be involved in the budget process even though they lack detailed knowledge of daily operations; the budget can still communicate company objectives and goals. Answer (D) is incorrect. The budget process is a part of the overall planning process.

5.2 The Budgeting Process

6. A planning calendar in budgeting is the

A. Calendar period covered by the budget.

B. Schedule of activities for the development and adoption of the budget.

C. Calendar period covered by the annual budget and the long-range plan.

D. Sales forecast by months in the annual budget period.

Answer (B) is correct. *(CMA, adapted)*
REQUIRED: The definition of a budget planning calendar.
DISCUSSION: The budget planning calendar is the schedule of activities for the development and adoption of the budget. It should include a list of dates indicating when specific information is to be provided by each information source to others. The preparation of a master budget usually takes several months. For instance, many firms start the budget for the next calendar year some time in September in hopes of having it completed by December 1. Because all of the individual departmental budgets are based on forecasts prepared by others and the budgets of other departments, it is essential to have a planning calendar to ensure the proper integration of the entire process.
Answer (A) is incorrect. The period covered by the budget precedes the events in the planning calendar. Answer (C) is incorrect. The period covered by the budget precedes the events in the planning calendar. Answer (D) is incorrect. The planning calendar is not associated with sales.

7. A budget manual, which enhances the operation of a budget system, is most likely to include

   A. A chart of accounts.

   B. Distribution instructions for budget schedules.

   C. Employee hiring policies.

   D. Documentation of the accounting system software.

Answer (B) is correct. *(CMA, adapted)*
   REQUIRED: The item normally included in a budget manual.
   DISCUSSION: A budget manual describes how a budget is to be prepared. Items usually included in a budget manual are a planning calendar and distribution instructions for all budget schedules. Distribution instructions are important because, once a schedule is prepared, other departments within the organization will use the schedule to prepare their own budgets. Without distribution instructions, someone who needs a particular schedule may be overlooked.
   Answer (A) is incorrect. A chart of accounts is included in the accounting manual. Answer (C) is incorrect. Employee hiring policies are not needed for budget preparation. They are already available in the human resources manual. Answer (D) is incorrect. Software documentation is not needed in the budget preparation process.

8. In developing the budget for the next year, which one of the following approaches would produce the greatest amount of positive motivation and goal congruence?

   A. Permit the divisional manager to develop the goal for the division that in the manager's view will generate the greatest amount of profits.

   B. Have senior management develop the overall goals and permit the divisional manager to determine how these goals will be met.

   C. Have the divisional and senior management jointly develop goals and objectives while constructing the corporation's overall plan of operation.

   D. Have the divisional and senior management jointly develop goals and the divisional manager develop the implementation plan.

Answer (D) is correct. *(CMA, adapted)*
   REQUIRED: The item that would produce the greatest amount of positive motivation and goal congruence.
   DISCUSSION: Joint development of goals is more conducive to motivation, as is allowing divisional managers to develop the implementation plan. Goal congruence is enhanced when senior management is involved in the budgeting process along with division managers.
   Answer (A) is incorrect. Using division managers to develop their goals does nothing for goal congruence. Answer (B) is incorrect. Having senior management set goals would not be as conducive to motivation as would having input from divisions. Answer (C) is incorrect. Senior management may not be in a position to develop an implementation plan.

9. Which one of the following is **not** an advantage of a participatory budgeting process?

   A. Coordination between departments.

   B. Communication between departments.

   C. Goal congruence.

   D. Control of uncertainties.

Answer (D) is correct. *(CMA, adapted)*
   REQUIRED: The item that is not an advantage of a participatory budgeting process.
   DISCUSSION: Uncertainties can be prepared for, but they cannot be subjected to human control through any budget process.
   Answer (A) is incorrect. Participatory budgeting involves extensive coordination between departments. Answer (B) is incorrect. Participatory budgeting involves extensive communication between departments. Answer (C) is incorrect. Goal congruence is one of the advantages of participatory budgeting.

10. Which one of the following statements concerning approaches for the budget development process is correct?

A. The top-down approach to budgeting will not ensure adherence to strategic organizational goals.

B. To prevent ambiguity, once departmental budgeted goals have been developed, they should remain fixed even if the sales forecast upon which they are based proves to be wrong in the middle of the fiscal year.

C. With the information technology available, the role of budgets as an organizational communication device has declined.

D. Since department managers have the most detailed knowledge about organizational operations, they should use this information as the building blocks of the operating budget.

Answer (D) is correct. *(CMA, adapted)*
REQUIRED: The correct statement concerning the budget development process.
DISCUSSION: Since department managers have the most detailed knowledge about organizational operations, they should use this information as the building blocks of the operating budget.
Answer (A) is incorrect. While a top-down approach can help make strategic goals more consistent, it cannot ensure adherence. Answer (B) is incorrect. Any budget should be adapted to changing circumstances. Answer (C) is incorrect. Information technology makes budgeting easier, not less relevant as a means of organizational communication.

11. Rock Industries has four divisions. In the quest to develop a more achievable budget for the coming year, the chief executive officer has elected to develop the company's budget by using a decentralized bottom-up budget approach. Chip Jarrett is production manager in one of the divisions. Jarrett's involvement in the budget process this year will probably

A. Be negligible.

B. Require development of a production budget that is forwarded to the Budget Department.

C. Require development of a production budget after receiving the division's projected sales forecast.

D. Require development of a production budget based on the prior year's manufacturing activity.

Answer (C) is correct. *(MA 0408 2-011)*
REQUIRED: The effect on Jarrett's involvement in the budget process.
DISCUSSION: Management of the division is responsible for setting the sales forecast. As production manager, Jarrett has the responsibility of ensuring the products are ready on schedule and in the right quantities.
Answer (A) is incorrect. The production manager must be involved in the budget process. Answer (B) is incorrect. A production manager cannot develop a budget for production until (s)he has been told what the sales forecast is. Answer (D) is incorrect. Current year projections are relevant to a budget, not prior year activity.

12. When developing a budget, an external factor to consider in the planning process is

A. A change to a decentralized management system.

B. The implementation of a new bonus program.

C. New product development.

D. The merger of two competitors.

Answer (D) is correct. *(CMA, adapted)*
REQUIRED: The external factor that should be considered during the budget planning process.
DISCUSSION: Several planning assumptions should be made at the beginning of the budget process. Some of these assumptions are internal factors; others are external to the company. External factors include general economic conditions and their expected trend, governmental regulatory measures, the labor market in the locale of the company's facilities, and activities of competitors, including the effects of mergers.
Answer (A) is incorrect. Changes in management is an internal factor. Answer (B) is incorrect. Employee compensation is an internal factor. Answer (C) is incorrect. A new product line is an internal factor.

5.3 Budgeting and Standard Costs

13. Jura Corporation is developing standards for the next year. Currently XZ-26, one of the material components, is being purchased for $36.45 per unit. It is expected that the component's cost will increase by approximately 10% next year and the price could range from $38.75 to $44.18 per unit, depending on the quantity purchased. The appropriate standard for XZ-26 for next year should be set at the

    A. Current actual cost plus the forecasted 10% price increase.

    B. Lowest purchase price in the anticipated range to keep pressure on purchasing to always buy in the lowest price range.

    C. Highest price in the anticipated range to ensure that there are only favorable purchase price variances.

    D. Price agreed upon by the purchasing manager and the appropriate level of company management.

Answer (D) is correct. *(CMA, adapted)*
REQUIRED: The appropriate standard for XZ-26 for next year.
DISCUSSION: Standard prices are designed for internal performance measurement. Standards should be attainable, but not so easily as to not provide motivation. Management should decide its objectives and set a standard that will achieve that objective when the standard is met. For example, the lowest price might not be selected if the company is using a JIT system, for which the primary objective is the minimization of inventories.
Answer (A) is incorrect. The actual cost could be more or less depending in the quantity purchased. Answer (B) is incorrect. The lowest price may not always be in the company's best interests if the quantity required to obtain the lowest price would lead to much higher carrying costs. Answer (C) is incorrect. Standards should be set tightly enough to provide motivation to purchasing management.

14. After performing a thorough study of Michigan Company's operations, an independent consultant determined that the firm's labor standards were probably too tight. Which one of the following facts would be inconsistent with the consultant's conclusion?

    A. A review of performance reports revealed the presence of many unfavorable efficiency variances.

    B. Michigan's budgeting process was well-defined and based on a bottom-up philosophy.

    C. Management noted that minimal incentive bonuses have been paid in recent periods.

    D. Production supervisors found several significant fluctuations in manufacturing volume, with short-term increases on output being followed by rapid, sustained declines.

Answer (B) is correct. *(CMA, adapted)*
REQUIRED: The fact inconsistent with the conclusion that the firm's labor standards were probably too tight.
DISCUSSION: It is highly unlikely that workers familiar with their own processes would set too-tight standards.
Answer (A) is incorrect. Many unfavorable efficiency variances would be an indicator of too-tight standards. Answer (C) is incorrect. The widespread failure for expected bonuses to be earned would be an indicator of too-tight standards. Answer (D) is incorrect. The situation described is indicative of rush jobs being too common, which is a result of poor production planning, not tight labor standards.

15. When compared with ideal standards, practical standards

    A. Produce lower per-unit product costs.

    B. Result in a less desirable basis for the development of budgets.

    C. Incorporate very generous allowance for spoilage and worker inefficiencies.

    D. Serve as a better motivating target for manufacturing personnel.

Answer (D) is correct. *(CMA, adapted)*
REQUIRED: The truth about practical standards when compared with ideal standards.
DISCUSSION: Practical standards, also called attainable standards, are more likely to meet with worker acceptance than standards based on an unachievable ideal.
Answer (A) is incorrect. The effect of one type of standard over another cannot guarantee lower costs. Answer (B) is incorrect. Practical standards are more appropriate in most cases than ideal standards in the development of budgets. Answer (C) is incorrect. An acceptance of high levels of spoilage and worker inefficiencies cannot be overcome through the use of standards.

16. Diana Stinson, Cherry Valley, Inc.'s factory manager, had lost her patience. Six months ago, she appointed a team from the production and service departments to finalize the allocation of costs and setting of standard costs. They were still feuding, so she hired Brennan and Rose, a large consulting firm, to resolve the matter.

All of the following are potential consequences of having the standards set by Brennan and Rose **except** that

    A. Brennan and Rose may not fully understand Cherry Valley's manufacturing process, resulting in suboptimal performance.

    B. Employees could react negatively since they did not participate in setting the standards.

    C. There could be dissatisfaction if the standards contain costs that are not controllable by the unit held responsible.

    D. The standards may appear to lack management support.

Answer (D) is correct. *(CMA, adapted)*
REQUIRED: What is not a potential consequence of having standards set by Brennan and Rose.
DISCUSSION: Of the choices listed, this one is not a potential consequence of having an outside consultant set standards. Since management did the hiring, the consultant's work product would naturally appear to have management support.
Answer (A) is incorrect. Brennan and Rose may not fully understand Cherry Valley's manufacturing process, resulting in suboptimal performance. Answer (B) is incorrect. Employees could react negatively since they did not participate in setting the standards. Answer (C) is incorrect. There could be dissatisfaction if the standards contain costs that are not controllable by the unit held responsible.

5.4 Correlation and Regression

17. Automite Company is an automobile replacement parts dealer in a large metropolitan community. Automite is preparing its sales forecast for the coming year. Data regarding both Automite's and industry sales of replacement parts as well as both the used and new automobile sales in the community for the last 10 years have been accumulated. If Automite wants to determine whether its sales of replacement parts are dependent upon the industry sales of replacement parts or upon the sales of used and new automobiles, the company should employ

    A. Simulation techniques.

    B. Correlation and regression analysis.

    C. Statistical sampling.

    D. Time series analysis.

Answer (B) is correct. *(CMA, adapted)*
REQUIRED: The technique to determine the variable to which sales are related.
DISCUSSION: Correlation and regression analysis can be used to determine whether a relationship exists among two or more variables. The degree of that relationship is assessed by means of correlation analysis. Thus, regressing sales (the dependent variable) on both sales of replacement parts and sales of automobiles (independent variables) determines the extent of the dependence.
Answer (A) is incorrect. Simulation is a means of experimenting with logical or mathematical models using a computer. Answer (C) is incorrect. Statistical sampling is a means of choosing and analyzing a sample to estimate population characteristics. Answer (D) is incorrect. Time series or trend analysis regresses the dependent variable on time (the independent variable).

18. A company has accumulated data for the last 24 months in order to determine if there is an independent variable that could be used to estimate shipping costs. Three possible independent variables being considered are packages shipped, miles shipped, and pounds shipped. The quantitative technique that should be used to determine whether any of these independent variables might provide a good estimate for shipping costs is

    A. Flexible budgeting.

    B. Linear programming.

    C. Linear regression.

    D. Variable costing.

Answer (C) is correct. *(CMA, adapted)*
REQUIRED: The quantitative technique that should be used to determine whether any of those independent variables might provide a good estimate for shipping costs.
DISCUSSION: Regression analysis, also called least-squares analysis, is the process of deriving the linear equation that describes the relationship between two (or more) variables with a nonzero coefficient of correlation.
Answer (A) is incorrect. Flexible budgeting is the calculation of the quantity and cost of inputs that should have been consumed given the achieved level of production. Answer (B) is incorrect. Linear programming is a mathematical technique used to optimize a linear function subject to certain constraints. Answer (D) is incorrect. Variable costing is a costing technique that treats only variable manufacturing costs as product costs.

19. The correlation coefficient that indicates the weakest linear association between two variables is

A. −0.73

B. −0.11

C. 0.12

D. 0.35

Answer (B) is correct. *(CMA, adapted)*
REQUIRED: The correlation coefficient that indicates the weakest linear association between two variables.
DISCUSSION: The correlation coefficient can vary from −1 to +1. A −1 relationship indicates a perfect negative correlation, and a +1 relationship indicates a perfect positive correlation. A zero correlation coefficient would indicate no linear association between the variables. Thus, the correlation coefficient that is nearest to zero indicates the weakest linear association. Of the options given in the question, the correlation coefficient that is nearest to zero is −0.11.
Answer (A) is incorrect. This figure signifies a strong negative correlation. Answer (C) is incorrect. This figure indicates a slightly stronger correlation than the weakest linear association. Answer (D) is incorrect. This figure indicates a considerably stronger correlation.

20. Correlation is a term frequently used in conjunction with regression analysis and is measured by the value of the coefficient of correlation, r. The best explanation of the value r is that it

A. Is always positive.

B. Interprets variances in terms of the independent variable.

C. Ranges in size from negative infinity to positive infinity.

D. Is a measure of the relative relationship between two variables.

Answer (D) is correct. *(CMA, adapted)*
REQUIRED: The best explanation of the coefficient of correlation (r).
DISCUSSION: The coefficient of correlation (r) measures the strength of the linear relationship between the dependent and independent variables. The magnitude of r is independent of the scales of measurement of x and y. The coefficient lies between −1.0 and +1.0. A value of zero indicates no linear relationship between the x and y variables. A value of +1.0 indicates a perfectly direct relationship, and a value of −1.0 indicates a perfectly inverse relationship.
Answer (A) is incorrect. The coefficient is negative if the relationship between the variables is inverse. Answer (B) is incorrect. The coefficient relates the two variables to each other. Answer (C) is incorrect. The size of the coefficient varies between −1.0 and +1.0.

21. All of the following are assumptions underlying the validity of linear regression output except

A. The errors are normally distributed.

B. The mean of the errors is zero.

C. Certainty.

D. The standard deviation of the errors is constant.

Answer (C) is correct. *(CMA, adapted)*
REQUIRED: The assumption that does not underlie linear regression.
DISCUSSION: Linear regression is based on several assumptions; for example, that there is no change in the environment, that errors in the values of the dependent variables are normally distributed with a mean of zero, that the standard deviation of these errors is constant, that the values of the dependent variables are statistically independent of each other, and that the independent variables are not correlated with each other. However, regression is only a means of predicting the future; it cannot provide certainty.

22. In the standard regression equation $y = a + bx$, the letter *b* is best described as a(n)

A. Independent variable.

B. Dependent variable.

C. Constant coefficient.

D. Variable coefficient.

Answer (D) is correct. *(CMA, adapted)*
REQUIRED: The meaning of the letter b in the standard regression equation.
DISCUSSION: In the standard regression equation, *b* represents the variable coefficient. For example, in a cost determination regression, *y* equals total costs, *b* is the variable cost per unit, *x* is the number of units produced, and *a* is fixed cost.
Answer (A) is incorrect. The independent variable is *x*. Answer (B) is incorrect. The dependent variable is *y*. Answer (C) is incorrect. The constant coefficient is *a*.

Questions 23 and 24 are based on the following information.

In preparing the annual profit plan for the coming year, Wilkens Company wants to determine the cost behavior pattern of the maintenance costs. Wilkens has decided to use linear regression by employing the equation $y = a + bx$ for maintenance costs. The prior year's data regarding maintenance hours and costs, and the results of the regression analysis, are given below and in the opposite column.

	Hours of Activity	Maintenance Costs
January	480	$ 4,200
February	320	3,000
March	400	3,600
April	300	2,820
May	500	4,350
June	310	2,960
July	320	3,030
August	520	4,470
September	490	4,260
October	470	4,050
November	350	3,300
December	340	3,160
Sum	4,800	$43,200
Average	400	$ 3,600

Average cost per hour	$9.00
a	684.65
b	7.2884
Standard error of a	49.515
Standard error of b	.12126
Standard error of the estimate	34.469
r^2	.99724

23. Based upon the data derived from the regression analysis, 420 maintenance hours in a month would mean that Wilkens Co.'s maintenance costs (rounded to the nearest dollar) would be budgeted at

A. $3,780

B. $3,600

C. $3,790

D. $3,746

Answer (D) is correct. *(CMA, adapted)*
REQUIRED: The budgeted maintenance costs given the activity level.
DISCUSSION: Substituting the given data into the regression equation results in a budgeted cost of $3,746 (rounded to the nearest dollar).

$$y = a + bx$$
$$y = 684.65 + 7.2884(420)$$
$$y = \$3,746$$

24. The percentage of Wilkens Co.'s total variance that can be explained by the regression equation is

A. 99.724%

B. 69.613%

C. 80.982%

D. 99.862%

Answer (A) is correct. *(CMA, adapted)*
REQUIRED: The percentage of Wilkens Co.'s total variance that can be explained by the regression equation.
DISCUSSION: The coefficient of determination (r^2) measures the percentage of the total variance in cost that can be explained by the regression equation. If the coefficient of determination is .99724, 99.724% of the variance is explained by the regression equation. Thus, the values in the regression equation explain virtually the entire amount of total cost.

25. The letter x in the standard regression equation is best described as a(n)

A. Independent variable.

B. Dependent variable.

C. Constant coefficient.

D. Coefficient of determination.

Answer (A) is correct. *(CMA, adapted)*
REQUIRED: The meaning of the letter x in the standard regression equation.
DISCUSSION: The letter x in the standard regression equation is the independent variable. For example, in a regression to determine the total cost of production, x equals units produced.
Answer (B) is incorrect. The dependent variable is y.
Answer (C) is incorrect. The constant coefficient is a.
Answer (D) is incorrect. The variable r^2 is the coefficient of determination.

5.5 Learning Curve Analysis

26. Corrigon Industries is preparing a bid for a special project requiring the production of 35,000 units. The engineering personnel have advised that the units can be produced in groups with the first group consisting of 1,000 units. A review of prior experience indicates that the direct labor time needed per unit will be progressively smaller by a constant percentage rate as experience is gained in the production process. The quantitative method that would best estimate Corrigon's total cost for the project is

A. Linear programming.

B. Dynamic programming.

C. Learning curve analysis.

D. Time series analysis.

Answer (C) is correct. *(CMA, adapted)*
REQUIRED: The quantitative method for estimating the decline in direct labor costs as production increases.
DISCUSSION: Learning curves reflect the increased rate at which people perform tasks as they gain experience. Thus, the time required to perform a given task becomes progressively shorter. Ordinarily, the learning curve is expressed as a percentage of reduced time to complete a task for each doubling of cumulative production.
Answer (A) is incorrect. Linear programming is an optimizing model used to determine a minimum or maximum, e.g., of a cost or revenue function, given certain constraints on resources. Answer (B) is incorrect. Dynamic programming is an approach to solving problems, not a particular algorithm. It divides a large mathematical model into smaller, more manageable pieces in such a way that, once the smaller problems have been solved, the result is the optimal solution to the overall model. Answer (D) is incorrect. Time series analysis applies to data gathered at successive moments in time. It is a forecasting technique in which the dependent variable is regressed on time.

27. The average labor cost per unit for the first batch produced by a new process is $120. The cumulative average labor cost after the second batch is $72 per product. Using a batch size of 100 and assuming the learning curve continues, the total labor cost of four batches will be

A. $4,320

B. $10,368

C. $2,592

D. $17,280

Answer (D) is correct. *(CMA, adapted)*
REQUIRED: The total labor cost assuming the learning curve continues.
DISCUSSION: The learning curve reflects the increased rate at which people perform tasks as they gain experience. The time required to perform a given task becomes progressively shorter. Ordinarily, the curve is expressed in a percentage of reduced time to complete a task for each doubling of cumulative production. One common assumption in a learning curve model is that the cumulative average time (and labor cost) per unit is reduced by a certain percentage each time production doubles. Given a $120 cost per unit for the first 100 units and a $72 cost per unit when cumulative production doubled to 200 units, the learning curve percentage must be 60% ($72 ÷ $120). If production is again doubled to 400 units (four batches), the average unit labor cost should be $43.20 ($72 × 60%). Hence, total labor cost for 400 units is estimated to be $17,280 (400 units × $43.20).
Answer (A) is incorrect. The cost of the items in the fourth batch equals $4,320. Answer (B) is incorrect. The amount of $10,368 is based on the assumption that the cumulative average unit labor cost is reduced by the learning curve percentage with each batch, not each doubling of output. Answer (C) is incorrect. The amount of $2,592 represents the labor cost of 100 units at the unit rate expected after another doubling of production to eight batches.

Questions 28 and 29 are based on the following information.

Moss Point Manufacturing recently completed and sold an order of 50 units that had costs as shown in the next column.

The company has now been requested to prepare a bid for 150 units of the same product.

Direct materials	$ 1,500
Direct labor ($8.50 × 1,000 hours)	8,500
Variable overhead (1,000 hours × $4.00)*	4,000
Fixed overhead**	1,400
	$15,400

*Applied on the basis of direct labor hours.
**Applied at the rate of 10% of variable cost.

28. If an 80% learning curve is applicable, Moss Point's total cost on this order would be estimated at

A. $26,400

B. $32,000

C. $38,000

D. $41,800

Answer (A) is correct. *(CMA, adapted)*
REQUIRED: The total cost of a new order given a learning curve percentage.
DISCUSSION: Assuming that the cumulative average time model applies, an 80% learning curve means that the cumulative average time per unit (and labor cost, given a constant labor rate) declines by 20% each time unit output doubles in the early stages of production. The first lot size was 50 units, which was produced at a total cost of $15,400 ($1,500 for materials and $13,900 for labor and overhead). Materials costs are strictly variable and should remain proportional to production. The labor ($8,500) and variable overhead ($4,000) costs (labor-related), however, will be affected by the learning curve. The average cost per lot for labor and variable overhead after 100 units have been produced should be 80% of the costs of the first lot of 50 units. Thus, the average labor and variable overhead cost per 50-unit lot will be $10,000 ($12,500 × 80%). If production doubles again (to a total production of 200 units or four lots of 50 each), the cumulative average cost for labor and variable overhead will be $8,000 per lot ($10,000 × 80%). Given four lots of 50 each, at an average cost of $8,000 per lot, the total cost for labor and variable overhead must be $32,000. Adding $6,000 for raw materials ($1,500 per 50-unit lot) gives a total variable cost of $38,000 for 200 units. Fixed overhead is 10% of total variable cost, so total cost is $41,800. The total cost for the last 150 units is $26,400 ($41,800 – $15,400).
Answer (B) is incorrect. The amount of $32,000 is the total cost for labor and variable overhead for 200 units. Answer (C) is incorrect. The amount of $38,000 is the total variable cost for 200 units. Answer (D) is incorrect. The amount of $41,800 is the total cost for 200 units.

29. If Moss Point had experienced a 70% learning curve, the bid for the 150 units would

A. Show a 30% reduction in the total direct labor hours required with no learning curve.

B. Include increased fixed overhead costs.

C. Be 10% lower than the total bid at an 80% learning curve.

D. Include 6.40 direct labor hours per unit at $8.50 per hour.

Answer (D) is correct. *(CMA, adapted)*
REQUIRED: The true statement about the bid for an incremental 150 units given a 70% learning curve effect.
DISCUSSION: The sum of the direct labor hours for the initial lot of 50 units was 1,000. A second lot of 50 would reduce the cumulative hours per lot to 700 (70% × 1,000 hours). A doubling to four lots would reduce the cumulative hours per lot to 490 (70% × 700 hours). Thus, for an output of 200 units, the total hours worked would be 1,960 (4 lots × 490 hours). Subtracting the 1,000 hours required for the first 50 units from the 1,960-hour total gives 960 hours for the last 150 units. Dividing 960 hours by 150 units produces a per-unit time of 6.4 hours.
Answer (A) is incorrect. With no learning curve effect, estimated total hours would be 4,000 instead of 1,960, a change of more than 50%. Answer (B) is incorrect. Fixed costs applied per lot would decline because they are based on labor hours, which are declining. Answer (C) is incorrect. Due to the cumulative nature of a learning curve, a 10% change in the learning curve does not result in a 10% change in direct labor costs. Given an 80% learning curve, estimated total hours would be 2,560 instead of 1,960.

30. Lake Corporation manufactures specialty components for the electronics industry in a highly labor intensive environment. Arc Electronics has asked Lake to bid on a component that Lake made for Arc last month. The previous order was for 80 units and required 120 hours of direct labor to manufacture. Arc would now like 240 additional components. Lake experiences an 80% learning curve on all of its jobs. The number of direct labor hours needed for Lake to complete the 240 additional components is

    A. 360.0

    B. 187.2

    C. 307.2

    D. 256.0

Answer (B) is correct. *(CMA, adapted)*
    REQUIRED: The number of labor hours needed to complete 240 additional components.
    DISCUSSION: One common assumption made in a learning curve model is that the cumulative average time per unit is reduced by a certain percentage each time production doubles. An 80% learning curve results in the following performance for the lots shown:

Units	Cumulative Average Hours
80	1.5 hours (120 ÷ 80)
160	1.2 hours (1.5 × .8)
320	.96 hours (1.2 × .8)

Thus, to produce 320 units, total production time will be 307.2 hours (320 × .96). The total time for the last 240 units will be 187.2 hours (307.2 − 120).
    Answer (A) is incorrect. Assuming no learning curve effect results in 360 hours. Answer (C) is incorrect. The total time for completing 320 units is 307.2 hours. Answer (D) is incorrect. The figure of 256 hours is a nonsense answer.

5.6 Time Series Analysis

31. Which one of the following is a sales forecasting technique that can be utilized in preparing the annual profit plan?

    A. Linear programming.

    B. Exponential smoothing.

    C. Queuing theory.

    D. Program Evaluation and Review Technique (PERT).

Answer (B) is correct. *(CMA, adapted)*
    REQUIRED: The sales forecasting technique that can be used in preparing the annual profit plan.
    DISCUSSION: Exponential smoothing is a sales forecasting technique used to level or smooth variations encountered in a forecast. It also adapts the forecast to changes as they occur. The simplest form of smoothing is the moving average, in which each forecast is based on a fixed number of prior observations. Exponential smoothing is similar to the moving average, but the term "exponential" means that greater weight is placed on the most recent data, with the weights of all data falling off exponentially as the data age.
    Answer (A) is incorrect. Linear programming is used to minimize a cost function or maximize a revenue or profit function, subject to constraints. Answer (C) is incorrect. Queuing is used to minimize the cost of waiting lines. Answer (D) is incorrect. PERT is used to monitor the progress of large multi-step projects, such as construction of a building.

32. The four components of time series data are secular trend, cyclical variation, seasonality, and random variation. The seasonality in the data can be removed by

    A. Multiplying the data by a seasonality factor.

    B. Ignoring it.

    C. Taking the weighted average over four time periods.

    D. Subtracting a seasonality factor from the data.

Answer (C) is correct. *(CMA, adapted)*
    REQUIRED: The means by which seasonality can be removed from time series data.
    DISCUSSION: Time series analysis relies on past experience. Changes in the value of a variable may have several possible components including secular trends, cyclical variation, seasonality, and random variation. Seasonal variations are common in many businesses. A variety of methods exist for including seasonal variations in a forecasting model, but most methods use a seasonal index. Alternatively, seasonal variations can be removed from data by using a weighted average of several time periods instead of data from individual periods.
    Answer (A) is incorrect. Adding a seasonality factor to, or subtracting it from, a forecast based on trend analysis is a means of adjusting for seasonality. Answer (B) is incorrect. Seasonality factors cannot be ignored; they are reflected in the data and must be considered for a model to be accurate. Answer (D) is incorrect. The seasonality adjustment for a single season's data may be an increase or a decrease.

33. A forecasting technique that is a combination of the last forecast and the last observed value is called

    A. Delphi.

    B. Least squares.

    C. Regression.

    D. Exponential smoothing.

Answer (D) is correct. *(CMA, adapted)*
    REQUIRED: The name of the forecasting technique that combines the last forecast with the last observed value.
    DISCUSSION: Exponential smoothing is a widespread technique for making projections because it requires less data be kept on hand than the moving average methods. The technique involves weighting the actual result for the previous period by a smoothing factor, weighting the forecast for the previous period by the smoothing factor's complement, and combining the two.
    Answer (A) is incorrect. Delphi is a decision-making approach in which the manager solicits opinions on a problem from experts in the field, summarizes the opinions, and feeds the summaries back to the experts; the process is then reiterated. This method is an attempt to avoid groupthink. Answer (B) is incorrect. Least squares is the process of using calculus to match a set of data to a straight line; it is used in regression analysis. Answer (C) is incorrect. Regression analysis is the process of deriving the linear equation that describes the relationship between two variables.

5.7 Expected Value

34. Philip Enterprises, distributor of video discs, is developing its budgeted cost of goods sold for next year. Philip has developed the following range of sales estimates and associated probabilities for the year:

Sales Estimate	Probability
$ 60,000	25%
85,000	40
100,000	35

Philip's cost of goods sold averages 80% of sales. What is the expected value of Philip's budgeted cost of goods sold?

    A. $85,000

    B. $84,000

    C. $68,000

    D. $67,200

Answer (D) is correct. *(CMA, adapted)*
    REQUIRED: The expected value of cost of goods sold.
    DISCUSSION: The expected value is calculated by weighting each sales estimate by the probability of its occurrence. Consequently, the expected value of sales is $84,000 [$60,000 × .25) + ($85,000 × .40) + ($100,000 × .35)]. Cost of goods sold is therefore $67,200 ($84,000 × .80).
    Answer (A) is incorrect. The amount of $85,000 is the sales estimate with the highest probability. Answer (B) is incorrect. The amount of $84,000 is the expected value of sales. Answer (C) is incorrect. The amount of $68,000 is 80% of the sales estimate with the highest probability.

35. The expected value of perfect information is the

    A. Same as the expected profit under certainty.

    B. Sum of the conditional profit (loss) for the best event of each act times the probability of each event occurring.

    C. Difference between the expected profit under certainty and the expected opportunity loss.

    D. Difference between the expected profit under certainty and the expected monetary value of the best act under uncertainty.

Answer (D) is correct. *(CMA, adapted)*
    REQUIRED: The true statement about the expected value of perfect information.
    DISCUSSION: Perfect information permits certainty that a future state of nature will occur. The expected value of perfect information determines the maximum amount a decision maker is willing to pay for information. It is the difference between the expected value without perfect information, that is, the expected value of the best action under uncertainty and the expected value under certainty. Under certainty, a decision maker knows in each case which state of nature will occur and can act accordingly.
    Answer (A) is incorrect. The expected value of perfect information is the difference between the expected profit under certainty and the profit from the best decision under uncertainty. Answer (B) is incorrect. The expected value of perfect information is the excess of the total conditional profits under certainty over the profit from the best decision under uncertainty. Answer (C) is incorrect. There is no expected opportunity loss under conditions of certainty.

Questions 36 through 38 are based on the following information. Butler and Burnside are projecting market conditions for the upcoming month. They have prepared the following payoff table:

Supply in Units	Demand in Units			
	0	2	4	6
	Probability of Demand			
	0.1	0.3	0.4	0.2
0	$ 0	$ 0	$ 0	$ 0
2	(80)	40	40	40
4	(160)	(40)	80	80
6	(240)	(120)	0	120

36. Butler and Burnside's expected profit when supply equals 4 units is

A. $(40)

B. $80

C. $20

D. $120

Answer (C) is correct. *(CMA, adapted)*
REQUIRED: The expected profit when supply equals 4 units.
DISCUSSION: The approach to the solution is to weight (multiply) the probabilities for each level of demand by the payoff for that level of demand.

Demand	Payoff		Probability		Weighted Payoffs
0	$(160)	×	.1	=	$(16)
2	(40)	×	.3	=	(12)
4	80	×	.4	=	32
6	80	×	.2	=	16
			Expected Profit		$ 20

Answer (A) is incorrect. This figure is the payoff amount when demand is 2 units. Answer (B) is incorrect. This figure is the payoff amount when demand is 4 or 6 units. Answer (D) is incorrect. This figure is calculated by adding the amounts in the column for a demand of 4 units.

37. Butler and Burnside's expected profit with perfect information is

A. $28

B. $20

C. $(36)

D. $68

Answer (D) is correct. *(CMA, adapted)*
REQUIRED: The expected profit with perfect information.
DISCUSSION: With perfect information, the seller could order the inventory each day to meet the exact demand. For example, if demand were zero, supply would be zero and the seller would not lose any money. If demand were 2 units, the seller would acquire an equal supply and make a profit of $40. The total profit can be calculated by weighting the payoff from each best option.

Demand	Payoff		Probability		Weighted Payoffs
0	$ 0	×	.1	=	$ 0
2	40	×	.3	=	12
4	80	×	.4	=	32
6	120	×	.2	=	24
			Expected Profit		$68

38. The price Butler and Burnside are willing to pay for perfect information is

A. $68

B. $40

C. $48

D. $104

Answer (B) is correct. *(CMA, adapted)*
REQUIRED: The price of perfect information.
DISCUSSION: The maximum amount the seller should pay for perfect information is the difference between the expected profit with perfect information and the expected profit if demand is not known. With perfect information, supply is the correct amount of units to maximize profit at each level of demand. Thus, the expected profit with perfect information is computed as follows: (.1 × $0) + (.3 × $40) + (.4 × $80) + (.2 × $120) = $68. Without perfect information, the seller should purchase the supply that will result in the maximum long-run profit. Using the information given, it can be determined that the profit will be $20 when the supply is 4 units. It is also evident that the profit is zero when the supply is zero. The expected profit must also be calculated for supply levels of 2 and 6 units. For a supply of 2 units, the expected profit is

.1(–$80) + .3($40) + .4($40) + .2($40) = $28

For a supply of 6 units, the expected loss is

.1(–$240) + .3(–$120) + .4($0) + .2($120) = $(36)

Thus, without perfect information, profits are maximized at $28 when the supply is 2 units. However, with perfect information, profits will be $68. Thus, a rational seller should therefore be willing to pay up to $40 ($68 – $28).
Answer (A) is incorrect. This figure is the amount of profit with perfect information. Answer (C) is incorrect. The price paid for perfect information equals the difference between profits expected with perfect information and profits without perfect information. Answer (D) is incorrect. The price paid for perfect information equals the difference between profits expected with perfect information and profits without perfect information.

39. The expected monetary value of an act is the

A. Sum of the conditional profit (loss) for each event.

B. Sum of the conditional profit (loss) for each event times the probability of each event's occurrence.

C. Conditional profit (loss) for the best event times the probability of each event's occurrence.

D. Revenue minus the costs for the act.

Answer (B) is correct. *(CMA, adapted)*
REQUIRED: The definition of the expected monetary value of an act.
DISCUSSION: Expected value analysis estimates future monetary value based on forecasts and their related probabilities of occurrence. The expected value under uncertainty is found by multiplying the probability of each outcome (event) by its payoff (conditional profit or loss) and summing the products.
Answer (A) is incorrect. The conditional profit or loss must be weighted by the probability of each event's occurrence. Answer (C) is incorrect. The best event will not occur every time; less desirable events will also occur and must enter into the calculation. Answer (D) is incorrect. Each event must be weighted by the probability of its occurrence.

5.8 Sensitivity Analysis

40. A widely used approach that managers use to recognize uncertainty about individual items and to obtain an immediate financial estimate of the consequences of possible prediction errors is

A. Expected value analysis.

B. Learning curve analysis.

C. Sensitivity analysis.

D. Regression analysis.

Answer (C) is correct. *(CMA, adapted)*
REQUIRED: The approach that gives an immediate financial estimate of the consequences of possible prediction errors.
DISCUSSION: Sensitivity analysis determines how a result varies with changes in a given variable or parameter in a mathematical decision model. For example, in a present value analysis, a manager might first calculate the net present value or internal rate of return assuming that a new asset has a 10-year life. The NPV or IRR can then be recalculated using a 5-year life to determine how sensitive the result is to the change in the assumption.
Answer (A) is incorrect. Expected value is the probabilistically weighted average of the outcomes of an action. Answer (B) is incorrect. Learning curve analysis quantifies how labor costs decline as employees learn their jobs through repetition. Answer (D) is incorrect. Regression, or least squares, analysis determines the average change in the dependent variable given a unit change in one or more independent variables.

41. Through the use of decision models, managers thoroughly analyze many alternatives and decide on the best alternative for the company. Often, the actual results achieved from a particular decision are not what was expected when the decision was made. In addition, an alternative that was not selected would have actually been the best decision for the company. The appropriate technique to analyze the alternatives by using expected inputs and altering them before a decision is made is

A. Expected value analysis.

B. Linear programming.

C. Program Evaluation Review Technique (PERT).

D. Sensitivity analysis.

Answer (D) is correct. *(CMA, adapted)*
REQUIRED: The technique that involves altering expected inputs during the decision process.
DISCUSSION: Sensitivity modeling can be used to determine the outcome of a variety of decisions. A trial-and-error method may be adopted, usually in a computer model, to calculate the sensitivity of the solution (variability of outcomes) to changes in a variable.
Answer (A) is incorrect. Expected value analysis is used to determine an anticipated return or cost based upon probabilities of events and their related outcomes. Answer (B) is incorrect. Linear programming optimizes a function given certain constraints. Answer (C) is incorrect. PERT is a network technique used to plan and control large projects.

Use Gleim **CMA Test Prep** Software for interactive testing with **additional multiple-choice questions**!

5.10 ESSAY QUESTION

Scenario for Essay Question 1

Video Recreation, Inc., (VRI) is a supplier of video games and equipment, such as large-screen televisions and DVD players. The company has recently concluded a major contract with Sunview Hotels to supply games for the hotel video lounges. Under this contract, a total of 4,000 games will be delivered to Sunview Hotels throughout the western United States, and all of the games will have a warranty period of 1 year for both parts and labor. The number of service calls required to repair these games during the first year after installation is estimated as follows:

Number of Service Calls	Probability
400	.1
700	.3
900	.4
1,200	.2

VRI's Customer Service Department has developed three alternatives for providing the warranty service to Sunview. These three plans are presented below.

Plan 1: VRI would contract with local firms to perform the repair services. It is estimated that six such vendors would be needed to cover the appropriate areas and that each of these vendors would charge an annual fee of $15,000 to have personnel available and to stock the appropriate parts. In addition to the annual fee, VRI would be billed $250 for each service call and would be billed for parts used at cost plus a 10% surcharge.

Plan 2: VRI would allow the management of each hotel to arrange for repair service when needed and then would reimburse the hotel for the expenses incurred. It is estimated that 60% of the service calls would be for hotels located in urban areas where the charge for a service call would average $450. At the remaining hotels, the charges would be $350. In addition to these service charges, parts would be billed at cost.

Plan 3: VRI would hire its own personnel to perform repair services and to do preventive maintenance. Nine employees located in the appropriate geographical areas would be required to fulfill these responsibilities, and their average salary would be $24,000 annually. The fringe benefit expense for these employees would amount to 35% of their wages. Each employee would be scheduled to make an average of 200 preventive maintenance calls during the year; each of these calls would require $15 worth of parts. Because of this preventive maintenance, it is estimated that the expected number of hotel calls for repair service would decline 30%, and the cost of parts required for each repair service call would be reduced by 20%.

VRI's Accounting Department has reviewed the historical data on the repair costs for equipment installations similar to those proposed for Sunview Hotels and found that the cost of parts required for each repair occurred in the following proportions:

Parts Cost per Repair	Proportion
$30	15%
$40	15%
$60	45%
$90	25%

Question

1.   Video Recreation, Inc., wishes to select the least costly alternative to fulfill its warranty obligations to Sunview Hotels. Recommend which of the three plans presented above should be adopted by VRI. Support your recommendation with appropriate calculations and analysis.

Essay Question 1 — Unofficial Answers

1. Video Recreation, Inc., should adopt Plan 3 as the least costly alternative. Calculations for all three plans are as follows:

Expected Number of Service Calls

Number of Service Calls	×	Probability	=	Expected Calls
400		.1		40
700		.3		210
900		.4		360
1,200		.2		240
		1.0		850

Expected Value of Parts Costs

Parts Cost per Repair	×	Proportion	=	Expected Cost
$30		.15		$ 4.50
40		.15		6.00
60		.45		27.00
90		.25		22.50
		1.00		$60.00

Plan 1

Vendor fees (6 × $15,000)	$ 90,000
Service calls (850 × $250)	212,500
Parts (850 × $60 × 1.1)	56,100
Estimated total cost	$358,600

Plan 2

Urban service calls (850 × $450 × .6)	$229,500
Rural service calls (850 × $350 × .4)	119,000
Parts (850 × $60)	51,000
Estimated total cost	$399,500

Plan 3

Employee salaries (9 × $24,000)	$216,000
Fringe benefits ($216,000 × .35)	75,600
Preventive maintenance parts (200 × 9 × $15)	27,000
Repair parts (850 × .7) × ($60 × .8)	28,560
Estimated total cost	$347,160

Use CMA Gleim Online and Essay Wizard to practice additional essay questions in an exam-like environment.

STUDY UNIT SIX
BUDGET METHODOLOGIES AND BUDGET PREPARATION

(30 pages of outline)

6.1	The Master Budget Process	209
6.2	Budget Methodologies	210
6.3	Static and Flexible Budgeting	213
6.4	Selecting the Budget Methodology	214
6.5	Overview of Master Budget Preparation	215
6.6	Operating Budget Calculations -- Production and Direct Materials	217
6.7	Operating Budget Calculations -- Others	218
6.8	Projecting Cash Collections	223
6.9	The Cash Budget	223
6.10	Pro Forma Financial Statements	225
6.11	Core Concepts	234
6.12	Essay Questions	250

This study unit is the **second of two** on **planning, budgeting, and forecasting**. The relative weight assigned to this major topic in Part 1 of the exam is **30%**. The two study units are

Study Unit 5: Budgeting Concepts and Forecasting Techniques
Study Unit 6: Budget Methodologies and Budget Preparation

After studying the outline and answering the questions in this study unit, you will have the skills necessary to address the following topics listed in the ICMA's Learning Outcome Statements:

Part 1 – Section A.3. Budget methodologies

For each of the budget systems identified [annual/master budgets, project budgeting, activity-based budgeting, zero-based budgeting, continuous (rolling) budgets, and flexible budgeting], the candidate should be able to:

    a.   define its purpose, appropriate use, and time frame
    b.   identify the budget components and explain the interrelationships among the components
    c.   demonstrate an understanding of how the budget is developed
    d.   compare and contrast the benefits and limitations of the budget system
    e.   evaluate a business situation and recommend the appropriate budget solution
    f.   prepare budgets on the basis of information presented
    g.   calculate the impact of incremental changes to budgets

Part 1 – Section A.4. Annual profit plan and supporting schedules

The candidate should be able to:

    a.   explain the role of the sales budget in the development of an annual profit plan
    b.   identify the factors that should be considered when preparing a sales forecast and evaluate the feasibility of the sales forecast based on business and economic information provided
    c.   identify the components of a sales budget and prepare a sales budget based on relevant information provided
    d.   explain the relationship between the sales budget and the production budget
    e.   identify the role that inventory levels play in the preparation of a production budget and define other factors that should be considered when preparing a production budget
    f.   prepare a production budget based on relevant information provided
    g.   demonstrate an understanding of the relationship between the direct materials budget, the direct labor budget, and the production budget
    h.   explain how inventory levels and procurement policies affect the direct materials budget

i. prepare direct materials and direct labor budgets based on relevant information and evaluate the feasibility of achieving production goals on the basis of these budgets

j. identify and describe alternative ways of allocating employee benefit expense

k. demonstrate an understanding of the relationship between the overhead budget and the production budget

l. separate costs into their fixed and variable components

m. prepare an overhead budget based on relevant information provided

n. identify the components of the cost of goods sold budget and prepare a cost of goods sold budget based on relevant information provided

o. demonstrate an understanding of contribution margin per unit and total contribution margin, identify the appropriate use of these concepts, and calculate both unit and total contribution margin

p. identify the components of the selling and administrative budget

q. explain how specific components of the selling and administrative budget may affect the contribution margin

r. prepare an operational (operating) budget

s. prepare a capital expenditure budget

t. demonstrate an understanding of the relationship between the capital expenditure budget, the cash budget, and the pro forma financial statements

u. define the purposes of the cash budget and describe the relationship between the cash budget and all other budgets

v. demonstrate an understanding of the relationship between credit policies and purchasing (payables) policies and the cash budget

w. prepare a cash budget

Part 1 – Section A.5. Top-level planning and analysis

The candidate should be able to:

a. define the purpose of a pro forma income statement, a pro forma statement of financial position, and a pro forma cash flow statement and demonstrate an understanding of the relationship among these statements and all other budgets

b. prepare pro forma income statements based on several revenue and cost assumptions

c. evaluate whether a company has achieved strategic objectives based on pro forma income statements

d. use financial projections to prepare a pro forma balance sheet and a statement of cash flows

e. identify the factors required to prepare medium- and long-term cash forecasts

f. use financial projections to determine required outside financing and dividend policy

g. determine the effect of financial forecasts on debt covenants, including debt ratio and coverage ratios (no calculations required)

h. forecast basic earnings per share (EPS) based on pro forma financial statements and other relevant information (calculation of basic EPS required)

6.1 THE MASTER BUDGET PROCESS

1. **Annual Profit Plan**

    a. The master budget, also called the comprehensive budget or annual profit plan, encompasses the organization's operating and financial plans for a specified period (ordinarily a year or single operating cycle).

    b. The importance of carefully drafting the budget calendar is illustrated here. The information contained in the lower-numbered budgets feeds the higher-numbered budgets.

       1) For example, the production budget cannot be prepared until after the sales budget. The direct materials budget and the direct labor budget cannot be prepared until after the production budget had been completed.

2. **Operating Budget**

    a. In the operating budget, the emphasis is on obtaining and using current resources.

       1) Sales budget
       2) Production budget
       3) Direct materials budget
       4) Direct labor budget
       5) Manufacturing overhead budget
       6) Ending finished goods inventory budget
       7) Cost of goods sold budget
       8) Nonmanufacturing budget

           a) Research and development budget
           b) Design budget
           c) Marketing budget
           d) Distribution budget
           e) Customer service budget
           f) Administrative budget

       9) Pro forma income statement

3. **Financial Budget**

    a. In the financial budget, the emphasis is on obtaining the funds needed to purchase operating assets. It contains the

       1) Capital budget (completed before operating budget is begun)
       2) Projected cash disbursement schedule
       3) Projected cash collection schedule
       4) Cash budget
       5) Pro forma balance sheet
       6) Pro forma statement of cash flows

Stop and review! You have completed the outline for this subunit. Study multiple-choice questions 1 through 4 beginning on page 236.

6.2 BUDGET METHODOLOGIES

1. **Project Budget**

    a. A project budget consists of all the costs expected to attach to a particular project, such as the design of a new airliner or the building of a single ship.

        1) While the project is obviously part of the company's overall line of business, the costs and profits associated with it are significant enough to be tracked separately.

    b. A project will typically use resources from many parts of the organization, e.g., design, engineering, production, marketing, accounting, and human resources.

        1) All of these aspects of the project budget must align with those of the firm's master budget.

    c. EXAMPLE of a project budget:

Function	1st Quarter	2nd Quarter	3rd Quarter	4th Quarter	Totals
Design	$ 800,000	$ 200,000	$ --	$ --	$1,000,000
Engineering	500,000	1,200,000	400,000	--	2,100,000
Production	--	2,100,000	1,500,000	1,500,000	5,100,000
Marketing	--	100,000	200,000	200,000	500,000
Accounting	100,000	100,000	100,000	100,000	400,000
Human Resources	20,000	20,000	20,000	20,000	80,000
Totals	**$1,420,000**	**$3,720,000**	**$2,220,000**	**$1,820,000**	**$9,180,000**

2. **Activity-Based Budgeting**

    a. Activity-based budgeting applies activity-based costing principles (see Study Unit 2, Subunit 3) to budgeting. Its greatest effect is on the application of indirect costs.

        1) A traditional budgeting system involves lumping all indirect costs into a single pool and allocating them to products based on a (usually arbitrary) driver such as volume or machine hours.

        2) EXAMPLE: A manufacturer produces two valves, a simple one and a complex one. It has budgeted production costs for the upcoming year using a volume-based budgeting system:

Cost Category	Simple Valve 50,000 Total	Per Unit	Complex Valve 10,000 Total	Per Unit	Total
Direct materials	$ 450,000	$ 9.00	$270,000	$27.00	$ 720,000
Direct labor	240,000	4.80	78,000	7.80	318,000
Total direct costs	$ 690,000	$13.80	$348,000	$34.80	$1,038,000
Allocated indirect costs	720,000	14.40	234,000	23.40	954,000
Total manufacturing costs	**$1,410,000**	**$28.20**	**$582,000**	**$58.20**	**$1,992,000**

    b. Activity-based budgeting involves defining the activities that drive indirect costs.

        1) A cost pool is established for each activity, and a cost driver is identified for each pool.

            a) The key to successful activity-based budgeting is selecting a driver for each pool that has a direct cause-and-effect relationship with the level of activity in that pool.

        2) The budgeted cost for each pool is determined by multiplying the demand for the activity by the estimated cost of a unit of the activity.

3) EXAMPLE: The manufacturer has designed an indirect-cost assignment system based on the following pools and drivers:

Indirect cost pool	Driver
Product design	Engineering hours
Production setup	Number of batches
Machining	Machine hours
Inspection & testing	Number of valves
Customer maintenance	Salesperson hours

c. Since activity-based budgeting employs multiple indirect cost pools, it provides far greater detail regarding indirect costs than traditional functional or spending-category budgeting (which only employs a single pool).

1) EXAMPLE: Note that, while the amounts of indirect costs assigned to the two products are different, indirect costs in total are (necessarily) the same as under the traditional system:

Cost Category	Estimated Driver Level	Cost per Unit of Driver	Simple Valve 50,000 Total	Simple Valve 50,000 Per Unit	Complex Valve 10,000 Total	Complex Valve 10,000 Per Unit	Total
Direct materials			$ 450,000	$ 9.00	$270,000	$27.00	$ 720,000
Direct labor			240,000	4.80	78,000	7.80	318,000
Total direct costs			**$ 690,000**	**$13.80**	**$348,000**	**$34.80**	**$1,038,000**
Indirect cost assignment:							
Product design:							
Simple valve	1,000 ×	$23.75 =	$ 23,750	$ 0.48			$ 90,250
Complex valve	2,800 ×	23.75 =			$ 66,500	$ 6.65	
Production setup:							
Simple valve	200 ×	21.00 =	4,200	0.08			4,620
Complex valve	20 ×	21.00 =			420	0.04	
Machining:							
Simple valve	2,000 ×	3.25 =	6,500	0.13			68,250
Complex valve	19,000 ×	3.25 =			61,750	6.18	
Inspection & testing:							
Simple valve	50,000 ×	12.50 =	625,000	12.50			750,000
Complex valve	10,000 ×	12.50 =			125,000	12.50	
Customer maintenance:							
Simple valve	1,500 ×	17.60 =	26,400	0.53			40,480
Complex valve	800 ×	17.60 =			14,080	1.41	
Total indirect costs			**$ 685,850**	**$13.72**	**$267,750**	**$26.78**	**$ 953,600**
Total manufacturing costs			**$1,375,850**	**$27.52**	**$615,750**	**$61.58**	**$1,991,600**

3. Zero-Based Budgeting

a. Zero-based budgeting (ZBB) is a budget and planning process in which each manager must justify his/her department's entire budget every budget cycle.

1) The concept originated in the U.S. Department of Agriculture in the early 1960s but was abandoned. Texas Instruments Corporation began using it in the late 1960s and early 1970s, as did the state of Georgia under Governor Jimmy Carter. Carter also tried to introduce the concept into the federal budget system when he served as president (1977–1980).

b. ZBB differs from the traditional concept of **incremental budgeting**, in which the current year's budget is simply adjusted to allow for changes planned for the coming year.

1) The managerial advantage of incremental budgeting is that the manager has to put forth less effort to justify changes in the budget.

    c.   Under ZBB, a manager must build the budget every year from a base of zero. All expenditures must be justified regardless of variance from previous years.

        1)   The objective is to encourage periodic reexamination of all costs in the hope that some can be reduced or eliminated.

    d.   ZBB begins with the deepest budgetary units of the entity.

        1)   It requires determination of objectives, operations, and costs for each activity and the alternative means of carrying out that activity.

        2)   Different levels of service (work effort) are evaluated for each activity, measures of work and performance are established, and activities are ranked according to their importance to the entity.

        3)   For each budgetary unit, a decision package is prepared that describes various levels of service that may be provided, including at least one level of service lower than the current one.

            a)   Accordingly, ZBB requires managers to justify each expenditure for each budget period and to review each cost component from a cost-benefit perspective.

    e.   The major limitation of ZBB is that it requires more time and effort to prepare than a traditional budget.

4. Continuous (Rolling) Budgeting

    a.   A continuous (rolling) budget is one that is revised on a regular (continuous) basis.

        1)   Typically, a company continuously extends such a budget for an additional month or quarter in accordance with new data as the current month or quarter ends.

        2)   For example, if the budget cycle is 1 year, a budget for the next quarter will be available continuously as each quarter ends.

    b.   EXAMPLE of rolling budget:

Product Line	Fiscal Year 1 1st Quarter	Fiscal Year 1 2nd Quarter	Fiscal Year 1 3rd Quarter	Fiscal Year 1 4th Quarter	Four Quarter Totals
Feed	$ 12,000	$ 10,000	$ 10,000	$ 14,000	$ 46,000
Animal health	2,000	1,200	800	1,000	5,000
Fertilizer	80,000	75,000	20,000	10,000	185,000
Crop protectants	74,000	76,000	41,000	11,000	202,000
Petroleum	120,000	20,000	14,000	100,000	254,000
Farm supplies	15,000	45,000	55,000	20,000	135,000
Totals	**$303,000**	**$227,200**	**$140,800**	**$156,000**	**$827,000**

Product Line	Fiscal Year 1 2nd Quarter	Fiscal Year 1 3rd Quarter	Fiscal Year 1 4th Quarter	Fiscal Yr 2 1st Quarter	Four Quarter Totals
Feed	$ 10,000	$ 10,000	$ 14,000	$ 9,000	$ 43,000
Animal health	1,200	800	1,000	2,200	5,200
Fertilizer	75,000	20,000	10,000	90,000	195,000
Crop protectants	76,000	41,000	11,000	90,000	218,000
Petroleum	20,000	14,000	100,000	85,000	219,000
Farm supplies	45,000	55,000	20,000	10,000	130,000
Totals	**$227,200**	**$140,800**	**$156,000**	**$286,200**	**$810,200**

    c.   The principal advantage of a rolling budget is that it requires managers always to be thinking ahead.

        1)   The disadvantage is the amount of time managers must constantly spend on budget preparation.

Stop and review! You have completed the outline for this subunit. Study multiple-choice questions 5 through 9 beginning on page 237.

6.3 STATIC AND FLEXIBLE BUDGETING

1. **Static Budgeting**

   a. A static budget is based on only one level of sales or production.

       1) EXAMPLE: A company has the following information for the period:

	Actual	Static Budget	Budget Variance
Production in units	1,000	1,200	200 U
Direct materials (units × $6)	$ 6,000	$ 7,200	$1,200 F
Direct labor (units × $10)	10,000	12,000	2,000 F
Variable overhead (units × $5)	5,000	6,000	1,000 F
Total variable costs	$21,000	$25,200	$4,200 F

   From these results, it appears that, although the production manager failed to achieve his/her production quota, (s)he did a good job of cost control.

   b. Contrast this with a **flexible budget**, which is a series of budgets prepared for many levels of activity.

       1) At the end of the period, management can compare actual performance with the appropriate budgeted level in the flexible budget.

       2) EXAMPLE: This is the flexible budget comparison for the company at the 1,000 unit level of production:

	Actual	Flexible Budget	Flexible Budget Variance
Production in units	1,000	1,000	--
Direct materials (units × $6)	$ 6,000	$ 6,000	$ --
Direct labor (units × $10)	10,000	10,000	--
Variable overhead (units × $5)	5,000	5,000	--
Total variable costs	$21,000	$21,000	$ --

   It is clear that the production manager merely incurred the expected costs for the production level that was actually achieved.

   c. Some organizations prepare only a static budget, which is based on a single level of sales and production.

Static Budget

	Units	Per Unit	Budgeted Amounts
Sales	900 ×	$120 =	$108,000
Beginning inventory	100 ×	$ 90 =	$ 9,000
Add: variable production costs	1,200 ×	$ 40 =	48,000
Goods available for sale			$57,000
Less: ending inventory	400 ×	$ 90 =	(36,000)
Cost of goods sold			(21,000)
Less: variable S&A expenses	900 ×	$ 12	(10,800)
Contribution margin			$ 76,200
Less: fixed production costs			(45,000)
Less: fixed S&A expenses			(10,000)
Operating income			**$ 21,200**

Rarely, however, do actual results adhere perfectly to budgets.

2.   **Flexible Budgeting**

   a.   Flexible budgeting uses knowledge of fixed and variable costs to allow firms to project potential results at multiple levels of sales and production.

      1)   In this scenario, sales and production are both lower than anticipated in the static budget, and the firm loses money:

Flexible Budget -- Scenario 1

	Units		Per Unit		Budgeted Amounts
Sales	700	×	$120	=	**$ 84,000**
Beginning inventory	100	×	$ 90	=	$ 9,000
Add: variable production costs	800	×	$ 40	=	32,000
Goods available for sale					$41,000
Less: ending inventory	200	×	$ 90	=	(18,000)
Cost of goods sold					(23,000)
Less: variable S&A expenses	700	×	$ 12		(8,400)
Contribution margin					$ 52,600
Less: fixed production costs					(45,000)
Less: fixed S&A expenses					(10,000)
Operating income					**$ (2,400)**

      2)   In this scenario, production far exceeds sales, resulting in a substantial rise in ending inventory. Since a large amount of variable cost is embedded in these units that are produced but not sold, operating income will rise over that of the static budget.

Flexible Budget -- Scenario 2

	Units		Per Unit		Budgeted Amounts
Sales	850	×	$120	=	**$102,000**
Beginning inventory	100	×	$ 90	=	$ 9,000
Add: variable production costs	1,400	×	$ 40	=	56,000
Goods available for sale					$65,000
Less: ending inventory	650	×	$ 90	=	(58,500)
Cost of goods sold					(6,500)
Less: variable S&A expenses	850	×	$ 12		(10,200)
Contribution margin					$ 85,300
Less: fixed production costs					(45,000)
Less: fixed S&A expenses					(10,000)
Operating income					**$ 30,300**

   b.   The knowledge gained through flexible budgeting can be used to compare the individual line items generated by the actual results in a process called variance analysis, discussed at length in Study Unit 7.

Stop and review! You have completed the outline for this subunit. Study multiple-choice questions 9 and 10 beginning on page 238.

6.4 SELECTING THE BUDGET METHODOLOGY

 CMA candidates must know how to both apply and select a specific budgeting method. They may also be required to explain a specific action, such as why a method should be selected. All topics are eligible to be tested on the multiple-choice section, the essay section, or both.

Some of the budget methodology questions that a candidate will encounter on the CMA exam focus on selection of the correct method for given circumstances rather than on the mechanics of applying it. This subunit consists entirely of such questions. Please review Subunits 6.2 and 6.3, paying special attention to the nature and purpose of each technique before attempting to answer the questions in this subunit.

Stop and review! You have completed the outline for this subunit. Study multiple-choice questions 11 through 14 beginning on page 239.

6.5 OVERVIEW OF MASTER BUDGET PREPARATION

 This study unit provides a brief overview of the master budget process. CMA candidates are expected to be able to prepare budgets based on relevant information. Take care to know the budget cycle and, especially, the order in which each budget is prepared.

The following is a brief introduction to the phases of drafting a master budget. Detailed descriptions follow in Subunits 6.6 and 6.7.

1. **Sales Budget**

    a. The sales budget is the first budget prepared because sales volume affects production and purchasing levels, operating expenses, and cash flow because sales volume affects production and purchasing levels, operating expenses, and cash flows.

        1) Thus, expectations about sales drive the entire budget process.

    b. Once a firm can estimate sales, the next step is to decide how much to produce or purchase.

        1) Sales are usually budgeted by product or department. The sales budget also establishes targets for sales personnel.

2. **Production Budgets**

    a. Production budgets (for manufacturing firms) are based on sales in units (not dollars) plus or minus desired inventory buildup or reduction.

        1) They are prepared for each department and each item. Production budgets are usually stated in units instead of dollars.

    b. When the production budget has been completed, it is used to prepare three additional budgets:

        1) Raw materials purchases, which is similar to the purchases budget of a merchandising firm

        2) Direct labor budget, which includes hours, wage rates, and total dollars

        3) Factory overhead budget, which is similar to a department expenses budget

3. **Purchases Budget**

    a. The purchases budget can follow after projected sales have been set. It is prepared on a monthly or even a weekly basis.

        1) Purchases can be planned so that stockouts are avoided. Inventory should be at an appropriate level to avoid unnecessary carrying costs.

4. **Expense Budgets**

    a. Expense budgets are prepared by department heads using the sales budget as a basis.

        1) Expense budgets are based on prior years' costs and adjusted for anticipated changes in prices, wages, and sales volume estimates.

5. Capital Budget

a. Equipment purchases (capital expenditures) are technically not part of the operating budget, but they must be incorporated into the preparation of the cash budget and pro forma financial statements.

b. Capital budgets may be prepared more than a year in advance to allow sufficient time to

1) Plan financing of major expenditures for equipment or buildings or
2) Receive custom orders of specialized equipment, buildings, etc.

6. Cash Budget

a. The cash budget is probably the most important part of a company's budget program.

1) Almost all organizations, regardless of size, prepare a cash budget. It is particularly important for organizations operating in seasonal industries.

2) An organization must have adequate cash at all times. Even with plenty of other assets, an organization with a temporary shortage of cash can be driven into bankruptcy. Proper planning can keep an entity from financial embarrassment.

b. A cash budget details projected cash receipts and disbursements. It cannot be prepared until the other budgets have been completed.

1) Cash budgeting facilitates loans and other financing. A bank is more likely to lend money to a firm if the money will not be needed immediately.

c. Below is an example of a cash budget for a company that had budgeted sales of $9,000 for January, $9,700 for February, and $13,950 for March.

Cash Budget
For Quarter Ending March 31

	January	February	March	Total
Beginning cash balance	$ 80	$ 20	$ 1,957	$ 80
Receipts:				
Collection from sales*	6,800	9,350	11,825	27,975
Total cash available	$6,880	$9,370	$13,782	$28,055
Payments:				
Purchases**	$3,150	$2,760	$ 3,960	$ 9,870
Sales salaries	1,350	1,455	2,093	4,898
Supplies	360	388	558	1,306
Utilities	120	110	100	330
Administrative salaries	1,800	1,800	1,800	5,400
Advertising	80	80	80	240
Equipment purchases	0	820	3,000	3,820
Total payments	$6,860	$7,413	$11,591	$25,864
ENDING BALANCE	$ 20	$1,957	$ 2,191	$ 2,191

* Sales are 50% cash sales and 50% on credit (net 30 days). Thus, 50% of each month's sales are collected in the month of the sale and 50% are collected in the following month. For example, the February collections were calculated as follows:

50% of January sales	$4,500
50% of February sales	4,850
	$9,350

** Purchases are on terms of net 30 days. Thus, purchases are paid for in the month following the purchase. The amount paid in February ($2,760) was the total purchases for January.

Stop and review! You have completed the outline for this subunit. Study multiple-choice questions 15 through 18 beginning on page 240.

6.6 OPERATING BUDGET CALCULATIONS -- PRODUCTION AND DIRECT MATERIALS

1. **Sales Budget**

   a. The sales budget, also called the revenue budget, is the starting point for the massive cycle that produces the annual profit plan (i.e., the master budget).

   b. The sales budget is an outgrowth of the sales forecast. The sales forecast distills recent sales trends, overall conditions in the economy and industry, market research, activities of competitors, and credit and pricing policies.

      1) For example,

         a) The company may determine that demand is highly elastic for its mature products and that growth will come only from new product introductions and from cost savings on existing products.

         b) At the same time, the company determines that a tight monetary policy on the Fed's part must cause the firm to tighten its credit standards.

         c) Simultaneously, a competitor that the firm knows is a low-cost producer is also considering moving into the markets that the budgeting company is considering.

      2) All of these factors must be taken into account when forming expectations about product sales for the coming budget cycle.

   c. The sales budget must specify both projected unit sales and dollar revenues.

   d. EXAMPLE of a sales budget. The demand for this firm's product is elastic, so the price cut in the third month is expected to boost sales.

	April	May	June	2nd Quarter Totals	Ref.
Projected sales in units	1,000	1,200	1,800	4,000	SB1
Selling price	× $400	× $400	× $380		
Projected total sales	$400,000	$480,000	$684,000	$1,564,000	SB2

2. **Production Budget**

   a. The production budget follows directly from the sales budget. To minimize finished goods carrying costs and obsolescence, the levels of production are dependent upon the projections contained in the sales budget.

      1) The production budget is concerned with **units only**. Product pricing is not a consideration since the goal is purely to plan output and inventory levels and the necessary manufacturing activity.

   b. EXAMPLE of a production budget:

	Source	April	May	June	2nd Quarter Totals	Ref.
Projected sales in units	SB1	1,000	1,200	1,800		
Add: desired ending inventory (10% of next month's sales)		120	180	200		
Total needed		1,120	1,380	2,000		
Less: beginning inventory		(100)	(120)	(180)		
Units to be produced		1,020	1,260	1,820	4,100	PB

3.   **Direct Materials Budget**

   a.   The direct materials budget follows directly from the production budget. It is concerned with both units and input prices.

      1)   To minimize raw materials carrying costs and obsolescence, the purchasing of inputs is tied closely to the projections contained in the production budget.

   b.   EXAMPLES of two direct materials budgets. Note that in the third month,

      1)   The process is expected to experience improved efficiency with regard to Raw Material A.

      2)   A price break on Raw Material B is expected.

Raw Material A	Source	April	May	June	2nd Quarter Totals	Ref.
Units to be produced	PB	1,020	1,260	1,820		
Raw material per finished product		× 4	× 4	× 3		DMB1
Total units needed for production		4,080	5,040	5,460		
Raw material cost per unit		× $12	× $12	× $12		DMB2
Cost of units used in production		$48,960	$60,480	$65,520	$174,960	DMB3
Add: desired units in ending inventory (20% of next month's need)		1,008	1,092	1,600		
Total needs		5,088	6,132	7,060		
Less: beginning inventory		(400)	(1,008)	(1,092)		
Raw material to be purchased		4,688	5,124	5,968		
Raw material cost per unit		× $12	× $12	× $12		
Cost of raw material to be purchased		**$56,256**	**$61,488**	**$71,616**		DMB4

Raw Material B	Source	April	May	June	2nd Quarter Totals	Ref.
Units to be produced	PB	1,020	1,260	1,820		
Raw material per finished product		× 2	× 2	× 2		DMB5
Total units needed for production		2,040	2,520	3,640		
Raw material cost per unit		× $10	× $10	× $8		DMB6
Cost of units used in production		$20,400	$25,200	$29,120	$74,720	DMB7
Add: desired units in ending inventory (20% of next month's need)		504	728	900		
Total needs		2,544	3,248	4,540		
Less: beginning inventory		(200)	(504)	(728)		
Raw material to be purchased		2,344	2,744	3,812		
Raw material cost per unit		× $10	× $10	× $8		
Cost of raw material to be purchased		**$23,440**	**$27,440**	**$30,496**		DMB8

Stop and review! You have completed the outline for this subunit. Study multiple-choice questions 19 through 22 beginning on page 241.

6.7   OPERATING BUDGET CALCULATIONS -- OTHERS

1.   **Direct Labor Budget**

   a.   The direct labor budget depends on wage rates, amounts and types of production, numbers and skill levels of employees to be hired, etc.

   b.   EXAMPLE of a direct labor budget. No new efficiencies are expected, and the wage rate is set by contract with the union.

	Source	April	May	June	2nd Quarter Totals	Ref.
Units to be produced	PB	1,020	1,260	1,820		
Direct labor hours per unit		× 2	× 2	× 2		DLB1
Projected total direct labor hours		2,040	2,520	3,640		DLB2
Direct labor cost per hour		× $18.64	× $18.64	× $18.64		
Total projected direct labor cost*		**$38,026**	**$46,973**	**$67,850**	**$152,849**	DLB3

*NOTE: For the remaining calculations, please round to the nearest whole number.

2. **Employee Fringe Benefits**

   a. The **cost of fringe benefits** must be derived once the cost of wages has been determined.

   b. EXAMPLE of an employee fringe benefit projection:

	Source	April	May	June	2nd Quarter Totals	Ref.
Projected direct labor wages	DLB3	$38,026	$46,973	$67,850	$152,849	
Employer FICA match (7.65%)		2,909	3,593	5,191	11,693	
Health insurance (12.1%)		4,601	5,684	8,210	18,495	
Life insurance (5%)		1,901	2,349	3,393	7,643	
Pension matching (4%)		1,521	1,879	2,714	6,114	
Total projected direct labor cost		**$48,958**	**$60,478**	**$87,358**	**$196,794**	**DLB4**

   c. The full per-hour cost of labor can now be determined. This will be used in determining the costs embedded in units remaining in ending finished goods inventory.

      1) Since a first-in, first-out (FIFO) assumption is used for all inventories and only units produced in June are expected to remain at the end of June, the calculation is only necessary for June's data.

Total projected direct labor cost	÷	Total projected direct labor hours	=	Full direct labor cost per hour	Ref.
$87,356	÷	3,640	=	$24	DLB5

   d. Whether employee fringes are included in direct labor costs or treated as overhead, the effect on cost of goods sold is the same. Both ways include the amounts in variable manufacturing costs.

3. **Variable Overhead**

   a. The manufacturing overhead budget reflects the nature of overhead as a mixed cost, i.e., one that has a variable component and a fixed component.

   b. Variable overhead contains those elements that vary with the level of production.

      1) Indirect materials
      2) Some indirect labor
      3) Variable factory operating costs (e.g., electricity)

   c. EXAMPLE of a variable overhead budget. Note that variable overhead will be applied to finished goods on the basis of direct labor hours.

Variable overhead	Source	April	May	June	2nd Quarter Totals	Ref.
Projected total direct labor hours	DLB2	2,040	2,520	3,640		
Variable OH rate per direct labor hour		× $2	× $2	× $2		MOB1
Projected variable overhead		**$4,080**	**$5,040**	**$7,280**	**$16,400**	**MOB2**

4. **Fixed Overhead**

   a. Fixed overhead contains those elements that remain the same regardless of the level of production.

      1) Real estate taxes
      2) Insurance
      3) Depreciation

b. EXAMPLE of a fixed overhead budget. Note that fixed overhead will be applied based on the number of units produced.

Fixed overhead	Source	April	May	June	2nd Quarter Totals	Ref.
Projected fixed overhead		**$9,000**	**$9,000**	**$9,000**	**$27,000**	**MOB3**
Projected unit production	PB	÷ 1,020	÷ 1,260	÷ 1,820		
Fixed OH applied per unit		$ 8.82	$ 7.14	$ 4.95		**MOB4**

5. **Ending Finished Goods Inventory Budget**

   a. The ending finished goods inventory budget can be prepared now that the components of finished goods cost have been projected.

      1) The end result will have a direct impact on the pro forma balance sheet. The higher the amount of costs capitalized in finished goods, the higher will be the firm's projected asset balance at year-end.

   b. EXAMPLE of a unit-cost calculation. Since a first-in, first-out (FIFO) assumption is used for all inventories and only units produced in June are expected to remain at the end of June, this calculation uses June's data.

	Source	Qty.	Source	Input cost	Cost per finished unit
Production costs in ending inventory:					
Direct materials -- raw material A	DMB1	3	DMB2	$12.00	$ 36.00
Direct materials -- raw material B	DMB5	2	DMB6	8.00	16.00
Direct labor	DLB1	2	DLB5	24.00	48.00
Variable overhead	DLB1	2	MOB1	2.00	4.00
Fixed overhead	--	1	MOB4	4.95	4.95
Finished goods cost					$108.95

   c. Now the total amount of cost embedded in ending inventory can be derived.

Total FIFO cost per finished unit	×	Projected units at June 30	=	Projected ending inventory	Ref.
$108.95	×	200	=	$21,790	EFGIB

6. **Cost of Goods Sold Budget**

   a. The cost of goods sold budget combines the results of the projections for the three major inputs (materials, labor, overhead).

      1) The end result will have a direct impact on the pro forma income statement. Cost of goods sold is the single largest reduction to revenues for a manufacturer.

   b. EXAMPLE of a cost of goods sold budget for the quarter:

	Source		Ref.
Beginning finished goods inventory		$ 16,200	
Manufacturing costs:			
Direct materials used -- A	DMB3	$174,960	
Direct materials used -- B	DMB7	74,720	
Direct labor employed	DLB4	196,794	
Variable overhead	MOB2	16,400	
Fixed overhead	MOB3	27,000	
Cost of goods manufactured		489,874	
Cost of goods available for sale		$506,074	
Ending finished goods inventory	EFGIB	(21,790)	
Cost of goods sold		**$484,284**	**CGSB**

c. Budgeted gross margin can now be calculated, the amount left over from sales revenue after the cost of the product:

	Source	
Sales	SB2	$1,564,000
Cost of goods sold	CGSB	(484,284)
Gross margin		**$1,079,716**

1) The calculation of gross margin is required for external financial reporting. Cost of goods sold for this purpose must be derived using absorption (full) costing, i.e., by including all manufacturing costs, both variable and fixed.

2) For internal reporting, variable (direct) costing, which includes only variable costs in cost of goods sold, is more useful than absorption costing.

7. **Variable Costing and Contribution Margin**

a. Contribution margin is the amount left over from sales after subtracting variable-basis cost of goods sold.

1) Although it is impermissible for external financial reporting, contribution margin is more useful to management accountants because it reveals more accurately the change in profitability resulting from a given change in output.

2) Absorption costing (required for external reporting) includes certain amounts in cost of goods sold that do not vary directly with the level of production, such as straight-line depreciation and property taxes.

b. Cost of goods sold calculated on a variable-costing basis, on the other hand, includes only those costs that vary directly with the level of production. The amount of sales left over after subtracting variable-basis cost of goods sold is contribution margin.

1) Because costs are accumulated so differently, inventory amounts as well as cost of goods sold are different under variable costing from what they are under absorption costing.

Sales		**$ X,XXX**
Beginning inventory	$X,XXX	
Add: variable manufacturing costs	X,XXX	
Goods available for sale	$X,XXX	
Less: ending inventory	(XXX)	
Variable-basis cost of goods sold		**$(X,XXX)**
Less: variable nonmanufacturing costs		(XXX)
Contribution margin		**$ X,XXX**

2) Contribution margin is the amount available for "contributing" to the covering of fixed costs and providing a profit (for a fuller discussion of absorption and variable costing, see Study Unit 3, Subunit 1).

c. The breakeven point is the level of production at which operating income equals zero, i.e., the level at which all fixed costs plus those variable costs incurred to that point have been covered.

1) Every sales dollar beyond breakeven provides operating profit.

$$Breakeven\ point = \frac{Total\ fixed\ costs}{Contribution\ margin\ per\ unit}$$

2) EXAMPLE: A manufacturer has budgeted total fixed costs of $1,240,000 and a budgeted contribution margin of $6.80 per unit. The breakeven point for the budget period is 182,353 units ($1,240,000 ÷ $6.80).

NOTE: Breakeven analysis, also called cost-volume-profit analysis, is tested in Part 2 of the CMA exam.

8. **Nonmanufacturing Budget**

    a. The nonmanufacturing budget consists of the individual budgets for R&D, design, marketing, distribution, customer service, and administrative costs.

        1) The development of separate R&D, design, marketing, distribution, customer service, and administrative budgets reflects a value chain approach.

        2) An alternative is to prepare a single selling and administrative budget for nonproduction costs.

    b. The variable and fixed portions of selling and administrative costs must be treated separately.

        1) Some S&A costs vary directly and proportionately with the level of sales. As more product is sold, sales representatives must travel more miles and serve more customers.

        2) Other S&A expenses, such as sales support staff, are fixed; they must be paid no matter the level of sales.

        3) As the variable portion of S&A costs increases, contribution margin, i.e., the amount available for covering fixed costs, is decreased.

    c. EXAMPLE of a nonmanufacturing costs budget. Note the separate treatment of the variable and fixed portions.

	Source	April	May	June	2nd Quarter Totals	Ref.
Variable nonmanufacturing costs:						
Projected sales in units	SB1	1,000	1,200	1,800		
Variable S&A expenses						
($3 per unit sold)		× $3	× $3	× $3		
Total variable nonmanufacturing costs		$ 3,000	$ 3,600	$ 5,400	$ 12,000	
Fixed nonmanufacturing costs:						
Research and development		$ 8,000	$ 8,000	$ 8,000	$ 24,000	
Design		4,000	4,000	4,000	12,000	
Marketing		7,000	7,000	7,000	21,000	
Distribution		10,000	10,000	10,000	30,000	
Customer service		11,000	11,000	11,000	33,000	
Administrative		50,000	50,000	50,000	150,000	
Total fixed nonmanufacturing costs		$90,000	$90,000	$90,000	$270,000	
Total nonmanufacturing costs		**$93,000**	**$93,600**	**$95,400**	**$282,000**	**NMB**

    d. Note that management can make tradeoffs among elements of selling and administrative expenses that can affect contribution margin.

        1) For example, use of fixed advertising expense will increase contribution margin, while the same sales level might be reached using variable sales commissions, a method that would reduce contribution margin.

9. **Pro Forma Operating Income**

    a. If the projected level of operating income is insufficient, the various components of the operating budget can be adjusted.

        1) EXAMPLE of pro forma operating income

	Source	
Sales	SB2	$1,564,000
Cost of goods sold	CGSB	(484,284)
Gross margin		$1,079,716
Nonmanufacturing costs	NMB	(282,000)
Operating income		**$ 797,716**

Stop and review! You have completed the outline for this subunit. Study multiple-choice questions 23 through 26 beginning on page 242.

6.8 PROJECTING CASH COLLECTIONS

1. **Capital Budget**

   a. Outside the annual financial budget cycle is the preparation of the capital budget, which often must be approved by the board of directors.

      1) The capital budget concerns financing of major expenditures for long-term assets and must therefore have a multi-year perspective. Productive machinery must be acquired to enable the company to achieve its projected levels of output.

   b. A procedure for ranking projects according to their risk and return characteristics is necessary because every organization has finite resources.

   NOTE: These procedures (net present value, internal rate of return, payback method, etc.) are tested in Part 2 of the CMA exam.

   c. The capital budget has a direct impact on the cash budget and the pro forma financial statements.

      1) Principal and interest on debt acquired to finance capital purchases require regular cash outflows. The acquired debt also appears in the liabilities section of the pro forma balance sheet.

      2) At the same time, the output produced by the new productive assets generates regular cash inflows. In addition, the new assets themselves appear in the assets section of the pro forma balance sheet.

2. **Cash Collections Schedule**

   a. The projected cash collections schedule is used to estimate the inflows of cash from customer payments.

      1) EXAMPLE of a cash collections schedule. Note the assumption that 5% of sales will prove to be uncollectible.

Projected February sales			$180,000		
Projected March sales			$220,000		

	Source	April	May	June	Ref.
Projected sales	SB2	$400,000	$480,000	$684,000	
Cash collections from sales:					
From 2nd prior month sales (30%)		54,000	66,000	120,000	
From prior month sales (50%)		110,000	200,000	240,000	
From current month sales (15%)		60,000	72,000	102,600	
Total cash collections from sales		**$224,000**	**$338,000**	**$462,600**	**PCCS**

Stop and review! You have completed the outline for this subunit. Study multiple-choice questions 27 through 30 beginning on page 244.

6.9 THE CASH BUDGET

1. **Cash Budget as Lynchpin of Budget Process**

    a. The cash budget is the part of the financial budget cycle that ties together all the schedules from the operating budget.

        1) A cash budget projects cash receipts and disbursements for planning and control purposes. Hence, it helps prevent not only cash emergencies but also excessive idle cash.

    b. A cash budget is vital because an organization must have adequate cash at all times. Almost all organizations, regardless of size, prepare a cash budget. Even with plenty of other assets, an organization with a temporary shortage of cash can be driven into bankruptcy.

        1) Proper planning can keep an entity from financial embarrassment. Thus, cash budgets are prepared not only for annual and quarterly periods but also for monthly and weekly periods.

            a) They are particularly important for organizations operating in seasonal industries.

            b) The factors needed to prepare a cash forecast include all other elements of the budget preparation process, plus consideration of collection policies, bad debt estimates, and changes in the economy.

        2) Credit and purchasing policies have a direct impact on the cash budget.

            a) Loose credit policies toward customers' credit result in delayed cash receipts.

            b) Taking advantage of purchase discounts results in accelerated cash outlays.

2. **Cash Disbursements Schedule**

    a. First, a projected cash disbursements schedule for raw materials is prepared.

        1) EXAMPLE of a raw materials cash disbursements schedule:

		March raw materials purchases -- A	$45,000		
		March raw materials purchases -- B	$17,000		

	Source	April	May	June	Ref.
Projected raw materials cost -- A	DMB4	$56,256	$61,488	$71,616	
Cash payments for purchases of A:					
For prior month purchases (40%)		18,000	22,502	24,595	
For current month purchases (60%)		33,754	36,893	42,970	
Total cash disbursements for A		**$51,754**	**$59,395**	**$67,565**	PCDS1
Projected raw materials cost -- B	DMB8	$23,440	$27,440	$30,496	
Cash payments for purchases of B:					
For prior month purchases (40%)		6,800	9,376	10,976	
For current month purchases (60%)		14,064	16,464	18,298	
Total cash disbursements for B		**$20,864**	**$25,840**	**$29,274**	PCDS2

3. **Cash Budget Preparation**

    a. The cash budget combines the results of the operating budget with the cash collection and disbursement schedules to produce a comprehensive picture of where the company's cash flows are expected to come from and where they are expected to go.

        1) The completed cash budget can be used to plan outside financing activities. For example, if the budget shows a cash deficit at some future date, the firm can plan ahead to borrow the necessary funds or sell stock.

        2) Dividend policy can also be planned using the cash budget. Dividend payment dates should correspond to a time when the firm has excess cash.

b.   EXAMPLE of a cash budget. The bottom section deals with the anticipated handling of the inevitable temporary excesses and deficiencies of cash.

	Source	April	May	June
Beginning cash balance		$ 50,000	$100,000	$130,767
Cash collections from sales	PCCS	224,000	338,000	462,600
Cash available for disbursement		$274,000	$438,000	$593,367
Cash disbursements:				
For raw material A	PCDS1	$ 51,754	$ 59,395	$ 67,565
For raw material B	PCDS2	20,864	25,840	29,274
For direct labor	DLB4	48,958	60,478	87,358
For variable overhead	MOB2	4,080	5,040	7,280
For fixed overhead	MOB3	9,000	9,000	9,000
For nonmanufacturing costs	NMB	93,000	93,600	95,400
For equipment purchases	Cap. Budg.	0	0	30,000
Total disbursements		$227,656	$253,353	$325,877
Surplus of cash available				
over disbursements		$ 46,344	$184,647	$267,490
Desired ending cash balance		(100,000)	(100,000)	(100,000)
Surplus (deficiency) of cash		**$ (53,656)**	**$ 84,647**	**$167,490**
Financing:				
Borrowings		$ 53,656	$ 0	$ 0
Repayments:				
Principal		0	(53,656)	0
Interest		0	(224)	0
Net financing		$ 53,656	$ (53,880)	$ 0
Ending cash balance		**$100,000**	**$130,767**	**$267,490**

Stop and review! You have completed the outline for this subunit. Study multiple-choice questions 31 through 34 beginning on page 246.

6.10 PRO FORMA FINANCIAL STATEMENTS

1.   **Pro Forma Statement of Income**

   a.   **Pro forma** is a Latin phrase meaning literally "according to form." It can be loosely translated "as if." Financial statements are referred to as pro forma when they reflect projected, rather than actual, results.

   1)   The pro forma income statement is used to decide whether the budgeted activities will result in an acceptable level of income. If the initial pro forma income shows a loss or an unacceptable level of income, adjustments can be made to the component parts of the master budget.

   2)   Other strategic objectives can also be observed from the pro forma income statement, such as desired rates of return, debt ratio, and the interest coverage ratio (times interest earned). The adequacy of earnings per share can also be observed from the pro forma income statement.

b.   EXAMPLE of a pro forma income statement:

Manufacturing Company
Pro Forma Statement of Income
2nd Quarter

Sales		$1,564,000
Beginning finished goods inventory	$ 16,200	
Add: cost of goods manufactured	489,874	
Goods available for sale	$506,074	
Less: ending finished goods inventory	(21,790)	
Cost of goods sold		(484,284)
Gross margin		$1,079,716
Less: selling and administrative expenses		(282,000)
Operating income		$ 797,716
Add: other revenues and gains		15,000
Less: other expenses and losses		(10,000)
Earnings before interest and taxes		$ 802,716
Less: interest expense		(224)
Earnings before income taxes		$ 802,492
Less: income taxes (40%)		(320,997)
Net income		**$ 481,495**

Basic earnings per share for 2nd quarter
(5,000,000 common shares issued and outstanding) $0.096

1)   Revenue and cost assumptions can be changed and their effects on pro forma net income observed.

a)   EXAMPLE: The company has projected gross margin to be 69% of sales ($1,079,716 ÷ $1,564,000). If gross margin is changed to 75% of sales ($1,564,000 × .75 = $1,173,000), the pro forma income statement will reflect a different bottom line.

Manufacturing Company
Pro Forma Statement of Income
2nd Quarter

Sales	$1,564,000
Cost of goods sold	(391,000)
Gross margin	$1,173,000
Less: selling and administrative expenses	(282,000)
Operating income	$ 891,000
Add: other revenues and gains	15,000
Less: other expenses and losses	(10,000)
Earnings before interest and taxes	$ 896,000
Less: interest expense	(224)
Earnings before income taxes	$ 895,776
Less: income taxes (40%)	(358,310)
Net income	**$ 537,466**

Basic earnings per share for 2nd quarter
(5,000,000 common shares issued and
outstanding) $0.107

2. **Pro Forma Balance Sheet**

   a. The pro forma balance sheet is prepared using the cash and capital budgets and the pro forma income statement.

      1) The pro forma balance sheet is the beginning-of-the-period balance sheet updated for projected changes in cash, receivables, payables, inventory, etc.

      2) If the balance sheet indicates that a contractual agreement may be violated, the budgeting process must be repeated.

         a) For example, some loan agreements require that owners' equity be maintained at some percentage of total debt or that current assets be maintained at a given multiple of current liabilities.

3. **Pro Forma Statement of Cash Flows**

   a. The pro forma statement of cash flows classifies cash receipts and disbursements depending on whether they are from operating, investing, or financing activities.

      1) The direct presentation reports the major classes of gross cash operating receipts and payments and the difference between them.

      2) The indirect presentation reconciles net income with net operating cash flow. Under GAAP, this reconciliation must be disclosed whichever presentation is chosen.

         a) The reconciliation requires balance sheet data, such as the changes in accounts receivable, accounts payable, and inventory, as well as net income.

   b. All the pro forma statements are interrelated (articulated), e.g., the pro forma cash flow statement will include anticipated borrowing. The interest on this borrowing will appear in the pro forma income statement.

4. **Financial Projections and Ratio Analysis**

   a. Pro forma financial statements are of interest to parties outside the organization as well as inside.

      1) Banks and stock analysts in particular want to know what the firm believes its results will be.

   b. Projections help the bank assess whether the company anticipates satisfying the requirements of debt covenants.

      1) Typically, a firm's financing agreement with its bank requires that its debt ratio remain below a certain threshold and that its coverage ratios remain above a threshold.

         a) The debt ratio is the portion of the firm's capital structure that consists of debt, i.e., total liabilities divided by total assets.

         b) The most common coverage ratio is times interest earned, i.e., earnings before interest and taxes divided by interest expense.

      2) Projection of satisfactory levels of these ratios provide the bank some assurance that the firm will remain solvent for the foreseeable future.

c.   Earnings per share (EPS) is probably the most heavily relied-upon performance measure used by investors.

1)   EPS states the amount of current-period earnings that can be associated with a single share of a corporation's common stock.

a)   EPS is only calculated for common stock because common shareholders are the residual owners of a corporation.

2)   Of the two versions of EPS required for external financial reporting (basic and diluted), only basic is needed on Part 1 of the CMA exam.

Basic Earnings per Share (EPS)

$$\frac{\textit{Income available to common shareholders (IACS)}}{\textit{Weighted-average number of common shares outstanding}}$$

a)   The claims of preferred shareholders must be satisfied before those of the residual owners. Thus, amounts associated with preferred stock are not available to the common shareholders and must be removed from the numerator.

Income Available to Common Shareholders (IACS)

Net income – Dividends on preferred stock

3)   In the sample pro forma income statements on page 226, the basic EPS figures were calculated as follows:

1st version: $\dfrac{\$481,496 \text{ net income} - \$0 \text{ preferred dividends}}{5,000,000 \text{ common shares}}$ = \$0.09630 per share

2nd version: $\dfrac{\$537,450 \text{ net income} - \$0 \text{ preferred dividends}}{5,000,000 \text{ common shares}}$ = \$0.10749 per share

a)   If any stock dividends or stock splits are declared during the reporting period, the number of shares outstanding must be weighted as if the additional shares had been outstanding for the whole period.

COMPREHENSIVE EXAMPLE of Pro Forma Financial Statement Preparation
from CMA exam

Jefferson Binders, Inc., is a manufacturer of notebooks with a comprehensive annual budgeting process that ends with the preparation of pro forma financial statements. All underlying budget schedules have been completed for the year ending December 31, Year 2, and selected data from these schedules are presented below.

To facilitate the budgeting process, Jefferson accumulates all raw materials, direct labor, manufacturing overhead (with the exception of depreciation), selling, and administrative costs in an account called expenses payable. The company's income tax rate is 40%, and income tax expense is classified as current income taxes payable.

Unit Sales	Unit Price	Total Revenue
9,500,000	$5.50	$52,250,000

Production Units	Unit Cost	Total Manufacturing Cost
9,640,000	$4.75	$45,790,000

Raw Materials	Quantity	Cost	Total Purchases
Ring Assembly	9,600,000	$.80	$7,680,000
Cover (2 per unit)	18,800,000	$.30	$5,640,000

Production Hours	Direct Labor Cost per Hour	Total Direct Labor Cost
2,410,000	$9.00	$21,690,000

Variable overhead	$ 5,790,000
Supervisory salaries	1,250,000
Depreciation	724,000
Other fixed costs	2,840,000
Total manufacturing overhead	$10,604,000

Selling expense	$1,875,000
Administrative expense	3,080,000
Total S&A expense	$4,955,000

Additional information:

- The majority of sales are on account.
- Each finished binder requires 15 minutes of direct labor time.
- Manufacturing overhead will be applied at the rate of $4.40 per direct labor hour ($10,604,000 ÷ 2,410,000 hours).
- Each semi-annual mortgage payment consists of interest plus an even principal reduction of $100,000. Interest payments for Year 2 are $250,000.

Jefferson has prepared the following pro forma statement of cash receipts and disbursements for the year ending December 31, Year 2, and pro forma statement of financial position as of December 31, Year 1. Jefferson uses the accrual basis of accounting.

Jefferson Binders, Inc.
Pro Forma Statement of Cash Receipts and Disbursements
For the Year Ending December 31, Year 2
($000 omitted)

Cash balance 1/1/Year 2 (estimated)	$ 565
Cash receipts:	
Cash sales	5,300
Collection of accounts receivable	46,600
Proceeds from sale of additional common stock (20,000 shares)	420
Total cash available	$52,885
Total cash available	
Cash disbursements:	
Raw materials	$13,380
Direct labor	21,640
Manufacturing overhead	9,650
Selling and administrative expense	4,980
Income taxes	860
Purchase of equipment	1,200
Cash dividends	320
Mortgage payment	450
Total disbursements	$52,480
Projected cash balance 12/31/Year 2	$ 405

Jefferson Binders, Inc.
Pro Forma Statement of Financial Position
as of December 31, Year 1
($000 omitted)

Assets

Cash	$ 565
Accounts receivable	825
Raw materials inventory*	301
Finished goods inventory**	608
Total current assets	$ 2,299
Land	$ 1,757
Property, plant, and equipment	12,400
Less: accumulated depreciation	2,960
Total long-term assets	$11,197
Total assets	$13,496

Liabilities and Equity

Expenses payable	$ 690
Mortgage payable	200
Income taxes payable	356
Total current liabilities	$ 1,246
Long-term mortgage payable	$ 2,700
Total liabilities	$ 3,946
Common stock (500,000 shares authorized, 300,000 shares outstanding, $10 par value)	$ 3,000
Paid-in capital in excess of par	5,400
Retained earnings	1,150
Total equity	$ 9,550
Total liabilities and equity	$13,496

*65,000 ring assemblies at $.80 each
830,000 covers at $.30 each
**128,000 units at $4.75 each

-- Continued on next page --

COMPREHENSIVE EXAMPLE -- Continued

Jefferson's pro forma statement of income for Year 2 is prepared as follows:

Jefferson Binders, Inc.
Pro Forma Statement of Income
For the Year Ending December 31, Year 2

Sales	$52,250,000
Cost of goods sold (9,500 units × $4.75)	(45,125,000)
Gross margin	$ 7,125,000
S&A expenses	(4,955,000)
Operating income	$ 2,170,000
Interest expense	(250,000)
Earnings before taxes	$ 1,920,000
Income tax expense (40%)	(768,000)
Net income	$ 1,152,000

For the pro forma statement of financial position for Year 2, current assets are calculated as follows:

Cash		$ 405,000
Accounts receivable		
Beginning balance		$ 825,000
Net increase for the year:		
Total sales	$52,250,000	
Less: collections on credit sales	(46,600,000)	
Less: cash sales	(5,300,000)	350,000
Ending balance		$ 1,175,000
Raw materials inventory		
Beginning balance		$ 301,000
Purchases:		
Ring assemblies	$ 7,680,000	
Covers	5,640,000	13,320,000
Used in production:		
Ring assemblies (9,640 × $0.80)	$ 7,712,000	
Covers (9,640 × 2 × $0.30)	5,784,000	(13,496,000)
Ending balance		$ 125,000
Finished goods inventory		
Beginning balance		$ 608,000
Completed (9,640 units × $4.75)		45,790,000
Goods available for sale		$46,398,000
Cost of goods sold (9,500 units × $4.75)		(45,125,000)
Ending balance		$ 1,273,000

Noncurrent assets are calculated as follows:

	Property, Plant, and Equipment	Accumulated Depreciation
Beginning balances	$12,400,000	$ 2,960,000
Activity for year	1,200,000	724,000
Ending balances	$13,600,000	$ 3,684,000

-- Continued on next page --

COMPREHENSIVE EXAMPLE -- Continued

Liabilities are calculated as follows:

Expenses payable
Beginning balance $ 690,000
Increases:
  Materials purchases $13,320,000
  Direct labor   21,690,000
  Manufacturing overhead:
    Total for year $10,604,000
    Less: depreciation   (724,000)   9,880,000
  Selling and administrative   4,955,000   49,845,000
Decreases:
  Materials purchases $13,380,000
  Direct labor   21,640,000
  Manufacturing overhead   9,650,000
  Selling and administrative   4,980,000   (49,650,000)
Ending balance $ 885,000

Income taxes payable
Beginning balance $ 356,000
  Add: current period expense   768,000
  Less: disbursements   (860,000)
Ending balance $ 264,000

Mortgage payable
Beginning balance $ 2,700,000
Less: reclassified as current liability   (200,000)
Ending balance $ 2,500,000

Stockholders' equity is calculated as follows:

Common stock
Beginning balance $ 3,000,000
Issuance of new shares (20,000 × $10 par value)   200,000
Ending balance $ 3,200,000

Paid-in capital in excess of par
Beginning balance $ 5,400,000
Issuance of new shares ($420,000 − $200,000)   220,000
Ending balance $ 5,620,000

Retained earnings
Beginning balance $ 1,150,000
  Add: net income   1,152,000
  Less: dividends   (320,000)
Ending balance $ 1,982,000

-- Continued on next page --

COMPREHENSIVE EXAMPLE -- Continued

Jefferson can now prepare its pro forma statement of financial position for Year 2:

Jefferson Binders, Inc.
Pro Forma Statement of Financial Position
As of December 31, Year 2

Current assets			Liabilities		
Cash		$ 405,000	Expenses payable		$ 885,000
Accounts receivable		1,175,000	Mortgage payable -- current		200,000
Raw materials inventory		125,000	Income taxes payable		264,000
Finished goods inventory		1,273,000	Mortgage payable -- noncurrent		2,500,000
Total current assets		$ 2,978,000	Total liabilities		$ 3,849,000
Noncurrent assets			Stockholders' equity		
Land		$ 1,757,000	Common stock		$ 3,200,000
Net prop., plant, and equipment:			Paid-in capital in excess of par		5,620,000
At historical cost	$13,600,000		Retained earnings		1,982,000
Less: accum. deprec.	(3,684,000)	9,916,000	Total stockholders' equity		$10,802,000
Total noncurrent assets		$11,673,000			
			Total liabilities and		
Total assets		$14,651,000	stockholders' equity		$14,651,000

Jefferson can now prepare its pro forma statement of cash flows for Year 2 using the indirect method of presentation for cash flows from operating activities:

Jefferson Binders, Inc.
Pro Forma Statement of Cash Flows
For the Year Ending December 31, Year 2

Cash flows from operating activities:		
Net income		$1,152,000
Adjustments to reconcile net income:		
Depreciation expense	$724,000	
Decrease in raw materials inventory	176,000	
Increase in finished goods inventory	(665,000)	
Increase in accounts receivable	(350,000)	
Increase in expenses payable	195,000	
Decrease in income taxes payable	(92,000)	
Net cash used in operating activities		(12,000)
Cash flows from investing activities:		
Purchase of equipment		(1,200,000)
Cash flows from financing activities:		
Reduction in mortgage principal	$(200,000)	
Issuance of common stock – par value	200,000	
Issuance of common stock – addl. PIC	220,000	
Dividends distributed	(320,000)	
Net cash used in financing activities		(100,000)
Net decrease in cash		$ (160,000)
Beginning balance		565,000
Ending balance		$ 405,000

5. **Graphical Depiction**

Master Budget Process

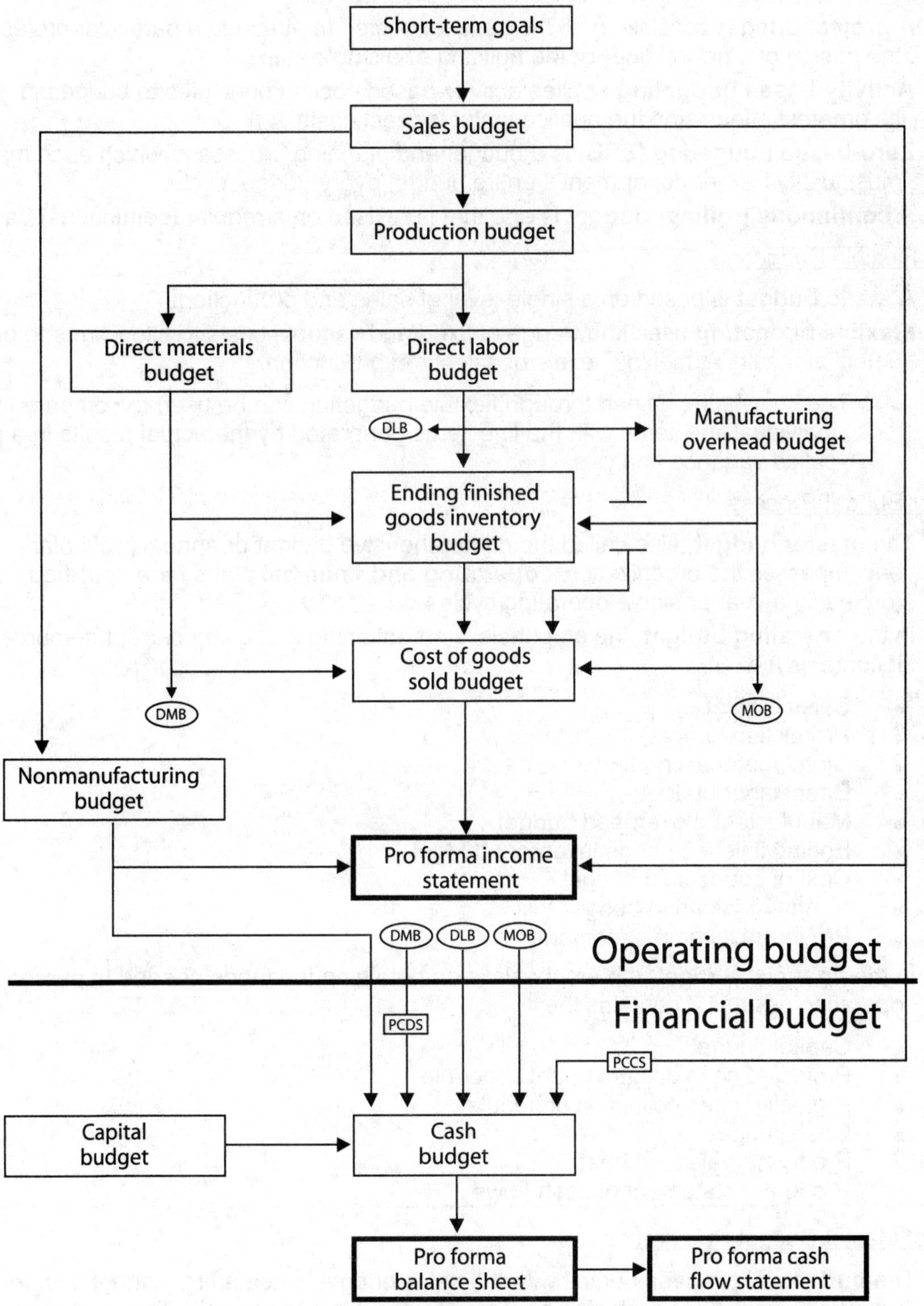

Figure 6-1

PCDS = projected cash disbursements schedule

PCCS = projected cash collection schedule

Stop and review! You have completed the outline for this subunit. Study multiple-choice questions 35 through 38 beginning on page 248.

6.11 CORE CONCEPTS

Budget Methodologies

- A **project budget** consists of all the costs expected to attach to a particular project, such as the design of a new airliner or the building of a single ship.
- **Activity-based budgeting** applies activity-based costing principles to budgeting. Its greatest effect is on the application of indirect costs.
- **Zero-based budgeting (ZBB)** is a budget and planning process in which each manager must justify his/her department's entire budget every budget cycle.
- A **continuous (rolling) budget** is one that is revised on a regular (continuous) basis.

Static and Flexible Budgeting

- A **static budget** is based on a single level of sales and production.
- **Flexible budgeting** uses knowledge of fixed and variable costs to allow firms to project potential results at multiple levels of sales and production.

  - The knowledge gained through flexible budgeting can be used to compare the individual line items with the line items generated by the actual results in a process called variance analysis.

The Master Budget Process

- The **master budget**, also called the comprehensive budget or annual profit plan, encompasses the organization's **operating and financial** plans for a specified period (ordinarily a year or single operating cycle).
- In the **operating budget**, the emphasis is on obtaining and using current resources. It contains the

  - Sales budget
  - Production budget
  - Direct materials budget
  - Direct labor budget
  - Manufacturing overhead budget
  - Ending finished goods inventory budget
  - Cost of goods sold budget
  - Nonmanufacturing budget
  - Pro forma income statement

- In the **financial budget**, the emphasis is on obtaining the funds needed to purchase operating assets. It contains the

  - Capital budget
  - Projected cash disbursement schedule
  - Projected cash collection schedule
  - Cash budget
  - Pro forma balance sheet
  - Pro forma statement of cash flows

Overview of Master Budget Preparation

- The **budgetary process** begins with the sales budget, since a firm cannot plan for production until it has projected how many units it intends to sell. The sales budget sets a target for sales personnel and affects every other element of the company.
- **Production budgets** are prepared in terms of units (not dollars) and are prepared for every production department. The production budget becomes the source for the raw material purchases budget, the direct labor budget, and the factory overhead budget.
- The **cash budget** is probably the most important part of a company's budget program.

Operating Budget Calculations -- Production and Direct Materials

- The **sales budget**, also called the revenue budget, is the starting point for the massive cycle that produces the annual profit plan (i.e., the master budget).
    - The sales budget is an outgrowth of the sales forecast. The sales forecast distills recent sales trends; overall conditions in the economy and industry; market research; activities of competitors; and credit and pricing policies.
- The **production budget** follows directly from the sales budget. It is concerned with units only.
- The **direct materials budget** follows directly from the production budget. It is concerned with both units and input prices.

Operating Budget Calculations -- Others

- The **direct labor budget** is also a direct outgrowth of the production budget.
    - The cost of fringe benefits must be derived once the cost of wages has been determined. Whether employee fringes are included in direct labor costs or treated as overhead, the effect on cost of goods sold is the same.
- The **manufacturing overhead budget** reflects the nature of overhead as a mixed cost, i.e., one that has a variable component and a fixed component.
    - **Variable overhead** contains those elements that vary with the level of production (indirect materials, indirect labor, variable factory operating costs).
    - **Fixed overhead** contains those elements that remain the same regardless of the level of production (real estate taxes, insurance, depreciation).
- The **ending finished goods inventory budget** can be prepared now that the components of finished goods cost have been projected.
- The **cost of goods sold budget** combines the results of the projections for the three major inputs (materials, labor, overhead).
- The **nonmanufacturing budget** consists of the individual budgets for R&D, design, marketing, distribution, customer service, and administrative costs.
    - The **variable and fixed portions** of selling and administrative costs must be treated separately.
- If **pro forma operating income** is insufficient, the various components of the operating budget can be adjusted.

Projecting Cash Collections

- Outside the operating budget cycle is the preparation of the **capital budget**, which must be approved by the board of directors.
- A **projected cash collection schedule** is prepared. It projects the inflows of cash from customer payments.

The Cash Budget

- The cash budget is the lynchpin of the financial budget. It combines the results of the operating budget with the cash collection and disbursement schedules to produce a comprehensive picture of where the company's cash flows are expected to come from and where they are expected to go.
    - The cash budget is not only the most important aspect of the entire budgetary process, it is also the most important from the viewpoint of CMA candidates. Candidates should be able to prepare detailed cash budgets.
    - A **projected cash disbursements schedule** must be prepared.

Pro Forma Financial Statements

- The **pro forma income statement** is used to decide whether the budgeted activities will result in an acceptable level of income.

- The **pro forma balance sheet** is prepared using the cash and capital budgets and the pro forma income statement.

- The **pro forma statement of cash flows** classifies cash receipts and disbursements depending on whether they are from operating, investing, or financing activities.

QUESTIONS

6.1 The Master Budget Process

1. In an organization that plans by using comprehensive budgeting, the master budget is

A. A compilation of all the separate operational and financial budget schedules of the organization.

B. The booklet containing budget guidelines, policies, and forms to use in the budgeting process.

C. The current budget updated for operations for part of the current year.

D. A budget of a not-for-profit organization after it is approved by the appropriate authoritative body.

Answer (A) is correct. *(CMA, adapted)*
REQUIRED: The nature of the master budget.
DISCUSSION: A company's overall budget, often called the master or comprehensive budget, encompasses the organization's operating and financial plans for a specified period, ordinarily a year. Thus, all other budgets are subsets of the master budget. In the operating budget, the emphasis is on obtaining and using current resources. In the financial budget, the emphasis is on obtaining the funds needed to purchase operating assets.
Answer (B) is incorrect. The booklet containing budget guidelines, policies, and forms to use in the budgeting process is the budget manual. Answer (C) is incorrect. The current budget updated for operations for part of the current year is a continuous budget. Answer (D) is incorrect. A master budget may be prepared by a for-profit entity.

2. While an operating budget is a key element in planning and control, it is **not** likely to

A. Establish a commitment of company resources.

B. Set out long-range, strategic concepts.

C. Integrate organizational activities.

D. Provide subsidiary planning information.

Answer (B) is correct. *(CIA, adapted)*
REQUIRED: What a budget is not likely to do.
DISCUSSION: Operating budgets seldom set out long-range strategic concepts because they usually deal with the quantitative allocation of people and resources. Strategic concepts are overall goals for the organization and are almost always stated in words.
Answer (A) is incorrect. Budgets do commit company resources in that the allotment of scarce resources is the primary purpose of a budget. Answer (C) is incorrect. Budgets do integrate organizational activities. Failure of a budget to integrate activities will result in the budgeting of more or less materials and resources than are available to the organization. Answer (D) is incorrect. Subsidiary plans can be made directly from overall budgets.

3. In preparing a corporate master budget, which one of the following is most likely to be prepared last?

A. Sales budget.

B. Cash budget.

C. Production budget.

D. Cost of goods sold budget.

Answer (B) is correct. *(CMA, adapted)*
REQUIRED: The last step in the typical corporate master budget.
DISCUSSION: The cash budget is the lynchpin of the financial budget. It combines the results of the operating budget with the cash collection and disbursement schedules to produce a comprehensive picture of where the company's cash flows are expected to come from and where they are expected to go. All the other budgets listed feed the cash budget in one way or another.
Answer (A) is incorrect. The sales budget precedes the cash budget. Answer (C) is incorrect. The production budget is the second step in the master budget, immediately following the sales budget. Answer (D) is incorrect. The cost of goods sold budget is completed well before the cash budget in the budgeting process.

4. Wilson Company uses a comprehensive planning and budgeting system. The proper order for Wilson to prepare certain budget schedules would be

A. Cost of goods sold, balance sheet, income statement, and statement of cash flows.

B. Income statement, balance sheet, statement of cash flows, and cost of goods sold.

C. Statement of cash flows, cost of goods sold, income statement, and balance sheet.

D. Cost of goods sold, income statement, balance sheet, and statement of cash flows.

Answer (D) is correct. *(CMA, adapted)*
    REQUIRED: The proper order in which budget schedules should be prepared.
    DISCUSSION: The pro forma cost of goods sold must be prepared before the pro forma income statement because it is a component of the income statement. Also, the income statement must be prepared before the pro forma balance sheet because net income is a necessary part of preparing the stockholders' equity section of the balance sheet. In turn, the income statement and the balance sheet are necessary for estimating cash flows. If the statement of cash flows is prepared using the indirect method, balance sheet data, e.g., the changes in accounts receivable, inventory, and accounts payable, must be available to determine the adjustments needed to reconcile net income to net cash flow.
    Answer (A) is incorrect. The balance sheet should not precede the income statement. Answer (B) is incorrect. The income statement cannot precede cost of goods sold. Answer (C) is incorrect. The statement of cash flows cannot precede the cost of goods sold. The latter is an input of the former.

6.2 Budget Methodologies

5. There are many different budget techniques or processes that business organizations can employ. One of these techniques or processes is zero-based budgeting, which is

A. Budgeting from the ground up as though the budget process were being initiated for the first time.

B. Budgeting for cash inflows and outflows to time investments and borrowings in a way to maintain a bank account with a minimum balance.

C. Using the prior year's budget as a base year and adjusting it based on the experiences of the prior year and the expectations for the coming year.

D. Developing budgeted costs from clear-cut measured relationships between inputs and outputs.

Answer (A) is correct. *(CIA, adapted)*
    REQUIRED: The true statement about zero-based budgeting.
    DISCUSSION: Zero-based budgeting (ZBB) is a planning process in which each manager must justify a department's entire budget every year (or period). Under ZBB, a manager must build the budget every year from a base of zero. All expenditures must be justified regardless of the variances from previous years' budgets. The objective is to encourage periodic reexamination of all costs in the hope that some can be reduced or eliminated.
    Answer (B) is incorrect. Zero-balance banking involves budgeting for cash inflows and outflows to time investments and borrowings in a way to maintain a bank account with a minimum balance. Answer (C) is incorrect. Using the prior year's budget as a base year and adjusting it based on the experiences of the prior year and the expectations for the coming year is an incremental budget process. Answer (D) is incorrect. Developing budgeted costs from clear-cut measured relationships between inputs and outputs is an adaptation of the definition of engineered costs, which forms the basis for the input-output approach to budgeting.

6. Which one of the following is **not** an advantage of activity-based budgeting?

A. Better identification of resource needs.

B. Linking of costs to outputs.

C. Identification of budgetary slack.

D. Reduction of planning uncertainty.

Answer (D) is correct. *(CMA, adapted)*
    REQUIRED: The factor not an advantage of activity-based budgeting.
    DISCUSSION: Activity-based budgeting applies activity-based costing principles to budgeting. It focuses on the numerous activities necessary to produce and market goods and services and requires analysis of cost drivers. Activity-based budgeting cannot reduce the level of uncertainty to which any large organization is subject.
    Answer (A) is incorrect. Better identification of resource needs is an advantage of any kind of budgeting. Answer (B) is incorrect. Linking costs to outputs is a feature of a cost accumulation system, such as job-order or process costing. Answer (C) is incorrect. Identification of budgetary slack can be built into any budget system, not just an activity-based one.

7. An advantage of incremental budgeting when compared with zero-based budgeting is that incremental budgeting

    A. Encourages adopting new projects quickly.

    B. Accepts the existing base as being satisfactory.

    C. Eliminates functions and duties that have outlived their usefulness.

    D. Eliminates the need to review all functions periodically to obtain optimum use of resources.

Answer (B) is correct. *(CMA, adapted)*
    REQUIRED: The advantage of incremental budgeting compared with zero-based budgeting (ZBB).
    DISCUSSION: Incremental budgeting simply adjusts the current year's budget to allow for changes planned for the coming year; a manager is not asked to justify the base portion of the budget. ZBB, however, requires a manager to justify the entire budget for each year. Incremental budgeting offers to managers the advantage of requiring less managerial effort to justify changes in the budget.
    Answer (A) is incorrect. Both types of budgets treat new projects in the same manner. Answer (C) is incorrect. Reexamining functions and duties that may have outlived their usefulness is an advantage of ZBB. Answer (D) is incorrect. Periodic review of functions is essential regardless of the budgetary system used.

8. A continuous profit plan

    A. Is a plan that is revised monthly or quarterly.

    B. Is an annual plan that is part of a 5-year plan.

    C. Is a plan devised by a full-time planning staff.

    D. Works best for a company that can reliably forecast events a year or more into the future.

Answer (A) is correct. *(CMA, adapted)*
    REQUIRED: The definition of a continuous profit plan.
    DISCUSSION: A continuous, or rolling, budget (profit plan) is one that is revised on a regular or continuous basis. Typically, a company that uses continuous budgeting extends the budget for another month or quarter in accordance with new data as the current month or quarter ends. For example, if the budget is for 12 months, a budget for the next year will always be available at the end of each interim period. Continuous budgeting encourages a longer-term perspective regardless of how little time remains in the company's current fiscal year.
    Answer (B) is incorrect. A continuous profit plan is one that is revised and extended as available information changes. Answer (C) is incorrect. A continuous plan can be prepared by either a full-time or part-time staff. Answer (D) is incorrect. It is the lack of reliable long-range information that makes the continuous profit plan so worthwhile.

6.3 Static and Flexible Budgeting

9. Barnes Corporation expected to sell 150,000 board games during the month of November, and the company's master budget contained the following data related to the sale and production of these games:

Revenue	$2,400,000
Cost of goods sold:	
Direct materials	675,000
Direct labor	300,000
Variable overhead	450,000
Contribution margin	$ 975,000
Fixed overhead	250,000
Fixed selling and administration	500,000
Operating income	$ 225,000

Actual sales during November were 180,000 games. Using a flexible budget, the company expects the operating income for the month of November to be

    A. $225,000

    B. $270,000

    C. $420,000

    D. $510,000

Answer (C) is correct. *(CMA, adapted)*
    REQUIRED: The expected operating income based on a flexible budget at a given production level.
    DISCUSSION: Revenue of $2,400,000 reflects a unit selling price of $16 ($2,400,000 ÷ 150,000 games). The contribution margin is $975,000, or $6.50 per game ($975,000 ÷ 150,000 games). Increasing sales will result in an increased contribution margin of $195,000 (30,000 games × $6.50). Since fixed costs are, by their nature, unchanging across the relevant range, net income will increase to $420,000 ($225,000 originally reported + $195,000).
    Answer (A) is incorrect. The net income before the increase in sales is $225,000. Answer (B) is incorrect. Net income was originally $1.50 per game. The $270,000 figure simply extrapolates that amount to sales of 180,000 games. Answer (D) is incorrect. Treating variable overhead as a fixed cost results in $510,000. Variable overhead is a $3 component ($450,000 ÷ 150,000 units) of unit variable cost.

10. Simson Company's master budget shows straight-line depreciation on factory equipment of $258,000. The master budget was prepared at an annual production volume of 103,200 units of product. This production volume is expected to occur uniformly throughout the year. During September, Simson produced 8,170 units of product, and the accounts reflected actual depreciation on factory machinery of $20,500. Simson controls manufacturing costs with a flexible budget. The flexible budget amount for depreciation on factory machinery for September would be

A. $19,475

B. $20,425

C. $20,500

D. $21,500

Answer (D) is correct. *(CMA, adapted)*
REQUIRED: The amount of depreciation expense shown on the flexible budget for the month.
DISCUSSION: Since depreciation is a fixed cost, that cost will be the same each month regardless of production. Therefore, the budget for September would show depreciation of $21,500 ($258,000 annual depreciation × 1/12).
Answer (A) is incorrect. Depreciation is a fixed cost that will be the same each month regardless of production. The budget for September would show depreciation of $21,500 ($258,000 × 1/12). Answer (B) is incorrect. The amount of $20,425 is based on the units-of-production method. Answer (C) is incorrect. The amount shown in the accounts is $20,500.

6.4 Selecting the Budget Methodology

11. The type of budget that is available on a continuous basis for a specified future period -- by adding a month, quarter, or year in the future as the month, quarter, or year just ended is dropped -- is called a(n)

A. Rolling budget.

B. Kaizen budget.

C. Activity-based budget.

D. Flexible budget.

Answer (A) is correct. *(CMA, adapted)*
REQUIRED: The budget type that involves continually adding new periods and dropping old ones.
DISCUSSION: A continuous (rolling) budget is one that is revised on a regular (continuous) basis. Typically, a company continuously extends such a budget for an additional month or quarter in accordance with new data as the current month or quarter ends. For example, if the budget cycle is 1 year, a budget for the next 12 months will be available continuously as each month ends. The principal advantage of a rolling budget is that it requires managers always to be thinking ahead.
Answer (B) is incorrect. A kaizen budget is one that assumes the continuous improvement of products and processes. Answer (C) is incorrect. An activity-based budget is one that applies activity-based costing principles to budgeting. Answer (D) is incorrect. A flexible budget consists of a series of budgets prepared for many levels of activity.

12. The use of the master budget throughout the year as a constant comparison with actual results signifies that the master budget is also a

A. Flexible budget.

B. Capital budget.

C. Zero-base budget.

D. Static budget.

Answer (D) is correct. *(CMA, adapted)*
REQUIRED: The type of budget that is used throughout the year for comparison with actual results.
DISCUSSION: If an unchanged master budget is used continuously throughout the year for comparison with actual results, it must be a static budget, that is, one prepared for just one level of activity.
Answer (A) is incorrect. A flexible budget can be used in conjunction with standard costs to provide budgets for different activity levels. Answer (B) is incorrect. A capital budget concerns only long-term investments. Answer (C) is incorrect. A zero-base budget is one that requires its preparer to fully justify every item in the budget for each period.

13. Which one of the following budgeting methodologies would be most appropriate for a firm facing a significant level of uncertainty in unit sales volumes for next year?

- A. Top-down budgeting.
- B. Life-cycle budgeting.
- C. Static budgeting.
- D. Flexible budgeting.

Answer (D) is correct. *(CMA, adapted)*
REQUIRED: The budgeting methodology most appropriate for a firm facing significant uncertainty about unit sales volumes.
DISCUSSION: With flexible budgeting, the firm prepares a series of budgets for many levels of sales and production. At the end of the period, management can compare actual sales performance with the appropriate budgeted level in the flexible budget.
Answer (A) is incorrect. Top-down budgeting entails imposition of a budget by top management on lower-level employees. It is the antithesis of participatory budgeting. Answer (B) is incorrect. Life-cycle budgeting estimates a product's revenues and costs for each link in the value chain from R&D and design to production, marketing, distribution, and customer service. The product life cycle ends when customer service is withdrawn. Answer (C) is incorrect. A static budget is for only one level of activity.

14. A plan that is created using budgeted revenue and costs but is based on the actual units of output is known as a

- A. Continuous budget.
- B. Flexible budget.
- C. Strategic plan.
- D. Static budget.

Answer (B) is correct. *(CMA, adapted)*
REQUIRED: The plan based on budgeted revenue and costs and actual output.
DISCUSSION: A flexible budget is a series of several budgets prepared for many levels of sales and production. A flexible budget is designed to allow adjustment of the budget to the actual level of activity before comparing the budgeted activity with actual results.
Answer (A) is incorrect. A continuous budget is revised on a regular (continuous) basis by extending it for another month or quarter in accordance with new data as the current month or quarter ends. Answer (C) is incorrect. A strategic plan is a long-term planning device. Answer (D) is incorrect. A static (fixed) budget is prepared for only one level of output. That level will probably not be the level of actual operations.

6.5 Overview of Master Budget Preparation

15. The foundation of a profit plan is the

- A. Capital budget.
- B. Sales forecast.
- C. Cost and expense budget.
- D. Production plan.

Answer (B) is correct. *(CMA, adapted)*
REQUIRED: The basis for a profit plan (budget).
DISCUSSION: The starting point for the annual budget is the sales forecast. All other aspects of the budget, including production, costs, and inventory levels, rely on projected sales figures.
Answer (A) is incorrect. A capital budget is only concerned with capital expenditures and cannot be prepared until it is known whether new equipment or facilities will be needed to service the expected sales for the upcoming period. Answer (C) is incorrect. This aspect of the budget cannot be prepared until sales have been estimated. Answer (D) is incorrect. Sales must be estimated before a production plan can be prepared.

16. Adams Manufacturing, Inc., produces farm tractors. The details of its budgeted cost of goods manufactured schedule should come from which of the following schedules?

- A. Cost of goods sold plus or minus the change planned in finished goods.
- B. Direct materials used, direct labor, manufacturing overhead, and work-in-process.
- C. Purchases, direct labor, manufacturing overhead, finished goods, and work-in-process.
- D. Purchases, raw material, work-in-process, and finished goods.

Answer (B) is correct. *(CMA, adapted)*
REQUIRED: The sources of the figures appearing on a budgeted cost of goods manufactured schedule.
DISCUSSION: Cost of goods manufactured equals all manufacturing costs incurred during the period, plus beginning work-in-process inventory, minus ending work-in-process inventory. The cost of goods manufactured schedule therefore includes direct materials, direct labor, factory overhead, and changes in work-in-process inventories.
Answer (A) is incorrect. Cost of goods sold equals the cost of goods manufactured adjusted for the change in finished goods. Also, finished goods are not a part of the cost of goods manufactured calculation. Answer (C) is incorrect. Purchases is a component of the raw materials budget, not the cost of goods sold schedule, and finished goods are not included in CGM. Answer (D) is incorrect. CGM includes direct materials used, not purchases or finished goods.

17. Which one of the following schedules would be the last item to be prepared in the normal budget preparation process?

A. Direct labor budget.

B. Cash budget.

C. Cost of goods sold budget.

D. Manufacturing overhead budget.

Answer (B) is correct. *(CMA, adapted)*
REQUIRED: The last item prepared in the normal budget preparation process.
DISCUSSION: The budget process begins with the sales budget, proceeds to the production and expense budgets, and eventually the cash budget. The cash budget cannot be prepared until the end of the process because all other budgets provide inputs to the cash budget.
Answer (A) is incorrect. A direct labor budget must be prepared before the cash budget. Answer (C) is incorrect. A cost of goods sold budget must be prepared before the cash budget. Answer (D) is incorrect. A manufacturing overhead budget must be prepared before the cash budget.

18. There are various budgets within the master budget cycle. One of these budgets is the production budget. Which one of the following best describes the production budget?

A. It summarizes all discretionary costs.

B. It includes required direct labor hours.

C. It includes required material purchases.

D. It is calculated from the desired ending inventory and the sales forecast.

Answer (D) is correct. *(CMA, adapted)*
REQUIRED: The best description of a production budget.
DISCUSSION: A production budget is based on sales forecasts, in units, with adjustments for beginning and ending inventories. It is used to plan when items will be produced. After the production budget has been completed, it is used to prepare materials purchases, direct labor, and factory overhead budgets.
Answer (A) is incorrect. A production budget is usually prepared in terms of units of output rather than costs. Answer (B) is incorrect. The direct labor budget is prepared after the production budget. Answer (C) is incorrect. The materials purchases budget is prepared after the production budget.

6.6 Operating Budget Calculations -- Production and Direct Materials

Questions 19 and 20 are based on the following information.

Daffy Tunes manufactures a toy rabbit with moving parts and a built-in voice box. Projected sales in units for the next 5 months are as follows:

Month	Projected Sales in Units
January	30,000
February	36,000
March	33,000
April	40,000
May	29,000

Each rabbit requires basic materials that Daffy purchases from a single supplier at $3.50 per rabbit. Voice boxes are purchased from another supplier at $1.00 each. Assembly labor cost is $2.00 per rabbit, and variable overhead cost is $.50 per rabbit. Fixed manufacturing overhead applicable to rabbit production is $12,000 per month. Daffy's policy is to manufacture 1.5 times the coming month's projected sales every other month, starting with January (i.e., odd-numbered months) for February sales, and to manufacture 0.5 times the coming month's projected sales in alternate months (i.e., even-numbered months). This allows Daffy to allocate limited manufacturing resources to other products as needed during the even-numbered months.

19. Daffy Tunes' unit production budget for toy rabbits for January is

A. 45,000 units.

B. 16,500 units.

C. 54,000 units.

D. 14,500 units.

Answer (C) is correct. *(CMA, adapted)*
REQUIRED: The unit production budget for January.
DISCUSSION: The production budget for January is 54,000 units (36,000 projected February sales × 1.5).
Answer (A) is incorrect. The figure of 45,000 is based on January sales. Answer (B) is incorrect. Budgeted production for February is 16,500 units. Answer (D) is incorrect. Budgeted production for April is 14,500 units.

20. Daffy Tunes' dollar production budget for toy rabbits for February is

A. $327,000

B. $390,000

C. $113,500

D. $127,500

Answer (D) is correct. *(CMA, adapted)*
REQUIRED: The dollar production budget for February.
DISCUSSION: The units to be produced in February equal 50% of March sales, or 16,500 units (33,000 × .5). The unit variable cost is $7.00 ($3.50 + $1.00 + $2.00 + $.50), so total variable costs are $115,500 (16,500 × $7). Thus, the dollar production budget for February is $127,500 ($115,500 variable + $12,000 fixed).
Answer (A) is incorrect. The amount of $327,000 is based on January sales. Answer (B) is incorrect. The production budget for January is $390,000. Answer (C) is incorrect. The production budget for April is $113,500.

Questions 21 and 22 are based on the following information.

Rokat Corporation is a manufacturer of tables sold to schools, restaurants, hotels, and other institutions. The table tops are manufactured by Rokat, but the table legs are purchased from an outside supplier. The Assembly Department takes a manufactured table top and attaches the four purchased table legs. It takes 20 minutes of labor to assemble a table. The company follows a policy of producing enough tables to ensure that 40% of next month's sales are in the finished goods inventory. Rokat also purchases sufficient direct materials inventory to ensure that direct materials inventory is 60% of the following month's scheduled production.

Rokat's sales budget in units for the next quarter is as follows:

July	2,300
August	2,500
September	2,100

Rokat's ending inventories in units for June 30 are

Finished goods	1,900
Direct materials (legs)	4,000

21. The number of tables to be produced by Rokat during August is

A. 1,400 tables.

B. 2,340 tables.

C. 1,440 tables.

D. 1,900 tables.

Answer (B) is correct. *(CMA, adapted)*
REQUIRED: The number of tables to be produced.
DISCUSSION: The company will need 2,500 finished units for August sales. In addition, 840 units (2,100 September unit sales × 40%) should be in inventory at the end of August. August sales plus the desired ending inventory equals 3,340 units. Of these units, 40% of August's sales, or 1,000 units, should be available from beginning inventory. Consequently, production in August should be 2,340 units.
Answer (A) is incorrect. The number of tables to be produced in July is 1,400. Answer (C) is incorrect. The figure of 1,440 tables is based on July's beginning inventory. Answer (D) is incorrect. July's beginning inventory equals 1,900 tables.

22. Assume Rokat's required production for August and September is 1,600 and 1,800 units, respectively, and the July 31 direct materials inventory is 4,200 units. The number of table legs to be purchased in August is

A. 6,520 legs.

B. 9,400 legs.

C. 2,200 legs.

D. 6,400 legs.

Answer (A) is correct. *(CMA, adapted)*
REQUIRED: The number of table legs to be purchased.
DISCUSSION: The August production of 1,600 units will require 6,400 table legs. September's production of 1,800 units will require 7,200 table legs. Thus, inventory at the end of August should be 4,320 legs (7,200 legs × 60%). The total of legs needed during August is 10,720 (6,400 + 4,320), of which 4,200 are available from the July 31 ending inventory. The remaining 6,520 legs must be purchased during August.
Answer (B) is incorrect. The figure of 9,400 legs is based on an ending inventory of 100% of September's production. Answer (C) is incorrect. Failing to consider the legs needed for the ending inventory results in 2,200 legs. Answer (D) is incorrect. The amount needed for August production is 6,400 legs.

6.7 Operating Budget Calculations -- Others

23. Which one of the following statements regarding selling and administrative budgets is most accurate?

A. Selling and administrative budgets are usually optional.

B. Selling and administrative budgets are fixed in nature.

C. Selling and administrative budgets are difficult to allocate by month and are best presented as one number for the entire year.

D. Selling and administrative budgets need to be detailed in order that the key assumptions can be better understood.

Answer (D) is correct. *(CMA, adapted)*
REQUIRED: The most accurate statement about selling and administrative budgets.
DISCUSSION: Sales and administrative budgets are prepared after the sales budget. Like the other budgets, they constitute prospective information based on the preparer's assumptions about conditions expected to exist and actions expected to be taken.
Answer (A) is incorrect. Selling and administrative budgets are no more optional than any other component of the master budget. Answer (B) is incorrect. Selling and administrative budgets have both variable and fixed components. Answer (C) is incorrect. Selling and administrative budgets should be prepared on the same basis as the remainder of the budget, typically on at least a monthly basis.

24. For the month of December, Crystal Clear Bottling expects to sell 12,500 cases of Cranberry Sparkling Water at $24.80 per case and 33,100 cases of Lemon Dream Cola at $32.00 per case. Sales personnel receive 6% commission on each case of Cranberry Sparkling Water and 8% commission on each case of Lemon Dream Cola. In order to receive a commission on a product, the sales personnel team must meet the individual product revenue quota. The sales quota for Cranberry Sparkling Water is $500,000, and the sales quota for Lemon Dream Cola is $1,000,000. The sales commission that should be budgeted for December is

A. $4,736

B. $82,152

C. $84,736

D. $103,336

Answer (C) is correct. *(CMA, adapted)*
REQUIRED: The budgeted sales commissions for the month.
DISCUSSION: The sale of 12,500 cases of Cranberry at $24.80 per case produces revenue of $310,000, an amount that does not qualify for commissions. The sale of 33,100 cases of Lemon at $32 per case produces revenue of $1,059,200. This amount is greater than the minimum and therefore qualifies for a commission of $84,736 ($1,059,200 × 8%). This calculation assumes that commissions are paid on all sales if the revenue quota is met.
Answer (A) is incorrect. The commission on $59,200 of Lemon sales is $4,736. Answer (B) is incorrect. The amount of $82,152 equals 6% of all sales. Answer (D) is incorrect. The amount of $103,336 assumes that a commission of $18,600 is paid on Cranberry.

Question 25 is based on the following information.

Rokat Corporation is a manufacturer of tables sold to schools, restaurants, hotels, and other institutions. The table tops are manufactured by Rokat, but the table legs are purchased from an outside supplier. The Assembly Department takes a manufactured table top and attaches the four purchased table legs. It takes 20 minutes of labor to assemble a table. The company follows a policy of producing enough tables to ensure that 40% of next month's sales are in the finished goods inventory. Rokat also purchases sufficient direct materials inventory to ensure that direct materials inventory is 60% of the following month's scheduled production.

Rokat's sales budget in units for the next quarter is as follows:

July	2,300
August	2,500
September	2,100

Rokat's ending inventories in units for June 30 are

Finished goods	1,900
Direct materials (legs)	4,000

---

25. Assume that Rokat Corporation will produce 1,800 units in the month of September. How many employees will be required for the Assembly Department? (Fractional employees are acceptable since employees can be hired on a part-time basis. Assume a 40-hour week and a 4-week month.)

A. 15 employees.

B. 3.75 employees.

C. 60 employees.

D. 600 employees.

Answer (B) is correct. *(CMA, adapted)*
REQUIRED: The number of employees required.
DISCUSSION: Each unit requires 20 minutes of assembly time, or 1/3 of an hour. The assembly of 1,800 units will therefore require 600 hours of labor (1,800 × 1/3). At 40 hours per week for 4 weeks, each employee will work 160 hours during the month. Thus, 3.75 employees (600 ÷ 160) are needed.
Answer (A) is incorrect. This number of employees assumes production occurs in a single 40-hour week. Answer (C) is incorrect. This number of employees assumes that each leg requires 20 minutes to assemble and that production occurs in a single 40-hour week. Answer (D) is incorrect. This number of employees is the number of hours needed, not the number of employees.

Question 26 is based on the following information.

Jordan Auto has developed the following production plan:

Month	Units
January	10,000
February	8,000
March	9,000
April	12,000

Each unit contains 3 pounds of direct materials. The desired direct materials ending inventory each month is 120% of the next month's production, plus 500 pounds. (The beginning inventory meets this requirement.) Jordan has developed the following direct labor standards for production of these units:

	Department 1	Department 2
Hours per unit	2.0	0.5
Hourly rate	$7.25	$12.00

26. Jordan Auto's total budgeted direct labor dollars for February usage should be

A. $164,000

B. $174,250

C. $184,500

D. $221,400

Answer (A) is correct. *(CMA, adapted)*
   REQUIRED: The total budgeted direct labor dollars for February.
   DISCUSSION: The standard unit labor cost is $20.50 [($7.25 × 2 hours in Department 1) + ($12 × .5 hour in Department 2)], so the total budgeted direct labor dollars for February equal $164,000 (8,000 units × $20.50).
   Answer (B) is incorrect. The amount of $174,250 is for 500 more units than budgeted usage. Answer (C) is incorrect. The amount for March is $184,500. Answer (D) is incorrect. The amount of $221,400 is for 120% of budgeted March production.

6.8 Projecting Cash Collections

27. Which one of the following is the best characteristic concerning the capital budget? The capital budget is a(n)

A. Plan to ensure that there are sufficient funds available for the operating needs of the company.

B. Exercise that sets the long-range goals of the company including the consideration of external influences caused by others in the market.

C. Plan that results in the cash requirements during the operating cycle.

D. Plan that assesses the long-term needs of the company for plant and equipment purchases.

Answer (D) is correct. *(CMA, adapted)*
   REQUIRED: The true statement about the capital budget.
   DISCUSSION: Capital budgeting is the process of planning expenditures for long-lived assets. It involves choosing among investment proposals using a ranking procedure. Evaluations are based on various measures involving the rate of ROI.
   Answer (A) is incorrect. Capital budgeting involves long-term investment needs, not immediate operating needs. Answer (B) is incorrect. Establishing long-term goals in the context of relevant factors in the firm's environment is strategic planning. Answer (C) is incorrect. Cash budgeting determines operating cash flows. Capital budgeting evaluates the rate of return on specific investment alternatives.

28. Which one of the following items would have to be included for a company preparing a schedule of cash receipts and disbursements for calendar Year 1?

A. A purchase order issued in December Year 1 for items to be delivered in February Year 2.

B. Dividends declared in November Year 1 to be paid in January Year 2 to shareholders of record as of December Year 1.

C. The amount of uncollectible customer accounts for Year 1.

D. The borrowing of funds from a bank on a note payable taken out in June Year 1 with an agreement to pay the principal and interest in June Year 2.

Answer (D) is correct. *(CMA, adapted)*
   REQUIRED: The item included in a cash budget for Year 1.
   DISCUSSION: A schedule of cash receipts and disbursements (cash budget) should include all cash inflows and outflows during the period without regard to the accrual accounting treatment of the transactions. Hence, it should include all checks written and all sources of cash, including borrowings. A borrowing from a bank in June Year 1 should appear as a cash receipt for Year 1.
   Answer (A) is incorrect. The cash disbursement presumably will not occur until Year 2. Answer (B) is incorrect. The cash flow will not occur until dividends are paid in Year 2. Answer (C) is incorrect. Bad debt expense is a noncash item.

29. DeBerg Company has developed the following sales projections for the calendar year.

May	$100,000
June	120,000
July	140,000
August	160,000
September	150,000
October	130,000

Normal cash collection experience has been that 50% of sales are collected during the month of sale and 45% in the month following sale. The remaining 5% of sales is never collected. DeBerg's budgeted cash collections for the third calendar quarter are

A. $427,500

B. $422,500

C. $414,000

D. $450,000

Answer (C) is correct. *(CMA, adapted)*

REQUIRED: The budgeted cash collections for the third quarter.

DISCUSSION: If 50% of sales are collected in the month of sale and 45% in the next month, with the balance uncollectible, collections during the third quarter will be based on sales during June, July, August, and September. As calculated below, total budgeted collections are $414,000.

June:	$120,000 × 45%	=	$ 54,000
July:	140,000 × (50% + 45%)	=	133,000
August:	160,000 × (50% + 45%)	=	152,000
September:	150,000 × 50%	=	75,000
Total			$414,000

Answer (A) is incorrect. The total cash expected to be collected from third calendar quarter sales is $427,500. Answer (B) is incorrect. The budgeted cash collections for August through October, not the third calendar quarter, is $422,500. Answer (D) is incorrect. The total budgeted sales for the third calendar quarter is $450,000.

30. The cash receipts budget includes

A. Funded depreciation.

B. Operating supplies.

C. Extinguishment of debt.

D. Loan proceeds.

Answer (D) is correct. *(CMA, adapted)*

REQUIRED: The item included in a cash receipts budget.

DISCUSSION: A cash budget may be prepared monthly or even weekly to facilitate cash planning and control. The purpose is to anticipate cash needs while minimizing the amount of idle cash. The cash receipts section of the budget includes all sources of cash. One such source is the proceeds of loans.

Answer (A) is incorrect. Funded depreciation involves cash outlays. Answer (B) is incorrect. Purchases of supplies involves cash outlays. Answer (C) is incorrect. The extinguishment of debt involves cash outlays.

6.9 The Cash Budget

Questions 31 and 32 are based on the following information.

The Raymar Company is preparing its cash budget for the months of April and May. The firm has established a $200,000 line of credit with its bank at a 12% annual rate of interest on which borrowings for cash deficits must be made in $10,000 increments. There is no outstanding balance on the line of credit loan on April 1. Principal repayments are to be made in any month in which there is a surplus of cash. Interest is to be paid monthly. If there are no outstanding balances on the loans, Raymar will invest any cash in excess of its desired end-of-month cash balance in U.S. Treasury bills. Raymar intends to maintain a minimum balance of $100,000 at the end of each month by either borrowing for deficits below the minimum balance or investing any excess cash. Expected monthly collection and disbursement patterns are shown in the column to the right.

- *Collections:* 50% of the current month's sales budget and 50% of the previous month's sales budget.
- *Accounts Payable Disbursements:* 75% of the current month's accounts payable budget and 25% of the previous month's accounts payable budget.
- All other disbursements occur in the month in which they are budgeted.

Budget Information

	March	April	May
Sales	$40,000	$50,000	$100,000
Accounts payable	30,000	40,000	40,000
Payroll	60,000	70,000	50,000
Other disbursements	25,000	30,000	10,000

31. In April, Raymar's budget will result in

A. $45,000 in excess cash.

B. A need to borrow $50,000 on its line of credit for the cash deficit.

C. A need to borrow $100,000 on its line of credit for the cash deficit.

D. A need to borrow $90,000 on its line of credit for the cash deficit.

Answer (C) is correct. *(CMA, adapted)*
REQUIRED: The effect on cash by the end of April.
DISCUSSION: Assuming Raymar maintained a $100,000 cash balance at the end of March, the amount to be borrowed or invested in April is the difference between cash receipts and disbursements. April's cash collections are $45,000 [($50,000 April sales × 50%) + ($40,000 March sales × 50%)]. Disbursements for accounts payable are $37,500 [($40,000 April payables × 75%) + ($30,000 March payables × 25%)]. In addition to the accounts payable disbursements, payroll and other disbursements will require an additional $100,000. Hence, total disbursements are estimated to be $137,500. The net negative cash flow (amount to be borrowed to reach the required minimum cash balance of $100,000) is $92,500 ($137,500 – $45,000). Because the line of credit must be drawn upon in $10,000 increments, the loan must be for $100,000.
Answer (A) is incorrect. Cash receipts equals $45,000. Answer (B) is incorrect. The cash deficit will be $92,500 without borrowing. Answer (D) is incorrect. A loan of only $90,000 would still leave a negative cash balance of $2,500.

32. In May, Raymar will be required to

A. Repay $20,000 principal and pay $1,000 interest.

B. Repay $90,000 principal and pay $100 interest.

C. Pay $900 interest.

D. Borrow an additional $20,000 and pay $1,000 interest.

Answer (D) is correct. *(CMA, adapted)*
REQUIRED: The transaction required in May.
DISCUSSION: The company will have to borrow $100,000 in April, which means that interest will have to be paid in May at the rate of 1% per month (12% annual rate). Consequently, interest expense is $1,000 ($100,000 × 1%). May receipts are $75,000 [($100,000 May sales × 50%) + ($50,000 April sales × 50%)]. Disbursements in May are $40,000 [($40,000 May payables × 75%) + ($40,000 April payables × 25%)]. In addition to the May accounts payable disbursements, payroll and other disbursements are $60,000, bringing total disbursements to $101,000 ($60,000 + $40,000 + $1,000). Thus, disbursements exceed receipts by $26,000 ($101,000 – $75,000). However, cash has a beginning surplus balance of $7,500 ($100,000 April loan – $92,500 negative cash flow for April calculated using the collections and disbursements information given). As a result, the company needs to borrow an additional $18,500 to eliminate its cash deficit. Given the requirement that loans be in $10,000 increments, the May loan must be for $20,000.
Answer (A) is incorrect. No funds are available to repay the loan. May receipts are less than May disbursements. Answer (B) is incorrect. No funds are available to repay the loan. May receipts are less than May disbursements. Answer (C) is incorrect. The 1% interest is calculated on a $100,000 loan, not a $90,000 loan.

Questions 33 and 34 are based on the following information.

Karmee Company has been accumulating operating data in order to prepare an annual profit plan. Details regarding Karmee's sales for the first 6 months of the coming year are as follows:

Estimated Monthly Sales		Type of Monthly Sale	
January	$600,000	Cash sales	20%
February	650,000	Credit sales	80%
March	700,000		
April	625,000		
May	720,000		
June	800,000		

Collection Pattern for Credit Sales	
Month of sale	30%
One month following sale	40%
Second month following sale	25%

Karmee's cost of goods sold averages 40% of the sales value. Karmee's objective is to maintain a target inventory equal to 30% of the next month's sales in units. Purchases of merchandise for resale are paid for in the month following the sale.

The variable operating expenses (other than cost of goods sold) for Karmee are 10% of sales and are paid for in the month following the sale. The annual fixed operating expenses are presented below. All of these are incurred uniformly throughout the year and paid monthly except for insurance and property taxes. Insurance is paid quarterly in January, April, July, and October. Property taxes are paid twice a year in April and October.

Annual Fixed Operating Costs	
Advertising	$ 720,000
Depreciation	420,000
Insurance	180,000
Property taxes	240,000
Salaries	1,080,000

33. The purchase of merchandise that Karmee Company will need to make during February will be

A. $254,000

B. $260,000

C. $266,000

D. $338,000

Answer (C) is correct. *(CMA, adapted)*
    REQUIRED: The purchase of merchandise for February.
    DISCUSSION: Purchases equal cost of goods sold, plus ending inventory, minus beginning inventory. Estimated cost of goods sold for February equals $260,000 ($650,000 sales × 40%). Ending inventory is given as 30% of sales in units. Stated at cost, this amount equals $84,000 ($700,000 March sales × 30% × 40%). Furthermore, beginning inventory is $78,000 ($260,000 COGS for February × 30%). Thus, purchases equal $266,000 ($260,000 + $84,000 – $78,000).
    Answer (A) is incorrect. The amount of $254,000 reverses the treatment of the change in inventory. Answer (B) is incorrect. February COGS is $260,000. Answer (D) is incorrect. The sum of COGS and beginning inventory equals $338,000.

34. The total cash disbursements that Karmee Company will make for the operating expenses (expenses other than the cost of goods sold) during the month of April will be

A. $255,000

B. $290,000

C. $385,000

D. $420,000

Answer (C) is correct. *(CMA, adapted)*
    REQUIRED: The total cash disbursements for operating expenses during April.
    DISCUSSION: Cash disbursements for variable operating expenses in April (excluding cost of goods sold) equal $70,000 ($700,000 March sales × 10%). Cash disbursements for fixed operating expenses (excluding depreciation, a noncash expense) include advertising ($720,000 ÷ 12 = $60,000), salaries ($1,080,000 ÷ 12 = $90,000), insurance ($180,000 ÷ 4 = $45,000), and property taxes ($240,000 ÷ 2 = $120,000). Hence, cash payments for April operating expenses are $385,000 ($70,000 + $60,000 + $90,000 + $45,000 + $120,000).
    Answer (A) is incorrect. The amount of $255,000 excludes variable selling expenses and advertising. Answer (B) is incorrect. The amount of $290,000 includes depreciation but excludes variable selling expenses and advertising. Answer (D) is incorrect. The amount of $420,000 includes depreciation.

6.10 Pro Forma Financial Statements

Questions 35 and 36 are based on the following information. Super Drive, a computer disk storage and back-up company, uses accrual accounting. The company's Statement of Financial Position for the year ended November 30 is as follows:

Super Drive
Statement of Financial Position
as of November 30

Assets		Liabilities and Stockholders' Equity	
Cash	$ 52,000	Accounts payable	$ 175,000
Accounts receivable, net	150,000	Common stock	900,000
Inventory	315,000	Retained earnings	442,000
Property, plant, and equipment	1,000,000	Total liabilities and stockholders' equity	$1,517,000
Total assets	$1,517,000		

Additional information regarding Super Drive's operations include the following:

- Sales are budgeted at $520,000 for December and $500,000 for January of the next year.
- Collections are expected to be 60% in the month of sale and 40% in the month following the sale.
- Eighty percent of the disk drive components are purchased in the month prior to the month of sale, and 20% are purchased in the month of sale. Purchased components are 40% of the cost of goods sold.
- Payment for the components is made in the month following the purchase.
- Cost of goods sold is 80% of sales.

35. Super Drive's projected balance in accounts payable on December 31 is

A. $161,280

B. $326,400

C. $166,400

D. $416,000

Answer (A) is correct. *(CMA, adapted)*
　　REQUIRED: The projected balance in accounts payable on December 31.
　　DISCUSSION: Payments are made in the month following purchase. The balance in accounts payable on November 30 is $175,000; this amount will be paid in December. The account is credited for purchases of a portion of components to be used for sales in December (20% of December components) and for sales in January (80% of January components). Cost of goods sold is 80% of sales, and components are 40% of cost of goods sold. Thus, December component needs are $166,400 ($520,000 sales × 80% × 40%), and January component needs are $160,000 ($500,000 sales × 80% × 40%). The December purchases of December component needs equal $33,280 ($166,400 × 20%). December purchases of January component needs are $128,000 ($160,000 × 80%). Hence, the total of December purchases (ending balance in accounts payable) equals $161,280 ($33,280 + $128,000).
　　Answer (B) is incorrect. The sum of the component needs for December and January equals $326,400. Answer (C) is incorrect. December component needs equals $166,400. Answer (D) is incorrect. Cost of sales for December equals $416,000.

36. Super Drive's projected gross profit for the month ending December 31 is

A. $416,000

B. $104,000

C. $134,000

D. $536,000

Answer (B) is correct. *(CMA, adapted)*
　　REQUIRED: The projected gross profit for December.
　　DISCUSSION: Given that cost of goods sold is 80% of sales, gross profit is 20% of sales. Consequently, pro forma gross profit is $104,000 ($520,000 × 20%).
　　Answer (A) is incorrect. Cost of goods sold is $416,000 (80% of sales). Answer (C) is incorrect. The amount of $134,000 equals 20% of the sum of November receivables and December sales. Answer (D) is incorrect. Gross profit cannot be greater than sales.

Questions 37 and 38 are based on the following information. Kelly Company is a retail sporting goods store that uses accrual accounting for its records. Facts regarding Kelly's operations are as follows:

- Sales are budgeted at $220,000 for December Year 1 and $200,000 for January Year 2.
- Collections are expected to be 60% in the month of sale and 38% in the month following the sale.
- Gross margin is 25% of sales.
- A total of 80% of the merchandise held for resale is purchased in the month prior to the month of sale and 20% is purchased in the month of sale. Payment for merchandise is made in the month following the purchase.
- Other expected monthly expenses to be paid in cash are $22,600.
- Annual depreciation is $216,000.

Below is Kelly Company's statement of financial position at November 30, Year 1.

Assets		Liabilities and Stockholders' Equity	
Cash	$ 22,000	Accounts payable	$ 162,000
Accounts receivable (net of $4,000		Common stock	800,000
allowance for uncollectible accounts)	76,000	Retained earnings	138,000
Inventory	132,000	Total liabilities and stockholders' equity	$1,100,000
Property, plant, and equipment (net of			
$680,000 accumulated depreciation)	870,000		
Total assets	$1,100,000		

37. Kelly's pro forma income (loss) before income taxes for December Year 1 is

A. $32,400

B. $28,000

C. $10,000

D. Some amount other than those given.

Answer (C) is correct. *(CMA, adapted)*
REQUIRED: The pro forma income (loss) before taxes for the month.
DISCUSSION: Sales are budgeted at $220,000. Given that cost of goods sold is 75% of sales, or $165,000, gross profit is $55,000. Deduct cash expenses of $22,600, depreciation of $18,000 ($216,000 ÷ 12), and bad debt expense of $4,400 ($220,000 × .02). This leaves an income of $10,000.
Answer (A) is incorrect. The amount of $32,400 does not reflect depreciation or bad debt expense. Answer (B) is incorrect. The amount of $28,000 does not consider depreciation. Answer (D) is incorrect. The correct amount is given in one of the other answer choices.

38. Kelly's projected balance in accounts payable on December 31, Year 1, is

A. $162,000

B. $204,000

C. $153,000

D. Some amount other than those given.

Answer (C) is correct. *(CMA, adapted)*
REQUIRED: The projected balance in accounts payable at the end of the month.
DISCUSSION: The balance is equal to the purchases made during December since all purchases are paid for in the month following purchase. Purchases for December is given as 20% of December's sales and 80% of January's sales. Thus, of the $220,000 of merchandise sold during December, 20%, or $44,000, would have been purchased during the month. January's sales are expected to be $200,000, so 80% of that amount, or $160,000, would have been purchased during December. December purchases are thus estimated as $204,000 at the company's selling prices. The merchandise costs only 75% of the marked selling prices, however. Therefore, the balance in the purchases account at month-end is projected to be $153,000 ($204,000 × 75%).
Answer (A) is incorrect. The accounts payable balance on November 30 is $162,000. Answer (B) is incorrect. Estimated purchases in December at the company's selling prices equals $204,000. Answer (D) is incorrect. The correct amount is given in one of the other answer choices.

Use the Gleim **CMA Test Prep** Software for interactive testing with **additional multiple-choice questions!**

6.12 ESSAY QUESTIONS

Scenario for Essay Questions 1, 2

Watson Corporation manufactures and sells extended keyboard units. Robin Halter, budget analyst, coordinated the preparation of the annual budget for the year ending August 31, Year 7. The budget was based on the prior year's activity. The pro forma statements of income and cost of goods sold are presented below.

Watson Corporation
Pro Forma Statement of Income
For the Year Ending August 31, Year 7
($000 omitted)

Net sales		$25,550
Cost of goods sold		16,565
Gross profit		$ 8,985
Operating expenses:		
Marketing	$3,200	
General and administrative	2,000	5,200
Income from operations		$ 3,785

Watson Corporation
Pro Forma Statement of Cost of Goods Sold
For the Year Ending August 31, Year 7
($000 omitted)

Direct materials:		
Materials inventory, 9/1/Year 6	$ 1,200	
Materials purchased	11,400	
Materials available for use	$12,600	
Materials inventory, 8/31/Year 7	1,480	
Direct materials consumed		$11,120
Direct labor		980
Factory overhead:		
Indirect materials	$ 1,112	
General factory overhead	2,800	3,912
Cost of goods manufactured		$16,012
Finished goods inventory, 9/1/Year 6		930
Cost of goods available for sale		$16,942
Finished goods inventory, 8/31/Year 7		377
Cost of goods sold		$16,565

On December 10, Year 6, Halter met with Walter Collins, vice president of finance, to discuss the results. After their discussion, Collins directed Halter to reflect the following changes to the budget assumptions in revised pro forma statements:

- The estimated production in units for the fiscal year should be revised from 140,000 to 145,000 units with the balance of production being scheduled in equal segments over the last 9 months of the year. The actual first quarter's production was 25,000 units.

- The planned inventory for finished goods of 3,300 units at the end of the fiscal year remains unchanged and will be valued at the average manufacturing cost for the year. The finished goods inventory of 9,300 units on September 1, Year 6, and dropped to 9,000 units by November 30, Year 6.

- Due to a new labor agreement, the labor rate will increase 8% effective June 1, Year 7, the beginning of the fourth quarter, instead of the previously anticipated effective date of September 1, Year 7, the beginning of the next fiscal year.

- The assumptions remain unchanged for direct materials inventory at 16,000 units for the beginning inventory and 18,500 units for the ending inventory. Direct materials inventory is valued on a first-in, first-out basis. During the first quarter, direct materials for 27,500 units of output were purchased for $2,200,000. Although direct materials will be purchased evenly for the last 9 months, the cost of the direct materials will increase by 5% on March 1, Year 7, the beginning of the third quarter.

- Indirect material costs will continue to be 10% of the cost of direct materials.

- One-half of general factory overhead and all of the marketing and general and administrative expenses are fixed.

Questions

1. Based on the revised data presented, calculate Watson Corporation's projected sales for the year ending August 31, Year 7, in

   a.   Number of units to be sold
   b.   Dollar volume of net sales

2. Prepare the pro forma statement of cost of goods sold for the year ending August 31, Year 7.

Essay Questions 1, 2 — Unofficial Answers

1. a. Based on the revised data presented, Watson Corporation's projected unit sales for the year ending August 31, Year 7, are calculated as follows:

Finished goods beginning inventory	9,300
Add: planned production	145,000
Units available for sale	154,300
Less: Finished goods ending inventory	(3,300)
Units to be sold	151,000

   b. Based on the revised data presented, Watson Corporation's projected dollar volume of net sales for the year ending August 31, Year 7, is $26,425,000 calculated as follows:

$$\text{Selling price per unit} = \text{Original projected sales dollars} \div \text{Original projected unit sales}$$
$$= \$25,550,000 \div (9,300 + 140,000 - 3,300) \text{ units}$$
$$= \$175 \text{ per unit}$$

$$\text{Dollar volume of projected net sales} = 151,000 \text{ units} \times \$175 \text{ per unit}$$
$$= \$26,425,000$$

2. Based on the revised data presented, Watson Company's pro forma statement of costs of goods sold for the year ending August 31, Year 7, is presented below. Supporting calculations are on the next page.

Watson Corporation
Pro Forma Statement of Cost of Goods Sold
For the Year Ending August 31, Year 7

Direct materials:		
Materials inventory, 9/1/Year 6		$ 1,200,000
Materials purchased[1]		12,120,000
Materials available for use		$13,320,000
Materials inventory, 8/31/Year 7[2]		1,554,000
Direct materials consumed		$11,766,000
Direct labor[3]		1,037,400
Factory overhead:		
Indirect material[4]	$1,176,600	
General factory overhead[5]	2,850,000	
Factory overhead applied		4,026,600
Cost of goods manufactured		$16,830,000
Add: finished goods inventory, 9/1/Year 6		930,000
Cost of goods available for sale		$17,760,000
Less: finished goods inventory, 8/31/Year 7[6]		383,028
Cost of goods sold		$17,376,972

Supporting Calculations

[1]Materials purchased:

1st quarter:	27,500 units @ $80 per unit	=	$ 2,200,000
2nd quarter:	40,000 units @ $80 per unit*	=	3,200,000
3rd quarter:	40,000 units @ $84 per unit**	=	3,360,000
4th quarter:	40,000 units @ $84 per unit	=	3,360,000
Total			$12,120,000

*$2,200,000 ÷ 27,500 units
**$80.00 × 1.05

[2]Materials inventory, 8/31/Year 7:

18,500 units @ $84 per unit	=	$ 1,554,000

[3]Direct labor:

1st quarter:	25,000 units @ $7 per unit*	=	$ 175,000
2nd quarter:	40,000 units @ $7 per unit	=	280,000
3rd quarter:	40,000 units @ $7 per unit	=	280,000
4th quarter:	40,000 units @ $7.56 per unit**	=	302,400
Total			$ 1,037,400

*$980,000 ÷ 140,000 units
**$7.00 × 1.08

[4]Indirect materials:

$11,766,000 × .10	=	$ 1,176,600

[5]General factory overhead:

Variable: 145,000 units × ($1,400,000 ÷ 140,000 units)	=	$ 1,450,000
Fixed: $2,800,000 ÷ 2	=	1,400,000
Total		$ 2,850,000

[6]Finished goods inventory, 8/31/Year 7:

3,300 units × ($16,830,000 ÷ 145,000 units)	=	$ 383,028

Use **CMA Gleim Online** and **Essay Wizard** to practice additional essay questions in an exam-like environment.

STUDY UNIT SEVEN
COST AND VARIANCE MEASURES

(21 pages of outline)

7.1	Variance Analysis Overview	256
7.2	Static and Flexible Budgeting	259
7.3	Direct Materials Variances	262
7.4	Direct Labor Variances	264
7.5	Mix and Yield Variances	265
7.6	Overhead Variances	267
7.7	Comprehensive Example	270
7.8	Sales Variances	271
7.9	Core Concepts	273
7.10	Essay Questions	289

Performance Management

Performance reporting is a major topic on the CMA exam. Factors to be analyzed for control and performance evaluation include revenues, costs, profits, and investment in assets. Variance analysis based on flexible budgets and standard costs is heavily tested, as is responsibility accounting for revenue, cost, contribution, and profit centers. The balanced scorecard and quality considerations are included in this coverage.

This study unit is the **first of two** on **performance management**. The relative weight assigned to this major topic in Part 1 of the exam is **25%**. The two study units are

Study Unit 7: Cost and Variance Measures

Study Unit 8: Responsibility Accounting and Performance Measures

After studying the outline and answering the questions in this study unit, you will have the skills necessary to address the following topics listed in the ICMA's Learning Outcome Statements:

Part 1 – Section B.1. Cost and variance measures

The candidate should be able to:

a. analyze performance against operational goals using methods based on revenue, manufacturing costs, non-manufacturing costs, and profit depending on the type of center or unit being measured

b. explain the reasons for variances within a performance monitoring system

c. prepare a performance analysis by comparing actual results to the master budget, calculate favorable and unfavorable variances from budget, and provide explanations for variances

d. identify the benefits and limitations of measuring performance by comparing actual results to the master budget

e. prepare a flexible budget based on actual sales (output) volume

f. calculate the sales-volume variance and the sales-price variance by comparing the flexible budget to the master (static) budget

g. calculate the flexible-budget variance by comparing actual results to the flexible budget

h. investigate the flexible-budget variance to determine individual differences between actual and budgeted input prices and input quantities

i. explain how budget variance reporting is utilized in a management by exception environment

j. define a standard cost system and identify the reasons for adopting a standard cost system

k.   demonstrate an understanding of price (rate) variances and calculate the price variances related to direct material and direct labor inputs

l.   demonstrate an understanding of efficiency (usage) variances and calculate the efficiency variances related to direct material and direct labor inputs

m.   demonstrate an understanding of spending and efficiency variances as they relate to fixed and variable overhead

n.   calculate a sales-mix variance and explain its impact on revenue and contribution margin

o.   demonstrate an understanding that the efficiency (usage) variances can be further analyzed as mix and yield variances

p.   explain how a mix variance results and calculate a mix variance

q.   calculate and explain a yield variance

r.   demonstrate how price, efficiency, spending, and mix variances can be applied in service companies as well as manufacturing companies

s.   analyze factory overhead variances by calculating variable overhead spending variance, variable overhead efficiency variance, fixed overhead spending variance, and production volume variance

t.   analyze variances, identify causes, and recommend corrective actions

7.1 VARIANCE ANALYSIS OVERVIEW

1.   **Uses of a Budget**

   a.   A budget communicates to employees the organization's operational and strategic objectives. The budget quantifies the operational steps that ultimately lead to the achievement of strategic objectives.

   b.   A performance evaluation system must be used to monitor progress toward the budget's objectives.

   c.   Feedback should be timely so that managers can take corrective action.

2.   **Variance Analysis**

   a.   Variance analysis is the basis of any performance evaluation system using a budget. Variances are the differences between the amounts budgeted and the amounts actually incurred (or earned in the case of revenues).

      1)   On the cost side, a favorable variance occurs when actual costs are less than standard costs. An unfavorable variance occurs when actual costs are greater than standard costs.

      2)   On the revenue side, a favorable variance occurs when actual revenues are greater than budgeted revenues. An unfavorable variance occurs when actual revenues are less than budgeted revenues.

         a)   Whether a variance is favorable or unfavorable depends on how it affects income. A favorable variance increases income, and an unfavorable variance decreases income.

      3)   EXAMPLE: Under efficient conditions, a worker should complete one unit of product per hour. If workers are normally paid $6 per hour, the standard labor cost per unit is $6 per unit.

         a)   If the actual per-unit amounts for a 1-week period were 1.1 hours at $6.25 per hour, or $6.88 per unit, the variance is $.88 per unit.

         b)   The variance is unfavorable because the actual cost exceeded the standard cost.

   b.   The significance of variances depends not only on their amount but also on their direction, frequency, and trend.

      1)   Persistent variances may indicate that standards need to be reevaluated.

c. Variance analysis is an important tool for the management accountant.

1) Variance analysis enables **management by exception**, the practice of giving attention primarily to significant deviations from expectations (whether favorable or unfavorable).

a) Managers must use their judgment to determine the most efficient use of their limited time.

b) Concentrating on operations that are not performing within expected limits is likely to yield the best ratio of benefits to costs.

3. **Assignment of Responsibility**

a. A crucial part of variance analysis is the **assignment of responsibility**. The performance measures on which managers are judged should be directly related to the factors that drive the element being measured, e.g., cost drivers and revenue drivers.

b. The goal is to assign responsibility for variances to those most likely to have information that will enable management to find solutions. A manager who does not control an activity may nevertheless be the individual who is best informed about it.

1) The constructive approach is to promote learning and continuous improvement in manufacturing operations, not to assign blame. However, variance analysis may be useful in evaluating managers' performance.

4. **Overview of Variances**

a. The following variances are covered in greater detail throughout this study unit. CMA candidates should be prepared to calculate and understand these variances.

b. **Static Budget Variance**

1) The beginning of variance analysis is the static budget variance.

2) The static budget variance measures the difference between the static (master) budget amount and the actual results. It is the total variance to be explained.

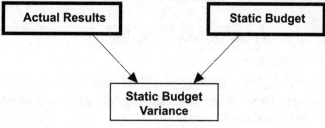

Figure 7-1

c. **Flexible budget variance and sales-volume variance**

1) The static budget variance consists of a flexible budget variance and a sales volume variance.

a) The **flexible budget variance** is the difference between the actual results and the budgeted amount for the actual activity level. It may be analyzed in terms of variances related to selling prices, input costs, and input quantities.

i) A **flexible budget** consists of the costs that should have been incurred given the actual level of production.

- The actual level of production is based on the actual output while still using the standard level of inputs.

ii) **Standard costs** should be established for direct materials, direct labor, and overhead. These standards can then be used to calculate variances.

b) The **sales-volume variance** is the difference between the flexible budget and static budget amounts if selling prices and costs are constant.

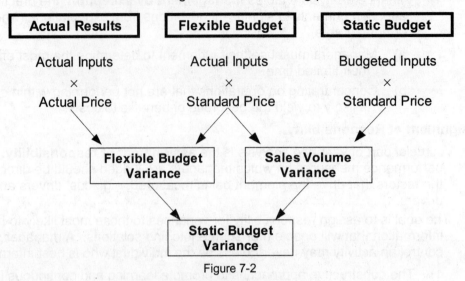

Figure 7-2

d. **Components of the Flexible Budget Variance**

1) The flexible budget variance consists of the following variances:

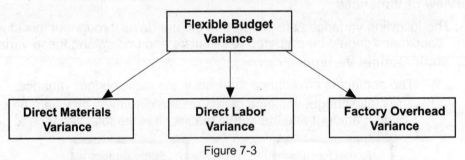

Figure 7-3

2) A **direct materials variance** includes a

a) Price variance

b) Quantity or usage variance (an efficiency variance for direct materials)

i) When a product has more than one input, the following variances can be calculated:

- Materials mix variance
- Materials yield variance

3) A **direct labor variance** includes a(n)

a) Rate variance (a price variance for direct labor).

b) Efficiency variance.

i) When labor rates vary, the following variances can be calculated:

- Labor mix variance
- Labor yield variance

4) **Factory overhead variances** have variable and fixed components. A four-way analysis includes two variable and two fixed components:

a) Variable overhead spending variance

b) Variable overhead efficiency variance

c) Fixed overhead spending variance (also known as a budget variance)

d) Fixed overhead production-volume variance

e. **Components of the Sales-Volume Variance**

1) When more than one product is made, the sales volume variance consists of the following variances:

 a) **Sales quantity variance**
 b) **Sales mix variance**

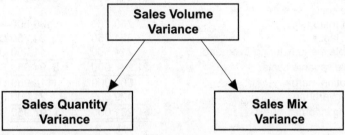

Figure 7-4

Stop and review! You have completed the outline for this subunit. Study multiple-choice questions 1 through 3 on page 276.

7.2 STATIC AND FLEXIBLE BUDGETING

1. **Static Budgeting**

a. A static budget is prepared before the budget period begins and is not changed.

1) The static budget reflects management's best estimates of, for example, sales, production, input prices, labor and overhead costs, and selling and administrative costs.

2) The static budget is based on the output planned at the beginning of the budget period.

3) Each element of the static budget is calculated using the appropriate cost driver.

a) A **cost driver** is used to assign costs to a cost object. It is a measure of activity, such as direct labor hours or machine hours, that has a cause-and-effect relationship with total cost.

Static Budget = (Standard Quantity × Standard Price) = (SQ × SP)

b. The **actual results** are prepared after the budget period ends.

1) The actual results reflect the revenues actually earned and the costs actually incurred.

2) The drivers are therefore adjusted to the actual amounts.

Actual Results = (Actual Quantity × Actual Price) = (AQ × AP)

c. The **static budget variance** is the difference between the static budget and the actual results for the period.

1) The static budget variance provides useful information, but it does not explain the cause of the variance.

Static Budget Variance = Actual Results − Static Budget = (AQ × AP) − (SQ × SP)

d.   EXAMPLE: At the end of the current period, ChowDown, Inc., a pet food manufacturer, prepared the following analysis of the static budget variance:

	AQ × AP Actual Results	Static Budget Variances	SQ × SP Static Budget
Units sold	16,500	1,500	18,000
Revenue	$1,947,000	$213,000 U	$2,160,000
Variable costs:			
Direct materials	750,750	160,500 F	911,250
Direct labor	321,750	24,750 U	297,000
Variable manufacturing overhead	214,500	41,700 U	172,800
Total variable costs	$1,287,000	$ 94,050 F	$1,381,050
Contribution margin	660,000	118,950 U	778,950
Fixed overhead	429,000	21,000 F	450,000
Operating income	$ 231,000	$ 97,950 U	$ 328,950

Total Static Budget Variance
$ 97,950 U

e.   Interpretation of the static budget variance can sometimes be misleading. For example, the above $160,500 variance on direct materials is labeled as favorable because actual cost was less than standard. However, the variance was mostly the result of production being lower than planned. Thus, the manager responsible did not do anything wonderful to generate the favorable variance. In fact, he may have been the cause of production delays, which led to the use of fewer materials.

f.   A flexible budget using standard costs helps management determine how much of the static budget variance arose from

1)   Inaccurate forecasts of output sold and
2)   Variations in the effectiveness and efficiency of actual output.

2.   Flexible Budgeting

a.   To create a flexible budget, **standard costs** are determined for the underlying cost drivers. They are budgeted unit costs established to improve productivity and efficiency.

1)   Standard costs are monetary measures with which actual costs are compared.
2)   A standard cost is not an average of past costs but an objectively determined estimate of what a cost should be. It may be based on accounting, engineering, or statistical quality control studies.
3)   A standard cost can be compared to "par" on a golf course.

b.   A standard-cost system alerts management when the actual costs of production differ significantly from standard costs.

1)   Because of the effects of fixed costs, standard costing is usually not effective without **flexible budgeting**.
2)   The purpose of standard costing is to control actual costs. Comparing actual and standard costs also permits an evaluation of managerial performance.
3)   Standard costs may be used with job-order and process costing to isolate variances.

    c.   **Ideal standards** are standard costs under optimal conditions. They are based on the work of the most skilled workers with no allowance for waste, spoilage, machine breakdowns, or other downtime.

        1)   These **tight standards** may have a positive behavioral effect if workers are highly motivated. However, they are not in wide use because they can have the opposite effect if the standards seem impossible to attain.

        2)   Ideal standards ordinarily are replaced by **practical standards** for cash budgeting, product costing, and budgeting departmental performance. Otherwise, accurate financial planning is very difficult.

        3)   Ideal standards have been adopted by some companies that apply continuous improvement and other total quality management (TQM) principles.

    d.   **Practical Standards** are defined as the performance that is reasonably expected to be achieved with an allowance for normal spoilage, waste, and downtime.

        1)   Practical standards represent possible but difficult to attain results.

    e.   Standard costs must be kept **current** to provide relevant information.

        1)   If prices have changed considerably for a particular material, a variance is always reported if the standard cost is not changed.

        2)   Much of the usefulness of standard costs is lost if a large variance is always expected.

        3)   The primary reason for calculating variances is to notify management whenever an unusual event has occurred.

    f.   A **flexible budget** adjusts for changes in the volume of activity. It can be adapted to any level of production. Budgeted revenues and costs are based on the actual quantities and standard costs.

$$Flexible\ Budget = (Actual\ quantity \times Standard\ Price) = (AQ \times SP)$$

    g.   Flexible budget variances and sales-volume variances are based on flexible budgets.

        1)   **Flexible budget variances** result from variations in the efficiency and effectiveness of producing actual output. They are the differences between actual results and flexible budget amounts.

$$\begin{aligned} Flexible\ Budget\ Variance &= Actual\ Results - Flexible\ Budget \\ &= (AQ \times AP) - (AQ \times SP) \\ &= AQ \times (AP - SP) \end{aligned}$$

        2)   Sales-volume variances result from inaccurate forecasts of output sold. They are the differences between flexible budget amounts and static budget amounts.

$$\begin{aligned} Sales\text{-}Volume\ Variance &= Flexible\ Budget - Static\ Budget \\ &= (AQ \times SP) - (SQ \times SP) \\ &= SP \times (AQ - SQ) \end{aligned}$$

The questions in this study unit use formulas written in different ways. For example, the flexible budget variance can be written in the following formats: AQ × (AP – SP), AQ × (SP – AP), (AP – SP) × AQ, or (SP – AP) × AQ. In each case, the absolute value is derived. The effect on income is then determined to decide whether the variance is favorable or unfavorable. Understanding the variances and understanding what each question is looking for will assist you in not becoming confused by the formulas being presented in different formats.

h.   EXAMPLE: At the end of the current period, ChowDown, Inc., prepared the following analysis of the flexible budget variance:

	AQ × AP Actual Results (AR)	AR – FB Flexible Budget (FB) Variances	AQ × SP Flexible Budget	FB – SB Sales Volume Variances	SQ × SP Static Budget (SB)
Units sold	16,500		16,500	1,500	18,000
Revenue	$1,947,000	$33,000 U	$1,980,000	$180,000 U	$2,160,000
Variable costs:					
Direct materials	750,750	84,563 F	835,313	75,937 F	911,250
Direct labor	321,750	49,500 U	272,250	24,750 F	297,000
Variable nonmanufacturing overhead	214,500	56,100 U	158,400	14,400 F	172,800
Total variable costs	$1,287,000	$21,037	$1,265,963	$115,087	$1,381,050
Contribution margin	660,000	54,037	714,037	64,913	778,950
Fixed overhead	429,000	21,000 F	450,000	0	450,000
Operating income	$ 231,000	$33,037	$ 264,037	$ 64,913	$ 328,950

Total Flexible Budget Variance   Total Sales Volume Variance
          $ 33,037 U $ 64,913 U

Total Static Budget Variance
          $ 97,950 U

i.   The next four subunits analyze the components of the flexible budget variance and the sales-volume variance. The following variances are typically calculated for this purpose:

1)   Flexible budget variances

a)   Direct materials variances

i)   Price
ii)   Quantity
iii) Mix and yield

b)   Direct labor variances

i)   Rate
ii)   Efficiency
iii) Mix and yield

c)   Factory overhead variances

i)   Variable overhead (spending and efficiency)
ii)   Fixed overhead (spending and production volume)

2)   Sales-volume variances

a)   Quantity
b)   Mix

Stop and review! You have completed the outline for this subunit. Study multiple-choice questions 4 through 8 beginning on page 276.

7.3 DIRECT MATERIALS VARIANCES

CMA candidates must be able to calculate and analyze variances. They must be able to identify causes and recommend corrective actions. Typically, a favorable variance is seen as desirable while an unfavorable one is undesirable, but this is not always the case. When taking the exam, it is easy to see a favorable variance and determine that this is desirable; however, as a CMA candidate, you will need to analyze the variances and determine their causes. You must be able to evaluate if they are desirable or not and recommend a course of action.

1.   Direct materials variances have price and efficiency components. Part of the total variance is attributed to using an amount of materials different from the standard quantity (the efficiency component). Part is attributed to a cost different from standard (the price component). These two sources of the total variance can be isolated.

2. **Direct Materials Price Variance**

    a.   The direct materials price variance equals the actual quantity of total input times the difference between the budgeted price and the actual price.

$$AQ \times (AP - SP)$$

    b.   The price variance may be isolated at the time of purchase or when materials are transferred to work-in-process.

        1)   A **purchase price variance** is a nonmanufacturing variance. It measures the difference between (a) the amount paid for **all** units of materials purchased during a specific period and (b) the amount expected to be paid. This formula can be used to calculate variances at the earliest time possible, which is at the time goods are purchased.

    c.   An unfavorable materials price variance results when the actual price is greater than the standard price.

    d.   Once a variance has been calculated, the next step is to analyze the reasons for the variance. In general, a favorable variance is desirable and an unfavorable variance is undesirable. But that is not always true:

        1)   An **unfavorable materials price variance** means that the actual price paid for materials is higher than the estimated standard price. This is usually undesirable. The purchasing function may be responsible under the assumption that it bought materials that cost too much. Thus, an unfavorable variance is not the fault of the production departments. However, the unfavorable variance may simply indicate that prices in the industry have risen, and standard costs should be updated.

        2)   A **favorable materials price variance** may mean that the purchasing function performed well by finding a lower-cost source for the materials. But, prices may have fallen, the purchasing function simply bought at the market price, and standard costs should be updated.

            a)   Another possibility is that the lower price may be attributable to lower quality materials. An analysis must be made to determine whether the lower quality materials result in a lower quality product or the use of excessive quantities in production. In these cases, the purchasing function is at fault.

3. **Direct Materials Quantity Variance**

    a.   The direct materials quantity variance (an efficiency or usage variance) equals the budgeted price times the difference between the actual quantity and the budgeted quantity.

$$SP \times (AQ - SQ)$$

        1)   The actual cost of the materials is ignored because the variance isolates the effect that would have occurred given no price variance.

        2)   An **unfavorable materials quantity variance** is usually blamed on the excessive use of materials by the production departments. It also may indicate theft of materials or other waste or shrinkage. However, the excessive use might be attributable to using lower quality materials that were purchased at a lower price.

            a)   An alternative explanation is that excessive usage may have been caused by using unskilled (and lower cost) labor. Thus, a favorable labor rate variance may have contributed to an unfavorable materials quantity variance.

3)   A **favorable materials quantity variance** may indicate that workers have been unusually efficient, for example, by reducing normal spoilage. But it may also indicate that they are producing lower-quality products with less than the standard quantity of materials.

   a)   Accordingly, a favorable variance is not always desirable. It may be as bad as, or worse than, an unfavorable variance. It may suggest that costs have been reduced at the expense of product quality.

4.   EXAMPLE: ChowDown, Inc., estimated output for the period of 18,000 units. However, actual output was 16,500 units. Standard direct materials per unit were estimated at 7.5, but the actual usage was 6.5 per unit. The standard price was budgeted at $6.75, but the actual price was $7.00. The direct materials variances are calculated as follows:

Direct Materials Variance	Units	Materials per Unit	Quantity	Price	Total
Static budget direct materials	18,000	7.5	135,000	$6.75	$911,250
Flexible budget direct materials	16,500	7.5	123,750*	$6.75	$835,313
Actual direct materials	16,500	6.5	107,250	$7.00	$750,750

Direct materials price variance	AQ × (AP – SP)**	$ 26,813 U
Direct materials quantity variance	SP × (AQ – SQ)***	111,375 F
Total materials variance		$ 84,562 F ($1 rounding difference)

* When calculating the quantity variance, the standard quantity equals actual units produced times the standard materials per unit. This equals the materials that should have been used given the actual level of production.
** 107,250 × ($7.00 – $6.75)
*** $6.75 × (107,250 – 123,750)

5.   **Service Organizations**

   a.   In a service organization, the direct materials variances are usually immaterial compared with the direct labor variances. The reason is that only a relatively small investment is made in direct materials because these organizations tend to be labor intensive.

Stop and review! You have completed the outline for this subunit. Study multiple-choice questions 9 through 28 beginning on page 277.

7.4 DIRECT LABOR VARIANCES

1.   The direct labor variance is similar to the direct materials variance. The total direct labor variance consists of the rate (price) variance and the efficiency (quantity) variance.

2.   **Direct Labor Rate Variance**

   a.   This variance equals the actual quantity times the difference between the actual rate and the standard rate.

$$AQ \times (AP - SP)$$

   b.   An **unfavorable labor rate variance** is usually caused by assigning skilled workers to a production process. The standard cost calculation may have assumed that unskilled (lower paid) workers could complete the job. But the greater efficiency of skilled workers might result in a favorable labor efficiency variance to offset the unfavorable labor rate variance.

      1)   Another explanation for an unfavorable labor rate variance is that a new union contract resulted in a higher wage to workers, in which case the standard costs should be updated.

   c.   A **favorable labor rate variance** is usually caused by assigning lower-skilled workers to a job. This may be desirable when they are qualified for the job. But the favorable rate variance may be offset by an unfavorable efficiency variance or lower quality products.

3. **Direct Labor Efficiency Variance**

    a. This variance equals the standard rate times the difference between the actual quantity and the standard quantity.

    $$SP \times (AQ - SQ)$$

    b. An **unfavorable labor efficiency variance** means that workers are spending too much time on a production process. This is normally undesirable, but it may be caused by using lower-skilled workers than anticipated, in which case the labor rate variance may be favorable.

        1) Another explanation is the use of low-quality materials that require extra time in the production process, in which case, the material price variance may be favorable.

    c. A **favorable labor efficiency variance** is almost always desirable. It means that employees are working efficiently and have been able to complete production in fewer hours than anticipated. It is considered a production department efficiency.

4. EXAMPLE: ChowDown, Inc., estimated output for the period of 18,000 units. However, actual output was 16,500 units. Standard direct labor was estimated at 3 hours per unit, but the actual usage was 3.25 hours per unit. The standard rate was $5.50, but the actual rate was $6.00. The direct labor variances are calculated as follows:

Direct Labor Variances	Units	Labor per Unit	Quantity	Price	Total
Static budget direct labor	18,000	3	54,000	$5.50	$297,000
Flexible budget direct labor	16,500	3	49,500*	$5.50	$272,250
Actual direct labor	16,500	3.25	53,625	$6.00	$321,750

Direct labor rate variance	AQ × (AP – SP)**	$26,813 U		
Direct labor efficiency variance	SP × (AQ – SQ)***	22,688 U		
Total labor variance		$49,501 U	($1 rounding difference)	

* When calculating the efficiency variance, the standard quantity equals actual units produced times the standard labor per unit. This equals the hours that should have been used given the actual level of production.

** 53,625 × ($6.00 – $5.50)
*** $5.50 × (53,625 – 49,500)

5. **Service Organizations**

    a. In a service organization, the direct labor variances are usually more relevant than the direct materials variances. A relatively large investment is made in direct labor and only a minor investment in direct materials.

Stop and review! You have completed the outline for this subunit. Study multiple-choice questions 29 through 41 beginning on page 281.

7.5 MIX AND YIELD VARIANCES

1. In some production processes, inputs are **substitutable**, for example, a baker of pecan pies may use pecans from Florida instead of Georgia or higher-skilled laborers instead of lower-skilled labor.

    a. Given substitutable inputs, the quantity and efficiency variances for direct materials and direct labor consist of a mix variance and a yield variance.

2.   To calculate these variances, the entity must determine the weighted-average standard price (a) using the standard mix of inputs **(SPSM)** and (b) using the actual mix of inputs **(SPAM)**.

    a.   EXAMPLE: A retail store budgets its employee hours for the upcoming month and calculates its weighted-average standard price of wages using the standard mix (SPSM) as follows:

	Budgeted Hours (SM)		Standard Wage (SP)		Subtotals
Managers	200	×	$22	=	$ 4,400
Sales associates	800	×	14	=	11,200
Warehouse	600	×	8	=	4,800
Totals	1,600				$20,400

SPSM = $20,400 ÷ 1,600 hours = $12.75 per hour

After month-end, the store employs the actual hours worked to calculate the weighted-average standard price using the actual mix (SPAM) as follows:

	Actual Hours (AM)		Standard Wage (SP)		Subtotals
Managers	220	×	$22	=	$ 4,840
Sales associates	800	×	14	=	11,200
Warehouse	480	×	8	=	3,840
Totals	1,500				$19,880

SPAM = $19,880 ÷ 1,500 hours = $13.2533 per hour

3.   The **mix variance** measures the relative use of higher-priced and lower-priced inputs in the production process based on standard input prices and **actual total quantity (ATQ)** of inputs. It isolates the effect of using the actual mix instead of the standard mix.

    Mix variance = ATQ × (SPSM – SPAM)

    a.   EXAMPLE: The store calculates its labor mix variance as follows:

        Labor mix variance = ATQ × (SPSM – SPAM)
                     = 1,500 hours × ($12.75 – $13.2533)
                     = 1,500 hours × –$0.5033
                     = $755 unfavorable

This variance was unfavorable because more highly-paid managers worked more hours and less highly-paid warehouse employees worked fewer hours than budgeted.

4.   The **yield variance** isolates the effect of the difference between the ATQ of inputs and the **STQ (standard total quantity)**. The calculation is based on standard input prices and the standard mix.

    Yield variance = (STQ – ATQ) × SPSM

    a.   EXAMPLE: The store calculates its labor yield variance as follows:

        Labor yield variance = (STQ – ATQ) × SPSM
                    = (1,600 hours – 1,500 hours) × $12.75
                    = 100 hours × $12.75
                    = $1,275 favorable

The variance was favorable because fewer hours than budgeted were used to produce the output. The sum of the mix and yield variances is the efficiency variance ($755 U + $1,275 F = $520 F).

5.   The same formulas can be applied to the mix and yield variances for direct materials.

Stop and review! You have completed the outline for this subunit. Study multiple-choice questions 42 through 45 beginning on page 284.

7.6 OVERHEAD VARIANCES

1. The total overhead variance consists of four variances. Two are calculated for variable overhead and two for fixed overhead.

2. **Variable Overhead**

    a. The total **variable overhead variance** is the flexible-budget variance. It is the difference between actual variable overhead and the amount applied based on the budgeted application rate and the standard input allowed for the actual output. It includes the following:

        1) The **spending variance** is the difference between (a) actual variable overhead and (b) the product of the budgeted application rate and the actual amount of the allocation base (activity level or amount of input).

            a) The variable overhead spending variance is favorable or unfavorable if production spending is less or more, respectively, than the standard.

        2) The **efficiency variance** is the budgeted application rate times the difference between (a) the actual input and (b) the standard input allowed for the actual output.

            a) Variable overhead applied equals the flexible-budget amount for the actual output level. The reason is that unit variable costs are assumed to be constant within the relevant range.

            b) If variable overhead is applied on the basis of output, not inputs, no efficiency variance arises.

            c) The variable overhead efficiency variance is related to the labor efficiency variance if overhead is applied to production on the basis of direct labor hours. For example, if the labor efficiency variance is unfavorable, the overhead efficiency variance also is unfavorable because they are based on the same number of input hours.

Variable Overhead Variances

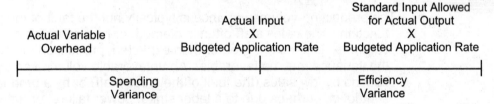

3) EXAMPLE: ChowDown, Inc., estimated output for the period of 18,000 units. However, actual output was 16,500 units. Standard processing time is 1.2 machine hours per unit. But actual usage was 1.3 machine hours per unit. The standard application rate was $8.00 per machine hour, but the actual rate was $10.00 per machine hour. The variable overhead variances are calculated as follows:

Variable Overhead Variances	Units	Machine Hours	Actual Quantity	Rate	Total
Static budget variable overhead	18,000	1.2	21,600	$ 8.00	$172,800
Flexible budget variable overhead	16,500	1.2	19,800	$ 8.00	$158,400
Actual variable overhead	16,500	1.3	21,450	$10.00	$214,500

Variable overhead spending variance	AQ × (AP – SP)*	$42,900 U	
Variable overhead efficiency variance	SP × (AQ – SQ)**	13,200 U	
Total variable overhead efficiency variances		$56,100 U	

*21,450 × ($10 – $8)
**$8 × (21,450 – 19,800)

3. **Fixed Overhead**

    a. The **total fixed overhead variance** is the difference between actual fixed overhead and the amount applied based on the budgeted application rate and the standard input allowed for the actual output. It includes the following:

        1) The **spending variance** (budget variance) is the difference between (a) actual fixed overhead and (b) the amount budgeted. This variance is the same as the fixed overhead flexible-budget variance. The reason is that the static budget lump-sum of fixed overhead is also the flexible budget amount over the relevant range of output. Moreover, the efficiency of production does not affect the fixed overhead variances.

            a) Thus, an efficiency variance is calculated for variable, but not fixed, overhead.

            b) The fixed overhead variance is simply attributable to more or less spending by the production function. Whether the difference is justified should be investigated.

        2) The **production-volume variance** (idle capacity variance or denominator-level variance) is the difference between (a) budgeted fixed overhead and (b) the product of the budgeted application rate and the standard input allowed for the actual output.

            a) This variance results when production capacity differs from capacity usage. A favorable (unfavorable) variance occurs when overhead applied is more (less) than budgeted fixed costs. For example, the variance is favorable when actual production exceeds planned production.

                i) EXAMPLE: If fixed cost is expected to be $10,000, and the expected (denominator) level of activity is 1,000 hours, the standard cost is $10 per hour. If actual production uses 1,100 hours, $11,000 of fixed overhead is applied to production (1,100 × $10). The production-volume variance is $1,000 favorable ($11,000 − $10,000).

            b) The production-volume variance is typically not the fault of the production function. The sales staff often is blamed, or rewarded, for a volume variance. If sales are greater than expected, production increases, and the variance may be favorable. An unfavorable volume variance may be caused by low sales (the fault of the sales staff) or by a production shutdown, perhaps due to a labor strike, power failure, or natural disaster. In these cases, the variance is attributable to actions of the general administration of the entity or to uncontrollable external factors.

Fixed Overhead Variances

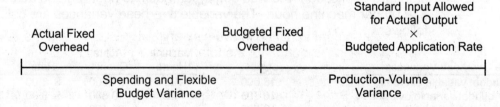

3) EXAMPLE: ChowDown, Inc., estimates output for the period of 18,000 units. However, actual output was 16,500 units. Fixed overhead is applied at $25 per unit sold. But actual cost per unit was $26. The fixed overhead variances are calculated as follows:

Fixed Overhead Variances	Units	Rate	Total	
Static and flexible budget fixed overhead	18,000	$25.00	$450,000	
Applied fixed overhead	16,500	$25.00	$412,500	
Actual fixed overhead	16,500	$26.00	$429,000	
Fixed overhead spending variance		Actual FO – Budgeted FO*	$21,000 F	
Fixed overhead production-volume variance		Budgeted FO – Applied FO**	37,500 U	

*($450,000 – $429,000)
**($450,000 – $412,500)

NOTE: The production-volume variance is unfavorable because it indicates that fixed overhead was underallocated to actual output. The variance is the amount of fixed overhead incurred for unused production capacity.

4. **Analysis of Overhead Variances**

   a. **Four-way overhead variance analysis** includes all four components of the total overhead variance.

Four-Way Analysis	Spending Variance	Efficiency Variance	Production Volume Variance
Variable OH	$42,900 U	$13,200 U	--
Fixed OH	$21,000 F	--	$37,500 U

   b. **Three-way overhead variance analysis** combines the variable and fixed spending variances and reports the other two variances separately.

Three-Way Analysis	Spending Variance	Efficiency Variance	Production-Volume Variance
Total OH	$21,900 U	$13,200 U	$37,500 U

   c. **Two-way overhead variance analysis** combines the spending and efficiency variances into one flexible-budget variance and reports the production-volume variance separately.

Two-Way Analysis	Flexible-Budget Variance	Production-Volume Variance
Total OH	$35,100 U	$37,500 U

   1) The flexible-budget variance in two-way analysis also is called the **controllable variance**. It is the portion of the total variance not attributable to the production-volume variance.

Stop and review! You have completed the outline for this subunit. Study multiple-choice questions 46 through 74 beginning on page 284.

7.7 COMPREHENSIVE EXAMPLE

As a CMA candidate, you will be expected to know and understand the different variance formulas. Take the time to memorize them but also to understand them. It may be useful to create notecards for these formulas to aid in retention. When you arrive at the exam, you will first be presented with a tutorial before your time for the exam begins. However, since you are using the Gleim Online and Test Prep Software, you will already be familiar with the information provided in the tutorial. Take these few minutes to write on your scrap paper any formulas or variances you can recall in that time. (Don't forget to pay attention to the time as once the time for the tutorial is up, your exam will begin.) This way, when you are presented with questions requiring you to calculate variances, you will be able to look at your scrap paper rather than trying to recall from memory during a time when you are stressed. This will help you keep the formulas straight and manage your time on the exam.

	STANDARD COSTS	ACTUAL COSTS
DIRECT MATERIALS	600,000 units of materials at $2.00 each	700,000 units at $1.90
DIRECT LABOR	60,000 hours allowed for actual output at $7 per hour	65,000 hours at $7.20
OVERHEAD	$8.00 per direct labor hour on normal capacity of 50,000 direct labor hours:	
	$6.00 for variable overhead	$396,000 variable
	$2.00 for fixed overhead	$130,000 fixed

MATERIALS VARIANCES

Price

$$AQ \times (SP - AP) = \text{Actual quantity} \times (\text{Standard price} - \text{Actual price})$$
$$= 700,000 \text{ units} \times (\$2.00 - \$1.90)$$
$$= 700,000 \times \$0.10$$
$$= \$70,000 \text{ F}$$

Quantity

$$(SQ - AQ) \times SP = (\text{Standard quantity} - \text{Actual quantity}) \times \text{Standard price}$$
$$= (600,000 \text{ units} - 700,000 \text{ units}) \times \$2.00$$
$$= -100,000 \times \$2.00$$
$$= \$200,000 \text{ U}$$

LABOR VARIANCES

Rate

$$AQ \times (SP - AP) = \text{Actual hours} \times (\text{Standard rate} - \text{Actual rate})$$
$$= 65,000 \text{ hours} \times (\$7.00 - \$7.20)$$
$$= 65,000 \times -\$0.20$$
$$= \$13,000 \text{ U}$$

Efficiency

$$(SQ - AQ) \times SP = (\text{Standard hours} - \text{Actual hours}) \times \text{Standard rate}$$
$$= (60,000 \text{ hours} - 65,000 \text{ hours}) \times \$7.00$$
$$= -5,000 \times \$7.00$$
$$= \$35,000 \text{ U}$$

VARIABLE OVERHEAD VARIANCES

Spending

$$(AQ \times SP) - AC = (\text{Actual hours} \times \text{Standard rate}) - \text{Actual costs incurred}$$
$$= (65,000 \times \$6.00) - \$396,000$$
$$= \$390,000 - \$396,000$$
$$= \$6,000 \text{ U}$$

Efficiency

$$(SQ - AQ) \times SP = (\text{Standard hours} - \text{Actual hours}) \times \text{Standard rate}$$
$$= (60,000 - 65,000) \times \$6.00$$
$$= -5,000 \times \$6.00$$
$$= \$30,000 \text{ U}$$

FIXED OVERHEAD VARIANCES

Spending

    Flexible/Static budget – Actual costs incurred = (50,000 hours × $2.00) – $130,000

                                        = $30,000 U

Production-Volume

    (Standard hours allowed for actual output × Standard rate) –

    Flexible/Static budget = (60,000 hours × $2.00) – (50,000 hours × $2.00)

                         = $120,000 – $100,000

                         = $20,000 F

NET MANUFACTURING VARIANCE $224,000 U

	Actual Output at Actual Input and Cost	Actual Output at Standard Input and Cost
Materials	$1,330,000	$1,200,000
Labor	468,000	420,000
Variable overhead	396,000	360,000
Fixed overhead	130,000	120,000
Net unfavorable variance		224,000
	$2,324,000	$2,324,000

Stop and review! You have completed the outline for this subunit. Study multiple-choice questions 75 through 83 beginning on page 287.

7.8 SALES VARIANCES

1. **Single Product Sales Variances**

    a. Variance analysis is useful for evaluating not only the production function but also the selling function.

        1) If sales differ from the amount budgeted, the difference could be attributable to either the **sales price variance** or the **sales volume variance** (sum of the sales quantity and mix variances).

        2) The analysis of these variances concentrates on **contribution margins** because fixed costs are assumed to be constant.

    b. EXAMPLE: A firm has budgeted sales of 10,000 units of its sole product at $17 per unit. Variable costs are expected to be $10 per unit, and fixed costs are budgeted at $50,000. The following compares budgeted and actual results:

	Budget Computation	Budget Amount	Actual Computation	Actual Amount
Sales	10,000 units × $17 per unit	$170,000	11,000 units × $16 per unit	$176,000
Variable costs	10,000 units × $10 per unit	(100,000)	11,000 units × $10 per unit	(110,000)
Contribution margin		$ 70,000		$ 66,000
Fixed costs		(50,000)		(50,000)
Operating income		$ 20,000		$ 16,000

Unit contribution margin (UCM) $70,000 ÷ 10,000 units = $7 $66,000 ÷ 11,000 units = $6

        1) Although sales were greater than budgeted, the contribution margin is less than budgeted. The discrepancy can be analyzed in terms of the sales price variance and the sales volume variance.

            a) For a single product, the **sales price variance** is the change in the contribution margin attributable solely to the change in selling price (holding quantity constant).

                i) In the example, the actual selling price of $16 per unit is $1 less than expected. Thus, the sales price variance is $11,000 U (11,000 actual units sold × $1).

      b)   For a single product, the **sales volume variance** is the change in the contribution margin attributable solely to the difference between the actual and budgeted unit sales (holding price constant).

          i)   In the example, it equals $7,000 F (1,000-unit increase in unit sales × $7 budgeted UCM).

          ii)   For a single product, the sales mix variance is zero (see the section on multiproduct sales variances). Thus, the sales volume variance equals the sales quantity variance.

      c)   The sales price variance ($11,000 U) plus the sales volume variance ($7,000 F) equals the total change in the contribution margin ($4,000 U).

  c.   A similar analysis may be done for **cost of goods sold**.

    1)   The average production cost per unit is used instead of the average unit selling price, but the quantities for unit production are the same.

    2)   Accordingly, the overall variation in gross profit is the sum of the variation in revenue plus the variation in cost of goods sold.

2.   Multiproduct Sales Variances

  a.   For two or more products, the multiproduct sales variances reflect not only the change in total unit sales but also the change in the sales mix.

    1)   The **multiproduct sales price variance** may be calculated as in the single-product case for each product. The results are then added.

      a)   An alternative is to multiply the actual total units sold times the difference between the following:

          i)   The weighted-average price based on actual units sold at actual unit prices.

          ii)   The weighted-average price based on actual units sold at budgeted prices.

    2)   The **multiproduct sales volume variance** may be calculated as in the single-product case for each product. The results are then added.

      a)   An alternative is to determine the difference between the following:

          i)   Actual total unit sales times the budgeted weighted-average UCM for the actual mix.

          ii)   Budgeted total unit sales times the budgeted weighted-average UCM for the budgeted mix.

    3)   The multiproduct sales volume variance consists of the sales quantity and sales mix variances.

      a)   The **sales quantity variance** is the difference between (1) the budgeted contribution margin based on actual unit sales and (2) the budgeted contribution margin based on budgeted unit sales. The calculation is based on the assumption that the budgeted sales mix is constant.

          i)   One way to calculate this variance is to multiply the budgeted UCM for each product times the difference between (a) the budgeted unit sales of the product and (b) its budgeted percentage of actual total unit sales. The results are then added.

             •   An alternative is to multiply the budgeted weighted-average UCM based on the budgeted mix times the difference between (1) total actual unit sales and (2) the total budgeted unit sales.

b) The **sales mix variance** is the difference between (1) the budgeted contribution margin for the actual mix and actual total unit sales and (2) the budgeted contribution margin for the budgeted mix and actual total unit sales.

   i) One way to calculate this variance is to multiply the budgeted UCM for each product times the difference between (a) actual unit sales of the product and (b) its budgeted percentage of actual total unit sales. The results are then added.

- An alternative is to multiply total actual unit sales times the difference between (1) the budgeted weighted-average UCM for the budgeted mix and (2) the budgeted weighted-average UCM for the actual mix.

4) **Comprehensive example:**

	Plastic	Metal	Total
Budgeted selling price per unit	$6.00	$10.00	
Budgeted variable cost per unit	3.00	7.50	
Budgeted contribution margin per unit	$3.00	$ 2.50	
Budgeted unit sales	300	200	500
Budgeted mix percentage	60%	40%	100%
Actual units sold	260	260	520
Actual selling price per unit	$6.00	$9.50	

a) As shown below (000 omitted), the **total contribution margin variance** was $100 unfavorable ($130 unfavorable sales price variance – $30 favorable sales volume variance).

Sales price variance:		
Plastic 260 × ($6.00 – $6.00)	$ 0	
Metal 260 × ($10 – $9.50)	(130)	$130 unfavorable
Sales volume variance:		
Plastic (260 – 300) × $3.00	$(120)	
Metal (260 – 200) × $2.50	150	$ 30 favorable
Total contribution margin variance		$100 unfavorable

b) The sales volume variance consists of the following:

Sales quantity variance:		
Plastic [(520 × .6) – 300] × $3.00	$ 36	
Metal [(520 × .4) – 200] × $2.50	20	$ 56 favorable
Sales mix variance:		
Plastic [260 – (520 × .6)] × $3.00	$(156)	
Metal [260 – (520 × .4)] × $2.50	130	$ 26 unfavorable
Sales volume variance		$ 30 favorable

Stop and review! You have completed the outline for this subunit. Study multiple-choice questions 84 through 99 beginning on page 288.

7.9 CORE CONCEPTS

Variance Analysis Overview

- **Budgets** are used to communicate to employees what an organization's operational and strategic goals are.
- **Variance analysis** is the foundation of any performance evaluation system based on a budget.
- A **favorable variance** increases income and an **unfavorable variance** decreases income.

- Variance analysis enables **management by exception**, the practice of giving attention primarily to significant deviations from expectations (whether favorable or unfavorable).
- A crucial part of variance analysis is the **assignment of responsibility**. The goal is to assign responsibility for variances to those most likely to have information that will enable management to find solutions.

Static Budgeting

- A **static budget** is prepared before the budget period begins and is left unchanged. The static budget reflects managements best estimate about sales, production, input prices, labor costs, overhead costs, selling and administrative costs, etc. The static budget is based on the level of output planned at the beginning of the budget period.
- The **actual results** are prepared after the budget period ends. The actual results reflect the revenues **actually earned** and the costs **actually incurred** during the period.
- The **static budget variance** is the difference between the static budget and the actual results for the period.

Standard Costs and Variances

- **Standard costs** are budgeted unit costs established to motivate optimal productivity and efficiency. When actual costs and standard costs differ, the difference is a variance. A variance is favorable when actual costs are less than standard costs. A variance is unfavorable when actual costs are greater than standard costs.
- **Ideal standards** are standard costs that are set for production under optimal conditions. **Practical standards** are the performance that is reasonably expected to be achieved with an allowance for normal spoilage, waste, and downtime.

Flexible Budgeting

- A **flexible budget** adjusts for changes in the volume of activity. It can be adapted to any level of production. Budgeted revenues and costs are based on the actual quantities and standard costs.
- Flexible budgets help management calculate flexible budget variances and sales-volume variances.
    - **Flexible budget variances** result from changes in the performance of manufacturing. They are the differences between actual results and flexible budget amounts.
    - **Sales-volume variances** result from inaccurate forecasts of output sold. They are the differences between flexible budget amounts and static budget amounts.

Direct Materials Variances

- The **total flexible budget variance** for direct materials can be stated as follows:

    Direct materials variance = Flexible budget – Actual results
    $$= (AQ \times SP) - (AQ \times AP)$$

- This total consists of a **price variance** and a **quantity variance**:

    Direct materials price variance = Flexible budget – Actual results
    $$= (AQ \times SP) - (AQ \times AP)$$
    $$= AQ \times (AP - SP)$$

    Direct materials quantity variance = Static budget – Flexible budget
    $$= (SQ \times SP) - (AQ \times SP)$$
    $$= (SQ - AQ) \times SP$$

- A **favorable materials quantity variance** indicates the use of less than the standard quantity of materials. A favorable quantity variance may therefore result from unusual efficiency or the production of lower quality products. An **unfavorable materials quantity variance** is usually caused by waste, shrinkage, or theft.

Direct Labor Variances

- The **total flexible budget variance** for direct labor can be stated as follows:

    Direct labor variance = Flexible budget − Actual results
    $$= (AQ \times SP) - (AQ \times AP)$$

- This total also consists of a **price (rate) variance** and a **quantity (efficiency) variance**:

    Direct labor rate variance = Flexible budget − Actual results
    $$= (AQ \times SP) - (AQ \times AP)$$
    $$= AQ \times (AP - SP)$$

    Direct labor efficiency variance = Static budget − Flexible budget
    $$= (SQ \times SP) - (AQ \times SP)$$
    $$= (SQ - AQ) \times SP$$

- A **favorable labor efficiency variance** indicates the use of less than the standard number of labor hours. A favorable variance may therefore result from unusual efficiency or the production of lower quality products. An **unfavorable labor efficiency variance** may be caused by production delays resulting from materials shortages, inferior materials, or excessive work breaks.

Mix and Yield Variances

- The quantity variance for materials and the efficiency variance for labor can be further subdivided into mix and yield variances:

    Mix variance = ATQ × (SPSM − SPAM)
    Yield variance = (STQ − ATQ) × SPSM

Overhead Variances

- A manufacturer's total overhead variance consists of **variable and fixed portions**.
- The **variable overhead variance** consists of a **spending variance** and an **efficiency variance**.

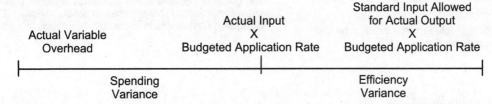

- The **fixed overhead variance** consists of a **spending variance** and a **production-volume variance**.

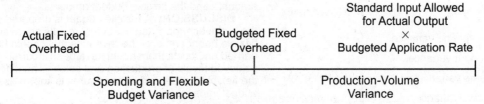

Sales Variances

- If a firm's **sales differ from the amount budgeted**, the difference could be attributable to either the sales price variance or the sale volume variance.
- For a single-product firm, the **sales price variance** is the change in the contribution margin attributable solely to the change in selling price.
- For a single-product firm, the **sales volume variance** is the change in the contribution margin caused by the difference between the actual and budgeted volume.
- If a company produces two or more products, the **multiproduct sales variances** reflect not only the effects of the change in total unit sales but also any difference in the mix of products sold.

QUESTIONS

7.1 Variance Analysis Overview

1. The purpose of identifying manufacturing variances and assigning their responsibility to a person/department should be to

A. Use the knowledge about the variances to promote learning and continuous improvement in the manufacturing operations.

B. Trace the variances to finished goods so that the inventory can be properly valued at year-end.

C. Determine the proper cost of the products produced so that selling prices can be adjusted accordingly.

D. Pinpoint fault for operating problems in the organization.

Answer (A) is correct. *(CMA, adapted)*
REQUIRED: The purpose of identifying and assigning responsibility for manufacturing variances.
DISCUSSION: The purpose of identifying and assigning responsibility for variances is to determine who is likely to have information that will enable management to find solutions. The constructive approach is to promote learning and continuous improvement in manufacturing operations, not to assign blame. However, information about variances may be useful in evaluating managers' performance.
Answer (B) is incorrect. Depending on a cost-benefit determination, variances either are adjustments of cost of goods sold or are allocated among the inventory accounts and cost of goods sold. Moreover, the accounting issues are distinct from supervisory considerations. Answer (C) is incorrect. Selling prices are based on much more than the cost of production; for instance, competitive pressure is also a consideration. Answer (D) is incorrect. By itself, pinpointing fault is not an appropriate objective. Continuous improvement is the ultimate objective.

2. A difference between standard costs used for cost control and the budgeted costs of the same manufacturing effort can exist because

A. Standard costs represent what costs should be, whereas budgeted costs are expected actual costs.

B. Budgeted costs are historical costs, whereas standard costs are based on engineering studies.

C. Budgeted costs include some slack, whereas standard costs do not.

D. Standard costs include some slack, whereas budgeted costs do not.

Answer (A) is correct. *(CMA, adapted)*
REQUIRED: The difference between standard costs and budgeted costs.
DISCUSSION: In the long run, these costs should be the same. In the short run, however, they may differ because standard costs represent what costs should be, whereas budgeted costs are expected actual costs. Budgeted costs may vary widely from standard costs in certain months, but, for an annual budget period, the amounts should be similar.
Answer (B) is incorrect. Standard costs are not necessarily determined by engineering studies. Answer (C) is incorrect. Standard costs are usually based on currently attainable standards applicable when a process is under control. They are set without regard to variances or slack. Answer (D) is incorrect. Budgeted costs include expected deviations from the standards.

7.2 Static and Flexible Budgeting

3. The difference between the actual amounts and the flexible budget amounts for the actual output achieved is the

A. Production volume variance.

B. Flexible budget variance.

C. Sales volume variance.

D. Standard cost variance.

Answer (B) is correct. *(CMA, adapted)*
REQUIRED: The term for the difference between the actual amounts and the flexible budget amounts.
DISCUSSION: A flexible budget is prepared at the end of the budget period when the actual results are available. A flexible budget reflects the revenues that should have been earned and costs that should have been incurred given the achieved levels of production and sales. The difference between the flexible budget and actual figures is known as the flexible budget variance.
Answer (A) is incorrect. The production volume variance equals under- or overapplied fixed overhead. Answer (C) is incorrect. The sales volume variance is the difference between the flexible budget amount and the static budget amount. Answer (D) is incorrect. A standard cost variance is not necessarily based on a flexible budget.

4. A manufacturing firm planned to manufacture and sell 100,000 units of product during the year at a variable cost per unit of $4.00 and a fixed cost per unit of $2.00. The firm fell short of its goal and only manufactured 80,000 units at a total incurred cost of $515,000. The firm's manufacturing cost variance was

A. $85,000 favorable.

B. $35,000 unfavorable.

C. $5,000 favorable.

D. $5,000 unfavorable.

Answer (C) is correct. *(CMA, adapted)*
REQUIRED: The manufacturing cost variance.
DISCUSSION: The company planned to produce 100,000 units at $6 each ($4 variable + $2 fixed cost), or a total of $600,000, consisting of $400,000 of variable costs and $200,000 of fixed costs. Total production was only 80,000 units at a total cost of $515,000. The flexible budget for a production level of 80,000 units includes variable costs of $320,000 (80,000 units × $4). Fixed costs would remain at $200,000. Thus, the total flexible budget costs are $520,000. Given that actual costs were only $515,000, the variance is $5,000 favorable.
Answer (A) is incorrect. The amount of $85,000 favorable is based on a production level of 100,000 units. Answer (B) is incorrect. The variance is favorable. Answer (D) is incorrect. The variance is favorable.

5. Based on past experience, a company has developed the following budget formula for estimating its shipping expenses. The company's shipments average 12 lbs. per shipment:

Shipping costs = $16,000 + ($0.50 × lbs. shipped)

The planned activity and actual activity regarding orders and shipments for the current month are given in the following schedule:

	Plan	Actual
Sales orders	800	780
Shipments	800	820
Units shipped	8,000	9,000
Sales	$120,000	$144,000
Total pounds shipped	9,600	12,300

The actual shipping costs for the month amounted to $21,000. The appropriate monthly flexible budget allowance for shipping costs for the purpose of performance evaluation would be

A. $20,680

B. $20,920

C. $20,800

D. $22,150

Answer (D) is correct. *(CMA, adapted)*
REQUIRED: The appropriate budgeted amount for shipping costs when 12,300 pounds are shipped.
DISCUSSION: The flexible budget formula is

Shipping costs = $16,000 + ($.50 × lbs. shipped)

Therefore, to determine the flexible budget amount, multiply the actual pounds shipped (12,300) times the standard cost ($.50) to arrive at a total expected variable cost of $6,150. Adding the variable cost to $16,000 of fixed cost produces a budget total of $22,150.
Answer (A) is incorrect. The amount of $20,680 is based on the actual number of sales orders, rather than on pounds shipped. Answer (B) is incorrect. The amount of $20,920 is based on the number of shipments, not the number of pounds shipped. Answer (C) is incorrect. The amount of $20,800 is based on planned pounds shipped of 9,600, not actual pounds shipped of 12,300.

7.3 Direct Materials Variances

6. Under a standard cost system, the materials efficiency variances are the responsibility of

A. Production and industrial engineering.

B. Purchasing and industrial engineering.

C. Purchasing and sales.

D. Sales and industrial engineering.

Answer (A) is correct. *(CMA, adapted)*
REQUIRED: The function(s) responsible for the materials efficiency (quantity) variance.
DISCUSSION: The materials efficiency variance is the difference between actual and standard quantities used in production, times the standard price. An unfavorable materials efficiency variance is usually caused by wastage, shrinkage, or theft. Thus, it may be the responsibility of the production department because excess usage would occur while the materials are in that department. In addition, industrial engineering may play a role because it is responsible for design of the production process.
Answer (B) is incorrect. Purchasing rarely can control the materials efficiency variance. Answer (C) is incorrect. Sales has no effect on the materials efficiency variance. Answer (D) is incorrect. Sales has no effect on the materials efficiency variance.

Questions 7 and 8 are based on the following information. Blaster, Inc., a manufacturer of portable radios, purchases the components from subcontractors to use to assemble into a complete radio. Each radio requires three units each of Part XBEZ52, which has a standard cost of $1.45 per unit. During May, Blaster experienced the following with respect to Part XBEZ52.

	Units
Purchases ($18,000)	12,000
Consumed in manufacturing	10,000
Radios manufactured	3,000

7. During May, Blaster incurred a purchase price variance of

   A. $450 unfavorable.

   B. $450 favorable.

   C. $500 favorable.

   D. $600 unfavorable.

Answer (D) is correct. *(CMA, adapted)*
   REQUIRED: The purchase price variance.
   DISCUSSION: Blaster's purchase price variance is calculated as follows:

$$\text{Purchase price variance} = AQ \times (SP - AP)$$
$$= 12{,}000 \text{ parts} \times (\$1.45 - \$1.50)$$
$$= 12{,}000 \times -\$0.05$$
$$= \$600 \text{ unfavorable}$$

   Answer (A) is incorrect. The standard quantity needed for the actual output times the $.05 unfavorable price variance per part equals $450 unfavorable. Answer (B) is incorrect. The variance is unfavorable, and $450 is the amount of the variance that relates only to the standard input for the actual output. Answer (C) is incorrect. The variance is unfavorable. Furthermore, the variance is based on the quantity purchased, not the quantity consumed. [Note: The materials price variance is sometimes isolated at the time of transfer to production.]

8. During May, Blaster incurred a materials efficiency variance of

   A. $1,450 unfavorable.

   B. $1,450 favorable.

   C. $4,350 unfavorable.

   D. $4,350 favorable.

Answer (A) is correct. *(CMA, adapted)*
   REQUIRED: The materials efficiency variance.
   DISCUSSION: Standard usage was three parts per radio at $1.45 each. For a production level of 3,000 units, the total materials needed equaled 9,000 parts, but materials actually used totaled 10,000 parts. Thus, the variance is $1,450 unfavorable {SP × (AQ – SQ) = [$1.45 standard cost per part × (10,000 actually used – 9,000 standard usage)]}.
   Answer (B) is incorrect. The variance is unfavorable. The actual quantity used exceeded the standard input allowed. Answer (C) is incorrect. Assuming that 12,000 parts were consumed results in $4,350 unfavorable. Answer (D) is incorrect. Assuming that 12,000 parts were consumed and that the variance is favorable results in $4,350 favorable.

9. Garland Company uses a standard cost system. The standard for each finished unit of product allows for 3 pounds of plastic at $0.72 per pound. During December, Garland bought 4,500 pounds of plastic at $0.75 per pound, and used 4,100 pounds in the production of 1,300 finished units of product. What is the materials purchase price variance for the month of December?

   A. $117 unfavorable.

   B. $123 unfavorable.

   C. $135 unfavorable.

   D. $150 unfavorable.

Answer (C) is correct. *(CMA, adapted)*
   REQUIRED: The materials purchase price variance.
   DISCUSSION: The materials purchase price variance equals the quantity purchased multiplied by the difference between the standard price and the actual price, or $135 unfavorable [4,500 lbs. × ($.75 – $.72)].
   Answer (A) is incorrect. The variance of $117 unfavorable is based on the standard input for 1,300 units. Answer (B) is incorrect. The variance of $123 unfavorable is based on the actual quantity used. Answer (D) is incorrect. The variance of $150 unfavorable is based on the assumption that 5,000 lbs. were purchased.

Questions 10 through 12 are based on the following information. ChemKing uses a standard costing system in the manufacture of its single product. The 35,000 units of direct materials in inventory were purchased for $105,000, and two units of direct materials are required to produce one unit of final product. In November, the company produced 12,000 units of product. The standard allowed for materials was $60,000, and the unfavorable quantity variance was $2,500.

10. ChemKing's standard price for one unit of direct materials is

    A. $2.00

    B. $2.50

    C. $3.00

    D. $5.00

Answer (B) is correct. *(CMA, adapted)*
    REQUIRED: The standard price for one unit of direct materials.
    DISCUSSION: Given that the company produced 12,000 units with a total standard cost for direct materials of $60,000, the standard cost must be $5.00 ($60,000 ÷ 12,000 units) per unit of finished product. Because each unit of finished product requires two units of direct materials, the standard unit cost for direct materials must be $2.50.
    Answer (A) is incorrect. The unit standard cost is $2.50. Answer (C) is incorrect. The actual cost per unit of direct materials is $3. Answer (D) is incorrect. The total standard cost of direct materials for each unit of finished product is $5.

11. ChemKing's units of direct materials used to produce November output totaled

    A. 12,000 units.

    B. 12,500 units.

    C. 23,000 units.

    D. 25,000 units.

Answer (D) is correct. *(CMA, adapted)*
    REQUIRED: The number of units of direct materials used to produce November output.
    DISCUSSION: The company produced 12,000 units of output, each of which required two units of direct materials. Thus, the standard input allowed for direct materials was 24,000 units at a standard cost of $2.50 each. An unfavorable quantity variance signifies that the actual quantity used was greater than the standard input allowed. The direct materials quantity variance equals the standard price per unit times the difference between actual and standard quantities. Consequently, because 1,000 ($2,500 U ÷ $2.50) additional units were used, the actual total quantity must have been 25,000 units (24,000 standard + 1,000).
    Answer (A) is incorrect. The number of units of finished product is 12,000. Answer (B) is incorrect. Assuming that each unit of finished product includes only one unit of direct materials results in 12,500 units. Answer (C) is incorrect. Assuming a favorable quantity variance results in 23,000 units.

12. ChemKing's direct materials price variance for the units used in November was

    A. $2,500 unfavorable.

    B. $11,000 unfavorable.

    C. $12,500 unfavorable.

    D. $3,500 unfavorable.

Answer (C) is correct. *(CMA, adapted)*
    REQUIRED: The direct materials price variance for the units used in November.
    DISCUSSION: Actual usage and the standard price were 25,000 units and $2.50, respectively. Actual price was $3.00 ($105,000 total cost ÷ 35,000 units purchased). Consequently, the direct materials price variance is $12,500 unfavorable {AQ × (AP – SP) = [25,000 units × ($3.00 – $2.50)]}.
    Answer (A) is incorrect. The direct materials quantity variance is $2,500 unfavorable. Answer (B) is incorrect. The price variance is $12,500, or $.50 per unit. Answer (D) is incorrect. The price variance is $12,500, or $.50 per unit.

13. A favorable materials price variance coupled with an unfavorable materials usage variance most likely results from

    A. Machine efficiency problems.

    B. Product mix production changes.

    C. The purchase and use of higher-than-standard quality materials.

    D. The purchase of lower than standard quality materials.

Answer (D) is correct. *(CMA, adapted)*
    REQUIRED: The cause of a favorable materials price variance coupled with an unfavorable materials usage variance.
    DISCUSSION: A favorable materials price variance is the result of paying less than the standard price for materials. An unfavorable materials usage variance is the result of using an excessive quantity of materials. If a purchasing manager were to buy substandard materials to achieve a favorable price variance, an unfavorable quantity variance could result from using an excessive amount of poor quality materials.
    Answer (A) is incorrect. Machine efficiency problems do not explain the price variance. Answer (B) is incorrect. A change in product mix does not explain the price variance. Answer (C) is incorrect. Materials of higher-than-standard quality are more likely to cause an unfavorable price variance and a favorable quantity variance.

14. Tower Company planned to produce 3,000 units of its single product, Titactium, during November. The standard specifications for one unit of Titactium include 6 pounds of materials at $.30 per pound. Actual production in November was 3,100 units of Titactium. The accountant computed a favorable direct materials purchase price variance of $380 and an unfavorable direct materials quantity variance of $120. Based on these variances, one could conclude that

    A. More materials were purchased than were used.

    B. More materials were used than were purchased.

    C. The actual cost of materials was less than the standard cost.

    D. The actual usage of materials was less than the standard allowed.

Answer (C) is correct. *(CMA, adapted)*
    REQUIRED: The meaning of a favorable direct materials purchase price variance and an unfavorable direct materials quantity variance.
    DISCUSSION: The direct materials purchase price variance may be isolated at the time of purchase or at the time of transfer to production. It equals the actual quantity of materials purchased or transferred times the difference between the standard and actual unit prices. Hence, a favorable direct materials purchase price variance means that materials were purchased at a price less than the standard price.
    Answer (A) is incorrect. No variance relates quantity purchased to quantity used. Answer (B) is incorrect. No variance relates quantity purchased to quantity used. Answer (D) is incorrect. The unfavorable quantity variance indicates that more materials were used than allowed by the standards. The direct materials quantity variance equals the standard unit price times the difference between the standard quantity allowed for the actual output and the actual quantity used.

15. David Rogers, purchasing manager at Fairway Manufacturing Corporation, was able to acquire a large quantity of direct materials from a new supplier at a discounted price. Marion Conner, inventory supervisor, is concerned because the warehouse has become crowded and some things had to be rearranged. Brian Jones, vice president of production, is concerned about the quality of the discounted materials. However, the Engineering Department tested the new materials and indicated that they are of acceptable quality. At the end of the month, Fairway experienced a favorable direct materials usage variance, a favorable direct labor usage variance, and a favorable direct materials price variance. The usage variances were solely the result of a higher yield from the new material. The favorable direct materials price variance is considered the responsibility of the

    A. Purchasing manager.

    B. Inventory supervisor.

    C. Vice president of production.

    D. Engineering manager.

Answer (A) is correct. *(CMA, adapted)*
    REQUIRED: The person responsible for a direct materials price variance.
    DISCUSSION: A direct materials price variance is the actual quantity used times the difference between the standard and actual prices. It is normally considered the responsibility of the purchasing manager because no one else has an opportunity to influence the price. In this case, the purchasing manager obtained the discount that led to the favorable price variance.
    Answer (B) is incorrect. An inventory supervisor has no influence over the price paid for materials. Answer (C) is incorrect. The vice president receives the materials without knowing the price. Answer (D) is incorrect. The engineering manager is concerned only with the quality of the materials.

16. Price variances and efficiency variances can be key to the performance measurement within a company. In evaluating the performance within a company, a materials efficiency variance can be caused by all of the following **except** the

   A. Performance of the workers using the material.

   B. Actions of the purchasing department.

   C. Design of the product.

   D. Sales volume of the product.

Answer (D) is correct. *(CMA, adapted)*
REQUIRED: The item not a cause of a materials efficiency variance.
DISCUSSION: An unfavorable materials quantity or usage (efficiency) variance can be caused by a number of factors, including waste, shrinkage, theft, poor performance by production workers, nonskilled workers, or the purchase of below-standard-quality materials by the purchasing department. Changes in product design can also affect the quantity of materials used. Sales volume of the product should not be a contributing factor to a materials efficiency variance.
Answer (A) is incorrect. Worker performance is a possible cause of a materials efficiency variance. Answer (B) is incorrect. Purchasing department actions are possible causes of a materials efficiency variance. Answer (C) is incorrect. Product design is a possible cause of a materials efficiency variance.

17. Todco planned to produce 3,000 units of its single product, Teragram, during November. The standard specifications for one unit of Teragram include six pounds of materials at $.30 per pound. Actual production in November was 3,100 units of Teragram. The accountant computed a favorable materials purchase price variance of $380 and an unfavorable materials quantity variance of $120. Based on these variances, one could conclude that

   A. More materials were purchased than were used.

   B. More materials were used than were purchased.

   C. The actual cost of materials was less than the standard cost.

   D. The actual usage of materials was less than the standard allowed.

Answer (C) is correct. *(CMA, adapted)*
REQUIRED: The implication of a favorable materials price variance or an unfavorable materials quantity variance.
DISCUSSION: A favorable price variance indicates that the materials were purchased at a price less than standard. The unfavorable quantity variance indicates that the quantity of materials used for actual production exceeded the standard quantity for the good units produced.
Answer (A) is incorrect. The quantity of materials purchased cannot be determined from the information given. Answer (B) is incorrect. The quantity of materials purchased cannot be determined from the information given. Answer (D) is incorrect. The actual usage was greater than standard.

7.4 Direct Labor Variances

18. The inventory control supervisor at Wilson Manufacturing Corporation reported that a large quantity of a part purchased for a special order that was never completed remains in stock. The order was not completed because the customer defaulted on the order. The part is not used in any of Wilson's regular products. After consulting with Wilson's engineers, the vice president of production approved the substitution of the purchased part for a regular part in a new product. Wilson's engineers indicated that the purchased part could be substituted providing it was modified. The units manufactured using the substituted part required additional direct labor hours resulting in an unfavorable direct labor efficiency variance in the Production Department. The unfavorable direct labor efficiency variance resulting from the substitution of the purchased part in inventory is best assigned to the

   A. Sales manager.

   B. Inventory supervisor.

   C. Production manager.

   D. Vice president of production.

Answer (D) is correct. *(CMA, adapted)*
REQUIRED: The person most responsible for an unfavorable direct labor efficiency variance caused by a part substitution.
DISCUSSION: An unfavorable direct labor efficiency variance is normally charged to the production manager, the person with the most control over the amount and kinds of direct labor used. However, that individual is not responsible. (S)he was told to use the nonconforming part that required extra labor time. Thus, the variance should be charged to the vice president of production, the individual who most influenced the incurrence of the cost.
Answer (A) is incorrect. The sales manager did not make the substitution decision. Answer (B) is incorrect. The inventory supervisor did not make the substitution decision. Answer (C) is incorrect. The production manager did not make the substitution decision.

19. Under a standard cost system, direct labor price variances are usually **not** attributable to

A. Union contracts approved before the budgeting cycle.

B. Labor rate predictions.

C. The use of a single average standard rate.

D. The assignment of different skill levels of workers than planned.

Answer (A) is correct. *(CMA, adapted)*
REQUIRED: The factor that usually does not affect the direct labor price variance.
DISCUSSION: The direct labor price (rate) variance is the actual hours worked times the difference between the standard rate and the actual rate paid. This difference may be attributable to (1) a change in labor rates since the establishment of the standards, (2) using a single average standard rate despite different rates earned among different employees, (3) assigning higher-paid workers to jobs estimated to require lower-paid workers (or vice versa), or (4) paying hourly rates, but basing standards on piecework rates (or vice versa). The difference should not be caused by a union contract approved before the budgeting cycle because such rates would have been incorporated into the standards.
Answer (B) is incorrect. Predictions about labor rates may have been inaccurate. Answer (C) is incorrect. Using a single average standard rate may lead to variances if some workers are paid more than others and the proportions of hours worked differ from estimates. Answer (D) is incorrect. Assigning higher paid (and higher skilled) workers to jobs not requiring such skills leads to an unfavorable variance.

Question 20 is based on the following information. Zazoo, Inc. specializes in reviewing and editing technical magazine articles. Zazoo sets the following standards for evaluating the performance of the professional staff:

Annual budgeted fixed costs for normal capacity level of 10,000 articles reviewed and edited	$600,000
Standard professional hours per 10 articles	200 hours
Flexible budget of standard labor costs to process 10,000 articles	$10,000,000

The following data apply to the 9,500 articles that were actually reviewed and edited during the current year.

Total hours used by professional staff	192,000 hours
Flexible costs	$9,120,000
Total cost	$9,738,000

20. Zazoo's labor efficiency variance for the year is

A. $100,000 unfavorable.

B. $238,000 unfavorable.

C. $380,000 favorable.

D. $500,000 favorable.

Answer (A) is correct. *(CMA, adapted)*
REQUIRED: The labor efficiency variance.
DISCUSSION: The labor efficiency variance is the standard cost per hour times the difference between standard and actual hour. The standard labor rate is $50 per hour, and the standard time allowed for 9,500 articles is 190,000 hours (9,500 × 20). Actual hours worked totaled 192,000. Thus, an unfavorable variance of 2,000 hours occurred. The unfavorable labor efficiency variance is therefore $100,000 (2,000 hours × $50).
Answer (B) is incorrect. The difference between the standard labor cost ($9,500,000) and total actual (fixed + variable) cost ($9,738,000) is $238,000. Answer (C) is incorrect. The variance is unfavorable. Answer (D) is incorrect. The efficiency variance is based on standard hours for actual production levels--in this case, 190,000 hours.

Questions 21 through 23 are based on the following information. Jackson Industries employs a standard cost system in which direct materials inventory is carried at standard cost. Jackson has established the following standards for the prime costs of one unit of product.

	Standard Quantity	Standard Price	Standard Cost
Direct materials	5 pounds	$ 3.60/pound	$18.00
Direct labor	1.25 hours	$12.00/hour	15.00
			$33.00

During May, Jackson purchased 125,000 pounds of direct materials at a total cost of $475,000. The total factory wages for May were $364,000, 90% of which were for direct labor. Jackson manufactured 22,000 units of product during May using 108,000 pounds of direct materials and 28,000 direct labor hours.

21. Jackson's direct materials usage (quantity) variance for May is

A. $7,200 unfavorable.

B. $7,600 favorable.

C. $5,850 unfavorable.

D. $7,200 favorable.

Answer (D) is correct. *(CMA, adapted)*
REQUIRED: The direct materials usage (quantity) variance.
DISCUSSION: This variance equals the standard unit cost times the difference between the actual quantity used and the standard quantity for good production. Consequently, the variance is $7,200 favorable {[(5 pounds × 22,000 units) – 108,000 pounds used] × $3.60}.
Answer (A) is incorrect. The variance is favorable. Answer (B) is incorrect. The variance is calculated by multiplying the quantity difference times the standard unit cost of $3.60, not the actual unit cost. Answer (C) is incorrect. The variance is favorable. Actual usage was less than the standard.

22. Jackson's direct labor price (rate) variance for May is

A. $8,400 favorable.

B. $7,200 unfavorable.

C. $8,400 unfavorable.

D. $6,000 unfavorable.

Answer (A) is correct. *(CMA, adapted)*
REQUIRED: The direct labor rate variance.
DISCUSSION: The direct labor rate variance equals the actual quantity of hours worked times the difference between the standard and actual labor rates. Total direct labor cost was $327,600 ($364,000 × 90%), and the actual unit direct labor cost was $11.70 ($327,600 ÷ 28,000 hours). Thus, the variance is $8,400 favorable [28,000 hours × ($12.00 – $11.70)].
Answer (B) is incorrect. The variance is favorable. The actual labor rate was less than the standard rate. Answer (C) is incorrect. The variance is favorable. The actual labor rate was less than the standard rate. Answer (D) is incorrect. The labor efficiency variance is $6,000, not the labor rate variance.

23. Jackson's direct labor usage (efficiency) variance for May is

A. $5,850 favorable.

B. $6,000 unfavorable.

C. $5,850 unfavorable.

D. $6,000 favorable.

Answer (B) is correct. *(CMA, adapted)*
REQUIRED: The direct labor usage (efficiency) variance.
DISCUSSION: The direct labor efficiency variance equals the standard unit cost times the difference between actual hours and standard hours. Accordingly, the variance is $6,000 unfavorable {[28,000 hours – (1.25 hours × 22,000 units)] × $12}.
Answer (A) is incorrect. The variance is unfavorable. More hours were worked than allowed by the standards. Answer (C) is incorrect. The labor efficiency variance is calculated using the standard labor rate, not the actual labor rate. Answer (D) is incorrect. The variance is unfavorable.

24. The flexible budget for the month of May was for 9,000 units with direct materials at $15 per unit. Direct labor was budgeted at 45 minutes per unit for a total of $81,000. Actual output for the month was 8,500 units with $127,500 in direct materials and $77,775 in direct labor expense. The direct labor standard of 45 minutes was maintained throughout the month. Variance analysis of the performance for the month of May shows a(n)

    A. Favorable direct materials usage variance of $7,500.

    B. Favorable direct labor efficiency variance of $1,275.

    C. Unfavorable direct labor efficiency variance of $1,275.

    D. Unfavorable direct labor price variance of $1,275.

Answer (D) is correct. *(CMA, adapted)*
    REQUIRED: The result of variance analysis based on a flexible budget for direct labor and materials.
    DISCUSSION: The static budget for direct materials is $127,500 (8,500 units × $15). Thus, no variance arose with respect to direct materials. Because direct labor for 9,000 units was budgeted at $81,000, the unit direct labor cost is $9. Thus, the direct labor budget for 8,500 units is $76,500, and the total direct labor variance is $1,275 ($77,775 − $76,500). Because the actual cost is greater than the budgeted amounts, the $1,275 variance is unfavorable. Given that the actual time per unit (45 minutes) was the same as that budgeted, no labor efficiency variance was incurred. Hence, the entire $1,275 unfavorable variance must be attributable to the direct labor rate (or price) variance.
    Answer (A) is incorrect. No direct materials variance occurred. The actual cost was equal to the budgeted cost for direct materials. Answer (B) is incorrect. No direct labor efficiency variance occurred. Budgeted hours were identical to actual hours for 8,500 units. Answer (C) is incorrect. No direct labor efficiency variance occurred. Budgeted hours were identical to actual hours for 8,500 units.

7.5 Mix and Yield Variances

25. The efficiency variance for either direct labor or materials can be divided into

    A. Spending variance and yield variance.

    B. Yield variance and price variance.

    C. Volume variance and mix variance.

    D. Yield variance and mix variance.

Answer (D) is correct. *(CMA, adapted)*
    REQUIRED: The components into which a direct labor or materials efficiency variance can be divided.
    DISCUSSION: A direct labor or materials efficiency variance is calculated by multiplying the difference between standard and actual usage times the standard cost per unit of input. The efficiency variances can be divided into yield and mix variances. Mix and yield variances are calculated only when the production process involves combining several materials or classes of labor in varying proportions (when substitutions are allowable in combining resources).
    Answer (A) is incorrect. A spending variance is not the same as an efficiency variance. Answer (B) is incorrect. A price variance is not the same as an efficiency variance. Answer (C) is incorrect. A volume variance is based on fixed costs, and an efficiency variance is based on variable costs.

7.6 Overhead Variances

26. If overhead is applied on the basis of units of output, the variable overhead efficiency variance will be

    A. Zero.

    B. Favorable, if output exceeds the budgeted level.

    C. Unfavorable, if output is less than the budgeted level.

    D. A function of the direct labor efficiency variance.

Answer (A) is correct. *(CMA, adapted)*
    REQUIRED: The effect on the variable overhead efficiency variance.
    DISCUSSION: The variable overhead efficiency variance equals the product of the variable overhead application rate and the difference between the standard input for the actual output and the actual input. Hence, the variance will be zero if variable overhead is applied on the basis of units of output because the difference between actual and standard input cannot be recognized.
    Answer (B) is incorrect. The variance will be zero. Answer (C) is incorrect. The variance will be zero. Answer (D) is incorrect. The correlation between the variable overhead and direct labor efficiency variances occurs only when overhead is applied on the basis of direct labor.

27. Variable overhead is applied on the basis of standard direct labor hours. If, for a given period, the direct labor efficiency variance is unfavorable, the variable overhead efficiency variance will be

A. Favorable.

B. Unfavorable.

C. The same amount as the labor efficiency variance.

D. Indeterminable because it is not related to the labor efficiency variance.

Answer (B) is correct. *(CMA, adapted)*
REQUIRED: The effect on the variable overhead efficiency variance of an unfavorable direct labor efficiency variance.
DISCUSSION: The calculation of the variable overhead efficiency variance is similar to that of the direct labor efficiency variance in that both measure the effect of the difference between actual and standard hours. Assuming overhead is applied on the basis of direct labor hours, both variance calculations will be based on the same number of hours. Thus, if the direct labor efficiency variance is unfavorable, the variable overhead efficiency variance will also be unfavorable.

28. Variable overhead is applied on the basis of standard direct labor hours. If, for a given period, the direct labor efficiency variance is unfavorable, the variable overhead efficiency variance will be

A. Favorable.

B. Unfavorable.

C. Zero.

D. The same amount as the direct labor efficiency variance.

Answer (B) is correct. *(CMA, adapted)*
REQUIRED: The effect on the variable overhead efficiency variance.
DISCUSSION: If variable overhead is applied to production on the basis of direct labor hours, both the variable overhead efficiency variance and the direct labor efficiency variance will be calculated on the basis of the same number of hours. If the direct labor efficiency variance is unfavorable, the overhead efficiency variance will also be unfavorable because both variances are based on the difference between standard and actual direct labor hours worked.
Answer (A) is incorrect. Both efficiency variances are based on the same number of hours worked. Thus, if one is unfavorable, the other will also be unfavorable. Answer (C) is incorrect. Both efficiency variances are based on the same number of hours worked. Thus, if one is unfavorable, the other will also be unfavorable. Answer (D) is incorrect. The amount of the variances will be different depending on the amount of the costs anticipated and actually paid.

29. Baltimore Products has an estimated practical capacity of 90,000 machine hours, and each unit requires two machine hours. The following data apply to a recent accounting period:

Actual variable overhead	$240,000
Actual fixed overhead	$442,000
Actual machine hours worked	88,000
Actual finished units produced	42,000
Budgeted variable overhead at	
90,000 machine hours	$200,000
Budgeted fixed overhead	$450,000

Of the following factors, Baltimore's production volume variance is most likely to have been caused by

A. A wage hike granted to a production supervisor.

B. A newly imposed initiative to reduce finished goods inventory levels.

C. Acceptance of an unexpected sales order.

D. Temporary employment of workers with lower skill levels than originally anticipated.

Answer (B) is correct. *(CMA, adapted)*
REQUIRED: The most likely cause of a production volume overhead variance.
DISCUSSION: Fixed overhead was budgeted based on a practical capacity of 90,000 machine hours. Because the actual hours used were 88,000, fixed overhead was underapplied, and an unfavorable production-volume variance resulted. The only one of the four actions that would result in fewer machine hours than were budgeted being consumed is the initiative to reduce finished goods inventory levels.
Answer (A) is incorrect. A wage hike to a production supervisor is a variable cost and would thus affect the variable, not the fixed, variance. Answer (C) is incorrect. An unexpected sales order would result in more machine hours than were budgeted, not fewer. In other words, an unexpected order would result in a variable volume variance. Answer (D) is incorrect. Worker wages are a variable cost and would thus affect the variable, not the fixed, overhead variance.

30. The fixed overhead volume variance is the

A. Measure of the lost profits from the lack of sales volume.

B. Amount of the underapplied or overapplied fixed overhead costs.

C. Potential cost reduction that can be achieved from better cost control.

D. Measure of production inefficiency.

Answer (B) is correct. *(CMA, adapted)*
  REQUIRED: The definition of fixed overhead volume variance.
  DISCUSSION: The fixed overhead volume variance is the difference between budgeted fixed costs and actual overhead applied, which equals the budgeted fixed overhead rate times the standard input allowed for the actual output. It is solely a measure of capacity usage and does not signify that fixed costs were more or less than budgeted.
  Answer (A) is incorrect. The fixed overhead volume variance concerns the application of fixed cost to product and does not encompass revenue or sales concepts in any way. Answer (C) is incorrect. The fixed overhead volume variance is calculated on the assumption that fixed costs are constant. Answer (D) is incorrect. The volume variance concerns output levels rather than the efficiency of production.

31. Which of these variances is **least** significant for cost control?

A. Labor price variance.

B. Materials quantity variance.

C. Fixed O/H volume variance.

D. Variable O/H spending variance.

Answer (C) is correct. *(CMA, adapted)*
  REQUIRED: The variance least significant for cost control.
  DISCUSSION: The fixed O/H volume variance occurs when actual activity levels differ from anticipated levels. It is an excellent example of cost allocation as opposed to cost control. Unlike other variances, the volume variance does not directly reflect a difference between actual and budgeted expenditures. The economic substance of this variance lies in the costs or benefits of capacity usage or nonusage. For example, idle capacity results in the loss of the contribution margin from units not produced and sold.
  Answer (A) is incorrect. A labor price variance reflects a difference between the actual price of labor and the budgeted price of labor, which is useful information for cost control. Answer (B) is incorrect. The materials quantity variance is the difference between budgeted and actual materials used during production. This is an important variance for cost control. Answer (D) is incorrect. The difference between actual variable O/H and the product of the actual input and the budgeted variable O/H rate is useful information for cost control.

32. Lee Manufacturing uses a standard cost system with overhead applied based upon direct labor hours. The manufacturing budget for the production of 5,000 units for the month of May included the following information:

Direct labor (10,000 hours at $15 per hour)	$150,000
Variable overhead	30,000
Fixed overhead	80,000

During May, 6,000 units were produced and the fixed overhead budget variance was $2,000 favorable. Fixed overhead during May was

A. Underapplied by $2,000.

B. Underapplied by $16,000.

C. Overapplied by $16,000.

D. Overapplied by $18,000.

Answer (D) is correct. *(CMA, adapted)*
  REQUIRED: The amount of overapplied overhead given relevant information.
  DISCUSSION: First, the actual production level for the month was 6,000 units of output. Second, the standard number of labor hours consumed per unit of output is 2 (10,000 budgeted direct labor hours ÷ 5,000 budgeted units output). Third, since fixed overhead for the month was budgeted at $80,000 and it is to be applied in proportion to 10,000 budgeted direct labor hours, the application rate is $8 per direct labor hour ($80,000 ÷ 10,000). Thus, the amount of fixed overhead applied for the month was $96,000 = (6,000 × $8 × 2). The fixed overhead budget variance was $2,000 favorable, which means the actual fixed overhead incurred for the month was $78,000 ($80,000 – $2,000). Thus, fixed overhead was overapplied by $18,000 ($96,000 – $78,000).
  Answer (A) is incorrect. Misinterpreting the $2,000 favorable budget (spending) variance results in $2,000 underapplied. Answer (B) is incorrect. Reversing the proper order of subtraction results in $16,000 underapplied. Answer (C) is incorrect. The production-volume variance is $16,000 overapplied.

7.7 Comprehensive Example

Questions 33 through 36 are based on the following information.

Ardmore Enterprises uses a standard cost system in its small appliance division. The standard cost of manufacturing one unit of Zeb is as follows:

Direct materials -- 60 pounds at $1.50 per pound	$ 90
Direct labor -- 3 hours at $12 per hour	36
Overhead -- 3 hours at $8 per hour	24
Total standard cost per unit	$150

The budgeted variable overhead rate is $3 per direct labor hour, and the budgeted fixed overhead is $27,000 per month. During May, Ardmore produced 1,650 units of Zeb compared with a normal capacity of 1,800 units. The actual cost per unit was as follows:

Direct materials (purchased and used) --	
58 pounds at $1.65 per pound	$ 95.70
Direct labor -- 3.1 hours at $12 per hour	37.20
Overhead -- $39,930 per 1,650 units	24.20
Total actual cost per unit	$157.10

33. Ardmore's total direct materials quantity variance for May is

A. $14,355 favorable.

B. $14,355 unfavorable.

C. $4,950 favorable.

D. $4,950 unfavorable.

Answer (C) is correct. *(CMA, adapted)*
REQUIRED: The direct materials quantity variance.
DISCUSSION: The direct materials quantity variance equals the difference between the standard and actual quantities times the standard price. Hence, the favorable direct materials quantity variance is $4,950 [1,650 units × (60 standard pounds – 58 actual pounds) × $1.50 standard].
Answer (A) is incorrect. The amount of the direct materials price variance is $14,355. Answer (B) is incorrect. The amount of the direct materials price variance is $14,355. Answer (D) is incorrect. A favorable variance exists. The standard amount for the actual output exceeded the actual amount.

34. Ardmore's direct materials price variance for May is

A. $14,355 unfavorable.

B. $14,850 unfavorable.

C. $14,355 favorable.

D. $14,850 favorable.

Answer (A) is correct. *(CMA, adapted)*
REQUIRED: The direct materials price variance.
DISCUSSION: The direct materials price variance equals the actual quantity used times the difference between the standard and actual price per unit. Thus, the unfavorable direct materials price variance is $14,355 [1,650 units × 58 actual pounds × ($1.50 standard price – $1.65 actual price)].
Answer (B) is incorrect. The variance of $14,850 is based on the standard unit quantity, not the actual quantity. Answer (C) is incorrect. The price variance is unfavorable. The actual price is greater than the standard price. Answer (D) is incorrect. The variance of $14,850 is based on the standard unit quantity, not the actual quantity.

35. Ardmore's direct labor rate variance for May is

A. $1,920 favorable.

B. $0

C. $4,950 unfavorable.

D. $4,950 favorable.

Answer (B) is correct. *(CMA, adapted)*
REQUIRED: The direct labor rate variance.
DISCUSSION: The direct labor rate variance equals the actual hours used times the difference between the standard and actual rates. Consequently, the direct labor rate variance is zero [1,650 units × 3.1 actual hours × ($12 per hour standard rate – $12 per hour actual rate)].
Answer (A) is incorrect. The amount of the flexible budget overhead variance is $1,920. Answer (C) is incorrect. The amount of the direct materials quantity variance is $4,950. Answer (D) is incorrect. The amount of the direct materials quantity variance is $4,950.

36. Refer to the information on the preceding page(s). Ardmore's flexible budget overhead variance for May is

    A. $3,270 unfavorable.

    B. $3,270 favorable.

    C. $1,920 unfavorable.

    D. $1,920 favorable.

Answer (D) is correct. *(CMA, adapted)*
    REQUIRED: The flexible budget overhead variance.
    DISCUSSION: The flexible budget overhead variance is the difference between actual overhead costs and the flexible budget amount for the actual output. Standard total fixed costs at any level of production are $27,000. Standard variable overhead is $9 per unit (3 labor hours × $3). Thus, total standard variable overhead is $14,850 for the actual output (1,650 units × $9), and the total flexible budget amount is $41,850 ($27,000 FOH + $14,850 VOH). Accordingly, the favorable flexible budget variance is $1,920 favorable ($41,850 flexible budget amount – $39,930 actual amount).
    Answer (A) is incorrect. The flexible budget amount for an output of 1,800 units is $3,270. Answer (B) is incorrect. The flexible budget amount for an output of 1,800 units is $3,270. Answer (C) is incorrect. A favorable variance exists. Actual overhead is less than the standard overhead at the actual production level.

7.8 Sales Variances

37. The variance that arises solely because the quantity actually sold differs from the quantity budgeted to be sold is

    A. Static budget variance.

    B. Master budget increment.

    C. Sales mix variance.

    D. Sales volume variance.

Answer (D) is correct. *(CMA, adapted)*
    REQUIRED: The variance that arises solely when actual sales differ from budgeted sales.
    DISCUSSION: If a firm's sales differ from the amount budgeted, the difference could be attributable either to the sales price variance or the sales volume variance. The sales volume variance is the change in contribution margin caused by the difference between the actual and budgeted sales volumes.
    Answer (A) is incorrect. A static budget variance is the difference between actual costs or revenues and those budgeted on a static budget. Answer (B) is incorrect. A master budget increment is an increase in a budgeted figure on the firm's master budget. Answer (C) is incorrect. The sales mix variance is caused when a company's actual sales mix is different from the budgeted sales mix.

38. In analyzing company operations, the controller of the Jason Corporation found a $250,000 favorable flexible-budget revenue variance. The variance was calculated by comparing the actual results with the flexible budget. This variance can be wholly explained by

    A. The total flexible budget variance.

    B. The total sales volume variance.

    C. The total static budget variance.

    D. Changes in unit selling prices.

Answer (D) is correct. *(CMA, adapted)*
    REQUIRED: The cause of a favorable flexible-budget revenue variance.
    DISCUSSION: Variance analysis can be used to judge the effectiveness of selling departments. If a firm's sales differ from the amount budgeted, the difference may be attributable to either the sales price variance or the sales volume (quantity) variance. Changes in unit selling prices may account for the entire variance if the actual quantity sold is equal to the quantity budgeted. None of the revenue variance is attributed to the sales volume variance because no such variance exists when a flexible budget is used. The flexible budget is based on the level of sales at actual volume.
    Answer (A) is incorrect. The total flexible budget variance includes items other than revenue. Answer (B) is incorrect. The sales volume variance represents the change in contribution margin caused by a difference between actual and budgeted units sold. However, given a flexible budget, there is no difference between budgeted and actual units sold. By definition, a flexible budget's volume is identical to actual volume. Answer (C) is incorrect. The total static budget variance includes many items other than revenue.

Use Gleim **CMA Test Prep** Software for interactive testing with **additional multiple-choice questions!**

7.10 ESSAY QUESTIONS

Scenario for Essay Questions 1, 2

The LAR Chemical Co. manufactures a wide variety of chemical compounds and liquids for industrial uses. The standard mix for producing a single batch of 500 gallons of one liquid is as follows:

Liquid Chemical	Quantity (in gallons)	Cost (per gallon)	Total Cost
Maxan	100	2.00	$200
Salex	300	.75	225
Cralyn	225	1.00	225
	625		$650

There is a 20% loss in liquid volume during processing due to evaporation. The finished liquid is put into 10 gallon bottles for sale. Thus, the standard material cost for a 10-gallon bottle is $13.00.

The actual quantities of materials and the respective cost of the materials placed in production during November were as follows:

Liquid Chemical	Quantity (in gallons)	Total Cost
Maxan	8,480	$17,384
Salex	25,200	17,640
Cralyn	18,540	16,686
	52,220	$51,710

A total of 4,000 bottles (40,000 gallons) were produced during November.

Questions

1. Calculate the total materials variance for the liquid product for the month of November and then further analyze the total variance into

   a. Materials price variance
   b. Materials mix variance
   c. Materials yield variance

2. Explain how LAR Chemical Co. could use each of the three materials variances – price, mix, yield – to help control the cost to manufacture this liquid compound.

Essay Questions 1, 2 — Unofficial Answers

1.   Total direct materials variance:

Static budget (SQ × SP):   4,000 bottles × $13.00   = $52,000
Less: actual cost   (51,710)
            Static budget variance $ 290 F

a.   Materials price variance

Chemical	Actual Quantity		Standard Price		Totals
Maxan	8,480 gallons	×	$2.00	=	$16,960
Salex	25,200 gallons	×	.75	=	18,900
Cralyn	18,540 gallons	×	1.00	=	18,540
Total AQ × SP					$54,400
Less: actual cost					(51,710)
Price variance					$ 2,690 F

b.   Materials mix variance

$$\frac{Standard\ weighted\text{-}average\ input\ cost\ per\ batch}{Standard\ input\ gallons\ per\ batch} = \frac{\$650}{625} = \$1.04\ per\ input\ gallon$$

Actual gallons × standard cost
    (calculated in a.) $54,400.00
Less actual quantity × standard weighted average cost per input gallon
    (standard proportion) (52,220 × $1.04)   54,308.80
Mix variance $ 91.20 U

c.   Materials yield variance

Expected quantity[1]   50,000   gallons
Less: actual quantity   (52,220) gallons
    Variance in input quantity   (2,220) gallons
Times: standard weighted average cost per input   × $1.04   per gallon
    Yield variance $2,308.80   U

[1] Every batch experiences a 20% loss in inputs due to evaporation. To generate 40,000 gallons of output, therefore, 50,000 gallons must be consumed.

2.   Before management can control costs, they need to know which costs are out of line, within whose area of responsibility has the variance appeared, what is the cause of the variance, and who has the responsibility to correct the cause. Variances help management to answer these issues. Specifically, the variances indicate where management should begin its investigation:

a.   Price variation – the information to identify the causes of the price variance usually can be obtained in the purchasing department. A review of purchasing procedures and records would disclose whether the variances were caused by permanent changes in prices, poor purchasing practices or poor production scheduling requiring incurrence of extra costs to expedite shipments. The information obtained will identify the department responsible for the extra cost and provide clues to improve the control.

b.   Mix and yield variances – the information to identify the cause of these variances can be obtained in production. A review of material records and handling procedure would disclose whether the mix variance was caused by the use of wrong proportions, entering excess materials into the process because of carelessness, or adjustment of the mix to accommodate off-standard material quality. Yield variance would often be explained by the same information. Nonstandard proportions would result in nonstandard yields and excess material inputs. The information obtained would identify the department responsible and provide clues to improve control.

STUDY UNIT EIGHT
RESPONSIBILITY ACCOUNTING
AND PERFORMANCE MEASURES

(19 pages of outline)

8.1	Responsibility Centers	292
8.2	Performance Measures -- Cost, Revenue, and Profit Centers	294
8.3	Performance Measures -- Investment Centers	296
8.4	Comparing Performance Measures for Investment Centers	298
8.5	Allocating Common Costs	299
8.6	Transfer Pricing -- Details	301
8.7	Transfer Pricing -- Selection	304
8.8	The Balanced Scorecard	305
8.9	Core Concepts	308
8.10	Essay Questions	323

This study unit is the **second of two** on **performance management**. The relative weight assigned to this major topic in Part 1 of the exam is **25%**. The two study units are

Study Unit 7: Cost and Variance Measures

Study Unit 8: Responsibility Accounting and Performance Measures

After studying the outline and answering the questions in this study unit, you will have the skills necessary to address the following topics listed in the ICMA's Learning Outcome Statements:

Part 1 – Section B.2. Responsibility centers and reporting segments

The candidate should be able to:

a. identify and explain the different types of responsibility centers

b. recommend appropriate responsibility centers given a business scenario

c. demonstrate an understanding of contribution margin reporting as used for performance evaluation and calculate a contribution margin

d. analyze a contribution margin report and evaluate performance

e. identify segments that organizations evaluate, including product lines, geographical areas, or other meaningful segments

f. explain why the allocation of common costs among segments can be an issue in performance evaluation

g. identify methods for allocating common costs, such as stand-alone cost allocation and incremental cost allocation

h. define transfer pricing and identify the objectives of transfer pricing

i. identify the methods for determining transfer prices and list and explain the advantages and disadvantages of each method

j. identify and/or calculate transfer prices using variable cost, full cost, market price, negotiated price, and dual-rate pricing

k. explain how transfer pricing is affected by business issues such as the presence of outside suppliers and the opportunity costs associated with capacity usage

l. describe how special issues such as tariffs, exchange rates, taxes, currency restrictions, expropriation risk, and the availability of materials and skills affect performance evaluation in multinational companies

Part 1 – Section B.3. Performance measures

The candidate should be able to:

a.   explain why performance evaluation measures should be directly related to strategic and operational goals and objectives; why timely feedback is critical; and why performance measures should be related to the factors that drive the element being measured, e.g., cost drivers and revenue drivers

b.   explain the issues involved in determining product profitability, business unit profitability, and customer profitability, including cost measurement, cost allocation, investment measurement, and valuation

c.   calculate product-line profitability, business unit profitability, and customer profitability given a set of data and assumptions

d.   evaluate customers and products on the basis of profitability and recommend ways to improve profitability and/or drop unprofitable customers and products

e.   define and calculate return on investment (ROI)

f.   analyze and interpret ROI calculations and evaluate performance on the basis of the analysis

g.   define and calculate residual income (RI)

h.   analyze and interpret RI calculations and evaluate performance on the basis of the analysis

i.   compare and contrast the benefits and limitations of ROI and RI as measures of performance

j.   explain how revenue and expense recognition policies may affect the measurement of income and reduce comparability among business units

k.   explain how inventory measurement policies, joint asset sharing, and overall asset measurement may affect the measurement of investment and reduce comparability among business units

l.   demonstrate an understanding of the effect international operations can have on performance measurement

m.   define critical success factors and discuss the importance of these factors in evaluating a firm

n.   define the concept of a balanced scorecard and identify its components

o.   identify and describe financial measures, customer satisfaction measures, internal business process measures, innovation and learning measures, and evaluate their relevance for a specific organization using the balanced scorecard

p.   identify and describe the characteristics of successful implementation and use of a balanced scorecard

q.   analyze and interpret a balanced scorecard and evaluate performance on the basis of the analysis

r.   recommend performance measures and a periodic reporting methodology given operational goals and actual results

8.1 RESPONSIBILITY CENTERS

1. **Decision Making and Decentralization**

   a.   The primary distinction between centralized and decentralized organizations is in the degree of freedom of decision making by managers at many levels.

       1)   In a centralized organization, decision making is consolidated so that activities throughout the organization may be more effectively coordinated from the top.

       2)   In a decentralized organization, decision making is at as low a level as possible. The premise is that the local manager can make more informed decisions than a manager farther from the decision.

2. **Responsibility Centers**

   a. A decentralized organization is divided into **responsibility centers** (also called **strategic business units**, or SBUs) to facilitate local decision making.

      1) Four types of responsibility centers are generally recognized.

   b. A **cost center**, e.g., a maintenance department, is responsible for costs only.

      1) Cost drivers are the relevant performance measures.

      2) A disadvantage of a cost center is the potential for cost shifting, for example, replacement of variable costs for which a manager is responsible with fixed costs for which (s)he is not.

         a) Another disadvantage is that long-term issues may be disregarded when the emphasis is on, for example, annual cost amounts.

         b) Yet another issue is allocation of service department costs to cost centers.

      3) Service centers exist primarily and sometimes solely to provide specialized support to other organizational subunits. They are usually operated as cost centers.

   c. A **revenue center**, e.g., a sales department, is responsible for revenues only.

      1) Revenue drivers are the relevant performance measures. They are factors that influence unit sales, such as changes in prices and products, customer service, marketing efforts, and delivery terms.

   d. A **profit center**, e.g., an appliance department in a retail store, is responsible for both revenues and expenses.

   e. An **investment center**, e.g., a branch office, is responsible for revenues, expenses, and invested capital.

      1) The advantage of an investment center is that it permits an evaluation of performance that can be compared with that of other responsibility centers or other potential investments on a return on investment basis, i.e., on the basis of the effectiveness of asset usage.

3. **Performance Measures and Manager Motivation**

   a. Each responsibility center is structured such that a logical group of operations is under the direction of a single manager.

      1) Measures are designed for every responsibility center to monitor performance.

   b. **Controllability.** The performance measures on which the manager's incentive package are based must be, as far as practicable, under the manager's direct influence.

      1) "Controllable" factors can be thought of as those factors that a manager can influence in a given time period.

         a) Inevitably, some costs, especially common costs such as the costs of central administrative functions, cannot be traced to particular activities or responsibility centers.

         b) The challenges associated with allocating common costs fully and fairly are discussed in Subunit 8.5.

      2) Controllable cost is not synonymous with variable cost. Often this classification is particular to the level of the organization.

         a) For instance, the fixed cost of depreciation may not be a controllable cost of the manager of a revenue center, but is controllable by the division vice president to which that manager reports.

    c.   **Goal congruence.** These performance measures must be designed such that the manager's pursuit of them ties directly to accomplishment of the organization's overall goals.

        1)   Suboptimization results when segments of the organization pursue goals that are in that segment's own best interests rather than those of the organization as a whole.

    d.   Along with the responsibility, a manager must be granted sufficient authority to control those factors on which his/her incentive package is based.

Stop and review! You have completed the outline for this subunit. Study multiple-choice questions 1 through 5 beginning on page 310.

8.2 PERFORMANCE MEASURES -- COST, REVENUE, AND PROFIT CENTERS

1.   **Cost Centers and Revenue Centers**

    a.   Since managers of cost and revenue centers can influence only one type of factor, variance analysis (see Study Unit 7) is the most appropriate performance measurement technique for these responsibility centers.

    b.   To be effective, a performance measure should be based on a cause-and-effect relationship between the outcome being measured and a driver that is under the manager's control.

        1)   An appropriate performance measure for a cost or revenue center might not even be financial. Examples might include number of invoices processed per hour or percentage of customer shipments correctly filled.

2.   **Profit Centers**

    a.   The contribution margin approach to reporting (in contrast to the financial reporting approach) is extremely useful in performance measurement for profit centers.

        1)   As described in Study Unit 3, Subunit 1, the contribution margin approach isolates the effects of variable and fixed costs, and thus highlights the effects of a manager's choices.

        2)   In addition to contribution margin and operating income, this approach can also be used to calculate multiple intermediate measures, as shown below:

Contribution Margin Income Statement

Sales		**$150,000**
Variable production costs		(40,000)
Manufacturing contribution margin		**$110,000**
Variable S&A expenses		(20,000)
Contribution margin		**$ 90,000**
Controllable fixed costs:		
Fixed production costs	$30,000	
Fixed S&A expenses	25,000	(55,000)
Short-run performance margin		**$ 35,000**
Traceable fixed costs:		
Depreciation	$10,000	
Insurance	5,000	(15,000)
Segment margin		**$ 20,000**
Allocated common costs		(10,000)
Segment operating income		**$ 10,000**

3. **Segment Reporting**

   a. A segment is a product line, geographical area, or other meaningful subunit of the organization.

     1) As the examples below illustrate, contribution margin reporting is extremely useful for manager decision making.

   b. **Product profitability analysis** allows management to determine whether a product is providing any coverage of fixed costs.

     1) EXAMPLE: At first glance, a dairy operation appears to be comfortably profitable.

Sales	**$540,000**
Variable costs	312,000
Contribution margin	**$228,000**
Other traceable costs:	
Marketing	116,000
R&D	18,000
Product line margin	**$ 94,000**
Fixed costs	24,000
Operating income	**$ 70,000**

A product profitability analysis shows an entirely different picture. Two product lines are losing money, and one is not even covering its own variable costs.

	Milk	Cream	Cottage Cheese	Total
Sales	**$300,000**	**$ 60,000**	**$180,000**	**$540,000**
Variable costs	110,000	62,000	140,000	312,000
Contribution margin	**$190,000**	**$ (2,000)**	**$ 40,000**	**$228,000**
Other traceable costs:				
Marketing	66,000	10,000	40,000	116,000
R&D	8,000	4,000	6,000	18,000
Product line margin	**$116,000**	**$(16,000)**	**$ (6,000)**	**$ 94,000**
Fixed costs				24,000
Operating income				**$ 70,000**

   c. **Area office profitability analysis** performs the same function on the segment level.

     1) EXAMPLE: A geographic profitability analysis for a company that provides research services allows management to see which branch offices are the most profitable.

	Cartagena	Riyadh	Mumbai	Osaka	Total
Sales	**$1,200,000**	**$800,000**	**$2,000,000**	**$4,600,000**	**$8,600,000**
Variable costs of sales	800,000	460,000	1,400,000	3,200,000	5,860,000
Other variable costs	256,000	176,000	320,000	544,000	1,296,000
Contribution margin	**$ 144,000**	**$164,000**	**$ 280,000**	**$ 856,000**	**$1,444,000**
Traceable fixed costs	150,000	100,000	160,000	220,000	630,000
Area office margin	**$ (6,000)**	**$ 64,000**	**$ 120,000**	**$ 636,000**	**$ 814,000**
Nontraceable fixed costs					200,000
Operating income					**$ 614,000**

d. **Customer profitability analysis** enables a firm to make decisions about whether to continue servicing a given customer.

1) EXAMPLE: At first, it might appear that the two unprofitable customers should be dropped.

	Gonzales	Abdullah	Patel	Kawanishi	Total
Sales	$10,000	$40,000	$62,000	$22,000	$134,000
Cost of goods sold	7,200	26,000	41,000	18,100	92,300
Other relevant costs	1,000	2,200	4,400	4,100	11,700
Customer margin	$ 1,800	$11,800	$16,600	$ (200)	$ 30,000
Allocated fixed costs	2,000	6,000	8,800	4,000	20,800
Operating income	$ (200)	$ 5,800	$ 7,800	$(4,200)	$ 9,200

Dropping Kawanishi makes sense. However, Gonzales is contributing to the coverage of fixed costs, costs that would have to be shifted to the other customers if Gonzales were dropped.

Stop and review! You have completed the outline for this subunit. Study multiple-choice questions 6 through 10 beginning on page 311.

8.3 PERFORMANCE MEASURES -- INVESTMENT CENTERS

1. **Purpose**

    a. Performance measures for investment centers reveal how efficiently the manager is deploying capital to produce income for the organization.

    b. Thus, most performance measures relate the center's resources (balance sheet) to its income (income statement).

2. **Return on Investment (ROI)**

    a. ROI is one of the two most widely used performance measures for an investment center.

$$\frac{Business\ unit\ profit}{Average\ total\ assets}$$

    b. EXAMPLE: The ROI calculations for the branch offices displayed in item 3.c.1) on the previous page are shown here:

	Cartagena	Riyadh	Mumbai	Osaka
Business unit profit	$ (6,000)	$ 64,000	$ 120,000	$ 636,000
Average total assets	121,000	825,000	1,015,000	9,900,000
Return on investment (ROI)	(5.0%)	7.8%	11.8%	6.4%

Even though the managers of the Osaka branch generated by far the largest contribution, they were not as efficient in the deployment of the resources at their disposal as were the managers of the Riyadh or Mumbai branches.

1) This example illustrates the principle that the appraisal of individual performance must consider more factors than simple dollars.

    c. A major problem with the application of ROI is that an investment center with a high ROI may not accept a profitable investment even though the investment's return is higher than the center's target ROI.

1) EXAMPLE: An investment center has an 8% ROI, and its investors expect 2%. If the decision makers look only at current ROI, they will reject a project earning 6%, even though that return exceeds the target.

3. **Residual Income**

    a. Residual income is a variation of ROI that measures performance in dollar terms rather than as a percentage return.

$$Business\ unit\ profit\ -\ (Average\ total\ assets\ \times\ Target\ rate\ of\ return)$$

1) Residual income is a significant refinement of the ROI concept because it forces business unit managers to consider the opportunity cost of capital.

b. EXAMPLE: The residual income calculations for the branch offices displayed in item 2.b. on the previous page are shown here:

	Cartagena	Riyadh
Business unit profit	$ (6,000)	$ 64,000
Average total assets	$121,000	$825,000
Times: target rate of return	× 6.0%	× 6.0%
Opportunity cost of capital	(7,260)	(49,500)
Residual income	**$(13,260)**	**$ 14,500**

	Mumbai	Osaka
Business unit profit	$120,000	$636,000
Average total assets	$1,015,000	$9,900,000
Times: target rate of return	× 6.0%	× 6.0%
Opportunity cost of capital	(60,900)	(594,000)
Residual income	**$ 59,100**	**$ 42,000**

This calculation reveals that, by employing the most resources, the Osaka branch has by far the highest threshold to clear for profitability.

4. **Comparability Issues with Investment Center Performance Measures**

a. Alternative income measurements include business unit profit, business unit profit adjusted for price level changes, cash flow, and earnings before interest and taxes (EBIT).

b. Invested capital may be defined in various ways, for example, as

1) Total assets available
2) Total assets employed, which excludes assets that are idle, such as vacant land
3) Working capital plus other assets, which excludes current liabilities (i.e., capital provided by short-term creditors)

a) This investment base assumes that the manager controls short-term credit.

c. Different attributes of financial information will also affect the elements of the investment base.

1) Historical cost
2) Replacement cost
3) Market value
4) Present value

d. The comparability of performance measures may be affected by differences in the accounting policies used by different business units.

1) For example, policies regarding depreciation, decisions to capitalize or expense, inventory flow assumptions, and revenue recognition can lead to comparability issues for performance measures.
2) These differences may be heightened for the business units of a multinational enterprise.

e. Issues other than accounting policy may also affect comparability.

1) Differences in the tax systems in the jurisdictions where business units operate
2) The presence of extraordinary items of profit or loss
3) Allocation of common costs
4) The varying availability of resources

Stop and review! You have completed the outline for this subunit. Study multiple-choice questions 11 through 15 beginning on page 313.

8.4 COMPARING PERFORMANCE MEASURES FOR INVESTMENT CENTERS

1. **ROI vs. Residual Income**

   a. Residual income is often considered preferable to ROI because it deals in absolute dollars rather than percentages.

      1) A manager with a 10% ROI would be reluctant to invest in a project with only an 8% return because his/her average overall return would decline. This would be detrimental to the company as a whole if the cost of capital were only 5%.

      2) However, under the residual income method, the manager would invest in any project with a return greater than the cost of capital or the hurdle rate that (s)he has been assigned.

      3) Thus, overall, the company would be better off even though the individual manager's ROI declined.

2. **Revenue and Expense Recognition Policies**

   a. A company's revenue and expense recognition policies may affect the measurement of income and thus reduce comparability among business units.

      1) For example, a company that uses last-in, first-out (LIFO) for inventory valuation will often show lower inventories and higher costs than a company that uses the first-in, first-out (FIFO) methodology. As a result, the LIFO company could appear to have a lower rate of return than if it had used the FIFO method.

      2) Other ratios would also be impacted, such as inventory turnover and asset turnover.

   b. Thus, when comparing companies or units on the basis of either return-on-investment or residual income, the analyst must be sure that both companies or units are using the same accounting policies in the determination of income.

   c. The sharing of assets by subunits within an organization may also affect measures of return.

      1) For instance, assets normally appear on the books of only one division, even though another division might have access to those assets. Therefore, the division that shares its assets with another division may find that it has a lower rate of return than the division that has access to the use of the assets.

   d. Similarly, a company or division that uses straight-line depreciation on its plant assets will have lower expenses in the early years of an asset's life than if an accelerated method were being used. Thus, the straight-line division would appear to be more profitable than the division using the accelerated method.

      1) Of course, the accelerated method may be preferred by top management because it results in a tax savings, but the implication of the ROI measure might be that the straight-line division is more profitable.

   e. International operations may not always be comparable to domestic divisions, since the complication of changes in foreign-currency exchange rates might make income comparisons difficult. Also, transfer pricing is complicated in the international arena, since differences in tax rates between countries may have a role in the selection of the transfer prices selected.

      1) For example, a company will set a transfer price at a level that will limit the profits in high-tax countries and shift that profit to the low-tax country.

      2) Similarly, high profits in a foreign country might not always be transferable to the home country; thus, to say that the foreign subsidiary is more profitable is meaningless if that profit cannot be enjoyed by the parent company.

Stop and review! You have completed the outline for this subunit. Study multiple-choice questions 16 through 20 beginning on page 314.

8.5 ALLOCATING COMMON COSTS

1. **Issues**

   a. Common costs are the costs of products, activities, facilities, services, or operations shared by two or more cost objects.

      1) The difficulty with common costs is that they are **indirect costs** whose allocation may be arbitrary.

   b. A direct cause-and-effect relationship between a common cost and the actions of the cost object to which it is allocated is desirable.

      1) Such a relationship promotes acceptance of the allocation by managers who perceive the fairness of the procedure, but identification of cause and effect may not be feasible.

   c. An alternative allocation criterion is the benefit received.

      1) For example, advertising costs that do not relate to particular products may increase sales of all products.

      2) Allocation based on the increase in sales by organizational subunits is likely to be accepted as equitable despite the absence of clear cause-and-effect relationships.

2. **Headquarters Costs**

   a. A persistent problem in large organizations is the treatment of the costs of headquarters and other central support costs. Such costs are frequently allocated.

      1) The allocation reminds managers that support costs exist and that the managers would incur these costs if their operations were independent. The allocation also reminds managers that profit center earnings must cover some amount of support costs.

   b. Research has shown that central support costs are allocated to departments or divisions for the following reasons:

      1) The allocation reminds managers that support costs exist and that the managers would incur these costs if their operations were independent.

      2) The allocation reminds managers that profit center earnings must cover some amount of support costs.

      3) Departments or divisions should be motivated to use central support services appropriately.

      4) Managers who must bear the costs of central support services that they do not control may be encouraged to exert pressure on those who do. Thus, they may be able to restrain such costs indirectly.

3. **Effects of Arbitrary Allocations**

   a. Managers' morale may suffer when allocations depress operating results.

   b. Dysfunctional conflict may arise among managers when costs controlled by one are allocated to others.

   c. Resentment may result if cost allocation is perceived to be arbitrary or unfair.

      1) For example, an allocation on an ability-to-bear basis, such as operating income, penalizes successful managers and rewards underachievers and may therefore have a demotivating effect.

4. **Allocation Alternatives**

a. If allocation is based on actual sales or contribution margin, responsibility centers that increase their sales (or contribution margin) will be charged with increased overhead.

b. If central administrative or other fixed costs are not allocated, responsibility centers might reach their revenue (or contribution margin) goals without covering all fixed costs (which is necessary to operate in the long run).

c. Allocation of overhead, however, is motivationally negative; central administrative or other fixed costs may appear noncontrollable and be unproductive.

d. A much preferred alternative is to budget a certain amount of contribution margin earned by each responsibility center to the central administration based on negotiation.

   1) The intended result is for each unit to see itself as contributing to the success of the overall entity rather than carrying the weight (cost) of central administration.

   2) Central administration can then make the decision whether to expand, divest, or close responsibility centers.

5. **Calculations**

a. Two specific approaches to common cost allocation are in general use.

   1) Under the **stand-alone method**, the common cost is allocated to each cost object on a proportionate basis.

   2) Under the **incremental method**, the cost objects are sorted in descending order by total traceable cost, and the common cost is allocated up to the amount of each.

EXAMPLE of Common Cost Allocation

The proportionate costs of servicing three customers are presented in the table below. The common cost of providing service to these customers is $8,000.

	Cost of Servicing	%
Luciano	$ 7,000	70%
Ratzinger	2,000	20%
Wojtyla	1,000	10%
Total	$10,000	100%

Stand-Alone Method

	Total Cost to Be Allocated		Allocation %		Allocated Cost
Luciano	$8,000	×	70%	=	$5,600
Ratzinger	8,000	×	20%	=	1,600
Wojtyla	8,000	×	10%	=	800
Total			100%		$8,000

Incremental Method

	Traceable Cost	Allocated Cost	Remaining Unallocated
To be allocated			$8,000
Luciano	$ 7,000	$7,000	1,000
Ratzinger	2,000	1,000	0
Wojtyla	1,000	0	
Total	$10,000	$8,000	

Stop and review! You have completed the outline for this subunit. Study multiple-choice questions 21 through 24 beginning on page 316.

8.6 TRANSFER PRICING -- DETAILS

1. **Purpose**

   a. Transfer prices are the amounts charged by one segment of an organization for goods and services it provides to another segment of the same organization.

      1) The principal challenge is determining a price that motivates both the selling and the buying manager to pursue organizational goal congruence.

   b. In a decentralized system, each responsibility center theoretically may be completely separate.

      1) Thus, Division A should charge the same price to Division B as would be charged to an outside buyer.

      2) The reason for decentralization is to motivate managers, and the best interests of Division A may not be served by giving a special discount to Division B if the goods can be sold at the regular price to outside buyers. However, having A sell at a special price to B may be to the company's advantage.

2. **Transfer Pricing Schemes**

   a. Four basic methods of transfer price setting are in common use: variable cost, full cost, market price, and negotiated price.

   b. **Variable Cost**

      1) By allowing the buyer to purchase at the selling division's variable cost, unused production capacity will be utilized (this method should only be used when the selling division has excess capacity).

      2) However, there is no incentive for the selling division, since it will be producing the products at a loss (even though the company as a whole will benefit from the arrangement).

         a) In practice, companies who wish to follow this philosophy actually adopt a negotiation policy wherein the transfer price will be something greater than variable costs but less than full costs. At least the seller would have a positive contribution margin if the price is set slightly above variable costs.

      3) The advantage of using variable costs is that the buyer is motivated to solve the company's excess capacity problem, even though that excess capacity is not in the buyer's division.

   c. **Full Cost**

      1) Full (absorption) cost includes materials, labor, and full allocation of manufacturing overhead.

      2) The use of full (absorption) cost ensures that the selling division will not incur a loss and provides more incentive to the buying division to buy internally than does use of market price.

         a) However, there is no motivation for the seller to control production costs since all costs can be passed along to the buying division.

   d. **Market Price**

      1) A market price is the best transfer price to use in many situations. For example, if the selling division is operating at full capacity and can sell all of its output at the market price, then there is no justification to use a lower price as the transfer price for intracompany transfers.

      2) Alternatively, if the selling division is not producing at full capacity, the use of market prices for internal transfers is not justified. A lower price might be more motivational to either the buyer or the seller.

e. **Negotiation**

1) A negotiated price may result when organizational subunits are free to determine the prices at which they buy and sell internally. Hence, a transfer price may simply reflect the best bargain that the parties can strike between themselves.

2) The transfer price need not be based directly on particular market or cost information.

3) A negotiated price may be especially appropriate when market prices are subject to rapid fluctuation.

3. **Choice of Transfer Pricing Policy**

a. The choice of a transfer pricing policy (which type of transfer price to use) is normally decided by top management at the corporate level. The decision typically includes consideration of multiple factors.

b. Goal congruence factors

1) The transfer price should promote the goals of the company as a whole.

c. Segmental performance factors

1) The segment making the transfer should be allowed to recover its incremental cost plus its opportunity cost of the transfer. The opportunity cost is the benefit forgone by not selling to an outsider.

   a) For this purpose, the transfer should be at market price.
   b) The selling manager should not lose income by selling within the company.

2) Properly allocating revenues and expenses through appropriate transfer pricing also facilitates evaluation of the performance of the various segments.

d. Negotiation factors

1) If the purchasing segment could purchase the product or service outside the company, it should be permitted to negotiate the transfer price.

2) The purchasing manager should not have to incur greater costs by purchasing within the company.

e. Capacity factors

1) If Division A has excess capacity, it should be used for producing products for Division B. If Division A is operating at full capacity and selling its products at the full market price, profitable work should not be abandoned to produce for Division B.

f. Cost structure factors

1) If Division A has excess capacity and an opportunity arises to sell to Division B at a price in excess of the variable cost, the work should be performed for Division B because a contribution to cover the fixed costs will result.

g. Tax factors

1) A wide range of tax issues on the interstate and international levels may arise, e.g., income taxes, sales taxes, value-added taxes, inventory and payroll taxes, and other governmental charges.

2) In the international context, exchange rate fluctuations, threats of expropriation, and limits on transfers of profits outside the host country are additional concerns.

   a) Thus, because the best transfer price may be a low one because of the existence of tariffs or a high one because of the existence of foreign exchange controls, the effect may be to skew the performance statistics of management.

b) The high transfer price may result in foreign management appearing to show a lower return on investment than domestic management, but the ratio differences may be negated by the fact that a different transfer pricing formula is used.

Transfer Price Decision Tree

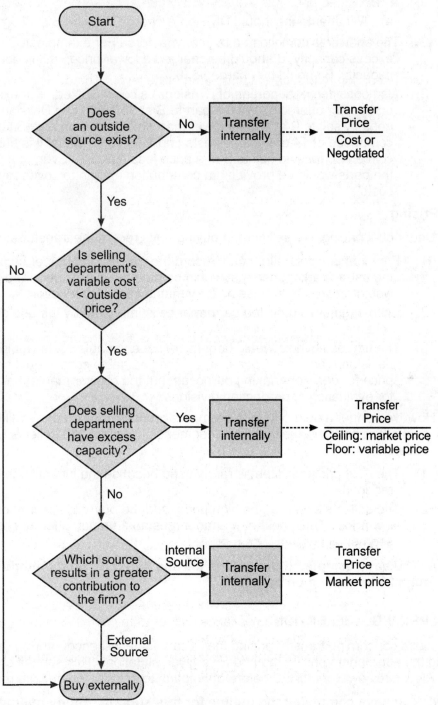

Figure 8-1

h.   EXAMPLE: Division A produces a small part at a cost of $6 per unit. The regular selling price is $10 per unit. If Division B can use the part in its production, the cost to the company (as a whole) will be $6.

    1)   Division B has another supplier who will sell the item to B at $9.50 per part. Division B wants to buy the $9.50 part from the outside supplier instead of the $10 part from Division A, but making the part for $6 is in the company's best interest.

        a)   What amount should Division A charge Division B?

    2)   The answer is complicated by many factors. For example, if Division A has excess capacity, B should be charged a lower price. If it is operating at full capacity, B should be charged $10.

    3)   Also consider what portion of Division A's costs is fixed. For example, if a competitor offered to sell the part to B at $5 each, can Division A advantageously sell to B at a price lower than $5? If Division A's $6 total cost is composed of $4 of variable costs and $2 of fixed costs, it is beneficial for all concerned for A to sell to B at a price less than $5. Even at a price of $4.01, the parts would be providing a contribution margin to cover some of A's fixed costs.

4.   **Dual Pricing**

a.   Under dual pricing, the selling and buying units record the transfer at different prices.

    1)   For example, the seller could record the transfer to another segment as a sale at the usual market price that would be paid by an outsider. The buyer, however, would record a purchase at the variable cost of production.

    2)   Each segment's reported performance is improved by the use of a dual-pricing scheme.

    3)   The firm as a whole would benefit because variable costs would be used for decision-making purposes. In a sense, variable costs would be the relevant price for decision-making purposes, but the regular market price would be used for evaluation of production divisions.

b.   However, under a dual-pricing system, the profit for the company will be less than the sum of the profits of the individual segments. In effect, the seller is given a corporate subsidy.

    1)   The dual-pricing system is rarely used because the incentive to control costs is reduced.

    2)   The seller is assured of a high price, and the buyer is assured of an artificially low price. Thus, neither manager must exert much effort to show a profit on segmental performance reports.

Stop and review! You have completed the outline for this subunit. Study multiple-choice questions 25 through 29 beginning on page 317.

8.7 TRANSFER PRICING -- SELECTION

Some of the questions concerning transfer pricing that a candidate will encounter on the CMA exam focus on selecting the appropriate pricing method for a given situation. This subunit consists entirely of such questions. Please review Subunit 8.6 before attempting to answer the questions in this subunit.

Stop and review! You have completed the outline for this subunit. Study multiple-choice questions 30 through 34 beginning on page 319.

8.8 THE BALANCED SCORECARD

1. **Critical Success Factors (CSFs)**

    a. The trend in performance evaluation is the balanced scorecard approach to managing the implementation of the firm's strategy.

        1) The balanced scorecard is an accounting report that connects the firm's critical success factors to measurements of its performance.

    b. Critical success factors (CSFs) are specific, measurable financial and nonfinancial elements of a firm's performance that are vital to its competitive advantage.

        1) Multiple measures of performance permit a determination as to whether a manager is achieving certain objectives at the expense of others that may be equally or more important. For example, an improvement in operating results at the expense of new product development would be apparent using a balanced scorecard approach.

    c. The balanced scorecard is a goal congruence tool that informs managers about the nonfinancial factors that top management believes to be important.

        1) Measures on the balanced scorecard may be financial or nonfinancial, internal or external, and short term or long term.

        2) The balanced scorecard facilitates best practice analysis. Best practice analysis determines a method of carrying on a business function or process that is considered to be superior to all other known methods. A lesson learned from one area of a business can be passed on to another area of the business or between businesses.

2. **SWOT Analysis**

    a. A firm identifies its CSFs by means of a SWOT analysis that addresses internal factors (its strengths and weaknesses) and external factors (its opportunities and threats).

        1) The firm's greatest strengths are its core competencies, which are functions the company performs especially well. These are the basis for its competitive advantages and strategy.

    b. Strengths and weaknesses are internal resources or a lack thereof, for example, technologically advanced products, a broad product mix, capable management, leadership in R&D, modern production facilities, and a strong marketing organization.

    c. **Opportunities and threats** arise from such externalities as government regulation, advances in technology, and demographic changes. They may be reflected in such competitive conditions as

        1) Raising or lowering of barriers to entry into the firm's industry by competitors
        2) Changes in the intensity of rivalry within the industry, for example, because of overcapacity or high exit barriers
        3) The relative availability of substitutes for the firm's products or services
        4) Bargaining power of customers, which tends to be greater when switching costs are low and products are not highly differentiated
        5) Bargaining power of suppliers, which tends to be higher when suppliers are few

    d. The SWOT analysis tends to highlight the basic factors of cost, quality, and the speed of product development and delivery.

3.   **Measures**

a.   Once the firm has identified its CSFs, it must establish specific measures for each CSF that are both relevant to the success of the firm and can be reliably stated.

   1)   Thus, the balanced scorecard varies with the strategy adopted by the firm.

   2)   For example, product differentiation or cost leadership either in a broad market or a narrowly focused market (a focus strategy). These measures provide a basis for implementing the firm's competitive strategy.

b.   The scorecard should include lagging indicators (such as output and financial measures) and leading indicators (such as many types of nonfinancial measures).

   1)   The latter should be used only if they are predictors of ultimate financial performance.

c.   The scorecard should permit a determination of whether certain objectives are being achieved at the expense of others.

   1)   For example, reduced spending on customer service may improve short-term financial results at a significant cost that is revealed by a long-term decline in customer satisfaction measures.

d.   By providing measures that are **nonfinancial as well as financial**, long term as well as short term, and internal as well as external, the balanced scorecard de-emphasizes short term financial results and focuses attention on CSFs.

e.   An effective balanced scorecard requires a vast amount of data of many different types.

   1)   For this reason, an enterprise resource planning (ERP) system is almost a necessity. An ERP integrates information systems across the organization by creating one database linking all of the firm's applications.

4.   **Possible CSFs and Measures**

a.   A typical balanced scorecard classifies objectives into one of four perspectives on the business.

b.   **Financial**

   1)   CSFs may be sales, fair value of the firm's stock, profits, and liquidity.

   2)   Measures may include sales, projected sales, accuracy of sales projections, new product sales, stock prices, operating earnings, earnings trend, revenue growth, gross margin percentage, cost reductions, return on investment (or any of its variants), residual income, cash flow coverage and trends, turnover (assets, receivables, and inventory), and interest coverage.

c.   **Customer Satisfaction**

   1)   **CSFs** may be customer satisfaction, dealer and distributor relationships, marketing and selling performance, prompt delivery, and quality.

   2)   **Measures**

      a)   **Financial.** These may include dollar amount of sales, trends in dollar amount of sales, dollar amount of returns, dollar amount of defects, and warranty expense.

      b)   **Nonfinancial.** These may include unit sales, trends in unit sales, market share, trend in market share, number of returns, rate of returns, customer retention rate, number of defects, rate of defects, number of warranty claims, rate of warranty claims, lead time, survey results, coverage and strength of distribution channels, market research results, training of marketing people, on-time delivery rate, service response time, and service effectiveness.

    d. **Internal Business Processes**

       1) **CSFs** may be quality, productivity (an input-output relationship), flexibility of response to changing conditions, operating readiness, and safety.

       2) **Measures**

          a) **Financial.** These may include such things as quality costs, scrap costs, and level of inventory carrying costs.

          b) **Nonfinancial.** These may include new products marketed, technological capabilities, rate of scrap and rework, survey results, field service reports, vendor defect rate, cycle time, labor and machine efficiency, setup time, scheduling effectiveness, downtime, capacity usage, maintenance, and accidents and their results.

    e. **Learning and Growth**

       1) **CSFs** may be development of new products, promptness of their introduction, human resource development, morale, and competence of the work force.

       2) **Measures**

          a) **Financial.** These may include financial and operating results, recruiting costs, orientation costs, and training costs.

          b) **Nonfinancial.** These may include number of design changes, patents and copyrights registered, R&D personnel qualifications, actual versus planned shipping dates, hours of training, skill set levels attained, personnel turnover, personnel complaints and survey results, organizational learning, and industry leadership.

5. **Functionality**

    a. Each objective is associated with one or more measures that permit the organization to gauge progress toward the objective.

       1) Achievement of the objectives in each perspective makes it possible to achieve the objectives in the next higher perspective.

       2) This chaining of objectives and perspectives embodies the implementation of a **strategy map**.

EXAMPLE of a Balanced Scorecard

Financial Perspective

    Objective: Increase shareholder value   **Measures:** Increase in common stock price
                                                Reliability of dividend payment

Customer Perspective

    Objective: Increase customer satisfaction   **Measures:** Greater market share
                                                Higher customer retention rate
                                              Positive responses to surveys

Internal Business Process Perspective

    Objective: Improve product quality   **Measures:** Achievement of zero defects

    Objective: Improve internal processes   **Measures:** Reduction in delivery cycle time
                                                  Smaller cost variances

Learning and Growth Perspective

    Objective: Increase employee confidence   **Measures:** Number of suggestions to
                                                  improve processes
                                              Positive responses to surveys

    Objective: Increase employee competence   **Measures:** Attendance at internal and external
                                                  training seminars

6.   **Development and Implementation**

    a.   The active support and participation of senior management are essential.

        1)   This involvement will in turn ensure the cooperation of lower-level managers in the identification of objectives, appropriate measures, targeted results, and methods of achieving the results.

    b.   The scorecard should contain measures at the detail level that permits everyone to understand how his/her efforts affect the firm's results.

        1)   The scorecard and the strategy it represents must be communicated to all managers and used as a basis for compensation decisions.

    c.   The following are problems in implementation of the balanced scorecard approach:

        1)   Using too many measures, with a consequent loss of focus on CSFs
        2)   Failing to evaluate personnel on nonfinancial as well as financial measures
        3)   Including measures that will not have long-term financial benefits
        4)   Not understanding that subjective measures (such as customer satisfaction) are imprecise
        5)   Trying to achieve improvements in all areas at all times
        6)   Not being aware that the hypothesized connection between nonfinancial measures and ultimate financial success may not continue to be true

Stop and review! You have completed the outline for this subunit. Study multiple-choice questions 35 through 38 beginning on page 321.

8.9 CORE CONCEPTS

Responsibility Centers

- A decentralized organization is divided into **responsibility centers** (also called **strategic business units**, or SBUs) to facilitate local decision making.

    •   A **cost center**, e.g., a maintenance department, is responsible for costs only.

    •   A **revenue center**, e.g., a sales department, is responsible for revenues only.

    •   A **profit center**, e.g., an appliance department in a retail store, is responsible for revenues and expenses.

    •   An **investment center**, e.g., a branch office, is responsible for revenues, expenses, and invested capital.

- Each responsibility center is structured such that a logical group of operations is under the direction of a single manager.

    •   **Controllability.** The performance measures on which the manager's incentive package are based must be, as far as practicable, under the manager's direct influence.

    •   **Goal congruence.** These performance measures must be designed such that the manager's pursuit of them ties directly to accomplishment of the organization's overall goals.

Performance Measures -- Cost, Revenue, and Profit Centers

- Since managers of **cost and revenue centers** can influence only one type of factor, variance analysis is the most appropriate performance measurement technique for these responsibility centers.

- The contribution margin approach to reporting (in contrast to the financial reporting approach) is extremely useful in performance measurement for **profit centers**.

- A **segment** is a product line, geographical area, or other meaningful subunit of the organization.

Performance Measures -- Investment Centers

- **Return on investment (ROI)** is one of the two most widely used performance measures of an investment center.

    Business unit profit ÷ Average total assets

    - A major problem with the application of ROI is that an investment center with a high ROI may not accept a profitable investment even though the investment's return is higher than the center's target ROI

- **Residual income** is a variation of ROI that measures performance in dollar terms rather than as a percentage return.

    Business unit profit – (Average total assets × Target rate of return)

    - Residual income is a significant refinement of the ROI concept because it forces business unit managers to consider the opportunity cost of capital.

Allocating Common Costs

- A persistent problem in large organizations is the treatment of the **costs of headquarters** and other central support costs. Such costs are frequently allocated.
- **Two specific approaches** to common cost allocation are in general use:
    - Under the **stand-alone method**, the common cost is allocated to each cost object on a proportionate basis.
    - Under the **incremental method**, the cost objects are sorted in descending order by total traceable cost, and the common cost is allocated up to the amount of each cost.

Transfer Pricing

- **Transfer prices** are the amounts charged by one segment of an organization for goods and services it provides to another segment of the same organization. The principal challenge is determining a price that motivates both the selling and the buying manager to pursue organizational goal congruence.
- **Methods** for determining transfer prices in common use include variable cost, full cost, market price, and negotiation.
- The **minimum price** that a selling division is willing to accept is the sum of the incremental cost of producing the unit so far plus the opportunity cost of selling the unit internally. The opportunity cost of selling internally varies depending on two factors: the existence of an external market for the product and whether the selling division has excess capacity.

The Balanced Scorecard

- **Critical success factors (CSFs)** are specific, measurable financial and nonfinancial elements of a firm's performance that are vital to its competitive advantage.
    - A firm identifies its CSFs by means of a **SWOT analysis** that addresses internal factors (its strengths and weaknesses) and external factors (its opportunities and threats).
- Once the firm has identified its CSFs, it must establish **specific measures** for each CSF that are both relevant to the success of the firm and can be reliably stated.
    - Measures must be both financial and nonfinancial, short-term and long-term.
- A typical balanced scorecard classifies objectives and measures into each of four perspectives on the business: **financial, customer satisfaction, internal business processes,** and **learning and growth**.
    - Each **objective** is associated with one or more **measures** that permit the organization to gauge progress toward the objective.
    - Achievement of the objectives in each perspective makes it possible to achieve the objectives in the **next higher perspective**.

QUESTIONS

8.1 Responsibility Centers

1. Fairmount, Inc., uses an accounting system that charges costs to the manager who has been delegated the authority to make the decisions incurring the costs. For example, if the sales manager accepts a rush order that will result in higher-than-normal manufacturing costs, these additional costs are charged to the sales manager because the authority to accept or decline the rush order was given to the sales manager. This type of accounting system is known as

A. Responsibility accounting.

B. Functional accounting.

C. Reciprocal allocation.

D. Transfer price accounting.

Answer (A) is correct. *(CMA, adapted)*
REQUIRED: The system in which additional costs are charged to the manager with authority for their incurrence.
DISCUSSION: In a responsibility accounting system, managerial performance should be evaluated only on the basis of those factors directly regulated (or at least capable of being significantly influenced) by the manager. For this purpose, operations are organized into responsibility centers. Costs are classified as controllable and noncontrollable, which implies that some revenues and costs can be changed through effective management. If a manager has authority to incur costs, a responsibility accounting system will charge them to the manager's responsibility center. However, controllability is not an absolute basis for establishment of responsibility. More than one manager may be able to influence a cost, and responsibility may be assigned on the basis of knowledge about the incurrence of a cost rather than the ability to control it.
Answer (B) is incorrect. Functional accounting allocates costs to functions regardless of responsibility. Answer (C) is incorrect. Reciprocal allocation is a means of allocating service department costs. Answer (D) is incorrect. Transfer price accounting is a means of charging one department for products acquired from another department in the same organization.

2. The basic purpose of a responsibility accounting system is

A. Budgeting.

B. Motivation.

C. Authority.

D. Variance analysis.

Answer (B) is correct. *(CMA, adapted)*
REQUIRED: The basic purpose of a responsibility accounting system.
DISCUSSION: The basic purpose of a responsibility accounting system is to motivate management to perform in a manner consistent with overall company objectives. The assignment of responsibility implies that some revenues and costs can be changed through effective management. The system should have certain controls that provide for feedback reports indicating deviations from expectations. Higher-level management may focus on those deviations for either reinforcement or correction.
Answer (A) is incorrect. Budgeting is an element of a responsibility accounting system, not the basic purpose. Answer (C) is incorrect. Authority is an element of a responsibility accounting system, not the basic purpose. Answer (D) is incorrect. Analysis of variances is an element of a responsibility accounting system, not the basic purpose.

3. In responsibility accounting, a center's performance is measured by controllable costs. Controllable costs are best described as including

A. Direct material and direct labor only.

B. Only those costs that the manager can influence in the current time period.

C. Only discretionary costs.

D. Those costs about which the manager is knowledgeable and informed.

Answer (B) is correct. *(CMA, adapted)*
REQUIRED: The elements of controllable costs.
DISCUSSION: Control is the process of making certain that plans are achieving the desired objectives. A controllable cost is one that is influenced by a specific responsible manager at a given level of production within a given time span. For example, fixed costs are often not controllable in the short run.
Answer (A) is incorrect. Many overhead costs are also controllable. Answer (C) is incorrect. Controllable costs need not be discretionary. Discretionary costs are characterized by uncertainty about the relationship between input and the value of the related output; they may or may not be controllable. Answer (D) is incorrect. Controllable costs are those over which a manager has control; the manager may be informed or know about costs that (s)he cannot directly regulate or influence.

4. A segment of an organization is referred to as a service center if it has

A. Responsibility for developing markets and selling the output of the organization.

B. Responsibility for combining the raw materials, direct labor, and other factors of production into a final output.

C. Authority to make decisions affecting the major determinants of profit including the power to choose its markets and sources of supply.

D. Authority to provide specialized support to other units within the organization.

Answer (D) is correct. *(CMA, adapted)*
REQUIRED: The definition of a service center.
DISCUSSION: A service center exists primarily and sometimes solely to provide specialized support to other units within the organization. Service centers are usually operated as cost centers.
Answer (A) is incorrect. A service center has no responsibility for developing markets or selling. Answer (B) is incorrect. A production center is engaged in manufacturing. Answer (C) is incorrect. A profit center can choose its markets and sources of supply.

5. The **least** complex segment or area of responsibility for which costs are allocated is a(n)

A. Profit center.

B. Investment center.

C. Contribution center.

D. Cost center.

Answer (D) is correct. *(CMA, adapted)*
REQUIRED: The least complex segment or area of responsibility for which costs are allocated.
DISCUSSION: A cost center is a responsibility center that is accountable only for costs. The cost center is the least complex type of segment because it has no responsibility for revenues or investments.
Answer (A) is incorrect. A profit center is a segment responsible for both revenues and costs. A profit center has the authority to make decisions concerning markets and sources of supply. Answer (B) is incorrect. An investment center is a responsibility center that is accountable for revenues (markets), costs (sources of supply), and invested capital. Answer (C) is incorrect. A contribution center is responsible for revenues and variable costs, but not invested capital.

8.2 Performance Measures -- Cost, Revenue, and Profit Centers

6. The segment margin of the Wire Division of Lerner Corporation should **not** include

A. Net sales of the Wire Division.

B. Fixed selling expenses of the Wire Division.

C. Variable selling expenses of the Wire Division.

D. The Wire Division's fair share of the salary of Lerner Corporation's president.

Answer (D) is correct. *(CMA, adapted)*
REQUIRED: The item not included in a statement showing segment margin.
DISCUSSION: Segment margin is the contribution margin for a segment of a business minus fixed costs. It is a measure of long-run profitability. Thus, an allocation of the corporate officers' salaries should not be included in segment margin because they are neither variable costs nor fixed costs that can be rationally allocated to the segment. Other items that are often not allocated include corporate income taxes, interest, company-wide R&D expenses, and central administration costs.
Answer (A) is incorrect. Sales of the division would appear on the statement. Answer (B) is incorrect. The division's fixed selling expenses are separable fixed costs. Answer (C) is incorrect. Variable costs of the division are included.

7. When using a contribution margin format for internal reporting purposes, the major distinction between segment manager performance and segment performance is

A. Unallocated fixed costs.

B. Direct variable costs of producing the product.

C. Direct fixed costs controllable by the segment manager.

D. Direct fixed costs controllable by others.

Answer (D) is correct. *(CMA, adapted)*
REQUIRED: The major distinction between segment manager performance and segment performance.
DISCUSSION: The performance of the segment is judged on all costs assigned to it, but the segment manager is only judged on costs that he or she can control. Some fixed costs are imposed on segments by the organization's upper management, and they are thus beyond the segment manager's control. These direct costs controllable by others make up the difference between segment manager performance and segment performance.
Answer (A) is incorrect. Unallocated fixed costs do not affect either performance measure. Answer (B) is incorrect. Direct variable costs affect both performance measures. Answer (C) is incorrect. Direct fixed costs controllable by the segment manager affect both performance measures.

8. Which of the following techniques would be best for evaluating the management performance of a department that is operated as a cost center?

A. Return on assets ratio.

B. Return on investment ratio.

C. Payback method.

D. Variance analysis.

Answer (D) is correct. *(CIA, adapted)*
REQUIRED: The best method for evaluating a cost center.
DISCUSSION: A cost center is a responsibility center that is responsible for costs only. Of the alternatives given, variance analysis is the only one that can be used in a cost center. Variance analysis involves comparing actual costs with predicted or standard costs.
Answer (A) is incorrect. Return on assets cannot be computed for a cost center. The manager is not responsible for revenue (return) or the assets available. Answer (B) is incorrect. Return on investment cannot be computed for a cost center. The manager is not responsible for revenue (return) or the assets available. Answer (C) is incorrect. The payback method is a means of evaluating alternative investment proposals.

9. Harris Co.'s income statement for profit center No. 12 for August includes

Contribution margin	$84,000
Manager's salary	24,000
Depreciation on accommodations	9,600
Allocated corporate expenses	6,000

The profit center's manager is most likely able to control which of the following?

A. $84,000

B. $68,400

C. $60,000

D. $44,400

Answer (A) is correct. *(Publisher, adapted)*
REQUIRED: The amount most likely subject to the control of the profit center's manager.
DISCUSSION: A profit center is a segment of a company responsible for both revenues and expenses. A profit center has the authority to make decisions concerning markets (revenues) and sources of supplies (costs). However, the profit center's manager does not control his/her salary, investment and the resulting costs (e.g., depreciation of plant assets), or expenses incurred at the corporate level. Consequently, profit center No. 12 is most likely to control the $84,000 contribution margin (sales - variable costs) but not the other items in the summarized income statement.
Answer (B) is incorrect. The profit center manager does not control depreciation on accommodations ($9,600) or the allocated corporate expenses ($6,000). Answer (C) is incorrect. The profit center manager does not control his/her $24,000 salary. Answer (D) is incorrect. The profit center's manager does not control the listed period expenses and therefore does not control the profit center's income.

10. Ordinarily, the most appropriate basis on which to evaluate the performance of a division manager is the division's

A. Contribution margin.

B. Net revenue minus controllable division costs.

C. Gross profit.

D. Net income minus the division's fixed costs.

Answer (B) is correct. *(CMA, adapted)*
REQUIRED: The most appropriate basis on which to evaluate the performance of a division manager.
DISCUSSION: Managerial performance should be evaluated on the basis of those factors controllable by the manager. Managers may control revenues, costs, and/or investment in resources. A well-designed responsibility accounting system establishes responsibility centers within the organization.
Answer (A) is incorrect. Contribution margin ignores the fixed costs of production; managers may control some fixed costs. Answer (C) is incorrect. Not everything included in the calculation of gross profit is controllable by the manager. Answer (D) is incorrect. Net income is computed after deducting fixed costs.

8.3 Performance Measures -- Investment Centers

11. A firm earning a profit can increase its return on investment by

A. Increasing sales revenue and operating expenses by the same dollar amount.

B. Decreasing sales revenues and operating expenses by the same percentage.

C. Increasing investment and operating expenses by the same dollar amount.

D. Increasing sales revenues and operating expenses by the same percentage.

Answer (D) is correct. *(CMA, adapted)*
REQUIRED: The means by which a profitable company can increase its return on investment (ROI).
DISCUSSION: ROI equals income divided by invested capital. If a company is already profitable, increasing sales and expenses by the same percentage will increase ROI. For example, if a company has sales of $100 and expenses of $80, its net income is $20. Given invested capital of $100, ROI is 20% ($20 ÷ $100). If sales and expenses both increase 10% to $110 and $88, respectively, net income increases to $22. ROI will then be 22% ($22 ÷ $100).
Answer (A) is incorrect. Increasing sales and expenses by the same dollar amount will not change income or ROI.
Answer (B) is incorrect. Decreasing revenues and expenses by the same percentage will reduce income and lower ROI.
Answer (C) is incorrect. Increasing investment and operating expenses by the same dollar amount will lower ROI. The higher investment increases the denominator, and the increased expenses reduce the numerator.

12. Which one of the following statements pertaining to the return on investment (ROI) as a performance measurement is **false**?

A. When the average age of assets differs substantially across segments of a business, the use of ROI may not be appropriate.

B. ROI relies on financial measures that are capable of being independently verified, while other forms of performance measures are subject to manipulation.

C. The use of ROI may lead managers to reject capital investment projects that can be justified by using discounted cash flow models.

D. The use of ROI can make it undesirable for a skillful manager to take on troubleshooting assignments such as those involving turning around unprofitable divisions.

Answer (B) is correct. *(CMA, adapted)*
REQUIRED: The false statement about ROI as a performance measurement.
DISCUSSION: Return on investment is the key performance measure in an investment center. ROI is a rate computed by dividing a segment's income by the invested capital. ROI is therefore subject to the numerous possible manipulations of the income and investment amounts. For example, a manager may choose not to invest in a project that will yield less than the desired rate of return, or (s)he may defer necessary expenses.
Answer (A) is incorrect. ROI can be misleading when the quality of the investment base differs among segments.
Answer (C) is incorrect. Managers may reject projects that are profitable (a return greater than the cost of capital) but would decrease ROI. For example, the managers of a segment with a 15% ROI may not want to invest in a new project with a 10% ROI, even though the cost of capital might be only 8%.
Answer (D) is incorrect. The use of ROI does not reflect the relative difficulty of tasks undertaken by managers.

13. Listed below is selected financial information for the Western Division of the Hinzel Company for last year.

Account	Amount (thousands)
Average working capital	$ 625
General and administrative expenses	75
Net sales	4,000
Average plant and equipment	1,775
Cost of goods sold	3,525

If Hinzel treats the Western Division as an investment center for performance measurement purposes, what is the before-tax return on investment (ROI) for last year?

A. 34.78%

B. 22.54%

C. 19.79%

D. 16.67%

Answer (D) is correct. *(CMA, adapted)*
REQUIRED: The before-tax ROI for an investment center.
DISCUSSION: An investment center is responsible for revenues, expenses, and invested capital. Given average plant and equipment of $1,775 and average working capital of $625, the net investment is $2,400. Before-tax profit is $400 ($4,000 sales – $3,525 cost of goods sold – $75 general expenses). If before-tax ROI equals before-tax profit divided by net investment, the answer is 16.67% ($400 ÷ $2,400).
Answer (A) is incorrect. This percentage results from subtracting working capital from plant and equipment in calculating the net investment. Answer (B) is incorrect. This percentage fails to include average working capital in the total for the net investment. Answer (C) is incorrect. This percentage results from not subtracting general and administrative expenses in the calculation of before-tax profit.

14. Which one of the following items would most likely **not** be incorporated into the calculation of a division's investment base when using the residual income approach for performance measurement and evaluation?

    A. Fixed assets employed in division operations.

    B. Land being held by the division as a site for a new plant.

    C. Division inventories when division management exercises control over the inventory levels.

    D. Division accounts payable when division management exercises control over the amount of short-term credit used.

Answer (B) is correct. *(CMA, adapted)*
    REQUIRED: The item most likely not incorporated into the calculation of a division's investment base.
    DISCUSSION: An evaluation of an investment center is based upon the return on the investment base. These assets include plant and equipment, inventories, and receivables. Most likely, however, an asset, such as land, that is being held by the division as a site for a new plant would not be included in the investment base because it is not currently being used in operations. Total assets in use rather than total assets available is preferable when the investment center has been forced to carry idle assets.
    Answer (A) is incorrect. Fixed operating assets are controlled by the division manager and contribute to profits. Answer (C) is incorrect. Inventories are operating assets that contribute to profits and are controlled by the division manager. Answer (D) is incorrect. The level of accounts payable is an operating decision that should be considered in the evaluation of the division manager.

15. The imputed interest rate used in the residual income approach to performance evaluation can best be described as the

    A. Average lending rate for the year being evaluated.

    B. Historical weighted-average cost of capital for the company.

    C. Target return on investment set by the company's management.

    D. Average return on investments for the company over the last several years.

Answer (C) is correct. *(CMA, adapted)*
    REQUIRED: The true statement about the imputed interest rate used in the residual income approach to performance evaluation.
    DISCUSSION: Residual income is the excess of the return on an investment over a targeted amount equal to an imputed interest charge on invested capital. The rate used is ordinarily set as a target return by management but is often equal to the weighted average cost of capital. Some enterprises prefer to measure managerial performance in terms of the amount of residual income rather than the percentage ROI because the firm will benefit from expansion as long as residual income is earned.
    Answer (A) is incorrect. The cost of equity capital must also be incorporated into the imputed interest rate. Answer (B) is incorrect. The current weighted-average cost of capital must be used. Answer (D) is incorrect. The rate should be based on cost of capital, not investment returns of preceding years.

8.4 Comparing Performance Measures for Investment Centers

16. REB Service Co. is a computer service center. For the month, REB had the following operating statistics:

Sales	$450,000
Operating income	25,000
Net profit after taxes	8,000
Total assets	500,000
Shareholders' equity	200,000
Cost of capital	6%

Based on the above information, which one of the following statements is true? REB has a

    A. Return on investment of 4%.

    B. Residual income of $(5,000).

    C. Return on investment of 1.6%.

    D. Residual income of $(22,000).

Answer (B) is correct. *(CMA, adapted)*
    REQUIRED: The true statement about the company's performance.
    DISCUSSION: Return on investment is commonly calculated by dividing pretax income by total assets available. Residual income is the excess of the return on investment over a targeted amount equal to an imputed interest charge on invested capital. The rate used is ordinarily the weighted-average cost of capital. Some companies measure managerial performance in terms of the amount of residual income rather than the percentage return on investment. Because REB has assets of $500,000 and a cost of capital of 6%, it must earn $30,000 on those assets to cover the cost of capital. Given that operating income was only $25,000, it had a negative residual income of $5,000.
    Answer (A) is incorrect. Although the firm's return on equity investment was 4%, its return on all funds invested was 5% ($25,000 pretax operating income ÷ $500,000). Answer (C) is incorrect. ROI is commonly based on before-tax income. Answer (D) is incorrect. The amount of $(22,000) equals the difference between net profit after taxes and targeted income.

17. Residual income is a better measure for performance evaluation of an investment center manager than return on investment because

A. The problems associated with measuring the asset base are eliminated.

B. Desirable investment decisions will not be neglected by high-return divisions.

C. Only the gross book value of assets needs to be calculated.

D. The arguments about the implicit cost of interest are eliminated.

Answer (B) is correct. *(CMA, adapted)*
 REQUIRED: The reason residual income is a better measure of performance evaluation than return on investment.
 DISCUSSION: Residual income is the excess of the amount of the ROI over a targeted amount equal to an imputed interest charge on invested capital. The advantage of using residual income rather than percentage ROI is that the former emphasizes maximizing a dollar amount instead of a percentage. Managers of divisions with a high ROI are encouraged to accept projects with returns exceeding the cost of capital even if those projects reduce the department's ROI.
 Answer (A) is incorrect. The methods use the same asset base. Answer (C) is incorrect. The methods use the same asset base. Answer (D) is incorrect. Use of the residual income method requires a knowledge of the cost of capital; thus, arguments about the implicit cost of interest may escalate with use of the residual income method.

Questions 18 and 19 are based on the following information. Edith Carolina, president of the Deed Corporation, requires a minimum return on investment of 8% for any project to be undertaken by her company. The company is decentralized, and leaves investment decisions up to the discretion of the division managers as long as the 8% return is expected to be realized. Michael Sanders, manager of the Cosmetics Division, has had a return on investment of 14% for his division for the past 3 years and expects the division to have the same return in the coming year. Sanders has the opportunity to invest in a new line of cosmetics that is expected to have a return on investment of 12%.

18. If the Deed Corporation evaluates managerial performance using residual income based on the corporate minimum required rate of return, what will be the preference for taking on the proposed cosmetics line by Edith Carolina and Michael Sanders?

	Carolina	Sanders
A.	Accept	Reject
B.	Reject	Accept
C.	Accept	Accept
D.	Reject	Reject

Answer (C) is correct. *(CMA, adapted)*
 REQUIRED: The preferences of the company and the division manager regarding a project with an ROI greater than the minimum return but less than the normal return if the manager is evaluated based on residual income.
 DISCUSSION: Residual income is the excess of the return on an investment over a targeted amount, which is equal to an imputed interest charge on invested capital (in this case, 8%). The rate is usually the weighted-average cost of capital. Some enterprises prefer to measure managerial performance in terms of the amount of residual income rather than the percentage ROI. The principle is that the enterprise is expected to benefit from expansion as long as residual income is earned. Using a percentage ROI approach, expansion might be rejected if it lowered ROI, even though residual income would increase. Using residual income, both Carolina and Sanders would accept the new project because residual income will increase if a 12% return is earned when the target ROI is only 8%.

19. If the Deed Corporation evaluates managerial performance using return on investment, what will be the preference for taking on the proposed cosmetics line by Edith Carolina and Michael Sanders?

	Carolina	Sanders
A.	Accept	Reject
B.	Reject	Accept
C.	Accept	Accept
D.	Reject	Reject

Answer (A) is correct. *(CMA, adapted)*
 REQUIRED: The preferences of the company and the division manager regarding a project with an ROI greater than the minimum return but less than the normal return.
 DISCUSSION: A company with an 8% ROI threshold should obviously accept a project yielding 12% because the company's overall ROI would increase. The manager being evaluated on the basis of ROI who is already earning 14% will be unwilling to accept a 12% return on a new project because the overall ROI for the division would decline slightly. This absence of goal congruence suggests a weakness in ROI-based performance evaluation.

20. Managerial performance can be measured in many different ways, including return on investment (ROI) and residual income. A good reason for using residual income instead of ROI is that

    A. Residual income can be computed without regard to identifying an investment base.

    B. Goal congruence is more likely to be promoted by using residual income.

    C. Residual income is well understood and often used in the financial press.

    D. ROI does not take into consideration both the investment turnover ratio and return-on-sales percentage.

Answer (B) is correct. *(CMA, adapted)*
    REQUIRED: The good reason for using the residual income method instead of ROI.
    DISCUSSION: Residual income is a significant refinement of the return on investment concept because it forces business unit managers to consider the opportunity cost of capital. The rate used is usually the weighted-average cost of capital. Residual income may be preferable to ROI because a business unit will benefit from expansion as long as residual income is earned. Using only ROI, managers might be tempted to reject expansion that would lower ROI, even though residual income would increase. Thus, the residual income method promotes the congruence of a manager's goals with those of the overall firm. Actions that tend to benefit the company will also tend to improve the measure of the manager's performance.
    Answer (A) is incorrect. An investment base is needed to calculate residual income. Answer (C) is incorrect. ROI and residual income calculations generally require the use of unpublished financial information. Answer (D) is incorrect. Both measures consider the same items.

8.5 Allocating Common Costs

21. Which one of the following firms is likely to experience dysfunctional motivation on the part of its managers due to its allocation methods?

    A. To allocate depreciation of forklifts used by workers at its central warehouse, Shahlimar Electronics uses predetermined amounts calculated on the basis of the long-term average use of the services provided.

    B. Manhattan Electronics uses the sales revenue of its various divisions to allocate costs connected with the upkeep of its headquarters building. It also uses ROI to evaluate the divisional performances.

    C. Rainier Industrial does not allow its service departments to pass on their cost overruns to the production departments.

    D. Tashkent Auto's MIS is operated out of headquarters and serves its various divisions. Tashkent's allocation of the MIS-related costs to its divisions is limited to costs the divisions will incur if they were to outsource their MIS needs.

Answer (B) is correct. *(CMA, adapted)*
    REQUIRED: The firm most likely to experience dysfunctional motivation on the part of its managers.
    DISCUSSION: Managerial performance ordinarily should be evaluated only on the basis of those factors controllable by the manager. If a manager is allocated costs that (s)he cannot control, dysfunctional motivation can result. In the case of allocations, a cause-and-effect basis should be used. Allocating the costs of upkeep on a headquarters building on the basis of sales revenue is arbitrary because cost may have no relationship to divisional sales revenues. Consequently, divisional ROI is reduced by a cost over which a division manager has no control. Furthermore, the divisions with the greatest sales are penalized by receiving the greatest allocation.
    Answer (A) is incorrect. Allocating depreciation on the basis of long-term average use is a reasonable basis of allocation. This basis is controllable by the division managers and reflects a causal relationship. Answer (C) is incorrect. A service department's cost overruns may not be attributable to any activities of production departments. Answer (D) is incorrect. Market-based allocations of costs of services are reasonable applications of the cause-and-effect principle.

22. Common costs are

    A. Direct costs.

    B. Current costs.

    C. Controllable costs.

    D. Indirect costs.

Answer (D) is correct. *(Publisher, adapted)*
    REQUIRED: The nature of common costs.
    DISCUSSION: Common costs are the cost of products, activities, facilities, services, or operations shared by two or more cost objects. They are indirect costs because they cannot be traced to a particular cost object in an economically feasible manner. Hence, they must be allocated.
    Answer (A) is incorrect. Direct costs can be traced to a particular cost object in an economically feasible manner. Answer (B) is incorrect. Current cost is an attribute used to measure assets. Answer (C) is incorrect. Controllable costs can be influenced by a particular manager.

23. A large corporation allocates the costs of its headquarters staff to its decentralized divisions. The best reason for this allocation is to

A. More accurately measure divisional operating results.

B. Improve divisional management's morale.

C. Remind divisional managers that common costs exist.

D. Discourage any use of central support services.

Answer (C) is correct. *(Publisher, adapted)*
    REQUIRED: The best reason for allocating headquarters costs.
    DISCUSSION: The allocation reminds managers that support costs exist and that the managers would incur these costs if their operations were independent. The allocation also reminds managers that profit center earnings must cover some amount of support costs.
    Answer (A) is incorrect. An arbitrary allocation may skew operating results. Answer (B) is incorrect. The allocation may create resentment and conflict. Answer (D) is incorrect. Efficient use of central support services should be encouraged.

24. Managers are most likely to accept allocations of common costs based on

A. Cause and effect.

B. Ability to bear.

C. Fairness.

D. Benefits received.

Answer (A) is correct. *(Publisher, adapted)*
    REQUIRED: The criterion most likely to result in acceptable allocations of common costs.
    DISCUSSION: The difficulty with common costs is that they are indirect costs whose allocation may be arbitrary. A direct cause-and-effect relationship between a common cost and the actions of the cost object to which it is allocated is desirable. Such a relationship promotes acceptance of the allocation by managers who perceive the fairness of the procedure, but identification of cause and effect may not be feasible.
    Answer (B) is incorrect. Allocation using an ability-to-bear criterion punishes successful managers and rewards underachievers. Answer (C) is incorrect. Fairness is an objective rather than a criterion. Moreover, fairness may be interpreted differently by different managers. Answer (D) is incorrect. The benefits-received criterion is preferable when a cause-effect relationship cannot be feasibly identified.

8.6 Transfer Pricing -- Details

25. A limitation of transfer prices based on actual cost is that they

A. Charge inefficiencies to the department that is transferring the goods.

B. Can lead to suboptimal decisions for the company as a whole.

C. Must be adjusted by some markup.

D. Lack clarity and administrative convenience.

Answer (B) is correct. *(CIA, adapted)*
    REQUIRED: The limitation of transfer prices based on actual cost.
    DISCUSSION: The optimal transfer price of a selling division should be set at a point that will have the most desirable economic effect on the firm as a whole while at the same time continuing to motivate the management of every division to perform efficiently. Setting the transfer price based on actual costs rather than standard costs would give the selling division little incentive to control costs.
    Answer (A) is incorrect. Inefficiencies are charged to the buying department. Answer (C) is incorrect. By definition, cost-based transfer prices are not adjusted by some markup. Answer (D) is incorrect. Cost-based transfer prices provide the advantages of clarity and administrative convenience.

26. An appropriate transfer price between two divisions of The Stark Company can be determined from the following data:

Fabricating Division:
Market price of subassembly	$50
Variable cost of subassembly	$20
Excess capacity (in units)	1,000

Assembling Division:
Number of units needed	900

What is the natural bargaining range for the two divisions?

A. Between $20 and $50.

B. Between $50 and $70.

C. Any amount less than $50.

D. $50 is the only acceptable price.

Answer (A) is correct. *(CMA, adapted)*
REQUIRED: The natural bargaining range for the transfer price.
DISCUSSION: An ideal transfer price should permit each division to operate independently and achieve its goals while functioning in the overall best interest of the firm. The production capacity of the selling division is always a consideration in setting transfer price. If Fabricating had no excess capacity, it would charge Assembling the regular market price. However, since Fabricating has excess capacity of 1,000 units, negotiation is possible because any transfer price greater than the variable cost of $20 would absorb some of the fixed costs and result in increased divisional profits. Thus, any price between $20 and $50 is acceptable to Fabricating. Any price under $50 is acceptable to Assembling because that is the price that would be paid to an outside supplier.
Answer (B) is incorrect. Assembling would not pay more than the market price of $50. Answer (C) is incorrect. Fabricating will not be willing to accept less than its variable cost of $20. Answer (D) is incorrect. Fabricating should be willing to accept any price between $20 and $50.

Questions 27 through 29 are based on the following information.

Parkside, Inc., has several divisions that operate as decentralized profit centers. Parkside's Entertainment Division manufactures video arcade equipment using the products of two of Parkside's other divisions. The Plastics Division manufactures plastic components, one type that is made exclusively for the Entertainment Division, while other less complex components are sold to outside markets. The products of the Video Cards Division are sold in a competitive market; however, one video card model is also used by the Entertainment Division.

The actual costs per unit used by the Entertainment Division are presented below.

	Plastic Components	Video Cards
Direct material	$1.25	$2.40
Direct labor	2.35	3.00
Variable overhead	1.00	1.50
Fixed overhead	.40	2.25
Total cost	$5.00	$9.15

The Plastics Division sells its commercial products at full cost plus a 25% markup and believes the proprietary plastic component made for the Entertainment Division would sell for $6.25 per unit on the open market. The market price of the video card used by the Entertainment Division is $10.98 per unit.

---

27. A per-unit transfer price from the Video Cards Division to the Entertainment Division at full cost, $9.15, would

A. Allow evaluation of both divisions on a competitive basis.

B. Satisfy the Video Cards Division's profit desire by allowing recovery of opportunity costs.

C. Provide no profit incentive for the Video Cards Division to control or reduce costs.

D. Encourage the Entertainment Division to purchase video cards from an outside source.

Answer (C) is correct. *(CMA, adapted)*
REQUIRED: The negative effect of a full-cost transfer price.
DISCUSSION: The use of full (absorption) cost ensures that the selling division will not incur a loss and provides more incentive to the buying division to buy internally than does use of market price. However, there is no motivation for the seller to control production cost since all costs can be passed along to the buying division.
Answer (A) is incorrect. Evaluating the seller is difficult if it can pass along all costs to the buyer. Answer (B) is incorrect. Transfers at full cost do not allow for a seller's profit. Answer (D) is incorrect. A full-cost transfer is favorable to the buyer. It is lower than the market price.

28. Assume that the Entertainment Division is able to purchase a large quantity of video cards from an outside source at $8.70 per unit. The Video Cards Division, having excess capacity, agrees to lower its transfer price to $8.70 per unit. This action would

    A. Optimize the profit goals of the Entertainment Division while subverting the profit goals of Parkside, Inc.

    B. Allow evaluation of both divisions on the same basis.

    C. Subvert the profit goals of the Video Cards Division while optimizing the profit goals of the Entertainment Division.

    D. Optimize the overall profit goals of Parkside, Inc.

Answer (D) is correct. *(CMA, adapted)*
    REQUIRED: The impact of lowering the transfer price to match an outside seller's price.
    DISCUSSION: If the selling division has excess capacity, it should lower its transfer price to match the outside offer. This decision optimizes the profits of the company as a whole by allowing for use of capacity that would otherwise be idle.
    Answer (A) is incorrect. This action is congruent with the goals of Parkside. The use of idle capacity enhances profits. Answer (B) is incorrect. The transfer is at a loss (relative to full cost) to the selling division, although the company as a whole will benefit. Answer (C) is incorrect. The buying division is indifferent as to whether to purchase internally or externally.

29. Assume that the Plastics Division has excess capacity and it has negotiated a transfer price of $5.60 per plastic component with the Entertainment Division. This price will

    A. Cause the Plastics Division to reduce the number of commercial plastic components it manufactures.

    B. Motivate both divisions as estimated profits are shared.

    C. Encourage the Entertainment Division to seek an outside source for plastic components.

    D. Demotivate the Plastics Division causing mediocre performance.

Answer (B) is correct. *(CMA, adapted)*
    REQUIRED: The effect of using a negotiated transfer price that is greater than full cost but less than market price.
    DISCUSSION: Given that the seller has excess capacity, transfers within the company entail no opportunity cost. Accordingly, the transfer at the negotiated price will improve the performance measures of the selling division. Purchasing internally at below the market price also benefits the buying division, so the motivational purpose of transfer pricing is achieved. The goal congruence purpose is also achieved because the internal transaction benefits the company.
    Answer (A) is incorrect. This arrangement creates no disincentive for the selling division. It will make a profit on every unit transferred. Answer (C) is incorrect. The market price charged by outside sources is higher than the negotiated price. Answer (D) is incorrect. Given idle capacity, selling at any amount in excess of variable cost should motivate the selling division.

8.7 Transfer Pricing -- Selection

30. The price that one division of a company charges another division for goods or services provided is called the

    A. Market price.

    B. Transfer price.

    C. Outlay price.

    D. Distress price.

Answer (B) is correct. *(CIA, adapted)*
    REQUIRED: The price that one division of a company charges another for goods or services provided.
    DISCUSSION: A transfer price is the price charged by one segment of an organization for a product or service supplied to another segment of the same organization.
    Answer (A) is incorrect. Market price is an approach to determine a transfer price. Answer (C) is incorrect. Outlay price is an approach to determine a transfer price. Answer (D) is incorrect. Distress price is an approach to determine a transfer price.

31. The most fundamental responsibility center affected by the use of market-based transfer prices is a(n)

    A. Production center.

    B. Investment center.

    C. Cost center.

    D. Profit center.

Answer (D) is correct. *(CMA, adapted)*
    REQUIRED: The most fundamental responsibility center affected by the use of market-based transfer prices.
    DISCUSSION: Transfer prices are often used by profit centers and investment centers. Profit centers are the more fundamental of these two centers because investment centers are responsible not only for revenues and costs but also for invested capital.
    Answer (A) is incorrect. A production center may be a cost center, a profit center, or even an investment center. Transfer prices are not used in a cost center. Transfer prices are used to compute profitability, but a cost center is responsible only for cost control. Answer (B) is incorrect. An investment center is not as fundamental as a profit center. Answer (C) is incorrect. Transfer prices are not used in a cost center.

32. In theory, the optimal method for establishing a transfer price is

   A. Flexible budget cost.

   B. Incremental cost.

   C. Budgeted cost with or without a markup.

   D. Market price.

Answer (D) is correct. *(CMA, adapted)*
   REQUIRED: The optimal method for establishing a transfer price.
   DISCUSSION: Transfer prices should promote congruence of subunit goals with those of the organization, subunit autonomy, and managerial effort. Although no rule exists for determining the transfer price that meets these criteria in all situations, a starting point is to calculate the sum of the additional outlay costs and the opportunity cost to the supplier. Given no idle capacity and a competitive external market (all goods transferred internally can be sold externally), the sum of the outlay and opportunity costs will be the market price.
   Answer (A) is incorrect. Using flexible budget cost as a transfer price provides no motivation to the seller to control costs and no reward for selling internally when an external market exists. Answer (B) is incorrect. Using incremental cost as a transfer price provides no motivation to the seller to control costs and no reward for selling internally when an external market exists. Answer (C) is incorrect. Market price is preferable to a budgeted or actual cost with or without a markup (unless the markup equals the profit earned by selling externally).

33. A carpet manufacturer maintains a retail division consisting of stores stocking its brand and other brands and a manufacturing division that makes carpets and pads. An outside market exists for carpet padding material in which all padding produced can be sold. The proper transfer price for padding transferred from the manufacturing division to the retail division is

   A. Variable manufacturing division production cost.

   B. Variable manufacturing division production cost plus allocated fixed factory overhead.

   C. Variable manufacturing division production cost plus variable selling and administrative cost.

   D. The market price at which the retail division could purchase padding.

Answer (D) is correct. *(CIA, adapted)*
   REQUIRED: The proper transfer price when an outside market exists
   DISCUSSION: The optimal transfer price of a selling division should be set at a point that will have the most desirable economic effect on the firm as a whole while at the same time continuing to motivate the management of every division to perform efficiently. The market price should be used as the transfer price to avoid waste and maximize efficiency in a competitive economy (an outside market in which all padding produced can be sold). This price also measures the product's profitability and the division managers' performance in a competitive environment.
   Answer (A) is incorrect. The market price will better achieve the goals of a transfer pricing system. The selling division would not have as strong an incentive to control costs if some variant of actual cost is used. The efficiency of the purchasing division is also promoted when it must treat the selling division as if it were an independent vendor. Answer (B) is incorrect. The market price will better achieve the goals of a transfer pricing system. The selling division would not have as strong an incentive to control costs if some variant of actual cost is used. Answer (C) is incorrect. The market price will better achieve the goals of a transfer pricing system. The selling division would not have as strong an incentive to control costs if some variant of actual cost is used.

34. The Eastern division sells goods internally to the Western division of the same company. The quoted external price in industry publications from a supplier near Eastern is $200 per ton plus transportation. It costs $20 per ton to transport the goods to Western. Eastern's actual market cost per ton to buy the direct materials to make the transferred product is $100. Actual per ton direct labor is $50. Other actual costs of storage and handling are $40. The company president selects a $220 transfer price. This is an example of

   A. Market-based transfer pricing.

   B. Cost-based transfer pricing.

   C. Negotiated transfer pricing.

   D. Cost plus 20% transfer pricing.

Answer (A) is correct. *(CIA, adapted)*
   REQUIRED: The type of transfer price.
   DISCUSSION: The optimal transfer price of a selling division should be set at a point that will have the most desirable economic effect on the firm as a whole while at the same time continuing to motivate the management of every division to perform efficiently. Because the $220 transfer price selected is based on the quoted external price (market), it is an example of market-based transfer pricing.
   Answer (B) is incorrect. The cost-based price would be $210 ($100 + $50 + $40 + $20). Answer (C) is incorrect. No negotiations took place. Answer (D) is incorrect. Cost plus 20% would be $252 ($210 × 1.20).

8.8 The Balanced Scorecard

35. The balanced scorecard provides an action plan for achieving competitive success by focusing management attention on critical success factors. Which one of the following is **not** one of the perspectives on the business into which critical success factors are commonly grouped in the balanced scorecard?

- A. Competitor business strategies.
- B. Financial performance.
- C. Internal business processes.
- D. Employee innovation and learning.

Answer (A) is correct. *(CMA, adapted)*
REQUIRED: The item not a perspective on the business as used on a balanced scorecard.
DISCUSSION: A typical balanced scorecard classifies critical success factors and measures into one of four perspectives on the business: financial, customer satisfaction, internal business processes, and learning and growth.
Answer (B) is incorrect. Financial performance measures are among the tools used in a typical balanced scorecard. Answer (C) is incorrect. A typical balanced scorecard contains critical success factors and measures focused on internal business processes. Answer (D) is incorrect. Employee innovation and learning is one of the perspectives on the business commonly used in a balanced scorecard.

36. Using the balanced scorecard approach, an organization evaluates managerial performance based on

- A. A single ultimate measure of operating results, such as residual income.
- B. Multiple financial and nonfinancial measures.
- C. Multiple nonfinancial measures only.
- D. Multiple financial measures only.

Answer (B) is correct. *(Publisher, adapted)*
REQUIRED: The nature of the balanced scorecard approach.
DISCUSSION: The trend in managerial performance evaluation is the balanced scorecard approach. Multiple measures of performance permit a determination as to whether a manager is achieving certain objectives at the expense of others that may be equally or more important. These measures may be financial or nonfinancial and usually include items in four categories: profitability; customer satisfaction; innovation; and efficiency, quality, and time.

37. On a balanced scorecard, which of the following would **not** be an example of a customer satisfaction measure?

- A. Market share.
- B. Economic value added.
- C. Response time.
- D. Customer retention.

Answer (B) is correct. *(Publisher, adapted)*
REQUIRED: The measure that is not an element of customer satisfaction on a balanced scorecard.
DISCUSSION: Customer satisfaction measures include market share, retention, response time, delivery performance, number of defects, and lead time. Economic value added, or EVA®, is a profitability measure.
Answer (A) is incorrect. Market share is a customer satisfaction measure. Answer (C) is incorrect. Response time is a customer satisfaction measure. Answer (D) is incorrect. Customer retention is a customer satisfaction measure.

38. On a balanced scorecard, which is more of an internal process measure than an external-based measure?

- A. Cycle time.
- B. Profitability.
- C. Customer satisfaction.
- D. Market share.

Answer (A) is correct. *(Publisher, adapted)*
REQUIRED: The measure that is more internal-process related on a balanced scorecard.
DISCUSSION: Cycle time is the manufacturing time to complete an order. Thus, cycle time is strictly related to internal processes. Profitability is a combination of internal and external considerations. Customer satisfaction and market share are related to how customers perceive a product and how competitors react.
Answer (B) is incorrect. Profitability is a measure that includes external considerations. Answer (C) is incorrect. Customer satisfaction is a measure that includes external considerations. Answer (D) is incorrect. Market share is a measure that includes external considerations.

Use Gleim **CMA Test Prep** Software for interactive testing with **additional multiple-choice questions!**

*Page
Intentionally
Left Blank*

8.10 ESSAY QUESTIONS

Scenario for Essay Questions 1, 2, 3, 4

Ajax Consolidated has several divisions; however, only two divisions transfer products to other divisions. The Mining Division refines toldine, which is then transferred to the Metals Division. The toldine is processed into an alloy by the Metals Division and is sold to customers at a price of $150 per unit. The Mining Division is currently required by Ajax to transfer its total yearly output of 400,000 units of toldine to the Metals Division at total manufacturing cost plus 10%. Unlimited quantities of toldine can be purchased and sold on the open market at $90 per unit. While the Mining Division could sell all the toldine it produces at $90 per unit on the open market, it would have to incur a variable selling cost of $5 per unit.

Brian Jones, manager of the Mining Division, is unhappy with having to transfer the entire output of toldine to the Metals Division at 110 percent of cost. In a meeting with the management of Ajax, he said, "Why should my division be required to sell toldine to the Metals Division at less than market price? For the year just ended, Metals' contribution margin was over $19 million on sales of 400,000 units while Mining's contribution was just over $5 million on the transfer of the same number of units. My division is subsidizing the profitability of the Metals Division. We should be allowed to charge the market price for toldine when transferring to the Metals Division."

Presented below is the detailed unit cost structure for both the Mining and Metals Divisions for the fiscal year ended May 31.

Cost Structure Per Unit

	Mining Division	Metals Division
Transfer price from Mining Division	--	$ 66
Direct material	$12	6
Direct labor	16	20
Manufacturing overhead	32[1]	25[2]
Total cost per unit	$60	$117

[1] Manufacturing overhead cost in the Mining Division is 25% fixed and 75% variable.
[2] Manufacturing overhead cost in the Metals Division is 60% fixed and 40% variable.

Questions

1. Explain why transfer prices based on cost are not appropriate as a divisional performance measure.

2. Using the market price as the transfer price, determine the contribution margin for both the Mining Division and the Metals Division for the year ended May 31.

3. If Ajax Consolidated were to institute the use of negotiated transfer prices and allow divisions to buy and sell on the open market, determine the price range for toldine that would be acceptable to both the Mining Division and the Metals Division. Explain your answer.

4. Identify which one of the three types of transfer prices -- cost-based, market-based, or negotiated -- is most likely to elicit desirable management behavior at Ajax Consolidated and thus benefit overall operations. Explain your answer.

Essay Questions 1, 2, 3, 4 — Unofficial Answers

1. Among the reasons transfer prices based on cost are not appropriate as a divisional performance measure are because they

    a. Provide little incentive for the selling division to control manufacturing costs as all costs incurred will be recovered

    b. Often lead to suboptimal decisions for the company as a whole

2. Using the market price as the transfer price, the contribution margin for both the Mining Division and the Metals Division for the year ended May 31 is calculated below.

    Ajax Consolidated Calculation of
    Divisional Contribution Margin
    For the Year Ended May 31

	Mining Division	Metals Division
Selling price	$ 90	$ 150
Less: variable costs		
Direct material	12	6
Direct labor	16	20
Manufacturing overhead	24[(1)]	10[(2)]
Transfer price		90
Unit contribution margin	$ 38	$ 24
Volume	× 400,000	× 400,000
Total contribution margin	$15,200,000	$9,600,000

    [(1)]   Variable overhead: $32 × 75% = $24
    [(2)]   Variable overhead: $25 × 40% = $10

    NOTE: The $5 variable selling cost that the Mining Division would incur for sales on the open market should not be included as this is an internal transfer.

3. If the use of a negotiated transfer price was instituted by Ajax Consolidated, which also permitted the divisions to buy and sell on the open market, the price range for toldine that would be acceptable to both divisions would be determined as follows:

    a. The Mining Division would like to sell to the Metals Division for the same price it can obtain on the outside market, $90 per unit. However, Mining would be willing to sell the toldine for $85 per unit as the $5 variable selling cost would be avoided.

    b. The Metals Division would like to continue paying the bargain price of $66 per unit. However, if Mining does not sell to Metals, Metals would be forced to pay $90 on the open market. Therefore, Metals would be satisfied to receive a price concession from Mining equal to the costs that Mining would avoid by selling internally. Therefore, a negotiated transfer price for toldine between $85 and $90 would benefit both divisions and the company as a whole.

4. A negotiated transfer price is the most likely to elicit desirable management behavior as it will

    a. Encourage the management of the Mining Division to be more conscious of cost control

    b. Benefit the Metals Division by providing toldine at less cost than its competitors

    c. Provide a more realistic measure of divisional performance

---

Use **CMA Gleim Online** and **Essay Wizard** to practice additional essay questions in an exam-like environment.

STUDY UNIT NINE
INTERNAL CONTROLS --
RISK AND PROCEDURES FOR CONTROL

(23 pages of outline)

9.1	Risk and the Control Environment	326
9.2	Control Procedures	333
9.3	Legal Aspects of Internal Control	338
9.4	Core Concepts	345
9.5	Essay Questions	361

Internal Controls

Management accountants are expected to have a thorough understanding of the risks inherent to, and the internal controls within, a business. Internal controls have always been a good idea in a well-run business, but with the passage of the Foreign Corrupt Practices Act in 1977, an effective internal control system became a legal requirement. The Sarbanes-Oxley Act of 2002 further enhanced the legal requirements for internal controls.

This study unit and the following study unit are on **internal controls**. The relative weight assigned to this major topic in Part 1 of the exam is **15%**.

After studying the outline and answering the questions in this study unit, you will have the skills necessary to address the following topics listed in the ICMA's Learning Outcome Statements:

Part 1 – Section D.1. Risk assessment, controls, and risk management

The candidate should be able to:

a. demonstrate an understanding of internal control risk and the management of internal control risk

b. identify and describe internal control objectives

c. explain how a company's organizational structure, policies, objectives, and goals, as well as its management philosophy and style, influence the scope and effectiveness of the control environment

d. identify the board of directors' responsibilities with respect to ensuring that the company is operated in the best interest of shareholders

e. describe how internal controls are designed to provide reasonable (but not absolute) assurance regarding achievement of an entity's objectives involving (i) effectiveness and efficiency of operations, (ii) reliability of financial reporting, and (iii) compliance with applicable laws and regulations

f. explain why personnel policies and procedures are integral to an efficient control environment

g. define and give examples of segregation of duties

h. explain why the following four types of functional responsibilities should be performed by different departments or different people within the same function: (i) authority to execute transactions, (ii) recording transactions, (iii) custody of assets involved in the transactions, and (iv) periodic reconciliations of the existing assets to recorded amounts

i. demonstrate an understanding of the importance of independent checks and verification

j. list examples of safeguarding controls

k. explain how the use of pre-numbered forms, as well as specific policies and procedures detailing who is authorized to receive specific documents, is a means of control

l.   define inherent risk, control risk, and detection risk

m.   describe the major internal control provisions of the Sarbanes-Oxley Act (Sections 201, 203, 302, and 404)

n.   identify the role of the PCAOB in providing guidance on the auditing of internal controls

o.   differentiate between a top-down (risk-based) approach and a bottom-up approach to auditing internal controls

p.   identify the PCAOB preferred approach to auditing internal controls as outlined in Auditing Standard #5

q.   identify and describe the major internal control provisions of the Foreign Corrupt Practices Act

r.   identify and describe the five major components of COSO's Internal Control Framework (the 92 model)

s.   assess the level of internal control risk within an organization and recommend risk mitigation strategies

t.   define and distinguish between preventive controls and detective controls

9.1 RISK AND THE CONTROL ENVIRONMENT

1.   **The Assessment and Management of Risk**

a.   Every organization faces risks, that is, unforeseen obstacles to the pursuit of its objectives. Risks take many forms and can originate from within or from outside the organization. Examples include the following:

1)   A hacker may break into a university's information systems, changing grades and awarding unearned degrees.

2)   The CEO may bribe a member of Congress to introduce legislation favorable to the firm's business.

3)   A foreign government may be overthrown in a *coup d'etat*, followed by the expropriation of the firm's assets in that country.

4)   An accounts payable clerk may establish fictitious vendors in the company's information systems and receive checks in payment for nonexistent goods or services.

5)   A spike in interest rates may make the firm's long-term capital projects unprofitable.

6)   The introduction of a new technology may make one of the firm's premier products obsolete.

7)   A reduction in government regulation brings a flood of new competitors into the firm's markets.

b.   **Risk assessment** is the process whereby management identifies the organization's vulnerabilities.

1)   All systems of internal control involve tradeoffs between cost and benefit. For this reason, no system of internal control can be said to be "100% effective." Organizations accept the fact that risk can only be mitigated, not eliminated.

2)   **Risk management** is the ongoing process of designing and operating internal controls that mitigate the risks identified in the organization's risk assessment.

c.   Risk can be quantified as a combination of two factors: the severity of consequences and the likelihood of occurrence. The expected value of a loss due to a risk exposure can thus be stated numerically as the product of the two factors.

1)   Risk can also be assessed in qualitative terms.

2) EXAMPLE: A company is assessing the risks of its systems being penetrated by hackers.

Event	Consequences	Likelihood
Minor penetration	Annoyance	90%
Unauthorized viewing of internal databases	Public embarrassment, Loss of customer confidence	8%
Unauthorized alteration of internal databases	PR crisis, Customer defection	2%

a) Although the occurrence of the annoyance level of incident is viewed as almost inevitable, the company will not find it worthwhile to institute the level of control necessary to prevent it.

b) By contrast, the occurrence of a disastrous level of incident is seen as remote, but the consequences are so severe that the company is willing to institute the costly internal controls that will ensure its prevention.

d. The AICPA audit risk model can be adapted to the system of internal control as follows:

1) Inherent risk (IR) is the susceptibility of one of the company's objectives to obstacles arising from the nature of the objective. For example, a uranium mine is inherently riskier than a strip mall.

2) Control risk (CR) is the risk that the controls put in place will fail to prevent an obstacle from interfering with the achievement of the objective. For example, a policy requiring two approvals for expenditures over a certain dollar amount could be bypassed by collusion.

3) Detection risk (DR) is the risk that an obstacle to an objective will not be detected before a loss has occurred. For example, an embezzlement that continues for a year before detection is much costlier than one that is discovered after 1 month.

4) Total risk (TR) may thus be stated as follows:

$$TR = IR \times CR \times DR$$

2. **The System of Internal Control**

a. An organization establishes a system of internal control to help it manage many of the risks it faces. The IMA's *Management Accounting Glossary* defines internal control as follows:

> *The whole system of controls (financial and otherwise) established by management to carry on the business of the enterprise in an orderly and efficient manner, to ensure adherence to management policies, safeguard the assets, and ensure as far as possible the completeness and accuracy of the records.*

b. The proper design and operation of an organization's system of internal controls is the responsibility of management.

1) Section 404 of the Sarbanes-Oxley Act of 2002 requires publicly traded companies to issue a report stating that

a) Management takes responsibility for establishing and maintaining the firm's system of internal controls, and

b) The system has been functioning effectively over the reporting period.

3. **PCAOB Approach**

    a. One of the requirements of the Sarbanes-Oxley Act is that the annual financial statement audit also address the firm's system of internal control.

        1) The PCAOB issued its Auditing Standard (AS) No. 5, "An Audit of Internal Control Over Financial Reporting That Is Integrated with An Audit of Financial Statements," to provide guidance when these two audits are integrated.

        2) AS 5 requires the external auditor to express an opinion on both the system of internal control and the fair presentation of financial statements.

    b. AS 5 focuses on the existence of material weaknesses in internal control:

        Because a company's internal control cannot be considered effective if one or more material weaknesses exist, to form a basis for expressing an opinion, the auditor must plan and perform the audit to obtain competent evidence that is sufficient to obtain reasonable assurance about whether material weaknesses exist as of the date specified in management's assessment. A material weakness in internal control over financial reporting may exist even when financial statements are not materially misstated.

        1) The AICPA's auditing standards define material weakness as follows:

            A material weakness is a deficiency, or combination of deficiencies, in internal control that results in a reasonable possibility that a material misstatement of the financial statements will not be prevented or timely detected and corrected.

        2) This financial reporting-oriented focus for internal controls stands in contrast with the broader view that internal controls are processes to aid the organization in achieving its goals.

4. **COSO Control Objectives**

    a. In its 1992 publication *Internal Control – Integrated Framework*, the Committee of Sponsoring Organizations of the Treadway Commission (COSO) defined internal control this way:

        Internal control is broadly defined as a process, effected by an entity's board of directors, management, and other personnel, designed to provide reasonable assurance regarding the achievement of objectives in the following categories:

        *   *Effectiveness and efficiency of operations*
        *   *Reliability of financial reporting*
        *   *Compliance with applicable laws and regulations*

        1) The following is the memory aid for the interrelated objectives:

E = Effective & Efficient	**E**verything
R = Reliability	**R**eally
C = Compliance	**C**ounts

    b. This classification is widely accepted, for example, by the AICPA in its model for external auditing.

c. **Effectiveness and Efficiency of Operations**

    1) Operational objectives relate to the achievement of the entity's mission.

    2) Effectiveness and efficiency of operations concern performance, including attainment of earnings objectives and the safeguarding of resources.

        a) Effectiveness and efficiency in meeting inappropriate objectives do not benefit the organization. Internal controls must be designed so that they focus effort on the achievement of the organization's objectives.

d. **Reliability of Financial Reporting**

    1) To make sound decisions, investors, creditors, and other users must have access to reliable financial reports, especially financial statements issued for general use.

        a) Reliable financial statements are fairly presented in conformity with the requirements of accounting standards setters.

e. **Compliance with Applicable Laws and Regulations**

    1) Entities must conduct their activities, and often take specific actions, in accordance with applicable laws and regulations.

    2) Entities are subject to laws at the local, state, and federal levels dealing with such matters as land use, waste disposal, wage and hour issues, and employee safety. In addition, numerous regulations govern individual industries, such as banking and trucking.

    3) Note that the Framework specifically cites reasonable, not absolute, assurance about the achievement of management's objectives. The benefits of internal controls must always exceed the costs of implementing them. A system of absolute assurance could only be implemented at prohibitively great expense [see item 1.b.1)].

5. **Components of Internal Control**

a. The COSO's internal control framework consists of the following five interrelated components:

    1) **The Control Environment**

        a) The control environment sets the tone of an entity and influences the control consciousness of personnel. It is the foundation for all other components of internal control, providing discipline and structure.

        b) To understand the control environment, the auditor considers programs and controls addressing fraud risk that have been implemented by management and those charged with governance. Their absence or inadequacy may be a material weakness.

    2) **Risk Assessment**

        a) Risk assessment is the identification and analysis of relevant risks to achievement of the objectives. It forms a basis for determining how the risks should be managed.

        b) Relevant risks include events and circumstances that may adversely affect an entity's ability to initiate, authorize, record, process, and report financial data consistent with financial statement assertions.

    3) **Control Activities**

        a) Control activities are the policies and procedures that help ensure management directives are carried out.

        b) These are the policies and procedures helping to ensure that actions are taken to address risks to achievement of objectives. Whether automated or manual, they have various objectives and are applied at various levels.

4)   **Information and Communication**

a)   Pertinent information must be identified, captured, and communicated in a form and timeframe that enable people to carry out their responsibilities.

i)   An information system consists of physical and hardware elements (infrastructure), software, data, manual and automated procedures, and people that interrelate to achieve a business goal.

ii) Communication includes providing an understanding to employees about their roles and responsibilities. For example, communication may be through policy manuals, financial reporting manuals, and memoranda. It also may be by electronic and oral means or by management actions.

5)   **Monitoring**

a)   Internal control systems need to be monitored. This process assesses the quality of the system's performance over time.

b)   Monitoring is management's timely assessment of internal control and the taking of corrective action so that controls operate as intended and are modified for changes in conditions. Establishing and maintaining internal control is management's responsibility.

b.   Graphical Depiction

1)   The COSO Framework may be represented as a cube, with rows, slices, and columns. The rows are the five components, the slices are the three categories of objectives, and the columns are the activities or units of the entity. The columns also may be viewed as a single dimension depicting the entity as a whole.

2)   The objectives should be examined for applicability to every identified activity and operating unit of the entity. Each combination of activity/unit and objective must address each of the five components.

COSO Internal Control Framework

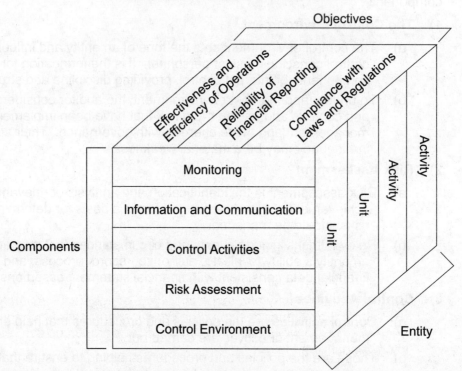

Figure 9-1

6. **The Control Environment**

    a. An organization's control environment encompasses the attitudes and actions of the board of directors and upper management regarding the significance of control, i.e., the "tone at the top." The components include

        1) Organizational structure. The structure of an entity is determined by its size and mission. The entity must be structured to best achieve its objectives, but structure is also a function of size. A large entity normally requires more formal reporting lines than a small one.

            a) An organization that is serious about internal control will design its lines of reporting and authority so that incompatible duties are not combined in the same job function and independent checks on performance are facilitated.

            b) EXAMPLE: An organization designs its system of internal control to separate the functions of recordkeeping, custody, and authority. For instance, the organization's accountants are responsible for keeping the books and report to the controller, while the daily bank deposits are prepared by employees who report to the treasurer.

        2) Policies are stated principles that require, guide, or restrict action. Policies should be designed to promote the conduct of authorized activities in an effective, efficient, and economical manner and to provide a satisfactory degree of assurance that the resources of the enterprise are suitably safeguarded. Procedures are the detailed steps that provide a guide for carrying out a policy.

            a) EXAMPLE: A policy can simply state, "All bank statements will be reconciled to the company's records on a monthly basis." A procedure consists of the detailed steps to be carried out in performing the reconciliation.

        3) Objectives and goals. An organization should set realistic, achievable goals that do not tempt managers to cross ethical boundaries.

            a) EXAMPLE: Pegging divisional vice-presidents' bonus schedules to a 25% growth in revenues in all product segments can lead managers to engage in unethical accounting practices.

        4) Management philosophy and operating style. Management's attitude toward sound risk management manifests itself in everyday actions in areas such as financial reporting, accounting estimates, and the selection of accounting principles.

            a) Integrity and ethical values are essential because they affect all aspects of control. Ethical behavior results from the entity's standards, the way they are transmitted, and how they are reinforced. Management creates an atmosphere conducive to better risk management by (1) removing incentives for dishonest, illegal, or unethical behavior, and (2) setting an example in its own behavior.

            b) EXAMPLE: When management routinely bypasses standing policies toward document approval, stretches accounting estimates, and encourages disregard of the principle of conservatism in financial reporting, risk is increased.

        5) Assignment of authority and responsibility. Management can improve the control environment by proper design of the organizational structure. Even when the number of personnel available is limited, lines of reporting can reinforce proper internal control.

      a)   EXAMPLE: The internal audit activity can report directly to the CEO and be viewed as an important tool for helping maintain a proper control environment. A less satisfactory position is for the internal audit to be viewed simply as an adjunct of the financial accounting function and be placed under the controller.

      b)   EXAMPLE: Management defines key areas of authority and responsibility by placing the information technology, financial accounting, and treasury functions under separate officers.

7.   **Board of Directors' Role**

   a.   Most publicly held corporations are required to have a board of directors, consisting of both inside members (officers and employees) and outside members (nonemployees who hold the company's stock).

      1)   The board is the governing authority of the corporation and is therefore responsible for establishing overall corporate policy. Day-to-day operations are delegated to management.

   b.   The directors have a fiduciary duty to the organization and its shareholders. They must exercise reasonable care in the performance of their duties, which entails being informed about and conversant with pertinent corporate information, attending meetings, analyzing corporate financial statements, etc.

      1)   Directors also owe a duty of loyalty, which prohibits dealing with the corporation unless full disclosure is made or usurping any corporate opportunity without giving the entity the right of first refusal.

      2)   Under the business judgment rule, however, a director will not have personal liability for his/her conduct if (s)he acts in good faith; is not motivated by fraud, conflict of interest, or illegality; and is not guilty of gross negligence.

         a)   Thus, honest errors of judgment do not result in liability. Moreover, a director may rely on information provided by an officer or an expert if the reliance is reasonable.

   c.   Directors typically

      1)   Select and remove officers
      2)   Determine the capital structure
      3)   Add, amend, or repeal bylaws
      4)   Initiate fundamental changes, such as mergers and divestitures
      5)   Declare dividends
      6)   Set the compensation of officers and management

8.   **Audit Committee's Role**

   a.   The audit committee is a subcommittee of the board of directors whose purpose is to help keep the external auditors independent of management. This is accomplished by assigning the selection, compensation, and oversight of the external auditors to the audit committee.

      1)   Many stock exchanges require a listed organization to have an audit committee.

      2)   A crucial aspect of the audit committee is that it be made up of outside directors, i.e., only shareholders who are not employed by the company. This custom was made compulsory by the Sarbanes-Oxley Act of 2002 (see item 2.a. in Subunit 9.3).

      3)   The audit committee also plays an important role in maintaining the control environment by approving the charter and overseeing the work of the internal audit activity.

   b.   A strong audit committee insulates both external and internal auditors from influences that may compromise their independence and objectivity.

9. **The Importance of Human Resources**

a. Human Resources policies and practices

1) Hiring standards should emphasize education, prior experience, past achievements, evidence of integrity and ethical behavior, and display a commitment to employing people who are competent and trustworthy.

2) Training policies should impart to employees a knowledge of their roles and responsibilities and expectations about their conduct and performance.

a) Human resource, or personnel, policies and procedures are an example of directive controls. Their objective is to cause a good event to occur rather than to stop a bad event from occurring.

b) Essentially, personnel policies and other directive controls are a special form of preventive controls in that errors are prevented through the proper selection and training of employees.

b. Commitment to competence

1) Competence consists of the knowledge and abilities necessary to complete required tasks. Simply having personnel in place who know what to do in a given situation is a crucial aspect of sound internal control.

2) Promotions based on periodic performance appraisals should reflect a commitment to rewarding competence.

Stop and review! You have completed the outline for this subunit. Study multiple-choice questions 1 through 6 beginning on page 347.

9.2 CONTROL PROCEDURES

1. **The Control Process**

a. Control requires feedback on the results of organizational activities for the purposes of measurement and correction.

b. The control process includes

1) Establishing standards for the operation to be controlled,
2) Measuring performance against the standards,
3) Examining and analyzing deviations,
4) Taking corrective action, and
5) Reappraising the standards based on experience.

c. An evaluation-reward system should be implemented to encourage compliance with the control system.

d. The costs of internal control must not be greater than its benefits.

2. **Types of Controls**

a. **Primary Controls**

1) Preventive controls deter the occurrence of unwanted events.

a) Storing petty cash in a locked safe and segregation of duties are examples of this type of control.

b) IT examples include (1) designing a database so that users cannot enter a letter in the field that stores a Social Security number and (2) requiring the number of invoices in a batch to be entered before processing begins.

2) Detective controls alert the proper people after an unwanted event. They are effective when detection occurs before material harm occurs.

    a) For example, a batch of invoices submitted for processing may be rejected by the computer system. A detective control provides for automatic reporting of all rejected batches to the accounts payable department.

    b) Hash totals are commonly used to detect data entry errors but may also be used to test for completeness.

    c) A burglar alarm is another example.

3) Corrective controls correct the negative effects of unwanted events.

    a) An example is a requirement that all cost variances over a certain amount be justified.

4) Directive controls cause or encourage the occurrence of a desirable event.

    a) Policy and procedure manuals are common examples.

b. **Secondary Controls**

1) Compensatory (mitigative) controls may reduce risk when the primary controls are ineffective. However, they do not, by themselves, reduce risk to an acceptable level.

    a) An example is supervisory review when segregation of duties is not feasible.

2) Complementary controls work with other controls to reduce risk to an acceptable level.

    a) For example, separating the functions of accounting for and custody of cash receipts is complemented by obtaining deposit slips validated by the bank.

c. **Time-Based Classification**

1) Feedback controls report information about completed activities. They permit improvement in future performance by learning from past mistakes. Thus, corrective action occurs after the fact. Inspection of completed goods is an example.

2) Concurrent controls adjust ongoing processes. These real-time controls monitor activities in the present to prevent them from deviating too far from standards. An example is close supervision of production-line workers.

3) Feedforward controls anticipate and prevent problems. These controls require a long-term perspective. Organizational policies and procedures are examples.

d. **Financial vs. Operating Controls**

1) Financial controls should be based on relevant established accounting principles.

    a) Objectives of financial controls may include proper authorization; appropriate recordkeeping; safeguarding of assets; and compliance with laws, regulations, and contracts. These are sometimes called "accounting controls."

2) Operating controls apply to production and support activities. They are sometimes called "administrative controls."

    a) Because they may lack established criteria or standards, they should be based on management principles and methods. They also should be designed with regard to the management functions of planning, organizing, directing, and controlling.

    e.   **People-Based vs. System-Based Controls**

        1)   People-based controls are dependent on the intervention of humans for their proper operation, for example, regular performance of bank reconciliations.

            a)   Checklists, such as lists of required procedures for month-end closing, can be valuable to ensure that people-based controls are executed when needed.

        2)   System-based controls are executed whenever needed with no human intervention.

            a)   An example is code in a computerized purchasing system that prevents any purchase order over a certain monetary threshold from being submitted to the vendor without managerial approval.

            b)   Other examples include control totals, reasonableness checks, and sequence tests.

3. Control Activities

    a.   Control activities are designed and placed in operation to ensure that management's directives are executed. Hence, they should include the requisite steps to respond to the risks that threaten the attainment of organizational objectives.

        1)   For this purpose, controls should be suitably designed to prevent or detect unfavorable conditions arising from particular risk exposures. They also should be placed in operation and operate effectively. If controls are not always in force, they cannot operate effectively, no matter how effective their design.

        2)   Control procedures are implemented to manage or limit risk in accordance with the entity's risk assessments whenever risk exposures exist that threaten loss of assets or misstatements of accounting or management information.

        3)   Controls can be identified in the following areas:

            a)   Segregation of duties, including four basic functional responsibilities
            b)   Independent checks and verification
            c)   Safeguarding controls
            d)   Prenumbered forms
            e)   Specific document flow

4. Segregation of Duties

This subunit describes the types and provides examples of segregation of duties. As a CMA candidate, you must be able to identify and explain proper segregation of duties procedures. However, you should also be able to apply this concept to many different functions within the internal control process.

    a.   Segregation of duties involves assigning different employees to perform functions such that an employee acting alone is prevented from committing an error or concealing a fraud in the normal course of his/her duties.

        1)   Four types of functional responsibilities should be segregated:

            a)   The authority to execute transactions
            b)   Recordkeeping of the transaction
            c)   Custody of the assets affected by the transactions
            d)   Periodic reconciliation of the existing assets to recorded amounts

2)   EXAMPLE in the purchases-payables cycle:

    a)   The authority to execute transactions is vested in the purchasing department, not, for example, the treasurer.

    b)   Recordkeeping is done by accounts payable, not purchasing.

    c)   Custody of the assets involved is vested in the warehouse, not inventory control.

    d)   Periodic reconciliation of the existing assets to recorded amounts is performed by inventory control, not the warehouse.

3)   EXAMPLE in the sales-receivables cycle:

    a)   The authority to execute transactions is vested in the sales department, not, for example, the treasurer.

    b)   Recordkeeping is done by accounts receivable, not sales.

    c)   Custody of the assets involved is vested in the warehouse (in the case of the merchandise) and the treasurer (in the case of the cash).

    d)   Periodic reconciliation of the existing assets to recorded amounts is performed by the general ledger accounting group, not the treasurer.

4)   EXAMPLE in the payroll cycle:

    a)   The authority to execute transactions is vested in the human resources department, which authorizes the hiring and termination of employees and their rates of pay and deductions.

    b)   Recordkeeping is done by the payroll department.

    c)   Custody of the assets involved is vested in the treasurer.

    d)   Periodic reconciliation of the existing assets to recorded amounts is performed by the general ledger accounting group.

5)   The following memory aid is for the functions that should be kept separate for proper segregation of duties:

A	Authorization
R	Recordkeeping
C	Custody
R	Reconciliation

5.   **Independent Checks and Verification**

  a.   The reconciliation of recorded accountability with the assets must be performed by a part of the organization either (1) unconnected with the original transaction or (2) without custody of the assets involved.

    1)   A comparison revealing that the assets do not agree with the recorded accountability provides evidence of unrecorded or improperly recorded transactions.

      a)   The converse, however, does not necessarily follow. For example, agreement of a cash count with the recorded balance does not provide evidence that all cash received has been properly recorded.

    2)   The frequency of such comparisons for the purpose of safeguarding assets depends on the nature and amount of the assets involved and the cost of making the comparison.

      a)   For example, cash may be counted daily but raw materials inventory only annually.

  b.   EXAMPLE: The general ledger group performs monthly reconciliations of bank statements to the company's records. This is an independent check on the work of the treasury function.

6. **Safeguarding Controls**

    a.   Safeguarding controls limit access to an organization's assets to authorized personnel. Access includes both direct physical access and indirect access through the preparation or processing of documents that authorize the use or disposition of assets.

        1)   EXAMPLES:

            a)   A lockbox system for collecting cash receipts from customers

            b)   Daily, intact deposit of cash receipts after preparation and verification by two treasury employees

            c)   Approval of credit memos by the credit department, not sales

            d)   Writeoffs of uncollectible accounts by the supervisor of the credit department manager

            e)   Unescorted access to computer operations center prohibited to (1) all non-information systems personnel and (2) all non-operations information system personnel, such as developers

            f)   Online access to production application libraries prohibited to developers; online access to production databases prohibited to all users except the organizational "owners" of the data elements

            g)   Direct deposit of pay in lieu of distribution of physical paychecks; unclaimed paychecks held by the treasurer, not payroll

            h)   Holding of securities in safe deposit box; two employees always present when box is accessed

            i)   Physical measures taken to protect assets from natural disasters, e.g., floods, wind damage, earthquakes

7. **Prenumbered Forms**

    a.   Sequentially prenumbered forms are the basis for a strong set of internal controls. Receiving reports in the warehouse and purchase orders in the sales department are common examples.

        1)   When every hardcopy form is prenumbered, all can be accounted for; e.g., the date of their use and the person who filled them out can be ascertained. Any document in the sequence that is missing can be flagged for special scrutiny when it is processed.

            a)   During the periodic reconciliation, the verifying party can detect unrecorded and unauthorized transactions.

        2)   This functionality can be achieved even in a paperless environment. Applications can be coded to sequentially number initiated transactions, and proper review and approval can be verified online.

        3)   In addition to prenumbered forms, procedures ensuring that personnel do not receive documents inappropriate to their duties enhance internal control.

            a)   For example, documents authorizing the writeoff of uncollectible receivables should not be routed to cashiers. These cashiers could later pocket the money if a written-off account was subsequently paid.

8. **Compensating Controls**

    a. Compensating controls replace the normal controls, such as segregation of duties, when the latter cannot feasibly be implemented.

        1) For example, in the finance and investment cycle, top management may authorize and execute investments and have access to the records, stock certificates, etc. The compensating control in this case is for at least two people to perform each function.

            a) An alternative to performance of each function by at least two people is to provide oversight. Thus, the board may authorize an investment, with other functions (custody of stock certificates, management of the portfolio, and oversight of record keeping) performed by a top manager.

        2) Other compensating controls in the finance and investment cycle include periodic communications with the board, oversight by a committee of the board, and internal auditing's reconciliation of the securities portfolio with the recorded information.

9. **Fraud**

    a. Fraud differs from error because it is intentional. It typically involves pressures or incentives to engage in wrongdoing and a perceived opportunity to do so.

    b. Examples are fraudulent financial reporting and misappropriation of assets.

    c. Internal controls are designed to, among other things, prevent fraud. However, because of the concealment aspects of fraudulent activity (e.g., collusion or falsification of documents), the controls cannot give absolute assurance that material fraud will be prevented or detected.

Stop and review! You have completed the outline for this subunit. Study multiple-choice questions 7 through 35 beginning on page 349.

9.3 LEGAL ASPECTS OF INTERNAL CONTROL

1. **Foreign Corrupt Practices Act**

    a. The Foreign Corrupt Practices Act (FCPA), enacted in 1977, had its origins in the Watergate investigations. The FCPA is designed to prevent secret payments of corporate funds for purposes that Congress has determined to be contrary to public policy.

        1) The Act amends the Securities Exchange Act of 1934 to prohibit a domestic concern, including any person acting on its behalf, whether or not doing business overseas and whether or not registered with the SEC, from offering or authorizing corrupt payments to any

            a) Foreign official
            b) Foreign political party or official thereof
            c) Candidate for political office in a foreign country

        2) Only political payments to foreign officials are prohibited. Payments to foreign business owners or corporate officers are not addressed by the FCPA.

        3) Corrupt payments are payments for the purpose of inducing the recipient to act or refrain from acting so that the domestic concern might obtain or retain business.

            a) The FCPA prohibits a mere offer or promise of a bribe, even if it is not consummated.

      b) The FCPA prohibits payment of anything of value. De minimis gifts and tokens of hospitality are acceptable.

      c) Payments are prohibited if the person making them knew or should have known that some or all of them would be used to influence a governmental official.

4) Foreign officials do not include clerical or ministerial employees.

      a) EXAMPLE: Payments made to a clerk to expedite the processing of goods through customs may not be prohibited by the Act.

      b) Such payments are not prohibited as long as the recipient has no discretion in carrying out a governmental function.

      c) Payments that are allowed under the written law of the foreign country are also not prohibited.

5) Regardless of whether they have foreign operations, all public companies must make and keep books, records, and accounts in reasonable detail that accurately and fairly reflect transactions and dispositions of assets.

6) All public companies registered under the 1934 Act must devise and maintain a system of internal accounting control sufficient to provide reasonable assurance that

      a) Transactions are executed in accordance with management's general or specific authorization.

      b) Transactions are recorded as necessary to

         i) Permit preparation of financial statements in conformity with generally accepted accounting principles (GAAP) or any other criteria applicable to such statements and

         ii) Maintain accountability for assets.

      c) Access to assets is permitted only in accordance with management's general or specific authorization.

      d) The recorded accountability for assets is compared with the existing assets at reasonable intervals, and appropriate action is taken with respect to any differences.

7) The penalties for an individual for each criminal violation of the corrupt practices provisions are a fine of up to $100,000 or imprisonment for up to 5 years, or both. A corporation may be assessed a fine of up to $2,000,000 for violation of the same section.

      a) Fines imposed upon individuals may not be paid directly or indirectly by an employer.

8) The implications of the Foreign Corrupt Practices Act of 1977 extend well beyond its anti-bribery provisions.

      a) All American businesses and business people are involved. Management is particularly affected. The responsibility for internal control is not new, but the potential for civil and criminal liabilities represents an added burden.

      b) The impact of the law and the threat its ambiguities pose may alter business operations. Management might decide to abandon direct selling operations in foreign countries in favor of the use of foreign agents in hopes that this might lessen their "reason to know."

9)   A written code of ethics and conduct is a necessity. This code should be communicated and monitored by internal auditors for compliance.

    a)   The code might include an explanation of the Foreign Corrupt Practices Act and its penalties. A firm may require written representations from employees that they have read and understood the provisions of the code.

    b)   Written representations regarding compliance might also be requested at future times. Foreign agents should be made aware of the prohibitions of indirect payments.

2.   **Sarbanes-Oxley Act**

  a.   The Sarbanes-Oxley Act of 2002 was a response to numerous financial reporting scandals involving large public companies. The Act contains provisions that impose new responsibilities on public companies and their auditors. The Act applies to issuers of publicly traded securities subject to federal securities laws.

    1)   The Act requires that each member of the audit committee, including at least one who is a financial expert, be an independent member of the issuer's board of directors. An independent director is not affiliated with, and receives no compensation (other than for service on the board) from, the issuer.

      a)   The audit committee must be directly responsible for appointing, compensating, and overseeing the work of the public accounting firm employed by the issuer. In addition, this audit firm must report directly to the audit committee, not to management.

      b)   Another function of the audit committee is to implement procedures for the receipt, retention, and treatment of complaints about accounting and auditing matters.

      c)   The audit committee also must be appropriately funded by the issuer and may hire independent counsel or other advisors.

    2)   Prohibited nonaudit services. Section 201 of the Act lists several activities that cannot be performed on behalf of audit clients. See item 3. on page 341 for the detailed explanation.

    3)   Audit partner rotation. Section 203 of the Act requires the lead auditor and the reviewing partner to be rotated off the audit. See item 4. on page 341 for the detailed explanation.

    4)   Corporate responsibility of a public company. Section 302 requires periodic statutory financial reports to include certain certifications. See item 5. on page 342 for the detailed explanation.

    5)   Internal control report. Section 404 of the Act requires management to establish and document internal control procedures and to include in the annual report a report on the company's internal control over financial reporting.

      a)   This report is to include

        i)   A statement of management's responsibility for internal control;

        ii)   Management's assessment of the effectiveness of internal control as of the end of the most recent fiscal year;

        iii) Identification of the framework used to evaluate the effectiveness of internal control (such as the report of the Committee of Sponsoring Organizations);

        iv)   A statement about whether significant changes in controls were made after their evaluation, including any corrective actions; and

    v)   A statement that the external auditor has issued an attestation report
         on management's assessment.

         •   Because of this requirement, two audit opinions are
             expressed: one on internal control and one on the financial
             statements.

   b)   The external auditor must attest to and report on management's
        assessment.

        i)   The auditor must evaluate whether the structure and procedures

             •   Include records accurately and fairly reflecting the firm's
                 transactions

             •   Provide reasonable assurance that transactions are recorded
                 so as to permit statements to be prepared in accordance with
                 GAAP

        ii) The auditor's report also must describe any material weaknesses in
             internal controls.

        iii) The evaluation is not to be the subject of a separate engagement but
             be in conjunction with the audit of the financial statements.

3. **Sarbanes-Oxley Section 201. SERVICES OUTSIDE THE SCOPE OF PRACTICE OF
    AUDITORS**

   (a) *PROHIBITED ACTIVITIES - Section 10A of the Securities Exchange Act of 1934 is
        amended by adding the following: It shall be unlawful for a registered public accounting
        firm (and any associated person of that firm) that performs for any issuer any audit
        required by the rules of the Commission to provide to that issuer, contemporaneously
        with the audit, any non-audit service, including:*

        *(1) bookkeeping or other services related to the accounting records or financial
              statements of the audit client;*
        (2) financial information systems design and implementation;
        (3) appraisal or valuation services, fairness opinions, or contribution-in-kind reports;
        (4) actuarial services;
        (5) internal audit outsourcing services;
        (6) management functions or human resources;
        (7) broker or dealer, investment adviser, or investment banking services;
        (8) legal services and expert services unrelated to the audit; and
        (9) any other services that the Board determines, by regulation, is impermissible.

        *PREAPPROVAL REQUIRED FOR NON-AUDIT SERVICES - A registered public
        accounting firm may engage in any non-audit service, including tax services, that is
        not described above, for an audit client only if the activity is approved in advance by
        the audit committee of the client.*

   (b) *EXEMPTION AUTHORITY - The Board may, on a case-by-case basis, exempt any
        issuer, public accounting firm, or transaction from the prohibition provision to the extent
        that such exemption is necessary or appropriate in the public interest and is consistent
        with the protection of investors, and subject to review by the Commission.*

4. **Sarbanes-Oxley Section 203. AUDIT PARTNER ROTATION**

   a.   CPA firms must rotate audit partners so that the same individual is not supervising a
        client's audit for an extended period of time.

   (j) *It shall be unlawful for a registered public accounting firm to provide audit services to
        an issuer if the lead (or coordinating) audit partner (having primary responsibility for the
        audit), or the audit partner responsible for reviewing the audit, has performed audit
        services for that issuer in each of the five previous fiscal years of that issuer.*

5.   **Sarbanes-Oxley Section 302. CORPORATE RESPONSIBILITY FOR FINANCIAL REPORTS**

    (a)   *REGULATIONS REQUIRED - The SEC shall require, for each company filing periodic reports under the Securities Exchange Act of 1934, that the principal executive officer or officers and the principal financial officer or officers, or persons performing similar functions, certify in each annual or quarterly report filed or submitted under the Act that--*

        (1)   *the signing officer has reviewed the report;*

        (2)   *based on the officer's knowledge, the report does not contain any untrue statement of a material fact or omit to state a material fact necessary in order to make the statements made, in light of the circumstances under which such statements were made, not misleading;*

        (3)   *based on such officer's knowledge, the financial statements, and other financial information included in the report, fairly present in all material respects the financial condition and results of operations of the issuer as of, and for, the periods presented in the report;*

        (4)   *the signing officers--*

            (A)   *are responsible for establishing and maintaining internal controls;*

            (B)   *have designed such internal controls to ensure that material information relating to the issuer and its consolidated subsidiaries is made known to such officers by others within those entities, particularly during the period in which the periodic reports are being prepared;*

            (C)   *have evaluated the effectiveness of the issuer's internal controls as of a date within 90 days prior to the report; and*

            (D)   *have presented in the report their conclusions about the effectiveness of their internal controls based on their evaluation as of that date;*

        (5)   *the signing officers have disclosed to the issuer's auditors and the audit committee of the board of directors (or persons fulfilling the equivalent function)--*

            (A)   *all significant deficiencies in the design or operation of internal controls which could adversely affect the issuer's ability to record, process, summarize, and report financial data and have identified for the issuer's auditors any material weaknesses in internal controls; and*

            (B)   *any fraud, whether or not material, that involves management or other employees who have a significant role in the issuer's internal controls; and*

        (6)   *the signing officers have indicated in the report whether or not there were significant changes in internal controls or in other factors that could significantly affect internal controls subsequent to the date of their evaluation, including any corrective actions with regard to significant deficiencies and material weaknesses.*

    (b)   *FOREIGN REINCORPORATIONS HAVE NO EFFECT- Nothing in this section 302 shall be interpreted or applied in any way to allow any issuer to lessen the legal force of the statement required under this section 302, by an issuer having reincorporated or having engaged in any other transaction that resulted in the transfer of the corporate domicile or offices of the issuer from inside the United States to outside of the United States.*

6.   **The Public Company Accounting Oversight Board (PCAOB)**

    a.   The PCAOB was vested with the authority to promulgate standards for the practice of auditing. PCAOB Auditing Standard 2 (issued in 2004) required that an audit of internal control be integrated with the audit of the financial statements. Although auditors are allowed to issue separate reports on the audits of financial statements and internal controls, in practice they are most often combined into a single report.

b. In 2007, Auditing Standard 2 was superseded by PCAOB Auditing Standard 5, which had similar requirements.

   1) Standard No. 5 is principles-based. It is designed to increase the likelihood that material weaknesses in internal control will be found before they result in material misstatement of a company's financial statements and, at the same time, eliminate procedures that are unnecessary.

   2) The final standard also focuses the auditor on the procedures necessary to perform a high quality audit tailored to the company's facts and circumstances. The new standard is more risk-based and scalable, which will better meet the needs of investors, public companies and auditors alike.

   3) The new auditing standard, by focusing the auditor's attention on those matters that are most important to effective internal control, presents another significant opportunity to strengthen the financial reporting process.

7. **Four objectives of Auditing Standard 5**

a. Focus the Internal Control Audit on the Most Important Matters

   1) The new standard focuses auditors on those areas that present the greatest risk that a company's internal control will fail to prevent or detect a material misstatement in the financial statements. It does so by incorporating certain best practices designed to focus the scope of the audit on identifying material weaknesses in internal control, before they result in material misstatements of financial statements, such as using a top-down (risk-based) approach to plan the audit. It also emphasizes the importance of auditing higher risk areas, such as the financial statement closing process and controls designed to prevent fraud by management.

   2) At the same time, it provides auditors a range of alternatives for addressing lower risk areas, such as by more clearly demonstrating how to calibrate the nature, timing, and extent of testing based on risk, as well as how to incorporate knowledge accumulated in previous years' audits into the auditors' assessment of risk and use the work performed by companies' own personnel, when appropriate.

b. Eliminate Procedures that Are Unnecessary to Achieve the Intended Benefits

   1) The Board examined every area of the internal control audit to determine whether the previous standard encouraged auditors to perform procedures that are not necessary to achieve the intended benefits of the audit. As a result, the new standard does not include the previous standard's detailed requirements to evaluate management's own evaluation process and clarifies that an internal control audit does not require an opinion on the adequacy of management's process.

   2) As another example, the new standard refocuses the multi-location direction on risk rather than coverage by removing the requirement that auditors test a "large portion" of the company's operations or financial position.

c. Make the Audit Clearly Scalable to Fit the Size and the Complexity of Any Company

   1) In coordination with the Board's ongoing project to develop guidance for auditors of smaller, less complex companies, Standard 5 explains how to tailor internal control audits to fit the size and complexity of the company being audited. Standard 5 does so by including notes throughout the standard on how to apply the principles in the standard to smaller, less complex companies, and by including a discussion of the relevant attributes of smaller, less complex companies as well as less complex units of larger companies.

    d.   Simplify the Text of the Standard

        1)   The Board's new standard is shorter and easier to read. This is in part because it uses simpler terms to describe procedures and definitions. It is also because the standard has been streamlined and reorganized to begin with the audit itself, to move definitions and background information to appendices, and to avoid duplication by cross-referencing to existing concepts and requirements that appear elsewhere in the Board's standards and relevant laws and SEC rules.

        2)   For example, the new standard eliminates the previous standard's discussion of materiality, thus clarifying that the auditor's evaluation of materiality for purposes of an internal control audit is based on the same longstanding principles applicable to financial statement audits.

        3)   Also, in order to better coordinate the final standard and the SEC's new rules and management guidance, the new standard conforms certain terms to the SEC's rules and guidance, such as the definition of "material weakness" and use of the term "entity-level controls" instead of "company-level controls."

8.   **Audit Approaches**

    a.   Essentially there are four different audit approaches:

        1)   The substantive procedures approach
        2)   The balance sheet approach
        3)   The systems-based approach
        4)   The risk-based approach

    b.   The substantive procedures approach is also referred to as the vouching approach or the direct verification approach. In this approach, audit resources are targeted on testing large volumes of transactions and account balances without any particular focus on specified areas of the financial statements.

    c.   Under the balance sheet approach, substantive procedures are focused on balance sheet accounts, with only limited procedures being carried out on income statement/profit and loss accounts. The justification for this approach is the notion that if the relevant management assertions for all balance sheet accounts are tested and verified, then the income figure reported for the accounting period will not be materially misstated.

    d.   The systems-based approach requires auditors to assess the effectiveness of the internal controls, and then to direct substantive procedures primarily to those areas where it is considered that systems objectives will not be met. Reduced testing is carried out in those areas where it is considered systems objectives will be met.

    e.   With the risk-based approach, audit resources are directed towards those areas of the financial statements that may contain misstatements (either by error or omission) as a consequence of the risks faced by the business.

        1)   Under a risk-based approach, every audit assignment presents a different challenge to an auditor, with no two audits being the same. For example, no two entities are the same in terms of business sector, location, size, employees, governance issues, ethos, and complexity of operations. There is no one single approach to auditing that ensures the performance of a perfect audit. However, it is generally accepted that for most entities, the risk-based audit approach will minimize the possibility of audit objectives not being met.

2) Auditors are required to make risk assessments of material misstatements at the financial statement and assertion levels, based on an appropriate understanding of the entity and its environment, including internal controls. As the auditor is required to focus on the entity and its environment when making risk assessments, this is known as the "top down" approach to identifying risks. The word "top" refers to the day-to-day operations of the entity and the environment in which it operates; "down" refers to the financial statements of the entity.

3) In summary, this approach requires auditors to identify the key day-to-day risks faced by a business, to consider the impact these risks could have on the financial statements, and then to plan their audit procedures accordingly. For this reason, the approach is often referred to as the "business risk approach." When adopting this approach, to facilitate the identification of risks and the assessment of their effect on the financial statements, risks are categorized as financial risks, such as cash flow risks, compliance risks, such as breaching of laws and regulations risk, and operational risks, such as loss of key employee risk and loss of data risk.

Stop and review! You have completed the outline for this subunit. Study multiple-choice questions 36 through 38 on page 359.

9.4 CORE CONCEPTS

Risk and the Control Environment

- All systems of internal control involve **tradeoffs between cost and benefit.** For this reason, no system of internal control can be said to be "100% effective." Organizations accept the fact that risk can only be **mitigated, not eliminated**.

- **Risk can be quantified** as a combination of two factors: the severity of consequences and the likelihood of occurrence. The expected value of a loss due to a risk exposure can thus be stated numerically as the product of the two factors.

- An organization establishes a **system of internal control** to help it manage many of the risks it faces. The IMA refers to internal control as "the whole system of controls (financial and otherwise) ..." The proper design and operation of an organization's system of internal controls is the **responsibility of management**.

- An organization's **control environment** encompasses the **attitudes and actions** of the board of directors and upper management regarding the significance of control, i.e., the "tone at the top." The components include organizational structure, policies, objectives and goals, management philosophy and operating style, and assignment of authority and responsibility.

- The **audit committee** is a subcommittee of the board of directors whose purpose is to help keep the external auditors independent of management. This is accomplished by assigning the selection, compensation, and oversight of the external auditors to the audit committee. Many stock exchanges require a listed organization to have an audit committee.

- In its 1992 publication *Internal Control – Integrated Framework*, the Committee of Sponsoring Organizations of the Treadway Commission **(COSO)** defined internal control as providing reasonable assurance about the achievement of objectives in the areas of **effectiveness and efficiency** of operations, **reliability** of financial reporting, and **compliance** with applicable laws and regulation. Note that the Framework specifically cites reasonable, not absolute, assurance about the achievement of management's objectives.

- COSO's internal control framework consists of five interrelated components: (1) control environment, (2) risk assessment, (3) control activities, (4) information and communication, and (5) monitoring.

Control Procedures

- Primary controls include **preventive controls**, **detective controls**, **corrective controls**, and **directive controls**.

- **Control activities** are designed and placed in operation to ensure that management's directives are executed. **Control procedures** are implemented to manage or limit risk in accordance with the entity's risk assessments whenever risk exposures exist that threaten loss of assets or misstatements of accounting or management information.

- Controls can be identified in **these areas**: segregation of duties, including the four basic functional responsibilities; independent checks and verification; safeguarding controls; prenumbered forms; and specific document flow.

- **Segregation of duties** involves assigning different employees to perform functions such that an employee acting alone is prevented from committing an error or concealing a fraud in the normal course of his/her duties. **Four types** of functional responsibilities should be segregated: the authority to execute transactions, the recording of transactions, custody of the assets affected by the transactions, and periodic reconciliation of the existing assets to recorded amounts.

- **Compensating controls** replace the normal controls, such as segregation of duties, when the latter cannot feasibly be implemented. For example, in the finance and investment cycle, top management may authorize and execute investments and have access to the records, stock certificates, etc. The compensating control in this case is for at least two people to perform each function.

- **Fraud** differs from error because it is intentional. It typically involves pressures or incentives to engage in wrongdoing and a perceived opportunity to do so. Examples are fraudulent financial reporting and misappropriation of assets. Internal controls are designed to, among other things, prevent fraud. However, because of the concealment aspects of fraudulent activity (e.g., collusion or falsification of documents), the controls cannot give absolute assurance that material fraud will be prevented or detected.

Legal Aspects of Internal Control

- The **Foreign Corrupt Practices Act (FCPA)** is designed to prevent secret payments of corporate funds for purposes that Congress has determined to be contrary to public policy. The Act prohibits bribery of any foreign **official**, foreign **political party** or official thereof, or **candidate for political office** in a foreign country. Only political payments to foreign officials are prohibited. Payment to foreign business owners or corporate officers are not addressed by the FCPA.

- Regardless of whether they have foreign operations, the FCPA requires all public companies to make and keep **books, records, and accounts in reasonable detail** that accurately and fairly reflect transactions and dispositions of assets. All public companies must devise and maintain a **system of internal accounting control** sufficient to provide reasonable assurance that the basic goals of transaction authorization, financial reporting, and safeguarding of assets are achieved.

- The **Sarbanes-Oxley Act of 2002** applies to issuers of publicly traded securities subject to federal securities laws. The Act requires that each member of the **audit committee**, including at least one who is a financial expert, be an **independent** member of the issuer's board of directors. An independent director is not affiliated with, and receives no compensation (other than for service on the board) from, the issuer.

    - **Section 201** limits the types of consulting services that a CPA firm may provide for an audit client.

    - **Section 203** requires audit firms to rotate their lead and reviewing partners at least every 5 years.

- **Section 302** requires periodic statutory financial reports to include certifications that:
  - The signing officers have reviewed the report
  - The report does not contain any material untrue statements or material omission or be considered misleading
  - The financial statements and related information fairly present the financial condition and the results of operations in all material respects
  - The signing officers are responsible for internal controls and have evaluated these internal controls within the previous 90 days and have reported on their findings
  - A list of all deficiencies in the internal controls and information on any fraud that involves employees who are involved with internal activities
  - Any significant changes in internal controls or related factors that could have a negative impact on the internal controls

  Organizations may not attempt to avoid these requirements by reincorporating their activities or transferring their activities outside of the United States.

- **Section 404** requires management to **establish and document internal control procedures** and to include in the annual report a report on the company's internal control over financial reporting. The **external auditor must attest** to and report on management's assessment.

QUESTIONS
9.1 Risk and the Control Environment

1. One of the financial statement auditor's major concerns is to ascertain whether internal control is designed to provide reasonable assurance that

A. Profit margins are maximized, and operational efficiency is optimized.

B. The chief accounting officer reviews all accounting transactions.

C. Corporate morale problems are addressed immediately and effectively.

D. Financial reporting is reliable.

Answer (D) is correct. *(CMA, adapted)*
REQUIRED: The objective of internal control.
DISCUSSION: Internal control is designed to provide reasonable assurance of the achievement of objectives in the categories of (1) reliability of financial reporting, (2) effectiveness and efficiency of operations, and (3) compliance with laws and regulations. Controls relevant to a financial statement audit ordinarily pertain to the objective of preparing external financial statements that are fairly presented in conformity with GAAP or another comprehensive basis of accounting.
Answer (A) is incorrect. Many factors beyond the purview of the auditor affect profits, and the controls related to operational efficiency are usually not directly relevant to an audit. Answer (B) is incorrect. The chief accounting officer need not review all accounting transactions. Answer (C) is incorrect. Controls relevant to a financial statement audit do not concern the treatment of corporate morale problems.

2. The primary responsibility for establishing and maintaining internal control rests with

A. The external auditor.

B. Management.

C. The controller.

D. The treasurer.

Answer (B) is correct. *(CMA, adapted)*
REQUIRED: The person primarily responsible for establishing and maintaining internal control.
DISCUSSION: Establishing and maintaining internal control is the responsibility of management. Internal control is intended to provide reasonable assurance that the entity's objectives are achieved. Achievement of these objectives is the basic function of management.
Answer (A) is incorrect. Auditors must consider internal control, but they do not establish and maintain it. Answer (C) is incorrect. The controller is responsible only to the extent that (s)he is a part of the management team. Answer (D) is incorrect. The treasurer is responsible only to the extent that (s)he is a part of the management team.

3. Risk assessment is a process

   A. Designed to identify potential events that may affect the entity.

   B. That establishes policies and procedures to accomplish internal control objectives.

   C. Of identifying and capturing information in a timely fashion.

   D. That assesses the quality of internal control throughout the year.

Answer (A) is correct. *(CMA, adapted)*
   REQUIRED: The essence of the risk assessment process.
   DISCUSSION: Every organization faces risks, that is, unforeseen obstacles to the pursuit of its objectives. Risks take many forms and can originate from within or from outside the organization. Risk assessment is the process whereby management identifies the organization's vulnerabilities.
   Answer (B) is incorrect. Internal control objectives cannot be formulated until the organization knows what its vulnerabilities are. Answer (C) is incorrect. Identifying and capturing information in a timely fashion is a function of an information system, not of risk assessment. Answer (D) is incorrect. Assessing the quality of internal controls is a portion of the internal control department's ongoing duties; it is not a definition of risk assessment.

4. When management of the sales department has the opportunity to override the system of internal controls of the accounting department, a weakness exists in

   A. Risk management.

   B. Information and communication.

   C. Monitoring.

   D. The control environment.

Answer (D) is correct. *(CMA, adapted)*
   REQUIRED: The conceptual location of a weakness when one department can override another's internal controls.
   DISCUSSION: An organization's control environment encompasses the attitudes and actions of the board of directors and upper management regarding the significance of control, i.e., the "tone at the top." One of the components of the control environment is the assignment of authority and responsibility. For example, management defines key areas of authority and responsibility by placing the information technology, financial accounting, and treasury functions under separate officers. When the management of one department can override the internal controls of another, authority and responsibility have not been properly assigned.
   Answer (A) is incorrect. Risk management is the ongoing process of designing and operating internal controls that mitigate the risks identified in the organization's risk assessment. Answer (B) is incorrect. Information and communication are ongoing processes in every organization; they are not the basis for internal control. Answer (C) is incorrect. Monitoring cannot prevent damage done due to a system design flaw, such as one department being able to override another's internal controls.

5. Some account balances, such as those for pensions or leases, are the results of complex calculations. The susceptibility to material misstatements in these types of accounts is defined as

   A. Audit risk.

   B. Detection risk.

   C. Sampling risk.

   D. Inherent risk.

Answer (D) is correct. *(CMA, adapted)*
   REQUIRED: The susceptibility to material misstatements in account balances resulting from complex calculations.
   DISCUSSION: Inherent risk is the susceptibility of an assertion to a material misstatement in the absence of related controls. This risk is greater for some assertions and related balances or classes than others. For example, complex calculations are more likely to be misstated than simple ones, and cash is more likely to be stolen than an inventory of coal. Inherent risk exists independently of the audit.
   Answer (A) is incorrect. Audit risk is the risk that the auditor may unknowingly fail to appropriately modify an opinion on financial statements that are materially misstated. Answer (B) is incorrect. Detection risk is the risk that the auditor will not detect a material misstatement that exists in an assertion. Answer (C) is incorrect. Sampling risk is the risk that a particular sample may contain proportionately more or fewer monetary misstatements or deviations from controls than exist in the population as a whole.

6. There are three components of audit risk: inherent risk, control risk, and detection risk. Inherent risk is

   A. The susceptibility of an assertion to a material misstatement, assuming that there are no related internal control structure policies or procedures.

   B. The risk that the auditor may unknowingly fail to appropriately modify his or her opinion on financial statements that are materially misstated.

   C. The risk that a material misstatement that could occur in an assertion will not be prevented or detected on a timely basis by the entity's internal control structure policies or procedures.

   D. The risk that the auditor will not detect a material misstatement that exists in an assertion.

Answer (A) is correct. *(CMA, adapted)*
REQUIRED: The definition of inherent risk.
DISCUSSION: According to AU 312, "Inherent risk is the susceptibility of an assertion to a material misstatement, assuming that there are no related internal control structure policies or procedures. The risk of such misstatement is greater for some assertions and related balances or classes than for others." Unlike detection risk, inherent risk and control risk "are independent of the audit." Furthermore, inherent risk and control risk are inversely related to detection risk. Thus, the lower the inherent risk, the higher the acceptable detection risk.
Answer (B) is incorrect. The risk that the auditor may unknowingly fail to appropriately modify his/her opinion on financial statements that are materially misstated is audit risk. Answer (C) is incorrect. The risk that a material misstatement that could occur in an assertion will not be prevented or detected on a timely basis by the entity's internal control structure policies or procedures is control risk. Answer (D) is incorrect. The risk that the auditor will not detect a material misstatement that exists in an assertion is detection risk.

9.2 Control Procedures

7. A proper segregation of duties requires that an individual

   A. Authorizing a transaction records it.

   B. Authorizing a transaction maintain custody of the asset that resulted from the transaction.

   C. Maintaining custody of an asset be entitled to access the accounting records for the asset.

   D. Recording a transaction not compare the accounting record of the asset with the asset itself.

Answer (D) is correct. *(CMA, adapted)*
REQUIRED: The item required by proper segregation of duties.
DISCUSSION: One person should not be responsible for all phases of a transaction, i.e., for authorization, recording, and custodianship of the related assets. These duties should be performed by separate individuals to reduce the opportunities for any person to be in a position of both perpetrating and concealing errors or fraud in the normal course of his/her duties. For instance, an employee who receives and lists cash receipts should not be responsible for comparing the recorded accountability for cash with existing amounts.
Answer (A) is incorrect. Authorization and recordkeeping should be separate. Answer (B) is incorrect. Authorization and asset custody should be separate. Answer (C) is incorrect. Recordkeeping and asset custody should be separate.

8. When considering internal control over securities, the auditor is especially concerned about

   A. Access to stock certificates by the corporate controller.

   B. Access to stock certificates by the corporate treasurer.

   C. Preparation of accrual adjustments on bonds by the corporate controller.

   D. Approval of temporary stock investment purchases by the corporate treasurer or company president.

Answer (A) is correct. *(CMA, adapted)*
REQUIRED: The major concern of an auditor considering internal control over securities.
DISCUSSION: Access to stock certificates by the controller is a breakdown of the fundamental segregation of duties needed for effective internal control. The controller, who performs the accounting function, should not have access to the assets.
Answer (B) is incorrect. The treasurer, in the normal performance of the custodianship function, rightly has access to stock certificates. Answer (C) is incorrect. The controller prepares accrual adjustments on bonds, e.g., discount (premium) amortization. Answer (D) is incorrect. The approval of temporary stock purchases by the treasurer or the president is a typical delegation of authority by the board. However, the directors should periodically review this activity.

9. The procedure that would best discourage the resubmission of vendor invoices after they have been paid is

A. A requirement for double endorsement of checks.

B. The cancellation of vouchers by accounting personnel.

C. The cancellation of vouchers by treasurer personnel.

D. The mailing of payments directly to payees by accounting personnel.

Answer (C) is correct. *(CMA, adapted)*
REQUIRED: The procedure best discouraging resubmission of vendor invoices after payment.
DISCUSSION: Canceling vouchers and supporting papers (with perforations, ink, etc.) upon payment prevents the payment of a duplicate voucher. If the person signing the check does the canceling, the documents cannot be recycled for duplicate payments. Securing the paid-voucher file from access by the accounts payable clerk is another effective control.
Answer (A) is incorrect. A single endorsement is not a control weakness if the person who signs does not have incompatible functions and if proper documentation is required before signing. Answer (B) is incorrect. The vouchers should not be canceled before payment. Answer (D) is incorrect. Mailing payments directly to payees does not prevent a second use of invoices by unethical personnel. Also, record keepers should not have access to signed checks.

10. Organizational independence in the processing of payroll is achieved by functional separations that are built into the system. Which one of the following functional separations is **not** required for internal control purposes?

A. Separation of timekeeping from payroll preparation.

B. Separation of personnel function from payroll preparation.

C. Separation of payroll preparation and paycheck distribution.

D. Separation of payroll preparation and maintenance of year-to-date records.

Answer (D) is correct. *(CMA, adapted)*
REQUIRED: The functional separation that is not required for internal control purposes.
DISCUSSION: Most companies have their payrolls prepared by the same individuals who maintain the year-to-date records. There is no need for this functional separation because both duties involve recordkeeping.
Answer (A) is incorrect. Separating timekeeping and payroll preparation is an effective control. It prevents one person from claiming that an employee worked certain hours and then writing a check to that employee. Payment to an absent or fictitious employee would therefore require collusion between two employees. Answer (B) is incorrect. Personnel should be separate from payroll. The former authorizes the calculation of the payroll by the latter. Answer (C) is incorrect. Separating paycheck preparation from distribution makes it more difficult for fictitious employees to receive checks.

11. Internal control should follow certain basic principles to achieve its objectives. One of these principles is the segregation of functions. Which one of the following examples does **not** violate the principle of segregation of functions?

A. The treasurer has the authority to sign checks but gives the signature block to the assistant treasurer to run the check-signing machine.

B. The warehouse clerk, who has the custodial responsibility over inventory in the ware house, may authorize disposal of damaged goods.

C. The sales manager has the responsibility to approve credit and the authority to write off accounts.

D. The department time clerk is given the undistributed payroll checks to mail to absent employees.

Answer (A) is correct. *(CMA, adapted)*
REQUIRED: The situation that does not violate the principle of segregation of functions.
DISCUSSION: Control procedures include segregation of duties to reduce the risk that any person may be able to perpetrate and conceal errors or fraud in the normal course of his/her duties. Different persons should authorize transactions, record transactions, and maintain custody of assets. The treasurer's department should have custody of assets but should not authorize or record transactions. Because the assistant treasurer reports to the treasurer, the treasurer is merely delegating an assigned duty related to asset custody. The use of the check-signing machine does not conflict with any other duty of the assistant treasurer and does not involve authorization or recording of transactions.
Answer (B) is incorrect. Authorization to dispose of damaged goods could be used to cover thefts of inventory for which the warehouse clerk has custodial responsibility. Transaction authorization is inconsistent with asset custody. Answer (C) is incorrect. The sales manager could approve credit to a controlled company and then write off the account as a bad debt. The sales manager's authorization of credit is inconsistent with his/her indirect access to assets. Answer (D) is incorrect. The time clerk could conceal the termination of an employee and retain that employee's paycheck. Recordkeeping is inconsistent with asset custody.

12. If internal control is well designed, two tasks that should be performed by different persons are

A. Approval of bad debt write-offs, and reconciliation of the accounts payable subsidiary ledger and controlling account.

B. Distribution of payroll checks and approval of sales returns for credit.

C. Posting of amounts from both the cash receipts journal and cash payments journal to the general ledger.

D. Recording of cash receipts and preparation of bank reconciliations.

Answer (D) is correct. *(CMA, adapted)*
REQUIRED: The tasks that should be performed by different persons if internal control is well designed.
DISCUSSION: Recording of cash establishes accountability for assets. The bank reconciliation compares that recorded accountability with actual assets. The recording of cash receipts and preparation of bank reconciliations should therefore be performed by different individuals since the preparer of a reconciliation could conceal a cash shortage. For example, if a cashier both prepares the bank deposit and performs the reconciliation, (s)he could embezzle cash and conceal the theft by falsifying the reconciliation.
Answer (A) is incorrect. There is no conflict between writing off bad debts (accounts receivable) and reconciling accounts payable, which are liabilities. Answer (B) is incorrect. Distribution of payroll checks and approval of sales returns are independent functions. People who perform such disparate tasks are unlikely to be able to perpetrate and conceal a fraud. In fact, some companies use personnel from an independent function to distribute payroll checks. Answer (C) is incorrect. Posting both ledgers would cause no conflict as long as the individual involved did not have access to the actual cash. If a person has access to records but not the assets, there is no danger of embezzlement without collusion.

13. Which one of the following situations represents an internal control weakness in the payroll department?

A. Payroll department personnel are rotated in their duties.

B. Paychecks are distributed by the employees' immediate supervisor.

C. Payroll records are reconciled with quarterly tax reports.

D. The timekeeping function is independent of the payroll department.

Answer (B) is correct. *(CMA, adapted)*
REQUIRED: The internal control weakness in the payroll department.
DISCUSSION: Paychecks should not be distributed by supervisors because an unscrupulous person could terminate an employee and fail to report the termination. The supervisor could then clock in and out for the employee and keep the paycheck. A person unrelated to either payroll recordkeeping or the operating department should distribute checks.
Answer (A) is incorrect. Periodic rotation of payroll personnel inhibits the perpetration and concealment of fraud. Answer (C) is incorrect. This analytical procedure may detect a discrepancy. Answer (D) is incorrect. Timekeeping should be independent of asset custody and employee records.

14. Which one of the following situations represents a strength of internal control for purchasing and accounts payable?

A. Prenumbered receiving reports are issued randomly.

B. Invoices are approved for payment by the purchasing department.

C. Unmatched receiving reports are reviewed on an annual basis.

D. Vendors' invoices are matched against purchase orders and receiving reports before a liability is recorded.

Answer (D) is correct. *(CMA, adapted)*
REQUIRED: The strength in internal control relevant to purchasing and accounts payable.
DISCUSSION: A voucher should not be prepared for payment until the vendor's invoice has been matched against the corresponding purchase order and receiving report. This procedure provides assurance that a valid transaction has occurred and that the parties have agreed on the terms, such as price and quantity.
Answer (A) is incorrect. Prenumbered receiving reports should be issued sequentially. A gap in the sequence may indicate an erroneous or fraudulent transaction. Answer (B) is incorrect. Invoices should not be approved by purchasing. That is the job of the accounts payable department. Answer (C) is incorrect. Annual review of unmatched receiving reports is too infrequent. More frequent attention is necessary to remedy deficiencies in internal control.

15. Auditors document their understanding of internal control with questionnaires, flowcharts, and narrative descriptions. A questionnaire consists of a series of questions concerning controls that auditors consider necessary to prevent or detect errors and fraud. The most appropriate question designed to contribute to the auditors' understanding of the completeness of the expenditure (purchases-payables) cycle concerns the

A. Internal verification of quantities, prices, and mathematical accuracy of sales invoices.

B. Use and accountability of prenumbered checks.

C. Disposition of cash receipts.

D. Qualifications of accounting personnel.

Answer (B) is correct. *(CMA, adapted)*
   REQUIRED: The most appropriate question designed to contribute to the auditors' understanding of the completeness of the expenditure cycle.
   DISCUSSION: A completeness assertion concerns whether all transactions and accounts that should be presented in the financial statements are so presented. The exclusive use of sequentially numbered documents facilitates control over expenditures. An unexplained gap in the sequence alerts the auditor to the possibility that not all transactions have been recorded. A failure to use prenumbered checks would therefore suggest a higher assessment of control risk. If a company uses prenumbered checks, it should be easy to determine exactly which checks were used during a period.
   Answer (A) is incorrect. Determination of proper amounts of sales invoices concerns the valuation assertion. Also, sales invoices are part of the sales-receivables (revenue) cycle. Answer (C) is incorrect. Cash receipts are part of the revenue cycle. Answer (D) is incorrect. Consideration of the qualifications of accounting personnel is not a test of controls over the completeness of any cycle. This procedure is appropriate during the consideration of the control environment.

16. When an organization has strong internal control, management can expect various benefits. The benefit **least** likely to occur is

A. Reduced cost of an external audit.

B. Elimination of employee fraud.

C. Availability of reliable data for decision-making purposes.

D. Some assurance of compliance with the Foreign Corrupt Practices Act of 1977.

Answer (B) is correct. *(CMA, adapted)*
   REQUIRED: The least likely benefit from a strong internal control.
   DISCUSSION: Even the best internal control cannot guarantee the complete elimination of employee fraud. Effective internal control will reduce the amount of employee fraud and probably detect losses on a timely basis.
   Answer (A) is incorrect. It is a benefit of strong internal control. The cost of the external audit will be lower because of the reduction of the audit effort related to substantive testing. Answer (C) is incorrect. It is a benefit of strong internal control. Management will have better data for decision-making purposes. Answer (D) is incorrect. It is a benefit of strong internal control. Management will have some assurance of compliance with the FCPA.

17. Which one of the following would **not** be considered an internal control structure policy or procedure relevant to a financial statement audit?

A. Maintenance of control over unused checks.

B. Periodic reconciliation of perpetual inventory records to the general ledger control account.

C. Comparison of physical inventory counts to perpetual inventory records.

D. Timely reporting and review of quality control results.

Answer (D) is correct. *(CMA, adapted)*
   REQUIRED: The example of a control unrelated to a financial statement audit.
   DISCUSSION: Policies and procedures relevant to a financial statement audit pertain to the entity's ability to record, process, summarize, and report financial data consistent with the assertions in the financial statements. Other policies and procedures may not be relevant to a financial statement audit, e.g., those concerning the effectiveness, economy, and efficiency of certain management decision-making processes (AU 319). Production controls, such as quality control reports, may fall in the latter category.

18. Which one of the following situations represents an internal control weakness in accounts receivable?

A. Internal auditors confirm customer accounts periodically.

B. Delinquent accounts are reviewed only by the sales manager.

C. The cashier is denied access to customers' records and monthly statements.

D. Customers' statements are mailed monthly by the accounts receivable department.

Answer (B) is correct. *(CMA, adapted)*
   REQUIRED: The internal control weakness in accounts receivable.
   DISCUSSION: Internal control over accounts receivable begins with a proper separation of duties. Hence, the cashier, who performs an asset custody function, should not be involved in recordkeeping. Accounts should be periodically confirmed by an auditor, and delinquent accounts should be reviewed by the head of accounts receivable and the credit manager. Customer statements should be mailed monthly by the accounts receivable department without allowing access to the statements by employees of the cashier's department. The sales manager should not be the only person to review delinquent accounts because (s)he may have an interest in not declaring an account uncollectible.

19. Control risk is the risk that a material misstatement in an account will not be prevented or detected on a timely basis by the client's internal control structure policies or procedures. The best control procedure to prevent or detect fictitious payroll transactions is

A. To use and account for prenumbered payroll checks.

B. Personnel department authorization for hiring, pay rate, job status, and termination.

C. Internal verification of authorized pay rates, computations, and agreement with the payroll register.

D. Periodic independent bank reconciliations of the payroll bank account.

Answer (B) is correct. *(CMA, adapted)*
REQUIRED: The best control procedure to prevent or detect fictitious payroll transactions.
DISCUSSION: The payroll department is responsible for assembling payroll information (recordkeeping). The personnel department is responsible for authorizing employee transactions such as hiring, firing, and changes in pay rates and deductions. Segregating the recording and authorization functions helps prevent fraud.
Answer (A) is incorrect. Prenumbering of payroll checks is a control procedure to ensure the completeness of accounting records, but it will not prevent fictitious or previously terminated employees from receiving checks. Answer (C) is incorrect. A test for mathematical accuracy does not prevent or detect fictitious transactions. Answer (D) is incorrect. Reconciling the accounting records to the bank statement is a test of the accuracy of the cash balance.

20. One characteristic of an effective internal control structure is the proper segregation of duties. The combination of responsibilities that would **not** be considered a violation of segregation of functional responsibilities is

A. Signing of paychecks and custody of blank payroll checks.

B. Preparation of paychecks and check distribution.

C. Approval of time cards and preparation of paychecks.

D. Timekeeping and preparation of payroll journal entries.

Answer (D) is correct. *(CMA, adapted)*
REQUIRED: The combination of responsibilities not considered a violation of the separation of duties requirement.
DISCUSSION: Combining the timekeeping function and the preparation of the payroll journal entries would not be improper because the employee has no access to assets or to employee records in the personnel department. Only through collusion could an embezzlement be perpetrated. Accordingly, the functions of authorization, recordkeeping, and custodianship remain separate.
Answer (A) is incorrect. Persons with recordkeeping but not custody of assets responsibilities should have access to blank checks, while the duty of signing checks (custodianship) should be assigned to persons (e.g., the treasurer) with no recordkeeping function. Answer (B) is incorrect. Payroll preparation and payment to employees should be segregated since they are incompatible recordkeeping and custodianship functions. Answer (C) is incorrect. Approval of time cards is an authorization function that is incompatible with the recordkeeping function of preparation of paychecks.

21. According to SAS 55 (AU 319), *Consideration of the Internal Control in a Financial Statement Audit*, an entity's internal control structure (ICS) consists of the policies and procedures established to provide reasonable assurance that specific entity objectives will be achieved. Only some of these objectives, policies, and procedures are relevant to a financial statement audit. Which one of the following would most likely be considered in such an audit?

A. Timely reporting and review of quality control results.

B. Maintenance of control over unused checks.

C. Marketing analysis of sales generated by advertising projects.

D. Maintenance of statistical production analyses.

Answer (B) is correct. *(CMA, adapted)*
REQUIRED: The procedure most likely relevant to a financial statement audit.
DISCUSSION: The policies and procedures most likely to be relevant to a financial statement audit pertain to the entity's ability to record, process, summarize, and report financial data consistent with the assertions embodied in the financial statements. Maintenance of control over unused checks is an example of a relevant procedure because the objective is to safeguard cash. The auditor must understand the ICS policies and procedures relevant to the assertions about cash in the financial statements. (S)he must then assess control risk for those assertions; that is, (s)he must evaluate the effectiveness of the ICS in preventing or detecting material misstatements in the assertions.

22. In an automated payroll processing environment, a department manager substituted the time card for a terminated employee with a time card for a fictitious employee. The fictitious employee had the same pay rate and hours worked as the terminated employee. The best control technique to detect this action using employee identification numbers would be a

   A. Batch total.

   B. Record count.

   C. Hash total.

   D. Subsequent check.

Answer (C) is correct. *(CMA, adapted)*
   REQUIRED: The control to detect a fictitious employee.
   DISCUSSION: A hash total of employee numbers would detect such a substitution although the termination had not yet been recorded. A hash total is an otherwise meaningless control total, such as the total of employee numbers or invoice numbers, that is used to verify data. Thus, the hash total for the employee listing by the personnel department could be compared with the total generated during the payroll run.
   Answer (A) is incorrect. A batch total, such as a financial total, summarizes one information field, such as pay or hours worked, in a group of documents. In this question, this item would have appeared to be correct. Answer (B) is incorrect. A record count is a control total of the number of records processed during the operation of a program. In this question, the number of documents was correct, assuming that the termination had not yet been recorded. Answer (D) is incorrect. A hash total would detect the irregularity more quickly and easily than a subsequent check.

23. Payroll systems should have elaborate controls to prevent, detect, and correct errors and unauthorized tampering. The best set of controls for a payroll system includes

   A. Batch and hash totals, record counts of each run, proper separation of duties, special control over unclaimed checks, and backup copies of activity and master files.

   B. Employee supervision, batch totals, record counts of each run, and payments by check.

   C. Passwords and user codes, batch totals, employee supervision, and record counts of each run.

   D. Sign tests, limit tests, passwords and user codes, online edit checks, and payments by check.

Answer (A) is correct. *(CMA, adapted)*
   REQUIRED: The best set of controls over payroll.
   DISCUSSION: Controls in a payroll system should include a proper separation of the functions of authorization, recordkeeping, and custody of assets; batch totals for such items as hours worked and payroll amounts; hash totals (e.g., of employee identification numbers) to test for completeness of processing; record counts for each run; special control over unclaimed checks (the person who distributes checks must not retain unclaimed checks); and backup copies of files to allow for reconstruction if information is lost.

24. Accounting controls are concerned with the safeguarding of assets and the reliability of financial records. Consequently, these controls are designed to provide reasonable assurance that all of the following take place **except**

   A. Permitting access to assets in accordance with management's authorization.

   B. Executing transactions in accordance with management's general or specific authorization.

   C. Compliance with methods and procedures ensuring operational efficiency and adherence to managerial policies.

   D. Comparing recorded assets with existing assets at periodic intervals and taking appropriate action with respect to differences.

Answer (C) is correct. *(CMA, adapted)*
   REQUIRED: The item for which an accounting control does not provide reasonable assurance.
   DISCUSSION: An accounting control is concerned with the safeguarding of assets and the reliability of financial records, whereas an operational or administrative control is concerned with operational efficiency and effectiveness. Thus, compliance with methods and procedures ensuring operational efficiency and adherence to managerial policies is an objective of an operational control.
   Answer (A) is incorrect. Control objectives concerning the entity's ability to record, process, summarize, and report financial data include management authorization of access to assets. Answer (B) is incorrect. Control objectives concerning the entity's ability to record, process, summarize, and report financial data include proper authorization of transactions. Answer (D) is incorrect. Control objectives concerning the entity's ability to record, process, summarize, and report financial data include comparison of recorded accountability with assets at reasonable intervals.

25. The reporting of accounting information plays a central role in the regulation of business operations. The importance of sound internal control practices is underscored by the Foreign Corrupt Practices Act of 1977 which requires publicly owned U.S. corporations to maintain systems of internal control that meet certain minimum standards. Preventive controls are an integral part of virtually all accounting processing systems, and much of the information generated by the accounting system is used for preventive control purposes. Which one of the following is **not** an essential element of a sound preventive control system?

A. Separation of responsibilities for the recording, custodial, and authorization functions.

B. Sound personnel practices.

C. Documentation of policies and procedures.

D. Implementation of state-of-the-art software and hardware.

Answer (D) is correct. *(CMA, adapted)*
REQUIRED: The item not an essential preventive control for an accounting system.
DISCUSSION: Preventive controls are designed to prevent an error or irregularity from occurring. State-of-the-art hardware and software would presumably incorporate the latest control features, but a less advanced system could very well contain a sound preventive control structure. Hence, state-of-the-art components are not essential for effective control.
Answer (A) is incorrect. Segregation of functions makes it more difficult for one person both to perpetrate and conceal an irregularity. Answer (B) is incorrect. Hiring honest and capable employees prevents many problems. Answer (C) is incorrect. Documentation provides a guide for conduct.

26. If employee paychecks are distributed by hand to employees, which one of the following departments should be responsible for the safekeeping of unclaimed paychecks?

A. Payroll Department.

B. Timekeeping Department.

C. Production Department in which the employee works or worked.

D. Cashier Department.

Answer (D) is correct. *(CMA, adapted)*
REQUIRED: The department that should be responsible for the safekeeping of unclaimed paychecks.
DISCUSSION: The responsibility for unclaimed paychecks should be given to a department that has no opportunity to authorize or write those checks. Because the treasury function serves only an asset custody function and thus has had no input into the paycheck process, it is the logical repository of unclaimed checks.
Answer (A) is incorrect. The Payroll Department was responsible for causing the check to be written. Answer (B) is incorrect. The Timekeeping Department authorized payment based on a certain number of hours worked. Answer (C) is incorrect. A production supervisor or fellow worker has an opportunity to intercept the check of a fictitious or terminated employee.

27. Organizational independence is required in the processing of customers' orders in order to maintain an internal control structure. Which one of the following situations is **not** a proper separation of duties in the processing of orders from customers?

A. Approval by Credit Department of a sales order prepared by the Sales Department.

B. Shipping of goods by the Shipping Department that have been retrieved from stock by the Finished Goods Storeroom Department.

C. Invoice preparation by the Billing Department and posting to customers' accounts by the Accounts Receivable Department.

D. Approval of a sales credit memo because of a product return by the Sales Department with subsequent posting to the customer's account by the Accounts Receivable Department.

Answer (D) is correct. *(CMA, adapted)*
REQUIRED: The situation not a proper separation of duties in the processing of customer orders.
DISCUSSION: Allowing a sales department to approve a credit memo without a receiving report would be dangerous. Sales personnel could overstate sales in one period and then reverse them in subsequent periods. Thus, a copy of the receiving report for returned goods should be sent to the billing department for preparation of a credit memo after approval by a responsible supervisor who is independent of the Sales Department.

Questions 28 through 31 are based on the following information.

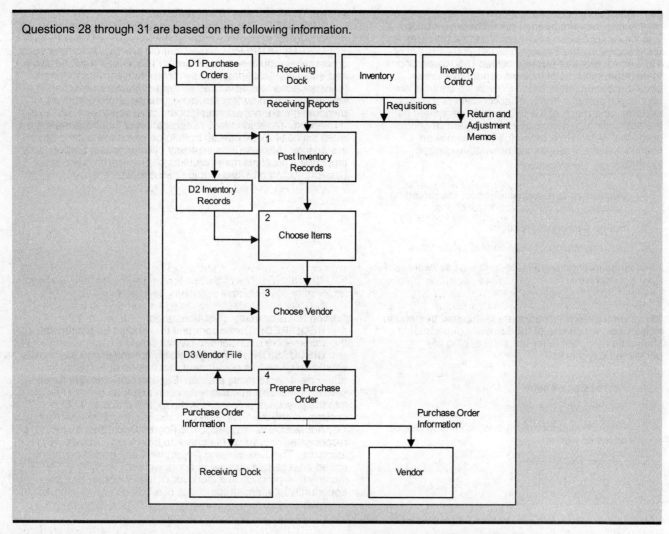

28. The initiation of the purchase of materials and supplies would be the responsibility of the

A. Purchasing Department.

B. Stores Control Department.

C. Inventory Control Department.

D. Production Department.

Answer (C) is correct.   *(CMA, adapted)*

REQUIRED: The department responsible for initiating the purchase of materials and supplies.

DISCUSSION: The Inventory Control Department would be responsible for initiating a purchase. It has access to the inventory records and would therefore know when stocks were getting low.

Answer (A) is incorrect. Purchasing places orders that have been initiated and authorized by others. Answer (B) is incorrect. Stores Control has custody of materials; it does not maintain inventory records. Answer (D) is incorrect. The Production Department manufactures goods and obtains materials from Stores Control.

29. Multiple copies of the purchase order are prepared for recordkeeping and distribution with a copy of the purchase order sent to the vendor and one retained by the Purchasing Department. In addition, for proper informational flow and internal control purposes, a version of the purchase order would be distributed to the

    A. Accounts Payable, Receiving, and Stores Control Departments.

    B. Accounts Payable, Receiving, and Inventory Control Departments.

    C. Accounts Payable, Accounts Receivable, and Receiving Departments.

    D. Accounts Payable, Receiving, and Production Planning Departments.

Answer (B) is correct. *(CMA, adapted)*
    REQUIRED: The recipients of purchase order copies.
    DISCUSSION: The Accounts Payable Department should receive a copy of the purchase order for internal control purposes to ensure that all invoices paid are for properly authorized items. The Receiving Department should receive a copy (with the quantity omitted to encourage an honest count) so that its employees will know that incoming shipments were authorized and should be accepted. In addition, the department issuing the purchasing requisition (the Inventory Control Department) should receive a copy as a notification that the order has been placed.
    Answer (A) is incorrect. Stores Control does not need to know that a purchase has been initiated. Answer (C) is incorrect. Accounts Receivable does not need a copy. Answer (D) is incorrect. Production Planning does not need a copy.

30. Responsibility for following up on any problems regarding orders of production materials and supplies, such as orders for which no acknowledgment has been received, orders overdue, partial orders, damaged or substandard merchandise received on an order, etc., would be entrusted to the

    A. Inventory Control Department.

    B. Stores Control Department.

    C. Production Planning Department.

    D. Purchasing Department.

Answer (D) is correct. *(CMA, adapted)*
    REQUIRED: The department responsible for following up on orders after the purchase order has been sent.
    DISCUSSION: The Purchasing Department is in the best position to follow up on purchase orders because it is the department closest to the vendors. In effect, the Purchasing Department is fully responsible for all communications with the vendor from the time a purchase order is issued until the goods are received.
    Answer (A) is incorrect. The Inventory Control Department should not have to follow up on orders once the purchase requisition has been sent. Answer (B) is incorrect. The Stores Department is responsible only for the security of goods once they are received. Answer (C) is incorrect. Production Planning is concerned only with the types and quantities of products to be produced.

31. The documents that the Accounts Payable Department must review before it can properly authorize payment for the purchase of materials and supplies are

    A. Vendor's invoice, purchase requisition, and acknowledgment purchase order.

    B. Vendor's invoice, acknowledgment purchase order, and receiving report.

    C. Vendor's monthly statement, purchase order, and voucher.

    D. Vendor's invoice, purchase order, and receiving report.

Answer (D) is correct. *(CMA, adapted)*
    REQUIRED: The documents that Accounts Payable must review before authorizing payment for purchases.
    DISCUSSION: The Accounts Payable Department prepares a voucher from a vendor's invoice only after examining supporting documents. These include a properly authorized purchase order and a receiving report stating quantities received and their condition.

32. The document that is the authorization to initiate the manufacture of goods is referred to as a

    A. Daily production schedule.

    B. Raw materials requisition.

    C. Bill of materials.

    D. Production order.

Answer (D) is correct. *(CMA, adapted)*
    REQUIRED: The document that is an authorization to initiate the manufacture of goods.
    DISCUSSION: The Production Planning Department uses a production order to authorize the Production Department to manufacture a specific product.
    Answer (A) is incorrect. The daily production schedule is used to plan a variety of manufacturing activities. Answer (B) is incorrect. A raw materials requisition is sent from the Production Department to inventory control to obtain materials needed for production. Answer (C) is incorrect. A bill of materials is a list of the components in a particular product.

33. For an internal audit department to be considered as a relevant internal control by the external auditor, the internal auditor must

   A. Be independent of the accounting function.

   B. Be cost effective.

   C. Perform operational audits.

   D. Use statistical sampling procedures.

Answer (A) is correct. *(CMA, adapted)*
   REQUIRED: The criterion the internal auditor must meet to be considered a relevant internal control by the external auditor.
   DISCUSSION: The internal auditor and the internal audit department can only be an effective control relevant to financial statement audits if the chief internal auditor reports to the board of directors or someone else outside the accounting function. Internal auditing must be independent to be effective.
   Answer (B) is incorrect. Intangible benefits may render an internal audit function an effective control even if it is not cost effective. It may not be good management to have an internal auditor who is not cost effective, but that does not affect the internal audit function's status as a control. Answer (C) is incorrect. Operational audits deal with effectiveness and efficiency and thus would not influence the effectiveness of the auditor as a control relevant to financial statement audits. Answer (D) is incorrect. An effective control need not use statistical procedures.

34. One of the steps in assessing control risk in a computerized information control system is identifying necessary controls to prevent data from being lost, added, duplicated, or altered during processing. An example of this type of control is the

   A. Authorization and approval of data in user departments and screening of data by data control groups.

   B. Review of data output by data control groups.

   C. Use of external and internal file labels.

   D. Use of control totals, limit and reasonableness checks, and sequence tests.

Answer (D) is correct. *(CMA, adapted)*
   REQUIRED: The control that will prevent data from being lost, added, duplicated, or altered during computer processing.
   DISCUSSION: A control total is an application control that may consist of a count of the number of records processed at different stages of the operation. Comparison of the counts indicates whether all records have been processed or some have been added. A control total might also consist of a total of one information field for all records processed, such as the total sales dollars for a batch of sales invoices. A limit or reasonableness check tests whether the value of a field falls outside a prescribed range. The range may be stated in terms of an upper limit, lower limit, or both. The loss, addition, etc., of data may result in an unreasonable value. A sequence test verifies the ordering of records and may therefore detect various anomalies.
   Answer (A) is incorrect. Authorization and approval by users and review by control groups are controls that do not function during processing. Answer (B) is incorrect. Review by control groups is a control that does not function during processing. Answer (C) is incorrect. Use of internal and external labels is an organizational, not a processing, control. External labels allow the computer operator to determine whether the correct file has been selected for an application. External labels are gummed-paper labels attached to a tape reel or other storage medium that identify the file. Internal labels perform the same function through the use of machine-readable identification in the first record in a file.

35. In a well-designed internal control structure in which the cashier receives remittances from the mail room, the cashier should **not**

   A. Endorse the checks.

   B. Prepare the bank deposit slip.

   C. Deposit remittances daily at a local bank.

   D. Post the receipts to the accounts receivable subsidiary ledger cards.

Answer (D) is correct. *(CMA, adapted)*
   REQUIRED: The activity that the cashier should not perform.
   DISCUSSION: The cashier is an assistant to the treasurer and thus performs an asset custody function. Individuals with custodial functions should not have access to the accounting records. If the cashier were allowed to post the receipts to the accounts receivable subsidiary ledger, an opportunity for embezzlement would arise that could be concealed by falsifying the books.

9.3 Legal Aspects of Internal Control

36. The requirement of the Foreign Corrupt Practices Act of 1977 to devise and maintain adequate internal control is assigned in the Act to the

A. Chief financial officer.

B. Board of directors.

C. Director of internal auditing.

D. Company as a whole with no designation of specific persons or positions.

Answer (D) is correct. *(CMA, adapted)*
REQUIRED: The person in a company responsible for compliance with the FCPA.
DISCUSSION: The accounting requirements apply to all public companies that must register under the Securities Exchange Act of 1934. The responsibility is thus placed on companies, not individuals.
Answer (A) is incorrect. Compliance with the FCPA is not the specific responsibility of the chief financial officer. Answer (B) is incorrect. Compliance with the FCPA is not the specific responsibility of the board of directors. Answer (C) is incorrect. Compliance with the FCPA is not the specific responsibility of the director of internal auditing.

37. The Sarbanes-Oxley Act has strengthened auditor independence by requiring that management

A. Engage auditors to report in accordance with the Foreign Corrupt Practices Act.

B. Report the nature of disagreements with former auditors.

C. Select auditors through audit committees.

D. Hire a different CPA firm from the one that performs the audit to perform the company's tax work.

Answer (C) is correct. *(CPA, adapted)*
REQUIRED: The Sarbanes-Oxley requirement that strengthened auditor independence.
DISCUSSION: The Sarbanes-Oxley Act requires that the audit committee of a public company hire and pay the external auditors. Such affiliation inhibits management from changing auditors to gain acceptance of a questionable accounting method. Also, a potential successor auditor must inquire of the predecessor auditor before accepting an engagement.
Answer (A) is incorrect. The SEC does not require an audit report in accordance with the FCPA. Answer (B) is incorrect. Reporting the nature of disagreements with auditors has been a long-time SEC requirement. Answer (D) is incorrect. The Sarbanes-Oxley Act does not restrict who may perform a company's tax work. Other types of engagements, such as the outsourcing of the internal audit function and certain consulting services, are limited.

38. A major impact of the Foreign Corrupt Practices Act of 1977 is that registrants subject to the Securities Exchange Act of 1934 are now required to

A. Keep records that reflect the transactions and dispositions of assets and to maintain a system of internal accounting controls.

B. Provide access to records by authorized agencies of the federal government.

C. Prepare financial statements in accord with international accounting standards.

D. Produce full, fair, and accurate periodic reports on foreign commerce and/or foreign political party affiliations.

Answer (A) is correct. *(CMA, adapted)*
REQUIRED: The major impact of the Foreign Corrupt Practices Act of 1977.
DISCUSSION: The main purpose of the Foreign Corrupt Practices Act of 1977 is to prevent bribery by firms that do business in foreign countries. A major ramification is that it requires all companies that must register with the SEC under the Securities Exchange Act of 1934 to maintain adequate accounting records and a system of internal accounting control.
Answer (B) is incorrect. Authorized agents of the federal government already have access to records of SEC registrants. Answer (C) is incorrect. Although some international accounting standards have been promulgated, they are incomplete and have not gained widespread acceptance. Answer (D) is incorrect. There are no requirements for providing periodic reports on foreign commerce or foreign political party affiliations.

Use Gleim **CMA Test Prep** Software for interactive testing with **additional multiple-choice questions!**

*Page
Intentionally
Left Blank*

9.5 ESSAY QUESTIONS

Scenario for Essay Questions 1, 2, 3

Micro Dynamics, a developer of database software packages, is a publicly held company whose stock is traded over the counter. The company recently received an enforcement release proceeding through an SEC Administrative Law Judge that cited the company for inadequate internal controls. In response, Micro Dynamics has agreed to establish an internal audit function and strengthen its audit committee.

A manager of the Internal Audit Department was recently hired as a result of the SEC enforcement action to establish an internal audit function. In addition, the composition of the audit committee has been changed to include all outside directors. Micro Dynamics has held its initial planning meeting to discuss the roles of the various participants in the internal control and financial reporting process. Participants at the meeting included the company president, the chief financial officer, a member of the audit committee, a partner from Micro Dynamics' external audit firm, and the newly appointed manager of the Internal Audit Department. Comments by the various meeting participants are presented below.

President: "We want to ensure that Micro Dynamics complies with the SEC's enforcement release and that we don't find ourselves in this position again. The Internal Audit Department should help to strengthen our internal control system by correcting the problems. I would like your thoughts on the proper reporting relationship for the manager of the Internal Audit Department."

Chief financial officer: "I think the manager of the Internal Audit Department should report to me since much of the department's work relates to financial issues. The audit committee should have oversight responsibilities."

Audit committee member: "I believe we should think through our roles more carefully. The Treadway Commission has recommended that the audit committee play a more important role in the financial reporting process; the duties of today's audit committee have expanded beyond the rubber-stamp approval. We need to have greater assurance that controls are in place and being followed."

External audit partner: "We need a close working relationship among all of our roles. The Internal Audit Department can play a significant role monitoring the control systems on a continuing basis and should have strong ties to your external audit firm."

Internal Audit Department manager: "The Internal Audit Department should be more involved in operational auditing, but also should play a significant monitoring role in the financial reporting area."

Questions

1. Describe the role of each of the following in the establishment, maintenance, and evaluation of Micro Dynamics' system of internal control:

    a. Management
    b. Audit committee
    c. External auditor
    d. Internal Audit Department

2. Describe the responsibilities that Micro Dynamics' audit committee has in the financial reporting process.

3. Discuss the characteristics of an audit committee in terms of the following:

    a. Composition, size, and term of membership
    b. Relationship with management, the external auditor, and the internal auditor

Essay Questions 1, 2, 3 — Unofficial Answers

1. a. Management has the overall responsibility for protecting company assets and, therefore, for establishing, maintaining, and evaluating the internal control system.

    b. The audit committee's primary responsibility involves assisting the board of directors in carrying out their responsibilities as they relate to the organization's accounting policies, internal control, and financial reporting practices. The audit committee assists management and the board in fulfilling their fiduciary and accountability responsibilities, and helps maintain a direct line of communication between the board and the external and internal auditors.

    c. The external auditor reviews the organization's control structure, including the control environment, accounting systems, and control procedures, in order to assess the control risks for financial statement assertions. In addition, the external auditor would inform the company of any material weaknesses found during the review.

    d. The Internal Audit Department performs both operational and financial audits to determine compliance with established policies and procedures, and reports its findings and recommendations to management or the audit committee for evaluation and corrective action. The Internal Audit Department may also assist the external auditors with their review of the internal control system.

2. The responsibilities of the Micro Dynamics' audit committee in the financial reporting process include

    a. Obtaining assurance that the organization's control system is adequate and effective, identifying risk and exposure, and ensuring that the financial disclosures made by management reasonably reflect the financial position, results of operations, and changes in cash flow

    b. Reviewing the progress of the audit and the final audit findings

    c. Acting as a liaison between the auditors and the board of directors

3. a. The audit committee should consist of at least three independent, outside directors. The maximum size may vary, but normally three to five members would be sufficient to allow each member to play an active role. The term is set by the board of directors and may vary but should include an arrangement to allow continuity to be maintained while rotating the membership.

    b. The audit committee is selected by the board of directors and assists the board of directors in carrying out their responsibilities concerning the organization's accounting policies, internal control, and financial reporting practices. The audit committee's oversight responsibilities that relate to the activities of management, the external auditor, and the internal auditor provide assurance to management and the public regarding the reliability and integrity of financial information. The audit committee also has the responsibility of selecting the external auditors, helping to resolve problems arising during the audit, and discussing the audit results with management and the external auditor.

Use **CMA Gleim Online** and **Essay Wizard** to practice additional essay questions in an exam-like environment.

STUDY UNIT TEN
INTERNAL CONTROLS --
INTERNAL AUDITING AND SYSTEMS CONTROLS

(22 pages of outline)

10.1 Internal Auditing 364
10.2 Systems Controls 369
10.3 Security Measures 376
10.4 Core Concepts 381
10.5 Essay Questions 397

This study unit concludes the material on **internal control (15%** of Part 1).

After studying the outline and answering the questions in this study unit, you will have the skills necessary to address the following topics listed in the ICMA's Learning Outcome Statements:

Part 1 – Section D.2. Internal auditing

The candidate should be able to:

a.   define the internal audit function and identify its functions and scope

b.   identify how internal auditors can test compliance with controls and evaluate the effectiveness of controls

c.   explain how internal auditors determine what controls to audit, when to audit, and why

d.   identify and describe control breakdowns and related risks that internal auditors should report to management or to the board of directors

e.   identify and define the objectives of a compliance audit and an operational audit

Part 1 – Section D.3. Systems controls and security measures

The candidate should be able to:

a.   describe how the segregation of accounting duties can enhance systems security

b.   identify threats to information systems, including input manipulation, program alteration, direct file alteration, data theft, sabotage, viruses, Trojan horses, and theft

c.   demonstrate an understanding of how systems development controls are used to enhance the accuracy, validity, safety, security, and adaptability of systems input, processing, output, and storage functions

d.   identify procedures to limit access to physical hardware

e.   identify means by which management can protect programs and databases from unauthorized use

f.   identify input controls, processing controls, and output controls and describe why each of these controls is necessary

g.   identify and describe the types of storage controls and demonstrate an understanding of when and why they are used

h.   identify and describe the inherent risks of using the Internet as compared to data transmissions over secured transmission lines

i.   define data encryption and describe why there is a much greater need for data encryption methods when using the Internet

j.   identify a firewall and its uses

k.   demonstrate an understanding of how flowcharts of activities are used to assess controls

l.   explain the importance of backing up all program and data files regularly, and frequently storing the backups at a secure remote site

m.   define the objective of a disaster recovery plan and identify the components of such a plan

10.1 INTERNAL AUDITING

1. **The Internal Audit Function**

   a. The growth and complexity of modern organizations has led to an accompanying growth in the field of internal auditing.

      1) An adequate internal audit activity is now considered to be so basic to the governance of a modern corporation that some stock exchanges require all companies registering to trade their stock to have one.

      2) Under the Foreign Corrupt Practices Act, organizations are expected to maintain reasonably detailed and accurate accounting records and a reasonably effective system of internal control. Maintaining an effective internal audit activity is an integral part of achieving this goal.

      3) Under the Sarbanes-Oxley Act of 2002, the CEO and CFO of a publicly traded company must certify to the effectiveness of the system of internal control.

   b. The Institute of Internal Auditors (The IIA), headquartered in Altamonte Springs, Florida, is the organization devoted to maintaining professional standards for the practice of internal auditing worldwide.

      1) The IIA defines internal auditing as follows:

         Internal auditing is an independent, objective assurance and consulting activity designed to add value and improve an organization's operations. It helps an organization accomplish its objectives by bringing a systematic, disciplined approach to evaluate and improve the effectiveness of risk management, control, and governance processes.

      2) The IIA's *International Standards for the Professional Practice of Internal Auditing* (the *Standards*) "provide guidance for the conduct of internal auditing at both the organizational and individual auditor levels."

      3) In addition, The IIA has issued numerous Practice Advisories, which it refers to as "concise and timely guidance to assist internal auditors in applying Code of Ethics and *Standards* and promoting good practices."

   c. The internal audit activity must be organizationally independent of the activities under audit. In addition, individual internal auditors must maintain an attitude of objectivity in carrying out their duties.

      1) Independence, therefore, is an attribute of the internal audit department as a whole, while objectivity is an attribute of the auditors themselves.

      2) Generally, the internal audit function is headed by the chief audit executive (CAE) who reports directly to the chief executive officer (CEO). The CAE also should have direct, unhindered access to the board of directors.

      3) The purpose, authority, and responsibility of the internal audit activity should be defined in a written charter. The charter should establish the internal audit activity's position within the organization; authorize access to records, personnel, and physical properties; and define the scope of internal audit activities.

2. **The Scope of Internal Auditing**

   a. The three principal functions of internal auditing within a modern organization are to aid

      1) Upper management in the maintenance of the firm's system of internal control
      2) Upper management in improving the efficiency of the firm's operations
      3) The external auditors in the conduct of the audit of financial statements

b.   The scope of work performed by an internal audit department is much broader than that performed by the independent external auditor. In carrying out its basic functions, the internal audit activity can perform a wide variety of specific tasks, such as

1)   Identifying and evaluating significant exposures to risk and contributing to the improvement of risk management and control systems

2)   Evaluating the adequacy and effectiveness of controls encompassing the organization's governance, operations, and information systems and the promotion of their continuous improvement

3)   Evaluating the reliability and integrity of financial and operational information

4)   Evaluating the effectiveness and efficiency of operations

5)   Evaluating the safeguarding of assets

6)   Evaluating compliance with laws, regulations, and contracts

7)   Ascertaining whether management has established adequate control criteria to evaluate the accomplishment of objectives and goals

8)   Preventing and detecting fraud

9)   Coordinating activities and sharing information with the external auditor

3.   **Incidents That Should Be Reported**

a.   The internal audit activity must report certain types of incidents that come to its attention to upper management and the board of directors. These include

1)   Fraud
2)   Illegal acts
3)   Material weaknesses and significant deficiencies in internal control
4)   Significant penetrations of information security systems

4.   **Reporting on Internal Control**

a.   The board and internal audit function have interlocking goals. The core role of the CAE is to ensure that the board receives the support and assurance services it requests.

b.   One of the primary objectives of the board is oversight of financial reporting processes to ensure their reliability and fairness. The board and senior management typically request that the internal audit activity perform sufficient audit work and gather other available information during the year to form an opinion on the adequacy and effectiveness of the internal control processes.

1)   The CAE normally communicates that overall evaluation, on a timely basis, to the board. The board will evaluate the coverage and adequacy of the CAE's report.

5.   **Financial Auditing**

a.   Internal auditors provide assurance regarding financial reporting to management and the board. For example, in many countries, laws require that management certify that the general-purpose financial statements are fairly stated in all material respects.

1)   Many countries also require management to provide an assessment of the organization's internal control over financial reporting. Internal auditors assist management in meeting these responsibilities.

b.   Reports of governance failures underscore the need for change to achieve greater accountability and transparency by all organizations. Senior management, boards, internal auditors, and external auditors are the basis of effective governance.

1)   The internal audit activity has a key role in improving operations by evaluating and improving the effectiveness of governance, risk management, and control.

        2)   Senior management has become more accountable (for example, as a result of legislation) for the information contained in financial reports. Thus, senior management and the board now tend to request more services from the internal audit activity.

             a)   These requests include evaluations of internal controls over financial reporting and the reliability and integrity of financial reports.

6. Compliance Auditing

   a.   Internal auditors should assess compliance in specific areas as part of their role in organizational governance.

        1)   They also should conduct follow-up and report on management's response to regulatory body reviews. Given the ever-expanding scope of governmental regulation, these duties of internal auditors have assumed increased importance.

7. Operational Auditing

   a.   *Sawyer's Internal Auditing: The Practice of Modern Internal Auditing* (Sawyer, Dittenhofer, and Graham, 5th ed., The IIA, 2003, p. 30) defines operational auditing as

> *The comprehensive review of the varied functions within an enterprise to appraise the efficiency and economy of operations and the effectiveness with which those functions achieve their objectives.*

Current pronouncements of The IIA no longer use the term "operational auditing." However, the term is included in the IMA's Learning Outcome Statements for Part 1 of the CMA exam.

---

   b.   An operational audit is thus a thorough examination of a department, division, function, etc. Its purpose is to appraise managerial organization, performance, and techniques.

        1)   An operational audit attempts to determine the extent to which organizational objectives have been achieved. It is a control technique that provides management with a method for evaluating the effectiveness of operating procedures and internal controls.

             a)   The focus is on efficiency, effectiveness, and economy (these terms are sometimes called the "three Es of operational auditing").

        2)   The report resulting from an operational audit consists primarily of specifying where problems exist or emphasizing the absence of problems.

        3)   The internal auditor compares a department's operations with company policies and procedures, industry averages, and departmental trends.

             a)   The basic tools of the internal auditor for operational auditing include

                 i)   Financial analysis
                 ii)   Observation of departmental activities
                 iii)   Questionnaire interviews of departmental employees

        4)   The operational audit evolved as an extension of the typical financial audit in that it goes beyond what is ordinarily considered to be the accounting function, e.g.,

             a)   Reviewing purchasing policies
             b)   Appraising compliance with company policies and procedures
             c)   Appraising safety standards and maintenance of equipment
             d)   Reviewing production controls and scrap reporting
             e)   Reviewing adequacy of facilities

c.   Internal auditors should not assume operating responsibilities. If senior management directs internal auditors to perform nonaudit work, they are not functioning as internal auditors.

d.   An operational audit is essentially a benchmarking activity. The auditor determines the standards in the form of industry averages, or information from competitors, and even common business sense, and assesses whether the department is operating efficiently, effectively, and economically.

8.   **Internal Control According to The IIA**

a.   The purpose of control is to support risk management and achievement of objectives. Control ensures

1)   The reliability and integrity of information;
2)   Efficient and effective performance;
3)   Safeguarding of assets; and
4)   Compliance with laws, regulations, contracts.

b.   Senior management oversees the establishment, administration, and assessment of risk management and control processes.

c.   Line managers assess control in their areas. Internal auditors provide assurance about the effectiveness of risk management and control.

d.   The chief audit executive (CAE) obtains sufficient audit evidence to form an overall opinion on the **adequacy and effectiveness** of control. This opinion is communicated to senior management and the board.

e.   The CAE develops the proposed internal audit plan to provide sufficient evidence to evaluate control. The plan should be flexible enough to permit adjustments during the year. It covers all major operations and functions. It also gives special consideration to operations most affected by recent or expected changes.

1)   Furthermore, the plan considers relevant work performed by others, including (a) management's assessments of risk management, control, and quality processes and (b) the work completed by external auditors.

f.   The CAE evaluates the plan's coverage. If the scope of the plan is insufficient to permit expression of an opinion about risk management and control, the CAE informs senior management and the board about gaps in audit coverage.

g.   The evaluation of control combines many individual assessments. Communication of findings to appropriate managers needs to be timely.

h.   The overall evaluation of control considers whether

1)   Significant weaknesses or discrepancies exist,
2)   Corrections or improvements were made, and
3)   A pervasive condition leading to unacceptable risk exists.

i.   Whether unacceptable risk exists depends on the nature and extent of risk exposure and level of consequences.

j.   The CAE's report on control processes is presented, usually once a year, to senior management and the board. It describes

1)   The role of control processes,
2)   The work performed, and
3)   Any reliance on other assurance providers.

k.   Control criteria. The first element of the control process is to establish standards for the program or operation to be controlled. Acceptable industry standards, standards developed by professional associations, standards in law and government regulations, and other sound business practices are usually deemed to be appropriate criteria. The IIA has addressed this subject as follows:

1)   Internal auditors should ascertain the extent to which operating and program goals and objectives have been established and conform to those of the organization.

    2)   Internal auditors should review operations and programs to ascertain the extent to which results are consistent with established goals and objectives to determine whether operations and programs are being implemented or performed as intended.

    3)   Adequate criteria are needed to evaluate controls. Internal auditors must ascertain the extent to which management has established adequate criteria to determine whether objectives and goals have been accomplished. If adequate, internal auditors must use such criteria in their evaluation. If inadequate, internal auditors must work with management to develop appropriate evaluation criteria.

    4)   During consulting engagements, internal auditors must address controls consistent with the engagement's objectives and be alert to significant control issues.

        a)   Internal auditors must incorporate knowledge of controls gained from consulting engagements into evaluation of the organization's control processes.

l.   Once the relevant internal controls have been identified, the internal auditor applies four types of procedures:

    1)   Make inquiries of appropriate personnel

        a)   While simple answers to verbal questions are not considered a strong form of evidence, they can nonetheless be very informative, especially when employees describe their ordinary duties or when they admit that a given control procedure is often not followed.

    2)   Examine documentation

        a)   Even in a computerized environment, some control procedures leave a paper trail. For example, purchases of capital equipment may require the signature of a regional vice president.

        b)   In some computerized environments, signatures and other approvals can be tracked electronically. The internal auditor may require specialized knowledge to determine whether these controls are functioning properly.

    3)   Observe control-related activities

        a)   Because some control procedures may leave no audit trail of any kind, the internal auditor may need to watch them being performed to gain assurance about them functioning properly.

    4)   Reperform client procedures

        a)   Some types of control procedures can be effectively tested simply by the internal auditor reperforming the activity. For example, the extended price of a line item on an invoice should equal the quantity shipped times the unit price. The auditor can reperform this multiplication on a sample of invoices to check for a computer error or unauthorized overrides.

9. **Due Care in Internal Auditing**

    a.   Attribute Standard 1220, *Due Professional Care*, states "Internal auditors must apply the care and skill expected of a reasonably prudent and competent internal auditor. Due professional care does not imply infallibility."

    b.   The IIA provides specifics about the application of due care in Practice Advisory 1220-1, *Due Professional Care*:

        1)   "Exercising due professional care involves internal auditors being alert to the possibility of fraud, intentional wrongdoing, errors and omissions, inefficiency, waste, ineffectiveness, and conflicts of interest, as well as being alert to those conditions and activities where irregularities are most likely to occur" (para. 1).

2) "Due professional care implies reasonable care and competence, not infallibility or extraordinary performance. As such, due professional care requires the internal auditor to conduct examinations and verifications to a reasonable extent. Accordingly, internal auditors cannot give absolute assurance that noncompliance or irregularities do not exist. Nevertheless, the possibility of material irregularities or noncompliance needs to be considered whenever an internal auditor undertakes an internal audit assignment" (para. 2).

c. The IIA provides the following Implementation Standards for the application of due care during assurance engagements.

1) Implementation Standard 1220.A1

Internal auditors must exercise due professional care by considering the

- Extent of work needed to achieve the engagement's objectives;
- Relative complexity, materiality, or significance of matters to which assurance procedures are applied;
- Adequacy and effectiveness of governance, risk management, and control processes;
- Probability of significant errors, fraud, or noncompliance; and
- Cost of assurance in relation to potential benefits.

2) Implementation Standard 1220.A2

In exercising due professional care, internal auditors must consider the use of technology-based audit and other data analysis techniques.

3) Implementation Standard 1220.A3

Internal auditors must be alert to the significant risks that might affect objectives, operations, or resources. However, assurance procedures alone, even when performed with due professional care, do not guarantee that all significant risks will be identified.

d. Any unexpected results from analytical procedures should be investigated and adequately explained.

e. Due professional care can be demonstrated if the auditor acted as any other auditor would have, given the same facts and circumstances.

Stop and review! You have completed the outline for this subunit. Study multiple-choice questions 1 through 4 beginning on page 384.

10.2 SYSTEMS CONTROLS

1. **Segregation of Duties**

a. The **segregation of accounting duties** can enhance systems security. Segregation of duties involves the separation of the functions of authorization, record keeping, and asset custody so as to minimize the opportunities for a person to be able to perpetrate and conceal errors or fraud in the normal course of his/her duties.

b. Thus, computer operators, programmers, analysts, and librarians should not have overlapping responsibilities.

2. **Three Goals of Information Security**

a. Availability is the ability of the intended and authorized users to access computer resources to meet organizational goals.

b. Confidentiality is assurance of the secrecy of information that could adversely affect the organization if revealed to the public or competitors.

c. Integrity is maintained by preventing the unauthorized or accidental modification of programs or data.

3. **Threats to Information Systems**

   a. Input manipulation is an intrusion into a system by exploiting a vulnerability in a legitimate electronic portal, such as the input boxes on a web page. An input box may call, for instance, for the user's address, but a knowledgeable hacker can implant HTML code in the input box that runs a system command giving him/her access to the organization's data.

   b. Program alteration is the deliberate changing of the processing routines of an application program. A famous, if apocryphal, example of long standing is a piece of code that directs all amounts less than one dollar to be directed to the malicious programmer's bank account.

   c. Direct file alteration is the deliberate changing of data in a database to the intruder's advantage. A common example is a hacker who uses unauthorized access to change his/her course grades while bypassing the normal audit trail.

   d. Data theft is the surreptitious copying of critical data elements from an organization's databases. Social Security and credit card numbers are common targets of this type of attack.

   e. Sabotage is the disruption of an organization's systems not for personal gain but simply for revenge or in the spirit of vandalism. Changing a company's website to include unflattering information that is not immediately noticeable is an example. Another example is a disgruntled programmer who injects a logic bomb (see item 3.g. below) into an application that will disrupt processing long after the programmer's departure from the company.

   f. Viruses are computer programs that propagate themselves from one computer to another without the user's knowledge. Some are written only for the programmer's amusement and are relatively harmless. This type of virus may cause a clever or annoying message to appear on the user's screen. Others are malicious and can cause great inconvenience and even loss of data to the user. A common way of spreading a virus is by email attachments and downloads.

   g. Logic bombs also destroy data but, unlike viruses, they remain on a single computer and do not replicate. Often they lie dormant until triggered by some occurrence, such as the arrival of a certain date.

   h. Worms are pieces of code that do not threaten the data on a computer (unlike viruses and logic bombs) but are destructive because of the rapidity with which they replicate themselves. A worm released onto the Internet will propagate from network to network, eventually overwhelming one or more servers with traffic.

   i. Trojan horses are voluntarily installed on a computer by the user because they are masquerading as programs the user wants. While the program may present the user with, for instance, an entertaining video game, behind the scenes, it contains codes that a hacker can activate later to take over the computer, retrieving sensitive data from it or using it to launch proxy attacks on other computers.

       1) Viruses, worms, Trojan horses, etc., are often collectively referred to as malicious software, or malware.

   j. Back doors are a means of obtaining access to a system while bypassing the usual password controls. IT personnel often deliberately design back doors into systems to allow system management during unusual circumstances. Hackers search for vulnerabilities in systems to exploit back doors for their own purposes.

   k. Theft becomes increasingly problematic with the higher portability of laptop and palmtop computers. All organizations must establish policies for the proper physical protection of computing infrastructure assets.

4. **Systems Development Controls**

    a. All information systems, automated or manual, perform four basic functions on information: input, processing, output, and storage.

        1) Proper management of the systems development process can enhance the accuracy, validity, safety, security, and adaptability of the controls over these functions.

    b. Effective systems development requires the setting of priorities. This can be achieved through a steering committee composed of managers from both the IT function and the end-user functions. The committee approves development projects, assigns resources, and reviews their progress.

        1) The steering committee also ensures that requests for new systems are aligned with the overall strategic plan of the organization.

        2) All newly developed systems should conform to established organizational standards for coding and documentation.

    c. Changes to existing systems should be subject to the same strict controls. Requests for changes should be initiated by an end user and authorized by management or the steering committee.

        1) All changes should be made to a working copy of the program. Production code should never be directly alterable by a programmer.

        2) All changes should be adequately tested before being placed in production. The test results should be demonstrated for and accepted by the user who requested the change.

            a) Adequate testing must involve the use of incorrect data. The program must be able to appropriately handle data that do not conform to the ideal.

        3) The changed program code should be stored in a secure library during testing and while awaiting migration into production.

    d. Unauthorized changes to programs can be detected by code comparison. The version in use compared electronically to an archived version known to be "clean."

5. **Physical Controls**

    a. Physical controls limit physical access and environmental damage to computer equipment and important documents.

        1) Physical access. Only operators should be allowed unmonitored access to the computer center. This can be accomplished through the use of a guard desk, a keypad, or a magnetic card reader.

        2) Environmental controls. The computer center should be equipped with a cooling and heating system to maintain a year-round constant level of temperature and humidity, and a fire-suppression system.

6. **Logical Controls**

    a. Logical controls are established to limit system access in accordance with the principle that all persons should have access only to those elements of the organization's information systems that are necessary to perform their job duties. Logical controls have a double focus, authentication and authorization.

        1) **Authentication** is the act of ensuring that the person attempting to access the system is in fact who (s)he says (s)he is. The most widespread means of achieving this is through the use of IDs and passwords.

            a) Anyone attempting access to one of the organization's systems must supply a unique identifier (e.g., the person's name or other series of characters) and a password that is known only to that person and is not stored anywhere in the system in unencrypted format.

          i)   Not even information security personnel should be able to view unencrypted passwords. Security personnel can change passwords, but the policy should require that the user immediately changes it to something secret.

    b)   Password optimization

          i)   Passwords should be difficult to guess.

- A dialog can be designed to query the user for common names in his/her life (children, pets, sports teams) so that these words can be stored and never permitted by the system to be used as that person's password.
- Ideally, passwords are at least eight characters long and contain both uppercase and lowercase letters and numerals.

          ii)   The system should force passwords to be changed periodically, e.g., every 90 days.

    c)   Password fatigue results when users must log on to several systems in the course of a day. Users are likely to write down their IDs and passwords in such cases, defeating the purpose of automated authentication.

          i)   Single sign-on can be the solution in well-managed systems environments. A single ID and password combination is required to allow a user access to all IT resources (s)he needs. A high level of maintenance and security consciousness is required to make single sign-on successful.

  2)   **Authorization** is the practice of ensuring that, once in the system, the user can only access those programs and data elements necessary to his/her job duties.

    a)   In many cases, users should be able to view the contents of some data fields but not be able to change them.

    b)   An example is an accounts receivable clerk who can view customers' credit limits but cannot change them. This same clerk can, however, change a customer's outstanding balance by entering or adjusting an invoice.

    c)   To extend the example, only the head of the accounts receivable department should be able to execute the program that updates the accounts receivable master balance file. An individual clerk should have no such power.

  7.   **Input, Processing, and Output Controls**

    a.   **Input controls** provide reasonable assurance that data submitted for processing are (1) authorized, (2) complete, and (3) accurate. These controls vary depending on whether input is entered in online or batch mode.

      1)   Online input controls can be used when data are keyed into an input screen.

        a)   Preformatting. The data entry screen mimics the old hardcopy document, forcing data entry in all necessary fields.

        b)   Edit checks. The data entry screen prevents certain types of incorrect data from entering the system. For example, the system rejects any attempt to enter numerals in the Name box or letters in the Amount box. Dropdown menus can restrict the user's choices to only valid selections.

        c)   Limit (reasonableness) checks. Certain amounts can be restricted to appropriate ranges, such as hours worked < 20 per day, or invoices over $100,000 requiring supervisor approval.

          d)   Check digits. An algorithm is applied to any kind of serial identifier to derive a check digit. During data entry, the check digit is recomputed by the system to ensure proper entry. Requiring the full number including check digit to be keyed in all future data entry operations eliminates the possibility of dropped or transposed digits, etc.

   2)   Batch input controls can be used when data are grouped for processing in "batches."

          a)   Management release. A batch is not released for processing until a manager reviews and approves it.

          b)   Record count. A batch is not released for processing unless the number of records in the batch, as reported by the system, matches the number calculated by the user.

          c)   Financial total. A batch is not released for processing unless the sum of the dollar amounts of the individual items as reported by the system matches the amount calculated by the user.

          d)   Hash total. The arithmetic sum of a numeric field, which has no meaning by itself, can serve as a check that the same records that should have been processed were processed. An example is the sum of all Social Security numbers.

              i)   This number is much too unwieldy to be calculated by the user, but once it is calculated by the system, it can follow the batch through subsequent stages of processing.

  b.   **Processing controls** provide reasonable assurance that (1) all data submitted for processing are processed and (2) only approved data are processed. These controls are built into the application code by programmers during the systems development process.

   1)   Some processing controls repeat the steps performed by the input controls, such as limit checks and control totals.

   2)   Validation. Identifiers are matched against master files to determine existence. For example, any accounts payable transaction in which the vendor number does not match a number on the vendor master file is rejected.

   3)   Completeness. Any record with missing data is rejected.

   4)   Arithmetic controls. Cross-footing compares an amount to the sum of its components. Zero-balance checking adds the debits and credits in a transaction or batch to ensure they sum to zero.

   5)   Sequence check. Computer effort is expended most efficiently when data are processed in a logical order, such as by customer number. This check ensures the batch is sorted in this order before processing begins.

   6)   Run-to-run control totals. The controls associated with a given batch are checked after each stage of processing to ensure all transactions have been processed.

   7)   Key integrity. A record's "key" is the group of values in designated fields that uniquely identify the record. No application process should be able to alter the data in these key fields.

  c.   **Output controls** provide assurance that processing was complete and accurate.

   1)   A complete audit trail should be generated by each process: batch number, time of submission, time of completion, number of records in batch, total dollars in batch, number of records rejected, total dollars rejected, etc.

          a)   The audit trail is immediately submitted to a reasonableness check by the user, who is most qualified to judge the adequacy of processing and the proper treatment of erroneous transactions.

      2)   Error listings report all transactions rejected by the system. These should be corrected and resubmitted by the user.

8.   **Computer-Assisted Audit Techniques (CAATs)**

    a.   Certain controls relating to the input, processing, and output of data are internal to the computer system. They should be tested by procedures that are not traditionally performed in a manual environment. Such techniques have been characterized as auditing around the computer or auditing through the computer.

    b.   Auditing around the computer is not appropriate when systems are sophisticated or the major controls are included in the computer programs. It may be appropriate for very simple systems that produce appropriate printed outputs.

        1)   The auditor manually processes transactions and compares the results with the client's computer-processed results.

        2)   Because only a small number of transactions can ordinarily be tested, the effectiveness of the tests of controls must be questioned.

        3)   The computer is treated as a black box, and only inputs and outputs are evaluated.

    c.   Auditing through the computer uses the computer to test the processing logic and controls within the system and the records produced. This approach may be accomplished in several ways, including

        1)   Processing test data
        2)   Parallel simulation
        3)   Generalized audit software
        4)   Data extraction techniques
        5)   Creation of an integrated test facility
        6)   Programming embedded audit modules
        7)   Others

    d.   Computer-assisted audit techniques may be systems- or transaction-based or may provide automated methods for extracting and analyzing data.

    e.   Test data, sometimes called a test deck, consist of a set of dummy inputs containing both good and bad data elements. This approach subjects auditor-created data to the client's programs.

        1)   The auditor can assess the controls embedded in the application by observing (a) whether the good data are correctly processed and (b) how well the system handles the bad input.

        2)   Test data must never be mingled with real data, and test data must not be allowed to interfere with production processing. Monitoring by IT personnel is crucial when the auditor employs a test deck.

    f.   Parallel simulation subjects client data to auditor-created programs.

        1)   The goal is to determine whether the data are subjected to the processes that the client claims the application performs.

        2)   Parallel simulation requires the auditor to have considerable technical knowledge. The auditor also must have extensive communications with client personnel to learn the designed functions of the application being imitated.

    g.   Generalized audit software (GAS) packages allow the auditor to load a copy of the client's production data onto the auditor's own computer and perform various analytical procedures.

        1)   The auditor can search for duplicate records, gaps in numerically sequenced records, high-monetary-amount transactions, suspect vendor numbers, etc. Control totals can be calculated, and balances can be stratified for receivables testing.

        2)   The leading GAS packages are ACL (Audit Command Language) and IDEA (Interactive Data Extraction and Analysis).

   h.   Data extraction techniques. The oldest form of data extraction is the manual copying of client records. Until the widespread use of photocopy machines, it was the only technique.

        1)   With the easy availability of computing, and especially networking, technology, data extraction can be performed quickly in very large volumes.

        2)   The hazards lie in ensuring that the data extracted are those required for the audit procedure being performed. Control totals and other methods are used for this purpose.

   i.   Spreadsheet analysis. Electronic spreadsheets, such as Microsoft Excel, permit easy analysis of huge amounts of client data and the performance of what-if scenarios.

   j.   Integrated test facility (ITF). In this approach, the auditor creates a fictitious entity (a department, vendor, employee, or product) on the client's live production system.

        1)   All transactions associated with the dummy entity are processed by the live system, and the auditor can observe the results.

        2)   Use of an ITF requires great care to ensure that no transactions associated with the dummy entity are included in production reports and output files.

   k.   An embedded audit module is an integral part of an application system. It is designed to identify and report actual transactions and other information that meet criteria having audit significance.

        1)   An advantage is that it permits continuous monitoring of online, real-time systems.

        2)   A disadvantage is that audit hooks must be programmed into the operating system and applications programs to permit insertion of audit modules.

   l.   Application tracing uses a feature of the programming language in which the application was written.

        1)   Tracing aids computer programmers in following the step-by-step operation of a computer program's source code. It can be used by auditors for the same purpose.

   m.   System mapping is similar to application tracing. But mapping is performed by another computer program instead of by the auditor.

9. **Storage Controls**

   a.   Dual write routines. The data can be stored on two separate physical devices (usually magnetic hard drives) so that a mishap to one does not destroy the organization's data set.

        1)   Especially important in this regard is the technology known as RAID (redundant array of inexpensive discs), a grouping of multiple hard drives with special software that allows for data delivery along multiple paths. If one drive fails, the other discs can compensate for the loss.

   b.   Validity checks. Hardware that transmits or receives data compares the bits in each byte to the permissible combinations in order to determine whether they constitute a valid structure.

   c.   Physical controls. Mounting hard drives in physically secure rooms and storing portable media (CD-ROMs, etc.) in locked storage areas are vital to preventing the compromise of confidential data.

Stop and review! You have completed the outline for this subunit. Study multiple-choice questions 5 through 30 beginning on page 385.

10.3 SECURITY MEASURES

1. **Inherent Risks of the Internet**

   a. Password Attacks

      1) A brute-force attack uses password cracking software to try large numbers of letter and number combinations to access a network. A simple variation is the use of password cracking software that tries all the words in a dictionary.

      2) Passwords also may be compromised by Trojan horses, IP spoofing, and packet sniffers. Spoofing is identity misrepresentation in cyberspace, (e.g., using a false website to obtain visitor information). Sniffing is the use of software to eavesdrop on information sent by a user to the host computer of a website.

   b. A man-in-the-middle attack takes advantage of networking packet sniffing and routing and transport protocols.

      1) These attacks may be used to steal data, obtain access to the network during a rightful user's active session, analyze the traffic on the network to learn about its operations and users, insert new data or modify the data being transmitted, and deny service.

      2) Cryptography is the effective response to man-in-the-middle attacks. The encrypted data will be useless to the attacker unless it can be decrypted.

   c. A denial-of-service (DoS) attack is an attempt to overload an organization's network with so many messages so that it cannot function (i.e., induce a system crash).

      1) A distributed denial-of-service (DDoS) attack comes from multiple sources, for example, the machines of several innocent parties infected by Trojan horses. When activated, these programs send messages to the target and leave the connection open.

      2) A DoS attack may establish as many network connections as possible to exclude other users, thus overloading primary memory or corrupting file systems.

2. **Use of Data Encryption**

   a. Encryption technology converts data into a code. Unauthorized users may still be able to access the data, but without the encryption key, they cannot decode it.

      1) Encryption technology may be either hardware- or software-based. Two major types of encryption software exist.

   b. **Public-key**, or asymmetric, encryption is the more secure of the two because it requires two keys: The public key for coding messages is widely known, but the private key for decoding messages is kept secret by the recipient.

      1) The parties who wish to transmit coded messages must use algorithmically-related pairs of public and private keys.

      2) The sender uses the recipient's public key, obtained from a directory, to encode the message, and transmits the message to the recipient. The recipient then uses the public key and the related private (secret) key to decode the message.

      3) Neither party knows the other's private key. The related public key and private key pair is issued by a certificate authority (a third-party fiduciary, e.g., VeriSign or Thawte). However, the private key is issued only to one party.

         a) RSA, named for its developers (Rivest, Shamir, and Adelman), is the most commonly used public-key method.

   c. **Private-key**, or symmetric, encryption is less secure because it requires only a single key for each pair of parties that want to send each other coded messages.

      1) Data Encryption Standard (DES), a shared private-key method developed by the U.S. government, is the most prevalent secret-key method. It is based on numbers with 56 binary digits.

2) The Advanced Encryption Standard (AES) is a recently adopted cryptographic algorithm for use by U.S. government organizations to protect sensitive information. The AES will be widely used on a voluntary basis by organizations, institutions, and individuals as well as by the U.S. government.

3. **Firewalls**

   a. A firewall is a combination of hardware and software that separates an internal network from an external network, such as the Internet, and prevents passage of specific types of traffic.

      1) Firewall systems ordinarily produce reports on organization-wide Internet use, exception reports for unusual usage patterns, and system penetration-attempt reports. These reports are very helpful as a method of continuous monitoring, or logging, of the system.

      2) A firewall alone is not an adequate defense against computer viruses. Specialized anti-virus software is a must.

4. **Flowcharting**

   a. Flowcharting is the representation of a process using pictorial symbols. Flowcharts can be useful in obtaining an understanding of internal control and in systems development.

      1) Flowcharting symbols have been standardized by both the American National Standards Institute (ANSI) and the International Organization for Standardization (ISO).

      2) Below are some standard flowcharting symbols representing process endpoints and connectors:

Starting or ending point

Connection between points on the same page

Connection between different pages of the flowchart

      3) Below are some standard flowcharting symbols representing processes:

Keying operation   Decision point

Computer operation   Manual operation

      4) Below are some standard flowcharting symbols representing input and output:

Generalized symbol for input or output used when the medium is not specified   Display on a video terminal

A document or report   Online storage (magnetic disk)

Database (magnetic disk)   Offline storage (file)

b. Vertical flowcharts present successive steps in a top-to-bottom format. Before the advent of object-oriented programming, flowcharts were a very common tool for computer programmers to design the flow of a new system. Below is an example of a simple vertical flowchart.

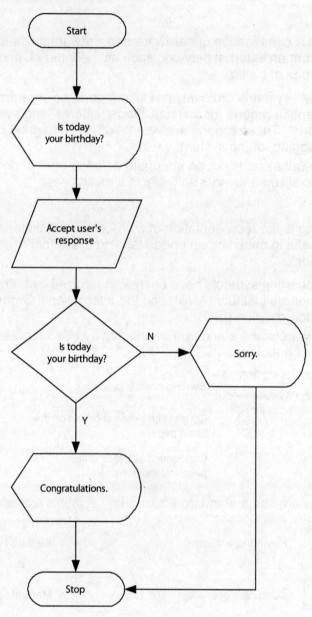

c. Horizontal flowcharts, also called systems flowcharts, depict areas of responsibility (departments or functions) in vertical columns. Activities and documents flow back and forth between departments across the page.

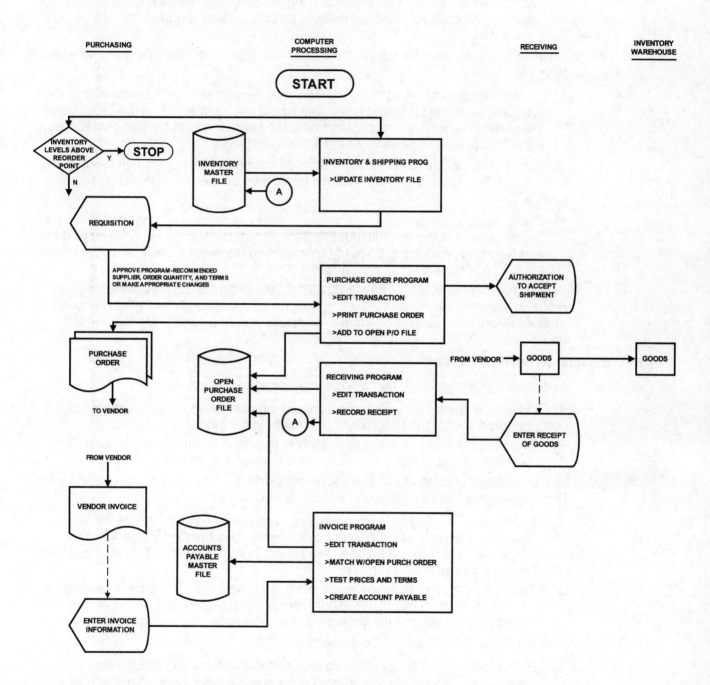

5. **Routine Backup and Offsite Rotation**

   a. It is a truth seldom grasped by those who are not computer professionals that an organization's data is more valuable than its hardware.

      1) Hardware can be replaced for a price, but each organization's data bundle is unique and is indispensable to carrying on business. If it is ever destroyed, it cannot be replaced. For this reason, periodic backup and rotation are essential.

   b. The offsite location must be temperature- and humidity-controlled and guarded against physical intrusion.

      1) Just as important, it must be geographically remote enough from the site of the organization's main operations that it would not be affected by the same natural disaster. It does the organization no good to have sound backup procedures if the files are not accessible or have been destroyed.

   c. A typical backup routine involves duplicating all data files and application programs once a month. (Application files must be backed up as well as data since programs change too.)

      1) Incremental changes, that is, only those data elements and programs that have changed since the last full monthly backup, are backed up every week and kept at the main processing center. (Transporting the weekly backups to the offsite location is generally not cost-effective.)

   d. In case of an interruption of normal processing, the organization's systems can be restored such that, at most, 3 weeks of business information is lost. This is not an ideal situation, but it is a far cry from a complete loss of a company's files, which could essentially put it out of business.

6. **Disaster Recovery Planning**

   a. Contingency planning is the name commonly given to this activity.

      1) Disaster recovery is the process of resuming normal information processing operations after the occurrence of a major interruption.
      2) Business continuity is the continuation of business by other means during the period in which computer processing is unavailable or less than normal.

   b. Two major types of contingencies must be planned for: those in which the data center is physically available and those in which it is not.

      1) Examples of the first type of contingency are power failure, random intrusions such as viruses, and deliberate intrusions such as hacking incidents. The organization's physical facilities are sound, but immediate action is required to keep normal processing going.
      2) The second type of contingency is much more serious. This type is caused by disasters such as floods, fires, hurricanes, earthquakes, etc. An occurrence of this type necessitates the existence of an alternate processing facility.

   c. Dealing with Specific Types of Contingencies

      1) Power failures can be guarded against by the purchase of backup electrical generators. These can be programmed to automatically begin running as soon as a dip in the level of electric current is detected. This is a widespread practice in settings such as hospitals where 24-hour system availability is crucial.
      2) Attacks such as viruses and denials-of-service call for a completely different response. The system must be brought down "gracefully" to halt the spread of the infection. The IT staff must be well trained in the nature of the latest virus threats to know how to isolate the damage and bring the system back to full operation.

3) The most extreme contingency is when the organization's main facility is rendered uninhabitable by flood, fire, earthquake, etc. It is to prepare for these cases that organizations contract for alternate processing facilities.

   a) An alternate processing facility is a physical location maintained by an outside contractor for the express purpose of providing processing facilities for customers in case of disaster.

   b) The recovery center, like the offsite storage location for backup files, must be far enough away that it will likely be unaffected by the same natural disaster that forced the abandonment of the main facility. Usually, companies contract for backup facilities in another city.

   c) Once the determination is made that processing is no longer possible at the principal site, the backup files are retrieved from the secure storage location and taken to the recovery center.

   d) Recovery centers can take many forms. Organizations determine which facility is best by calculating the tradeoff between the cost of the contract and the cost of downtime.

      i) A hot site is a fully operational processing facility that is immediately available. A flying-start site is a hot site with the latest data and software that permit startup within a few minutes or even a few seconds.

      ii) A warm site is a facility with limited hardware, such as communications and networking equipment, already installed but lacking the necessary servers and client terminals.

      iii) A cold site is a shell facility lacking most infrastructure but readily available for the quick installation of hardware.

Stop and review! You have completed the outline for this subunit. Study multiple-choice questions 31 through 39 beginning on page 393.

10.4 CORE CONCEPTS

Internal Auditing

- An adequate **internal audit activity** is now considered to be so basic to the governance of a modern corporation that some stock exchanges require all companies registering to trade their stock to have one.

- The Institute of Internal Auditors (The IIA) provides the following definition: "Internal auditing is an **independent, objective assurance and consulting activity** designed to add value and improve an organization's operations."

- The internal audit activity must be **organizationally independent** of the activities under audit. In addition, individual internal auditors must maintain an **attitude of objectivity** in carrying out their duties. Independence, therefore, is an attribute of the internal audit department as a whole, while objectivity is an attribute of the auditors themselves.

- Generally, the internal audit function is headed by the **chief audit executive (CAE)** who reports directly to the chief executive officer (CEO). The CAE also should have direct, unhindered access to the board of directors. The purpose, authority, and responsibility of the internal audit activity should be defined in a **written charter**.

- The **three principal functions** of internal auditing within a modern organization are to aid (1) upper management in the maintenance of the firm's system of internal control, (2) upper management in improving the efficiency of the firm's operations, and (3) the external auditors in the conduct of the audit of financial statements.

- The internal audit activity **must report** certain types of **incidents** that come to its attention to upper management and the board of directors. They include fraud, illegal acts, material weaknesses and significant deficiencies in internal control, and significant penetrations of information security systems.

- Internal auditors should **assess compliance** in specific areas as part of their role in organizational governance. They also should conduct follow-up and report on management's response to **regulatory body reviews**. Given the ever-expanding scope of governmental regulation, these duties of internal auditors have assumed increased importance.

- **Operational auditing** is a review of a function within an enterprise to appraise the **efficiency** and economy of operations and the **effectiveness** with which those functions achieve their objectives.

- **Senior management** oversees establishment, administration, and assessment of the system of risk management and control. **Line managers** assess control in their areas.

- The **internal auditors** provide assurance about the effectiveness of risk management and control.

- The CAE obtains sufficient evidence to assess the adequacy and effectiveness of control. This assessment is communicated to management and the board.

Systems Controls

- The three **goals** of information security are **availability, confidentiality, and integrity**.

- **Threats** to information systems include input manipulation, program alteration, direct file alteration, data theft, sabotage, viruses / logic bombs / worms / Trojan horses (known collectively as malware), back doors, and theft.

- **Physical controls** limit physical access and environmental damage to computer equipment and important documents. They consist of

  - **Physical access** (i.e., who can get into a room with computer equipment), and
  - **Environmental controls** (i.e., maintaining the computer equipment room with a constant level of temperature and humidity, and a fire-suppression system).

- **Logical controls** are established to limit access in accordance with the principle that all persons should have access only to those elements of the organization's information systems that are necessary to perform their job duties. Logical controls have a double focus:

  - **Authentication** is the act of ensuring that the person attempting to access the system is in fact who (s)he says (s)he is. The most widespread means of achieving this is through the use of IDs and passwords.
  - **Authorization** is the practice of ensuring that, once in the system, the user can only access those programs and data elements necessary to his/her job duties. In many cases, users should be able to view the contents of some data fields but not be able to change them.

- **Input, Processing, and Output Controls**

  - **Input controls** vary depending on whether input is entered in online or batch mode. **Online input controls** can be used when data are keyed into an input screen. Among them are preformatting, edit checks, limit (reasonableness) checks, and check digits. **Batch input controls** can be used when data are grouped for processing in "batches." Commonly used ones are management release, record counts, financial totals, and hash totals.
  - **Processing controls** include validation, completeness, arithmetic controls, sequence checks, run-to-run control totals, and key integrity.
  - **Output controls** include a complete audit trail and error listings.

- ■ **Computer-assisted audit techniques** are used to test controls related to the input, processing, and output of data that are internal to the computer.

  - ● **Generalized audit software** packages allow an auditor to load a copy of the client's production data onto the auditor's own computer and perform various analytical procedures.
  - ● **Integrated test facility** is an approach where auditors create a fictitious entity on a client's live production system. All transactions are processed with the dummy entity by the live system, and the auditor can observe the results.
- ■ **Storage controls** consist of dual write routines, validity checks, and physical controls.

Security Measures

- ■ Certain security **risks are inherent** in use of the **Internet**. Listed here are some of the forms that attacks over the Internet can take.

  - ● **Password attacks.** A brute-force attack uses password cracking software to try large numbers of letter and number combinations to access a network. Passwords also may be compromised by Trojan horses, IP spoofing, and packet sniffers.
  - ● A **man-in-the-middle attack** takes advantage of networking packet sniffing and routing and transport protocols.
  - ● A **denial-of-service (DoS)** attack is an attempt to overload an organization's network with so many messages that it cannot function (i.e., induce a system crash).
- ■ **Data encryption** is a very powerful tool in counteracting Internet attacks. Encryption technology converts data into a code. Two major types of encryption software exist.

  - ● **Public-key**, or **asymmetric**, encryption is the more secure of the two because it requires two keys: The public key for coding messages is widely known, but the private key for decoding messages is kept secret by the recipient. The parties who wish to transmit coded messages must use algorithmically-related pairs of public and private keys. Neither party knows the other's private key. The related public key and private key pair is issued by a certificate authority; the private key is issued only to one party.
  - ● **Private-key**, or **symmetric**, encryption is less secure because it requires only a single key for each pair of parties that want to send each other coded messages.
- ■ A **firewall** is a combination of hardware and software that separates an internal network from an external network, such as the Internet, and prevents passage of specific types of traffic. A firewall alone is not an adequate defense against computer viruses. Specialized anti-virus software is a must.
- ■ **Flowcharting** is the representation of a process using pictorial symbols.

  - ● **Vertical flowcharts** present successive steps in a top-to-bottom format.
  - ● **Horizontal flowcharts**, also called systems flowcharts, depict areas of responsibility (departments or functions) in vertical columns. Activities and documents flow back and forth between departments across the page.
- ■ **Periodic backup and rotation** are essential. The offsite location must be temperature- and humidity-controlled and guarded against physical intrusion. Just as important, it must be geographically remote enough from the site of the organization's main operations that it would not be affected by the same natural disaster.
- ■ A typical **backup routine** involves duplicating all data files and application programs once a month. Incremental changes, that is, only those data elements and programs that have changed since the last full monthly backup, are backed up every week and kept at the main processing center.

- **Disaster recovery** planning is also called **contingency** planning. Disaster recovery is the process of resuming normal information processing operations after the occurrence of a major interruption. Business continuity is the continuation of business by other means during the period in which computer processing is unavailable or less than normal. **Two major types** of contingencies must be planned for: those in which the data center is physically available (power failure, viruses, hacking) and those in which it is not (floods, fires, hurricanes, earthquakes).

- An **alternate processing facility** is a physical location maintained by an outside contractor for the express purpose of providing processing facilities for customers in case of disaster. The recovery center, like the offsite storage location for backup files, must be far enough away that it will likely be unaffected by the same natural disaster that forced the abandonment of the main facility. Usually, companies contract for backup facilities in another city.

QUESTIONS

10.1 Internal Auditing

1. From a modern internal auditing perspective, which one of the following statements represents the most important benefit of an internal auditing activity to management?

A. Assurance that published financial statements are correct.

B. Assurance that fraudulent activities will be detected.

C. Assurance that the organization is complying with legal requirements.

D. Assurance that there is reasonable control over day-to-day operations.

Answer (D) is correct. *(CMA, adapted)*
REQUIRED: The most important benefit of an IAA.
DISCUSSION: According to the definition of internal auditing, "Internal auditing is an independent, objective assurance and consulting activity designed to add value and improve an organization's operations. It helps an organization accomplish its objectives by bringing a systematic, disciplined approach to evaluate and improve the effectiveness of risk management, control, and governance processes." Thus, it helps the organization to maintain effective controls by evaluating their effectiveness and efficiency and by promoting continuous improvement (Standard 2120).
Answer (A) is incorrect. Published financial statements are only required to be fairly presented. Internal audit activities cannot ensure correctness. Answer (B) is incorrect. Internal auditing's responsibility with respect to fraud detection is to examine and evaluate the adequacy and effectiveness of internal control. Answer (C) is incorrect. Internal auditing evaluates and contributes to the improvement of risk management, control, and governance processes, but it cannot ensure compliance with legal requirements.

2. Of the following, the primary objective of compliance testing is to determine whether

A. Procedures are regularly updated.

B. Financial statement line items are properly stated.

C. Controls are functioning as planned.

D. Collusion is taking place.

Answer (C) is correct. *(CMA, adapted)*
REQUIRED: The primary objective of compliance testing.
DISCUSSION: Internal auditors should assess compliance in specific areas as part of their role in organizational governance. Compliance testing can be used to determine whether laws and regulations are being adhered to, as well as whether internal controls are functioning as designed.
Answer (A) is incorrect. Compliance testing involves assessing the everyday functioning of internal controls. Answer (B) is incorrect. The proper statement of financial statement line items is the purview of a financial audit, not a compliance audit. Answer (D) is incorrect. No type of testing can be sure of detecting instances of collusion.

3. Which of the following is most likely to be regarded as a strength in internal control in a traditional external audit?

A. The performance of financial audits by the internal audit activity.

B. The performance of operational engagements by internal auditors.

C. The routine supervisory review of production planning.

D. The existence of a preventive maintenance program.

Answer (A) is correct. *(CMA, adapted)*
REQUIRED: The activity most likely regarded as a strong internal control in a traditional external audit.
DISCUSSION: The external auditor's traditional role is to perform an audit to determine whether the externally reported financial statements are fairly presented. Thus, a financial audit by the internal audit activity is relevant to the traditional external audit because it is an engagement in which the reliability and integrity of financial information is evaluated. Such an engagement is consistent with internal auditing standards. According to Standard 2130.A1, the internal audit activity must evaluate the adequacy and effectiveness of controls in responding to risks within the organization's governance, operations, and information systems. This evaluation extends to the (1) reliability and integrity of financial and operational information; (2) effectiveness and efficiency of operations; (3) safeguarding of assets; and (4) compliance with laws, regulations, and contracts.
Answer (B) is incorrect. Operational engagements are concerned with operational efficiency and effectiveness, matters that are not the primary focus of an external audit of financial statements. Answer (C) is incorrect. Routine supervisory review of production planning is a concern of management but does not directly affect the fair presentation of the financial statements. Answer (D) is incorrect. The existence of a preventive maintenance program is not directly relevant to a financial statement audit.

4. Which one of the following forms of audit is most likely to involve a review of an entity's performance of specific activities in comparison to organizational-specific objectives?

A. Information system audit.

B. Financial audit.

C. Operational audit.

D. Compliance audit.

Answer (C) is correct. *(CMA, adapted)*
REQUIRED: The type of audit most likely to involve a review of an entity's performance of specific activities.
DISCUSSION: An operational audit is a thorough examination of a department, division, function, etc. Its purpose is to appraise managerial organization, performance, and techniques. An operational audit attempts to determine the extent to which organizational objectives have been achieved.
Answer (A) is incorrect. An information system audit involves examining the specific controls over information systems. Answer (B) is incorrect. A financial audit involves assessing the fair presentation of financial statements in accordance with U.S. GAAP. Answer (D) is incorrect. A compliance audit involves assessing the everyday functioning of internal controls.

10.2 Systems Controls

5. Data processed by a computer system are usually transferred to some form of output medium for storage. However, the presence of computerized output does not, in and of itself, ensure the output's accuracy, completeness, or authenticity. For this assurance, various controls are needed. The major types of controls for this area include

A. Transaction controls, general controls, and printout controls.

B. Activity listings, echo checks, and pre-numbered forms.

C. Tape and disk output controls and printed output controls.

D. Input controls, tape and disk output controls, and printed output controls.

Answer (D) is correct. *(CMA, adapted)*
REQUIRED: The major types of controls to ensure that computerized output is accurate, complete, and authentic.
DISCUSSION: Input controls provide reasonable assurance that data received for processing have been properly authorized, converted into machine-sensible form, and identified, and that data have not been lost, suppressed, added, duplicated, or otherwise improperly changed. Input controls also relate to rejections, correction, and resubmission of data that were initially incorrect. Output controls provide assurance that the processing result is accurate and that only authorized personnel receive the output.
Answer (A) is incorrect. General, transaction, and print-out controls do not ensure accuracy of inputs. Answer (B) is incorrect. An echo check, which is an input control over transmission along communications lines, does not ensure proper authorization of data. Neither do the other techniques ensure completeness of data. Answer (C) is incorrect. Output controls are insufficient to ensure completeness and accuracy of output. Input controls are also needed.

6. In the organization of the information systems function, the most important separation of duties is

A. Not allowing the data librarian to assist in data processing operations.

B. Assuring that those responsible for programming the system do not have access to data processing operations.

C. Having a separate information officer at the top level of the organization outside of the accounting function.

D. Using different programming personnel to maintain utility programs from those who maintain the application programs.

Answer (B) is correct. *(CMA, adapted)*
REQUIRED: The most important separation of duties in the information systems function.
DISCUSSION: Separation of duties is a general control that is vital in a computerized environment. Some separation of duties common in noncomputerized environments may not be feasible in a computer environment. However, certain tasks should not be combined. Systems analysts, for example, should be separate from programmers and computer operators. Programmers design, write, test, and document specific programs required by the system developed by the analysts. Both programmers and analysts may be able to modify programs, data files, and controls and should therefore have no access to computer equipment and files or to copies of programs used in production. Operators should not be assigned programming duties or responsibility for systems design and should have no opportunity to make changes in programs and systems.
Answer (A) is incorrect. Librarians maintain control over documentation, programs, and data files; they should have no access to equipment, but they can assist in data processing operations. Answer (C) is incorrect. A separate information officer outside of the accounting function would not be as critical a separation of duties as that between programmers and processors. Answer (D) is incorrect. Programmers usually handle all types of programs.

7. Data input validation routines include

A. Terminal logs.

B. Passwords.

C. Hash totals.

D. Backup controls.

Answer (C) is correct. *(CMA, adapted)*
REQUIRED: The example of a data input validation routine.
DISCUSSION: Application controls, including input controls, are designed to ensure the accuracy and completeness of data entered into the computer. Input controls provide assurance that data have not been lost, suppressed, added, duplicated, or otherwise improperly changed. A hash total is an example of a data input validation routine. A hash total is a control total without a defined meaning, such as the total of employee numbers or invoice numbers, that is used to verify the completeness of data. Thus, the hash total for the employee listing by the personnel department could be compared with the total generated during the processing run.
Answer (A) is incorrect. Terminal logs are access controls. Answer (B) is incorrect. Passwords are access controls. Answer (D) is incorrect. Backup controls are general controls.

8. An accounting system identification code that uses a sum-of-digits check digit will detect all of the following errors **except**

A. Completeness errors.

B. Transcription errors.

C. Transposition errors.

D. Validity errors.

Answer (C) is correct. *(CMA, adapted)*
REQUIRED: The error not detected by a sum-of-digits check digit.
DISCUSSION: Self-checking digits may be used to detect incorrect identification numbers. The digit is generated by applying an algorithm to the ID number. During the input process, the check digit is recomputed by applying the same algorithm to the code actually entered. If the check digit is merely a sum, transposition errors will not be detected because the sum will be unaffected.
Answer (A) is incorrect. Completeness errors will be detected. The sum will be different if such errors occur.
Answer (B) is incorrect. Transcription errors will be detected. The sum will be different if such errors occur. Answer (D) is incorrect. Validity errors will be detected. The sum will be different if such errors occur.

9. In order to prevent, detect, and correct errors and unauthorized tampering, a payroll system should have adequate controls. The best set of controls for a payroll system includes

    A. Batch and hash totals, record counts of each run, proper separation of duties, passwords and user codes, and backup copies of activity and master files.

    B. Employee supervision, batch totals, record counts of each run, and payments by check.

    C. Passwords and user codes, batch totals, employee supervision, and record counts of each run.

    D. Batch totals, record counts, user codes, proper separation of duties, and online edit checks.

Answer (A) is correct. *(CMA, adapted)*
    REQUIRED: The best set of controls over payroll.
    DISCUSSION: Controls in a payroll system should include a proper separation of the functions of authorization, record keeping, and custody of assets; batch totals for such items as hours worked and payroll amounts; hash totals (e.g., of employee identification numbers) to test for completeness of processing; record counts for each run; special control over unclaimed checks (the person who distributes checks must not retain unclaimed checks); and backup copies of files to allow for reconstruction if information is lost.
    Answer (B) is incorrect. Separation of duties and backup procedures are not mentioned. Answer (C) is incorrect. Separation of duties and backup procedures are not mentioned. Answer (D) is incorrect. Special controls over unclaimed checks and backup procedures are omitted.

10. An employee in the receiving department keyed in a shipment from a remote terminal and inadvertently omitted the purchase order number. The best systems control to detect this error would be

    A. Batch total.

    B. Completeness test.

    C. Sequence check.

    D. Reasonableness test.

Answer (B) is correct. *(CMA, adapted)*
    REQUIRED: The best systems control to detect the omission of a purchase order number on a receiving report keyed in from a remote terminal.
    DISCUSSION: A completeness test checks that all data elements are entered before processing. An interactive system can be programmed to notify the user to enter the number before accepting the receiving report.
    Answer (A) is incorrect. A batch total is a total of one information field (such as sales on invoices) for all records in a batch. Answer (C) is incorrect. A sequence check tests for the ordering, not omission, of records. Answer (D) is incorrect. A limit or reasonableness test checks the values of data items against established limits.

11. Which one of the following statements concerning concurrent auditing techniques is **false**?

    A. They allow monitoring a system on a continuous basis for fraudulent transactions.

    B. They are most useful in complex online systems in which audit trails have either become diminished or are very limited.

    C. They allow faster detection of unauthorized transactions.

    D. They are standard components of generic software packages.

Answer (D) is correct. *(CMA, adapted)*
    REQUIRED: The false statement concerning concurrent auditing techniques.
    DISCUSSION: The primary use of generalized audit software (GAS) is to select and summarize a client's records for additional testing. These packages permit the auditor to audit through the computer; to extract, compare, analyze, and summarize data; and to generate output for use in the audit. They allow the auditor to exploit the computer to examine many more records than otherwise possible with far greater speed and accuracy. Hence, GAS facilitates analysis of all sources of potential error. However, concurrent auditing techniques are not included because they must be incorporated into the client's systems. For example, embedded audit data collection is a transaction selection approach incorporated within the regular production programs to routinely extract transactions meeting certain criteria for further testing. In effect, it provides a window through which the auditor can access the process.
    Answer (A) is incorrect. Dubious transactions can be immediately identified and reported to the auditor (rather than the user) for review and investigation, without waiting for the scheduled audit. Answer (B) is incorrect. Embedded audit modules and the like compensate for the loss of the traditional paper audit trail. Answer (C) is incorrect. Dubious transactions can be immediately identified and reported to the auditor (rather than the user) for review and investigation, without waiting for the scheduled audit.

12. In auditing computer-based systems, the integrated test facility (ITF)

    A. Allows the auditor to assemble test transactions and run them through the computer system to test the integrity of controls on a sample data base.

    B. Is a set of specialized software routines that are designed to perform specialized audit tests and store audit evidence.

    C. Is a concurrent audit technique that establishes a special set of dummy master files and enters transactions to test the programs using the dummy files during regular processing runs.

    D. Uses an audit log to record transactions and data having special audit significance during regular processing runs.

Answer (C) is correct. *(CMA, adapted)*
    REQUIRED: The true statement about an ITF.
    DISCUSSION: An ITF involves the use of a fictitious entity, such as a dummy customer in accounts receivable, against which data transactions are processed. Results are compared with previously determined results. This procedure is used within the framework of regular production, frequently without computer operator knowledge. The use of an ITF enables testing of a system as it routinely operates. The cost of using an ITF is low. The disadvantages of the ITF include the need to later nullify the data put into the system and the possibility of contaminating a database.
    Answer (A) is incorrect. An ITF includes a dummy entity as well as test data. Answer (B) is incorrect. Generalized audit software is a set of specialized software routines that are designed to perform specialized audit tests and store audit evidence. Answer (D) is incorrect. The ITF does not use an audit log.

13. The most critical aspect of separation of duties within information systems is between

    A. Project leaders and programmers.

    B. Programmers and computer operators.

    C. Management and users.

    D. Programmers and systems analysts.

Answer (B) is correct. *(CMA, adapted)*
    REQUIRED: The most critical aspect regarding separation of duties within information systems.
    DISCUSSION: The computer operator should not be assigned programming responsibility and have the opportunity to make changes in programs as (s)he operates the equipment. In general, achieving control through separation of duties in the EDP department requires that EDP personnel have no access to assets and that access to computer operation, possession of files, and development of program logic be strictly separated.
    Answer (A) is incorrect. Combining the duties of project leaders and programmers affords less opportunity to commit irregularities than combining programming and computer operation, although separation of these duties might enhance control. Answer (C) is incorrect. Combining the duties of management and users affords less opportunity to commit irregularities than combining programming and computer operation, although separation of these duties might enhance control. Answer (D) is incorrect. Combining the duties of programmers and systems analysts affords less opportunity to commit irregularities than combining programming and computer operation, although separation of these duties might enhance control.

14. Which one of the following input validation routines is **not** likely to be appropriate in a real-time operation?

    A. Sign check.

    B. Reasonableness check.

    C. Sequence check.

    D. Redundant data check.

Answer (C) is correct. *(CMA, adapted)*
    REQUIRED: The input validation routine not appropriate in a real-time operation.
    DISCUSSION: All of the terms listed refer to program controls to prescreen or edit data prior to processing, but the sequence check is most likely to be used only in batch processing. A sequence check tests to determine that records are in proper order. For example, a payroll input file would be sorted into Social Security number order. A sequence check could then be performed to verify record order. This control would not apply in a real-time operation because records would not be processed sequentially.
    Answer (A) is incorrect. Sign checks test data for the appropriate arithmetic sign. For instance, hours worked in a payroll should always be a positive number. Answer (B) is incorrect. Reasonableness tests verify that the amounts of input or output fall within predetermined limits. Answer (D) is incorrect. A redundancy check requires transmission of additional data items to check a previously received data item; for example, a few letters of a customer's name could be matched against the name associated with the customer number.

15. The online data entry control called preformatting is

A. A program initiated prior to regular input to discover errors in data before entry so that the errors can be corrected.

B. A check to determine if all data items for a transaction have been entered by the terminal operator.

C. A series of requests for required input data that requires an acceptable response to each request before a subsequent request is made.

D. The display of a document with blanks for data items to be entered by the terminal operator.

Answer (D) is correct. *(CMA, adapted)*
REQUIRED: The definition of preformatting.
DISCUSSION: To avoid data entry errors in online systems, a screen prompting approach may be used. The dialogue approach, for example, presents a series of questions to the operator. The preformatted screen approach involves the display on the CRT of a set of boxes for entry of specified data items. The format may even be in the form of a copy of a transaction document.
Answer (A) is incorrect. It describes an edit routine.
Answer (B) is incorrect. It describes a completeness check.
Answer (C) is incorrect. It describes prompting.

16. Which one of the following represents a lack of internal control in a computer-based system?

A. Any and all changes in applications programs have the authorization and approval of management.

B. Provisions exist to ensure the accuracy and integrity of computer processing of all files and reports.

C. Provisions exist to protect data files from unauthorized access, modification, or destruction.

D. Programmers have access to change programs and data files when an error is detected.

Answer (D) is correct. *(CMA, adapted)*
REQUIRED: The example of a lack of internal control in a computer system.
DISCUSSION: A functional separation of EDP activities is necessary. A programmer designs program flowcharts and writes the computer programs as required by the system. Once the program has been debugged and the documentation prepared, the programmer should have no further access to it or to data files. A librarian is responsible for permitting only computer operators, not programmers, to have access to programs.
Answer (A) is incorrect. A basic tenet of internal control is that all activities should be executed in accordance with management's express or implied authorization. Answer (B) is incorrect. Effective internal control ensures the reliability of records. A control group (clerk) should perform a continuous review function by supervising and monitoring input, operations, and distribution of output. Answer (C) is incorrect. Security is a proper concern of internal control. Restricted access and passwords are examples of controls to secure data files.

17. Edit checks in a computerized accounting system

A. Are preventive controls.

B. Should be performed on transactions prior to updating a master file.

C. Must be installed for the system to be operational.

D. Should be performed immediately prior to output distribution.

Answer (B) is correct. *(CMA, adapted)*
REQUIRED: The true statement about edit checks in a computerized accounting system.
DISCUSSION: Edit checks are those that are programmed into the software. They include error listings, field checks, financial totals, hash totals, limit and range checks, preformatting, reasonableness (relationship) tests, record counts, self-checking digits, sequence checks, sign checks, and validity checks. Such checks should be performed on transactions before the master file is updated.
Answer (A) is incorrect. Edit checks also include detective and corrective controls. Answer (C) is incorrect. Edit checks are not necessary for a system to run; they are purely for internal control purposes. Answer (D) is incorrect. Edit checks are normally performed at the time of input or during manipulation of data, not at the time of output.

18. The use of a generalized audit software package

A. Relieves an auditor of the typical tasks of investigating exceptions, verifying sources of information, and evaluating reports.

B. Is a major aid in retrieving information from computerized files.

C. Overcomes the need for an auditor to learn much about computers.

D. Is a form of auditing around the computer.

Answer (B) is correct. *(CMA, adapted)*
REQUIRED: The true statement about the use of a generalized audit software package.
DISCUSSION: The primary use of generalized computer programs is to select and summarize a client's records for additional testing. Generalized audit software packages permit the auditor to audit through the computer, to extract, compare, analyze, and summarize data and generate output as part of the audit program. They allow the auditor to exploit the computer to examine many more records than otherwise possible with far greater speed and accuracy.
Answer (A) is incorrect. The auditor must still use audit judgment. Answer (C) is incorrect. An auditor must have a knowledge of computer auditing to use a generalized software package. Answer (D) is incorrect. Using a generalized software package is a means of auditing through the computer.

19. Which one of the following is the best reason for developing a computer security plan?

A. All possible threats associated with the data processing equipment are identified.

B. Recovery from the damage associated with any identified threats can be assured.

C. A company can select the set of control policies and procedures that optimize computer security relative to cost.

D. The user departments can be assured that control policies are in place and their data files are secure.

Answer (C) is correct. *(CMA, adapted)*
REQUIRED: The best reason for developing a computer security plan.
DISCUSSION: A comprehensive computer security plan should be developed to safeguard physical facilities and hardware and provide for the privacy and integrity of data. Such a plan assists management in ensuring that benefits exceed costs.
Answer (A) is incorrect. Identification of all threats is not possible. Answer (B) is incorrect. Reasonable but not absolute assurance can be provided. Answer (D) is incorrect. The development of a plan is not the same as its successful implementation.

20. An online data entry technique that can be employed when inexperienced personnel enter data is the use of

A. Overflow procedures.

B. Prompting.

C. Compatibility tests.

D. Checkpoints.

Answer (B) is correct. *(CMA, adapted)*
REQUIRED: The online data entry technique used when inexperienced personnel enter data.
DISCUSSION: An online, real-time system permits interaction between the system and the user. Such a system can be designed to guide data entry by prompting (asking questions of) the user. Automatic teller machines are common examples.
Answer (A) is incorrect. Overflow occurs when too large a number is attempted to be stored in the CPU's memory, but an overflow control does not provide assistance to the inexperienced user. Answer (C) is incorrect. It is an access control. Answer (D) is incorrect. Checkpoints are "snapshots" of data values and program indicators taken periodically in a batch processing run. They are useful as a means of recovery in the event of a temporary hardware failure.

21. Routines that use the computer to check the validity and accuracy of transaction data during input are called

A. Operating systems.

B. Edit programs.

C. Compiler programs.

D. Integrated test facilities.

Answer (B) is correct. *(CMA, adapted)*
REQUIRED: The routines that check the validity and accuracy of transaction data during input.
DISCUSSION: Special programs validate (edit) input data for completeness, validity, and accuracy. The edited data are then used in processing. The errors, omissions, or exceptions are printed on a report.
Answer (A) is incorrect. The operating system controls the overall functioning of the CPU and its online peripheral equipment. Answer (C) is incorrect. A compiler translates source programs written in a higher level language into machine language. Answer (D) is incorrect. An ITF uses simulated transactions to audit the processing system.

22. An example of an internal check is

A. Making sure that output is distributed to the proper people.

B. Monitoring the work of programmers.

C. Collecting accurate statistics of historical transactions while gathering data.

D. Recalculating an amount to ensure its accuracy.

Answer (D) is correct. *(CMA, adapted)*
REQUIRED: The example of an internal check.
DISCUSSION: Arithmetic proof checks (recalculations) are performed by edit routines before data are processed. A simple example is comparing total debits and total credits.

23. A control designed to catch errors at the point of data entry is

A. A batch total.

B. A record count.

C. A self-checking digit.

D. Checkpoints.

Answer (C) is correct. *(CMA, adapted)*
REQUIRED: The control designed to catch errors at the point of data entry.
DISCUSSION: A check digit, or self-checking number, is an input control to determine if an error might have been made on an identification number. The digit is an extra number on the end of the identification number (creating a new ID number) that is calculated by an algorithm on the original part of the ID number. If the ID is miskeyed, the algorithm will produce a number different from the check digit and an error will be detected and reported.
Answer (A) is incorrect. A batch total is the total of an information field in a batch of records. Answer (B) is incorrect. A record count is a control total using a count of records processed during the various phases of the operation of a program. Answer (D) is incorrect. A checkpoint is a point in a program at which data are recorded for backup purposes.

24. Program documentation is a control designed primarily to ensure that

A. Programmers have access to the tape library or information on disk files.

B. Programs do not make mathematical errors.

C. Programs are kept up to date and perform as intended.

D. Data have been entered and processed.

Answer (C) is correct. *(CMA, adapted)*
REQUIRED: The purpose of program documentation.
DISCUSSION: Complete, up-to-date documentation of all programs and associated operating procedures is necessary for efficient operation of a computer installation. Maintenance of programs is important to provide for continuity and consistency of data processing services to users. Program documentation (the program run manual) consists of problem statements, systems flowcharts, operating instructions, record lay-outs, program flowcharts, program listings, test data, and approval and change sheets.
Answer (A) is incorrect. Programmers should not have access to operational materials. Answer (B) is incorrect. Editing routines check for arithmetic errors prior to processing, and debugging should uncover errors in programs. Answer (D) is incorrect. The control group exists to supervise input, processing, and output.

25. Compatibility tests are sometimes employed to determine whether an acceptable user is allowed to proceed. In order to perform compatibility tests, the system must maintain an access control matrix. The one item that is **not** part of an access control matrix is a

A. List of all authorized user code numbers and passwords.

B. List of all files maintained on the system.

C. List of all programs maintained on the system.

D. Limit on the number of transaction inquiries that can be made by each user in a specified time period.

Answer (D) is correct. *(CMA, adapted)*
REQUIRED: The item not a part of an access control matrix.
DISCUSSION: Compatibility tests restrict access to the computer system by determining whether access by a given user (or device) is compatible with the nature of the attempted use. A series of passwords or identification numbers may be required to gain access to the system, to examine data files, and to perform processing using particular programs. Thus, a clerk might be authorized only to read the data in a given file while using a specified terminal, but his/her superior might be able to update the file. Compatibility tests require online storage of authorization tables or matrices that specify the access permitted to specified codes and devices. The number of authorized inquiries per user is not included in such a table.

26. Whether or not a real-time program contains adequate controls is most effectively determined by the use of

    A. Audit software.

    B. An integrated test facility.

    C. A tagging routine.

    D. A tracing routine.

Answer (B) is correct. *(CMA, adapted)*
    REQUIRED: The audit technique that best determines whether a real-time program contains adequate controls.
    DISCUSSION: An integrated test facility involves the use of a fictitious entity, such as a dummy customer in accounts receivable, against which data transactions are processed. The results are then compared with those previously determined. This technique can be used without computer operator knowledge during routine system operation. The ITF is relatively inexpensive and requires no special processing. It is employed in auditing online, real-time systems.
    Answer (A) is incorrect. Audit software is used with batch processing systems. Answer (C) is incorrect. Tagging requires the generation of a complete audit trail and is used in advanced systems. Tagging electronically identifies the items to be traced (tracked) by means of a special code. These transactions are processed normally but are monitored to determine if the program logic is handled appropriately. Answer (D) is incorrect. Tracing requires the generation of a complete audit trail and is used in advanced systems. Tracing (tracking) is an audit technique that provides an electronic walk-through of the data processing system.

27. The most critical aspect of the separation of duties within a mainframe information systems environment is between

    A. Programmers and project leaders.

    B. Programmers and systems analysts.

    C. Programmers and users.

    D. Programmers and computer operators.

Answer (D) is correct. *(CMA, adapted)*
    REQUIRED: The most critical aspect of the separation of duties in a mainframe environment.
    DISCUSSION: Segregation of duties is important in any environment in which control is a concern. In particular, programmers and computer operators should be kept separate because programmers have the ability to modify programs, files, and controls. Thus, they should not be allowed to also operate the computer.
    Answer (A) is incorrect. Neither programmers nor project leaders have access both to programs and computers; thus, danger of control breakdowns is minimal. Answer (B) is incorrect. Systems analysts are specifically qualified to analyze and design computer systems; the work of the systems analyst is used to guide the work of programmers. The two need to work together. Answer (C) is incorrect. Neither programmers nor users of computer output have access to the operating computer; thus, danger is minimal.

28. Control procedures over accounting information systems are referred to as general controls or application controls. The primary objective of application controls in a computer environment is to

    A. Maintain the accuracy of the inputs, files, and outputs for specific applications.

    B. Ensure the separation of incompatible functions in the data processing departments.

    C. Provide controls over the electronic functioning of the hardware.

    D. Plan for the protection of the facilities and backup for the systems.

Answer (A) is correct. *(CMA, adapted)*
    REQUIRED: The primary objective of application controls in a computer environment.
    DISCUSSION: Application controls relate to specific tasks performed by the IT department. Their function is to provide reasonable assurance that recording, processing, and reporting of data are performed properly. Application controls are often categorized as input controls, processing controls, and output controls.
    Answer (B) is incorrect. Separation of incompatible functions is a general, not an application, control. Answer (C) is incorrect. Hardware controls are general controls. Answer (D) is incorrect. Operating controls are general controls.

29. A company employing an online computer system has terminals located in all operating departments for inquiry and updating purposes. Many of the company's employees have access to and are required to use the terminals. A control the company would incorporate to prevent an employee from making an unauthorized change to computer records unrelated to that employee's job would be to

A. Restrict the physical access to terminals.

B. Establish user codes and passwords.

C. Use validity checks.

D. Apply a compatibility test to transactions or inquiries entered by the user.

Answer (D) is correct. *(CMA, adapted)*
REQUIRED: The control to prevent an unauthorized change in a computer record by an employee with online access.
DISCUSSION: A compatibility test is an access control used to ascertain whether a code number is compatible with the use to be made of the information requested. For example, a user may be authorized to enter only certain kinds of transaction data, to gain access only to certain information, to have access to but not update files, or to use the system only during certain hours.
Answer (A) is incorrect. The employees must have access to the system. Thus, the restriction of access would not solve the problem. Answer (B) is incorrect. The employees must have access to the system. Thus, user codes and passwords would not solve the problem. Answer (C) is incorrect. A validity check is used to compare input identification numbers with acceptable numbers.

30. In entering the billing address for a new client in Emil Company's computerized database, a clerk erroneously entered a nonexistent zip code. As a result, the first month's bill mailed to the new client was returned to Emil Company. Which one of the following would most likely have led to discovery of the error at the time of entry into Emil Company's computerized database?

A. Limit test.

B. Validity test.

C. Parity test.

D. Record count test.

Answer (B) is correct. *(CMA, adapted)*
REQUIRED: The best computerized control for preventing an erroneous zip code from being entered.
DISCUSSION: In validity tests, values entered into the system are compared against master files of valid data. In this case, a master file of all zip codes recognized in the U.S. is held in memory and each time a clerk enters data in the zip code field, the clerk's entry is compared to the list of valid values. If the zip code entered does not match any entry in the master file, data entry is halted and the clerk is advised to reenter the data.
Answer (A) is incorrect. A limit test deals with quantified data, such as preventing hours worked in a single week from exceeding 100 without special authorization. Answer (C) is incorrect. A parity test is a means of ensuring whether the correct number of binary bits has been transmitted. Answer (D) is incorrect. A record count test is a batch-level control for ensuring that the correct number of records has been processed in a batch.

10.3 Security Measures

31. The graphic portrayal of the flow of data and the information processing of a system, including computer hardware, is best displayed in a

A. Data-flow diagram.

B. System flowchart.

C. Gantt chart.

D. Program flowchart.

Answer (B) is correct. *(CMA, adapted)*
REQUIRED: The best method of displaying the flow of data and the information processing of a system.
DISCUSSION: A system flowchart is a graphic analysis of a data processing application, usually prepared by a systems analyst. The system flowchart is general and stresses flows of data, not computer program logic. A program flowchart is a graphic representation of the detailed steps and logic of an individual computer program.
Answer (A) is incorrect. A data-flow diagram would show only the flow of data, not the total system. Answer (C) is incorrect. A Gantt chart is a bar chart used to monitor the progress of large projects. Answer (D) is incorrect. A program flowchart shows only the details of a single program, not the entire computer system.

32. A critical aspect of a disaster recovery plan is to be able to regain operational capability as soon as possible. In order to accomplish this, an organization can have an arrangement with its computer hardware vendor to have a fully operational facility available that is configured to the user's specific needs. This is best known as a(n)

A. Uninterruptible power system.

B. Parallel system.

C. Cold site.

D. Hot site.

Answer (D) is correct.   *(CMA, adapted)*
REQUIRED: The fully operational facility that is configured to the user's specific needs.
DISCUSSION: A disaster recovery plan may include a contract with an external contingency facility vendor. Depending on the organization's needs, the contingency facility may be a hot site or a cold site. A hot site is an arrangement with a vendor for a fully operational facility that is configured to the user's specific needs and that will be available within 24 hours. A hot site may also be fixed or portable and is recommended for an organization that cannot afford for its computer system to be down for even one day.
Answer (A) is incorrect. An uninterruptible power system is a system that is fully protected by a generator or battery backup to prevent data destruction and downtime from electrical power outages. Answer (B) is incorrect. A parallel system exists if a company maintains an identical system to the main system. Answer (C) is incorrect. A cold site is a cheaper alternative to a hot site. It is a shell facility suitable for the quick installation of computer equipment. It provides a prebuilt, environmentally controlled area with raised flooring, electrical power, and appropriate plumbing.

Questions 33 through 37 are based on the following information. This flowchart depicts the processing of daily cash receipts for Rockmart Manufacturing.

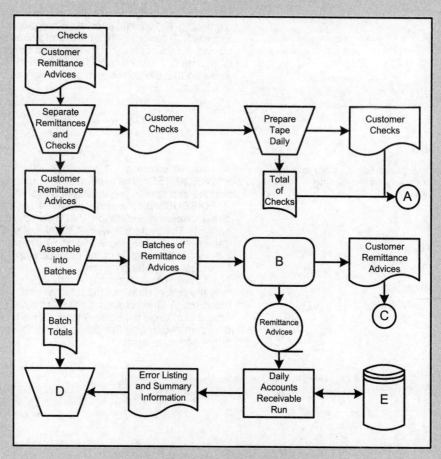

33. The customer checks accompanied by the control tape (refer to symbol A) are

A. Forwarded daily to the billing department for deposit.

B. Taken by the mail clerk to the bank for deposit daily.

C. Forwarded to the treasurer for deposit daily.

D. Accumulated for a week and then forwarded to the treasurer for deposit weekly.

Answer (C) is correct. *(CMA, adapted)*
REQUIRED: The proper procedure for handling customer checks and the related control tape.
DISCUSSION: Symbol A is a connector between a point on this flowchart and another part of the flowchart not shown. The checks and the adding machine control tape should flow through symbol A to the treasurer's office. The treasurer is the custodian of funds and is responsible for deposit of daily receipts.
Answer (A) is incorrect. Record keepers perform functions that should be separate from custody of assets. Answer (B) is incorrect. The mail clerk should prepare a list of checks received before they are forwarded to the treasurer for deposit. Answer (D) is incorrect. Daily receipts should be deposited intact daily and then reconciled with the bank deposit records. Prompt deposit also safeguards assets and avoids loss of interest income.

34. What is the appropriate description that should be placed in symbol B?

A. Keying and verifying.

B. Error correction.

C. Collation of remittance advices.

D. Batch processing.

Answer (A) is correct. *(CMA, adapted)*
REQUIRED: The appropriate description for symbol B.
DISCUSSION: Because the figure below symbol B signifies magnetic tape, the operation represented by symbol B must be keying the information onto the tape. Verifying the keyed data would also occur at this step.
Answer (B) is incorrect. Error correction occurs subsequently except for keying errors. Answer (C) is incorrect. Collation has already occurred. Answer (D) is incorrect. Batch processing describes the entire system.

35. The next action regarding the customer remittance advices (refer to symbol C) is to

A. Discard them immediately.

B. File them daily by batch number.

C. Forward them to the internal audit department for internal review.

D. Forward them to the treasurer to compare with the monthly bank statement.

Answer (B) is correct. *(CMA, adapted)*
REQUIRED: The action taken regarding the customer remittance advices at symbol C.
DISCUSSION: All activity with respect to the paper documents most likely ceases at symbol C. Accordingly, the batched documents must be filed.
Answer (A) is incorrect. The documents should be kept for reference and audit. Answer (C) is incorrect. Internal auditors cannot feasibly review all documents regarding transactions even in an audit. Answer (D) is incorrect. Comparison by the treasurer would be inappropriate. (S)he has custody of cash.

36. What is the appropriate description that should be placed in symbol D?

A. Attach batch total to report and file.

B. Reconcile cash balances.

C. Compare batch total and correct as necessary.

D. Proof report.

Answer (C) is correct. *(CMA, adapted)*
REQUIRED: The appropriate description for symbol D.
DISCUSSION: This flowcharting symbol indicates a manual operation or offline process. Because the input to this operation consists of an adding machine tape containing batch totals and a document containing summary information about the accounts receivable update and an error listing, the operation apparently involves comparing these items.
Answer (A) is incorrect. No filing symbol is given. Answer (B) is incorrect. The flowchart concerns daily receipts, not the reconciliation of cash balances. Answer (D) is incorrect. Symbol D indicates a comparison, not output in the form of a report.

37. What is the appropriate description that should be placed in symbol E?

A. Accounts receivable master file.

B. Bad debts master file.

C. Remittance advice master file.

D. Cash projection file.

Answer (A) is correct. *(CMA, adapted)*
REQUIRED: The appropriate description of symbol E.
DISCUSSION: The flowcharting figure at symbol E indicates magnetic disk storage. Because it is an input and output for the daily computer processing of accounts receivable, it must be the accounts receivable master file.
Answer (B) is incorrect. Bad debts are not a part of processing daily receipts. Answer (C) is incorrect. The remittance advice master file was not used for the daily accounts receivable run. Answer (D) is incorrect. The cash projection file was not used for the daily accounts receivable run.

38. A company's management is concerned about computer data eavesdropping and wants to maintain the confidentiality of its information as it is transmitted. The company should utilize

    A. Data encryption.

    B. Dial back systems.

    C. Message acknowledgment procedures.

    D. Password codes.

Answer (A) is correct. *(CMA, adapted)*

REQUIRED: The most effective countermeasure against data eavesdropping.

DISCUSSION: The most effective preventive measure against unauthorized interception of data is encryption. Encryption technology converts data into a code. Unauthorized users may still be able to access the data, but without the encryption key, they will be unable to decode the information. Encryption technology may be either hardware- or software-based.

Answer (B) is incorrect. Dial back systems are a primitive countermeasure that are only appropriate to old-style dialup modem connections. Answer (C) is incorrect. Message acknowledgment procedures are a means only for affirming that a message has been received by the intended party; they do not provide any means of alert in case of interception by an unintended party. Answer (D) is incorrect. Password codes must be assigned and saved on specific systems; they are not applicable to ongoing electronic transmission.

39. Which one of the following would most compromise the use of the grandfather-father-son principle of file retention as protection against loss or damage of master files?

    A. Use of magnetic tape.

    B. Inadequate ventilation.

    C. Storing of all files in one location.

    D. Failure to encrypt data.

Answer (C) is correct. *(CMA, adapted)*

REQUIRED: The practice most likely to compromise computer file backup-and-rotation procedures.

DISCUSSION: The offsite location where an organization's computer backup files are kept must be temperature- and humidity-controlled and guarded against intrusion just as the main processing center is. Just as important, it must be geographically remote enough from the site of the organization's main operations that it would not be affected by the same natural disaster. It does an organization no good to have sound backup procedures if the files are not accessible or have been destroyed.

Answer (A) is incorrect. Magnetic tape is a sound, though slow, medium for the storage of backup files. Answer (B) is incorrect. Inadequate ventilation, while undesirable, is not the most compromising of the choices. Answer (D) is incorrect. If data will only be used on equipment owned by the organization and will not be transmitted over network lines, leaving it unencrypted will not compromise the soundness of backup-and-rotation procedures.

Use Gleim **CMA Test Prep** Software for interactive testing with **additional multiple-choice questions**!

10.5 ESSAY QUESTIONS

Scenario for Essay Questions 1, 2, 3

Brawn Technology, Inc., is a manufacturer of large wind energy systems. The company has its corporate headquarters in Buenos Aires and a central manufacturing facility about 200 miles away. Since the manufacturing facility is so remote, it does not receive the attention or the support from the staff that the other units do. The president of Brawn is concerned about whether proper permits have been issued for new construction work being done to handle industrial waste at the facility. In addition, he wants to be sure that all occupational safety laws and environmental issues are being properly addressed. He has asked the company's internal auditor to conduct an audit focusing on these areas of concern.

Questions

1. Internal auditors conduct many types of audits, including financial audits and fraud audits. Identify and describe the two other fundamental types of internal audits. Using examples, describe two situations where each of these additional types of audit would be applicable.

2. Referring to Brawn Technology,

    a. Identify the type of audit that would best address the concerns of the president.
    b. Identify the objective of this audit.
    c. Give two reasons why this type of audit would best address the concerns of the president.

3. Recommend two procedures that could be implemented at Brawn's manufacturing plant that would lessen the president's concerns. Explain each of your recommendations.

Essay Questions 1, 2, 3 — Unofficial Answers

1. The two additional fundamental types of internal audits are operational audits and compliance audits.

    An operational audit is a comprehensive review of the varied functions within an enterprise to appraise the efficiency and economy of operations and the effectiveness with which those functions achieve their objective. An example would be an audit to assess productivity. Other examples could include an evaluation of processes to reduce rework, or reduce the time required to process paperwork or goods.

    A compliance audit is the review of both financial and operating controls to see how they conform to established laws, standards, regulations, and procedures. An environmental audit would be an example of a compliance audit. Other examples of compliance audits could include the review of controls over industrial wastes or the review of procedures ensuring that proper disclosure is made regarding hazardous materials on site.

2. A compliance audit would best fit the requirements of the president of Brawn.

    a. The objective of this compliance audit is to assure the president that the manufacturing facility has appropriate policies and procedures in place for obtaining the needed permits, has obtained all the required permits in accordance with the law, and that environmental and safety issues are being properly addressed.

    b. The assignment specifically is to address the proper use of permits, compliance with safety regulations, and compliance with environmental standards. These issues can only be properly addressed by conducting a compliance audit. Although financial and operational areas might be involved, they would be secondary to the compliance issues. For example, a financial impact could result from the evaluation of compliance with safety regulations. The findings might result in additional expenditures for safety precautions or a reduction in the company's risk of being fined for lack of compliance.

3. To mitigate the president's concern, the following activities and procedures could be implemented:

    a. Set the tone at the top. The president should communicate to all employees that the company expects appropriate business practices on the part of all employees in all divisions.

    b. Ensure that all employees have the necessary information to perform their duties. Keep the lines of communication open. For example, involve senior managers from the manufacturing facility in monthly operational meetings for the whole company.

    c. Conduct regularly scheduled audits of compliance with applicable laws, regulations, and standards.

    d. Periodically review and update policies, rules, and procedures to ensure that internal controls prevent or help to detect material risks. Make sure all employees have access to the relevant policies and procedures. For example, post the policies and procedures on the company's intranet.

Use **CMA Gleim Online** and **Essay Wizard** to practice additional essay questions in an exam-like environment.

APPENDIX A
ICMA CONTENT SPECIFICATION OUTLINES AND CROSS-REFERENCES

The following pages consist of a reprint of the ICMA's Content Specification Outlines (CSOs) and related information for Part 1, effective May 1, 2010. In addition, we have provided cross-references to the Gleim CMA study units. Please use these CSOs as reference material only. The ICMA's CSOs have been carefully analyzed and have been incorporated into Study Units 1 through 10 to provide systematic and rational coverage of exam topics.

We believe we provide comprehensive coverage of the subject matter tested on the CMA exam. If, after taking the exam, you feel that certain topics, concepts, etc., tested were not covered or were inadequately covered, please go to www.gleim.com/feedbackCMA1 or scan the QR code below with your mobile device. We do not want information about CMA questions, only information/feedback about our CMA Review System's coverage.

Be part of something!

Help make Gleim even better with your feedback.

www.gleim.com/feedbackCMA1

Effective May 1, 2010

Content Specification Outlines
Certified Management Accountant (CMA) Examinations

The content specification outlines presented below represent the body of knowledge that will be covered on the CMA examinations. The outlines may be changed in the future when new subject matter becomes part of the common body of knowledge.

Candidates for the CMA designation are required to take and pass Parts 1 and 2.

Candidates are responsible for being informed on the most recent developments in the areas covered in the outlines. This includes understanding of public pronouncements issued by accounting organizations as well as being up-to-date on recent developments reported in current accounting, financial, and business periodicals.

The content specification outlines serve several purposes. The outlines are intended to:

- Establish the foundation from which each examination will be developed.
- Provide a basis for consistent coverage on each examination.
- Communicate to interested parties more detail as to the content of each examination part.
- Assist candidates in their preparation for each examination.
- Provide information to those who offer courses designed to aid candidates in preparing for the examinations.

Important additional information about the content specification outlines and the examinations is listed below and on the following page.

1. The coverage percentage given for each major topic within each examination part represents the relative weight given to that topic in an examination part. The number of questions presented in each major topic area approximates this percentage.

2. Each examination will sample from the subject areas contained within each major topic area to meet the relative weight specifications. No relative weights have been assigned to the subject areas within each major topic. No inference should be made from the order in which the subject areas are listed or from the number of subject areas as to the relative weight or importance of any of the subjects.

3. Each major topic within each examination part has been assigned a coverage level designating the depth and breadth of topic coverage, ranging from an introductory knowledge of a subject area (Level A) to a thorough understanding of and ability to apply the essentials of a subject area (Level C). Detailed explanations of the coverage levels and the skills expected of candidates are presented on the following page.

4. The topics for Parts 1 and 2 have been selected to minimize the overlapping of subject areas among the examination parts. The topics within an examination part and the subject areas within topics may be combined in individual questions.

5. With regard to U.S. Federal income taxation issues, candidates will be expected to understand the impact of income taxes when reporting and analyzing financial results. In addition, the tax code provisions that impact decisions (e.g., depreciation, interest, etc.) will be tested.

6. Candidates for the CMA designation are assumed to have knowledge of the following: preparation of financial statements, business economics, time-value of money concepts, statistics and probability.

7. Parts 1 and 2 are four-hour exams and each contains 100 multiple-choice questions and 2 essay questions. Candidates will have three hours to complete the multiple-choice questions and one hour to complete the essay section. A small number of the multiple-choice questions on each exam are being validated for future use and will not count in the final score.

8. For the essay questions, both written and quantitative responses will be required. Candidates will be expected to present written answers that are responsive to the question asked, presented in a logical manner, and demonstrate an appropriate understanding of the subject matter. It should be noted that candidates are expected to have working knowledge in the use of word processing and electronic spreadsheets.

9. Ethical issues and considerations are tested in both Parts 1 and 2. In Part 1, ethics will be tested from the perspective of the individual and in Part 2, from the perspective of the organization.

In order to more clearly define the topical knowledge required by a candidate, varying levels of coverage for the treatment of major topics of the content specification outlines have been identified and defined. The cognitive skills that a successful candidate should possess and that should be tested on the examinations can be defined as follows*:

Knowledge: Ability to remember previously learned material such as specific facts, criteria, techniques, principles, and procedures (i.e., identify, define, list).

Comprehension: Ability to grasp and interpret the meaning of material (i.e., classify, explain, distinguish between).

Application: Ability to use learned material in new and concrete situations (i.e., demonstrate, predict, solve, modify, relate).

Analysis: Ability to break down material into its component parts so that its organizational structure can be understood; ability to recognize causal relationships, discriminate between behaviors, and identify elements that are relevant to the validation of a judgment (i.e., differentiate, estimate, order).

Synthesis: Ability to put parts together to form a new whole or proposed set of operations; ability to relate ideas and formulate hypotheses (i.e., combine, formulate, revise).

Evaluation: Ability to judge the value of material for a given purpose on the basis of consistency, logical accuracy, and comparison to standards; ability to appraise judgments involved in the selection of a course of action (i.e., criticize, justify, conclude).

The three levels of coverage can be defined as follows:

Level A: Requiring the skill levels of knowledge and comprehension.

Level B: Requiring the skill levels of knowledge, comprehension, application, and analysis.

Level C: Requiring all six skill levels – knowledge, comprehension, application, analysis, synthesis, and evaluation.

The levels of coverage as they apply to each of the major topics of the Content Specification Outlines are shown on the following pages with each topic listing. The levels represent the manner in which topic areas are to be treated and represent ceilings, i.e., a topic area designated as Level C may contain requirements at the "A," "B," or "C" level, but a topic designated as Level B will not contain requirements at the "C" level.

*A more thorough explanation of these skills is presented in Appendix C, Types and Levels of Exam Questions.

CMA Content Specification Overview

Part 1   *Financial Planning, Performance and Control*
(4 hours – 100 questions and 2 essay questions)

Planning, Budgeting and Forecasting	**30%**	**Level C**
Performance Management	**25%**	**Level C**
Cost Management	**25%**	**Level C**
Internal Controls	**15%**	**Level C**
Professional Ethics	**5%**	**Level C**

Candidates for the CMA designation are assumed to have knowledge of the following: preparation of financial statements, business economics, time-value of money concepts, statistics and probability. Questions in both parts of the CMA exam will assume that the successful candidate can effectively integrate and synthesize this knowledge with the specific topics covered in the content specification outline.

Below and on the following pages, we have reproduced verbatim the ICMA's Content Specification Outlines (CSOs) for Part 1. We also have provided cross-references to the study units and subunits in this book that correspond to the CSOs' coverage. If one entry appears above a list, it applies to all items in that list.

Part 1 – Financial Planning, Performance and Control

A. **Planning, Budgeting, and Forecasting (30% - Levels A, B, and C)**

1. *Budgeting concepts*

    a. Operations and performance goals (5.1)
    b. Characteristics of a successful budget process (5.2)
    c. Resource allocation (5.2)
    d. Other budgeting concepts (5.3)

2. *Forecasting techniques*

    a. Regression analysis (5.4)
    b. Learning curve analysis (5.5)
    c. Exponential smoothing (5.6)
    d. Time series analysis (5.6)
    e. Expected value (5.7)

3. *Budgeting methodologies*

    a. Annual business plans (master budgets) (6.1)
    b. Project budgeting (6.2, 6.4)
    c. Activity-based budgeting (6.2, 6.4)
    d. Zero-based budgeting (6.2, 6.4)
    e. Continuous (rolling) budgets (6.2, 6.4)
    f. Flexible budgeting (6.3, 6.4)

4. *Annual profit plan and supporting schedules*

    a. Operational budgets (6.5 – 6.7)
    b. Financial budgets (6.8, 6.9)
    c. Capital budgets (6.5)

5. *Top-level planning and analysis*

    a. Pro forma income (6.8)
    b. Financial statement projections (6.10)
    c. Cash flow projections (6.10)

B. **Performance Management (25% - Levels A, B, and C)**

  1. *Cost and variance measures*

     a. Comparison of actual to planned results (7.1)
     b. Use of flexible budgets to analyze performance (7.2)
     c. Management by exception (7.1)
     d. Use of standard cost systems (7.2)
     e. Analysis of variation from standard cost expectations (7.3 – 7.8)

  2. *Responsibility centers and reporting segments*

     a. Types of responsibility centers (8.1)
     b. Transfer pricing models (8.6, 8.7)
     c. Reporting of organizational segments (8.2, 8.3)

  3. *Performance measures*

     a. Product profitability analysis (8.2)
     b. Business unit profitability analysis (8.2)
     c. Customer profitability analysis (8.2)
     d. Return on investment (8.3, 8.4)
     e. Residual income (8.3, 8.4)
     f. Investment base issues (8.3, 8.4)
     g. Effect of international operations (8.4)
     h. Critical success factors (8.8)
     i. Balanced scorecard (8.8)

C. **Cost Management (25% - Levels A, B, and C)**

  1. *Measurement concepts* (1.1, 1.5, 1.6)

     a. Cost behavior and cost objects (1.2 – 1.4)
     b. Actual and normal costs (1.6, 3.4, 3.5)
     c. Standard costs (1.6, 3.4, 3.5)
     d. Absorption (full) costing (3.1, 3.2)
     e. Variable (direct) costing (3.1, 3.2)
     f. Joint and by-product costing (3.3)

  2. *Costing systems*

     a. Job order costing (2.1)
     b. Process costing (2.2)
     c. Activity-based costing (2.3)
     d. Life-cycle costing (2.4)

  3. *Overhead costs*

     a. Fixed and variable overhead expenses (3.4, 3.5)
     b. Plant-wide versus departmental overhead (3.4)
     c. Determination of allocation base (3.4, 3.5)
     d. Allocation of service department costs (3.6, 3.7)

  4. *Operational efficiency*

     a. Just-in-time manufacturing (4.1)
     b. Material requirements planning (MRP) (4.2)
     c. Theory of constraints and throughput costing (4.3)
     d. Capacity management and analysis (4.4)

5. ***Business process performance***

    a.   Value chain analysis (4.5)
    b.   Value-added concepts (4.5)
    c.   Process analysis (4.6)
    d.   Benchmarking (4.6)
    e.   Activity-based management (4.6)
    f.   Continuous improvement concepts (4.6)
    g.   Best practice analysis (4.6)
    h.   Cost of quality analysis (4.6)

D. Internal Controls (15% - Levels A, B, and C)

1. ***Risk assessment, controls, and risk management***

    a.   Internal control structure and management philosophy (9.1)
    b.   Internal control policies for safeguarding and assurance (9.2)
    c.   Internal control risk (9.1, 9.2)
    d.   Implications of the Sarbanes-Oxley Act of 2002 (9.3)
    e.   U.S. Foreign Corrupt Practices Act internal control requirements (9.3)
    f.   COSO Internal Control Framework (9.1)

2. ***Internal auditing***

    a.   Responsibility and authority of the internal audit function (10.1)
    b.   Types of audits conducted by internal auditors (10.1)

3. ***Systems control and security measures***

    a.   General accounting system controls (10.2)
    b.   Application and transaction controls (10.2)
    c.   Network controls (10.3)
    d.   Flowcharting to assess controls (10.3)
    e.   Backup controls (10.3)
    f.   Disaster recovery procedures (10.3)

E. Professional Ethics (5% - Levels A, B, and C)

1. ***Ethical considerations for management accounting and financial management professionals***

    a.   Provisions of IMA's "Statement of Ethical Professional Practice" (1.1)
    b.   Evaluation and resolution of ethical issues such as:

        ■ Fraudulent reporting
        ■ Manipulation of analyses and results
        ■ Unethical behavior in developing budgets and standards
        ■ Manipulation of decision factors (1.1)

APPENDIX B
ICMA SUGGESTED READING LIST
(As printed in the ICMA's 2012 Resource Guide)

The ICMA suggested reading list that follows is reproduced to give you an overview of the scope of Part 1. You will not have the time to study these texts. Our CMA Review System is complete and thorough and is designed to maximize your study time. Candidates are expected to stay up-to-date by reading articles from journals, newspapers, and professional publications.

Part 1 – Financial Planning, Performance and Control

Planning, Budgeting and Forecasting

Blocher, Edward J., Stout, David E., and Cokins, Gary, *Cost Management: A Strategic Emphasis*, 5th edition, McGraw Hill, New York, NY, 2010.

Horngren, Charles T., Datar, Srikant, and Rajan, Madhav, *Cost Accounting: A Managerial Emphasis*, 14th edition, Prentice-Hall, Upper Saddle River, NJ, 2012.

Anderson, David R., Sweeney, Dennis J., Williams, Thomas A., Camm, Jeff, and Martin, R. Kipp, *Quantitative Methods for Business, 11th Edition*, Mason, Ohio: South Western, 2010.

Performance Management

Blocher, Edward J., Stout, David E., and Cokins, Gary, *Cost Management: A Strategic Emphasis*, 5th edition, McGraw Hill, New York, NY, 2010.

Horngren, Charles T., Datar, Srikant, and Rajan, Madhav, *Cost Accounting: A Managerial Emphasis*, 14th edition, Prentice-Hall, Upper Saddle River, NJ, 2012.

Cost Management

Blocher, Edward J., Stout, David E., and Cokins, Gary, *Cost Management: A Strategic Emphasis*, 5th edition, McGraw Hill, New York, NY, 2010.

Horngren, Charles T., Datar, Srikant, and Rajan, Madhav, *Cost Accounting: A Managerial Emphasis*, 14th edition, Prentice-Hall, Upper Saddle River, NJ, 2012.

Internal Controls

Bodnar, George H., and Hopwood, William S., *Accounting Information Systems*, 10th edition, Prentice-Hall, Upper Saddle River, NJ, 2010.

Sawyer, Lawrence B., Dittenhofer, Mortimer A., and Graham, Anne, eds., 2003. *Sawyer's Internal Auditing: The Practice of Modern Internal Auditing*, 5th edition, The IIA, Altamonte Springs, FL, 2003.

Simkin, Mark G., Rose, Jacob M., Norman, Carolyn S., *Core Concepts of Accounting Information Systems*, 12th edition, John Wiley & Sons, Hoboken, NJ, 2012.

Professional Ethics

IMA, 2005, *IMA Statement of Ethical Professional Practice*,
http://www.imanet.org/PDFs/Statement of Ethics_web.pdf.

APPENDIX C
TYPES AND LEVELS OF EXAM QUESTIONS

The following is based on an excerpt from the ICMA's Resource Guide for the CMA exam, printed in 2012.

TYPES OF EXAM QUESTIONS

All multiple choice items within the CMA parts 1 and 2 are of the 4-option multiple-choice type, with one and only one correct answer for each question. There are, however, a number of variations on this type of item used in the CMA exams. In the examples below, the term "stem" refers to all the information that precedes the answer options or alternatives.

Closed Stem Item

This item type is characterized by a stem that is a complete sentence which concludes with a question mark. The options may be complete or incomplete sentences.

Example:

Which one of the following would have the effect of increasing the working capital of a firm?

a.   Cash payment of payroll taxes payable.
b.   Cash collection of accounts receivable.
c.   The purchase of a new plant, financed by a 20-year mortgage.
d.   Refinancing a short-term note with a 2-year note.

Key = d

Sentence Completion Item

This type of item is characterized by a stem that is an incomplete sentence. The options represent conclusions to that sentence.

Example:

If a product's elasticity coefficient is 2.0, this means the demand is

a.   perfectly elastic.
b.   elastic.
c.   inelastic.
d.   perfectly inelastic.

Key = b

Except Format

This type of item is employed when you are required to select the option that does not "fit." In this case, three of the options will fit or be defined by the stem, and one option (the correct option) will not fit. A variation on this type of question is to use the word **not** instead of **except** in the stem, in the form of "Which one of the following is **not**...".

Example:

All of the following are considered tangible assets **except**

a. real estate.
b. copyrights.
c. prepaid taxes.
d. accounts receivable.

Key = b

Most/Least/Best Format

This type of item requires you to select an option which is either better or worse than the others. In all cases, the correct answer represents the collective judgment of experts within the field.

Example #1:

Which one of the following **best** describes a production budget?

a. It is based on required direct labor hours.
b. It includes required material purchases.
c. It is based on desired ending inventory and sales forecasts.
d. It is an aggregate of the monetary details of the operating budget.

Key = c

Example #2:

Which one of the following is **least** likely to help an organization overcome its communication problems between the Accounting Department and other departments?

a. Job rotation.
b. Cross-functional teams.
c. Written policies and procedures.
d. Performance appraisals.

Key = d

QUESTION LEVELS

In addition to the variety of item formats previously described on the previous pages, the CMA exams present test items at varying cognitive levels. These levels range from questions that require a recall of material to questions that require a sophisticated understanding such that you must apply your knowledge to a novel situation, or judge the value of information as it may apply to a particular scenario. A description of each of these levels, along with sample questions, appears below and on the following pages. The cognitive level required for each major topic area of the CMA exams is shown in the Topic/Resource outline.

Level A

This cognitive level represents the "lowest" or most basic level, and includes items that require the recall of facts and the recognition of principles. This level includes the categories of knowledge and comprehension.

Knowledge: This is the lowest level of learning. Items in this category are those that require the recall of ideas, material, or phenomena related to the topic of interest. In these questions, you will be asked to define, identify, and select information.

Example:

A market situation where a small number of sellers comprise an entire industry is known as

    a.   a natural monopoly.
    b.   monopolistic competition.
    c.   an oligopoly.
    d.   pure competition.

Key = c

To correctly respond to the item above, you must recall the textbook definition of an oligopoly.

Comprehension: Items in this category require you to grasp the meaning of the material presented in some novel way. A question testing for comprehension describes some principle or fact in words different from those used in textbooks and often uses a situation as a way to present the idea. In order to answer the item correctly, you must recognize the principle demonstrated in the problem; memory alone will not be sufficient for identifying the correct answer.

Example:

Social legislation is frequently criticized for being inefficient because the agencies

    a.   use flexible rather than rigid standards.
    b.   rely heavily on the free market to allocate resources.
    c.   rarely consider the marginal benefits relative to the marginal costs.
    d.   enforce their policies too leniently.

Key = c

In order to answer this item correctly, you must know something about the issues or principles in connection with social legislation. Other questions dealing with this level of testing are those that ask you to identify an option which best explains, illustrates, or provides an example of the concept in question.

Level B
This cognitive level includes items that test for the application of material to novel situations and the ability to analyze or break down information into its component parts. Items that require application or analysis are included in this level.

Application: Items in this category measure understanding of ideas or content to a point where you can apply that understanding to an entirely new situation. The objective of these items is to test whether you can use the knowledge in an appropriate manner in a real-life situation.

Example:

The balance sheet for Miller Industries shows the following.

Cash	$ 8,000,000
Accounts Receivable	13,500,000
Inventory	7,800,000
Prepaid Expenses	245,000
Property, Plant, & Equipment	4,700,000

Based on this information, what are the Total Current Assets for this firm?

a. $21,500,000.
b. $29,300,000.
c. $29,545,000.
d. $34,245,000.

Key = c

Rather than rely on memory or comprehension alone, the situation presented in this item requires you to draw on your knowledge of the calculation of Total Current Assets and apply that knowledge to the particular data presented in the problem. Other items dealing with this level of testing might ask you to identify a specific situation requiring a certain course of action, or the most appropriate procedure or steps to apply to a particular problem.

Analysis: Analysis involves the ability to break down material into its component parts so that its organizational structure can be understood. It involves the ability to recognize parts, as well as the relationships between those parts, and to recognize the principles involved. Items in this category ask you to differentiate, discriminate, distinguish, infer, and determine the relevancy of data.

Example:

A firm is considering the implementation of a lock-box collection system at a cost of $80,000 per year. Annual sales are $90 million, and the lock-box system will reduce collection time by 3 days. The firm currently is in debt for $3,000,000. If the firm can invest the funds designated for the lock-box at 8%, should it use the lock-box system? Assume a 360-day year.

a.   Yes, it will produce a savings of $140,000 per year.
b.   Yes, it will produce a savings of $60,000 per year.
c.   No, it will produce a loss of $20,000 per year.
d.   No, it will produce a loss of $60,000 per year.

Key = c

In this item, you are presented with a novel situation, and asked to identify the data that are relevant to the problem at hand, which in this case involves the determination of the savings or loss of implementing a lock-box type of collection system. You are required to apply principles to determine savings or loss, and then to make an analysis of the outcomes of the alternative courses of action.

Level C

This cognitive level is considered the "highest" or most challenging level, and includes items that require you to evaluate information.

Evaluation: Items in this category are those that require the ability to judge the value of material for a given purpose, based on definite criteria. These questions include those that ask you to appraise, conclude, support, compare, contrast, interpret, and summarize information.

Example:

A home services organization has been using the straight-line depreciation method for calculating the depreciation expenses of its equipment. Based on recently acquired information, the firm's assistant controller has altered the estimated useful lives of the equipment. The corresponding changes in depreciation result in a change from a small profit for the year to a loss. The assistant controller is asked by the controller to reduce by half the total depreciation expense for the current year. Believing he is faced with an ethical conflict, the assistant controller reports the problem to the Board of Directors. In accordance with **IMA's Statement of Ethical Professional Practice**, which one of the following is the correct evaluation of the assistant controller's action?

a.   The assistant controller's action was appropriate as an immediate step.

b.   The assistant controller's action would have been appropriate only if other alternatives had first been tried.

c.   The assistant controller's action was not appropriate under any circumstances.

d.   Not enough information has been given to evaluate the assistant controller's action.

Key = b

The situation presented in this item requires you to evaluate the course of action that the assistant controller has taken. Option b is the correct option. While the assistant controller's action is appropriate, the situation may be resolved by less drastic means first. You are asked to make a judgment on the appropriateness of the actions to the situation described, and answer the question on the basis of this information.

INDEX

Abnormal spoilage
    Definition of 30
    Job-order costing 57
    Process costing 62
Absorption (full) costing 31, 91
Activity
    Analysis 65, 149
    -Based
        Budgeting 210
        Costing (ABC) 32, 63
            And TOC 143
            Overhead allocation 105
        Management (ABM) 68, 149
        Systems 65
    Drivers 66
Actual costing 32
After-purchase costs 70
AICPA audit risk model 327
Allocation base 102
Analysis
    Best practice 152
    SWOT 305
Annual profit plan 209
Area office profitability analysis 295
Asymmetric encryption 376
Audit
    Committee 332
    Compliance 366
    Operational 366
    Trail 373
Auditing Standard
    2 342
    5 . . . . 328, 343
Authentication 371
Authorization 372
Avoidable costs 28

Back doors 370
Backlash effect 147
Backup 380
Balanced scorecard 152, 305
Batch-level activities 65
Benchmarking 150
Benefit received 299
Best practice analysis 152
Bill of materials (BOM) 138
Board of directors 172, 332
Bottleneck 140, 148
Brute-force attack 376

Budget 169, 209
    Breakeven point 221
    Capital 223
    Cash
        Example of 225
        Order of preparation 216
        Purpose of 223
    Committee 172
    Continuous (rolling) 212
    Contribution margin 221
    Controllability 174
    Cost of goods sold, example of 220
    Cycle 233
    Direct
        Labor, example of 218
        Materials, example of 218
    Ending finished goods inventory 220
    Expense, order of preparation 215
    Financial 209, 223
    Fixed overhead, example of 220
    Flexible 214
    Gross margin 221
    Manual 172
    Master (comprehensive) 209
    Nonmanufacturing, example of 222
    Operating 209, 217
    Participation 172
    Planning calendar 172
    Production
        Example of 217
        Order of preparation 215
    Project 210
    Purchases, order of preparation 215
    Revisions 174
    Sales
        Example of 217
        Order of preparation 215
    Static 213
    Variable overhead, example of 219
Budgetary slack 173
Budgeting 167
    Activity-based 210
    Incremental 211
    Process 173
    Zero-based (ZBB) 211
Bullwhip effect 147
Business
    Continuity 380
    Judgment rule 332
    Process reengineering (BPR) 150
By-products 29, 100

Capacity
    Expansion 144
    Factors, transfer pricing 302
    Normal 30
    Planning 143
    Practical 30
    Theoretical (ideal) 30
Capital expenditures 216

Carrying costs 30
Cash
 Budget 223, 224
  Order of preparation 216
 Collection schedule. 224
 Disbursements schedule 224
Cellular organization 136
Certificate authority 376
CIA exam. 15
Coefficient of
 Correlation. 176
 Determination. 177
Cold site 381
Committed costs. 28
Common costs
 Allocation of 299
 Definition of 24
Compensating controls 338
Compensatory (mitigative) controls 334
Competence. 20
Complementary controls 334
Compliance 329
Computer-assisted audit techniques (CAATs). . . . 374
Concurrent controls. 334
Confidentiality. 20
Conformance costs 152
Constant gross-margin percentage NRV
 method 34, 99
Constraint 139
Contingency planning 380
Contribution margin. 31
Control 169
 Activities 329, 335
 Compensatory (mitigative) 334
 Complementary 334
 Corrective 334
 Criteria 367
 Detective 334
 Environment. 329, 331
 Feedback. 334
 Financial 334
 Internal 340, 364
 Operating. 334
 People-based 335
 Preventive 333
 Risk (CR). 327
 System-based 335
Controllability 293
Controllable costs 28
Controls
 Compensating 338
 Safeguarding 337
Conversion costs 22
Corrective controls 334
Correlation analysis. 176
Corrupt payments 338
COSO, definition of control. 328
Cosourcing 139

Cost 21
 Accounting. 21
 Accumulation systems 53
 Behavior 24
 Center. 293
 Driver
  Activity-based costing 67
  Definition of 22
  Overhead allocation 102
 Historical 29
 Incurrence 148
 Management terminology. 21
 Objects 22, 66
 Of goods
  Manufactured 27
  Sold 27
   Budget 220
 Pools. 23, 65, 66
 Standards 174
 Structure, transfer pricing. 302
 Target 71
Costing
 Absorption (full) 31, 91
 Activity-based (ABC) 32, 63
  Overhead allocation 105
 Actual 32
 Extended normal 32
 Job-order. 32, 54
 Life-cycle 33, 70, 148
 Normal 32
  Example 107
 Peanut-butter 63
 Process. 32, 57
 Standard 33
 Target 35
 Throughput (supervariable) 140
 Variable (direct) 31, 91
Costs
 After-purchase 70
 Avoidable. 28
 Carrying. 30
 Central
  Administration 300
  Support 299
 Committed 28
 Common
  Allocation of 299
  Definition of 24
 Conformance 152
 Controllable 28, 174
 Conversion 22
 Currently attainable (practical) standards . . . 175
 Differential 28
 Direct 23
 Discretionary 28
 Economic. 29
 Engineered 28
 Environmental 153
 Fixed. 25
 Fringe benefits 219
 Full absorption 301

Costs (continued)
Ideal (theoretical) standards 175
Imputed 29
Incremental 28
Indirect 23, 299
Joint (common) 97
Allocation of 33
Definition of 29
Locked-in (designed-in) 148
Manufacturing 22
Marginal 27
Mixed (semivariable) 25
Nonconformance 152
Noncontrollable 28, 174
Nonmanufacturing 22
Nonvalue-added 149
Opportunity 29, 143
Outlay (out-of-pocket) 28
Overhead 101
Period 23
Prime 22
Product (inventoriable) 23
Quality 152
Relevant 29
Resource 66
Selling (marketing) 22
Separable 29, 97
Service (support) 108
Sunk 29
Transferred-in 30
Value-adding 30, 149
Variable 24, 301
Credibility 20
Critical success factors (CSFs) 147, 305
Currently attainable (practical) standards 175
Customer profitability analysis 296

Data theft 370
Denial-of-service (DoS) attack 376
Detection risk (DR) 327
Detective controls 334
Differential costs 28
Direct
Costs 23
File alteration 370
Labor 22
Variances 264
Materials 22
Variances 262
Method
Calculation of 109
Definition of 34
Directive controls 334
Disaster recovery 380
Discretionary costs 28
Drum-buffer-rope (DBR) 141
Dual
Pricing 304
-Rate method 112

Economic costs 29
Effectiveness and efficiency 329
Electronic data interchange (EDI) in JIT 135

Encryption 376
Engineered costs 28
Environmental controls 371
Equipment purchases 216
Equivalent units of production (EUP) 59
Error listings 374
Estimated net realizable value (NRV) method . . 34, 99
Expected value 184
Of perfect information (EVPI) 186
Expenses, administrative 22
Extended normal costing 32

Facility-sustaining activities 65
Factory operating costs 22
Feedback controls 333, 334
Feedforward controls 334
Financial
Accounting 21
Auditing 365
Controls 334
Firewall 377
First-in, first-out (FIFO), EUP 60
Fixed
Costs 25
Overhead variance 268
Flesher, Dale L. iii
Flexible budget 214
Variance
Definition of 257
Formula 261
Flowcharting 377
Forecasting 176
Foreign Corrupt Practices Act of 1977 338
Four-way overhead variance analysis 269
Fraud 338
Fringe benefits, cost 219

Gleim, Irvin N. iii
Goal
Budget 171
Congruence 152, 302
Goal congruence 294
Gross margin 31

High-low method 26
Historical cost 29
Homoscedasticity 179
Hot site 381

Ideal (theoretical) standards 175
IMA Statement of Ethical Professional Practice . . . 18
Imputed costs 29
Income, residual 296
Incremental
Costs 28
Method 300
Indirect
Costs 23
Labor 22
Materials 22

Industry situation, budget 173
Information
    And communication. 330
    Security 369
Inherent risk (IR) 327
Input
    Controls. 372
    Manipulation. 370
Insourcing 139
Institute of Internal Auditors (IIA) 364
Integrity 20
Internal
    Auditing. 364
    Control 340, 364
        Components 329
        Monitoring 330
Invested capital 297
Investment
    Bases 297
    Center 293

Job
    Cost sheets 54
    -Order costing 32, 54
Joint (common) costs 97
    Allocation of 33
    Definition of 29
Joint products
    Allocation of 98
    Definition of 97
Just-in-time (JIT) 134

Kaizen 149
Kanban 135

Lagging indicators 306
Leading indicators 306
Lean operation 134
Learning
    Curve analysis 180
    Model
        Cumulative average-time 181
        Incremental unit-time 181
Least-squares analysis 178
Life-cycle costing 33, 70
Linear-cost functions 26
Locked-in (designed-in) costs 148
Logic bombs 370
Logical controls 371

Malicious software (malware) 370
Man-in-the-middle attack 376
Management
    Accounting. 21
    By exception 33
    Plan 170

Manufacturing
    Cells 136
    Costs 22
    Overhead. 22, 54
    Resource planning (MRP II) 138
Marginal costs 27
Market price 301
Master production schedule (MPS) 137
Material weaknesses 328, 341
Materials requirements planning (MRP) 137
Mix variance. 266
Mixed (semivariable) costs 25
Monitoring 150, 330
Motivation 169

Negotiation 302
Nonconformance costs 152
Noncontrollable costs 28
Nonlinear-cost function 26
Nonmanufacturing costs 22
Nonvalue-added
    Activity 67, 149
    Costs 149
Normal
    Costing 32
        Example 107
    Spoilage
        Definition of 30
        Job-order costing 56
        Process costing 62

Offsite location 380
Operating controls. 334
Opportunity costs 29
Outlay (out-of-pocket) costs 28
Output controls 373
Outsourcing 139
Overhead. 101
    Application rate
        Calculation of 103
        Departmental vs. plantwide 107
        In ABC 105
        Single-rate vs. dual-rate 112
    Application rate in job-order costing. 55
    Variances 267

Password. 371
    Attacks 376
    Fatigue 372
    Optimization 372
Payoff table 184
PCAOB 342
Peanut-butter costing 63
People-based controls 335
Perfect information 186
Performance measures 294, 296
Period costs 23
Physical
    Access 371
    Controls. 371
    Unit method 33

Planning 170
  Capacity 143
Porter, Michael E. 144
Preventive controls 333
Prime costs 22
Private-key encryption 376
Process 150
  Analysis 148
  Costing 32, 57
  Value analysis 67, 149
Processing controls 373
Product
  -Cost cross-subsidization 63
  (Inventoriable) costs 23, 91
  Profitability analysis 295
  -Sustaining activities 65
Profit
  Center 293
  Plan 169
    Annual 209
Pro forma
  Balance sheet 227
  Income statement 225
  Operating income 222
  Statement of cash flows 227
Program alteration 370
Public-key encryption 376
Pull system 135
Push system 137

RAID 375
Reasonable assurance 339
Reciprocal method
  Calculation of 111
  Definition of 35
Regression analysis 178
Relevant costs 29
Relevant range 24, 27
Reliability 329
Residual income 296
Resolution of ethical conflict 21
Resource
  Costs 66
  Drivers 66
Responsibility centers 292
Return on investment (ROI) 296
Revenue center 293
Rework 30
Risk 326
  Assessment 326, 329
  Management 326

Sabotage 370
Safeguarding controls 337
Sales
  Forecast 217
  Value at split-off method 33, 98
  Variances 271
  -Volume variance
    Definition of 258
    Formula 261
Sarbanes-Oxley Act 327, 340, 342
Scrap 30

Security 376
Segment reporting 295
Segmental performance 302
Segregation of duties 335
Sensitivity analysis 186
Separable costs 29
Service (support) department costs 108
Single sign-on 372
Sniffing 376
Split-off point 29, 97
Spoilage
  Definition of 30
  Job-order costing 56
  Process costing 62
Spoofing 376
Stand-alone method 300
Standard
  Costs 174
  Setting 176
Statement on Management
  Accounting (SMA) 143, 145, 150, 152
Static budget 213, 259
  Variance
    Definition of 257
    Formula 259
Step-
  Cost function 26
  Down method
    Calculation of 110
    Definition of 34
Storage controls 375
Strategic business units 293
Sunk costs 29
Supervariable costing 140
Supply chain 147
Symmetric encryption 376
System
  -Based controls 335
  Of internal control 327
Systems development controls 371

Target
  Cost 71
  Costing 35
  Price 71
Tax factors, transfer pricing 302
Theft 370
Theory of constraints (TOC)
  And ABC 143
  Definition of 139
  Example of 142
  Steps in an analysis 139
Three-way overhead variance analysis 269
Throughput
  Costing 140
  Margin 140
Time series analysis 181
  Exponential smoothing 183
  Simple moving average 182
  Weighted moving average 182
Total
  Industry capacity 144
  Quality management (TQM) 150
  Risk (TR) 327

Traditional (volume-based) costing system. . . .   63, 65
Transfer pricing 301, 302
Transferred-in costs 30
Trojan horses. 370
Two-way overhead variance analysis 269

Unit-level activities 65

Value
  -Adding
    Activity 67, 149
    Costs 30, 149
  Chain 70, 145
    Analysis. 145
  Engineering 71, 148
  Expected 184
Variable
  Costs 24
  (Direct) costing 31, 91
Variance
  Analysis. 256
  Direct
    Labor 264
    Materials 262
  Mix and yield 265
  Overhead. 267
  Sales. 271
Viruses 370
Volume-based systems 63, 65

Warm site 381
Waste 30
Weighted-average, EUP 60
Whole-life costs 71
Worms 370

Yield variance. 266

GLEIM CPA REVIEW SYSTEM

All 4 sections, including Gleim Online, Review Books, *Test Prep Software Download*, *Simulation Wizard*, Audio Review, *CPA Review: A System for Success* Booklet, plus bonus Book Bag.

$989.95 x _____ = $_____

Also available by exam section (does not include Book Bag).

GLEIM CMA REVIEW SYSTEM

Includes: Gleim Online, Review Books, *Test Prep Software Download*, Audio Review, *Essay Wizard*, *CMA Review: A System for Success* Booklet, plus bonus Book Bag.

$739.95 x _____ = $_____

Also available by exam part (does not include Book Bag).

GLEIM CIA REVIEW SYSTEM

Includes: Gleim Online, Review Books, *Test Prep Software Download*, Audio Review, *CIA Review: A System for Success* Booklet, plus bonus Book Bag.

$824.95 x _____ = $_____

Also available by exam part (does not include Book Bag).

GLEIM EA REVIEW SYSTEM

Includes: Gleim Online, Review Books, *Test Prep Software Download*, Audio Review, *EA Review: A System for Success* Booklet, plus bonus Book Bag.

$629.95 x _____ = $_____

Also available by exam part (does not include Book Bag).

"THE GLEIM EQE SERIES" EXAM QUESTIONS AND EXPLANATIONS

Includes: 5 Books and *Test Prep Software Download*.

$112.25 x _____ = $_____

Also available by part.

GLEIM ONLINE CPE

Try a FREE 4-hour course at gleim.com/cpe
- Easy-to-Complete
- Informative
- Effective

Contact
GLEIM PUBLICATIONS
for further assistance:

gleim.com
800.874.5346
sales@gleim.com

SUBTOTAL $_____

Complete your order on the next page

GLEIM PUBLICATIONS, INC.

P. O. Box 12848   Gainesville, FL 32604

TOLL FREE:	800.874.5346	Customer service is available (Eastern Time):
LOCAL:	352.375.0772	8:00 a.m. - 7:00 p.m., Mon. - Fri.
FAX:	352.375.6940	9:00 a.m. - 2:00 p.m., Saturday
INTERNET:	gleim.com	Please have your credit card ready,
EMAIL:	sales@gleim.com	or save time by ordering online!

SUBTOTAL (from previous page) $_____

Add applicable sales tax for shipments within Florida. _____

Shipping (nonrefundable) 14.00

TOTAL $_____

Email us for prices/instructions on shipments outside the 48 contiguous states, or simply order online.

NAME (please print) _____

ADDRESS _____ Apt. _____
(street address required for UPS/Federal Express)

CITY _____ STATE _____ ZIP_____

____ MC/VISA/DISC/AMEX ____ Check/M.O. Daytime Telephone (_____)_____

Credit Card No. _____ - _____ - _____ - _____

Exp. _____/_____ Signature _____
    Month / Year

Email address _____

1. We process and ship orders daily, within one business day over 98.8% of the time. Call by 3:00 pm for same day service.

2. Gleim Publications, Inc. guarantees the immediate refund of all resalable texts, unopened and un-downloaded Test Prep Software, and unopened and un-downloaded audios returned within 30 days. Accounting and Academic Test Prep online courses may be canceled within 30 days if no more than the first study unit or lesson has been accessed. In addition, Online CPE courses may be canceled within 30 days if no more than the Introductory Study Questions have been accessed. Accounting Practice Exams may be canceled within 30 days of purchase if the Practice Exam has not been started. Aviation online courses may be canceled within 30 days if no more than two study units have been accessed. This policy applies only to products that are purchased directly from Gleim Publications, Inc. No refunds will be provided on opened or downloaded Test Prep Software or audios, partial returns of package sets, or shipping and handling charges. Any freight charges incurred for returned or refused packages will be the purchaser's responsibility.

3. Please PHOTOCOPY this order form for others.

4. No CODs. Orders from individuals must be prepaid.

Subject to change without notice. 07/12

For updates and other important information, visit our website.

GLEIM
KNOWLEDGE
TRANSFER
SYSTEMS®

gleim.com